JEAN RENOIR
Letters

JEAN RENOIR
Letters

Edited by
David Thompson and Lorraine LoBianco

Translations by
Craig Carlson
Natasha Arnoldi
Michael Wells

Translations of the letters of François Truffaut by
Anneliese Varaldiev

faber and faber
LONDON · BOSTON

First published in Great Britain in 1994
by Faber and Faber Limited
3 Queen Square
London WC1N 3AU

Photoset by Parker Typesetting Service, Leicester
Printed in England by Clays Ltd, St Ives plc

A CIP record for this book is available from the British Library

ISBN 0-571-17298-9

2 4 6 8 10 9 7 5 3 1

To Dido Freire Renoir, without whom
this book would not have been possible

Contents

List of Illustrations

All photographs appear by permission of the Jean Renoir Estate and are
from the Renoir Papers, Arts Special Collection, UCLA, except for:
François Truffaut with Jean Renoir on location for *Le Déjeuner sur
l'Herbe* (28) and the cast of *Le Caporal Epinglé* (29) from the National
Film Archive; the photograph of Henri Cartier-Bresson in *Une Partie de
Campagne* (32) was taken by Elie Lotar, and is reproduced by permission
of Henri Cartier-Bresson.

1 Jean Renoir at home in Beverly Hills in the 1960s. The bust behind him is of
his mother, sculpted by his father.

Foreword

In 1974 I was in Los Angeles casting *1900*, and somebody told me that Jean Renoir had seen *The Conformist,* and perhaps he would like to meet me. At that time I didn't even know he was still alive, so both myself and my wife Clare were very excited. We went up to his rather anonymous house in Beverly Hills and were taken into the drawing room. At the end of the room there was a kind of jungle of plants, and he was sitting there in a wheelchair with a blanket on his knee.

He looked at us and smiled, and I panned from his face to just behind him, where I saw what looked like a little bronze head of Jean, aged five or six, made by his father Auguste. It was extraordinary to see this old man of eighty and the bust of the smiling little boy, for they were the same person, with the same incredible joy in their smile. So even before we started to talk I was taken by a kind of dizziness thinking about the father and the son. Pierre-Auguste Renoir was an extraordinary painter, one of the real monuments of the nineteenth century, and there next to one of his sculptures was his son, now an old man. I thought there was this incredible link, because they both represented the reality of their days in the most human and dramatic way. I don't know about the relationship between Jean and Pierre-Auguste, but in Jean's films there was a great affinity to his father's art, sometimes visually, by penetrating the world of his father with his camera, making fun of it and at the same time adoring it. Jean was often discovering the same world of his father in the world around him.

We started to speak and immediately I felt I was talking with a young director of my own generation, like Truffaut or Godard. His vision of cinema was as modern and as contemporary and as hungry as those film-makers who considered him a master. I remember he said that when he chose actors, the first thing was to go against the obvious idea one has of a certain character. It was a kind of declaration of war against conventions and clichés. We spoke about sound, and how he was strongly against dubbing. Then we discussed improvisation, and the more he was talking, the more we became absorbed in the magic of that meeting.

I told him that when I started to make movies in the 1960s, it was important for us not only to be telling a story through cinema, but also to analyse cinema while we were making it. From his smile it was clear that he had accomplished that over thirty years earlier, with a complete knowledge and lucidity about what he was doing. Then he said something that has become famous in our lives – he said, 'You must always leave a door open on the set. Somebody can come in, completely unexpected.' This idea, that you cannot lie to the camera, that the camera is always telling the truth, that reality is the real object of the desire of the camera, is something I will never forget.

After an hour he seemed a bit excited and tired, maybe tired because he was excited, and we decided to leave as we were even more tired and excited than him. I remember very well that he made a gesture with his arm and asked me, 'Can I give you a kiss, may I embrace you?' So we embraced. And when I kissed his bald head, the smell was exactly like the head of my grandfather when I was six or seven.

When I am asked to list my ten best films of all time, in general I try to avoid the torture of making such a choice. But I know that number one used to be and will always be *La Règle du Jeu*. It was made in 1939, and I think Renoir was very conscious of the fact that Europe was on the verge of war. This film, which is about a weekend in a country château where people who we would today call Eurotrash gather, was in fact a supreme prophecy of the reality of that time. This film that I consider to be the ultimate achievement in cinema was a complete flop, it didn't work at all with audiences when it was first released. I remember that Renoir told me he was surprised at this reception, as he thought he had made such a light film, a social comedy in the style of Marivaux or Beaumarchais. He was still amazed by that rejection, wounded even, and it reminded me of the misery we often have to cope with as film-makers.

I'm not a Buddhist. I was born a Catholic and then became a kind of non-believer, and though I've made a film on Buddhism it would be a lie to say I'm a Buddhist. I would be talking about my desire, not my reality. But Buddhists believe that everything has a mind, not only people, and I believe films are living things. Renoir's films have a mind, a heart, bones, guts, genitals, and of course they have Karma. For Buddhists the Karma is what we call in Western terms destiny, but destiny in the West is something written by an outside force, probably in Heaven. For a Buddhist, you are the writer of your Karma, the writer of your destiny – and the script of your destiny is the story of your behaviour.

Renoir was capturing life ('always leave a door open on your set'), for his camera was never objective towards that life. The camera of Renoir was enjoying a love affair with that life and these people, all of them, by choosing them, abandoning them, discovering them, and forgetting them. His stories float on the liquid surface of his style, between dead calm and a typhoon. Perhaps in this respect Renoir had a little Buddha in him. His style could only express love all the time. He even loves the ugly characters in his movies. He cannot make a final judgement on anybody, and he offers a chance for forgiveness towards his bad characters because he's curious about them, their reasons for their life story. The important thing for him was always the reality in front of the camera. His style is every style, because cinema is made up of paintings, of sculpture, of architecture, of music, of poetry, of literature.

He would create the most fantastic shots, as if he could forget the general meaning of a film and just focus on that one shot. There are shots by Renoir that are films with a beginning, a middle and an end, and then they go to another shot which is another film. And always you have this incredible *joie de vivre*, the joy of film-making, and an invincible curiosity for exploring other styles. He was falling in love with faces, landscapes, a corner of a room or a mechanical music box. That was his profession, always to fall in love with what was in front of his camera.

Renoir films are as real as life, and at the same time they are supremely cinema. How did he do it? Let's all try harder to learn from his lesson.

Bernardo Bertolucci
January 1994

Introduction

François Truffaut, Orson Welles and Charles Chaplin all said, at one time or another, that the greatest film director who ever lived was Jean Renoir. It is a fine accident of history that his centenary is also that of the art form he mastered. Such events traditionally bring out more words on their subject. Many books have already been written on his films, and will – we hope – continue to be written. At least two full-length biographies have been published. But to date, although they have been referred to in previous books, and a selection of the 1940s correspondence in French has been available, this is the first comprehensive collection of his letters to be published.

All the letters used in the making of this book came from the Arts Special Collections Library of the University of California at Los Angeles. They were a large part of the Renoir papers and memorabilia donated by Alain Renoir, Jean Renoir's son, following the death of Jean's widow Dido and the sale of their Beverly Hills home in the autumn of 1990. These materials were catalogued by Lorraine LoBianco, one of the editors of this book, from May 1991 to August 1993. The other editor, David Thompson, came from London to research the collection for a BBC documentary on Jean Renoir's life and work. She felt that these letters were so warm, witty and full of spontaneous thoughts and detail that they painted a more immediate and intimate portrait of the man than any book on him had yet achieved. He agreed. They are a vivid record of just how his films came to be made, which is far removed from the common misconception of the smooth transition of idea to celluloid. And in their shifts in tone, according to who he was addressing, a more complex man emerged, warts and all. Out of our excitement at this discovery came the idea to produce an edition of these letters that would tell the story of Jean Renoir's life from a new angle, and make these precious documents available to a wider public.

The letters in the collection fill over thirty boxes and span sixty years; the very first letter (not, alas, an original but a smudged photocopy) in this volume was handwritten by Jean Renoir in 1913; the last was typed, probably by his secretary, in 1978, six months before his death. However, the vast majority of the letters cover the years following 1939. Why are there not more letters from the 1930s, which were, for most people, Renoir's greatest years as a film-maker? The most logical guess would be that until 1938, Jean simply did not keep copies of his correspondence. One thing is clear: the existence of copies of letters from 1939 onwards is due to one person, Dido Freire Renoir. When she entered Renoir's personal life, probably in 1938, she also fully entered his professional life, which included acting as his translator (she was nearly fluent in at least five languages thanks to her background as the daughter of a diplomat) and typing his letters and scripts. She also kept the carbon copies of every item of correspondence, as well as telegrams, bills, receipts, tickets, and books. Thanks to Dido's thoroughness, many letters written to Renoir were also preserved, some of which we are pleased to include in this selection.

Although she only received one credit on a Renoir film – as script girl on *La Règle du Jeu* – Dido was far more than an efficient housewife and a superlative secretary. She was a constant adviser to him in his choice of subjects, in the writing of his scripts, and in the management of his financial affairs (Renoir was not a particularly worldly man when it came to business, as some of the letters also reveal). She also kept a close watch on his circle of friends. For friends were very important to Jean Renoir. He would often say, in the numerous interviews he gave when his film career was almost over, that the true subject of his films was the contact between people and the importance of friendship. Certainly this is borne out in the letters by the regularity with which certain names reappear, especially – since most of them date from after his arrival in the United States – the screenwriter Dudley Nichols, the playwright Clifford Odets, and the actress Ingrid Bergman. He would also keep up correspondence with his oldest friends, such as the artist Albert André, the writer Pierre Lestringuez, and the producer Pierre Braunberger. His immediate family was also important to him, especially his younger brother Claude Sr (who failed to match the levels of success achieved by his elder siblings) and his nephew Claude Jr, the outstanding cinematographer. To Ginette Doynel, his representative in Paris from the late 1950s until her death in 1989, he would regularly write about everything from the current state of his projects (and as in the later career of many an established film director, there were plenty of unrealized projects) to his health problems. When in his last decade Renoir was virtually housebound because of Parkinson's disease, he formed a close bond with director François Truffaut, whom he saw as a kind of spiritual heir in the realm of cinema.

But what particularly emerges from these letters is the importance to

Renoir of his marriage to Dido. Not only did she give him the love that proved so difficult in the past – his first wife Catherine Hessling was highly strung, emotionally unstable and extremely ambitious, a disturbing cocktail – but also the solid foundation that gave his creativity a freer hand. Much of Renoir's correspondence is, in tone, respectful and generous. But when he was separated from Dido, such as when he was making *The Golden Coach* in Rome and *Le Caporal Epinglé* in Vienna, then he would write to her regularly in a much freer, more gossipy style, clearly compensating for the absence of her conversation. This also helps to explain other gaps in the collection, such as the years spent filming *French Cancan, Eléna et les Hommes* and *Le Déjeuner sur l'Herbe*: Dido was by his side throughout the shooting of these films. When she was absent and Renoir felt the need to let off steam about the problems created by difficult producers or temperamental actors, these letters provided such a platform. But true to the man who, through his own character of Octave in *La Règle du Jeu*, said that everybody has their reasons, he is ready to acknowledge that such people might be good at their job even when at their most impossible. There are few hints of the bitterness or despair that many film-makers might have expressed as the difficulties of the profession mounted up in their later years.

There has always been conjecture as to Renoir's true political standing. Unfortunately, the letters that remain from the 1930s do not shed much light in this area, other than an obvious tendency to side with the left for humanitarian reasons. It is easy to forget that fascism in this period had many human faces. In the US, it appears that no-one ever drew attention to his support of the Communist Party in France in the mid-1930s. What might surprise some is Renoir's repudiation of the Gaullists during World War Two. Certainly after the war Renoir was heavily criticized in France for remaining in America. These letters do spell out clearly most of the reasons just why he stayed in California, although a primary one is never mentioned. Dido herself never felt particularly accepted by Jean's French comrades, and surely her feelings on this subject – and her reluctance to visit Paris – played a large part in Renoir's decision to become a naturalized American.

Just as Jean Renoir chose to live a life of two languages, so the collection of letters contains many written in English, mostly composed with Dido's help. Writing in a second language, however, seems to bring no special constraints. By putting all the letters into chronological order, with a brief commentary to fill in gaps and explain movements and key events, we hope that a narrative will emerge that gives a fuller sense of

Renoir's development as man and film-maker than was previously possible. It certainly shows how an artist in the film industry is always struggling with a machine that will probably undermine his intentions and desires. Renoir's wry accounts of the Hollywood system – a dominion ruled by executives and agents – shows that little had changed since the 1940s.

What the letters also reveal is how a man comes to terms with the ageing process within changing environments. Renoir always considered himself to be formed by the pre-World War One era, the *Belle Epoque* that his father recorded in paint, as well as the dignified military code of the period which he showed most eloquently in *La Grande Illusion*. However, the expressions of understanding and emotion in these letters speak across time, and go some way to explaining why Renoir's films still appear so contemporary and direct in feeling. Renoir would often say that for him, the real joy of film-making was in the act of creation, working closely with actors and technicians. Watching the films immediately conveys that communal celebration of life through art. Just as collaboration was so important to him, we hope that the readers of these letters, as they journey through eight decades, will feel themselves becoming part of that precious circle of friendship and artistic activity.

Lorraine LoBianco
David Thompson
January 1994

Acknowledgements

Jean Renoir always claimed he never made a film on his own, but that he worked in conjunction with people he called 'my accomplices' or 'my collaborators'.

The same applies to this book. There were many collaborators who helped with its creation and certainly deserve a public 'thank you'. Alain Renoir approved of our project with the kind of enthusiasm every editor dreams of, as well as supplying us with information on names and events mentioned in the correspondence. Brigitte J. Küeppers and UCLA Arts Special Collections granted permission to use the letters from the Jean Renoir Papers. Also to be thanked are Walter Donohue and Kevin MacDonald, our editors at Faber and Faber, for believing in the book. For their kindness in granting permission for the publication of letters written to Jean Renoir, we would like to thank the following: for a letter from Roberto Rossellini and the letters of Ingrid Bergman, her family and especially Isabella Rossellini and Pia Lindstrom; for the letters of Clifford Odets, his son, Dr Walt Odets; for the letters of François Truffaut, Madeleine Morgenstern, her daughters Eva and Laura Truffaut, and Josephine, daughter of Fanny Ardant; for the letters and telegrams of Robert Flaherty, his daughter Monica Flaherty Frassetto; for her own letter, Leslie Caron; for the letter by Henry Miller, Anthea Morton-Saner and Georges Hoffman at Curtis Brown. For the letters of Dudley Nichols, we were unable to locate anyone responsible for the administration of his estate. For this case, and others that may arise, we would be interested to hear from any concerned parties.

Both the Foreword by Bernardo Bertolucci and the concluding Memoir by Henri Cartier-Bresson were adapted from interviews conducted by David Thompson for the BBC *Omnibus* documentary on Jean Renoir. We would like to thank both of them for agreeing to participate in this volume and for spending time refining their texts.

A large part of our gratitude goes to the team of translators who worked very hard within a very tight schedule to deal with a huge pile of letters. Craig Carlson left his warm home in sunny California to join us in cold, sometimes snowy, London to do translations. Natasha Arnoldi spent most of her Christmas in Los Angeles similarly employed. Michael

Wells delivered his translations by computer link-up from Paris. Anneliese Varaldiev faxed her translations of François Truffaut's letters over from a Los Angeles traumatized by the January earthquake. Others helped in their research, in particular Vincent Jacquet-Françillon, Catherine Ancian, David Watson and especially Alan Dingle.

David Thompson would like to thank Lenny Borger, Alexander and Elizabeth Whitelaw, Ronald Bergan, Gilbert Adair and Paul Ryan for their help and support, freely and gladly given.

Lorraine LoBianco would like to thank Brigitte J. Küeppers for the privilege of cataloguing Jean Renoir's papers and for her understanding of the importance of such a collection. Ray Soto at the UCLA Arts Library provided access to much-needed information, Genevieve Fong spent hours photocopying letters and shared not only her enthusiasm, but her apartment for two hectic weeks in LA, and Dawn Becker typed endless letters into a database over Christmas. From Jean and Dido Renoir, I inherited a close friend, Nick Frangakis, whose encouragement is gratefully acknowledged. My parents, John and Nancy LoBianco, provided love, support . . . and a fax machine, all of which was vital. And David Thompson took an idea and helped transform it into a book.

Editors' Note

In assembling this collection of letters, our aim was to provide translations that honoured the original texts and were comparable with the style
of those letters already existing in English. Inevitably the latter include
some eccentricities of expression that where possible we have retained.
Renoir's spelling – in particular of people's names – was erratic, to say
the least, and in many instances these have been reproduced and duly
acknowledged. We have also sought to leave in both the French and
English letters some of Renoir's emphases made through the use of
capitals and the layout of text, while standardizing titles of films, plays,
books, journals etc. The original language title has been used where it
was most appropriate. Any editorial changes have been made using
square brackets; [. . .] indicates a cut, usually made to avoid repetitions of
information, very occasionally to avoid remarks of a personal nature that
we felt inappropriate to this publication.

This selection of letters represents only a fraction of the thousands
available to us, and our choice was based on their content and value in
elucidating Jean Renoir's life and career. In general we selected those
which contributed to such a narrative, and rejected those which repeated
the same stories or would be of interest only to their recipients. Consequently we have also supplied biographical information where this could
not be deduced from the letters themselves, or where there were signifi-
cant gaps in the collection. We have made annotations to all names that
were known to us, and regret that some of them appear to be lost in time.

Biographical Information

Occupation: Film director and author
Real Name: Jean Renoir
Height: 6 feet
Colour of hair: White
Eyes: Blue
Birthplace: Paris, France
Date of Birth: 15 September 1894
Father's name: Auguste Renoir
Occupation: Painter
Mother's name: Aline Charigot
Towns lived in, for what period: Nearly all life in Paris and father's estate at Cagnes-sur-Mer, south of France
Favourite childhood memory: Going to theatre on Sundays and to vaudeville
College: Bachelier en lettres
Athletic or other achievements: Aviation, automobile racing, horse riding
Youthful ambition: To be a cavalry officer
What studies best in: Latin and French literature
Military record if any: Cavalry lieutenant, then in air force in first World War, 1914
Travel: France, Great Britain, North Africa, the desert, Belgium, Italy, Switzerland, Portugal, Germany, Russia, India, Greece, Ireland
Present residence: Beverly Hills
Married to: Dido Renoir, 6 February 1944
Children: Alain Renoir, teaching literature at the University of California at Berkeley
Favourite scent: Smell of tar in Paris streets
Favourite superstition: None
Favourite flower: Rose
Favourite classical author: Rabelais
Favourite playwright: Courteline
Favourite orchestration: Mozart's *Don Giovanni*
Favourite modern author: Saint-Exupéry
Favourite modern playwright: Giraudoux

Favourite modern painter: Braque
Favourite historical character: St Francis of Assisi
Favourite illustrator: Daumier
First picture was: La Fille de l'Eau (1924)
Producing firm: My own, produced by self at Gaumont studio, Paris, Cagnes-sur-Mer (Alpes Maritimes), France, 1919 to 1924
Activities aside from pictures: Writing
What living personality do you most admire: Igor Stravinsky
Favourite exercise: None
Favourite animals: Dachshunds
Lives at: Beverly Hills and Paris
Type of home: Beverly Hills, hillside home; Paris, former home of Alexandre Dumas Sr in Montmartre
How did you get into pictures: During father's illness my brother and I projected Chaplin's comedies to amuse him and I was converted
Recreation: To enjoy life
Favourite play: Julius Caesar by Shakespeare
Favourite picture: Greed directed by Erich Von Stroheim
What is favourite picture you directed: The River
Favourite colour: White
Favourite menu: Charcoal broiled steak and green salad
Favourite type of man or woman: Types are indifferent to me, only interested in personalities
Pet aversion: Snobs
Do you believe in hunches: Yes
Favourite vacation: Country life with country people
Greatest disappointment: I try to forget them

[Personally compiled by Jean and Dido Renoir for publicity purposes, 27 March 1958]

Chère maman—

Je vois bien que maintenant le sort en est jeté. Nous partirons pour Luçon— Seulement, comme les quartiers ne sont pas finis, on nous logera d'abord dans des baraquements aux sables d'Olonnes.

Ce que je vois de plus ennuyeux dans ce départ, c'est que le corps des officiers va se trouver complètement changé— On n'envoie pas un bon officier à Luçon! Tous les gens remarquables qui nous commandent s'en vont pour aller soit dans l'est, soit dans des garnisons près de Paris— Seuls des incapables resteront.

Je vois bien, comment va mon père?

Je vous embrasse tous

Jean.

Letter written by Jean Renoir to his mother in early 1914. (See page 6.)

18 Mai 1974

Cher François

Ma main tremble mais j'éprouve le besoin de communiquer avec vous sans l'intermédiaire d'une machine à écrire, froid objet mécanique, sans âme, aux lettres dures comme de l'acier ou plutôt comme du chrome

Puisse cette petite note vous apporter le message manuel de mon amitié.

· Vivent les sens
· A bas le cerveau

Dido se joint à moi pour vous embrasser.

Vivent les mistons.

Jean Renoir.

Merci pour votre collaboration à l'ouvrage sur la Grande Illusion et pour les livres. Fidèles messagers de la pensée.

P.P.S. votre passage sur les élections me désopilant.

Letter written by Jean Renoir to François Truffant on 18 May 1974. (See page 522.)

LETTERS

2 Pierre-Auguste Renoir and Aline Renoir, c. 1910

1894–1912

1894: *Jean Renoir is born in the Paris house known as the Château des Brouillards, off the rue Girardon, in Butte-Montmartre on 15 September 1894. He is the second son of the artist Pierre-Auguste Renoir (1841–1919) and Aline Charigot (1862–1915); the first is Pierre (1885–1952). Gabrielle Renard (1879–1959), a cousin of Jean's mother and a model for his father, becomes nurse to the young boy, and together they appear in many of Pierre-Auguste's paintings.*

1897: *Jean Renoir has his first experience of the cinema when Gabrielle takes him to the Grand Magasin Dufayel, an episode recounted in* My Life and My Films. *The young Jean also becomes a fan of the Guignol puppet theatre in the Tuileries gardens.*

1898: *Pierre-Auguste Renoir buys a house in Essoyes, the village in Burgundy where Aline and Gabrielle were born. This becomes a regular summer home for the Renoirs, and Essoyes is the site of the family grave.*

1901: *The third Renoir son, Claude (1901–69), is born in Essoyes. Nicknamed Coco, he is subsequently referred to as Claude Sr, to distinguish him from Pierre's son Claude (1913–93), known as Claude Jr.*

1907: *After spending many summers on the Côte d'Azur, the Renoirs purchase the estate in Cagnes-sur-Mer known as Les Collettes, which later becomes the painter's permanent residence as he is crippled with arthritis.*

1912: *After attending the Ecole Masséna, Nice, Jean studies philosophy and mathematics. But his chief ambition is to enter military service.*

1913

On 17 February, Jean Renoir enlists in the First Regiment of Dragoons. After attending Cavalry School at Saumur, he is stationed at Joigny.

To Aline Renoir   *[1913?]*

Dear Maman,

If you have some shopping to do, could you at the same time buy me a sleeping bag big enough for my long legs – and a grey blanket, or one that won't soil easily.

[Jean]

To Claude Renoir Sr   *19 May 1913*

Dear Coco,

Thursday's your First Communion – I'm very happy and will think of you on that day. Moreover, I think about it every day.

At the moment of the great event, I will be, without a doubt, on a horse in the fields.

Pray to the Good Lord for your Papa and your Maman.

Your big brother who loves you very much.

[Jean]

3 Pierre-Auguste Renoir with his third son Claude Sr (Coco) at Les Collettes in 1913

1914

To Aline Renoir

Dear Maman,

I really believe that now the die has been cast. We are leaving for Luçon – however, since the quarters are not finished, they will lodge us first in the barracks at Sables d'Olones [sic].

The most annoying thing I can see in our departure is that the officer corps are going to find themselves completely changed – good officers don't get sent to Luçon!

All the good people who command us will either go East or to the garrisons near Paris – only the incompetents will stay.

I'm doing well, how's my father?

Love to everyone.

Jean

To Aline Renoir

9 April 1914
4th Squadron Hospital

Dear Maman,

The Major insists that I completely relax and only leave the hospital when capable of resuming my duties – and without fatigue.

Therefore, I won't be able to leave the hospital until next Monday.

The Station Hotel is not as good as the Duc de Bourgogne Hotel – as for the food, I don't know.

I still have a good appetite and I am treating myself to jams.

I received quite a nice letter from Mrs Lestringuez[1] who sent me some brochures. I have also received a letter from Dr Baudot.[2] It appears my godmother[3] is terribly busy with the cathedrals.

I hope Papa is doing quite well now and that he hasn't had a recurrence of his rheumatism.

My love to you as well as Papa and Coco

Jean

[6]

1 Mother of Pierre Lestringuez. For description, see *Renoir, My Father*.
2 Family doctor and friend. For description, see *Renoir, My Father*.
3 Jeanne Baudot, daughter of Dr Baudot, was a student of Pierre-Auguste Renoir.

To Albert André[1]   *10 April [1914]*

Sir,

I was very happy to receive your letter. I'm doing very well at the moment, although still in the hospital. I'll be leaving Monday.

I am in isolation and no one can see me for fear of contagion. Thank you very much for all the kind words you've written. My illness hasn't been too unpleasant.

For the last few days, my friend Maleissye has come to see me, so that I'm not bored any more. We sing together at the top of our lungs, improvising duos and studying theory. The Colonel comes by from time to time to boost morale.

As soon as I can, perhaps Sunday at eight, I'll come to see you. You will see that I am not dead and you can give me some details about the exhibition. Isolated as I am, I have not been able to get hold of any magazines so that I don't know anything about anything.

Nevertheless, from your short letter I can see that you are pleased.

My father had an attack of rheumatism. He's fine now.

My kind regards to you and Mrs André –

Jean Renoir

Ist Drag.

4th Squadron

1 Albert André (1869–1954), minor Impressionist painter and close friend of Pierre-Auguste Renoir.

World War One breaks out on 4 August. In September, Jean Renoir is briefly hospitalized for gonorrhea, described in cavalry slang as a coup de pied de Vénus, *and is visited by Aline.*

4 Jean Renoir (on the far right, marked by a cross) in the uniform of the First Dragoons at Les Sables d'Olonnes. His friend Maleissye is on the far left. The inscription reads: 'Several Luçon officers encamped at Les Sables'.

1915

As a second lieutenant, Jean Renoir is transferred at his own request to the 6th Battalion of the Chasseurs Alpins (Alpine Infantry) and sent to the front. On 17 April, in the Vosges region, he is shot and wounded in the right femur by a Bavarian sniper. He is hospitalized at Gérardmer. Although she has recently been diagnosed as a diabetic, Aline Renoir makes the journey to Alsace to see her wounded son. She pleads with the doctors not to amputate Jean's leg, even though he is suffering from gangrene. The chief physician at the hospital has just been replaced by Professor Laroyenne, who has devised an alternative procedure involving the circulation of distilled water through the wound. The gangrene subsides, Jean recovers, but for the rest of his life he will limp and suffer from recurrent infections.

To Georges Rivière[1]   *15 May 1915*
                                                    Gérardmer

My dear Rivière,

Jean is better. I don't know whether I can claim victory yet, but this evening [his temperature] was only 37.7 and at lunchtime he was hungry for the first time since the wound and today is the nineteenth day.

It really is a miracle. One day I'll tell you about the phases he's been through.

Most affectionately,
Aline Renoir

1 Georges Rivière, friend and biographer of Pierre-Auguste Renoir. His daughter Renée married Paul Cézanne Jr.

To Georges Rivière   *19 May 1915*
                                                    Gérardmer

My dear Rivière,

Last night Jean underwent a serious operation which lasted more than an hour. When they brought him back to his bed he was very ill and I left

[9]

him feeling very worried, so I was in a hurry to see him this morning. I found him very much better than I dared hope. His fever at eight this morning was 39.4 but you see how little that is.

The doctor I saw last night did not hide from me the fact that Jean's condition is still very serious. An infection is still to be feared, but if he continues to be improving in ten days time we can consider him saved. Happily he was in good health when this bullet hit him. Oh I wish I was eighteen days older [!]

I will keep you up to date and thank you for all the trouble you've gone to and I believe that time is on our side.

Most affectionately,
Aline Renoir

To Georges Rivière

22 May 1915
Gérardmer

My dear Rivière,

I am leaving Gérardmer on Monday evening and will spend a few days at Essoyes and will be in Paris next Saturday – the 29th – in the evening. My leaving means that Jean is well. The poor thing has still another forty-five days here, so I promised to come back to see him. As soon as I arrive at Cagnes I shall hasten my preparations to return, because it's impossible for me to be at Gérardmer while Renoir[1] is at Cagnes. It's really too far.

Goodbye, with all my affection,
Aline Renoir

1 Aline Renoir always referred to her husband as 'Renoir'.

To Georges Rivière

26 May 1915
Gérardmer

My dear Rivière,

I am leaving Jean this evening. I'm going to Essoyes where I'll arrive tomorrow evening at nine o'clock and will be in Paris on Monday evening for a few days only. Would you like to come and dine with me on Monday evening? I shall arrive home at about seven in the evening. If you can come I'll tell you about Jean's condition. He is suffering much less.

I hope to see you soon, my dear Rivière. Jean and I send our affectionate greetings.

Aline Renoir

To Aline Renoir

Dear Maman,

   Papa's letter dated the 19th told me that you are ill. I hope that it isn't anything serious. The fact that you are thinking of undertaking the journey makes me think you aren't suffering too much. Nevertheless, I wouldn't like you to tire yourself out needlessly. I'm doing very well – they take me down to the garden in a chaise-longue.

   The best hotel here is the Hôtel d'Europe, rue de la République.

   Love to you both,

   Jean

To Aline Renoir

Dear Maman,

   I am writing to Paris and Cagnes at the same time.

   I am doing very well here, spending pleasant afternoons in the shade of cherry trees laden – though not for much longer – with beautiful cherries. Yesterday I inaugurated the chaise-longue.

   I am doing very well here – sleeping well.

   The treatments are not the same as those of Professor Laroyenne but they're sufficient for what I have now. My wound can be looked after by anyone, it's an easy dressing to do.

   Of all things Miss Tititi has been replaced by an even more repulsive sister who is looking to impose convent discipline on us. That doesn't please us after having lived so freely in the woods, and I am afraid the good sister will only become tormented by the friskiness of the Chausseur Officers being cared for here.

   Love to you all.

   Jean

   I received the telegram the same day you sent it.

To Aline Renoir

Dear Maman,

   I'm still doing very well. Now it's your turn to take care of yourself, not I, who do no more than lie in bed, which I have now got used to and find almost agreeable.

Try to get well soon and especially don't worry about me.

My wound is healing. There is already a centimetre of new flesh growing around it. I'm still oozing pus, but it's not leaking through my bandage.

I must confess that I am not reassured to know that Papa is going to travel alone with Louise.[1] How are they going to get to Besançon station? And change trains??

I would be very sorry if Papa, by coming to see me, were to tire himself out.

Much love to you all,

Jean

---

1 The Renoir family cook, usually referred to as 'Grand' Louise'.

Aline Renoir returns to Les Collettes and, exhausted and sick from the journey, takes to bed. She dies on 27 June.

To Pierre-Auguste Renoir

[1915]
[Gérardmer]

Dear Papa,

I'm doing very well and not suffering at all. I have to relieve myself into a portable throne with my leg propped up on a chair. I'm able to get myself into an easy chair for a few moments while they remake my bed. I need some help with this because if I stand on my leg, the pain is awful.

But I have learned to consider my leg as a useless piece of meat which little by little will regain strength and mobility.

Not knowing if you are in Cagnes or in Paris, I'll write to both places.

Love to you all,

Jean.

To Commandant [name unknown]

[late 1915]
[Paris]

Commandant,

Dr Elie Faure[1] has written to my father to say that I could contact you if in need. I am following his advice and that is why I am bothering you.

A month ago, I applied for tank duty. But having never received a response, I have abandoned hope of returning to this branch of the service, and this is why I have asked to enter the air force.

Being unable to fight on foot because of my serious leg wound, it would be for me the only way not to rot in the barracks and still be of some service to my country.

My application for the air force was sent two weeks ago. I would be happy if you could advise me on this matter or tell me if there is any hope.

Forgive the liberty I am taking, but my only excuse is my strong desire to return in this interesting branch of service.

Respectfully yours,

Jean Renoir

1 Philosopher and writer, friend to Pierre-Auguste Renoir.

5 Jean Renoir in the uniform of the French Flying Corps with (from the left) Georges Rivière and Paul Cezanne Jr. The children are Jean-Pierre and Aline Cézanne.

1916–1923

1916: *After a convalescence spent in Paris to be close to his father, Jean Renoir begins to make regular visits to the cinema. When he recovers, Jean transfers to the French Flying Corps. Initially as an observer with aerial reconnaissance billeted at Champagne, then as a qualified pilot, he sees action and makes the acquaintance of Major Pinsard, whose stories of escape from prison camps will be a source for* La Grande Illusion. *After crashing his plane, Jean is posted to Paris, where he spends more time at the cinema, becoming a fan of Charlie Chaplin and American films in particular.*

1917: *Pierre-Auguste Renoir finds a new model in Andrée Heuschling, known as 'Dédée' (1900–1979).*

1918: *When the war ends on 11 November, Jean Renoir returns to live at Les Collettes.*

1919: *Together with his brother Claude, the artist Albert André and his wife Maleck, and Andrée Heuschling, Jean Renoir works as a potter and ceramist. Pierre-Auguste dies on 3 December.*

1920: *On 24 January, Jean Renoir marries Andrée Heuschling. They buy a house, the Villa St El, in Marlotte, located south of the forest of Fontainebleau on the river Loing. Jean's close friend, Paul Cézanne Jr (son of the artist), moves close by on a property known as La Nicotière.*

1921: *On 31 October, Jean's son Alain is born.*

1922/23: *Jean Renoir continues to work in ceramics, but is spending more time seeing films. He is particularly impressed by* Le Brasier Ardent *(Ivan Mosjoukine/Alexander Volkov), but his preference is for American over French cinema. Andrée models herself after American film actresses like Gloria Swanson and aspires to be a star.*

1924: *Intent on becoming a film-maker, Jean Renoir shoots his first film in March:* Catherine, *or* Une Vie Sans Joie, *with Albert Dieudonné as director, Jean as writer and producer, and Andrée – changing her name to Catherine Hessling – in the title role. Also collaborating on this film are the writer Pierre Lestringuez, Pierre Champagne and as cameraman, Jean Bachelet.* Catherine *does not receive a public screening for three years, and Jean, frustrated by Albert Dieudonné's intransigence, decides to direct his next film. Inspired by repeated viewings of* Foolish Wives *(Erich Von Stroheim, 1921), he develops a screenplay by Pierre Lestringuez,* La Fille de l'Eau *(known in UK as* Whirpool of Fate*). Filmed around Marlotte in the summer with Catherine in the lead role, the film is previewed in Paris on 12 December.*

1925

To Claude Renoir Sr   *16 February 1925*

My dear Claude,

La Fille de l'Eau is finally going to be released at the Corso and although this comes a little late, it opens up some foreign and domestic business opportunites for me. This cinema is obviously one of the smallest on the boulevards, but it's very well located and *La Fille de l'Eau* can, if business is good, play there for a month. Furthermore, the owner of the Corso has eight other cinemas, some more attractive than others, which will be available to me in the future.

The early disappointments of my film career have not been in vain, after all.

I believe that I can now enter this field with some chance of success.

How well a film does depends only on how it's released (assuming, of course, that the film itself is not a crashing bore). One can be sure of doing good box-office returns in the provinces and good sales overseas if, immediately after the film's opening, it is shown exclusively on the boulevard, accompanied by a large amount of publicity about the film's success, whether real or imaginary.

I've studied the progress of all the films released this winter. Only those released under these conditions have had positive financial results. That's why I have decided to do the same this summer and as soon as *La Fille de l'Eau* has started its run, that is to say on 3 April, I will start looking for a way to ensure that my film will have a cinema where it can be shown until the end of the year.

Now let's move on to more serious things: the last time you were in Paris you told me you would like to work in the Cinema and I told you it would be better if you'd wait so that you don't risk having the terrible experiences that I've had. Along with Pierre, I am in the midst of looking into a business which might make it very easy for us to distribute and exhibit films that either of us would like to make. It's a question of purchasing the assets of the Folies Dramatiques. Please don't tell anyone about this, for it is an excellent opportunity and could be arranged for very little money. From the public's point of view, this cinema is superbly

[17]

located. The box-office receipts of the neighbouring establishments are very high. What's more, if I can be sure that the receipts will be good, the building could be enlarged and become one of the biggest cinemas in Paris.

Here at last is a solid foundation which will allow us to earn some money and to meet on equal footing with the distributors for our future productions, because one must not forget that it is the exhibitors who have the upper hand.

If the idea interests you, each of us will have to put in 100,000 francs. It's possible that this sum may not be necessary, for there are other interested parties who might want to go into business with us. In any case, get back to me quickly.

If you see Pierrot, tell him that I am in the process of finding a way for him to have exclusive representation of my film from Cannes to Menton.

Give Paulette[1] a kiss for Dédée and me, with our fondest wishes,
Jean Renoir

---

1 Wife of Claude Renoir Sr.

No distributor is found for La Fille de l'Eau. *Disappointed with the cinema, Jean Renoir opens a shop near the Place de la Madeleine to sell pottery. He and Catherine also take an apartment in Paris at 30 rue de Miromesnil. A growing friendship with Pierre Braunberger, who has just returned from Hollywood, leads Jean to make a lavish film adaptation of Emile Zola's* Nana, *with Catherine in the title role. Braunberger brings in German finance, and shooting begins in October.*

6 Jean Renoir in the 1920s

7 Catherine Hessling in *Sur un Air de Charleston*

1926–1933

1926: Nana *is premiered at the Moulin Rouge in Paris in June. It is a commercial failure, and Jean Renoir is forced to sell several of his father's paintings to pay his debts. Despite this flop, Jean goes on to make a short film with Catherine,* Sur un Air de Charleston, *and then directs* Marquitta. *It is around this time that he becomes friends with Jacques Becker and Carl Koch. With Catherine, Jean acts in a short film by Alberto Cavalcanti,* La P'tite Lili, *which features nineteen-year-old Dido Freire in a small role. The editor on this film is Marguerite Houllé.*

1927: Jean Renoir makes his final important film with Catherine Hessling, La Petite Marchande d'Allumettes.

1928: Jean Renoir undertakes projects not originated by him, directing Tire au Flanc, *produced by Braunberger and including in its cast Michel Simon, and* Le Tournoi *(or* Le Tournoi dans la Cité).

1929: Jean Renoir directs his last silent film, Le Bled, *with exteriors shot in Algeria.*

1930: Jean Renoir separates from Catherine. She goes on to make only two films of note, Du Haut en Bas *(G. W. Pabst, 1933) and* Crime et Châtiment *(Pierre Chenal, 1935).*

1931: After two years absence from film-making, Jean Renoir is offered the direction of his first sound production, On Purge Bébé, *a Feydeau farce starring Michel Simon, for the Braunberger-Richebé company. Shot at Billancourt studios in six days, and released quickly afterwards to immediate box-office success, it proves Jean to be an able film-maker. He is allowed to direct his first major film that summer,* La Chienne, *again with Michel Simon.*

1932: After purchasing the rights from Georges Simenon to a Maigret story, La Nuit du Carrefour, *Jean Renoir shoots the film with his brother Pierre in the lead role. He follows this with another collaboration with Michel Simon,* Boudu Sauvé des Eaux, *which is a commercial and critical success. At the end of the year he makes* Chotard et Cie *as a 'director for hire'.*

[21]

1933: Jean Renoir films Madame Bovary, *with his brother Pierre as Charles, in the autumn. The original version is three hours long, causing the distributors to cut the film down to two hours. It is released in January 1934, but is not successful.*

1934

To Jacques Mortier[1]

9 *May 1934*
Meudon-Bellevue

My dear Mortier,

The high hopes I had when I came to see you at Easter on the subject of *Toni* and, in general, a possible collaboration with the NRF[2] seems to me to be crumbling every day. I gave them *L'Epingle dans la Neige* to read some days after my return. And they haven't responded. I haven't seen Gallimard[3] again and I have the distinct feeling that there is an obstacle which is preventing my access to his office and the opportunity for a face to face conversation with him. I don't know if all this has come from ARON[4] but it's possible.

In the making and then the sale of *Madame Bovary* there have been some ... blunders ...? extremely prejudicial to the interests of the backing company. Each time I wanted to open either Gallimard or Aron's eyes, I found myself up against a brick wall. I'm learning frightening things every day. Some foreigners' offers to buy were rejected out of hand, for example. I don't think ARON is dishonest. I think, instead, that he is a sort of dreamer little suited to direct business affairs. What's more, he governs his life by following personal sympathies or antipathies. A person's value doesn't count in his eyes. He always supports his friends. He's sentimental. For example, I suspect that he hates BRAUN-BERGER[5] and rejects all proposals from him, even interesting ones, without even thinking about them. On the other hand, he must have a high regard for certain smaller merchants, real shysters to whom he gives preference. Because all this produces bad results, it may be opportune for the NRF to leave the real causes of these bad results in the dark, and to let a cloud of suspicion hang over my responsibility in this matter.

There is also something else. ARON had written a play that I thought excellent and which I had shown to my brother Pierre at the Comédie des Champs Elysées and asked him to read carefully. Well, my brother didn't share my enthusiasm; frankly, he found the play bad and ARON must realize this. I don't believe he had in his mind the least idea of exchange, and that the literature which I recommended to his company might suffer from my brother's coldness in regard to his. But I don't believe that this

[23]

state of things can advance our interests, and, one thing leading to another, I feel myself rather powerless. I'm struggling with a very difficult situation. I'm having all sorts of problems and I'm really afraid of not being in a position to foist the production of *Toni* upon any company whatsoever. I would be only too happy if some sort of work allowed me to earn a living this summer. Being able to choose a screenplay is a dream that will have to wait for better times.

All these problems are rather depressing and I feel I'm losing my confidence, which is so vital for success. Boring and humiliating administrative matters keep me in Paris. If not, I would love to have gone and spent some time with you. I would have asked you to do some articles for the magazine *VU* and we would have illustrated these articles with some very attractive photographs. Perhaps we might have done a lot of other things, but all of that really is hypothetical.

If you pass through Paris, remember that I have a place for you to stay at my house in MEUDON. If you see Jeannot[6] give him my regards.

My love to you and Madeleine,[7]

Jean Renoir

1 Jacques Mortier, old school friend and chief of police in Nice who gave Jean Renoir the story on which *Toni* is based. He wrote thrillers under the pseudonym Jacques Levert.
2 *Nouvelle Revue Française*, the distinguished literary journal. The company that produced *Madame Bovary*, the NSF, was an associated enterprise so named to recall the NRF, and foundered after the failure of the film.
3 Gaston Gallimard, the publisher of the NRF and producer of *Madame Bovary*.
4 Robert Aron, executive producer of *Madame Bovary*.
5 Pierre Braunberger (1905–91), film producer whose career spanned the period from the 1920s to the 1970s, including *Un Chien Andalou* (Luis Buñuel/Salvador Dali, 1928), *Vivre Sa Vie* (Jean-Luc Godard, 1962), and *Un Homme et Une Femme* (Claude Lelouch, 1966). He produced several of Jean Renoir's films including *Nana*, *Tire au Flanc*, and *Une Partie de Campagne*.
6 Jean Mortier, son of Jacques Mortier. He was Jean Renoir's godson.
7 Wife of Jacques Mortier.

To Mr Berthomieu
Syndicat des Chefs Cinéastes Français

22 May 1934
Meudon-Bellevue

My dear friend,

The other day I announced to you my intention to hand in my resignation if the assembly ratifies the proposed demonstration against Foreigners.

I had wavered a little for, frankly, it pained me to leave a group of such good friends, with whom it will now be difficult for me to meet. One of the advantages of these unions – and certainly not the least – is fostering amicable relations between people who otherwise would never see each other. But I must be consistent with myself and that is why I made the decision to lie low and wait for better days.

I have also given my resignation to L'Association des Auteurs de Films. I have an excellent reason which is the Sauvage affair,[1] but between us, the real reason is that having been nominated to the Comité de la rue Ballu by and for our Union, it wouldn't seem right for me, now that I am leaving our group, to continue sitting on the other side.

I hope soon, dear friend, to have the pleasure of seeing you again in private, and please be so kind as to pass on to our friends the enclosed letter, in which I give my resignation.

Cordially,
Jean Renoir

---

1 Renoir is probably alluding to the case of André Sauvage, director of poetic documentaries in the late 1920s, whose potential masterpiece, *La Croisière Jaune*, was ruined in November 1933 when his producers, André Citroën – the automobile manufacturer – and Bernard Nathan – the head of Pathé – seized all the materials after the first screening and had another director recut the film. The above-mentioned Association failed to come to the aid of Sauvage or defend his rights.

To The Members of Le Syndicat des Chefs Cinéastes Français

23 May 1934
Meudon-Bellevue

My dear Comrades,

I perfectly understand the reasons which drove you to share the view of other Unions concerning Foreigners working in French studios, and to help those struggling to decide whether or not to participate in a public demonstration.

The situation is tragic and French artists need to earn a living. If I disassociate myself from you, it is because to fight against the foreigners in our guild seems to me a bad way to improve the situation.

It is my conviction that in France an artistic industry can only work if it acquires a certain influence in the world. Paris is not a provincial city, it's one of the World capitals and its influence has stemmed from its absorption of many foreign elements.

Throughout our history we can see that the most brilliant periods of Art, Literature and Industry are those where our schools have welcomed many non-French elements. I do, of course, use the word 'Schools' in the sense of groups, even of doctrines.

I believe that film must be national in its spirit (as in American and Russian films, and as German films used to be before producers' simple-mindedness made them a dubious commodity), and this must be uncompromising. But that's not the case now. We allow ourselves to be invaded by the American spirit. This is bad because Americans will always make American films better than we do.

We must make French films, because we make them better than anyone else. We must create a School which will influence the world as does, for example, L'Ecole Picturale Française Moderne, which adopted foreign elements and used them to create this type of international relationship so necessary for the effectiveness and greatness of an industry.

I fear that by working in a different way, we work against the genuine interests of French cinema. For as long as we, the French, are holding on to a small leftover bone for ourselves to eat, the situation will not get any better, because this bone is so small that it can't possibly feed us all. What must be done is to transform this bone into a succulent piece of meat to nourish all our comrades, and this can only happen by working together in an entirely different spirit from the one which inspired the vote for the demonstration.

That is why, being consistent with myself, and seeing that I can only oppose this very strong tendency, which I believe to be false, I prefer to step down and I ask you to accept my resignation.

Best regards,
Jean Renoir

To Carl Koch[1]   *1 June 1934*

My dear Carl,
I still don't have any news from NRF. The reason must be that ARON still owes me a little money and has the firm intention of not giving it to me. I've learned that they are finally going to make their film *IO* [sic] by cashing the drafts for *Madame Bovary*. As they must know that I am aware of this, they are preferring to play dead. Thus, I haven't been able to mention what you wrote to me about, and I am very sure that it is now useless to talk about anything with these nice people. Or perhaps I need to be more forceful in order to make them afraid. This is why this

company does business through 'Gentlemen's Agreements', which allows them to do things without a contract, and so gives them the upper hand.

I think that my only recourse vis-à-vis NRF is to try and forget them. I wrote a personal letter to Gaston GALLIMARD who has not replied. That is a very clear sign.

I'm glad to hear that Lotte[2] has some work. That's the rarest thing at the moment. Take advantage of it and do something beautiful. I have no doubts as to the results, and I know very well that if Lotte is able to have a little peace and quiet, her films will be successful.

I have only received one serious proposition, from someone you know well. It's Carl EINSTEIN[3] who used to frequent WASSMUTH and ZUCKI. If you see that delightful family as well as his brother, don't forget to say that I often think of them and that I send them all my regards.

Carl EINSTEIN has a friend who may put a little money in a film. He's a very serious man and, above all, very intelligent. He doesn't have, like Gaston Gallimard, his intelligence spoiled by a kind of constant fear. He's very sporty, flies a lot. He's a former officer who still belongs to patriotic organizations, which doesn't prevent him being a lot more liberal than certain intellectuals we know at NRF.

If I don't find any more money to add to what this man wants to put in as business capital, it is obvious I won't be able to make a film. But it's already a lot to have a base, and this gives me the courage to look, or rather to help EINSTEIN with his search because he has a lot more connections than I do.

The film which we want to make would be a kind of chronicle of characters on an average Paris street from just after the war until the present. If we find enough money, I would love to have you come and help us because it is perfect for you. Unfortunately, nothing has been done yet, and what I've told you is purely in the realm of conjecture. We would also like to bring to this film a mixture of lively characters and caricatures. One of the unlucky characters in our story is 'journalism'. I believe that the only way of expressing this is with a trick film.

But all this is still far from being realized and it was our hope to make the Martigues[4] film before *Bovary*.

Write to me from time to time, it makes me happy. I would be glad to hear that the Germans are becoming very rich. That would be different from what is happening here, where really business is very difficult.

Kiss LOTTE. Marguerite[5] sends her love to you both.

With my warm regards,

Jean Renoir

PS. Say hello to STECHEL and also tell him that my house is beginning to be full of cats. I had quite a scare because ALAIN was operated on for appendicitis. He's fine now and I am a little more reassured.

1 Carl Koch (1892–1963) worked as Jean Renoir's assistant on *La Grande Illusion* and *La Règle du Jeu*. He also co-wrote *Madame Bovary* and *La Marseillaise*.
2 Lotte Reiniger (1899–1981), wife of Carl Koch. She was famous for her silhouette animation films such as *The Adventures of Prince Achmed* (1926), and responsible for the section using this technique in *La Marseillaise*.
3 Carl Einstein, art critic who co-wrote the screenplay of *Toni* with Renoir.
4 *Toni* (1934).
5 Marguerite Houllé, who later adopted the name 'Renoir'. She was editor on all of Jean Renoir's films from 1932 to 1939. Following his separation from Catherine Hessling, he lived with Marguerite until the filming of *La Règle du Jeu*.

With production facilities provided by Etablissements Marcel Pagnol, Jean Renoir films Toni *at Les Martigues, near Marseilles, during the summer.*

1935–1936

1935: Jean Renoir collaborates with Jacques Prévert and the October Group, a notable left-wing theatre ensemble, to make Le Crime de Monsieur Lange *in Paris during October and November. This venture brings Jean closer to the Front Populaire.*

1936: Commissioned by the Parti Communiste Français, Jean Renoir oversees and co-directs La Vie est à Nous *in February. The film is refused a certificate of censorship, but is shown at party meetings and film societies. Jean contributes articles to the newspaper* Ciné-Liberte, *expressing his views on how French cinema may be aided. In July he begins shooting* Une Partie de Campagne *on the banks of the Loing near Montigny and Marlotte. Bad weather causes lengthy delays, and eventually Jean abandons the film in order to honour his commitment to make* Les Bas-Fonds. *This film, which marks his first collaboration with Jean Gabin, opens in Paris in December, and wins the Prix Louis-Delluc.*

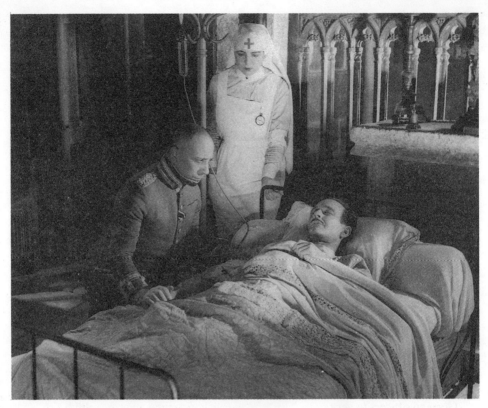

8 Erich Von Stroheim (Captain Von Rauffenstein) and Pierre Fresnay (Captain
de Boeldieu) in *La Grande Illusion*

<u>1937</u>

At the beginning of the year, Jean Renoir begins filming La Grande
Illusion. *The premiere is held in Paris on 4 June. The film provokes an
accusation of plagiarism by Jean des Vallières, author of* Kavalier
Scharnhorst, *published by Albin Michel in 1931, and Jean receives a
detailed letter of the specific complaints.*

To Albin Michel and Jean des Vallières

[June] 1937
Meudon-Bellevue

ORIGINS OF SCENES FROM LA GRANDE ILLUSION
CALLED INTO QUESTION BY ALBIN MICHEL &
DES VALLIERES

In the book

1 – A French aircraft is shot
down. The pilot is received by the
German officers (a very
exceptional event). They have
lunch.

2 – He is surprised that one of the
German officers speaks fluent
French; the one in question
replies that he was a mechanic at
Blériot.

Origins

1 – Fact recounted to Charles
Spaak[1] by Fonck, Hervitaux, and
Gerlich, wartime aviators with
whom he had been in contact to
study the possibilities of a film on
dogfights during the war.

2– On this point, I must respond
by invoking the general subject of
the film *La Grande Illusion*. The
goal of this film is not to describe
the life of French prisoners in
German camps during the war.
It is a confrontation between
different types of men. Using the
world of the prisoner of war
camps appeared to us an
excellent way of revealing the
characters.
The President of the League of

[31]

Wartime Escapees, Mr Richard, and a commission of escapees, with whom we had important discussions before starting the film, know this very well as we agreed with them that the scenes which later would allow Commandant Von Rauffenstein and Capt de Boeldieu to confront each other had no place in a purely documentary account of the lives of prisoners. But given the nature of the film, knowing the measure of the different types of humanity at a certain epoch, they considered this scene perfectly valid in the film. Consequently when it was a question of presenting in the German camp opposing types brought together in groups, we found it necessary to show a contrast in the characters of the two officers, at the same time noblemen and career officers. Given that we were dealing with the air force it was inevitable that we would set on each side of the scale two former mechanics. And, given that in a French film, a pretext must be found to have the actors speak in a language understandable to the audience, we had imagined that the German had worked in France. I must say that many similar facts have been reported to me and, when I was myself a prisoner of the Germans for three weeks during the battle of the Marne, I

3 – Each of the German officers tells of French aircraft that he has shot down. (In the film, they bring out a wreath of honour for a French crew which has been shot down.)
4 – Transfers to the interior of Germany, searches . . .

5 – In a series of camps and barracks, the characters include: An actor from the Odéon, a Roads and Bridges engineer, a Russian with whom one of the Frenchmen had walked in the courtyard, a real Street Parisian etc.

saw how in the hospital ward at Amiens where I was recovering, two former mechanics, one French, the other German, discovered that they had worked at the same factory in France without ever having met, and exchanged memories in common. I don't think that his account can constitute a monopoly.
3 – Memories of the German ace Von Richtoffen [sic].

4 – About fifty accounts from fifty comrades who had been prisoners. In particular, the account of Mr Buno-Varilla [sic].
5 – As for the actor, we really couldn't use our comrade Maurice Chevalier.[2]
As for the other professions, they were composed from a thousand conversations with comrades who had lived these lives, and by taking account of the usual kinds of officers found in every country in the world.
What's more, there isn't a Russian in our barracks. We have them in the camp because it would have been inaccurate to show a prison camp without Russians. As for the deceived husband, I prefer to believe for the honour of French wives that this rare exception was the pure invention of both Mr des Vallières and ourselves.

6 – Construction of an escape tunnel (under the direction of the engineer).

6 – Formal account of Col. Pinsard and a reading of the documented account in the book by Lieutenant Bastain, *My Ten Escapes*. Speaking of this book, I should say what valuable reading it was for the preparation of our work.

7 – Trapdoor in the floor of the Gymnasium (in the film the floor of the barracks).

7 – See 6.

8 – Description of the work and suffocation in the tunnel. The plan fails through discovery (in the film, the plan fails because of a change of camps).

8 – See 6.

9 – Scenes of the distribution of parcels and their being opened.

9 – Reported by Mr Aget, former prisoner of war, who in his concentration camp had been forced to help the sub-officer responsible for the distribution of parcels.

10 – Scene of the camp theatre in a camp where there are a majority of English prisoners and some of them dress up as girls.

10 – Account of Mr Spaak, Belgian Minister of Foreign Affairs, brother of the co-author and a prisoner during the war.

11 – Successive changes of camp with various escapes, for which the repeat offenders are placed in an especially secure camp from which they will not be able to escape.

11 – See any account by any prisoner of war.

12 – Record or descriptions of different types of escapes which the officers have tried: as German soldiers, as women, hiding in dirty laundry. (In the film, recalled in the course of the reception given by the commandant.)

12 – Type of reception cited several times by some prisoners, notably by Mr Buno-Varilla [sic]. Equally to be found in Lieutenant Bastin's book.
The escape attempts cited in this scene are similar to some famous cases and are cited by everyone. In this scene, we mention several others.

[34]

13 – The *Kavalier Scharnhorst* fortress was the only one of its kind in Germany, created especially for the troublemakers and the repeat escapees.

13 – This analogy stemmed, without a doubt, from the fact that this type of reprisal camp had really existed in Germany and this is well known by all prisoners.

Besides, the fortress in the film, even if it is equally designated to serve as a reprisal camp, had nothing in common with the *Kavalier Scharnhorst*. Instead, it resembles a castle in Southern Germany which several prisoners had spoken of to us.

Whereas, if I'm not mistaken, the *Kavalier Scharnhorst* is a fortress in the style of Vauban.[3]

14 – New searches.

14 – See 4.

15 – The camp commandant evokes Montmartre and the women.

15 – Account of my personal friend, the Uhlan[4] Captain Alfred Flechteim, who, in meeting French prisoners in Belgium, had immediately asked them about Maxim's.

16 – He wears jewels with a gaudy affectation that shows bad taste.

16 – Commandant Von Rauffenstein's costume (which I found in excellent taste) was put together by Mr Von Stroheim[5] according to precise documentation. 1 – from the personal memory of a former Austrian officer; 2 – From the memoirs of the German ace Von Richtoffen [sic]. The chain he wears on his arm personally belongs to Mr Von Stroheim. He wore a similar one when he was an officer.

[35]

17 – A character seen: an entomologist studying butterflies (in the film: a scholar translating Pindar).

17 – Remembrance of my cousin Edmond Renoir, a schoolteacher in Versailles, who was not a prisoner but who, despite the contingencies of wartime, never ceased to translate writers even more secret than Pindar.

18 – Belligerent and rebellious attitude of the officers who ridicule the guards and plot escapes.

18 – How could it be otherwise?

19 – The episode of the fire started by the officers and the alarm given by the *boche* guard.

19 – This episode was recounted to me by Dr Zederbaum, former doctor-major in the Russian army. What's more, in our film, there is no '*boche*' guard; there is a *German* guard, which has no connection, and indicates the profound difference between the book and the film.

20 – Organization of monstrous din with boxes, pans and anything with which one might make a noise, to try the patience of the Germans. Several escapes.

20 – Authentic story, related by several escapees and approved by the representatives of the League of Escapees.
We asked these men the question: Are the remembrances of these escapees exaggerated, or is this act of provocation realistic as presented in our film? They responded favourably.

21 – The same chronological sequence of events in the book and the film show that the latter etc . . .

21 – How could the chronological sequence of events in the life of an officer prisoner be very different from the chronological sequence of events in the life of all the other prisoners?

22 – For example, the effect of the word *verboten*; the surprise that the Germans didn't pillage the tins of food. The reflection 'it's my duty' by the German who torments the officers.

22 – For *verboten*, remembrance of the brother of Mr Matras, cameraman on the film. The rest from documentation by Mr Koch, former artillery lieutenant in the German Army, and assistant on the film on matters concerning the German atmosphere.

23 – Various types of officers who indulge in minor activities, studying maps. The same scenes of camp life, roll-call, food, town bells sounding the victories (effect on the prisoners), same setting of the escape preparations, of the idleness and the feverish activity of the officers during the last hours, the incidents of escapes, etc. . . . etc . . .

23 – I'm not able to state exactly the origins of the information cited opposite. I think that almost all of the wartime escapees consulted had given it to us.

CONCLUSION

Our principal sources are: the remembrances of Colonel Pinsard, Mr Aget, Mr Buno-Varilla [sic], Mr Spaak, brother of the co-author, Mr Gaudet and the members of the League of Escapees who did us the kindness of verifying our work and allowed us, through their memories, to realize in this film a sufficiently exact atmosphere for Mr des Vallières to find the details of what he had experienced.

Amongst these men, allow me to cite Mr Etevenon, who was kind enough to furnish us with written notes which we drew on a lot; and I must add that, on the advice of the President of the League of Escapees, Mr Richard, we used Lieutenant Bastin's book *My Ten Escapes* to check the exactitude of all the events presented in the film.

What's more, throughout the writing of the screenplay, the shooting of the film and the editing, we had the constant collaboration of Mr Karl Koch [sic], former lieutenant in the German Army, who furnished us with all the details necessary for the exact reconstruction of the German atmosphere during the war.

I think that, although other people could bear witness to our good faith, it would suffice to cite one of the members of the League of

Escapees who studied with us, point by point, our shooting script, which helped us make quite a few modifications, giving the film a certain authenticity. Besides, it was these gentlemen who advised us to read *Kavalier Scharnhorst* by Mr des Vallières, a book which neither Mr Spaak nor I knew. We have glanced through it to satisfy our conscience, but whatever the coincidences indicated by Messrs Albin Michel and des Vallières, I affirm that all the incriminating facts were acquired elsewhere.

Moreover, as I have already said earlier, our film is not a film about escapes. If it were, we would have given it a much greater documentary exactitude. It's the story of a conflict between men, and we have situated this action in a group of German prisons during the war.

Out of respect for the men who suffered in these prisons, we wanted this framework to be reconstructed with the greatest possible exactitude. From great desire for documentation and our research, we finally arrived at a knowledge of events similar to those related by Mr des Vallières.

It must not be forgotten that the life of prisoners of war was extremely limited and that the witnesses whom we interviewed had sometimes, no doubt, lived through the same experiences as Mr des Vallières.

[Jean Renoir]

1 Charles Spaak (1903–75), screenwriter who co-scripted with Jean Renoir *Les Bas-Fonds* and *La Grande Illusion*. He also wrote *La Kermesse Héroique* (Jacques Feyder, 1935), *La Belle Equipe* (Julien Duvivier, 1936), and many others.
2 Maurice Chevalier (1888–1972), entertainer and actor, whose films included *The Love Parade* (Ernst Lubitsch, 1929), *A Bedtime Story* (Norman Taurog, 1933), and *Gigi* (Vincente Minnelli, 1958).
3 Vauban, military engineer and architect.
4 German cavalryman.
5 Erich Von Stroheim (1885–1957), director whose films included *Foolish Wives* (1922), *The Merry Widow* (1925) and *Greed* (1925). As an actor: *La Grande Illusion* and *Sunset Boulevard* (Billy Wilder, 1950).

To Louis Aragon[1]
Ce Soir
Paris

25 June 1937
Paris

My dear Aragon,

Something rather troubling has happened to me. I apologize for speaking to you about it but I believe it's an attack on me more general than mere blackmail.

I based *La Grande Illusion* on the stories which my comrades had told me about their captivity. Their accounts moved me, and together with

Spaak, we fashioned a screenplay. Moreover, Spaak for his part had some reminiscences from his brother, a Belgian minister who had been imprisoned during the war.

The right-wing newspapers *Candide, Action Française*, etc ... noted the success of this film, but with reservations, astonished to see an individual considered a dangerous revolutionary take on a national subject and shape it into a form which appeals to the majority of audiences of all political opinions.

In some of the newspapers (I believe in an article by young Fayard) an allusion had been vaguely made to the fact that I had, perhaps, drawn my documentation from a book by a friend of Fayard called Desvallières [sic]. This allusion made me seem ridiculous, because the book by Desvallières (*Kavalier Scharnhorst*) is a rather hateful book, written in a spirit of mean and narrow-minded nationalism, in which he speaks of '*boches*'. Whereas I did everything possible to make a film which, by being totally national, would be absolutely international.

Naturally, I also recount certain stories that Desvallières recounted, for the simple reason that they are true stories, and these true stories are just a few of dozens of examples which have been told over and over again in prisoner of war camps and which are very similar.

Now the threat is becoming clear: Desvallières is accusing me of plagiarism! I am naturally going to defend myself, and my producers have decided to sue him for blackmail as well as his publisher, Albin Michel.

The incriminating events are true events, therefore in the public domain, and Mr Desvallières has absolutely no reason to lay claim to them exclusively, any more than the prisoners to whom these experiences happened and who recounted them to me.

I believe that you understand the danger:

1 – Desvallières, who is a former prisoner, regards everything involving prisoners of war as belong to him;

2 – His friends from *Candide, Gringoire, L'Action Française*, are only too happy to support him in his attempt to prove that an author classified as left-wing can't produce a national subject without stealing it from them.

In conclusion, once again, it's a question of insinuating that all which is national (La Marseillaise, the Unknown Soldier, prisoners of war in this case) belongs exclusively to the fascists.

My dear friend, I don't know what is going to become of this whole affair, but if need be I will ask you for advice.

[39]

Give my best to your wife and see you soon.

Jean Renoir

1 Louis Aragon (1897–1982), early Surrealist and novelist (*Le Paysan de Paris*, 1926) who was also director of the Communist weekly *Ce Soir*, for which Jean Renoir contributed regular articles in 1937.

To Mr Rappoport [1]   29 June 1937
                                                          Paris

Dear Sir,

Here is the little work you asked me for.

For witnesses, up to now I have only found a few members of the League of Escapees, but I think that, given the seriousness of this League, their testimony will carry considerable weight.

Many of these gentlemen are willing to affirm that they had read our screenplay before it was filmed, that they criticized it, that they led us to make some judicious changes and that, during this collaboration, they didn't think for an instant about any similarity to *Kavalier Scharnhorst*.

The author of the book, Mr des Vallières, being part of this League, knows that these gentlemen would not fail to indicate anything that they thought, with the release of this film, would harm the interests of their comrades.

With my sincere regards,

Jean Renoir

1 Lawyer representing Jean Renoir.

To André Hirschmann[1]   2 July 1937

Dear friend,

I discovered the following in the 25 June *Paris Soir*:

'Four French films have just been banned by the Yugoslav censors: *Marthe Richard*,[2] *La Grande Ilusion*, *L'Homme à abattre*[3], *Soeurs d'Armes*,[4] without doubt because these four productions deal with the Great War and counter-espionage.'

Although it is a little late, perhaps we could respond.

1 – Say that *La Grande Illusion* has nothing at all to do with counter-espionage films.

2 – If this decision by the Yugoslav censors is wrong, refute it.

I'm writing to you because I think it is always worth taking any opportunity to talk about a film in the newspapers.

Best regards,

Jean Renoir

1 Film publicist.
2 *Marthe Richard au Service de La France* (Raymond Bernard, 1937).
3 *L'Homme à abattre* (*The Marked Man*) (Léon Mathot, 1936).
4 *Soeurs d'Armes* (Léon Poirier, 1937).

To Mr Rappoport   *10 July 1937*

Dear Sir,

I managed to contact Mr Etevenon of the League of War Escapees. He passed on to me an article he wrote about *La Grande Illusion* which proves that, within the circle of war escapees, they don't think that *La Grande Illusion* plagiarizes *Kavalier Scharnhorst*. I'm passing this article, of which I'm keeping a copy, on to you so that you'll have it before Monday. Mr Etevenon has also given me several examples from the newspaper *L'Evadé* which could be helpful to us.

As he works for a large company, he isn't sure if he can come in person on Tuesday morning to the hearing. But he asks me to call him instead and maybe he will be able to join us around 11 o'clock, if the arbitration hasn't already ended.

Mr Bunau-Varilla, who gave us some other details about his own escape, will testify.

I wasn't able to meet up with Colonel Pinsard, who is on military exercises, but Mr Gaut,[1] the former officer who introduced him to me, will testify; he will be able to give a very precise idea of Pinsard's account which constitutes the principal framework of *La Grande Illusion*.

I am also writing to Mr Aget, a war escapee who is in Paris and who has given us some other information, as well as putting us in touch with the League of Escapees. I don't know yet if he'll be able to testify.

Yours sincerely,

Jean Renoir

1 Pierre Gaut was the producer of *Toni*.

To Edouard Aget[1]

Dear Mr Aget,

Have you received my letter advising you to get in direct contact with Mr Rollmer Sr?[2] Believe me, if you haven't already done so, you should speak to him about your meeting. In case you did not get my letter, I will remind you of the address and telephone number of his office: RAC, 19 rue de Lisbonne, Paris VIIIème – Telephone: Laborde 85–84 and 85. You'll have a better chance of finding him in the morning around eleven o'clock or late in the afternoon.

This isn't the only reason I am writing to you, but also because we are going into arbitration about our disagreement with Mr Albin Michel and des Vallières.

I believe that you are in the know about this? Spaak told me that Gabin[3] spoke to you about it. It's a very simple thing: these gentlemen think that we have drawn the details of our film from the book *Kavalier Scharnhorst*. We want to prove our good faith by affirming that we drew our information, not from the book, but from absolutely direct sources. I already have with me the best witness to the story, Colonel Pinsard himself, whose story I closely followed in *La Grande Illusion*.

Would you be able to do us the kindness of testifying that we had dealings with you and subsequently, through your intermediary, several members of the League of Escapees and that you yourself and these gentlemen had some conversations with us about the life of Allied prisoners in Germany during the war? This would add to the testimony of Pinsard.

The person who has been most surprised by this whole ridiculous affair is Pinsard, because all of his officers who have seen the film constantly tell him: 'Colonel, we just saw you on the screen.'

I understand the feelings of des Vallières, who believes that the release of *La Grande Illusion* is going to prevent him from selling the film rights of his book *Kavalier Scharnhorst*. But he is wrong, because in his very richly documented book there is enough to make a good half-dozen films which are very different from *La Grande Illusion*.

He is also wrong because his actions could lead one to suppose that what he recounted was invented. We are simply among that large group of authors, of both film and books, who have based our work on accounts of real events, which, because they are real, are in the public domain. The lives of prisoners of war no more belong to des Vallières than to d'Harcourt, Bastaing or to many others who told their own adventures, or those of their comrades. They belong to history.

I apologise, dear Mr Aget, for these long digressions. It's only to tell you that Spaak and I would be very happy if you could leave your business for a moment, though it may not be convenient, and tell the arbitrators about this difference of opinion, what you know about it.

This arbitration[4] will take place on Tuesday, 13 July at 9.30 in the morning, at the Société des Auteurs, 9 rue Ballu, Paris IXème. If you cannot come, could you please send me a letter in your place? It would not be as valuable as your presence, but since you are so busy, it may be too difficult for you to get away.

Thanking you in advance and with my best regards.

Jean Renoir

1 Prisoner of war in World War One who contributed ideas to *La Grande Illusion*.
2 Frank Rollmer, producer at RAC (Réalisation d'Art Cinématographique) who produced *La Grande Illusion* and distributed *La Marseillaise*.
3 Jean Gabin (1904–76), actor in Jean Renoir's *Les Bas-Fonds, La Grande Illusion* and *French Cancan*. His other major roles were in *La Belle Equipe* (Julien Duvivier, 1936), *Pépé le Moko* (Julien Duvivier, 1937), *Quai des Brumes* (Marcel Carné, 1938), *Le Jour se Lève* (Marcel Carné, 1939), and many films in the 1950s and 1960s.
4 The decision of the court on 28 July was that the film was not even a partial plagiarism of the book by des Vallières.

Filming begins on La Marseillaise *in September. Commissioned by the Communist trade union, the* CGT, *the film is partly financed by public subscription.*

[43]

1938

To Jean Rollmer[1]
Société RAC

31 January 1938
Paris

Sir,

In the course of several discussions with your publicity services, I have decided that I must call to the attention of those responsible the fact that the public loathes films which are called 'historical', and that any advertising which makes the public believe that *La Marseillaise* could be classified in this category is not, I believe, in the best interest of the film.

Since filming ended I have, in all my discussions and the different articles I have published, constantly defended this point of view. Thus, the posters that I saw today in vast numbers on the walls of Paris in my opinion reinforce the idea that *La Marseillaise* will be a so-called historical epic, that it to say, it will belong to a genre that the public, for good reason, detests.

Moreover, it seems to me that some of the posters are of inferior artistic quality. They portray characters who are inhumane, unpleasant and pompous. Whereas, in the film, we tried to show humane, likeable and unaffected characters.

Since all this publicity is working against the interests of the film, I insist, as someone whose public career is only just beginning, on telling you of my impressions, and protesting against this publicity which I believe is harmful to our common interests.

Yours sincerely,
Jean Renoir

1 Son of Frank Rollmer.

To André Hirschmann
16 February 1938
Paris

My dear Hirschmann,

I am so sorry that you worried yourself needlessly over this old business. I would be ungrateful if, on the pretext that our tastes had for an instant differed on a small detail, I were to forget the enormous amount of work that you put in, and the wonderful results you obtained.

I hope to have the pleasure of seeing you soon. Maybe we could meet one night for dinner, with my brother Claude, and we would talk not about *La Marseillaise*, but about the next film, which for me is much more interesting.

I send you many thanks for the care and attention you took on my behalf with this specially-drawn programme. I am very touched by it.

Sincerely,

Jean Renoir

Telegram to Albert Pinkevitch[1]   *17 February 1938*
Hotel Lafayette
New York

NEW VERSION[2] READY MONDAY HAVE CUT ABOUT 700 METRES STOP REMOVING SECOND PART VERSAILLES ENTIRE SECOND REEL AND BEGINNING TUILERIES TOCSIN UP TO SHOT [OF] THE QUEEN AND LA CHESNAYE EXPLAINING DEFENCE BY WINDOW

LOTS OF LOVE

JEAN

1 Co-producer at RAC of *La Grande Illusion* and distributor of *La Marseillaise*. For description, see *My Life and My Films*.
2 New version of *La Marseillaise*.

Telegram to Albert Pinkevitch   *19 February 1938*
Beverly Wilshire Hotel   *Paris*
Beverly Hills

RAC INCAPABLE [OF] DEFENDING MARSEILLAISE VIOLENTLY ATTACKED BY RIGHT WING PRESS STOP ILL WILL AND BACKING OUT STOP RAC ATTITUDE WILL FORCE ME PERHAPS TO SIGN AGREEMENT ELSEWHERE STOP DYING TO KNOW ABOUT YOUR PROJECTS

LOTS OF LOVE

JEAN

Telegram to Albert Pinkevitch   *23 February 1938*
Beverly Wilshire Hotel
Beverly Hills

HAVE ALREADY ABANDONED SEA RESCUE SUBJECT STOP WORKING
ON ORIGINAL SCREENPLAY DARDANELLES WAR ADVENTURE RE-
COUNTED BY SAILORS [FROM] ANTIBES STOP WHEN ARE YOU COM-
ING BACK
    LOVE
    JEAN

To Frank Rollmer   *5 March 1938*
                           Paris

Dear Mr Rollmer,

I hope that you have received my letters of 31 January and 21 February.

I would be particularly happy if you could answer the question concerning English rights for *La Grande Illusion*.

I write to you today to keep you up to date about the state of my work and that of my collaborators.

After Albert left, we worked on a subject which he asked us to look at, knowing that a screenplay could serve the cause of Peace. Applying ourselves to this goal, we had found a maritime story that Albert, who was familiar with it, asked us to abandon. I suppose the reason for this change of plan has something to do with the state of his negotiations in America; he must have been obliged to alter his intentions, because in the same telegram he asked us to think about a small subject, a drama or a comedy.

Having nothing of this sort in my mind, we proposed looking at a subject which we had previously discussed in Antibes, and which he had agreed with, which took place during the war either in Salonica or the Dardanelles.

He replied by telegram saying that he accepted the idea, although the general story line seemed a little complicated to him.

Since exchanging telegrams, we now think it's better to forget such a huge undertaking, and to try to present to the public an adventure on a smaller scale than *La Grande Illusion* or *La Marseillaise*.

After having looked at different projects, we decided on two which seemed superior to the others.

The first is *Diary of a Chambermaid*[1] by Octave Mirbeau, a project which I worked on before with Mr Koch.

Naturally the treatment we made didn't follow all of Mirbeau's plot – though the original work didn't have much plot anyway. We contented ourselves with using certain major characters and certain first-rate situations throughout a story which we composed ourselves, but put off finishing until later; if, when Albert returns, you decide that this project is interesting, we must first work on acquiring the rights.

The second project is an original story. That doesn't mean that it won't be necessary to buy some rights to have peace of mind and not risk what happened with *La Grande Illusion*. In fact, there is an analogy between our story and a silent American film by the German director MURNAU[2] which previously had been very successful under the title of *Sunrise*. This film was based on a novel by SUDERMAN, entitled *The Journey to Tilsit*. Nevertheless, even if a lawyer advises us to acquire these rights, it's less important than securing those for *Diary of a Chambermaid* by Octave Mirbeau.

We think that we can work on this story. If, when Albert returns, it doesn't please you, I will keep it for myself, and I will be ready to look at something else with you.

It's a drama about love in the country. The action happens amongst simple peasants. There's a section that takes place in a large city, at a fun fair. It could be advantageous to situate this story in the Midi. This is why my collaborators and I thought that our work would perhaps be more productive if we were to continue with it there. All the more because, so far, the publicity for *La Marseillaise*: articles, press conferences, radio, has taken up a lot of my time; my life in Paris has often been disrupted, so that I have trouble working there; and in the country I will have a better opportunity, with the help of my collaborators, of starting quickly on the work, which we want to show you very soon.

With my best regards,
Jean Renoir

1 *Le Journal d'une Femme de Chambre*, written by Octave Mirbeau (1850–1917) in 1900. Jean Renoir eventually filmed his version in Hollywood in 1946; Luis Buñuel filmed a very different adaptation in France in 1964.
2 F. W. Murnau (1888–1931), German director famous for *Nosferatu* (1922) and *The Last Laugh* (1924), who left his homeland for Hollywood, where he made *Sunrise* (1927).

To Frank Rollmer

5 *March 1938*
Paris

Dear Mr Rollmer,

I am enclosing a letter from Hollywood which might interest you. It is interesting because it proves that people over there, who are not blinded by the mean little political campaigns here, saw nothing tendentious in this film.

Sincerely yours,
Jean Renoir

To Samuel Goldwyn[1]
United Artists
Hollywood

7 *March 1938*
Paris

Dear Mr Goldwyn,

I was overcome by your proposition that I should work at your studio. I am very flattered that you thought of me, and I thank you for it.

I am unable to accept your friendly invitation because I am under contract to Mr Albert PINKEVITCH, for whom, moreover, I am shortly going to start a film.

My best regards.
Jean Renoir

1 Noted Hollywood producer Sam Goldwyn (1882–1974) was responsible for such films as *Dodsworth* (William Wyler, 1936), *Stella Dallas* (King Vidor, 1937), *The Little Foxes* (William Wyler, 1941), and *The Best Years of Our Lives* (William Wyler, 1946).

In August, Jean Renoir begins filming La Bête Humaine, *based on the novel by Emile Zola, at Billancourt studios and on location at the Gare St Lazare in Paris, and Le Havre. The production company is Paris Film Production (Robert Hakim).*

To Mr Cornet
Station Master, Le Havre

6 *September 1938*
Paris

Dear Sir,

This little note is to tell you that, thanks to your kindness, we have been able to film some very interesting shots at Le Havre railway station.

We are starting work at the studio, and we have a month and a half to go before finishing the film.

Enclosed is a small clipping from *Ce Soir* that I wrote to let the mechanics who helped us so much know that we had no part in the stupidities published in certain newspapers.

Yours sincerely,
Jean Renoir

To Mr Reverdy[1]

6 September 1938
Paris

My dear Reverdy,

Have a good rest. I believe that we are going to start the Le Havre Depot Refectory scene on Monday. Of course your advice would be indispensable in this matter. Before that, I am going to shoot the dance. But I suspect that a railwaymen's ball looks very much like any other ball, and the scenes that I shoot there will above all deal with the emotional states of Lantier and Séverine.

I am sending you the issue of *Ce Soir* in which I published a small rectification of the absurdities in *Paris Soir*. If you think that I should send it to some of your comrades, you only have to give me their names and addresses.

See you soon, my dear Comrade.

Best wishes,
Jean Renoir

1 Presumably an employee at Le Havre railway station.

Prior to the signing of the Munich agreement on 30 September, the atmosphere in Europe suggests war is imminent, and Jean Renoir reacts accordingly.

To Mr Daladier[1]

14 September 1938
Paris

Dear Minister,

I beg leave to request admission to the army film corps.

In the event of war, I must rejoin the cavalry as a lieutenant of the 4th division in ALENÇON. I am forty-four years old and was wounded in the last war, and finished behind the lines. I seriously fear that my physical state and my age will affect my performance in almost any capacity. I never finished my tour of duty, and my military knowledge has deteriorated to next to nothing. In the current situation, I therefore risk giving a rather poor service to my country.

On the other hand, I am extremely familiar with the cinema. For more than fifteen years my life has been totally devoted to this profession. I have done art direction, camera work; I was an electrician, and I was the first in France to manufacture lighting equipment for use with panchromatic film. I've done trick effects and I know a little about laboratory work. Allow me to list some of the films I've done since 1925 as author or director: *Nana* – *Le Tournoi dans la Cité* – *La Petite Marchande d'Allumettes* – *La Chienne* – *Les Bas-Fonds* – *La Grande Illusion* – *La Marseillaise*.

At the moment, I am at Joinville studios where I am filming an adaptation of Zola's[2] *La Bête Humaine*.

I have the firm conviction that I can usefully serve my country with my camera. Moreover, I have always been excited by the idea of shooting documentary footage in wartime at the front. This is why I'm drawing your attention to my case.

Respectfully yours,

Jean Renoir

---

1 Edouard Daladier (1884–1970), Minister of War in 1938, had been leader of the Radical party and Premier three times during the 1930s. He was ousted from power in March 1940.
2 Emile Zola (1840–1902), author of *L'Assommoir* (1877), *Nana* (1880) and *La Bête Humaine* (1890).

To Raymond Blondy[1]

20 September 1938
Paris

My dear Raymond Blondy,

Further to our conversation yesterday, I agree to consider, as far as my affairs will allow me at this time, collaborating on the script for the film *Chicago Frenchman*[2] (working title), which Jacques BECKER[3] will direct by next November on behalf of 'HAUSSMAN FILMS'.

Failing that, I will be happy to help the début of my assistant Jacques Becker by giving my patronage and advice as a sort of supervisor for his film.

In either case, you may mention my name in the ads for the film's release and eventually in the credits.

Concerning my remuneration, I accept the offer, made in the name of 'HAUSSMAN FILMS', to pay me: -

In the first case (collaboration on the script and dialogue), a sum of *25,000 frs* (twenty-five thousand francs) in cash, and *25,000 frs* (twenty-five thousand francs) in a 'HAUSSMAN FILMS' draft (a total of fifty thousand francs).

In the second case (simple supervision of the film), a sum of *25,000 frs* (twenty-five thousand francs) in cash.

These terms obviously do not correspond to those which are usually made for me by producers; however, on the understanding that they remain confidential between us, I willingly subscribe to them in order to help my friend Jacques BECKER start his career as a director.

I add that all that's been written in this letter is valid only if the film is directed by Jacques BECKER, and only by him.

I look forward to the confirmation by 'HAUSSMAN FILMS' so that the definitive agreement can be signed.

Sincerely yours,

[Jean Renoir]

1 Production manager on *La Grande Illusion*.
2 An unrealized project. Becker repudiated his first film as director – *Tête de Turc* in 1935 – and his first completed feature was *Le Dernier Atout* (1942).
3 Jacques Becker (1906–60) graduated from being Jean Renoir's first assistant to make some important films, such as *Casque d'Or* (1952), *Touchez Pas au Grisbi* (1954) and *Le Trou* (1960).

To Maurice Leblond[1]

22 November 1938
Meudon

My dear friend,

Thank you for thinking of sending me the photograph of Emile ZOLA on the train. It's an excellent idea to have it published as you indicate. I am going to take care of it.

I am very happy and proud that the few words I was able to say the other night interested people. It's a great joy for me to have participated in this ceremony.[2]

La Bête Humaine will not be released as soon as we thought. I am still editing, surrounded by tiny pieces of film. The music isn't composed yet, and there's still a lot of work to do on the sound. Of course, we are going as quickly as we can, but it will take a miracle for us to be ready before 25 December.

As soon as I'm able to project the entire film, I will let you and Madame Leblond know, and perhaps we will be able to arrange a screening together at your convenience.

In about eight days, I will be a little more calm, and I hope that we'll be able to see each other.

My warm regards, and please give my respects to Madame Leblond-Zola.

Jean Renoir

1 Writer and husband of Denise Zola, daughter of the author. She wrote the titles for Jean Renoir's film of *Nana*, and collaborated on the script of *La Bête Humaine*.
2 Jean Renoir had given a short lecture to the Zola Society in November 1938 at the Sorbonne.

In November, Jean Renoir sets up his own production company, La Nouvelle Edition Française ('NEF'), with Claude Renoir Sr, Camille François, Andre Zwoboda and Olivier Billou. La Bête Humaine opens in Paris on 29 December, and is an immediate box-office hit.

9   The trade announcement of the filming of *La Règle du Jeu*

10 Robert Flaherty

1939

In January, Jean Renoir goes to Marlotte to work on the screenplay of La Règle du Jeu *with Carl Koch and Camille François. At the end of the month, he goes to London, where he meets the documentary film-maker Robert Flaherty. In February, filming on* La Règle du Jeu *begins at Sologne, and is completed in June. The script girl on the film is Dido Freire (1907–1990), with whom he has fallen in love.*

To Robert Flaherty[1] [*Original in English*]   *14 February 1939*
Chelsea, London   *Brinon-sur-Sauldre*

Dear Flaherty,

I left Paris on Monday afternoon and am now in Sologne with Jean Renoir.

We have been talking about you a great deal and Jean Renoir has told me his opinion on the best way to produce in France your tiger story.

The Gaumont Company are very much interested in any film produced by you.

Concerning the possibility of giving money in advance, it is probable they shall wait until the film Jean Renoir is starting now has been shown. Not because they are short of capital, but because it is the first time they have done this sort of thing, and they are wanting some results of this first experience before starting on anything else of the kind.

Jean Renoir also tells me he hopes that in a few months his film Company, 'La NEF',[2] will be stronger, and when that happens he will gladly help you himself. Also Mr Jay, Director of the Gaumont Company, who has great confidence in 'La NEF', will be able, at that moment, to do what it is impossible, as far as capital is concerned, to do at the present moment.

In short, Jean Renoir thinks that he is unable to help you a great deal just now, but he hopes to do so in a few months' time, arranging for your film to be distributed by 'La NEF', who would bring to you their knowledge of the French circuits and so on.

If they did that now, it would not be to the best of your interests, as their positions will only be really strong after their first film has been shown.

If you could first produce a film in England, the story of the Boy and the Pony, for instance, it would give us time to talk of our prospects of collaboration at a later date, on firmer ground.

In any case, Jean Renoir's collaborators all agree to work in conjunction with you as soon as they are certain to be able to do so.

Jean Renoir very much regretted to have to leave Paris while you were there.

As regards TECHNICOLOR,[3] Jean Renoir tells me he starts his next film in 8 days time.[4] It would be a marvellous subject for a colour film, particularly as La Sologne is a unique country to be shown in colour during the winter months. If TECHNICOLOR wishes to take an interest in the film, paying all extra expenses that add up to an ordinary black and white film, (technical, extra number of collaborators, added length of time for actors, studio, technicians, etc.) and if TECHNICOLOR can be ready to start work in one week's time in Paris, Jean Renoir would agree to the arrangement. But he fears the delay is too short. Such important concerns need a long time to act, they are not like the 'NEF', where everything is done quickly.

Jean Renoir would be very happy if in the near future you could work with us, and 'La NEF' would be very proud to add the name of Flaherty to that of Jean Renoir.

On 20 February we start working at the Pathé Studios in Joinville, and when you come to Paris, please consider it as belonging to you, and come to see us.

With best regards from Jean Renoir.

Affectionately,

Dido Freire

1 Robert Flaherty (1884–1951) was one of the most influential documentary film-makers in the history of cinema. His films included *Nanook of the North* (1922), *Moana* (1926), *Tabu* (co-directed with F. W. Murnau, 1933), *Man of Aran* (1934) and *Louisiana Story* (1948).
2 La Nouvelle Edition Française.
3 Technicolor, in its full-colour glory, was first used in *Becky Sharp* (Rouben Mamoulian, 1935). At this time it was necessary to hire the equipment from Technicolor, and have one of their advisers in attendance on set.
4 *La Règle du Jeu.*

To Dido Freire [*Original in English*]   *20 February 1939*
Paris   *London*

My dear Dido,

To begin with please thank Jean Renoir for the most interesting letter he has written to me through you. I shall watch the progress of his film company, la 'NEF' with the greatest interest. It will be marvellous if he can develop the kind of distribution that will allow one to make the films one wants to do.

I am going to go ahead with the coal mine-boy and pony picture. It looks fairly certain now that the money will be obtained for it within the next week or so. By the time I have completed this picture, I shall look forward eagerly to joining you all in France.

I believe that today is the day you start your production. My best wishes go with it. You will be hearing from me from time to time, and the first news will be, I hope, that my own film has started.

With all good wishes to Jean Renoir and to yourself.

As ever,

Robert Flaherty

To Camille François[1]   *1 June 1939*

My dear Camille,

CLAUDE[2] has kept you abreast of the various thoughts I've recently been having, along with my production assistant, concerning the film we are completing, *La Règle du Jeu*, and our future work.

With regard to *La Règle du Jeu*, I believe that we have made a good film; in any case, it is finished, and that, in part, is thanks to your courage and that of Olivier BILLOU. Nevertheless, we are in a line of work where there is never a complete victory, and where one must be sure of the trump cards in the next hand before laying down all the cards from the previous one.

Now that I am more relaxed and can reflect upon the work we've done, I believe I can tell you that from a production point of view, everything worked out very well. The bad weather made us go over budget, but there was nothing we could do, and no human power exists which could have enabled us to get around this grave inconvenience. At all events, none of our collaborators, all of whom carried out their jobs magnificently, are at fault. It's even possible that, in good conditions, the way they work would have enabled us to make a film for below the usual

11 Jean Renoir with his assistant and script girl, Dido Freire, on location for
La Règle du Jeu

cost. The only error that I can point out was mine. This was to have agreed to write the script for *L'Or du Cristobal*,[3] which delayed the script of *La Règle du Jeu* and made us start out with an incomplete draft. This draft wasn't good; I had to do several revisions during the shooting, and if *La Règle du Jeu* is not well received by the public, I think we must attribute it to that alone. It's a lesson for next time: we must never again start without being thoroughly prepared.

There are still some pieces to shoot. After the first screening of the film, my collaborators and I were convinced that the characters in the film are not justifiable to the public without these details.

That takes care of the past. As far as the future is concerned, my problem is to set up, as quickly as possible, a big film in colour. Colour, at the present time, is the biggest problem: foreigners will beat us to it if we don't take stock quickly.

On the other hand, I have been devoting myself to an examination of my situation. The fact is, I feel that, at my age, I am no longer a youngster still with the power to undertake projects in the hope of making money, but a man who has worked for fifteen years and is obliged to live off the proceeds from past efforts. Nothing is for ever, and I'm no longer at a point in my life when one can count on the future. Because of that, with my next film I must make some money.

On the other hand, if we want to guarantee a budget for a film in colour, we will need a very expensive star. Combining all these elements (which seem to me necessary): colour, my salary and a big star, means that the film that I must do now will have to be a big budget film.

Therefore you must seriously examine the situation, and choose between two lines of action:

Either you feel very sure about throwing yourself into this enterprise right away: this means a lot because, as it unfolds, we will be confronted with other stages in the development of the NEF: the planning and acquisition of our own technical facilities, which means at least what is needed for filming and recording sound, the planning of a workplace in North Africa, which is even more necessary as filming in colour requires a lot of light, and finally bringing together new producers willing to make films with us. All this is very grand and ambitious, and cannot be done in a day. I must next see Duvivier,[4] as it's possible that he'll be interested. Don't forget that in creating the NEF, my far-off goal was to form something like a French 'United Artists', that is to say, a much larger and more fair-minded business than the kind that exists simply for distribution.

Another line of action might be that you consider it more prudent to wait until the results obtained are definite, in other words, you ask for a breather. I would consider that an extremely sensible idea, and while waiting I would make the film in colour for another company.

For a moment, and I have spoken of this to you, I had the idea of making a film in America, which could have led me to further my valuable international connections; but I've rejected it for the moment because, even while taking the first steps, which was contact with an agent in charge of negotiations, I was asked to commit myself too much, and I wish to remain free to pursue our work.

Therefore, if I had to make my next film outside the NEF, I would prefer to do it closer to home, with either a French or English production company. We must not forget that I cannot come to a standstill, and since I don't work like the majority of my comrades, who shoot a completed screenplay written by experts in the field, I am led to surround myself with a group of assistants who form a kind of a regular office staff for the research and development of ideas for screenplays. This also costs money, all the more since it means my assistants and myself will spend some months on subjects which may later prove to be of little interest. Sometimes we revive them; for example, right now I am in the middle of reviving an old idea which had once seemed bad because it wasn't well thought-out, but now seems good, no doubt because it has matured in my mind.

All that certainly presents problems; I don't pretend to resolve them here, but it seems to me a good idea to put them down on paper in order to have, in a few months time, a testimony of our mental state after our first stage. Perhaps you too could put some similar thoughts down on paper. It's too bad we can't include photographs with this letter; we'll all have a good laugh over this in a few years' time.

Very sincerely yours,
Jean Renoir

1 Camille François, producer of *La Règle du Jeu*, and song-writer.
2 Claude Renoir, Sr, production manager on *La Règle du Jeu*.
3 This film, with its script credited to Carl Koch, was begun by Jacques Becker in 1939, but abandoned by him when the war began. It was completed by Jean Stelli and released in April 1940.
4 Julien Duvivier (1896–1967) was one of the major French directors of the 1930s, whose films included *Pépé le Moko* (1937) and *Un Carnet du Bal* (1937). He worked in Hollywood during World War Two.

On 7 July, La Règle du Jeu *opens in Paris to a disastrous reception. Audiences are confused and offended, necessitating various cuts to the film in an attempt to make it more palatable to the public, but without success. It is eventually banned by the French government for being 'demoralizing'. On 14 July, Jean Renoir and Dido Freire arrive in Rome, at the request of the Italian government and Scalera Films, to work with Carl Koch on the screenplay of* La Tosca.

To Commander Calve
Army Film Service

27 August 1939
Cagnes-sur-Mer

Commander,

I have left Italy, where I was in the process of preparing a film, and I have come to continue my work at my brother's house in Cagnes-sur-Mer.

I am at your disposal, and ask you to trust in my loyalty.

Jean RENOIR

'Les Collettes'

Cagnes-sur-Mer (A.M.)

P.S. I left Italy in an atmosphere of absolute calm; to me the people seemed very friendly and during the car journey from Rome to here, I didn't hear a single disagreeable remark against France, in fact quite the contrary.

I relayed my impressions to my friends at the Information Service at the border. They didn't seem at all surprised by the neutral and very peaceable description I gave them of my trip.

However, all this doesn't necessarily mean anything. It is possible that during my stay in Italy since the beginning of August, there have been troop movements so secret I haven't caught wind of them, but I've heard no mention of this.

As far as the call-up is concerned, of the hundred or so persons employed at the studio where I worked, there were four or five men mobilized as specialists.

[Jean Renoir]

Jean Renoir and Dido Freire return to Paris and take up residence at 7 avenue Frochot, which becomes their permanent residence in Paris. With

Hitler's invasion of Poland and the declaration of war by Britain and France on 3 September, Jean enters the Service Cinématographique de l'Armée as a lieutenant, with duties to make a propaganda film.

To Dido Freire [*Original in English*]   *18 September 1939*
                                                       The Spaulding Hotel
                                                       Duluth, Minnesota

My dear Dido,

It was wonderful to get the postcard from Rome from you, and Jean Renior [sic]. I suppose your project to do a film in Italy is now scattered to the winds through this terrible war. Up to the last minute I did not believe it would happen. I did not believe there could be such colossal stupidity. As I read the war news this morning about Poland being torn to pieces in two weeks, it makes me despair. I cannot tell you how concerned I am about you all. My own daughter Barbara is down in India with her two children. It seems to me impossible that she can continue living there for I am afraid India is no longer safe.

I am addressing this letter in care of Olwyn Vaughan[1] as I have not your Paris address with me here. Please write often and let me know how you are and what you are going to do.

I started the film for the American Government three weeks ago, and have already shot some 15,000 feet. I have a staff of six men, motor cars, camera equipment, etc. Have been slowly travelling through the country. It will involve several thousand miles before the film is done. If it wasn't for the war and all the worry about you all over in Paris and London, it would have been a pleasure to do, but as it is, one has no enthusiasm left for anything any more. Do give my love to Jean and to all my friends. And please write as soon as you can and let me know what is happening to you all.

With much love.

As ever,

Robert Flaherty

PS. Al Lewin[2] sends his love to you all.

R.F.

1 Olwyn Vaughan, a friend to both Flaherty and Renoir, was Secretary of the British Film Institute from 1935–45 and ran Le Petit Club Français in London.
2 Albert Lewin (1894–1968) was a distinguished Hollywood producer who became a director of highly 'literary' films, the most famous being *The Picture of Dorian Gray* (1945) and *Pandora and the Flying Dutchman* (1951).

12 Jean Renoir in his army uniform for the Service Cinématographique

To Robert Flaherty [*Original in English*]   *8 October 1939*

My dear Bob,

Your letter made me very happy, I feel rather downhearted with all these ghastly things happening . . . It is the first time I am glad you are not near us, away from all this.

We had to leave Italy when there was the *mobilisation générale*. Jean Renoir is now a lieutenant in the French Army, and doing his bit in the Service Cinématographique de l'Armée.

Most of the time he stays in Paris, and I am most pleased to be still able to help him with his work.

It was rather sad having to leave Italy, we were very happy there, it is such a wonderful country.

Like you I did not believe such colossal stupidity could happen, I felt very optimistic until the last minute, and even now I can hardly believe it.

Paris is very quiet, at times we have air-raid warnings which get us out of bed in the middle of the night. But so far no air-raids.

Jean Renoir is probably going to shoot a propaganda film, he is busy now on the script, and I think it is a good story.

I am glad you are working. We are all looking forward to seeing your film, and hope to be once more together in happier circumstances.

Please give my love to Monica,[1] don't worry and don't forget us. You know how fond we are of you.

As ever,
Dido [Freire]

1 Daughter of Robert Flaherty.

To Robert Flaherty [*Original in English*]   *8 October 1939*

Dear Bob,

We are not too unhappy and we live in the hope of better days. The moral [sic] is good and that's the important thing.

Warmest regards to you and Monica and yours,
Jean Renoir

[*Jean Renoir added in French*]
Dear old Bob who I love much,

I am going to make films which enchant me – no longer with actors, but with *men, real ones*.

Love to all,
Jean Renoir

To Mr Ringel   *12 December 1939*
                                                Paris

Lieutenant RENOIR to Mr RINGEL

Charged with an urgent mission in Italy, I solicit your support in rapidly obtaining an exit visa for myself and my secretary, whom I need for my work.

NATURE OF THE MISSION:

It's a matter of establishing artistic contact between the two countries through the cinema, and doing so by using technicians and artists from the two nations.

For the last five weeks, Mr Vittorio MUSSOLINI,[1] the President of Era-Film Corporation, has been calling on me to develop the first film, which could, no doubt, be followed by many others.

Mr FRANÇOIS-PONCET, Ambassador to Rome, wanted very much to intervene and advise the Information Commissioner in Paris that he would consider my presence in Rome very useful.

My military superiors have asked me to be assigned to the French Embassy in Rome.

This proposition was delivered on 12 November 1939.

Since the waiting period necessary for this assignment has turned out to be very long, and this lateness risks being counter to the Propaganda which is the reason for my dispatch to Italy, and moreover because the technical and material conditions for the execution of the film are becoming difficult because of this delay, the costs are rising, etc . . . the Commissioner of Information has decided to give me a Mission Order allowing me to leave in the normal way while waiting for my assignment.

[signed:]

Last Name: RENOIR
First Name: JEAN
Born in Paris (18th) on 15 September 1894
Residence: 7 avenue Frochot PARIS (9th)
Itinerary: By way of the border at VINTIMILLE
Destination: ROME (Italy)

Last Name: FREIRE
First Name: DIDO
Born in PARA (Brazil) on 4 April 1907
Residence: 7 avenue Frochot Paris (9th)

References: His Excellency Mr de SOUZA-DANTAS, Brazilian Ambassador in Paris

1 Benito Mussolini opened the Rome studios known as Cinecittà on 27 April 1937, and his son Vittorio worked as a producer there.

To Attorney Pierre Loewel   *19 December 1939*

Dear Sir,

I've just learned that Henri Jeanson[1] is going on trial for an article he wrote at the beginning of the war. I am not acquainted at all with this article. For some time now, Jeanson and I haven't been on good terms. Moreover, the reason for this 'coldness' between us rests on the shoulders of Henri Jeanson: I put some hope in Russian collaboration in the event of 'hard times', he stubbornly insisted on not believing in it. The events split us apart, and I am happy, with this letter, publicly to make honourable amends to him.

But this is a mere detail. What's important in my eyes is that Henri Jeanson is one of the best servants of my craft (the cinema).

You should know, Dear Sir, that in the last few months the French cinema has been in the process of regaining its rightful place in the world. I'm not stressing the value of this as French propaganda. This success has uniquely relied upon the works of a small group of authors, of directors, and of actors respected and acclaimed in all foreign countries. Jeanson was one of the heads of this small group, and if some event were to get in the way of him maintaining his place in this struggle, it would be a serious loss to our country's artistic success abroad.

In concluding this letter, may I add that I hold Henri Jeanson to be a perfectly honourable man, and I would voluntarily, without fear of regret, offer my personal guarantee of his moral standards.

Best regards.

[Jean Renoir]

1 Henri Jeanson (1900–1970) was a Communist journalist who collaborated with Jean Renoir on the journal *Ciné-Liberté*. Their attempts to work on *La Marseillaise* together came to nothing. As the film critic of the satirical newspaper *Le Canard Enchaîné*, he would later accuse Renoir – on dubious evidence – of making anti-Semitic remarks while in Lisbon in November 1940. As a screenwriter his credits included *Pépé le Moko* (Julien Duvivier, 1936) and *Hotel du Nord* (Marcel Carné, 1938).

1940

With the encouragement of the French government, who hope to keep good relations with Italy, Jean Renoir and Dido Freire leave for Rome in January to teach at the Centro Sperimentale and film La Tosca.

To Robert Flaherty [*Original in English*]   *2 May 1940*
US Film Service   *Rome*
Washington DC

Dear Bob,

We heard from you by de Rochemont[1] who passed through Rome on his way to Paris.

Even if I don't write, I think there is not one day in which your name is not mentioned either by Jean or by myself.

Do tell us how you are getting on with your film. We have had many worries with our *La Tosca*. It is such a long story that I think I had better spare you. But this time everything seems to be settled, and we shall probably start next week.

How is Monica?

Dear Bob, as I told you in Paris, I still want Jean to go to America, specially now as it will also mean being together with you once more.

We have had a telegram from de Rochemont on behalf of Lois Jacoby,[2] Hotel Royalton, New York, with a proposition from [a] major studio providing 500 dollars per week during three months' acclimatization period, and 1,500 dollars per week during the actual work of the film.

Jean is interested, and has answered favourably, only asking a few extra things like voyage payd [sic] from Europe and back for himself and secretary, this secretary to be appointed by the society engaging him, etc. etc.

Jean thinks he could better serve the Propaganda of his country in USA than anywhere else.

Of course he should have to be asked by Diplomatic channels or by the US Government.

During the war Jean is affected to the Ministry of Information and they

13 Dido Freire and Jean Renoir in Rome

are the only ones who can give him the authorization to go to America.

Let me know if you think this offer is a good thing for Jean. We are waiting for your letter. Perhaps, dear Bob, if it is not too much trouble, and if you are in New York, you could call on Lois Jacoby. We count on you like a friend. That is why I have made bold to ask you to help us.

My very fond love to you and Monica.

Dido

1 Richard de Rochemont, who with his brother Louis produced the *March of Time* newsreels.
2 New York agent.

Filming finally begins on La Tosca, *but Jean Renoir only manages to shoot five sequences by 10 May, when Germany invades Belgium and Holland. Jean returns to France, but Dido remains behind until 10 June, when Mussolini declares his allegiance to Hitler. Carl Koch stays on to complete the film.*

To Dido Freire
[Rome]

30 May 1940
[Paris]

Dear Dido,

Here is a copy of the letter I sent to Barattolo.

To be brief, you should know that I found everybody here in a very different state from when we left. Everybody told me plainly: 'It's not right to make *La Tosca* when the Germans are 120 kilometres from Paris.' Furthermore, we mustn't forget that I am in the military, and in view of the very clear advice that was given to me in Nice about having to take orders in Paris, I had absolutely no choice but to obey them.

The events taking place in France at this moment are extraordinary. I am full of hope and when I see people so full of resolve I believe that we are going to pull through.

I hope that Barattolo will understand that my duties keep me here. I'm asking you to speak to him to that effect, and to tell him that I haven't any choice, but that this doesn't alter my sincere desire to meet up with him some day.

Today I am going to work on getting you your return visa for France, because you must come and help me with this new work which events oblige me to undertake.

I saw Alain. He is in great form.

I will write you a longer letter tomorrow because today I am having a very hectic day.

Fondest love,

Jean Renoir

Dear Dido. Ask for your French visa. For my part, I'm doing my best in Paris. I'm eager to see you again and send my love. Jean R.

Jean and Dido decide to leave Paris, which is preparing to defend itself against German occupation (the Nazis march in on 14 June), and take refuge with the Cézanne family in Marlotte. With the Cézannes they take flight, stopping off at La Creuse.

To Robert Flaherty [*Original in English*]   *8 July 1940*
Chénérailles (Creuse)

Dear Bob,

We have been able to leave Paris, and, after an eventful voyage, we have taken refuge in a baking room and a haystack of a small country place in Limousin (Old province of the Centre of France and, by coincidence, the birthplace of my Father).

Dido and I are in very good health. We are rather worried of the future, because we wonder what will become of the film industry in Europe after all these happenings.

Affectionately yours,

Jean Renoir

This is my address for the present but my mail will be forwarded.

Darling Bob. I am longing to see you and to hear from you.

Fond love to you and Monica.

Dido[1]

1 Since Jean Renoir's English was virtually non-existent before his arrival in the USA, it can be assumed the translation of these letters in English is by Dido Freire.

Telegram to Jean Renoir [*Original in English*]   *27 July 1940*
Chénérailles   *Washington DC*

OVERJOYED HEAR FROM YOU CAN YOU AND DIDO COME OVER IF I
ARRANGE WITH HOLLYWOOD YOUR SERVICES AS DIRECTOR
BELIEVE I CAN ARRANGE ADVANCE FUNDS IF YOU NEED THEM MUCH
LOVE YOU BOTH CABLE VIA WESTERN UNION
   ROBERT FLAHERTY

*At the end of July, Jean Renoir and Dido Freire arrive at Les Collettes
and contemplate their next move in the Vichy-controlled South.
Attempts are made by representatives of Nazi interests to persuade Jean
to make films for the 'New France'.*

Telegram to Robert Flaherty   *6 August 1940*
[*Original in English*]   *Les Collettes*
Washington DC   *Cagnes-sur-Mer*

WARM THANKS IMPOSSIBLE LEAVE FRANCE WITHOUT SPECIAL
AUTHORIZATION LOVE
   JEAN RENOIR

To Robert Flaherty [*Original in English*]   *8 August 1940*
US Film Service   *Cagnes-sur-Mer*
Washington DC

My dear Bob,

I am deeply moved by this one more proof of your friendship, and I
shall never forget that you have remembered us and tried to help us in the
unhappy circumstances we are living through.

If it was in my power I would gladly go to you immediately, and I
would accept your generous offer. But certain obligations keep me in
France. They are of two kinds: firstly I am under contract with SCALERA
FILM Society in Rome. Because of the war I was unable to fulfil my
engagements with them. As no one is to blame in this case, and as, on the
contrary, they have always been extremely decent to me, I want to give
them a chance of disposing of me before I start on another work. Then,
of course, I think of our French Cinema in such a state of confusion after

[71]

our disaster. If I can help in some way, I think it is my duty to do so. I would be ashamed to leave my fellow-countrymen when everything goes wrong.

On the other hand if I realize that there is nothing I can do out here: I may not be wanted, or it may be impossible to make films in France. If also my Italian producers do not need me, then I would consider myself free to act as I wish, and I would not hesitate any longer to appeal to your friendship and to go to you.

The best solution would be to work here for a while, and when things become once more really normal, and the fact of leaving France a natural phase in my profession, then I could join you and try to make a film in a far away country, as I have longed for all my life.

I would like to keep in touch with you and I hope the day will not be far off that will bring us together. I know I can depend on you for that.

Thank you once more, dear Bob, please believe in my very true friendship.

Jean Renoir

To Robert Flaherty [*Original in English*]   *10 August 1940*
Cagnes-sur-Mer

Dear Bob,

It was so nice of you to try to help us out of all this mess. Your cable made us both very happy. How are you getting on Bob dear, do write us a nice long letter. We speak of you almost every day, it was such a happy time when we were together. Is Monica with you? Please give her my love.

We are in the south of France, in the home of Jean's father. It now belongs to his younger brother. It is all very beautiful, but our hearts are full of sadness. Jean's son is also here, he enlisted in the beginning of the war and had a very hard time of it, poor kid. Anyway we have him safe and sound once more.

After living for nearly two months in our barn, sleeping in the hay and so forth, we managed to reach Cagnes. All the experiences we have lived through would make a most exciting film and we hope to be able to realize it one day.

Of course Jean believes his duty is to stay here, but in my opinion it is quite useless as he will not be able to work for a long time, and in every way it is tragic for him to be idle. My wish is to go to America, but it is difficult to leave France just at present as a special permit is needed which is very hard to obtain. In my case I could naturally go to America. I have my visa and also full attorney's power to sign a contract in Jean's name.

I think he will realize after a while that there is nothing to do out here, and when it happens, he will not refuse a concrete offer coming from America. I am very worried about my Mother and sister who are still in England.[1] They are having a tough time. When is all this madness going to finish. Bob dear, I am so happy you are out of it all.

My very fond love to you and Monica,
Dido

---

1 Dido's father had been Brazilian consul in Liverpool, where her widowed mother and sister Dirce continued to live.

Telegram to Jean Renoir [*Original in English*]   *12 August 1940*
Les Collettes   *Washington*
Cagnes-sur-Mer

HAVE CONFERRED WITH STATE DEPARTMENT AND AL LEWIN HOLLY-WOOD STATE DEPARTMENT ADVISES YOU GO NEAREST AMERICAN CONSULATE NICE OR MARSEILLES CABLE IF YOU DECIDE TO DO THIS WHEREUPON CONFIRMING CABLES WILL BE SENT CONSULATE FROM STATE DEPARTMENT MYSELF AND AL LEWIN LEWIN'S HOLLY-WOOD AGENT SURE CAN OBTAIN POSITION FOR YOU HE IS WORKING ON IT NOW DO YOU WANT WE ALSO CONFER WITH LOIS JACOBY IN NEW YORK LOVE FROM US ALL
    ROBERT FLAHERTY

Telegram to Robert Flaherty   *14 August 1940*
US Film Service   *Cagnes-sur-Mer*
Washington, DC

IMPOSSIBLE TO MAKE A DECISION WITHOUT CONSULTING VICHY MINISTRY WILL CABLE REPLY THANKS TO YOU AND LEWIN
JEAN RENOIR

To Robert Flaherty [*Original in English*]   *14 August 1940*
                                                       Les Collettes
                                                       Cagnes-sur-Mer

Dear Bob,

We have just received your long cable of August 12th. How nice of you and Al Lewin to take so much trouble over us. Jean is deeply grateful to

[73]

you and longing to be near you, even more so at present after the many proofs of friendship you have given him.

Jean has written to you telling you his wish to help in the reorganization of the film industry in France. But, sad to say, war is not ended in Europe and there is very slight hope of anyone bothering about our film industry when there are so many more important things to worry about, for instance the food problem etc. etc.

I must say that Jean begins to lose hope of arriving at some result, and of being useful in his work. He was so happy on receiving your telegram and wrote at once to Mr Tixier Vignancourt who is responsible for the film industry in the Vichy Government, exposing [sic] him all the facts. Of course Jean should not act without the approval of this Service. If Tixier Vignancourt advises him to work in America, no doubt that at the same time he will make it easy for Jean to obtain his French visa to leave the country.

If we receive a favourable answer, we shall cable to you at once, and ask for the help you so kindly offer in your cable. I am afraid we shall also be obliged to ask you for our fares to America. Really Bob, I wonder what we should do without you.

Another important matter is the question of the contract with the Italian firm in Rome. We have also written to them, but as Italy is in war I do not think they shall want Jean to fulfil his engagements just at present. At any rate we expect an answer shortly.

As regards Lois Jacoby, considering she is a friend of Rochemont's who as a matter of fact cabled us recently saying she was working on a job for Jean, it is perhaps better to keep in touch with her. But then Al Lewin's agent and Lois Jacoby, I am sure, can easily establish a sort of understanding between them.

As I told you before, dear Bob, as soon as everything is settled we shall send you a cable and go to the American Consulate in Nice.

I can hardly believe I may soon see you again, it would be the happiest day for me in a long time. Jean also looks forward to seeing you and sends his best love to you and sincere regards to Al Lewin.

Write soon dear Bob, remember me to Monica.

Fondly yours,

Dido

To the Director of Radio and Cinema[1]

Dear Sir,

I have two very good friends in America, Mr de Rochemont, who with his brother produces *The March of Time*, and Robert Flaherty, the author of *Nanook, Moana, Elephant Boy, Man of Aran*, who works with the US Film Service in Washington. They have strongly insisted that I go to make a film in America. These are very responsible people and sincere friends of France.

I told them that I had to abide by your decision.

I am sure that they understand my desire to be involved with the rebirth of our national cinema. But they have the impression that film production in our country won't be able to start up again for several months.

I would like to offer you my feelings on this subject: here on the Riviera, it is a lamentable sight. Apart from certain of my friends who are true professionals, the riff-raff known to you continue to cause trouble. And I still don't foresee a way of getting rid of them. The only proper way to make a film is to find a backer outside these people. This isn't convenient, and even then it will be necessary to involve some undesirables in order to get access to a studio and technical equipment.

Finally, it would be disastrous to make a poor film and give the world the impression that French cinema has become second rate.

Moreover, I attempted to communicate with Italian producers on the subject we talked about. I still have no response from my friends in Rome. I suppose that at the moment they must have other things on their minds.

Of course, my intention is not to do anything until I receive their opinion. I insist on that for ethical reasons, as our collaboration over there has developed into a friendship, and for material reasons, the activities of the Ministry of Information during the war having prevented me from fulfilling my contract.

The advantage of America is that I could work there right away. I must work if I am to sustain the modest influence I have with the public and the financiers.

But if there is a chance of making something quickly in France, it is very obvious that I must stay. I ask you to tell me if you believe such an opportunity exists. You are in charge of our profession, it is up to you to dictate my conduct. I apologize for bothering you, I know that your time is precious, but I am convinced that any cinema business, no matter how small, is of concern to you.

I sent a telegram to America in response to the urgent one that I received today. I am asking my colleagues over there to be patient and to wait for your response.

Yours sincerely,
Jean Renoir

1 Tixier Vignancourt.

To the Director of Radio and Cinema

24 *August 1940*
Cagnes-sur-Mer

Dear Sir,

I received your letter of 19 August, and I thank you for replying so promptly.

I have already advised the American Consul in Nice, who has received instructions from the State Department in Washington to help me through the formalities regarding my American visa, that I am now in a position to travel to America.

Also, I have filled in the forms for an exit visa from France at the Police Headquarters in Nice. This request needs to be conveyed to the Ministry of the Interior in Vichy. I am a disabled war veteran and unsuited to active service, but I am not yet forty-eight years old, after which age an exit visa would not be required.

My aim is to make a film in America and to try to profit from my stay over there, in order subsequently to help the commercial distribution of a film I want to make here in France at a later date, and which is very close to my heart. The actor Jean Gabin is equally enthusiastic about this project. Both of us are completely in agreement about working with all our energies to produce a film of great scope to serve the spirit of France in the world.

Allow me to add to this letter a brief outline of our story.[1] If one day you have the opportunity to talk to the Marshal[2] about it, it would make me very proud. I believe that the project would please him. It would be a mistake to start up our industry once again with films about defeat. And the painting of religious heroism is perhaps even more timely than that of military triumphs of the past. But such a project requires a lot of money and the organization of an extremely onerous colonial expedition, and as a result could only be undertaken when the commercial market has sorted itself out and when we have found foreign clients who would make up our strength; in short, when we could offer the greatest possible reassurances to the silent partners I will be attempting to deal with at that time. On the other hand, an idea like this ought to be nurtured a little. The cause that we would present is too great a cause for us to allow ourselves to fail.

All these considerations make it very wise [for me], I believe, while waiting for the right moment, to go and serve an apprenticeship in America that could only be of benefit to this future project. Jean Gabin thinks as I do. Twentieth Century-Fox has advertised a film set in Hudson's Bay[3] in which he will probably play the part of a French-Canadian. But both of us have decided to work together as soon as possible and to throw ourselves into the making of the story which is so close to our hearts.

Besides, I am convinced that you will end up by consolidating all the resources available in French cinema and that it will be easier to do good work within a new structure than on the crumbling ruins of a make-believe industry.

If I obtain my French exit visa, before leaving I would like to pay a brief visit to Vichy and ask you for instructions. In the current climate every Frenchman who is abroad, whether he likes it or not, has a part to play. If you could spare me a few minutes, perhaps they would not be wasted.

If I don't receive my visa, I will try just the same to set something up here, for it is essential that I ply my trade since I haven't amassed a private fortune. But this little solution doesn't seem to me to suit the serious conditions in which we live.

I apologize for this long letter.

Yours sincerely,

Jean Renoir

1 *Le Magnificat*, the story of French missionaries in an uncharted region of the Amazon.
2 Pétain.
3 *Hudson's Bay* (Irving Pichel, 1940), which did not star Jean Gabin but Paul Muni.

To Robert Flaherty [*Original in English*]

US Film Service
Washington DC

24 August 1940
Les Collettes
Cagnes-sur-Mer

Dear Bob,

I have written to the Ministry responsible for the film industry in France asking them if they need me at the present moment to work on a French film.

Mr Tixier Vignancourt, who is at the head of this Service, has answered that I can (for a certain lapse of time) work with you in the United States. Of course this authorization is only a moral one which I wanted naturally to obtain. But it does not exempt me from taking other steps of an administrative order.

I must, first of all, obtain from the Home Secretary my visa to leave France. I am 46 years old and it is only after 48 that one is allowed out of the country.

I have applied for a permit through the police headquarters in Nice who have sent all particulars to the Home Secretary. It is this Ministry that can give or refuse me the authorization to go abroad.

As soon as I receive an answer I shall cable, and also accept your kind offer to help us financially as I have not the necessary dollars to pay my trip and Dido's. Please tell us if it does not inconvenience you too much to lend us the necessary amount.

At the American Consulate in Nice the employee whom we saw advised us to travel by Clipper.[1] They had received instructions from Washington and have been very helpful. I know it is to you I owe all this and I am happy to possess a friend like you.

At the American Express on the other hand they advise me to go by sea. There will probably be room on a ship by the end of October. It does not matter one way or the other, the main thing is to see you soon again. I am very impatient, but can do nothing but wait this answer from the Home Secretary in Vichy. Only then we shall know what we can do.

Dear Bob, please believe in my very sincere friendship.

Jean Renoir

1 Air service.

To Robert Flaherty [*Original in English*]   *4 September 1940*
US Film Service   *Cagnes-sur-Mer*
Washington DC

Dear Bob,

Jean has left for Vichy to see about his French visa at the Ministère de l'Intérieur. It is the only document we still need, as at the American Consulate in Nice, thanks to you, they are quite willing to do what is necessary once we have all the required documents.

Everything is terribly long and difficult. There is such a crowd at the

American Consulate that I waited a whole week before being able to be received. As we do not live in Nice, and as I have to go by bus, who pass me by most of the time full up from Cannes (no more motor cars are allowed to run), I arrive when a compact crowd is already waiting; and although patiently I stand and wait until closing time I don't manage to get through. Perhaps if you send them a word saying we are wanted urgently in the US and to treat us differently from the waiting mob, it would mean a great gain of time.

I sent you a cable advising you of Jean's trip to Vichy, I think myself that it is going to be difficult, perhaps impossible to obtain his French visa. He is two years short of the age required to be allowed to leave the country (48), but then as he was so badly wounded in the 1914 war perhaps it will be taken into consideration. He limps very badly and is unfit for any kind of active service in the Army.

I would really be disappointed not to be able to go over. I am so much looking forward to it.

We received a cable from Rochemont, saying none of our letters have reached him. I suppose the same must have happened in your case. It is very worrying as I had explained how things stand so that you could help and act when you think so fit. I am trying once more, hoping for better results. I wanted to write through the American Consulate, but they only accept correspondence from American subjects.

Jean has now received an answer from Tixier-Vignancourt who is at the head of the Film Industry in the Vichy Government. He encourages Jean's departure for America for a certain lapse of time as there seems no probability at present of making films in France. There are other and more important questions to see to first. But of course his authorization is only a moral one, and everything depends on the Home Secretary (Minis-tère de l'Intérieur).

If this question is settled favourably I shall cable asking you or Lois Jacoby to see to our fares at the American Express, who has a branch in Nice that could be advised by cable. I should ask you to pay our fares from Nice to the States as we are practically penniless, no money being allowed out of Paris where we have everything we possess. Perhaps they could immediately reserve two tickets either on the Clipper or on a ship, whichever you think best. It would mean gaining time as I believe everything is full up for months to come. I am ashamed to give you so much trouble my dear Bob. And there is still one more thing: before giving the visa the American Consulate requires financial guaranty [sic] of relatives or friends living in the US with documents proving same. I know we can count on you and Rochemont for this. So I trust you will do what is best. We have also written to Rochemont, but if this letter reaches you please let him know all the news, and Al Lewin, and please tell them how grateful we are for their interest and friendship.

I don't send cables more often, they are terribly expensive and we are rather short of money.

Dear Bob, I hope to see you very soon. I am so worried about my Mother and sister. They are in Liverpool and I read continually in the papers of the heavy bombardments over the town. Really it is dreadful not to be able to write or to receive letters. Well, so is life, if at least I could be near you . . .

My love to Monica,
Dido

Telegram to Jean Renoir [*Original in English*] 6 September 1940
Cagnes-sur-Mer   *Washington*

AL LEWIN'S AGENT DEVERICH HOLLYWOOD NEGOTIATING FOR JEAN AT LEWIN'S SUGGESTION AGENT OPTIMISTIC ABOUT MAKING IMPORTANT DEAL VERY SOON BUT NOW FINDS FRANCES MANSON OF FELDMAN BLUM AGENCY CLAIMS THE AGENT FOR JEAN IN HOLLYWOOD IS THIS SO CABLE LEWIN'S AGENT WOULD LIKE OPTION ON JEAN FOR SIXTY DAYS WOULD ADVISE DOING THIS AS I HAVE GREAT CONFIDENCE IN LEWIN WHOSE ONLY INTEREST IS LIKE MINE OVERJOYED TO KNOW YOU AND JEAN CAN LEAVE YOUR CABLE NOT CLEAR BUT AM CABLING AMERICAN CONSUL NICE AS UNDERSTANDING OF IT HOW SOON ARE YOU READY LEAVE LOVE
  ROBERT FLAHERTY

Telegram to Robert Flaherty   *18 September 1940*
[*Original in English*]   *Cagnes-sur-Mer*
Washington DC

FELDMAN BLUM ENTIRELY UNKNOWN LEWIN'S PROPOSITION VERY INTERESTING CONSULT JACOBY YOURSELF DECISION OBTAINED FRENCH VISA PLEASE SECURE PASSAGES WITH ROCHEMONT REGARDS
  JEAN RENOIR

[80]

To Richard de Rochemont
Hotel Algonquin
New York

19 September 1940
Cagnes-sur-Mer

Dear Rochemont,

I've arrived from Vichy. The French authorities have approved my trip to America. They think that it will take some time for the European Cinema to reorganize itself, and that, while waiting, it would be better for me to go to America where I could continue what I'm doing rather than stay here and do nothing.

Dido is delighted with this decision, but unfortunately there are still several obstacles to overcome. The most important is the question of places on the boat or the Clipper. When we have these places we will be able to obtain Spanish and Portuguese visas, which we can get only at the last moment and only for transit.

With regard to the American visa, it's a long and complicated story but the Consul at Nice has received instructions to give us one.

To return to the voyage itself, the two current practical ways are by the American Export Line boat or the Clipper. Both of these leave from Lisbon and both are full until the end of December and probably January. Do you think it would be possible to get a complimentary ticket from America, which is impossible to get in France? If not, perhaps I can obtain some places for 12 November on a Spanish boat which leaves from Bilbao for Havana. From Havana, we could easily travel to New York by plane.

It is wonderful that Lois Jacoby can advance us the money for the trip. She must be so kind to put us in touch with Flaherty. We left Paris with very little on us, and we are flat broke. In any case, we are incapable of paying for a journey as far as America.

Also, she must look into our problems with work. Bob Flaherty cabled me about a proposition from Al Lewin's Hollywood agent, and I asked him to consult Lois Jacoby.

Dear Rochemont, I desperately want to see you soon and make the acquaintance of Lois Jacoby. Dido is equally impatient. Thanks to Flaherty and you, perhaps this will happen. Even if this fails, I will never forget it.

Very truly yours,
Jean Renoir

To Robert Flaherty [*Original in English*]   *5 October 1940*
US Film Service   *Cagnes-sur-Mer*
Washington DC

My dear Bob,

Dido and I have finally obtained our American visas, and we hope soon to drink a few whiskys in Washington with you. I have to go there to present myself to the French Ambassador. I would like to avail myself of this opportunity to try to bring nearer to all Americans my country of France. We need so much, at the present moment, to find sympathy and friendship outside our frontiers.

We expect to have room either on an American Export Liner or on a Clipper before the end of the month. It would mean that the great reunion would take place in November. There is only one drawback, I am obliged to leave my son, Alain, as he is too young to obtain an authorization to go abroad.

Rochemont must have explained to you all about the Feldman Agency. Four or five months ago I signed an understanding with Lois Jacoby, a friend of Rochemont's, leaving her free to take the decisions she found best. On account of the war I had not heard from Jacoby for a long while and ignored[1] what steps she had taken.

I regret the Al Lewin offer as I had learnt to appreciate him on our few meetings, but this understanding with Lois Jacoby binds me. Nevertheless I am certain that the decisions she has taken are good. Rochemont is at the bottom of all this, and I trust him absolutely.

We have received a charming letter from Monica. Dido has started to teach me English. I already know the alphabet. It is not sufficient to hold a conversation, but I am firmly decided to work and make some progress.

A bientôt, dear Bob.

Affectionately yours,

Jean Renoir

Fond love to you and Monica. My dear Bob, I am so happy to see you all soon.

Dido

---

1 Meaning 'was unaware of'.

Telegram to Feldman Blum Agency
[*Original in English*]
Hollywood

6 *October 1940*
Cagnes-sur-Mer

ACCEPT YOUR TERMS REGARDING AMERICAN ENGAGEMENT
THROUGH JACOBY
    JEAN RENOIR

Telegram to Robert Flaherty
[*Original in English*]
Washington DC

19 October 1940

STAYING HOTEL TERMINUS MARSEILLES TO OBTAIN SPANISH TRAN-
SIT VISA NECESSARY AMERICAN AMBASSADOR MADRID CLAIMS US
FROM SPANISH GOVERNMENT CAN YOU OBTAIN THIS LOVE
    DIDO FREIRE

*In November, Jean Renoir and Dido Freire, acting on advice that travel-
ling in Spain is difficult, decide to embark from Lisbon instead of
Madrid, making their way there via Tangier. Money is sent from New
York to cover the extra expense of these journeys. Jean arrives in Lisbon
ahead of Dido, who has to remain behind in Tangier.*

To Dido Freire
Tangier

[November?] 1940
Hotel Metropole
Lisbon

Dear Dido,

I am suffering terribly without you. Even so, everything is beautiful
here and pleases me no end.

I am going to have dinner with an extremely nice Portuguese director
who showed me a highly accomplished documentary on some typical
villages.

I still haven't seen your Ambassador, nor anyone else for that matter.
It's Saturday and everyone is away. The police formalities kept me busy
all morning and afternoon. I saw that film and a film by Metro[1] with
Robert Montgomery, *The Earl of Chicago*.[2] Very good film – too well
made – too well acted, but with a very moving ending which made me
forget the all-too-obvious nature of the beginning.

[83]

I love you with all my heart and I am waiting for you,
Jean Renoir

1 MGM.
2 Directed by Richard Thorpe in 1940. A Chicago mobster inherits an English title.

To Dido Freire
Tangier

[November?] 1940
Hotel Metropole
Lisbon

Dear Dido,

I am still missing you and it's getting even worse.

I went to lunch at your friend's place. Such charming people. Such beautiful children. A beautiful house. Your friend is truly a wonderful woman. One that adores you. Her husband is a Portuguese 'Pierre Fighiera'.[1] I love that kind of person.

Impossible to see the fellow from the American Export Line for whom Hollen gave me a letter. I gave the letter to an employee who handed it over to him, but he hasn't shown up.

On the Clipper, on the other hand, they were expecting me and made me feel part of the family.

We are only waiting for you and the formalities will be done quickly. I myself am quite hopeful.

Did you see the bombing of Marseilles? It seems it was a plane that made a mistake. Alain must have had a good laugh.

Come quickly. All my love from the bottom of my heart.

Jean Renoir

Find out from Cook about direct flights Tangier–Lisbon.

At the Brazilian Embassy, I saw an attaché. He promised me that he would telegraph your colleagues in Madrid so that they would recommend you to the Spanish visas service. [. . .][2]

1 Pierre Fighiera was a close friend of Jean Renoir.
2 The rest of this letter is illegible.

To Dido Freire

26 November 1940
Lisbon

Dear Dido,

I got your three letters at the same time. I hope that you never get this one, or rather, that it will reach you much later in California. Because you must come here quickly. First of all because I am so alone and Lisbon, wonderful though I find it, isn't quite the same without you. Furthermore, of the two the Clipper seems the more reliable, despite what everyone says here, namely that the Pan-American [Line] are full of good intentions but never keep their promises, and people have been known to leave up to a month after the scheduled date. If you were here, it would be all the same to me. We will wait patiently here, as that's all we can do.

You are right to think that it may take ages to get the Spanish visa. The attaché from your Embassy whom I saw was very nice. But this friendliness was by no means any guarantee of his willingness to act quickly. 'Don't make trouble and we'll sort out the obstacles with some choice words.' That's the motto of all petty officials these days. Give me David's address, who I hope to find at Metro Goldwin [sic] and who remains mysteriously elusive. Give the Posners my regards and tell them that being here would not improve their situation. The boats are full and American Export seems to me to be having a bit of a clean-out before taking any more reservations. Life is so out of control here, it may be worth the wait in Tangier.

Dear Dido, I love you with all my heart.

Jean Renoir

To Tixier Vignancourt

9 December 1940
Lisbon

Dear Sir,

I am about to leave Lisbon. My address in New York will be c/o Richard de Rochemont, The Algonquin Hotel, or the French Embassy where I will present myself just as we agreed that I would at Vichy.

Here in Lisbon I have been in touch with my Portuguese colleagues. I held a screening of *La Grande Illusion* with a discussion, which went very well. I have received an honorary membership of the Portuguese Cinema Union (up till now, I am the first foreigner to have been accepted). I explained to them my ideas about a 'Latin' cinema and we have consequently decided to form a committee to pursue this idea. We have asked certain Spanish and Italian individuals to be part of this committee.

On all matters concerning the Portuguese cinema I would advise you to contact the President of the Union: Antonio LOPES RIBEIRO, c/o 'ANIMATOGRAFO' Lisbon.

All these events, which proved that French ideas are well received here, have been much aided by Mr WARNIER, the Director of the French Institute in Lisbon. I must give another talk to the students at this Institute.

Please give my regards to Madame TIXIER VIGNANCOURT and my best wishes to PRADE and to Madame PRADE if you should be seeing them.

Yours as ever,
Jean Renoir

After being reunited on 5 December, Jean Renoir and Dido Freire finally embark on 20 December on the SS Siboney, headed for New York. On the voyage, Jean shares a suite with celebrated writer Antoine de St Exupéry.

Telegram to Jean Renoir
[*Original in English*]
SS Siboney

25 December 1940
Washington DC

WAITING FOR YOUR ARRIVAL OVERJOYED LOVE TO YOU AND DIDO THIS CHRISTMAS DAY
  ROBERT FLAHERTY

1941

Jean Renoir and Dido Freire arrive in New York on New Year's Eve. They stay for five days at the Royalton Hotel with Robert Flaherty, then travel on to Washington DC. On 10 January, they arrive in Hollywood, temporarily staying at the Sunset Towers, 8358 Sunset Boulevard.

To Jean Renoir and Dido [*Original in English*]   *10 January 1941*
Hollywood   *Washington*

Dear Jean and Dido,

Dido, I could take you over my knee and spank you for not waking me.

I rarely sleep so late as I did the morning Jean and you left. I was <u>really</u> disappointed. There were so many little things I wanted to say at this last moment.

Our thoughts were with you as you flew across the country. I just know that you must be thrilled at being in California.

I enclose a letter from David and another that came through the mail yesterday.

Floyd Crosby[1] will be calling on you. He is an old protégé of mine and did the camerawork on *Tabu*.[2]

I am asking him to have you meet Cedric Belfrage,[3] an old friend of mine who is an Englishman [and] lives in Hollywood. He is a writer but has nothing to do with films. Belfrage will have you meet Theodore Dreiser[4] who I know you will both enjoy.

You will be meeting so many interesting people, and I am sure you will like California. Let me know if there is any little thing I can do.

Much love to you both.

As ever,

Bob [Flaherty]

1 Floyd Crosby (1899–1985), cinematographer whose credits included *Tabu* (1931), *High Noon* (1952), and *The Fall of the House of Usher* (1960).
2 Directed by Robert Flaherty and F. W. Murnau (1931).
3 Cedric Belfrage, English-born editor of a left-wing national weekly published in New York. He was later deported as a victim of HUAC.
4 Theodore Dreiser (1871–1945), author of *An American Tragedy* (1925) and *The Stoic* (1947).

14 Jean Renoir and Dido Freire on board the SS *Siboney* for New York

To Robert Flaherty
[*Original in English*]

Dear Bob,

Dido is writing to you and explaining much better than I could do with my poor English how we are busy – and the clam showder [sic] where we are living.

I got the same difficulties you did with our Hungarian people and I have no more a bit of hope to make the picture I wanted to make when I was with you in New York.

Dear Bob, I would like to see you making a new picture. I miss you on the screen. The pictures they are making now seem to me so annoying, and flat, and poor. I am sure they are killing the interest of the audience for the movies and very soon, people will prefer the merry go rounds or the Whorehouses and we will have to find another job.

With my love,
Jean Renoir

To Robert Flaherty [*Original in English*]

Dear Bob,

Jean just went out to the Universal Studios to have lunch with René Clair.[1] I did not go as this is the only free time I could manage to write to you which I wanted to do very badly.

The day flight to Hollywood is very tiring. Of course the plane arrives here at one o'clock in the morning, but it really means about twenty hours flying as it is 4 o'clock by Washington time. Anyway here we are. I wish we could be together. We both miss you so much.

Yesterday we saw Daven[2] and Charlie Feldman.[3] Before we even mentioned Jacoby they asked us what all this nonsense meant, and we told them the whole story. I believe they never had anything to do with them and want to get rid of them straight away. Feldman asked Jean to relax, rest for awhile, and then they would settle together all this unpleasant affair. I am so glad, Bob. I could never forgive anyone for telling me such silly things about you.

Jean is going to sign with Zanuck.[4] There is no choice as Daven, who works with Fox and advanced money for our trip etc. has already arranged everything with Feldman. He wants to become Jean's producer in the Fox outfit. Everyone seems to help Jean only to get something out of it. Still it is in human nature, and not everyday in life does one meet a friend like you. In any case I think this is quite an acceptable combination. We have told Feldman to decide himself as he has had other propositions.

We are anxious to see your film when it is finished.

I believe Jean forgot the photographs of his boy in your apartment and I must have left my fountain pen somewhere. If you find them could you please post them on to us.

We were so glad to meet Frances.[5] Please give our love.

Fondly yours,
Dido

Feldman promised to get an affidavit for Alain and a contract. Isn't it marvellous! As soon as we have the two documents we shall send them on to you.

1 René Clair (1898–1981), director, whose major films included *The Italian Straw Hat* (1927), *Sous les Toits de Paris* (1930), and *Le Million* (1931). He spent the war making films in Hollywood, returning to France in 1945.
2 André Daven (1900–81), producer.
3 Charles K. Feldman (1904–68), leading agent in the 1940s who became a producer.
4 Darryl F. Zanuck (1902–79), production chief at Twentieth Century-Fox from 1934 to 1956.
5 Frances Flaherty, wife of Robert.

Jean Renoir and Dido Freire move into a house at 8150 Hollywood Boulevard. On 15 January, Jean signs a one-year contract with Twentieth Century-Fox, with the intention of directing two films. He tries to arrange a contract for his son Alain, still in the defeated French army, to be a cameraman at the studio.

To Alain Renoir

8 March 1941
Hollywood

My dear Alain,

The American Consul in Nice seems like a strange creature. Unfortunately, in his job he can do things his own way, and, since your contract requires a visa, I can only do one thing: ask for this visa and send it to you.

I'm sure this will be sorted out quickly, on the one hand because Flaherty is taking care of it at the State Department, and on the other because Mr Sidney Kent, President of Fox, who lives in New York, was told about your problem and is going to act on it.

I am eager to see you arrive because Dido and I are a little troubled without you. Life here is not unpleasant, as long as one can be together in a big enough family. We're rented a rather large house and you must hurry over here and help us fill it. Especially since I started out with the idea of making a film and then going back. But I had to sign a contract including an option for a second film. Moreover, you can't learn English overnight. I've worked tremendously hard for the past two months, and I am just beginning to understand a normal conversation. I still have not grasped all that the actors in films are saying to each other on the screen. If I want to make a good film, I must be able to give instructions to actors and technicians, and because of this, I do not believe that they will let me start right away.

Therefore, I ask you to do your best to join up with me, since here you will earn a living, whereas in France you are your uncle's responsibility, and you don't contribute anything.

What will definitely interest you here are the possibilities in South America. Outside of your contract with Fox, which foresees in particular lots of films in Brazil, Ivens[1] is going to make a documentary in the wildest part of Bolivia, and he offered to take you along.

I do not yet know all the possibilities of Hollywood, because it's a place where you never see anyone. I saw the heads of Fox one or two times for a few minutes and that was all. If there weren't such formalities over your visa and all the problems with the Bank and Taxes, which are very complicated, we would only see a few friends and that's all.

David Flaherty lives with us. He's Bob's brother, and he is helping me write a story which I'm counting on for your uncle Claude.

I wrote this story once before but some friends dissuaded me from doing it because they thought it would be rejected. I have started work on it again with the help of David Flaherty.

From time to time we meet up with his friends, who are mostly cameramen or technicians who have worked with Bob and have been all around the least civilized parts of the world. In general, they are very charming people.

We live in a very pretty house, with a rather large garden, built on a hill which overlooks the whole city. It is in Hollywood which, it seems, is not very elegant at all. The high-class people live in Beverly Hills, or further west, towards the sea. The most expensive villas are in Santa Monica.

Dido and I are very pleased with this house, which is a little old and sort of an American Marlotte. We have housekeepers, Harry and Grace. He is rather black, she is a curious mix of Negro and Irish: she is light-skinned with freckles and very pretty. He was a bus driver in Pasadena. They are very nice and friendly. He loves helping out by saying OK and by giving us slaps on the back. They have a splendid, brand-new Chevrolet, for everyone has a car here. Even the most wretched newspaper vendors go to work in a *jallopy*[2] [sic] (which means *tacot* in American). It's because the distances are so enormous. My friends often tell me that I'm right next door to my studio. When, in fact, I'm ten kilometres from it.

I wanted to buy myself a Chevrolet, but my agent Feldman told me not to. It seems that in my situation, I must have at least a Buick. I therefore bought myself a Buick convertible, which is horrible, but which runs very well. Dido drives like Nuvolari,[3] and bought herself an old Packard convertible, a great bargain, which is a lot prettier than my Buick. I am very jealous.

The streets here are very long. For example, we live at 8150 Hollywood Boulevard. And before you reach us, on our side of the street, there really are 8148 houses.

Hollywood Boulevard is the Boulevard des Capucines of Hollywood. But that part is around three kilometres from our house. Then it gets lost in the hills, and becomes a very small road. That is where we are. Our place slightly resembles the set-up we had in Les Collettes, though with a few more neighbours. At the bottom of the hill, at the same distance as Le Beal is from les Collettes, there are lots of shops and even some restaurants, doctors, dentists, and markets.

At the very end of this little area, which is the intersection of Laurel Canyon and Sunset Boulevard, is Schwab's Drug Store. One finds everything there, even medicine. They sell cigarettes, bras, newspapers, fountain pens, lingerie, sweets, dishes, wine, and alcohol. There is a huge counter where they serve you strange food. I will not tell you much about the food because I want you to be surprised. Americans cook like little girls playing with their toy plates, making themselves dishes with whatever they can steal from their mothers' kitchens: a raw carrot, a piece of chocolate, a leftover cauliflower, and some currant jelly.

Dido and I sometimes come across some extremely funny combinations which make us laugh like lunatics. She won't touch them, whereas I try everything.

I've had a pain in my leg, which, adding to the diverse administrative complications, has kept me in the house. I'm doing better, and we are going to take some strolls downtown.

A few hours from here is a desert as beautiful as the Sahara. A little further are some Indian reservations which, it seems, have not changed. And above all, there remain some entirely Mexican areas which must be wonderful. In the old part of Los Angeles, one can see some far from ordinary characters.

In short, my dear Alain, it is a large country both grandiose and ridiculous, and one must become familiar with it. I must say that I like Americans a lot. One can get along well with them and can work with them. Come quickly, for I am starting to miss you terribly, and it really bothers me to know you have nothing to do. Here you will find work that will excite you. That's just about the best thing one can do in life.

Sending you my love,

[Jean]

P.S. I have sometimes run into Lucachevich[4] who drives around in his spats in a hermetically sealed Cadillac sedan. That's because of a certain kind of *racket*[5] which is practised a lot here: taking advantage of a car stopping, some people climb inside next to the driver, and threaten him with a revolver, asking for his money. At the next stop, they get out and calmly take off.

Lucachevich is against this behaviour.

---

1 Joris Ivens (1898–1989), documentary film-maker, whose films included *Spanish Earth* (1937) – for which the French commentary was spoken by Jean Renoir and the English by Ernest Hemingway – and *The 400 Million* (1938).
2 Originally in English
3 Italian champion racing driver.
4 Joseph Lucachevich, producer.
5 Original in English.

To Sidney Kent [*Original in English*]   *19 March 1941*
New York   *Hollywood*

Dear Mr Kent,

I know, through André DAVEN, that you have been kind enough to intervene in behalf of my son Alain, and that you have asked His Excellency Admiral LEAHY[1] to use his good offices in obtaining for him both French and American visas.

I want you to be assured of my deep and lasting gratitude. At the moment I have only one means of proving it to you: by working with my whole heart and soul for your Company, and that I should have done in any case. But your kind gesture is to me a stronger bond even than a contract, and I shall do my utmost to show my appreciation in a tangible way.

It is more than likely that, sooner or later, you will meet my son. If I may say it, he is a fine boy, who has played his part in this war in a particularly valiant way. Though barely eighteen years old, he saw active fighting from the outset, being one of a cavalry regiment of which only a handful returned alive.

Your understanding of my paternal anxiety is quite in keeping with the humane attitude I have found in the American authorities generally, and as far as I am concerned, it contributes enormously toward strengthening my attachment to your country.

With my kindest feelings,

Jean Renoir

1 William Daniel Leahy (1875–1959), American admiral and diplomat. In 1940, he was named ambassador to Vichy France.

To Charles Feldman[1] [*Original in English*]   *9 April 1941*
Beverly Hills   *Hollywood*

Dear Mr Feldman,

Following the conference of 31 March between yourself, Mr Dover and Mr Ned Marin, and Dido Freire and myself (I was very sorry that Mr Blum could not be there), I have carried out your instructions and have done everything in my power to help our mutual friend Daven. I have done it, indeed, with pleasure, since he is my compatriot who has helped me with regard to my son, and I am happy to do him a good turn. But, as you know, this has led me finally to accept the idea of doing *Venezuela*.[2]

There is no doubt that this is a very good subject. Mr Nunnally Johnson[3] has written a remarkable screenplay, and Mr Zanuck is particularly anxious that I do it. This latter circumstance impresses me very much, for Mr Zanuck knows his business and must surely have good reasons for his choice. But this is not my kind of film, and in making it I am almost sure of compromising gravely my career in America. In this whole matter my own personality may have been a little neglected, and the fact overlooked that the author of *La Grande Illusion* can do more exceptional and personal things. All my life I have missed out with ordinary films, and succeeded only with films which seemed impossible. I have taken the liberty of calling your attention to this point, which must interest you since our interests are the same.

As I have told you, I have full confidence in Mr Blum and in you; this I have already demonstrated. But I have less confidence in my success with *Venezuela*; and I wish that you would, from this moment, try to find a means to offset the consequences of the mistake, not material but psychological, of my first film in America. I see a way of doing this. It is to have me sign a contract at once for *I Wake Up Screaming*[4] with Dwight Taylor[5] and Milton Sperling.[6] Taylor is now developing some excellent ideas, and I feel that my collaboration with him can produce great results. And while I am making these two films I wish you would study thoroughly the question of *Wind, Sand and Stars*,[7] and persuade either Mr Zanuck or an independent producer to take up this great idea – the only one which has presented itself up to now that is capable of placing me in the front rank of Hollywood directors, and of giving me in the United States the place I occupied in Europe.

I should like this setup to be ready before the release of *Venezuela*, for I am afraid that the effect of this first film will be detrimental to my future projects.

You must not read into this letter any expression of hard feelings. I am very pleased with the idea of beginning *Venezuela* in an atmosphere which promises to be most friendly. But I am most anxious, before making it, that you know my exact state of mind.

Very cordially yours,

Jean Renoir

1 Charles Feldman and Ralph Blum were Jean Renoir's first American agents.
2 Unrealized project.
3 Nunnally Johnson (1897–1977), screenwriter whose credits included *The Grapes of Wrath* (John Ford, 1940), *Roxie Hart* (William Wellman, 1942), and *The Dark Mirror* (Robert Siodmak, 1946).
4 *I Wake Up Screaming* was eventually directed by Bruce Humberstone in the same year. Also known as *Hot Spot*.
5 Dwight Taylor (1902–86), screenwriter whose credits included *Pick-up on South Street* (Sam Fuller, 1953) and *Interlude* (Douglas Sirk, 1957).
6 Milton Sperling, producer and screenwriter, whose credits included *Sun Valley Serenade* (Bruce Humberstone, 1941) and *I Wake Up Screaming*.
7 English title of *Terre des Hommes*, a novel by Antoine de Saint-Exupéry.

To Mr Avronsart[1]

My dear Avronsart,

If I haven't written to you until now, it's because I was truly ashamed of discovering my total lack of power in all areas.

Hollywood is an immense land in which no one is in contact with anyone else. This is why agents are the kings of the country. It is they who secure your contracts and who introduce you to the studios.

My agent, Feldman, arranged a contract for me at Fox, and no doubt I will start work in a month. But I can say that, during the three months which have just elapsed, I have truly only become acquainted with my agent, my English teacher, and my doctor, because I've had a terribly serious case of rheumatism from my old war wound. Outside of these three people, I visit the numerous French people who are here and who are in the same boat.

For the last two weeks, I've started jabbering on a little in English and making a few more friends. I am still not at the point where I can do you even the slightest favour, but I'm hoping that once I've made my film, if it is successful my position will change completely. Here, one has to prove oneself. The reception that one might have had abroad, as is my case, can allow one to find satisfactory employment here (and this is what happened to me). That's quite something in itself, but having taken this first step, people look for a chance to trip you up and it is useless to ask them for anything until one has entered into their circles, and this is achieved through the work.

This said, I like Americans a lot. Their spirit pleases me, and I bow before the necessities of life in a country where I am a foreigner.

What complicates things even more is that there are many unemployed, and each time that one suggests anyone coming from abroad, one is aware of a very natural kind of *self-defence*[2] which comes into play. For example, I decided to talk about your article to some journalists. And each time they told me that they themselves and many of their American colleagues had dozens of very interesting articles ready for print which they counted on for a living, but hadn't been able to place.

My dear Avronsart, I am in the middle of finding out one thing, that here I am not Jean Renoir doing his tenth film in his country but a newcomer, very warmly received, having found employment that many Americans wouldn't be able to find, and who is making his <u>first</u> film in America. If this debut film is good, I will be able to do lots of things. For example, I will be able to bring my brother over, which is impossible for me to do right now.

There is another way to look at things. And I admit that I am often this way inclined. That is to consider my trip here as a study trip. That having done one or two films under technical conditions unknown in Europe, I will learn a lot, and that, after this, I will return to my country where I will be able to make our own industry profit from the knowledge I have gained.

I apologize for all this rambling on about myself . . . Pray to God that peace arrives soon, and that communication is resumed once more. We live in uncertain times, and that prevents so many things from happening.

Jean Renoir

1 Journalist.
2 Originally in English.

To Eugène Lourié[1]
Bormes

12 May 1941
Hollywood

Dear Lourié,

I would have liked to have answered by saying that I've done a lot for you. Alas, despite my desire to see you here, there was nothing I could do. I have to tell you that my attempts have been restricted to small talk. I have been in contact with some people who want to help you, but who seem as helpless as myself.

In order to do something here, it is necessary to have proved oneself. It is possible that, after one or two films, I will have a little more influence. But, for the moment, I am still getting out of this slack period in which other people do me favours.

Because life here is impossible without a *job*.[2] It's the first thing that I would have wanted to guarantee you, even something minor.

When I tell you that I still haven't been able to hire Dido as my secretary, and that the American Consul in Nice has refused Alain a visa because the papers I sent to him weren't sufficient, I hope you will understand.

It is possible 'the opportunity' will arrive. When it comes, you have to jump aboard. Maybe this opportunity will present itself tomorrow, with a producer telling me: 'I love the art direction on your films, let's bring over the artist that did it.'

My biggest misfortune is that I don't speak English, which condemns me to live a very isolated life. I don't have the ease of conversation that opens so many doors.

Concerning normal affidavits: they are very difficult to get because they must be supplied by American citizens. The 'Unions' mistrust any possible foreign competition, which makes getting affidavits in our milieu rather difficult.

I have become so depressed by the idea of my son, as well as my brother, being far away from me for such a potentially long period that several times I've almost tried to go home. The obstacle is that I have a contract, that I've been paid, and it would not be very honourable to fail to observe my professional commitments.

I have the impression that everything will return to normal, and that either myself or some other friend will suddenly find a way to bring you here.

None of this would matter if we were in a period where you could earn a normal living.

I often think of you and your problem (to say the least) of being out of work, and of your wife's courage in putting up with this situation.

I feel helpless and stupid, incapable of offering you the simplest words of encouragement.

Write me a short letter when you have the time. Simply tell me how you are doing.

I continue to hope that one day I will be able to write you a more cheerful letter

Warmest regards,

Jean Renoir

---

1 Eugène Lourié (1905–91), art director, whose credits included many of Jean Renoir's films: *Madame Bovary, Les Bas-Fonds, La Bête Humaine, La Grande Illusion, La Règle du Jeu, This Land is Mine, The Southerner, Diary of a Chambermaid*, and *The River*. He later became a director.

2 Originally in English.

To Charles Feldman and Ralph Blum   *14 May 1941*
[*Original in English*]   *Hollywood*
Beverly Hills

Gentlemen,

I have been informed, by a telephone call from Mr Blum, of the proposals of Twentieth Century-Fox to postpone the starting date of my work.

This doesn't suit me at all, for I have every interest in getting through with *Venezuela* quickly, and I was all ready to begin it as soon as the script was finished and the casting assured. But I am anxious to please them, since they have been first-rate toward me, and I am particularly grateful to them for all they have done in the matter of my son.

This is why I ask your advice on these proposals for an arrangement.

The greatest risk for me is the breaking of my contract through the entry of the United States into the War. I should like you to try to obtain from these gentlemen the principle of an indemnity, to be fixed, in the event of a sudden stoppage of my salary payments because of war.

Another question is that of my first film. You know how little enthusiasm I have for *Venezuela*. the only thing which seems to me to redeem this subject is the admirable script of Mr Nunnally Johnson. But even this does not alter the fact that my speciality is not great spectacle films; and I should be happy if Mr Zanuck would consent to entrust another subject to me.

Of the two subjects which he has proposed, *Venezuela* and *I Wake Up Screaming*, there is one which quite pleases me; this is the second, with Charles Laughton,[1] Henry Fonda[2] and Alice Faye.[3]

This is evidence of my good-will, and I should be very happy if it were decided that this would be my first assignment.

I now come to the most important point. When I came to Hollywood, it was in the hope of bringing to Americans the best of myself. Now, rightly or wrongly, I have the conviction that I can make a good thing with *Wind, Sand and Stars*, by St Exupéry.[4]

I should like, then, that after *I Wake Up Screaming*, you find me a possibility for making *Wind, Sand and Stars*. This book could first be proposed to Fox. But in case the subject does not please Mr Zanuck, it would be a very good thing if he would consent to give me my freedom to make this film with another producer. In this case, the option which Fox has on my second film would be applicable after a normal time has been allowed me in which to make *Wind, Sand and Stars* or any other film. (I say 'any other film' because, if no producer should want to make *Wind, Sand and Stars*, I should not have to remain all this time without doing anything.)

In the event that Fox should give up the idea of making *I Wake Up Screaming*, I should like the subject to replace it to be chosen by mutual agreement. The same would apply to the second subject in the event of the option being taken up.

I should be equally happy if you would be good enough to draw the attention of my future producers to the fact that I am much more an author of films than a director, and that the several successes I have had, I have obtained above all through my work on the scripts. Certainly, I do not pretend to be able to do in English what I have done in French: that is, the adaptation of a story (which often was my own, as in the case of *La Grande Illusion*), the screenplay, the dialogue, and everything except the production, in which I do not claim to be a master.

But there would be an advantage for the producer in allowing me at least to collaborate. I should certainly make a much better job of directing scenes in whose creation I had participated.

To arrive at such an arrangement, which seems more suitable to my temperament, I should not be tied up too long with Fox.

I beg you, gentlemen, to see in this letter only the desire to seek the right means of assuring the quality of my work in America. I am delighted with my present situation, and these few suggestions are made simply to set at rest my professional conscience.

In that which concerns questions of money – reservation made for the precaution to which I have referred in case of war – I should be delighted to accept the settlement of which you have spoken to me.

Sincerely yours,

Jean Renoir

1 Charles Laughton (1899–1962), actor whose credits included *The Private Life of Henry VIII* (Alexander Korda, 1933), *The Hunchback of Notre Dame* (William Dieterle, 1939), and *Advise and Consent* (Otto Preminger, 1960). He also directed *The Night of the Hunter* (1955).
2 Henry Fonda (1905–82), actor whose credits included *Young Mr Lincoln* (John Ford, 1939), *The Lady Eve* (Preston Sturges, 1941), and *12 Angry Men* (Sidney Lumet, 1957).
3 Alice Faye (b.1912), singer-actress whose credits include *George White's Scandals* (George White, 1934), *Alexander's Ragtime Band* (Henry King, 1938), and *Hello, Frisco, Hello* (Bruce Humberstone, 1943).
4 Antoine de Saint-Exupéry (1900–44), author of *The Little Prince* (1943), *Night Flight* (1931), and *Terre des Hommes (Wind, Sand and Stars)* (1939).

To Darryl F. Zanuck [*Original in English*]   *23 May 1941*
Twentieth Century-Fox Film Corporation   *Hollywood*
Los Angeles

Dear Mr Zanuck,

I thank you for having thought of me for *Swamp Water*. This is exactly the subject I would have chosen for myself if I had been my own producer.

I am not yet capable of discussing Dudley Nichols'[1] screenplay in detail. As I read English too slowly, it is my collaborator, Miss Dido Freire, who has translated it for me page by page, during the night. She shares my enthusiasm.

I am a great admirer of Dudley Nichols, who collaborated with John Ford on one of the world's best films, *The Informer*, and I shall be so glad to meet him Tuesday at the conference.

Perhaps certain parts of this screenplay are a little long. Not that they are not interesting, but they risk involving us in too much footage. In a week, when I have studied the question carefully, I will offer a few suggestions to Dudley Nichols.

I am delighted that you have thought of giving me Irving Pichel[2] to help me on my first American picture. I am so delighted that I ask you to let me study, with him, a plan of work which will permit us not to be separated. I have the impression that between now and the 14th of July (a very good date for a Frenchman!) we have time, the two of us, to do together the swamp views, and also to prepare the work in the studio.

I am thoroughly happy with the casting which you propose. Permit me, nevertheless, to express one regret, which is not to be making this magnificent production with Tyrone Power,[3] whom I like tremendously, not only as an actor, but also as a man.

I do not say this in disparagement of Dana Andrews,[4] whom I know too little through his brief performance in *Tobacco Road*,[5] in which he was excellent.

Sincerely yours,
Jean Renoir

1 Dudley Nichols (1895–1960), screenwriter who won an Academy Award for *The Informer* (John Ford, 1935). His other major credits include: *Bringing Up Baby* (Howard Hawks, 1938) and *Stagecoach* (John Ford, 1939).
2 Irving Pichel (1891–1954), actor, producer and director. His directorial credits include: *The Most Dangerous Game* (1930) and *The Moon is Down* (1943).
3 Tyrone Power Jr (1913–58), actor whose credits included: *Alexander's Ragtime Band* (Henry King, 1938) and *Blood and Sand* (Rouben Mamoulian, 1941).
4 Dana Andrews (1909–92), actor whose credits included *Swamp Water, The Ox-Bow Incident* (William Wellman, 1943), and *The Best Years of Our Lives* (William Wyler, 1946).
5 *Tobacco Road* (John Ford, 1941).

To Antoine de Saint-Exupéry

New York

Dear Saint-Ex,

In my letter yesterday, I forgot to explain to you a point which I believe is very important and about which you should speak to Becker.[1] It is that projects which are a little different from the Film Industry norm are not given the go-ahead in Hollywood, but in New York.

I have absolutely no proof to support this theory, but I have the feeling that here, it's a Factory, with workers, engineers, and important Managing Directors; in short, people who follow orders. But the financiers, those who feed the machine and reap the rewards, are in New York.

Of course, the Studio heads here are extremely important and can decide everything. But they hold back from jumping into projects which are outside of the ordinary and which, if they were to fail, would cause them to be blamed by New York without being able to defend themselves with the same old argument which is: How could I foresee that this story wouldn't please the public, since so many films like it made a lot of money last year?

Let's take the case of Orson Welles,[2] for example. He could handle an unusual story as well as use completely different techniques to those practised here. But this is because he was known by one of the heads of Radio who happened to have found himself with considerable financial interests at RKO,[3] which allowed Welles to do what he wanted at this studio.

I hope that *Wind, Sand and Stars* can come together without us having to grease the wheels as much. But, all the same, I really wanted to share my thoughts with you, which perhaps could be very useful for Becker.

As always, keep this secret and discreet. Hollywood is a small town.

With all my love,

Jean Renoir

1 Maximilian Becker, literary agent.
2 Orson Welles (1915–85), actor and director, whose films included *Citizen Kane* (1941), *The Magnificent Ambersons* (1943), and *The Lady From Shanghai* (1948). His contract at RKO gave him unprecedented freedom as a studio director.
3 Radio-Keith-Orpheum (RKO) Studios.

On 5 June, Twentieth Century-Fox announces that Jean Renoir will direct Swamp Water. *He and Dido fly with Irving Pichel (designated producer and dialogue director) to Waycross, Georgia, to scout locations.*

To Darryl F. Zanuck [*Original in English*]   *7 June 1941*
Twentieth Century-Fox Film Corporation
Los Angeles

Dear Mr Zanuck,

I have seen *Blood and Sand*,[1] as you had recommended me to do because of Linda Darnell.[2] She is still better in it than she was in *Chad Hannah*,[3] and if the audience near me did not show very much enthusiasm for her, perhaps it was because she is a little too charming in tragic situations.

Before beginning the splendid story that you have been good enough to assign to me, and which pleases me still more now that I have seen Georgia, I feel it is my duty to tell you frankly my impression of this actress. She is very beautiful, very sympathetic, very sweet – too sweet, in my opinion, to represent a young girl who, at an age when the others are experiencing the joys and the protection of family life, is obliged to earn her own living as a maid-of-all-work in the home of the village grocers. The McCords are evidently good folks, but they are incapable of taking the place of Julie's dead mother and of her hunted father. Now, Linda Darnell radiates happiness and health. She is so charming that in this village of good, simple folk she would be treated like a little queen. I assume that the public will want a contrast between Julie and Mabel, and it seems clear to me that the more humble we make Julie, the greater will be the force of her victory over this daughter of well-to-do farmers who is so sure of herself.

On the other hand, rightly or wrongly, I am full of confidence in Ann [sic] Baxter.[4] I have seen some of her tests, and they have been a revelation to me with regard to the role of Julie. I think that her person would suggest to the public the whole pathetic and tragic situation of Ben's little sweetheart, without our being obliged to explain it by long-drawn-out scenes, or too lengthy dialogue.

I should be very grateful if you would authorize me to make a test with Ann Baxter. This is perhaps the best way of judging the situation clearly.

I have read your letter on tempo. I agree with you completely, and I hope in *Swamp Water* to give you satisfaction in this respect.

Sincerely yours,
Jean Renoir

Zanuck added the following note to this letter:

Dear Jean,
    It is okay to make tests of Darnell and Baxter.
    D.F.Z.

1 *Blood and Sand* (Rouben Mamoulian, 1941).
2 Linda Darnell (1921–65), actress whose credits included *Blood and Sand* (Rouben Mamoulian, 1941), *Hangover Square* (John Brahm, 1945), and *Unfaithfully Yours* (Preston Sturges, 1948).
3 *Chad Hannah* (Henry King, 1940).
4 Anne Baxter (1923–85), actress whose credits included *Swamp Water, The Razor's Edge* (Edmund Goulding, 1946), and *All About Eve* (Joseph L. Mankiewicz, 1950).

To Pierre Fighiera[1]

20 *June 1941*
Hollywood

Dear Pierrot,
    I am trying to imagine what kind of life you may be living now. Here we have a French newspaper called *Le Courrier du Pacifique*, which contains all the Havas news items and some news about France. There was recently a study on the conditions of horticulturists in the Midi, and the author of the article was forced to conclude that the situation, although a little brighter, nevertheless remains only bearable. I would like to think the article expresses the real state of things.
    When you write to me again (and I hope that you will), tell me a little about all this. And especially, tell me about yourself, Alice[2] and Mr Burfin, and friends from over there. Often I reproach myself and I think of my stupidity in the past. In France, it was so easy to see each other . . . and yet we didn't get around to it. Now that I have a vague idea of America, I have the impression that, when I return, I will want to go all over France . . . and above all, constantly stay in touch with the people who are dear to me.
    I am going to start a film called *Swamp Water* (*Marécage*). The subject matter seems quite good, [but] I had to fight ferociously to rid myself of some problems more ridiculous than anything in life. Here, one doesn't make what one wants to. The studios are run in a military way, and a director is nothing more than an employee among many other employees. Nevertheless, I am not unhappy. If the system is bad, the people are charming and even the most powerful people will still talk to you. Perhaps I will end up getting out while the going is good. I am going

to film some exteriors in Georgia. It's a 5,000-kilometre trip. I already went there to look around, it's a fascinating place. Of course, we travel there by plane, which takes a long day and night. But after the monotonous trip above the clouds, one arrives in a country completely different from Hollywood. It's no longer a region under construction like here, where cardboard houses grow like mushrooms, it's old country, with old wooden farms and country folk who resemble those from our country. I met, moreover, many people of French descent. I could see why, in the rest of America, the Georgians are considered as a rather backward people. Perhaps I love backward people, but down there, I made lots of charming friends. I don't know if you've read the stories of Mark Twain,[3] such as *Tom Sawyer* or *Huckleberry Finn*. If you have read them, you know my rapture at finding myself suddenly in the setting of these stories which cradled my youth.

I am going there mainly for the swamp, which is called Okefenokee Swamp and has remained extremely wild. One finds there a great number of crocodiles, otters, coypus, vultures and black bears. It's a kind of tropical Sologne. We will reconstruct a large portion of this countryside in the studio, but I can film some shots on location. I achieved something else: that is, to film with young actors who are not well known but are full of enthusiasm, and who will do just about all I want. I'm starting to speak a little English and I can give them instructions directly. When I make a big mistake in English, everybody is amused. They aren't nasty and don't have the sort of stupid hostility against foreigners that one encounters in lots of countries.

I am very happy in my dealings with the technicians and crew. They are truly very devoted and their work is first rate. I feel they are trying to help me. In sum, all of this would be perfect if all the companies here hadn't become so big. The studios are like huge factories, and the way they are organized is remarkable. One only has to express a wish for it instantly to be realized, but one has more the impression of working in a shoe factory than in the cinema.

I don't know if I will make good films here, but at least I'm not wasting my time. I'm learning so many things. I am especially learning to discipline myself, which perhaps is necessary.

My old friend Pierrot, all this does not make up for our olive trees. There are some nice olive trees here, but they are very small and seem to me to be less silver-coloured. Above all, their trunks are not as knotty nor their shapes as bizarre as ours. Californian wine isn't bad, but it's not as good as le Bellet ... The climate is magnificent, but it brings on rheumatism. For the first time in twenty-five years, I suffer from my old war wound. But most important of all, none of this matters ... and I know well that when I have done what I have to do here, I will return to France and all my friends.

.With much love,

Jean Renoir.

1 Pierre Fighiera, florist and old friend of Jean Renoir.
2 Alice Fighiera, wife of Pierre.
3 Mark Twain (Samuel Clemens) (1835–1910), author.

To Jean Renoir [*Original in English*]   *6 July 1941*
Hollywood   *New Milford, Connecticut*

Dear Jean Renoir,

Not until now has there been enough time for us to catch our breath and settle down to saying hello to our friends. And you and Dido are first in our minds. How can we tell you what a pleasure it was to find such new friends in Hollywood, where always in the past Esta[1] has found social life so uncongenial? I shall say nothing. You both know how we felt and what joy it was to mingle our sense of living, even so briefly. I have never seen Esta respond so quickly to people who were, for the first moment at least, strangers. Dido, we press your hand. Esta admires you deeply, and I say that light shines upon you both. Even in this shadowed world.

By this time you must be in the thick of Hollywood's 'factory life'. I had a note from Mr Zanuck upon arrival here saying he was pleased with the final script. Thank goodness <u>somebody</u> was pleased. We all know what happens to scripts and films and from long experience I say there is no use complaining about it. One must simply do the best one can. Once in a blue moon there comes a time when by scheming and planning you can make your own sort of picture. And until those times come one must meantime live.

I saw in the papers that you had got Walter Huston[2] to play Thursday. I have always believed him to be a grand actor, with real power and sincerity, though he has not frequently been permitted to use his gifts. Whether or not you got Miss Gish[3] I haven't heard. A sweet woman indeed. Perhaps you will find use for her in a later picture. Mr Z[anuck] said you were leaving for Georgia and I rather worried, for we were in the midst of a wretched heat wave and the humid weather continued until only a few days ago. I feared you would be having the devil's own time down there, with those man-eating flies and the like. It was even too hot to work here. I tried but even the paper in the typewriter would get limp and wet and then I would go dripping out to the lake to get dry. That sounds like a joke but it is true. A plunge in the water and then one could dry off for a while.

[. . .] Dido, I know Jean Renoir is too busy, but you must find time to scribble us a note and tell us how you are and how the film is going. We look forward eagerly to see you again in the fall, unless you will take a trip east when the film is finished and see how fine Connecticut is.

With warm thoughts for you,
Dudley (+ Esta) Nichols

1 Esta V. Nichols (1889–1968), wife of Dudley.
2 Walter Huston (1884–1950), actor whose credits included *Dodsworth* (William Wyler, 1936), *Swamp Water*, and *Treasure of the Sierra Madre* (John Huston (son of Walter), 1948).
3 Lillian Gish (1894–1993), actress whose credits included *Birth of a Nation* (D. W. Griffith, 1915), *Way Down East* (Griffith, 1920), and *Night of the Hunter* (Charles Laughton, 1955).

To Fritz Lang[1]

9 *July 1941*
Hollywood

Dear Sir,

I was truly very happy to receive such a kind letter from you. Your thoughts are those of a good friend, and I thank you for them. I know nothing of the article which you refer to regarding *Swamp Water*.[2] I am too much of a beginner in English to read anything but the main news of the war in the daily newspapers.

I hope that our relationship will go beyond this, and that I will have the great joy of meeting you.

I'm writing to you in French, knowing that you speak my language perfectly. In a short time, I hope that I will be able to address you in English. As for German, my efforts to learn English have made me forget almost all of it.

Best regards,
Jean Renoir

1 Fritz Lang (1890–1976), director whose credits included *Dr Mabuse* (1922), *Metropolis* (1927), *M* (1931), and *Fury* (1936). He remade *La Chienne* as *Scarlet Street* (1945) and *La Bête Humaine* as *Human Desire* (1954).

2 An article had been published which suggested that Lang was angry at having been replaced by Jean Renoir on *Swamp Water*. Lang wrote to Renoir to deny the article.

To Jean Renoir [*Original in English*]   *Bastille Day [14 July 1941]*
Hollywood   *New Milford, Connecticut*

Dear Jean,

This day of all others I must write to you. And imagine that your letter should arrive on this day! Esta and I have both enjoyed your fine letter to her, and it delighted her the more being in French. She will treasure it. Soon she will reply and write to Dido. Esta has not been well and I am worried: ever since that serious operation several years ago she has not been herself. What can one do? I don't know. Perhaps we should go to one of the great clinics, the Mayos or Johns Hopkins, and have searching diagnosis. Ah, well, we go on as best we can.

[...] I am eager to learn how *Swamp Water* goes. But don't take any time from your work for writing notes; once you are in the swing of things it consumes all energy, I know. I'm sorry it was not a better script for you. Had we been able to work the first script over ourselves for several weeks, it would have been a different story. Zanuck is a remarkable and strange man in many ways; but I will confess to you in confidence that at heart there is no rapport between this type of man and myself; it has been a painful struggle for me to adapt myself to work and get along with the Hollywood executive; now I do it too well and that is probably a bad sign for me, shows a loss of personal integrity. But there is no point in speaking of these things openly and one should avoid it. My salvation now lies in staying away from Hollywood as much as possible and trying to write in other forms. Unfortunately I love the cinema form too much.

Soon I shall take some snapshots of our place here and send them on so you and Dido may have a notion of Connecticut. It is like living in a deep green forest here, with a little lake before the house, and nothing to disturb our tranquillity except the things that happen within – and the anguish of the world which one cannot put out of mind. If one only had some certain news about the Soviet war. I am so distrustful of the British leaders; now is the time to strike and they are not striking. I cannot help fearing that some deal was made through Hess and that a fascist world is rushing upon us unawares. When one can no longer

15 Jean Renoir on the set of *Swamp Water*. On the far left is Irving Pichel; in the centre the actors Walter Huston (Thursday Ragan) and Mary Howard (Hannah)

trust one is finished. Nietzsche's[1] hatred of love is storming across the world.

Dudley Nichols

1 Friedrich Nietzsche (1844–1900), German philosopher whose works included *The Birth of Tragedy* (1872) and *Beyond Good and Evil* (1886). His theories of a 'superman' were seriously distorted by the Nazis.

To Dudley Nichols [*Original in English*]   21 *July 1941*
New Milford, Connecticut   *Hollywood*

Dear Dudley,

[...] I am not at all enthusiastic about my work at Fox. For a lazy director, it would be ideal. It consists of being seated in an armchair and saying, 'Action!' and 'Cut!' It is useless to tire oneself out trying to present the scenes according to a personal conception, for everything is decided by Zanuck, and when the rushes don't conform to his ideas, he has the scenes reshot.

I'm afraid you will be disappointed in *Swamp Water*. I ask you not to judge my work in America from this film, which will be Mr Zanuck's and not mine.

I have two ideas which haunt me. The first is the story you have told me. The other is St Exupéry's *Wind, Sand and Stars* (I wish you would read this book). If I can't do either one of them, I'm going to try to write, to commit to paper the heap of ideas I have in my head. In any case, I would rather sell peanuts in Mexico than make films at Fox. I am not a eunuch, and the joys of the harem do not constitute an idea which can satisfy me.

My dear Dudley, your letter has been for me a ray of light in the darkness. I've said to myself, 'So there are still good souls who honestly love our poor medium!' With all my heart, I want to work with you. If this does not come to pass, I want at least the boon of seeing you often.

You have made mention of your wife's health. I would like so much to hear that she is quite well now. I have a great affection for her, and it would distress me very much to know that she was ill. Don't fail to tell her how much I am hoping – in a few weeks, when this film is finished – to find the occasion of spending some good evenings with the two of you.

With all my affection,
Jean Renoir

To Jean Renoir [*Original in English*]   29 *July 1941*
Hollywood   *New Milford*

Dear Jean,

Your letter brings both melancholy and wry laughter. At your comparison of Fox studio with a harem I looked back on studios I have worked in and saw those offices of writers and directors as curtained cubicles where the coy wives and concubines wait for the head pasha to come every Wednesday afternoon with his little gifts of paper, large gilt-edged checks for the favorites and a few scattered coins for the ageing and less talented. Is it some new perversion Pasha Gildwyn [sic] or Pasha Zanuck wishes this afternoon? Very well – we'll put our souls into impossible positions! Tell lies? Surely, a thousand and one! Corrupt life, deny reality – anything to keep on getting those paper gifts. Don't go out in the world, dear ladies, or you might get impregnated by life. Just sit tight and wait for the royal sperm of money.

But it's really worse than that, for the pashas control the mechanism of procreation, and the girls can't leave the seraglio and give birth to anything, no matter how much the desire.

That being the case at present, I hope you will find strength to stick it out. I don't care a damn about the script. Make the film. Don't be driven out. There will be a little of Renoir at the heart of it, even though it wear[s] the skin of Zanuck. As I wrote Dido, the people who count will judge not you but Hollywood in this film, for your achievements are clearly recorded elsewhere . . . Yes, a story teller, a dramatist at heart; it is simply that you chose a medium one step nearer the imagination than the word to work in. To do that you had to master the medium of the word first. Certainly you can step back to it. The eloquence of your writing, and its simplicity, are added proof of that.

I had a nice letter from Irving Pichel. I wish I could tell you the fine things he speaks of you. He is very devoted. Please believe that when I write that he would not fight in the making of a picture, I meant no criticism, he knows he is not in a position to make any fight and being a man with a family he is anxious about his security. The old demon that gets everyone in this present world – security – as if there were any such thing save within our own souls.

[. . .] I've felt that if you finished *Swamp Water* and got some sort of successful film out of it, regardless how far it fell short of being Renoir, we could take a story and go to Wanger,[1] and get a producing setup for ourselves, first to make one picture and then further ones if it turned out well. And we'd make it turn out well.

If we cannot get *Hunky*[2] we shall find something else when you are ready to make another film. I've not yet read St Ex's book but I promise you I shall very shortly. Will write you then. If it impresses you so much as film material I feel sure it will impress me. For myself (unless one is ready to make the film of all time, of heroic proportions and intensity) I prefer material that is not 'dispersed', a story that focuses as much as possible in one or two characters, with everyone else incidental to the fabric of the unfolding drama. That was what I sought in *The Informer*. *Hunky* has the same thing. *The Baker's Wife*[3] had it in the comedy vein. *La Bête Humaine* had it. *La Grande Illusion* was a larger story, and the same attention was given to the group as if they were individuals in a smaller drama; yet the drama peaked in Gabin . . . Never mind, we shall find story material, or originate it ourselves. Perhaps that would be most exciting of all – to originate a film. You can do it alone. But perhaps in an alien environment I can be of great aid. I feel I would learn much about film writing in such a collaboration. I feel I am only at the rudiments of screen writing, for one has no chance to expand and develop in the Hollywood setup. For we only grow in any art form by <u>doing</u>. From living the material, from doing the mastery . . . There are plenty of great topics in these times; we can find the theme and then what matters is how it is handled, how deeply and emotionally – and then how skilfully – it is developed in terms of cinematic art.

Esta has had some bad days but she is feeling better at the moment, thank God. Here is a complicated affliction in which one does not know what is psychic and what is organic. [. . .] She is an intense being and like all such people must have a strong meaning in life or things go ill. Lacking religion or a clear aim, and unable to find any pride in my work any more than I could myself, she came to a sort of psychic bewilderment. If I can make my life mean more, she can make hers mean more, and she will be better. She certainly is improving here.

I'd intended writing more and telling you about our life here, but the telephone repair man has just driven up the lane and now I must show him what I want done; and I must get this in the mailbox or it will not go off for another day. Soon I'll take some snaps and show you what a serene place we live in. You and Dido must come and visit us when the damned film is wound up. Forgive this sudden haste, and thanks again for your fine letter.

Our warmest greetings,
Dudley [Nichols]

1 Walter Wanger (1894–1968), producer whose credits included: *Queen Christine* (Rouben
Mamoulian, 1934), *Stagecoach* (John Ford, 1939), and *I Want to Live!* (Robert Wise, 1958)
2 Nichols' unrealized project.
3 *The Baker's Wife (La Femme du Boulanger)* (Marcel Pagnol, 1938).

To Darryl F. Zanuck [*Original in English*]

1 August 1941
Twentieth Century-Fox Film Corporation   *Hollywood*
Los Angeles

Dear Zanuck,

I have received your note regarding backgrounds and my excessive
slowness in the film *Swamp Water*. This letter, and our previous conversation about the acting of Walter Huston, have made me feel that our
association is a mistake, both for you and for me. The fact is, I have been
too long in this profession to change the methods in which I have come to
believe sincerely, and which, in any case, are adapted to my temperament.
You yourself have very definite ideas on the direction of films, and these
ideas have stood the test. Since my methods seem to be at such variance
with your ideas, why prolong a collaboration which gives no enthusiasm
to either of us? As you well know, in our profession it is only through
enthusiam and sincerity that one is able from time to time to move the public.

Rest assured, my dear Zanuck, that if you ask me to give up the direction
of the film, I will do so ungrudgingly.

Cordially yours,
Jean Renoir

To Charles Boyer[1]

3 August 1941
Hollywood

Dear Charles,

I find myself in a rather unfortunate situation which, without a doubt, is
going to force me to leave our very pleasant club, La Cienega.[2]

I'm having a tough time with the work Zanuck has entrusted me with.
He would have liked me to make this film very quickly, and be contented
with shooting what is in the screenplay without bringing anything of
myself to it. I know nothing of this type of work. In France, rather than
being a director, I was a story teller, transforming a sheet of paper on to a
screen. The outcome of this wrong way of thinking about my work is that I
am in the process of driving Zanuck to despair by my slowness. Any
moment now I expect him to dispense with my services for which I can
hardly blame him.

[113]

16 French exiles in Hollywood: from left to right, M. Pizella, Julien Duvivier,
René Clair, François Prieur and Jean Renoir

This deplorable state of affairs unfortunately coincides with a painful new outbreak of my old wound from the last war.

All this makes me think that very soon I am going to have to break with this life, gather together some money I've put aside, and bury myself in some little provincial hole-in-the-wall town where I can replace the camera with the pen, and try writing a book.

Dear Charles, I am very busy right now, and this prevents me from telling you everything face to face.

I've received a new letter from my friend in London[3] who is doing so much for the French over there. I believe that she deserves recognition from the Hollywood Chapter.

My best wishes to both you and Pat Patterson.[4]

Regards,

Jean Renoir

1 Charles Boyer (1897–1978), actor whose credits included: *Mayerling* (Anatole Litvak, 1936), *Tovarich* (Anatole Litvak, 1937), *Gaslight* (George Cukor, 1944), and *Madame de . . .* (Max Ophuls, 1953).
2 Boyer founded the French Research Foundation during World War Two, which served as a library and a meeting place for the French in Hollywood. He received a special Oscar for this work in 1942.
3 Olwyn Vaughan.
4 Pat Patterson (1911–78), actress, wife of Boyer.

Telegram to Darryl F. Zanuck   *18 August 1941*
[*Original in English*]
Twentieth Century-Fox Film Corporation
Los Angeles

ALTHOUGH MR KOENIG FINALLY ADMITTED IN HIS CONVERSATION WITH ME TODAY THAT THE REAL REASON WHY I WAS BEING TAKEN OFF DIRECTION OF SWAMP WATER WAS BECAUSE MR ZANUCK CONSIDERS THE PICTURE IS PROGRESSING TOO SLOWLY. NEVERTHELESS IN VIEW OF MR KOENIGS INSINUATION EARLIER IN CONVERSATION THAT I WAS NOT WELL ENOUGH TO CONTINUE PICTURE I AM COMPELLED TO INFORM YOU THAT I AM READY WILLING AND ABLE BOTH FROM STANDPOINT OF MY HEALTH AND OTHERWISE TO CONTINUE WITH THE RENDITION OF MY SERVICES AND I SHALL OF COURSE EXPECT TO BE COMPENSATED IN FULL IN ACCORDANCE WITH THE TERMS OF MY CONTRACT WITH YOU
SINCERELY
JEAN RENOIR

To Dudley Nichols

Dear Dudley,

I haven't kept you up to date about what's happened during these last weeks because things change every day, and it's only now that I'm beginning to see the situation clearly.

Let me go back earlier in the story. A little more than a week ago the situation was very tense. So much so that Koenig asked me not to continue the film for health reasons. This was a deplorable solution for me because I wouldn't have been paid, and I would have been tied to Fox by an option for another film. My agent advised Fox that I wanted to quit working, but that I wasn't sick and I would have to be paid. In the middle of the night, they telephoned me about coming back to work the next morning, and this occasion was one of the greatest joys of my life. When I arrived on the set, the workers, technicians and actors gave me a round of applause and came over and shook my hand. Dear Dudley, this moment made me love the American people even more. Now I have definitely been conquered. My greatest desire is to suceed at something here. And I would very much like that something to be with you.

The last days of work were spent in a delicious peace. Next we showed the film to Zanuck. He was not satisfied with the end. And I believe that he is right. Our fight scene and our crocodiles, filmed at the studio in a fake jungle with a little dirty water, were rather poor. He gave his very definite ideas to Irving Pichel, who wrote an ending conforming to his wishes, which is in the process of being filmed. I've been present at the shoot without intervening, because all that needs to be done is to execute Zanuck's strict orders. I'm happy to give a little direction to the actors, who are very pleasant and with whom I have a marvellous collaboration. It's just a matter of four long days from eight in the morning until midnight and then I will be free. I will send you a copy of this ending, as another one was needed anyway. Zanuck is not a bad screenwriter. He is full of logical ideas and has a certain dramatic sense. He lacks only a sensibility.

After this film, I will be free. My agents asked Goetz[1] not to use the option they have on me. They were very nice and agreed to give me any freedom.

The possibilities on offer to me are the following:
– Selznick,[2] who wants to film a love story divided into three different parts, each filmed by a different director, and no doubt written by a different writer. In all probability the directors would be Hitchcock,[3] Capra[4] and myself. Outside this project, it seems that he is terrifically

interested in a collaboration between you and me.

– Al Lewin-Leow [sic].[5] Al is a very good friend of mine. I've dealt with him directly rather than through my agents. He has just had a failure, and he is now convinced that the only way for independents to be successful is to go completely outside the Hollywood system, to change everything, both the spirit of films and the way they are made. He has some money through his association with Leow [sic]. If he really feels like making something new, it could be a good solution for us.

– Korda,[6] who theoretically has arranged to let me make a film.

Everyone is very excited by a complete collaboration between you and me. And my agents Feldman-Blum even more so.

As usual, please don't talk about these projects, especially Selznick's, which was offered to me under a veil of secrecy. On the other hand, since I don't yet have assurance in writing that I am actually released from Fox, I prefer not to talk too much about future projects.

I'm not sure what to say to you about the film. I believe that I got good performances from Dana Andrews and Anne Baxter, I also believe that Walter Brennan[7] is very good. I like Virginia Gilmore[8] a lot. I believe that Zanuck is wrong about the specific criticism he made to me of Walter Huston. In the final editing, he gave a certain dignity to the film. This is certainly due to the quality of your dialogue. I don't know if the film will appeal to the public or not. I like it well enough, despite the fact I didn't direct it at all the way I felt it. I also like it because it has given me my first contact with you and with the crew of an American studio.

My greatest desire now is to meet up with you, to see Esta in good health, and for us to have a wonderful time together, talking about everything we love about the world. I will write to you after my last four days on *Swamp Water*. Dido is in the process of finishing reading the subjects which you spoke to her about. She is translating them for me as she reads them. *Black Narcissus*[9] is obviously something big. Soon I will be familiar with the others as well.

From Dido and myself, affectionately yours,

Jean Renoir

1 William Goetz (1906–69), executive at 20th Century-Fox.

2 David O. Selznick (1902–65), independent producer, most notably of *Gone with the Wind* (Victor Fleming, 1939), *Rebecca* (Alfred Hitchcock, 1940), and *Duel in the Sun* (King Vidor, 1946).

3 Alfred Hitchcock (1899–1980), director famous for his 'suspense' films, including *The 39 Steps* (1935), *The Lady Vanishes* (1938), *Spellbound* (1945), and *North by Northwest* (1959).

4 Frank Capra (1897–1991), director whose films included *It Happened One Night* (1934), *Mr Smith Goes to Washington* (1939), and *It's a Wonderful Life* (1947).

5 David L. Loew (1897–1973), independent producer and film company executive.

6 Alexander Korda (1893–1956), director and producer whose films included *The Private Life of Henry VIII* (1933) and *The Thief of Bagdad* (1940).

7 Walter Brennan (1894–1974), actor whose credits included *Swamp Water*, *My Darling Clementine* (John Ford, 1946), and *Rio Bravo* (Howard Hawks, 1959).

8 Virginia Gilmore (1919–86), actress whose credits included *Swamp Water* and *Pride of the Yankees* (Sam Wood, 1942).

9 *Black Narcissus*, written by Rumer Godden (b.1907), would eventually be filmed by Michael Powell (1905–90) and Emeric Pressburger (1902–87) in 1948.

To Jean Renoir [*Original in English*]   *8 September 1941*
Hollywood   *New Milford, Connecticut*

Dear Jean,

How curious, I was just sitting down to write you a letter when your own letter arrived in the morning post. I wince with compassion at the brief account you give, and I am sure it has been a painful time for you. I can look back on most of my years in Hollywood as times of quiet desperation, and yet there were good moments too. I know what joy you must have experienced on returning to the set and being greeted with such warmth by the cast and crew. There are good people in Hollywood, people who are eager to give you their best. Even some of the people at the top are not bad: it is the power of money that corrupts most of them. Money, when it breaks away from its true service to mankind – that of being a medium of circulation, a necessity for truly social activities – acquires an evil spirit of its own and becomes anti-life. And it transfers that spirit to the men who control it: really it controls them. Yet we have the problem of money and must face it as artists as best we can. I agree with you about Mr Z[anuck]. He has a clever and imaginative brain, but power has atrophied his feeling for human beings. Under a different system he could have been a most useful and important man to society. But it is not enough to use the head, real wisdom lies in the heart; in the loving heart I should say – for all the terror of hell crouches in the unloving heart . . . I do not worry about the film. I know there will [be] some of Jean Renoir in it, and we can measure the errors of Hollywood by any falsities that appear. Do not bother to send me the revised climax of the scenario. I was none too satisfied with it in the truncated script which we finally turned in, for it had a smell of contrivance. Yet I thought your style would take that curse off it. Never mind, let us not worry about anything like that.

[. . .] The other projects you mention (and of course I treat our discussions as matters of strict confidence) are interesting. I think you would get along well with David S[elznick]. He is the only producer I know who seems infused with artistic feeling, whose goal is not money. Money has come to him but I doubt if he has ever worked solely for it. This is my observation at a distance, as I have never worked for David. But I respect him very much. He is wise enough to know that if you make distinguished films you cannot avoid making money also. Do I understand correctly that it would be <u>one film</u> directed by three men on the subject of love? Or three films, a trilogy? (Incidentally, you might tell David that one of the finest titles I have ever seen was on a novel I came across in Russia, a slim book whose title translated into *I Love*. I don't know why the title fascinates me so. It so simple and compelling. I don't see why it could not be used on the right film in America; the Russian novel itself could never be filmed, not the right subject-matter.)

Hitchcock to my way of thinking is an extremely clever man but a trickster. Mere sleight-of-hand but no understanding of reality or insight into human beings. Frank Capra I like personally and he is a great technician, but (I say to you privately) all surface. He never fails to make a picture that moves, but it never moves one's heart. Either he has not suffered in himself or he has always fled from facing it. Something has to happen inside him before he will make a picture <u>I</u> will call great. But he is an honest man and has not Hitchcock's charlatanism. The Englishman I am sure is a mountebank; which does not mean that he cannot make highly successful films. The way audiences are trained nowadays he is more likely to succeed than the rest of us. But a film on one subject by the three of you would be an exciting challenge. You make something to tear the heart and let them tickle them the ribs.

Al Lewin I like, too. He is that rare thing among producers, a man of literary perception. He has a flair for quality. It seems to me he has never yet found the right men to work with .

I too wish we might see you and Dido. Do you contemplate a trip east after finishing the film? I wish you might see the tranquillity we have here. Connecticut is beautiful in September and early October. That is one reason why we hate to think of leaving for the west before the end of October. They are the finest months of the year, even though the drowsy days of lounging in the sun and swimming in the brook are past. About your release from your option for a second film, I am sure your agents have done the right thing; though of course you must see that you receive all moneys that are due you. Anyway I am happy that you are seeing

Swamp Water through to the finish. I think it was essential for you to go through with it to the bitter end. That is why I kept urging you to stick it out. For the only place to make films in the world, perhaps for some years to come, is in America. Even here the future seems to be closing in for free artists. But, here and now, there are good people to work with in Hollywood – and why not make good films? One must surmount the difficulties somehow.

As for ourselves, we have had a trying time lately. Esta was quite ill and I was so worried that I completely stopped working. But now she is better and I really think she will continue to improve from now on. Really she looks better than at any time for several years. So there is cheer in the house. She needs faith in life, in me, and some expression for her vital urges. In highly strung people it is not easy to tell where the psychic ends and the psychological begins.

Let me hear your future plans. Love from us,
Dudley Nichols

To Dudley Nichols [*Original in English*]   *13 September 1941*

Dear Dudley,

I think I have finished *Swamp Water*. I don't know the latest change-ments [sic] made by Zanuck, I only know the ones he made before. They consist in the suppression of all the important central scene between Tom Keefer and Ben in the swamp: the coal in the hand, the story of the murder, and all the night scene. The deer sequence was not shot at all. All this is replaced by a scene between Ben and Jesse Wick, and during the scene Ben understands that the Dorsons are the murderers.

The scene is good, like all Zanuck's ideas, which are good in them-selves, but they destroy the films, bringing them back solely to an ingenious report of events.

I have the impression that one of the possibilities for success of *Swamp Water* could be in the strangeness of this story. And the strangeness was based partly on the character of Tom Keefer. In spoiling this c[h]aracter I think that the success of the film is compromised.

[. . .] With Dido, we have read your statement on aid to Russia. I have found it extremely interesting. It answers the thoughts of many people. I have felt it during my work at the studio. Most of those around me are astonished by the Russian resistance, and they admire even more the Red Army, having long been persuaded that it was worthless. On the other hand, in the 'high circles' (I can only speak of Zanuck's environment), one affects not to speak of Russia. It is as if this country did not exist. This 'decent' silence makes me think of the attitude of an honourable family, obliged to accept, for a while, the help of a relative who has bad habits and a bad reputation. Articles like yours are indispensable just now, to bring these people to a more realistic conception of the present situation.

We are happy to know that Esta is feeling better. We are trying very hard to go to see you, but I think, before we can do that, I must sign for another film. It will be necessary to blot out the bad impression my difficulties at Fox could leave in the Hollywood people.

I may have to go to Washington to try to get my boy over from Morocco.[1] If I go East, I will go to Connecticut, and I think Dido will come with me. It would be wonderful to go for long walks with Esta, in the country, and to find you in the evening, after your work, and have long talks all of us together.

My dear friends, we think of you every day with all our affection.

Love from both of us,

Jean Renoir

---

1 Alain Renoir had escaped from France to Casablanca.

To Dudley Nichols [*Original in English*] 27 *September 1941*
New Milford, Connecticut *Hollywood*

Dear Dudley

To sum up the situation, it boils down, in my opinion, to three possibilities. The other propositions I have had are very interesting from a financial standpoint, but absolutely commonplace.

These three possibilities are:

1 – Pare Lorentz,[1] producer at RKO. He has worked for the American Government, and arrives with new ideas. It seems that they have enough respect for him at RKO to grant him a certain freedom. His tendency is towards the documentary in films. He thinks, for instance, of making films in South America, with real local characters, not transposed for Hollywood. He has no definite idea, and I have to see him again. I had the impression of an interesting personality; later, perhaps, we could meet him together.

2 – David Selznick. He has excellent ideas, but very definite. I intend to

propose to him a very difficult and dangerous story: *Le Roman d'une Femme de Chambre* [sic] (The Diary of a Chambermaid) by Octave Mirbeau; also, another story in his line: *Margoton La Gardeuse de Poules* (Poultry Meg's Family) by Anderson. He will be long to decide anything. After his last successes he is uneasy, and possessed by the desire of making still better.

By what I have heard of him, he is a sort of intelligent dictator, and a tyrant. On the other hand, like you told me in your letter, he certainly is not only after money.

3 – A producer by the name of Harry Eddington who actually works for RKO. He may leave them to go to United Artists.

He wants to remake my old film *La Chienne* (The Bitch). At RKO he is rather independent on account of a contract he has with Cary Grant.[2] I think it is Cary Grant, who, being crazy about *La Chienne*, made him buy the story.

By principle I am against remaking the film, particularly when it has been a successful film, but *La Chienne* is a strange enterprise. Ten years ago I fought bitterly for this film, and I won, after many painful incidents. It was my first important talkie and it was also the first French *naturaliste* talking picture, [a] style so often copied since.

During two or three years, producers, in spite of its financial success, bitterly criticized *La Chienne*, and then they started working on the same line. We can say that *Quai des Brumes*[3] is a result of this series.

I am interested because I know that this story carries in it a kind of virtue, and I am curious to see if its influence will be the same here as in France.

In case you don't know it, I will try to give you an idea of the story:

Maurice Legrand is cashier in a wholesale drapery situated in an old quarter of Paris. The employees are reunited in a Montmarte restaurant to commemorate the *Légion d'Honneur* just given to the boss. After the banquet the party decides to go on to a whorehouse. Only Legrand, whom it does not amuse, walks home.

At the bottom of the street, all in stairs, like the streets of Paris under the Sacré Coeur, he comes upon a young pimp named Dédé who is beating a girl named Lulu. Legrand separates them and easily throws Dédé down, as he is completely drunk. Lulu, distracted, fears that her friend is hurt, and Legrand is obliged to help her to put Dédé to bed in a dingy hotel of the neighbourhood. He then offers to take her home.

Legrand and Lulu walk through the Montmartre streets, and the young woman, understanding she has to do with a very naïve man, plays the innocent young thing, tells him how strict her family is, speaks of propriety, of Dédé's qualities, etc. etc.

I linger on this because the interest of this film is that our characters are not innocents, or idiots, or villains (I told as much in a prologue played by puppets), Lulu is not a vamp, and if she pretends to be innocent, it corresponds simply to the expression of an atavism of small 'bourgeois' which awakens in her in front of a man in dress coat.

Legrand is married to a shrew, widow of a sergeant-major killed in the 1914 war. His only amusement is to paint. His wife cannot bear it, and she despises him completely, comparing this stupid mania of putting colours on a canvas to the habits of the sergeant-major. He used to drink, he used to play cards, in other words he was a 'real' man.

The story is very simple. Legrand sets up Lulu in a small apartment, in which he is perfectly happy, in which he loves the young woman, and in which he paints. Lulu, following Dédé's advice, takes all the money she can from him, and, calmly, Legrand draws in the cash-box of his boss.

Then he steals some shares that his wife had hidden under the linen in the cupboard. But all this is not enough for Dédé who tries selling the pictures that Legrand has painted and left at Lulu's apartment. We must say that to show off in front of Lulu, Legrand passes himself for a painter, and hides from her the fact of being a simple cashier. We must also say that he belongs to the category of Frenchmen called the Sunday painters, among whom several great talents were revealed. Legrand has talent, and his paintings, presented under a false name (a woman's name so that Lulu can play the part), begin to interest many amateurs and to be really worth money. Evidently Legrand ignores[4] all that. He continues to paint and to love Lulu, explaining as best he can his frequent absences to his wife.

Lulu, on her side, hides Dédé from him, and speaks of him as of her brother Fernand.

One day Legrand meets the sergeant-major, his wife's first husband. He is not at all a hero but a deserter hiding under a false name. He tries to blackmail Legrand and to get some money out of him, but Legrand plots an extravagant and burlesque farce to bring the sergeant-major back into his wife's arms. He is now free.

He takes his belongings and definitely leaves his home to go to Lulu. It is raining heavily, but Legrand is happy and sings walking along in the empty streets. He arrives at Lulu's house, runs up the stairs, opens the door, and finds Lulu in bed with Dédé. He goes away, desperate, and wanders endlessly.

[123]

Dédé, furious, beats Lulu, accusing her of destroying a situation which was beginning to become very profitable, and he leaves the girl taking what is left of Legrand's paintings, excepting one that is unfinished.

After having wandered a few days, Legrand comes back to see Lulu. He has arrived at an explanation of everything. His version is that Lulu, being terrorized by Dédé, obeys him only through fear. On the other hand he also understands what happened to his paintings, having seen one hanging on the front window of an Art Gallery. He tells Lulu he will take her away, far from Paris, and from Dédé. They will live together in the country, he will paint, and they will be happy. Lulu is lying on a bed cutting the pages of a book. Street-singers are outside. Whilst he paces up and down in the room, their voices reach him through an open window. He is trying to understand what is going on in the girl[']s head. And suddenly he understands she does not love him, has never loved him. He tells her so, and it makes her laugh. She cannot stop. And this laugh is so exasperating that he kills her with the paper-knife.

He then leaves the house, unnoticed, as the janitors are very much interested by the street-singers.

Dédé returns to see Lulu, he is more noticeable than Legrand, and the janitors see him.

I pass the details of the trial. Dédé is sentenced to death. The attitude of Legrand has largely contributed to this result. He avenges himself of his scoffed love. He takes his revenge of this man, stupid, with no education, ugly and heartless, and who nevertheless succeeded in gaining the total love of Lulu.

Dédé is guillotined.

Legrand is thrown out of his wholesale drapery and his heart is not in painting any more.

Many years later the epilogue shows him dragging along the Paris streets. He has become a beggar, and he picks up old cigarette-ends. An argument on who is to open the door of an automobile brings him face to face with the sergeant-major. His wife is dead, and he, also, has become a beggar. The two men laugh heartily, finding this meeting rather comical. They get a few cents after closing the door of an automobile in which a very opulent-looking man deposits a picture. This picture is a self-portrait of Legrand. We saw him painting it during the film, and I finished, framing this last image of a Paris street in the small puppet theatre of the beginning, and the curtain falls.

Dear Dudley, first of all I would like you to tell me if this story is capable of exciting you. If you like it, I think that together we can make something good. I am going to have another meeting with Eddington. If he decides to make this film, it should be around the beginning of January.[5]

I forgot to tell you in my résumé that one of the peculiarities of the film, which greatly helped to its success, was that everything around Dédé was spoken in a very authentic slang. Especially so, as for playing Dédé, I had taken, not an actor, but an authentic character who brought me his true way of speaking.[6]

I would very much like to know what Esta thinks of it all. I hope she is quite well now, and that she is enjoying the country that must be so beautiful around you. I am now going to think of a practical way of going to see you. I have so many things to tell you, and, more than that, I want to hear you.

My affection to you both,
Jean Renoir

PS. I told Eddington, who is terribly excited at the idea of our collaboration, that you would be here possibly at the end of October. J.R.

1 Pare Lorentz (1905–62), documentary film-maker and producer whose films included: *The Plow That Broke the Plains* (1936) and *The River* (1937).
2 Cary Grant (1904–86), actor whose films included *Topper* (Norman Z. McLeod, 1937) and *Bringing Up Baby* (Howard Hawks, 1938).
3 *Quai des Brumes* (Marcel Carné, 1938).
4 Meaning 'is ignorant of'.
5 *La Chienne* was remade by Fritz Lang as *Scarlet Street* in 1945 with Edward G. Robinson and Joan Bennett. Dudley Nichols wrote the screenplay.
6 Georges Flamant (1904–90), actor, who also appeared in *Les 400 Coups (The 400 Blows)* (François Truffaut, 1959).

Swamp Water *opens in New York on 16 November. It proves to be Fox's most profitable film of the year, but chastened by his difficulties with Zanuck (for Zanuck's side of the story, see Rudy Behlmer's* Memo from Darryl F. Zanuck*), Jean Renoir terminates his contract.*

On 7 December, the Japanese attack Pearl Harbor, causing the United States to declare war on Japan the following day. Three days later Germany and Italy declare war on the United States, just as Alain Renoir is arriving in New York. Once in Hollywood, Alain enlists in the US Army, Field Artillery, despite the fact that he does not speak a word of English. After training, he is sent to fight in the Pacific.

17 Dido Freire with Alain Renoir in his army uniform on the lawn at their
Hollywood Boulevard home

1942

On 21 February, Jean Renoir signs a contract with Universal Studios. He and Dido Freire move into their new home at 1615 North Martel Avenue in Hollywood.

To Antoine de Saint-Exupéry
New York

2 June 1942
Hollywood

Dear Saint-Ex,

For a long time I've wanted to write to you: ever since the day after our last telephone call. It must have been months. It seems like years.

I loved your book so much. I don't know if it's good or bad, but I am sure that it is honest. My thirst to be around honest people is very great. The honest man is becoming a rarity. Perhaps it's because genius is becoming a rarity. Genius and honesty are such close cousins. They are so alike that I believe them not to be two brothers, but to be one and the same. As Cézanne, who was very religious, once said: 'I will go to heaven, but my heaven will not be the same as the one of my gardener, who is a bad gardener and doesn't know how to grow a single bean.' The honesty of imbeciles is of no interest to us.

My dear Saint-Ex, I have a new house; it is small and modest, but the garden resembles the one at Paradou described by Emile Zola when he was honest and wrote *La Faute de L'Abbé Mouret*.[1] I am with Dido, and I'm writing to you in the room which serves as the dining room, all the while contemplating a wood fire which burns as high as a table. For I have made a Provençal style fireplace, enough to grill steaks without getting down on all fours or getting stiff in the joints.

Everyone has told you that your book is extraordinary. It is obviously true. For me it is better than that. It is the book I would have written if I had the courage and honesty to go deep inside myself, painfully to extract what little truth there is from among all the falsehood, and to place it completely raw on a table like a butcher wraps your steak in thick yellow paper.

Since I last saw you I've realized something very important: I hate the

[127]

French who live in America, except for you, Lamotte, Gabrielle[2] and perhaps others like Lazareff,[3] Charles David,[4] and René Clair. I especially detest the Gaullists. Because the Pétainists at least try to stand up for the modest scraps normally left over for a civil servant. But the others seem to me truly to represent the dregs of the shabby-looking candidates for the aforementioned scraps. 'If Uncle Sam recognizes de Gaulle, perhaps I would be named Consul and I would earn 200 dollars a month. But let's guard against the Communists. Evidently the Russians fight well, but all the same tomorrow, after victory, we don't want them to be in power. No, the law still belongs to the same benefactors, and we will be there, our traps wide open, to gather up the crumbs.' Good old Boyer invited us to a meeting where he made us sign a ridiculous manifesto under all kinds of pretexts, ranging from: 'I belong to the FBI, and if you don't sign you will go to a concentration camp,' to 'sign, in order to save some unfortunate comrades who have thoughtlessly made remarks which could be taken as Nazi.' And all of us French *petit bourgeois*, some scared by concentration camps, others moved, as in the good old days of the Montmartre theatre, by the innocent comrade who's fallen into bad ways, we signed. Personally, I did it with joy, the last, or rather next to the last one to sign, because René Clair, with his critical spirit, didn't go for it. As far as I'm concerned, I say with joy, because I am truly happy to break away from all things political concerning my ex-country. I love Mr Roosevelt, and I like neither Vichy, which allows things to get into too much of a mess, nor de Gaulle, who looks a little too much like a profiteer.

But enough of politics, I hate all that. I am going to give you some news about myself and people who are dear to me, hoping you will do the same, for despite my silence, I am very concerned. First off, my son. His American adventures are very straightforward. He enlisted in the American Army, wanting to go quickly into battle, and refusing to choose any specialization as long as they sent him to the front. As luck would have it, he was placed on tractor duty in the Field Artillery, which he detests because he only likes horses. But the lack of horses at his new post was compensated by the possibility of leaving swiftly for the front, which was his wish. Right now, he is somewhere in the Pacific I presume, but the wonderful discretion of military correspondence doesn't allow me to suspect where. Dido is doing well. She worked hard putting the house in order. She isn't with me on the film which I'm making at Universal[5] with Deanna Durbin,[6] because we prefer her to be free to prepare the next film that I must make right away afterwards, and which is more or less the story which I told you about in New York, but free from the Central European influences which spoiled it a little at the beginning, and re-drafted under an original form which allows me to be free, and to avoid the rights of respect and constraint to whoever. Dudley Nichols is helping me with this second *job*.[7] He's a terrific guy, and I am full of hope. For right now, I'm just starting to shoot my film with Deanna Durbin. It's a mish-mash of joys and sorrows. My producer is Bruce Manning.[8] He's a sweet character. He is from New Orleans, that's to say, a creole. Deanna Durbin is probably the best friend I've encountered among film actresses. Also she has talent, but this hasn't spoiled her.

My dear Saint-Ex, I believe that I've told you enough useless stuff. But this evening I felt like gabbing with you. I'm sending only a small part of my affection with this letter. If I had to send you all of it, it would be far too much work. It would also represent a kind of talent which I have from time to time, perhaps, but not tonight. For however much electricity you are charged with, nothing is more difficult than establishing contact without resorting to silly sentimentality.

Best wishes,
Jean Renoir

1 *The Sin of Father Mouret.*
2 Gabrielle Renard Slade (1879–1959), Jean Renoir's former nurse, who left France with her husband, the American painter Conrad Slade, and their son, Jean (known as Jeannot), soon after Renoir.
3 Pierre Lazareff, owner of *France-Soir* before the war. In Hollywood he ran an agency for French actors. After the war, he returned to France to set up the journal *Libération*.
4 Charles David, director and third husband of Deanna Durbin. He was production manager on Renoir's *On Purge Bébé* and *La Chienne*.
5 Originally titled *Forever Yours*, Jean Renoir worked for two months on the film before withdrawing for 'health' reasons. It was completed by Bruce Manning and released as *The Amazing Mrs Halliday* in 1942. Cinephiles claim to detect the Renoir style in some scenes of the film.
6 Deanna Durbin (b.1921), actress and singer whose credits included *Three Smart Girls* (Henry Koster, 1936) and *It Started with Eve* (Henry Koster, 1941).
7 Originally in English.
8 Bruce Manning, scriptwriter whose credits included *Mad About Music* (Norman Taurog, 1938), *Guest Wife* (Sam Wood, 1945), and *Never Can Say Goodbye* (Jerry Hopper, 1955).

To Alain Renoir [*Original in English*]   6 July 1942
US Army   *Hollywood*

Dear Alain,

I write in English because I think the letters in a foreign language have to go to some censure[1] commission, I don't know where, maybe in Washington. It is perhaps the reason for the lack of news about yourself. I am not worried, but I think now it is about time we should be able to correspond without disturbing the national defence. I hope you are all right and that you found some good friends. Personally I am in the middle of my Deanna Durbin picture (she is a very good comrade). Till now I was shooting in the back lot of Universal with plenty of Chinese children. They are very nice but without any respect for my person. They want me to play with them exactly as if I was their own age. I don't know if I am making a good picture. I have a lot of doubts because of the lack of screenplay. I am shooting in the dark, and I don't know whether, at the end of the picture, Deanna Durbin marries the leading man or gets killed by some Japanese bomb (I guess she will marry the leading man). The only definite result so far is that I got beautifully sunburned. I look like a lobster after it is cooked.

All the time I am thinking of you. We are living in an amazing time, probably a hot spot in the history of the world, the only fault of this historical moment is to make people live too far away the ones from the others.

With my love,
Jean Renoir

1 Renoir here means 'censorship'.

To Dudley Nichols [*Original in English*]   26 July 1942
New Milford, Connecticut   *Hollywood*

My dear Dudley

Thank you for your letter. Please do not think for a moment that Dido and I were disturbed by this last meeting at your house. On the contrary, we absolutely wanted to see Esta and you before you left. And the only thing which worried us a little was the idea of troubling you in your last minute preparations.

I followed your advice of frankly stating the question of my replacement by another as director of the Deanna Durbin film. I had, and I still have, a very good reason for this. It is that I truly suffer a great deal with my bad leg, and that this constant impression of dragging a painful limb cuts off all my inspiration. Well, I spoke to Bruce Manning and told him that my present physical condition makes me a bad director, and that, on the other hand, in a film where improvisation plays such a big part, perhaps it is better that the one who improvises hold all strings in his own hand. He will then find himself more or less in the position of a painter who starts on a canvas without a certain definite conception. This canvas may become a masterpiece providing he be alone to follow his instinct, and that the colours shall be put by him on the canvas, in direct relation with his creative dreaming. And the details of his material work will help his imagination and allow him gradually to define his subject. In other words, instead of starting from the screenplay to arrive at the shooting, the artist can start from the shooting to arrive at the screenplay. But this system, I think, excludes the idea of collaboration.

Perhaps I did not use exactly these words in trying to convince Bruce Manning, but this was the basis of my chain of reasoning. He nearly agreed with me on the necessity for him to direct the picture and to write it at the same time, and I offered to stay with him and help him at the beginning, then, when he would feel sure enough of himself, I would go and rest, follow a treatment for my leg, and prepare my work with you.

Unluckily he could not adopt all this without the authorization of the executives of Universal, who declared themselves completely against it. They immediately called Ralph Blum, who arrived post-haste, had a conference with them, then with me. He told me, from them, that if I abandoned the picture, they themselves would stop it, and that it would probably mean the end of Bruce Manning as producer. It would also probably mean my own end as director in Hollywood. Never would I be forgiven for abandoning a picture because it is in difficulties.

This second argument did not worry me greatly, but the first one, I confess, impressed me. I have not the right to do such harm to Bruce Manning, who, besides his drawbacks due to a certain slowness of creation and perhaps a little laziness, is a brilliant man, full of talent, and who behaved extremely well towards me. So I declared I would continue the film to the best of my ability.

This is where I stand, and I ignore[1] absolutely where it is going to lead me. Bruce says we have sixty more days of shooting. But how can we know for certain in an enterprise in which everything is left to chance? And we must not forget that this picture may be saved by giving great attention to the cutting and by retakes that can reinforce weak situations.

[131]

Dear Dudley, all this seems very much like a catastrophe, but I am powerless. The whole thing seemed so simple at the beginning, and now has become so difficult. I started this picture thinking I was going into an easy and agreeable story, with a talented actress whom I like, and to be executed with the help of a perfect and rapid mechanism, since in this studio it is the eighth Deanna Durbin film, and that they have the advantage of experience. In my idea I was going to start on 1 June, and finish on 1 August, more or less the time when your diverse commitments would set you free. It all seemed easy and harmonious.

I can only state the situation to you, not being able myself to foresee any solution. Ralph Blum pretends[2] everything can be settled, but I don't see how. I am going to wait one week, and next Sunday I shall write you my new impressions. Meanwhile please tell Esta we think of her. I hope the trip did not tire you, and that you found again with joy your dear Connecticut.

Our affection to you both,

Jean Renoir

1 Meaning 'do not know'.
2 Meaning 'claims'.

Telegram to Dudley Nichols
[*Original in English*]
New Milford, Connecticut

6 *August 1942*
Hollywood

FOR REASONS OF HEALTH I HAD TO STOP TODAY MY WORK AT UNIVERSAL. SHALL WRITE YOU TOMORROW. LOVE TO YOU BOTH.

JEAN RENOIR

Telegram to Jean Renoir
[*Original in English*]
Hollywood

7 *August 1942*
New Milford, Connecticut

DEAR JEAN MANY THANKS FOR WIRE. AM SURE THE THERAPY YOU NEED AWAITS US AT RKO. WILL WIRE YOU DATE OF MY RETURN AS SOON AS GET TRANSPORTATION. LOVE TO YOU AND DIDO FROM BOTH.

DUDLEY

Telegram to Dudley Nichols
[*Original in English*]
New Milford, Connecticut

I HAD WRITTEN YOU A LONG LETTER YESTERDAY. DIDO IS TRANS-
LATING IT BUT WE WILL KEEP IT HERE AND READ IT TOGETHER. AS
FOR MY HEALTH YOUR WIRE WAS A WONDERFUL CURE ALREADY.
LOOKING FORWARD TO SEEING YOU. LOVE TO YOU BOTH.
    JEAN

To Dudley Nichols [*Original in English*]
New Milford, Connecticut

My dear Dudley,

As I wrote to you in my last letter, things did not work out too well in my Universal picture. Was it my lack of energy caused by my bad state of health, or was it the invincible laziness of Bruce Manning – whatever it may have been, the work kept on being slow and vague. One day Bruce would tell me that the story would play around the children, the next day he would assure me that the children could only form a background to the only important point, the love story. Yesterday when we parted, he told me that he was not able to tell me the story but that he hoped that during shooting, by itself, the story would take shape.

Although work was very slow, he had such difficulties with the writing of the story that I happened to be catching up, even overtaking the script, and one day the entire crew was sent home for the afternoon as we had nothing written to shoot.

Before we started to shoot I told Bruce several times that a good story somehow is conceived with ease, and that all these delays and difficulties in working the story out, gave me doubts about the idea from which he started out. If it had only been to give me confidence, I should have liked a written continuity of scenes however rough, even if during the shooting we might have made changes. This would have convinced me that this story could be told with a beginning, a middle and an end.

Personally I love to improvise. Improvisation often helps to better adapt the idea of a scene to the personality of an actor, to the character of a set, of a landscape or of a prop, the meaning of which one sometimes only discovers at the last moment on the set. But this kind of improvisation is only possible when it applies to the improvement of something already existing, a kind of basis; in other words, if it is a modification of

[133]

the shape, not of the idea. When improvisation handles the actual invention of the story, I consider it bad. The only way to save a picture based on such principles is giving the picture to an improviser who is a writer and director at the same time. This man handling the actors on the set may be able to get the spark which leads to invention.

What made matters at Universal still more complicated was the fact that Bruce Manning is a most charming man, and that for nothing in the world I should want to harm him. You are the only person to whom I frankly express my doubts on his present power of invention, knowing your discretion.

Sometime ago I already had explained to Bruce all the above and I had also asked him to take over the directing of the picture. I had written you after this discussion. You can imagine my joy when yesterday I understood that he agreed with me. He told me that in agreement with the front office and with Deanna Durbin I was authorized to stop my work on account of the state of my health. By the way, this reason happened to have become the truth. Never has my leg given me as much trouble. My old war wound kind of revolted against the stupidities I had to do. Universal are very happy about this solution too, they asked me not to tell anybody that I felt disgusted with the picture, but to put it all exclusively on the state of my health. On their side, they have agreed not to blame me for the slow pace of the work. I gladly accepted this, as it sets me free. However I must say that I cannot reproach myself for being slow. They could see it themselves that under the special conditions under which I was working, with an ever changing and improvised script no one could work any quicker.

What must have caused their decision is the showing of the first rough cutting [sic], which bored me to tears and which must have come as a great disappointment to them. How can one interest the people when one has nothing to tell them? The most daring camera movements, the sweetest and cutest close-ups cannot possibly fill the space left by the absence of any ideas.

Dear Dudley, I think I have bored you enough with my adventures. At the present moment, I am looking after myself and I'll do it thoroughly, as I want to be in the best shape physically and morally for the collaboration with you.

Your Connecticut must be wonderful. You are sure to appreciate the shadow of the beautiful trees and the coolness of the waters. I am sure Esta is happy to be back in these familiar landscapes, so civilized after the irrigated desert which makes California.

Please write to me. Dido and I often think of you and regret that you cannot be with us, now when we could make the best of it.

Yours as ever,
Jean Renoir

To Robert Flaherty [*Original in English*]   *8 August 1942*
Black Mountain Farm   *Hollywood*
Brattleboro, Vermont

Dear Bob,

David,[1] whom I saw yesterday, told me that you would perhaps come to California. How wonderful to see you again. I also learnt that you had recuperated[2] your children from India. I can imagine how you feel about it. And I also heard all the difficulties you have been having with your plans for making pictures. When we see each other you will tell me all about it, and I will tell you my troubles. We will console each other before a good bottle of Scotch, and we will be happy to arrive at the conclusion that the Hollywood people are more and more sinking in their own dirt.

Dear Bob, Dido and I think of you very often and we send you our best love,

Jean Renoir

PS. Please remember us to your wife and to those of your children that you happen to have around you.

1 David Flaherty, younger brother of Robert.
2 Meaning 'retrieved'.

To Charles Laughton[1]   *24 August 1942*

Dear Charles Laughton,

I tried to speak to you by telephone today. Too late. You had left. I would only like to say to you that Dudley Nichols and I have truly started working together and that it's not coming along too badly. I believe that we are helping to bring to life a rather amusing character. I am very anxious to meet you and tell you all about it. Let me know as soon as you've returned.

Sincerely yours,
Jean Renoir

1 Jean Renoir became friends with Laughton, another new resident in Hollywood. For some time, Renoir had been developing a film about conditions in Occupied France. He co-wrote a screenplay with Dudley Nichols which would become *This Land is Mine*.

To Alain Renoir

27 August 1942
Hollywood

Dear Alain,

Well, here I am back again in the movies. Forget about writing books, I no longer have the time to think about anything but the film. RKO seems to have a very pleasant and calm atmosphere. From time to time they fire all the people, like those to whom I offered my story a few months ago, and now I have to work with people I don't know. None of this is of any importance because the man who is sitting in the president's seat wears the same suit, smokes the same cigars, and talks the same talk as the man before him. I believe that they are going to use Lourié for the art direction. Besides Charles Laughton, I will have a gracious young lady named Maureen O'Hara.[1] The French collaborator will be played by a pretentious sort of fop, but a very good actor nevertheless, by the name of George Sanders.[2] I have just finished a letter to my old friend Stroheim, asking him to join us and play the role of the German officer who uses all his charms in vain to conquer Charles Laughton. I don't know my cameraman yet. I just hope that he will be a little quicker than the usual ones in Hollywood.

I hope that you continue to get along well with the snakes and other strange animals that inhabit the region.

With all my love,

Jean Renoir

1 Maureen O'Hara (b.1920), actress whose credits include *The Hunchback of Notre Dame* (William Dieterle, 1939), *How Green Was My Valley* (John Ford, 1941), and *Sitting Pretty* (Walter Lang, 1948).
2 George Sanders (1906–72), actor whose credits included *Foreign Correspondent* (Alfred Hitchcock, 1940), *The Picture of Dorian Gray* (Albert Lewin, 1945), and *All About Eve* (Joseph L. Mankiewicz, 1950).

To Erich Von Stroheim [*Original in English*]   *27 August 1942*
Fulton Theatre   *Hollywood*
New York City

Dear Eric [sic],

I have never written to you because I didn't want to do it without having something worthwhile to tell you. Now, for the first time since I arrived here, I foresee a possibility of working with you. It is not something important, but I believe it can interest you.

In a few words here is what I have done in Hollywood so far, it may help you to better understand the situation. I first had a contract with Fox, and there made one picture, *Swamp Water*. But I was very unhappy, and did everything I could to break my contract. Luckily Zanuck's interest in me was very mild, and he gave me my liberty. After that I stayed one year without working, but the money I had from this first film kept me going. Finally I started something at Universal, your old studio, with Deanna Durbin. There I did not find Zanuck's authority, but disorganization and weakness to a point that I felt certain of making a very bad film. But I became ill and did not finish it.

Now here I am in a totally different situation, and for the first time in Hollywood with hopes of making a film like I used to make them in France.

Dudley Nichols had written the screenplay of *Swamp Water*, very much changed by Zanuck, but since that collaboration, we had the desire of one day working together. I had the idea of a story happening in our time, in Europe, under Nazi occupation. Dudley liked this story and he is writing a very good screenplay. We shall make it at RKO, and he will be the producer. Dudley Nichols is a wonderful man, a great writer, and I have full confidence in him. In this story there is a part of a German officer. It is not big. He is more spoken of than seen. But the main scene in the film is between him and the principal character, which will be played by Charles Laughton. This German officer is not commonplace. The idea for this part came to us while remembering a dinner I had with an important German agent in Lisbon. He pretended to be a Swiss, but later I learnt he was German, and that he made little mystery about it. During this dinner he recited French poetry with barely an accent. He knew everything concerning French culture, and declared himself a passionate admirer of it. His ideal was a Europe where the Germans would be the organizers and the French the artists. Probably he was sincere. This refined and cultivated man impressed me as being far more dangerous than a brutal Nazi.

This is more or less the starting point of the character, and the motive of the scene with Laughton playing the part of a schoolmaster whose collaboration would be precious to the Germans.

Perhaps it can amuse you to come again to Hollywood in circumstances that, due to the personality of Dudley Nichols, may allow you to say something on the screen, and to remind people here who you are. The other actors will be: Maureen O'Hara, in the part of a teacher loved by Laughton, and George Sanders who plays the part of a French collaborator. The art director will be Lourié who was with us in *La Grande Illusion*. We shall start shooting around 1 November.

Dear Eric [sic], I write without great hopes, as I know you are doing interesting things in the theatre. If the part does not interest you, please tell me so frankly, I shall understand perfectly. In any case it will have given me the pleasure of imagining the possibility of again being with you on a stage. On the other hand if it does interest you, I shall write you more details.[1]

Dido sends you her best regards. My son Alain, whom you know, is in the American army and actually somewhere in the Pacific.

With my sincerest affection,

Jean Renoir

1 Von Stroheim was unable to accept the role, as he was then appearing on Broadway in *Arsenic and Old Lace*.

To Private Alain Renoir

13 September 1942
Hollywood

Dear Alain,

To write to you I've interrupted a very interesting conversation with Dido. It's a question of who is the proudest, Dido because of her skill in driving gasoline-powered automobiles, or myself for repairing a 50-cent lighter which looks like one of Stephenson's locomotives and, I blushingly confess, is more valuable for its aesthetic properties than for its ability to light cigarettes.

I've finished writing the script which I'm doing with Dudley Nichols for Laughton. We are enchanted. It is strong stuff and clearly shows, I hope, that some European leaders preferred to see the Nazis taking over their country than to grant privileges to their workers. It's the whole history of collaboration, conscious or unconscious, honest or dishonest, which we are trying to explain.

I finally know the name of the mysterious sickness which for ages has made me listless, tired, spent and incapable of any true effort. It's a chronic appendicitis which I will have to have operated on after the Laughton film, that's to say, in four or five months. So I've been put on a strict diet. No more wonderful *potées* of beans in bacon fat, and especially no more slices of sausage accompanied by a good red wine, with Gabrielle, while we talk about you.

Dido and I are expecting all the Slade family.[1] I believe they are going to buy a house 800 metres from here. I will be awfully pleased by that. There'll be the chance to see them without having to get the car out of the garage.

I'm including with this letter an article on the Zazous.[2] It seems that they now constitute a movement in France which annoys the Germans a lot. That is how I understood it when you told me about it, and we differed in our opinions on this matter. It didn't seem possible to me that people who love Negro music could, at the same time, be admirers of racist theories whose perfect musical expression is Richard Wagner.[3] I believe that the article in question will amuse you.

Here things continue to roll as usual. Because of my appendicitis, I no longer go out. Dido, as you know, loves staying in the house. So that the evenings calmly flow by with the two of us together, thoughts of you by our side. It's been such a long time since we've had any news from you, but I think that you have other things to do besides writing, so we are not worried.

With our love,
Jean Renoir

1 Gabrielle, her husband the painter Conrad Slade, and their son Jean (Jeannot) had lived in the USA since 1941.
2 The Zazous were cabaret singers who performed satirical songs, and who Alain Renoir thought might in fact be collaborators.
3 Richard Wagner (1813–83), German composer of music dramas, including *Tristan and Isolde* and *The Ring of the Nibelungs*. His popularity with the Nazis, along with his infamous anti-Semitic pronouncements, have tainted his personality and, for some, his music.

To Erich Von Stroheim
[*Original in English*]

28 September 1942
Hollywood

Dear Eric [sic],

I have to start my film immediately, and because of that RKO rapidly decided on all the actors. Sorry not to have you, we changed the part and engaged Walter Slezach[1] [sic]. Here at RKO everyone regrets you are not in our picture. They are really very nice, and very different from what I have encountered in other studios. But they have to reckon with the competition of other films on similar subjects that are being made all around; for instance *Moon is Down*[2] at Fox. That is the reason they want me to begin at once.

[...] I just got a letter from the Captain of my son telling me he is an exceptional soldier and that I should be proud of him. I do not need to tell you how happy it has made me.

I don't know when I shall go to New York. When the film is completed I must undergo an operation for appendicitis. After that we shall see. Perhaps the opportunity I now miss will come my way again, and we will find ourselves together once more on a studio set.

Best of luck and very sincerely yours,
Jean Renoir

1 Walter Slezak (1902–83), actor whose credits included *Lifeboat* (Alfred Hitchcock, 1944) and *The Inspector General* (Henry Foster, 1949).
2 *The Moon is Down* (Irving Pichel, 1943), based on the John Steinbeck novel about the Nazi invasion of Norway.

From October to December, Renoir films This Land is Mine *at RKO Studios.*

18 On the set of *This Land is Mine*: from left to right, Maureen O'Hara (Louise Martin), Dudley Nichols, Jean Renoir and Charles Laughton (Albert Lory)

1943

To Maximilian Becker [*Original in English*]   *15 March 1943*
AFG Literary Agency   *Hollywood*
New York City

Cher Becker,

I received your letter and your story, *White Shore of Olinda*. I have not yet begun to read it, but I hope to find a little time this week and will let you know what I think of it.

Your sending this made me think of the scenario which you sent me last year. I have forgotten the title. It is a story which takes place in a village of Northern Canada, and it is about a policeman who places a microphone in a confessional in order to overhear the confession of an assassin. At RKO they are asking me for suggestions as to stories either to be made by me or by others. As well as I can remember this story is good and I might be able to suggest it. Could you tell me if it is still available, and in case it should interest them, give me some vague idea of what it might cost. It must not be too expensive because they would not even consider it. They do not wish to spend a great deal of money except for best sellers which bring with them publicity already made.

Now to speak of my book. I am very touched that Mr Hitchcock[1] is still interested. Alas, I am no further advanced than the last time I wrote you. The reason for this is my film, *This Land is Mine*, which has taken all my time and all my thought for a much longer period than I had expected. The preparation took a long time. Dudley Nichols and I examined a great many stories having to do with the Occupation but finally decided to invent our own action which would correspond better with our own ideas of the *rapport entre occupants et occupés*.[2] After all, this terrible question of the enemy *à domicile* is probably the most important of those presented by our unfortunate time, and our work was very delicate and very difficult even after the first print was made, during the cutting when it was necessary to soften some of the too brutal passages and, by contrast, to give more importance to certain parts which we had neglected. Constantly we believed that the cutting was finished but a projection of the complete film showed that we were mistaken and we had to make other changes. The result was that in the matter of the book about my father I have a quantity of notes which will permit me, if I have two months of tranquillity, to write the book, perhaps maladroit, perhaps uninteresting, but full of facts. Unfortunately, I do not know how I am going to find those two months, as I am immediately beginning again a film with Dudley Nichols for RKO. I am very happy about it because working with this remarkable man gives me great pleasure, but it does not leave my mind free to write.

If you reply soon give me news of Saint Ex. Gabin told me that he had perhaps gone to Africa, but I find it difficult to believe because modern warfare is waged with such young men. No matter how magnificent the vitality of our friend, it is a fact that he has passed the age of the pilot of modern war. Then, too, since he has so much talent no doubt he can serve his country better by writing fine books.[3]

Cher Becker, I await news of you. Aside from the question of the film all goes well here. My son is still 'somewhere in the Pacific'. I often hear from him in letters which are full of optimism.

With kindest regards,

Jean Renoir

1 Publisher. The book in question is about Pierre-Auguste Renoir, which he would write in the late 1950s.
2 'The relationship between the occupiers and the occupied'.
3 Antoine de Saint-Exupéry joined the Free French forces and disappeared while on a reconnaissance mission in North Africa, on 31 July 1944.

To Robert Flaherty
[*Original in English*]

15 March 1943
RKO Radio Pictures, Inc
Los Angeles

Dear Bob,

I am — at least I hope so — completely finished with the work on *This Land is Mine*, the film about which you wrote me such a nice letter. Now Dudley Nichols and I, before beginning another story, must forget all our preoccupation with that one. For years I haven't consecrated myself so completely to any work, forgetting everything else in life, except the war because this film is about the war.

However, it is done. It has not yet been presented to the public, but the people who are occupying themselves with selling it and convincing the public that it is good have seen it and have decided to back it. Now we can think of other things.

Circumstances have recently brought me in contact with the people of the Hays Office.[1] This organization seems to be completely allied with the government. I believe that Washington would like to try by this intermediary to influence the cinema of Hollywood toward a better comprehension of the war effort. One of their present preoccupations is with South America and it is my understanding that they would like to have pictures made in South America by directors from the United States. Could you perhaps have some information regarding this through some of our friends in Washington? It all seems to me somewhat confused, but perhaps it is the beginning of some very interesting work to be done in the future. Personally, if I were not so occupied here, I should like very much to make a trip in a country a bit more primitive than Hollywood.

Joris Ivens has just arrived here. He gave me news of you indirectly, having met in New York some friends of yours who told him that you were writing a book in Vermont. That interests me very much because now I can read in English. In a few days Joris will show me the film which he made with the Canadian Navy.[2] He appears to be very enthusiastic and very pleased with it.

Dear Bob, do give me some news of yourself from time to time. Dido and I both send our best regards.

Sincerely,
Jean Renoir

---

1 The Hays Office (The Motion Picture Producers Distributors Association) was a censorship board for American films, which was controlled by former Postmaster General Will H. Hays. The Hays Office was responsible for designating a 'Production Code', which specified what could and could not be shown in motion pictures. The board was terminated in 1945, but the Code remained in place until 1966.
2 *Action Stations!* (1943).

To Jean Renoir [*Original in English*]
Hollywood

23 *March 1943*
Black Mountain Farm
Brattleboro, Vermont

Dear Jean,

With haste and some concern I answer your letter which arrived yesterday. Think twice before you tie yourself with a government film.

The politics in Washington can break your heart.

Hollywood I think is far far better if you can get anything like a story that you have the feeling to do. Even wait for the right story in Holly-wood, but do not go to Washington to make a film.

I have no doubt the film you have just made will be a real contribution to the war effort – it will be seen by millions of people. Do more films like that and you will surely be doing the best that you can do for everyone.

You say in your letter that 'Washington would like to try by this intermediary to influence the cinema of Hollywood toward a better comprehension of the war effort'. I wish to heaven that someone could influence Washington!

I sound embittered, dear Jean. I am! I have had enough of Washington.

Would it not be wise for you to wait until your film comes out? Come to New York then. Maybe then something could be done there about South America and I will gladly go with you to Washington if in any way I can help you. Your success is very dear to me.

It is wonderful news to hear that now at last the company is going to back your film, we shall pray for its success.

Forgive my not answering your first good letter – I've been glued to my writing – caught in it – all tangled – writing is to me so very hard.

And I have been like a wounded elephant.

David is with Duranty in New York – He has been up twice to see us here.

I have not seen New York all winter. What one does not know never hurts one!!

I shall be very anxious to hear from you.

Much love to Dido and you.

As ever,

Bob [Flaherty]

To Private Robert Feld [*Original in English*]   *17 May 1943*
Camp Blanding, Florida   *Hollywood*

Dear Mr Feld,

Dudley Nichols and I, authors of the film *This Land is Mine*, were very happy upon reading your letter. Such appreciations are, for us, the best reward and a great encouragement. Personally I come of a country, France, where one could witness Nazis at work, and where the results of their propaganda are tangible. I am able, knowing the question, to tell my American friends where, if one listens, it can lead. We really are at a turning point of history, and we are the spectators of one of the most horrible battles between good and evil. Unfortunately, we are no more at the time of the Bible, when an angel, sent from Heaven, or a prophet showed men the way to follow. We are in doubt, and sometimes, evil disguises itself under appearances of good. That is why, when we believe we have seized a little corner of the truth, we must quickly tell it to other men; by books if one is a writer, by a film, if one is a film-maker. This is what Dudley Nichols and myself have tried to do. Thank you for having understood it so well, and thank you for having written it to us.

Sincerely yours,
Jean Renoir

This Land is Mine *opens in New York on 27 May. In his search for new projects, Jean Renoir holds discussions with David O. Selznick and the star he currently has under contract, Ingrid Bergman. The Swedish-born actress came to Hollywood to make* Intermezzo *(Gregory Ratoff, 1939), and subsequently has had a great success with* Casablanca *(Michael Curtiz, 1943) and* For Whom the Bell Tolls *(Sam Wood, 1943). She and her husband, Dr Peter (also spelled Petter) Lindstrom, become close friends of Jean.*

1944

To Ingrid Bergman[1] [*Original in English*]   *9 January 1944*
183rd Station Hospital   *Hollywood*
c/o Postmaster, Seattle, Washington

Dear Ingrid,

What joy we had to get a letter from you, specially written from where you are. It brought us the feeling of a pure snow breeze and transported us in white landscapes where only very fragile and delicate flowers grow. In our time one must go very far to find 'mystery'. Formerly, as soon as one was leaving the friendly village to wander in the neighbouring forest, immediately elves and fairies were surrounding the traveller and trying to get in touch with him. Now, to meet them requires a far greater effort. They are shy creatures, and our noisy modern world frightens them. They have retired very far to the north. And as it is hardly possible to go farther than you went, I am sure you must have met a few of them, and you will come back from your voyage with unforgettable recollections.

And above all else you will carry with you the joy of having brought some happiness to 'fine guys' who must feel a little lost so far from home.

I hope we shall soon see you again, and that you will tell us all your adventures.[2] Dido sends you her love.

Affectionately yours,

Jean Renoir

PS. We are now, with Ruth[3] and Dudley Nichols, the four owners of the option for *Precious Bain* [sic]![4]

1 Ingrid Bergman (1915–82), actress whose credits included *Casablanca* (Michael Curtiz, 1943), *Notorious* (Alfred Hitchcock, 1946), and *Eléna et les Hommes*.
2 Ingrid Bergman was in Alaska to do a travelling USO show for the troops.
3 Ruth Roberts, Ingrid Bergman's dramatic coach.
4 *Precious Bane*, the novel by Mary Webb, was a project conceived by Nichols and Renoir for Bergman. David O. Selznick objected to the fact that the heroine had to sport a hare lip, though this did not apparently worry Bergman.

On 4 February, Jean Renoir marries Dido Freire at Charles Laughton's house, with Dudley Nichols acting as best man. Jean also changes agents, from Feldman-Blum to Berg-Allenberg.

To Bert Allenberg [*Original in English*]
Beverly Hills

19 February 1944
Hotel Algonquin
New York

Dear Bert,

I just received the following cable from my friend Louis Jouvet[1] in Mexico City:

'DEAREST JEAN WELL ARRIVED EVERYTHING ALL RIGHT HERE THANKS YOUR LETTER STOP PLEASE DO TRY TO COME A MOST SERIOUS PROPOSITION TO MAKE GENUINE FRENCH FILM HERE ACCORDING YOUR STYLE AND SPIRIT STOP THINK IT OVER STOP EVERYTHING PLANNED FOR MAY STOP YOUR COLLABORATION NEEDED AND ASKED STOP WISH YOU COULD AFFORD SUCH AN IMPORTANT OPPORTUNITY STOP PLEASE ANSWER QUICKLY STOP HOPE WILL LEAVE FOR ALGER AFTERWARDS TO GO ON AFFEC-TIONATELY – LOUIS JOUVET'

I answered right away as follows:

'BUSY IN NEW YORK FOR THREE MONTHS STOP HAVE ALSO SIGNED FOR FILM IN HOLLYWOOD STARTING NEXT AUGUST STOP AM WRITING TO MY AGENT BERT ALLENBERG 121 SOUTH BEVERLY DRIVE BEVERLY HILLS ASKING HIM TO GET IN TOUCH WITH YOU LOVE – JEAN RENOIR'

Louis Jouvet is our best stage director. What he made in Paris in his own theatre is probably superior to anything similar made in England, Germany, Russia, or anywhere else in Europe. He was the champion of several of our best authors like: Marcel Achard, Jules Romains, Jean Giraudoux. One year ago I asked for a visa for Jouvet to enter the US because I believed this man, who is also one of our greatest actors, could make a good job in any Hollywood studio.

The visa was not granted for some reason I failed to understand, but probably the real reason was Jouvet himself was not over anxious to get it. Since two years he is travelling all over Latin America with a big part of the stock company of his Parisian theatre. They made a great patriotic job for their home country showing the best French plays in many districts where they hardly knew what any kind of theatre is.

And I believe he feels responsible for the actors who were with him during this pretty tough trip. I don't think he would like to come to the US without them.

I give you these details because it is possible you hear many contradictory stories about Jouvet, and I want you to know my personal feeling about the matter. In any case I believe the man is a 'good man', and if he is thinking of a picture in French, made in Mexico, it must be something worthwhile.

I shall write and ask him to send to us both more informations [sic] about his project. If it sounds all right, perhaps we could find a few months between my Government picture and the Hakim[2] picture.

I hope the actual[3] one can be made in two months, and on the other hand Hakim told me several times McCrea[4] would be happy to postpone the starting date of *Hold Autumn in Your Hand*.[5]

Of course I leave everything up to you, and I will follow your advice.

We had a fine trip my wife and I. While in Chicago we payd [sic] a visit to the Art Institute where the collection of Modern French Art is really wonderful.

I am back in New York for two days, then once more I shall go to the country house of Burgess Meredith,[6] fourty [sic] miles from the town. It is there we are working on the screenplay with Burgess Meredith, who is the producer, and Maxwell Anderson[7] who is the writer. The place is very beautiful, and both my wife and I are happy to know this part of the US.

Dear Bert, I hope I shall see you soon. Even with all the excitements of New York I miss my friends in California.

Sincerely yours,

Jean Renoir

---

1 Louis Jouvet (1887–1951), theatre director and actor, whose film credits included: *La Kermesse Héroique* (Jacques Feyder, 1935), *Les Bas-Fonds, Drôle de Drame* (Marcel Carné, 1937), *La Marseillaise*, and *Quai des Orfèvres* (Henri-Georges Clouzot, 1947).

2 Robert Hakim (1907–92), producer whose films included *La Bête Humaine, The Southerner, A Double Tour* (Claude Chabrol, 1959), *Le Plein Soleil* (René Clement, 1960), *Eva* (Joseph Losey, 1962), *Belle de Jour* (Luis Buñuel, 1967), and *Isadora* (Karel Reisz, 1969).

3 Meaning 'present'.

4 Joel McCrea (1905–90), actor whose credits included *Foreign Correspondent* (Alfred Hitchcock, 1940) and *The Palm Beach Story* (Preston Sturges, 1942).

5 Original title of *The Southerner*.

6 Burgess Meredith (b.1908), actor whose credits include *Winterset* (Alfred Santell, 1936), *The Diary of a Chambermaid*, and *Rocky* (John Avildsen, 1976).

7 Maxwell Anderson (1888–1959), playwright and screenwriter whose film credits included *What Price Glory?* (Raoul Walsh, 1926), *Winterset* (Alfred Santell, 1936), and *Key Largo* (John Huston, 1948).

To Jean Renoir [*Original in English*]   *26 February 1944*

Dear Dad,

I just received your letter from 6 February.

You give me there the best news I've had for many moons and I should say that I've been wishing this to happen for a long while but I didn't dare to ask you about it in my letters.

I'm only sorry that I can't be there to give you my congratulations but I hope that you'll wait for me before to have the 'big party'.[1] I, too, would like to celebrate — by the way, I consider this requires some big cigars? What about that? I've received 2 packages of film but I couldn't write to thank you because I was away with the forward party and the mail was dropped to us by plane and it is much easier for a cub to drop the mail to us than for us to throw it up to that so called aircraft.

Anyway I wish you and Dido the very best luck and my best love to you two. (I think you're a very lucky man.)

Your son,

A[lain] Renoir

1 Celebrating Jean Renoir and Dido Freire's marriage.

From February to April, Jean Renoir answers a call to help in an instruction film for American troops going to France produced by the Office of War Information, Salute to France. *The film is made in New York, and Jean works in collaboration with Philip Dunne, Garson Kanin and Burgess Meredith.*

To Jean Renoir [*Original in English*]   *24 March 1944*
Washington DC   *RKO Radio Pictures, Inc.*
                                           Los Angeles

Dear Jean and Dido,

I have only just returned to the office. Worry finally put me in bed, though the doctor called it lumbago, or spastic condition or some such thing. I was laid up ten days, which accounts for my silence. Meantime a wire came from OWI[1] about outtakes from TLIM[2] and Eddie[3] said he would take care of it. Seems it had to be cleared through [the] legal department. Now he tells me that when they looked for the outtakes, they had been destroyed. That seems rash to me, but Eddie explains they have too little storage space for film at this studio. Anyway that seems to scotch the hope, and I'm most sorry.

[...] Incidentally, [Gregory] Peck,[4] when I talked with him the other night, spoke about your farmer script.[5] Evidently he has been approached in case they cannot get Joel McCrea. Perhaps that means there is some hitch about getting Joel. Might be worth your inquiring. I know you would be happy with Peck. He is fine. And he will have a good name after *Keys to the Kingdom*[6] comes out; he's in it now, at Fox. At 15th Century Fox![7] Peck said he had read the novel, not the script, and liked it very much.

Dear Jean, we miss you. And dear Dido, ditto. The absence of both of you is a double ache. I miss you, Esta misses you, everyone misses you. It's as if the fire had gone out on the hearth. May all go well with you but come back soon.

Dudley [Nichols]

1 Office of War Information.
2 *This Land is Mine.*
3 Edward Donahoe, associate producer of Dudley Nichols' directorial debut, *Government Girl* (1943), and subsequently *Sister Kenny* (1944). He was assistant director to Renoir on *This Land is Mine.*
4 Gregory Peck (b.1916), actor whose credits include *Spellbound* (Alfred Hitchcock, 1945) and *Roman Holiday* (William Wyler, 1953).
5 *The Southerner*, at this stage called *Hold Autumn in Your Hand.*
6 *Keys to the Kingdom* (John M. Stahl, 1944).
7 This refers to a joke attributed to Renoir in reaction to his dealings with the studio, 'It has been a pleasure working for 15th Century Fox.' It may have been said to a) a publicist (the version recounted by Renoir himself), b) a journalist, or c) Zanuck himself. Renoir blamed his poor English for the error.

To Dudley Nichols [*Original in English*]

24 *March 1944*
Hotel Algonquin
New York City

Dear Dudley,

I just received a letter from Eddie, and he tells me your health has not been too good since you returned from the East. I hope you feel better by now. Dido and I have been very worried thinking of your voyage to Ohio under such sad circumstances.

We hope to see you very soon. The production on which we are working having many collaborators, Dido and I think that in a few weeks we shall not be needed any more. The set-up was charming and congenial until a lady you know came along and vamped the male elements of the production. I am speaking of Marlene Dietrich,[1] unemployed because of Gabin's departure. Since she has been around our young men think only of things not at all connected with the picture. When we arrived in New York she played the part of the 'distressed widow'. Now she is playing the part of 'Messaline'.[2] For me, I think she will always remain an extremely boring lady.

[...] Please tell Esta we are anxious to see her once more, and that we miss your house, our dinners together, and our meetings.

Best regards to Mr and Mrs Francis and Eddie.

Love to Esta and you,

Jean Renoir

1 Marlene Dietrich (1901–92), German-born actress whose credits included: *The Blue Angel* (Josef Von Sternberg, 1930), *Shanghai Express* (Josef Von Sternberg, 1932), and *Destry Rides Again* (George Marshall, 1939).
2 Messalina (AD c.22–48), wife of Roman Emperor Claudius I, famed for her ruthless ambition and promiscuity.

To Dudley Nichols [*Original in English*] 2 April 1944
New York City

Dear Dudley,

I don't know all the details of the story of Sister Kenny,[1] but the little I know makes me certain there is in it the material of a great film. In France I had already been impressed by a similar story; a fisherman's wife in Berck-Plage, on the Channel, who, about eighty years ago, with a Doctor from Paris, started the new methods for curing tuberculosis of the bones. This is only to tell you that the adventure of Sister Kenny corresponds to old preoccupations of mine. Furthermore, as you say, this film would fit in the frame of our common aspiration: to show the life of a saint, in a time when materialism seems (perhaps only outwardly) to be gaining. It is good in a time like this to exalt pure spiritualism, self-devotion, and renouncement of the easy pleasures of this world. I also see in it the exaltation of the safeguard of one of God's best creations: I speak of the human body.

Dear Dudley, if I can work with you on this exciting project, I would be a very happy man. You can count on me and on all my enthusiasm.

Concerning my commitment with Hakim and David Loew, I think I can consider myself as free. Nevertheless, to be prudent, perhaps you could contact Allenberg. I am writing to him today. Of course I don't want to act badly towards Hakim or anybody, but I have the conviction that *Hold Autumn in Your Hand* doesn't hold at all.

We hope to be back in Hollywood pretty soon. I am lucky to have an associate in this Government film.[2] This associate is Garson Kanin.[3] Already now he has taken the direction of the cutting, while I am doing the shooting. As he is in the Army, and it is part of his duties, I think I can consider my part as finished with the actual shooting. This would allow me, in case Sister Kenny is only started in November, and while you are working on *Hunky*, to try and make something in those empty months. I have an idea for a comedy, perhaps Koerner[4] will be interested. Of course the ideal would be to start at once, and together, on Sister Kenny.

We have not yet received Johnny A.[5] I am a little worried.

Dear Dudley, Dido and I see with joy the day approaching of our return to Hollywood. We realize now that with you and Esta, Gabrielle and her family, our fat Charles,[6] and a few others, we have found there 'home'.

Our love to you both,
Jean Renoir

1 Elizabeth Kenny (1886–1952), Australian nurse who developed a method of physical therapy to treat polio victims. Renoir and Nichols planned to make the film together, but Nichols eventually directed the film, *Sister Kenny* (1946), starring Rosalind Russell.
2 *Salute to France*, which starred Burgess Meredith.
3 Garson Kanin (b.1912), director and screenwriter, whose credits include, as screenwriter, *Born Yesterday* (George Cukor, 1950); as director, *The Great Man Votes* (1939).
4 Charles Koerner, head of production at RKO from 1942 until his death in 1946.
5 A project about Johnny Appleseed (John Chapman, 1774–1845), an American folk hero who roamed the United States, planting apple trees.
6 Charles Laughton.

To Dudley Nichols [*Original in English*]   *9 April 1944*
Hotel Algonquin,
New York

Dear Dudley,

We received your letter dated 5 April and your wire just after we ourselves had wired you the date of our return to Hollywood.

After knowing your projects of stopping in Minneapolis, we thought the best would be to join you there on our way back, providing of course Koerner and Allenberg arrive at an understanding in their meeting next Tuesday. If I am going to direct the picture I am very anxious to meet Miss Kenny with you.

[. . .] If the deal is made I hope I will know soon when they plan to start the shooting of *Sister Kenny,* and whether you shoot *Thieves Like Us*[1] before. If so I would like to be back quickly in Hollywood and to try to make a picture myself while you are busy with *Thieves*. I have some ideas for a light comedy which could maybe interest Koerner. If we start *Sister Kenny* earlier I will be happy to forget about that and to get busy right now with you.

Finally we received Johnny A. Dido read it yesterday evening and told me the story. I will start to read it myself today, but through the explanations Dido gave me I can feel there the basis of a great poetic subject. The love of this man for squirrels, and his passion for apple trees makes me remember a character which attracts me so much, St Francis of Assisi.

I am quite tired of politics after two months spent with furious de Gaullists and sincere but a little annoying theorists. More and more I believe the only people which count in the history of a nation are the saints; these saints being artists, peasants, statesmen, or workers, but being always preoccupied by small, casual, daily questions which seem vulgar to the theorists.

I keep the newspaper clipping you sent us about aristocrats in Paris, it is very interesting and confirms many things I am feeling about the situation in France.

I hope your trip will be easy. I am sure Esta will enjoy to see again her New Milford house.

Love to you and Esta from us both.

Jean Renoir

PS. Dear Dudley. What an exciting adventure it would be to go to England with you. I believe frankly *Precious Bane* would gain if made over there, not because of the landscapes or of any other physical reason, but because of the inspiration you and I would find after a few drinks in some quiet Shropshire inn. Of course the picture can also be made in Hollywood, and I will follow your decision about it.

Love,

Jean

1 Edward Anderson's novel was eventually made as *They Live by Night* (Nicholas Ray, 1948) and subsequently under its original title by Robert Altman in 1974.

To Jean Renoir [*Original in English*]   *16 May 1944*
Hollywood   *New Milford, Connecticut*

Dear Jean and Dido,

   Forgive my not writing sooner but I have been ill. I buried my father on
the way East. He died the day after I left Los Angeles. I arrived at the old
home the day after his death and buried him on a sunny morning, on
Saturday, when the daffodils were aglow with new life and the blackbirds
were crying in the trees around the grave. It is a hard thing to return your
father to the earth. The day before he died he kept murmuring,
unconsciously, 'I am going outside, I am going outside, I am going
outside ... and then I'm going to stay outside all the time.' Whether he
meant escape from the body into God again or simply going out into the
Spring to sleep again in the earth for ever, keeps me wondering. Ah well,
he lived a good life and now he is gone.

   I enclose a letter from Sister Kenny (Will you return it please, as I must
write her as soon as I am well enough. I forgot to say I was very ill when I
got here and only rested since. Soon I shall be very well again.)

   She seems to have misunderstood what I wrote about Jean, briefly
before I left Los Angeles. I told her that I had seen him on his return and
she takes it for a first meeting. I said I knew she would be glad he was to
direct the film because he was among other things a very fine honest man.
I explain this so you will understand her remarks.

   Now Jean, I propose we meet in Minneapolis 18 June, and spend a
week or ten days close to her, hear her lectures, watch her work et cetera.
I have written NY[1] just now for transportation 16 June. I will put Esta
on the Chief[2] in Chicago, the 17th, then catch a train for Minneapolis, to
be there not later than the morning of the 18th. If this meets with your
approval please ask the studio to arrange your transportation. Also they
can reserve a couple of rooms for us, from the 18th on, at a Minneapolis
hotel. I shan't write E. Kenny until I hear from you. You can check the
matter with Joe Nolan or Charlie Koerner.

   I shan't write you about the farm now. It is wonderful and I begin to
get well in mind as well as body. A kind of ugliness enters one in
Hollywood. Here it sweats out and the self becomes sweet again.

   Love to you both, from us both,
   Dudley [Nichols]

1 New York, meaning RKO's New York business offices.
2 Train.

Dear Dudley,

Dido and I had learnt by Mr Francis the death of your father. We hesitated to write, fearing it to be uselessly painful for you. We cannot, alas, do anything against this common law. We shall go through it ourselves when our time comes. The consolation is in the certainty that the moral worth of our dear ones, who leave us, ensures them of a bearable life in the hereafter, whatever this hereafter may be. It is even probable that this future life is better than the one men have so stupidly fashioned for themselves on this earth. Dear Dudley, our thoughts have been with you during your ordeal, believe we are with you with all our heart.

It is with pleasure that I shall go on the 18th to Minneapolis. Eddie has seen Nolan about it, and in the beginning of next week I shall go to RKO to inquire if everything is arranged for your transportation and mine. Eddie was in town for a few days, having lost his father-in-law. He has now gone back to Texas to shoot the second unit of an important Western.

I have not yet studied the material on *Sister Kenny* which is on your desk. I was, and still am, preoccupied by the picture I have to make with David Loew. It is a subject which could be great if treated with the certain sense of humour so common with the people of the soil in America. I fear the author of the screenplay is rather theoretic. He is coming today, and I am impatient to see the results of our first day of collaboration.

I liked Sister Kenny's letter, it is the letter of a person who has known how to limit the world to her mission. How exciting it is to make a film about such a character.

We have seen Mary McCarthy[1] two or three times. But I have neglected her due to occupations around the David Loew film. A complete silence has succeeded to an avalanche of phone calls. I hope she is not vexed and that she understands.

Allenberg has probably explained to you the situation on *Precious Bane*. My ideas are not very definite on this subject, and the one thing which really holds me back is the fear to miss my son if he comes back on furlough. By his letters it seems they are in need of well-trained elements in his sector for at least one year more.

I am happy of the good impression you have of your farm. Spring must be marvellous in the East, and all this beauty has certainly soothed you during the bad moments you have gone through and helped you to get well.

I am sure Esta is enjoying Connecticut, especially as a contrast to California. I would like to tell her what Claude Monet[2] told me a short time before he died, one day when coming from the sunburnt south of France I visited him in his estate of Giverny in blue-green Normandy: 'It must do you good to see a little lettuce.'

Our love to you both,

Jean Renoir

1 Mary McCarthy (1912–89), noted writer of novels such as *The Group* (1954), and also a screenwriter who co-wrote *Sister Kenny* with Nichols and Alexander Knox.
2 Claude Monet (1840–1926), Impressionist painter.

To Dudley Nichols [*Original in English*]   7 *June* 1944
New Milford, Connecticut

Dear Dudley,

I lunched with Eddie yesterday and you surely know already that everything is fixed for our transportation. I am very happy to meet you in Minneapolis, and the thought of making this great film with you also fills me with happiness.

I had thought for a moment to ask Eddie to help me with *Hold Autumn in Your Hand*. But I do not think this is a reasonable thing to do. *Sister Kenny* will claim him completely, and I need someone in *Hold Autumn* able to prepare this film, and to be busy with it, probably at the same time as *Sister Kenny* is being prepared. Eddie promised to give me the name of an assistant he knows well, and certainly this will be very satisfactory.

Yesterday morning I had a meeting with Allenberg on the question of *Precious Bane*. He took the decision to send the money back to Ingrid Bergman as he feels we are losing our time with her.

He is against the fact of going to England, no doubt fearing we might find complications out there. I told him my personal opinion which is that after our last conversations, both you and I had come to think that such a story would gain a great deal if shot on the actual spots described in the book. But the last news I received from my son does not incite me to leave the US. He tells me trained soldiers are badly needed in the Pacific, and that he does not think they will send him back on furlough before another year. The poor boy adds that he has caught a disease called 'jungle rot' and that the doctor had to paint him completely in blue from head to foot. I do not want to miss him on any account when at last he does return. However great my desire to make *Precious Bane*, I prefer to miss this picture than to miss Alain.

As for making the film in America, it seems to me that lately you have told me such wonderful stories, purely American, which would be much easier to do over here than *Precious Bane*. For instance: *The Little Wife* – your crime in the suburbs of New York – *The Domesday Book* – This does not mean that I do not want to make *Precious Bane* in England, but simply that I would prefer to make it later.

We are continually listening to the radio to hear the news about the invasion. Provided our hopes do not meet with disappointment. Dido and I are optimistic, and wait soon for the end of this nightmare.

Love to Esta from both of us.

With all our friendship,

Jean Renoir

Following the Allied landing in Normandy in June, German troops are driven out of Paris by the end of August.

His casting difficulties resolved, Jean Renoir begins shooting The Southerner *in September, on location near Madera, California.*

To Bert Allenberg [*Original in English*]   10 November 1944
Beverly Hills   *Hollywood*

Dear Bert,

I think I have found a story for Paulette Goddard.[1] I mentioned it to her and she seemed interested. It is *The Diary of a Chambermaid* by Octave Mirbeau. This novel has been translated into English and published as a rather 'sexy' book. But beside this characteristic, which can easily be made more acceptable for the screen, there is also in it the basis of a great and dramatic love story.

Could you please ask someone at your organization to find out some information about this book, and if need be to take an option. I imagine the editor of the translation in this country knows something concerning the rights for a motion picture. There exists also in New York a representative of the 'Société des Auteurs Français' (Authors' League of France).

[158]

19 From left to right, David L. Loew, Robert Hakim and Jean Renoir, on
location for *The Southerner*

Thank you, dear Bert, I am anxious to be fixed on this subject as I believe this is the great film for Paulette and myself.

Sincerely yours,

Jean Renoir

Octave Mirbeau: *Le Journal d'une Femme de Chambre* (*The Diary of a Chambermaid*).

Publisher: Eugène Fasquelle, 11 rue de Grenelle, Paris.

The book I have here was printed in 1918, but I believe it was published before that date.

1 Paulette Goddard (1911–90), actress whose credits included *Modern Times* (Charles Chaplin, 1936), *The Great Dictator* (1941), and *Kitty* (Mitchell Leisen, 1946). She was married to Burgess Meredith from 1944 to 1950.

To Pierre Blanchar[1]
Beverly Hills Hotel
Beverly Hills

31 December 1944
Hollywood

Dear Pierre Blanchar,

René Clair, Julien Duvivier and myself all need to agree upon what you asked us about the dubbing of French films for the American market. Apart from this statement, in which we will try to remain objective, I cannot resist the desire to let you know my personal feelings, without concerning myself about preserving a balanced view.

I believe that the success of French films in America comes from the fact that in them, people speak <u>in French</u>. In other words, the 'star' attraction which draws a sympathetic public to French films is not X or Y, not Raimu[2] or Danielle Darrieux,[3] Boyer, Gabin or yourself; it's the French language. I've had discussions in this matter with Americans of all classes and backgrounds. These conversations have led me to the conclusion that the only way to retain the favoured position of French cinema in America is to avoid at all costs having the actors speak in English. If we commit this error we will fall from the pedestal on which a particular audience has placed us through their friendly admiration. These people who like us will cease going to see our films. We will lose their custom and probably fail to win over the mass audience, who will always prefer to see home products.

In the case of Americans who go to see our films, there is something more serious than the desire just to be entertained. I would like to think that in their appreciation of them is a genuine love. And this love is simultaneously a very powerful and a very fragile thing. A brunette who dyes her hair red to attract a larger number of admirers risks losing a sincere man who was ready to dedicate his life to her.

Apart from this 'American' reason which leads me to question the dubbing of our films, there is also a 'French' reason. The dubbing of French films in English will draw us fatally towards the dubbing of American films in French. Well, nothing is as dangerous for a nation in a state of recovery as becoming accustomed to such a sub-standard product as a dubbed film. Countries like Italy readily accept the monstrosity of transforming an actor's personality through the substitution of another voice (in the Middle Ages, criminals would have been burnt at the stake for committing the sacrilegious act of grafting two souls on a single body); this has allowed foreign companies, French, American or German, to flood the Italian market and even suffocate Italian cinema. I take the example of Italy because it's there above all that the public have lost their dignity, and have become the least aware of the mess into which their industry has fallen. It is easy to get a bewildered country used to dubbing. At first the public feel that something sounds wrong, but little by little they become used to this jarring tone, and then one fine day you have a country defenceless against foreign productions. At the moment, things are only semi-bad, American productions being pure and of genuine quality, but were the face of the world to change once again, perhaps it will not be the fine films from Hollywood that our public will be lapping up, but less innocent productions from other countries.

I believe that today's leading figures in French cinema must not allow our audience to become accustomed to dubbing. Giving in to dubbed films is what happens to a country that has been economically conquered, and is morally weak. I am sure that the American public will reject foreign productions dolled up in this way. The youthful spirit and robust health of these people will know how to stop short of this grave mistake (I ought to say, this sin).

What seems right to me would be complete freedom in importing and exporting films to all countries on condition that these films be honestly presented in a form that doesn't falsify the product. French films must be shown to Americans in French, and American films shown in English to the French, without any restrictions or any regulations limiting such exchanges. This would function as propaganda for the English language and American culture in France. This would also be a good way of spreading the language and culture of France in America. But for the love of God, in a time when this world could lose itself by reverting to the commercial lies that existed before the war, let us not be blinded by the obvious financial advantages of a combination that is perfectly disgusting, as much from the point of view of humanity as of art.

France has just suffered terrible losses. We have fewer men, fewer factories, fewer oil wells and fewer aircraft than our powerful friends. Let's show them that at least there is a treasure which our enemies have not been able to take from us, and that is our artistic integrity.

Yours faithfully,

Jean Renoir

1 Pierre Blanchar (1892–1963), theatre and screen actor, whose credits included *L'Atlantide* (G. W. Pabst, 1932), *Crime et Châtiment* (Pierre Chenal, 1935), and *La Symphonie Pastorale* (Jean Delannoy, 1946).

2 Raimu (1883–1946), popular French actor especially remembered for his roles in Pagnol's Marseilles Trilogy and *La Femme du Boulanger* (Marcel Pagnol, 1938).

3 Danielle Darrieux (b.1917), French actress whose credits include *Mayerling* (Anatole Litvak, 1936), *Le Plaisir* (Max Ophuls, 1952), and *Madame de* . . . (Max Ophuls, 1953).

1945

To David L. Loew [*Original in English*]   *17 February 1945*
New York City

Dear Dave,

Thank you for your authorization to show the picture[1] to the French journalists. Three of them attended the projection, among them Mrs Andrée Viollis, who is the most important personality of the group. They enjoyed it very much, and certainly will write about it when they are back in Europe.

The next day Gregg[2] had a nice surprise when he took back the print. The projectionist of RCA told him it was the first time, since long ago, he was looking at a picture through his little window. Usually he just reads a magazine. But his wife, who was waiting for him, told him in the middle of the first reel that the picture didn't look like the other ones he is used to project, and he said he was so much attracted by the story he simply couldn't go back to his magazine during the whole show. If we have many people thinking this way, maybe the picture will be more commercial than one expects. I believe the publicity will play a big part in its destiny. If we attract the public inside the theatre the fight is won. The problem is how to attract it. That is why the title is also so important. With *Down by the River* I think you have a good one.

Yesterday, as Sam told you, the agents of Miss Goddard, Dudley Nichols, and myself had a meeting with RKO. Charlie Koerner was very nice and seems to be interested in the project.

I hope you arrive soon at the end of your sojourn in the East. We miss you and are anxious to see you back. We both wish Meta[3] and you plenty of fun during your last New York days and an easy and pleasant return trip.

Jean Renoir

1 *The Southerner.*
2 Gregg Tallas, editor on *The Southerner.*
3 Meta Loew, wife of David.

To Jean Renoir [*Original in English*]   *28 June 1945*
Hollywood   *Paris*

Dear Jean,

I saw your brother the very first night I was here, which was yesterday. I happened to ask the right man about Pierre, he knew him and took me to his house. What a strange but lovely place you had there. I enjoyed seeing both Pierre and Claude – also Claude's son and Pierre's very pretty wife. Pierre was working in 2 pictures and was in bed when we arrived, but we dragged him out. I saw a painting of you sewing, you had long beautiful hair which made me laugh. Your brothers looked very well, it seems food is not to [sic] well and it is hard to get enough to get along. Clothes are terribly expensive, shoes look awful with high wooden soles. Stockings don't exist. I have to take mine off because I can't stand all the dirty looks I receive from the French women looking at my legs. Your brothers were anxious to know about your son and I like a fool didn't have any information about him, I didn't ask you. Please tell them in letters. France and Paris looks same (I am sorry I haven't seen France!) but still is not the same. The people look different which is understandable. Paris is much quieter than I remember it. People go early to bed – I guess night life is too expensive. Montparnasse and Montmartre are still lively and it is funny to see all these American boys trying to understand the French girls. Our soldiers are very upset that everything is so high. A bottle of champagne is $18–20 and just admission to night-clubs is 500 francs. I am leaving for Germany tomorrow where I'll stay most of the time.

My very best to you and good luck on the picture.
Ingrid [Bergman]

To Ingrid Bergman [*Original in English*]   *14 July 1945*
USO Camp Service   *Hollywood*
New York City

Dear Ingrid,

I just received your letter, and believe me, it was a great pleasure to read it. I felt as if some part of my brothers, whom I miss so much, had been brought to me. From the way you write about them and about Paris, I guess several things they themselves would never have mentioned. It is most kind of you to have given some of the few spare moments you had to my family. I am anxiously waiting for the time you will be back here to thank you in person.

I believe that your tour will bring you great happiness. Your trip in Alaska already was a magnificent experience. I wish you less hardship and even more personal success on this one.

Hoping to see you soon.

Jean Renoir

To John Huston[1] [*Original in English*]   *21 July 1945*
Tarzana, California   *Hollywood*

Dear John,

I tried to get in touch with you in Hollywood, some time ago, but you had already left for the East. I wanted to tell you how much I appreciated your film *San Pietro*.

Right now I am in the midst of a picture and I know I shall not be able to see you before several weeks. That is why, between two shots, I am sending you this note, to express my admiration for your work.

I hope *San Pietro* will be shown everywhere. It is splendid propaganda against future wars. I believe it is even superior to your *Report from the Aleutians* which, before I saw your last film, I used to consider as the finest of the pictures this war has produced.

Sincerely yours,

[Jean Renoir]

1 John Huston (1906–87), in 1945 a major in the Signal Corps, was the son of Walter Huston and a noted director whose films included *The Maltese Falcon* (1941), *The Treasure of the Sierra Madre* (1948), and *Fat City* (1972). During the war he made a number of documentaries, including the two mentioned by Renoir.

Shooting begins in July on The Diary of a Chambermaid, *starring Paulette Goddard with Burgess Meredith as producer as well as playing a lead role. On 26 August* The Southerner *opens in New York.*

To Paulette Goddard and   *3 October 1945*
Burgess Meredith [*Original in English*]   *Hollywood*

Dear Paulette,

I believe that our picture[1] has now reached its final form. When you and Burgess see it your first reaction will probably be to regret some of the things which required so much work from us, but I believe that

[165]

20 Jean Renoir and Paulette Goddard during the filming of *The Diary of a Chambermaid*.

ultimately both of you will happy and proud of our common child.

Paulette, each time I see this picture I become a little prouder of my collaboration with you. You are just wonderful, how wonderful I cannot even tell you. I have ruthlessly cut anything slowing down the action, and now Celestine walks through the film with the impetuosity of a force of nature. What you have done makes me absolutely happy and I don't believe any other girl has ever attempted to realize this kind of expression on the screen since the motion pictures talk.

Burgess, when you'll see the picture you will enjoy the screenplay you have established, the words you put in the actors' mouths, as much as if you hadn't written them yourself. But what will surprise you above everything is Captain Mauger. After my cuts the character acquired a stronger unity without losing its amazing tempo, and expresses danger even more perfectly. I think that after Celestine it is Mauger who leads the picture. Right now I am working on the music with Michelet,[2] I am sure it will be perfect but I shall probably have to discuss somewhat; to have the recordings made as soon as possible, Michelet and his crew are being driven too fast, but you can count on me, I would rather fight with the whole world than yield an inch of the picture's quality.

Dear Paulette, I did not phone, I hate telephones specially on long distance calls. Nothing seems to give me a worse letdown than to hear a dear friend's voice as if he were inside the room, and to know at the same time that 3,500 miles are between us. I am very anxious to see you back to tell you lots of things, and specially to talk about a Paulette Goddard picture directed by Jean Renoir from a subject I know very well and which I believe is at least as good for you as *The Diary of a Chambermaid*.

Dear friends, I see only one more thing to add: that I miss you terribly and that I send you all my love.

Jean Renoir

1 *The Diary of a Chambermaid*
2 Michel Michelet, composer who later worked on a number of Fritz Lang films.

To Burgess Meredith [*Original in English*]   *27 October 1945*
Hollywood

Dear Burgess,

The Varsovie Hospital people are hanging on the phone to proclaim their enthusiasm about your name and Paulette's name printed on the mail paper. I feel the same and hope we will very soon get the necessary money to help these Spanish Partisans who, in the real beginning of the war, were the first defenders of our liberties.

Monday I am going to see our first complete print. I think it will be all right. The boys in the mixing room did a wonderful job and very quickly. Ben Bogeaus[1] was afraid of the strike and we did it in a hurry. The last reel which without the added sound tracks was a little flat, is now very impressing [sic], especially the part concerning the death of Joseph.

Did you get a call from some publisher – or stage producer, I don't know – who wants you to read a play written by a Frenchman I know who is living here: Louis Verneuil. He is very proud of this play because in three long acts he shows only two characters. He asked me whether you got the book.

Dear Burgess, I hope your projects won't keep you too much away from here. I am anxious to see you and Paulette. I must say that in about two weeks I will be shooting again. You know what it means – living in a little world by itself, with very little connection with the other planets.

Dido and me, we send you our love.

Jean Renoir

1 Benedict Bogeaus, co-producer of *Diary of a Chambermaid*. A former Chicago real-estate dealer, he came to Hollywood in 1940 to become a producer.

To Paulette Goddard and Burgess Meredith [*Original in English*]

7 November 1945
RKO Radio Pictures, Inc.
Los Angeles

Dear Paulette and Burgess,

Our preview was very successful. The manager of the Academy, a 20th Century-Fox Theatre in Inglewood,[1] said it was the most successful preview he's had for over a year. Everybody seems to be perfectly happy, starting with Ben Bogeaus and finishing with Mr Leserman of United Artists. I am the only one who doesn't feel absolutely satisfied with myself.

Paulette dear, you are amazing in this picture and Celestine is exactly the girl I had dreamt of. Everybody is raving about your being absolutely great – and much better in this picture than in your previous Paramount ones. This is probably true; but, to me, it's not sufficient. I think the fault is with the way your part is designed all through the screenplay, and I cannot forgive myself for not having seen it. Perhaps I am the only one who does see this now, but I'm quite sure that Burgess and you will understand what I mean. Believe me, I have learnt the lesson and the next time I will know how to build a part for you.

Dear Burgess, our story is powerful and I think you will find the just reward of your stubbornness when you decided to rescue our enterprise from the RKO shipwreck. You will enjoy the lines you put into the mouths of our people and, above all, you will be terribly happy about Captain Mauger. This strange neighbour is not only thoroughly accepted by the public, but it certainly looks like a kind of triumph for you.

Probably Ben has already told you about Hurd[2] and Francis.[3] It is hard to say which was more loved, or more hated, by the public. As for Irene, she never appears without starting a riot of laughter, making it impossible to get even a bit of her dialogue. Of course the character the public follows most closely is Paulette's. And the doubts I expressed apropos of her role are purely my own. Maybe these doubts come from the fact I discovered, only when finding myself in the midst of an audience, that this picture was not a 'star' picture, but actually an 'ensemble' picture, with Paulette playing the most important part. And I must admit that my ambition was to make a 'star' picture with her.

After the first preview, I cut a little of Francis and certain other things which caused the public to laugh. They followed the picture so intently that any small mistake becomes grave, and I had to be very severe. Now, they still follow it with passion, but they do not laugh at the wrong moments. That's about all I can tell you.

Dear Paulette, please wire me if I may show the film to Charlie Chaplin.[4] I'm certain he will love it, maybe even more because of the facts I told you above.

I'm working much too hard at RKO, and am thinking of you almost all the time.

My dearest love to you both,
Jean Renoir

1 Suburb of Los Angeles.
2 Hurd Hatfield (b.1918), actor whose credits include *Picture of Dorian Gray* (Albert Lewin, 1945) and *King of Kings* (Nicholas Ray, 1961).
3 Francis Lederer (b.1906), actor whose credits include *Pandora's Box* (G. W. Pabst, 1927) and *Midnight* (Mitchell Leisen, 1939).
4 Charles Chaplin (1889–1977), actor-director of such classics as *The Gold Rush* (1925), *City Lights* (1931), *The Great Dictator* (1940), and *Monsieur Verdoux* (1947). He was married to Paulette Goddard from 1936 to 1942.

In December, Alain Renoir finally returns home from Japan. During his service he has become a naturalized American.

To Mrs Preston Sturges[1]   *11 December 1945*
[*Original in English*]   *Hollywood*
Hollywood

Dear Mrs Sturges,

My wife and I are not very lucky with your Sunday parties. My boy being here, we find ourselves involved in so many engagements, dinners or just drinks with old friends he knew before getting into the Army, that we don't know when we will find any free time for a while.

But that is not all. Something else is happening to me which seems to be taken from a Preston Sturges picture. It's long story, but I must tell it because I know you will appreciate it ... My grandfather, the father of my mother, decided about ninety years ago not to stay with his wife. My grandmother was apparently a very nice woman, but a little temperamental and her husband, being a quiet man, left her without saying goodbye. The only thing we knew about him was the country where he was living, Canada. A few days ago, I received a letter, signed by many cousins, now living in Santa Monica. You may imagine our excitement. The first meeting will be Sunday, and I am terribly anxious to know this part of my family.

So, you must excuse us. We hope some day to be free of the family complication, and we will see you again.

Sincerely yours,

[Jean Renoir]

1 Wife of Preston Sturges (1898–1959), writer/director famous for such screwball comedies as *The Lady Eve* (1941), *Sullivan's Travels* (1941), and *The Palm Beach Story* (1942).

To Betty Field[1] [*Original in English*]   *18 December 1945*

Dear Betty,

I did not answer immediately your kind letter. When I received it, I was still completely absorbed in the cutting of my other picture: *The Diary of a Chambermaid*. And you know that each production is just like a small separate world from which it is very difficult to escape, even if it is to answer the friendly and thoughtful letter of a person of whom you are very fond.

You said in your letter that 'ill and worn out during our work, you did not contribute as much as you would have wished'. It is very modest of you to say so. Personally I cannot even dream of another Nona and every time I see the picture again, I admire you more and more. The real way to show me how you act when you are not 'worn out' would be to make another picture with me, if your great success in *Dream Girl*[2] does not tie you for ever to the stage. I am very sorry I am not in New York now and cannot go and applaud you.

Will you please give your husband my congratulations for this common success of you both. I am very happy he has not forgotten our short meeting at the house of Dwight Taylor in Hollywood.

My wife and I hope we shall meet again very soon and send you our best wishes for a Merry Christmas.

Sincerely yours,

Jean Renoir

1 Betty Field (1918–73), actress whose credits included: *Of Mice and Men* (Lewis Milestone, 1940), *The Southerner*, and *The Great Gatsby* (Elliott Nugent, 1949).
2 Stage production on Broadway.

1946

Under contract to RKO Studios to turn out a low-budget film, Jean Renoir begins shooting Desirable Woman, *later to be re-titled* Woman on the Beach.

To Claude Renoir Sr   *26 January 1946*
Paris

Dear Claude,
  [. . .]
  I have just finished shooting the exteriors for my film.[1] I don't know what they'll be like. I am a little afraid about not having had enough time to write the script. On the other hand, I'm shooting in ideal conditions, at the Pathé studios which belong to RKO. I very rarely see the production people. Moreover, all I have to do is ask them for something necessary for the production and they give it to me. Joan Bennett[2] is charming.
  There was a *press preview*[3] of *Diary of a Chambermaid*. I was too tired from my current work to go to it. Dido and Ingrid Bergman went in my place and told me that it went well.
  I write to you on a set supposed to represent a little house on the dunes, and my shoes are full of sand.
  My love to you all,
  Jean Renoir

1 *The Woman on the Beach*
2 Joan Bennett (1910–90), actress whose credits included *Man Hunt* (Fritz Lang, 1941) and *Father of the Bride* (Vincente Minnelli, 1950).
3 Originally in English.

Diary of a Chambermaid *premieres in Chicago on 15 February.*

To Marie Lestringuez[1]
Neuilly-sur-Seine

Dear Marie,

It's been a long time since I've written to you. It's because I'm shooting a film called *Desirable Woman*. It's taken almost all my time during these last months, but I don't regret it, as everything is happening in a perfectly pleasant atmosphere. Joan Bennett, the 'desirable woman', is the devoted wife of one of my friends, and the mother of numerous children. This frightening 'vamp' divides her time between knitting and child-rearing. She knows how to make fun of her screen personality and doesn't waste a single ironic allusion to her false eyelashes or any other artifices of make-up. The other actors, camera crew, technicians, also form an excellent company, the sort that has me returning home from this adventure almost regretting that it's going to end.

Dido hasn't been able to take part in my work, too busy with domestic problems which have become more acute since Alain's return, and complicated by the total absence of domestic servants.

Alain is doing well. By not touching a single drop of alcohol, even wine or beer, he is pretty sure of getting rid of his bout of malaria. He had wanted to go to university, but all the soldiers returning from the war had the same idea and anything that resembles a school is full to breaking point. He hopes to be luckier next semester, and while waiting he is trying to earn some money from photography. Because of this the house has taken on a very technical aspect; the conversations revolve around questions of cameras, light meters, developer, emulsions, etc. . . .

[. . .]

Here, there's no mistake about it, life resembles the way we were in France after the 1918 armistice. The country is bigger. Because of this fact, reactions are perhaps a little slower. But I seem to be reliving certain moments, coming across ideas which are only too familiar to me. The left-wing groups which in France are called 'socialists' and 'communists' are represented here by certain unions. The right wing, as in our country twenty-five years ago, set out to absorb the former soldiers and pit them against the workers. *L'Action Française* is replaced by movements more or less derived from the Ku Klux Klan and instead of wanting to gut a Jew, the same kind of fools manifest a strange desire to burn Negroes. Fortunately, as I said earlier, the country is large and this size gives it a wisdom which may perhaps be the wisdom of slowness but which can stop these people on the threshold of excessive dangers. Regardless of a movement's strength in the United States, one can always find some corner of the country a few thousand miles away, which is not affected by it. This allows another movement to spring up in reaction to the first one and create a balance. In conclusion, to sum up my opinion about the post-war United States, I believe that the horrible development of machines is less dangerous here than in a small country because there still remains more space around the monsters.

Dear Marie, I will not ask you to write to us for I know that when one has to work and be busy in the house and, I hope, also a little with oneself, one hardly has the time to be side-tracked by letter-writing. Your interrupted letter says a lot about your situation. But finally, you know the pleasure all of us had in sharing a moment with you.

Everyone in the house joins me in sending their love.

Jean Renoir

1 Marie Lestringuez, sister of Pierre. Childhood friend of Jean Renoir.

To Louis Guillaume[1]
Paris

8 May 1946
Hollywood

Dear Mr Guillaume,

I received your letter of 29 April. Dido and I are terribly sorry to learn that the situation in France is not getting better and that you are still struggling with the same supply problems. To add to these difficulties are problems that I'm posing for you, the lengthy errands, the waiting, the tedious discussions necessitated by court action for my divorce,[2] and by the defence of my interests in general.

In your letter one sentence struck me, it's the one where you told me that you couldn't take what you need from the consignments of money which I have been sending you. Please, Mr Guillaume, you have to take what is due to you. We have never settled accounts, and if we must do it, you know better than I how and in what manner to do it. But for each cheque that I'm sending you, please subtract the amount that you judge normal for you. If you weren't in Paris, I would have to pay someone to represent me.

[. . .]

Concerning my divorce case, your letter grieves me, both for your sake and mine. What a complicated business for something so simple. My point of view hasn't changed. Since they want to blackmail me, I don't see why I should continue to help Catherine financially as she has taken such a hostile position. According to my view on the separation, I don't owe her anything, and I have definitely decided to give her nothing.

I am probably going to ask for American naturalization. Will you tell me what you think about this?

Concerning the insurance on *Le Chasseur*,[3] I'm going to try to do it here (Los Angeles) with Lloyds of London. Would you get a valuation by a recognized dealer who is an expert? Bignou[4] would be well served by having a representative in New York, George Keller, who is a very good man and well respected. I believe that if this painting was sold in the United States, an art lover would have to pay around $75,000. The expert mustn't give too low an estimate, that would be awful. I don't plan on selling this painting but I'm keen on having its great value established. Moreover, the insurers would be happy to insure it below its value if I find the premium too expensive.

Next I would ask you to ascertain how it can be brought over to America. In that Bignou can give you good advice as well. But we're not at that stage yet.

Thank Aline[5] for the great mark of friendship that she gave me by helping you preserve this painting.

In addition to the certification by an expert, could you send me right away Aline's exact address (the insurance company must know where the painting is located), the dimensions of the painting and a photograph if you have one; if not, I will find a reproduction in America.

I have bought a lot in Beverly Hills and as soon as I am allowed and the materials are available, I will have a house built there which is not too big but a space worthy to hang *Le Chasseur*.

My dear Guillaume, I will quickly end this letter, having as usual rambled on; I believe I've told you what's essential for the moment, the most important thing being my determination (following, in part, your advice) to stay in this country which isn't mine, but where through my work I can hope to find a calmer life and perhaps a happier one than I've known until now. Our wish, Dido's and mine, would be to see you and spend a vacation with you. Perhaps one day that will be less complicated than now.

Yours sincerely,
Jean Renoir

1 Louis Guillaume was the Renoir family lawyer until his death in 1956.
2 According to French law, Renoir was still not legally divorced from his first wife, Catherine Hessling.
3 Painting of Jean Renoir by his father (c.1908) which was bequeathed to the Los Angeles Country Museum of Art in 1979.
4 Art dealer.
5 Aline Cézanne, daughter of Paul Cézanne Jr, hid *Le Chasseur* from the Nazis, who had special orders from Hermann Goering to capture it.

To Pierre Lestringuez[1]
Paris

11 May 1946
Hollywood

My dear Pierre,

What's become of you, are you continuing to hack out screenplays by the dozen, as you would say? My brother Pierre writes to me that he has to make film after film in order to pay his taxes. And above all, what's become of the theatrical projects which were so close to your heart? I also hope that the film project which was born from our conversations about the armistice at Les Collettes will see the light of day.

Here, I have just experienced a period of confusion. My film *The Diary of a Chambermaid* was rather badly received, especially by the critics. It wasn't a financial failure, but it was perhaps a moral one. There is always something just in this kind of penalty. I believe that the post-war period is going to bring to us bigger changes than the last one, of 1918; changes in life and manners, and therefore changes in taste. I don't want to lose contact, but from time to time I feel that I've lost it. I feel out of step with the immense childishness of the new generations, whether French or American. I am indifferent to the preoccupations of most of my comrades, and it is possible that certain problems that seem fundamental to me seem futile to them. On the other hand, I am too accustomed to doing everything in my films to be happy with directing in a pure and simple way while leaving others the ideas and task of creating sources of emotion. Soon I will have been playing a jack-of-all-trades for twenty years. I don't want to subject myself to change now.

All my best to our friends.

Sincerely yours,

Jean Renoir

1 Pierre Lestringuez, writer who collaborated on scripts for Jean Renoir and occasionally appeared as an actor (under the name Pierre Philippe) in his films *Catherine*, *La Fille de l'Eau*, *Nana*, and *Une Partie de Campagne*. For description, see *My Life and My Films*.

To Claude Renoir Jr[1]
Paris

My dear Claude,

In your last letter, the one which I never answered, you dissuaded me from returning home. Your advice only confirmed my own feelings. Not that I'm afraid of working in material conditions less satisfactory than here, but more simply because the day that I make films again in France, I want to make them about my own subjects, and not simply adapt some book or play, even if they're excellent. Since the war ended, my ideas have been very confused. They are barely beginning to become clear and I don't think that if I went to Paris now, I would have anything worthwhile to offer a producer. I probably have more ideas which could apply to America, and that is why I want to try and make a good film here, taken from a personal story. The only work which fully satisfied me here was *The Southerner*, which you might have seen. If you haven't seen it, try to have it screened at United Artists.

A while ago I received a photograph of your kid.[2] He looks very handsome and healthy. You have my compliments.

With much love,

Jean Renoir

1 Claude Renoir Jr (1913–93), son of Pierre Renoir, having distinguished himself as a cinematographer on his uncle's films *Toni* and *Une Partie de Campagne*, as well as assisting on *La Bête Humaine* and *La Grande Illusion*, would go on to an international career after the war. Renowned for his work with Technicolor, his later credits included: *The River, The Golden Coach, Eléna et les Hommes, Le Mystère Picasso* (Henri-Georges Clouzot, 1956), *Une Vie* (Alexandre Astruc, 1958), *French Connection II* (John Frankenheimer, 1975), and *The Spy Who Loved Me* (Lewis Gilbert, 1977).
2 Jacques Renoir (b.1942), who became a cameraman with Jacques Cousteau.

To Claude Renoir Sr
Paris

My dear Claude,

In your letter of 22 April you spoke to me about *La Partie de Campagne*,[1] but as you also told me about the death of poor Mr Dupre,[2] this bad news made me forget the rest of the letter.

I don't think that the release of this uncompleted film can do me any good. In order to complete it, Pierre Braunberger will have to resort to some expedient measures. On the other hand, I'd be very sorry to take away from him this hope of recouping a little of the money which he put into it. The poor boy must have had such a hard time and I pity him with all my heart. And you know that I've always had a weak spot, if not a real affection, for this charming joker straight out of the novel *Les Linotettes* by Courteline.[3] Therefore, my dear Claude, do whatever seems best to you. From here, I am really incapable of expressing the slightest opinion.

With all my love,

Jean Renoir

1 *Une Partie de Campagne* was finally released in Paris on 8 May 1946.
2 Grandfather of Claude Jr's wife, Denise. He was also the father of Paulette, wife of Claude Sr.
3 Georges Courteline (1858–1929), French journalist and dramatist of the bourgeoisie.

To Mrs Louise Chevallier-Munier   *15 May 1946*
Essoyes   *Hollywood*

My dear Louise,

[...]

I left France in 1940 with the idea that, being in America myself, I could make it easier for my son to come over. I also succumbed, let's be frank about it, to an attack of fear. Some of my films, and also some newspaper articles which I wrote, were clearly anti-Nazi and I knew I was a marked man. On the one hand, I knew that the Germans would ask me to make films in brilliant conditions. I was afraid of being suddenly faced with a dilemma: be a traitor or be a hero and, not knowing if I'd have the courage to be the latter, I thought that it would be better to accept the offer from the American Government which put a passport at my disposal. After that, it took me almost a year to be able to get Alain over here. When he arrived, America was just entering the war. He hesitated between de Gaulle's army and the American Army. Unfortunately, as far as the first was concerned, we knew of many young Frenchmen who were enlisted and were fretting with impatience in English or African camps, not being able to fight. He therefore enlisted in the American army, and this gesture, made at a time when the only thing that counted was to fight against our enemies, probably set his life off towards an unexpected destiny. He fought a very tough war in New Guinea and the Philippines in an infantry division. During the armistice, he was an artillery lieutenant in Japan. The dangers experienced alongside young men from here, and almost four years without speaking a word of his mother tongue, made him into a curious mix of Frenchman and American and it is very probable that the future direction of his life lies here.

But if your letters are short, mine are easily too long. You believe my time is precious; yours, in the middle of all your work, is certainly much more. This is why I'll leave you here.

One more thing. As you guessed, I have remarried. My wife's name is Dido Danin-Freire, her maiden name. She is Brazilian and as brown as you.

Ask us frankly for anything that can be of help to you. Here, the stores are out of stock (strikes, rehabilitation) but it's not the total emptiness that you are familiar with in France, and despite the chicanery of the postal service, one can still arrange to send certain things.

I send all my best wishes to your husband and your boys. I hope some day to get to know your daughter-in-law and your grandson.

With love.

Jean Renoir

P.S. Gabrielle, who is here, wishes to be remembered to you.

To Robert Hakim [*Original in English*]   *8 June 1946*
RKO Radio Pictures Inc   *Hollywood*
Hollywood

Dear Robert,

Pursuant to the decision we came to after our meeting with Mr Joseph Breen,[1] I am writing you this letter in which I shall point out and try to explain the lines along which we could set up a scenario of *Madame Bovary*.

The first point I wish to stress is the necessity for our following Flaubert's[2] book with absolute fidelity, however, the subject being a vast one – of much greater scope than that usually covered in a picture – I think we can, without taking liberties with the story, bring out certain elements very forcibly, and leave certain others in obscurity.

We must also attempt to deduce a moral lesson from the unfortunate Emma's emotional experiences. Flaubert succeeds in doing this very well by means of the novel itself, taking full advantage of commentary and description. A film being limited to dialogue and photography, some other way of bringing out this moral lesson must be found.

[179]

At the start I would emphasize Emma's early training and certain facts which were responsible for the moulding of her character: the great mistake her father made in sending her to a fashionable college where she came in contact with girls much wealthier than herself, thereby rubbing shoulders with a world that was far from being her own; it was there too that she learned to despise her father, a simple Norman farmer. I should like to lay stress on her dreams, the books she read, and also perhaps on the superficial aspect of her religious feeling. With the help of these elements, I might be able to begin the creation of the picture on a solid basis – one with which audiences are quite familiar. The refusal to face facts and look at life from the realistic standpoint is quite a common failing among the young girls of today. And in America particularly, if so many women jump from one divorce into another, and end by living an extremely unhappy life, it is really because, like Emma Bovary, they waste their time hunting for an impossible ideal man, all the more impossible and unattainable because he exists only in their imagination.

To show Madame Bovary's fundamental mistake in a vivid light, I should like the actor playing her husband's part to be a man of normal appearance, giving, in addition to his great qualities – good-heartedness and good-nature – the impression of also being a man of normal intelligence. By marrying Emma to an old gentleman who is both ugly and stupid to a revolting degree, it seems to me we destroy the message of moral significance which I should like the picture to deliver. Such a repugnant husband as this would be entirely sufficient, in the eyes of the majority of our audiences, to absolve Madame Bovary from all blame. I want to show that Emma's mistake lies in herself, that she is the victim of herself, her own worst enemy; and that if her life had been built on sounder principles, she would have been perfectly happy with her husband.

I cannot give you a clear idea of a plot for the picture until after I have written the screen play, but I can tell you now that the line which seems best to me is the one given us by the author himself, with this difference that everything should be seen or rather _felt_ by Emma and from Emma's standpoint. The novel gives us a general description in which the heroine is simply one of the objects described. Flaubert dissects Emma and explains her like a surgeon analysing a corpse during a lesson on anatomy. Instead of the audience's contemplating this case with cold scrutiny, I should like it to participate more intimately in this woman's experience, and by so doing, to feel more deeply the disastrous results of her mistake.

[. . .]

Please consider this letter, Robert, as the hasty expression of my first reaction. Everything I have said needs to be reviewed and discussed. Nevertheless, I hope that this first effort on my part will be satisfactory to you.

Cordially yours,
Jean Renoir

1 Director of the Code Administration, ie the American censor. His son, Thomas Breen, acted in *The River*.
2 Gustave Flaubert (1821–80), French novelist whose other major works include *L'Education Sentimentale* (1869) and the unfinished *Bouvard et Pécuchet* (1881).

To Claude Renoir Sr
Paris

26 July 1946
Hollywood

Dear Claude,

I am sorry to hear the bad news you gave me about your film, and I only wish that soon you will send me better news. You came across such a good subject, and I was so full of hope for what you could have done with it that it really distresses me to know that you have missed this opportunity.

I am afraid that the new conditions created in the French cinema by the Blum/America agreements are only serving to slow down your work of salvage. I would like you to give me news of your case in particular and the results of these new agreements. Here, together with some friends, we are going to try and influence the opinion of Hollywood to make the studios less demanding. But I am very afraid that once again our government has sacrificed an industry that it always despised, that it still despises and will always despise. This makes me want to stay here more and more. The cinema is my craft, and I'm afraid that in France, unless there's a total change, it will become more and more difficult to practise it.

If you must give up hope of directing films in France, tell me what your intentions are. What you wrote to me about 'Antipolis'[1] seems to indicate that it's going rather well over there, for I have no doubt that if these new agreements are unfavourable to production, they are infinitely favourable to exhibition. Maybe your idea is, if things don't work out on one side to change over completely to the other. It's perhaps the simplest solution. The other solution would perhaps be to come here and try your luck. In that case I would be all too happy to help you out with the cost of the trip

[181]

and offer to put you up until you've found your feet. If you came here, I would advise you wholeheartedly to do as if you were starting in the cinema again and begin from that point. Apart from René Clair, Duvivier and myself, whose films were vaguely recognized here and who were able to practise their craft as 'directors for hire', nearly all the French who came to Hollywood failed completely because they wouldn't accept small *jobs*.[2] If they had forgotten their past in France and started again as a third assistant in some *westerns*,[3] Moguy,[4] Schwab, Kessel, Michel Bernheim and others would now be *directors*.[5] They would be assigned to crime thrillers shot in eight days or to big films, depending on their luck and talent, but they would be working and earning a living, which is just as important. That's what Siodmak[6] did, agreeing five years ago to make whatever film Universal gave him. After two years they had put him on miserable 'B' pictures. Now he's doing much better than me financially and can choose the subjects that he likes.

If such an adventure appeals to you, namely starting right from the beginning in America, I believe that now I could help you here, and that it would represent a stopgap measure in which you could find great rewards.

I hope that you will not need all this, and that you will come here just to sightsee and have a little fun. After all, *Les Eaux Printanières* isn't the only film being made in France, and if it fails you will probably find another story and another plan of action. But in the end, should the occasion arise, I would rather explain to you once more what I think the chances are for a kid in your situation here in Hollywood.

I am going to remake *Madame Bovary* with Robert Hakim, who has become a producer at RKO. More precisely, he has found private capital and has made an agreement with RKO for their studio facilities and distribution. He is very nice, very agreeable, and gets along very well with Rathvon, the new president. I am as free as if I was the producer myself, with the advantage of not having to worry about business problems. Besides, I wouldn't have the time, because I'm busy working. I'm finishing the music and sound mix on *Woman on the Beach*; I ought to work on the *Bovary* screenplay; and I'm trying to create a story which would be satisfying to Ingrid Bergman and Walter Wanger.[7]

I am not surprised that you haven't seen Paulette Goddard. She and her husband, Burgess Meredith, are the busiest people in the world. Their lives are like an American magazine article on *movie stars*.[8] That doesn't stop them from being charming, if very restless.

[...]

Dido and I send you and Paulette much love.
Jean Renoir

PS. Just as I was dropping this letter in the mailbox, I read in a Holly-wood newspaper that *This Land Is Mine* was very badly received in Paris[9] because the subject of the resistance was treated in an unorthodox way in the film. I won't hide from you how unpleasant this news is to me. I made this film with all my heart and sincerity. It wasn't easy for me to subject people to a topic of this kind at a time when everything French was considered in America to be in the service of the enemy. It seemed to me that my first duty was to explain to Americans through the medium of film, which is 'my medium', that an anti-Nazi feeling also existed in occupied Europe. I believe I succeeded in that, and I had proof of it in the numerous letters written by soldiers, which I can sum up in these few words: 'Until now, I believed that all the French were bastards; your film made me reflect on that, and I think now that perhaps my opinion was exaggerated.'

Furthermore Resistance fighters from different countries, among them a delegation of Russian cameramen sent on leave of absence to America for heroic acts during the war, saw this film and confirmed to me that the state of mind of an occupied town, and the insinuating way the Germans had acted in certain places, were very well represented.

1 A large cinema and entertainment complex built in Antibes. Unfortunately for Claude, he had to sell off his interest just before the venture became profitable.
2 Originally in English.
3 Originally in English.
4 Léonide Moguy (1899–1976), director whose credits included: *Paris After Dark* (1943).
5 Originally in English.
6 Robert Siodmak (1900–73), German director (actually born in the USA) whose credits included *Son of Dracula* (1943), *Spiral Staircase* (1945), and *The Killers* (1946).
7 Walter Wanger (1894–1968), producer.
8 Originally in English.
9 *This Land is Mine* opened in Paris in a dubbed version on 10 July.

To Louis Guillaume   *27 July 1946*
Paris   *Hollywood*

Dear Mr Guillaume,
I'm adding a little more to the letter that I sent to you the day before yesterday. I just read in the American newspapers that my film *This Land*

is Mine with Charles Laughton has been very badly received in Paris. This really hurt me, for this film, made in 1942, was very good propaganda for France at a moment when it was badly needed in America. In fact, at that time the general opinion of Americans was that the French were collaborating with the Germans. If one believes the numerous letters RKO received especially from soldiers, this film led many audiences to reflect upon this question and, together with other facts, even made them revise their judgement. This incident has increased my mistrust of the unhealthy sensitivity which is so evident in the French nowadays. I understand them and I pity them, but, regarding the question about which I spoke to you the day before yesterday, namely domestic help, I would be grateful if you would pay attention to that. It would bother me enormously to have to deal with people who, each time I gave them instructions, would answer me: 'You can shut up, Sir, I am a war hero, but during the war you became a fat cat in Hollywood.'

I would also like you to find a way for me to obtain newspaper clippings that could interest me professionally. Perhaps Devalde,[1] who after all is my agent in France, could be of service in this matter?

That's it for today, dear Mr Guillaume. Thank you for all your patience. Dido and I send you our best.

Jean Renoir

PS. I believe, furthermore, that RKO were wrong to show a piece of work that was topical in 1942. But that doesn't alter the fact that, if what I read is true, I am not prepared to forget the deep anguish caused by my fellow countrymen's lack of understanding towards me. I said in the beginning of my letter that I was feeling a great desire to stay here. This incident can only reinforce this desire not to go where I will find men whose heroism during the war obliges me to admire them but whose sensitivity seems regrettable to me.

1 The name of Jean Renoir's agent in France is correctly spelled Jean Dewalde.

To Louis Guillaume
Paris

21 August 1946
Hollywood

Dear Mr Guillaume,

Mr Gang[1] received a long letter from Mr Masse[2] with the findings. He can only give me his advice when everything has been translated. In case

Mr Masse was unaware of it, tell him that the witness for my divorce was Gabrielle Slade, who was also the witness for my legal separation in Paris.

We are really in an odd situation. At one time Dido and I thought about divorcing, which would have made our situation in France legal and would have allowed me, without any possible objection, to request a divorce. But we didn't have any motive whatsoever for divorce to present to the California tribunal, and they would have denied this loophole to us. The only thing to do would be for Dido to claim to be the injured party for having married a gentleman who wasn't free. But California law would not recognize this reason, since it is she who set me free.

Do you have any news about the export licence for *Le Chasseur*? I'm eager to receive this painting. I am sure I'll be staying here for several years yet, and I want, as quickly as possible, to gather together the things that matter to me most.

[...]

Dido and I send you our best wishes,

Jean Renoir

1 Martin Gang, Jean Renoir's American lawyer.
2 Jean Renoir's French lawyer.

To Alain Renoir
King City, California

23 *August 1946*
Hollywood

Dear Alain,

I am very happy to learn that you found a *job*[1] in a place which you seem to like. I know King City because I went there with Dudley Nichols and Lou Shapiro. Lou Shapiro is probably the only Jewish cowboy in the two Americas. He's a great guy who in his later years has become the manager for exteriors at RKO. We only stayed in King City for about fifteen minutes, and our acquaintance with the city is limited to a long, narrow bar located on the outside of the turn the road takes when it leaves the city to go south.

[...]

Woman on the Beach proved to be rather catastrophic. I had a bad preview in Santa Barbara.[2] There was a lot of bad blood and I worked like a galley slave editing and re-editing. Now, I've decided to stick with the current structure, which will still take me another two weeks to complete. If this doesn't work, I will ask RKO to entrust the film to someone else.

    With much love,
    Jean Renoir

1 Originally in English.
2 City located north of Los Angeles.

To Pierre Lestringuez   *27 August 1946*
Paris   *Hollywood*

My dear Pierre,

Don't think that I haven't thought about the story which you told me about in your letter, which is already three months old. It's a shame that it wasn't the subject of the film I just finished, which was also about an old gentleman, a young man and a woman. But there you have it: there was a novel published and barely read, and it was this miserable plot which RKO decided to give me to direct. I accepted, I don't know why, no doubt in order to pay my taxes, and it added a few miles of film to our good city's annual output. Here, as used to happen in Paris, they want a book and stars. The world is so small, we speak different languages, but all men are the same. The only way to present your story would be to have a good English translation made of it, in the form of a novel or a tale. Something that wouldn't resemble a screenplay. If you still feel excited by the subject, why not write it? You would probably find a good translator in Paris. It is important that it has a literary quality and not a cinematic one. As for screenplays, they have lots of them here and they never read them. Whereas I can bring a short story to some producer and I know he will read it. I love your idea and I know how to persuade them.

    [...]

I have just spent four months of absolutely mind-numbing editing and re-editing on my last film. Finally I had to ask for help, since I went stupid in the head and I was no longer clear-sighted about anything.

Dido is doing well and sends you and your relations her best. Alain is wandering around somewhere in California, earning a living at a ranch or a gas station. I just sent him some books to help him prepare him for his exam in the Fall. It seems he hasn't given up his idea of English. As for the cinema, even if he once thought about it, with the return of the veterans who had worked in Hollywood before the war, the studios are full to bursting point. One couldn't fit a pin in there, and the unions categorically refuse to admit anyone new.

These rambling lines bring me closer to you.

With all my love to you and those close to you,

Jean Renoir

To Jean Lauer[1]   28 August 1946
Grimaud-Var   Hollywood

My dear Jean,

Even here, in this city so different from everything around it, I badly feel the gap left by Monique's departure.[2] I would like very much to see you and spend some time with you in the garden she loved so much. Alas, it's going to be impossible for me to enter France, at least for some time. Dido and I were married here by Californian state law, and one year before, I had filed for divorce from Catherine, by Californian state law as well. Unwittingly, I committed an error. Having been separated from Catherine for almost fifteen years, the formality for transforming this separation into a divorce was very simple, but I had neglected it. Since my Californian divorce has been granted for reasons which are not recognized by French law, it turns out that in America I am an honourable citizen and in France I am a bigamist. If I cross the borders of my country, I seriously risk being sent to prison. Of course, this whole situation is caused by Catherine, who is asking for a settlement in exchange for financial compensation. At the beginning I said yes, and immediately the sum went up. It's hard enough earning money nowadays, and I don't have the means to give in to what seems to me a kind of blackmail. That is why, my dear Jean, I won't be able to see you and, please believe me, I feel very deprived. In place of being reunited in person, my heart is with you. I understand your pain, hoping that this house so full of Monique's presence, those beautiful horizons which she so often contemplated, and your work, will help you get through this.

With warm regards,

Jean Renoir

1 Old friend of Jean Renoir.
2 Monique, Jean Lauer's wife, had recently died of cancer.

To Louis Guillaume
Paris

My dear Guillaume,

You have probably already received my letter in which I gave you the latest information which I could obtain concerning the shipping and travel insurance for *Le Chasseur*. I've added to this the authorization to move the wardrobes. If this paper should be notarized, let me know.

I will now answer the rest of your letter of 30 August. Regarding *Whisky*, thanks for sending me the book. Before you begin taking any steps, which are always tiring and time consuming, it is better that I first reread the book. My ideas on making a film from it are still rather vague. I will probably often be asking you to send me some books and information on various subjects, until I find that rare bird capable of being of interest to producers, actors, and, if possible, the public as well. More and more, I'm counting on doing lots of research work before deciding on a story.

Thank you as well for *Prenez Garde à la Peinture*. That isn't for me, but for a colleague at RKO who hopes to convince this studio about the subject.

As for *La Femme Nue de Goya*, it is possible that my memory serves me wrong. I am trying at this very moment to assemble documentation about the adventures of Goya and the Duchess of Alba,[1] as I think that the role of the latter would be very good for Paulette Goddard. If you have any ideas about books which could give me information on this subject, buy them and send them to me. Here, at the municipal library, I have already found a fair amount of information. Of course, I'm trying to be discreet about this subject, as with my other projects, because Hollywood, like Paris, is a city where you can quickly have an idea swiped from you.

As for Mamee's[2] tombstone, I leave that to you.

Concerning your expenses being deductible from my income tax return, here as in France, that happens in the month of March. The next time I see the expert who helps Dido in these matters, I will ask him exactly in what form that must be drawn up. The letters which you frequently addressed to me on your letterhead are already a justification. No doubt it will be necessary to add to it a summary of my professional expenses in France during the year gone by, drawn up in a book of accounts. I will tell you more about this subject at the appropriate time.

Concerning the inventory and shipment of my furniture, I am waiting for the former in order to help me recall what I own and decide what I want brought over. But you already have so much to do with *Le Chausseur* . . . please take your time with the rest. The only thing I fear would be for Catherine to find some way of foreclosing on everything I own in France. But if I have *Le Chasseur* I will consider that I have saved the most important thing. Since the rest has much less value, if things turn bad, you can always buy back the few objects I am most attached to.

[. . .]

Thanks for your news about the revival of *La Grande Illusion*.[3] It was very pleasing for us to know that it went well. I needed this encouragement, being a little depressed by certain difficulties surrounding my last film.

Received a letter from Mr Gang which complimented the work of Mr Masse. He advised me to make a list of valuable things which Catherine could take from me. I can only think of the portrait of my mother, the sketch of *Le Jugement de Paris* which was above the salon mirror at Marlotte, and a landscape. Perhaps there are other things which you remember? Nothing is pressing, as you said, and I think that Gang considers this list to be a defensive weapon in case we lose and we're asked for money. You can always put this idea to Mr Masse.

Since we are on the subject, I must tell you something which I haven't told a soul, not even my lawyers, just Dido. It is that, if Catherine makes an appeal, and if I see things being prolonged, I have decided on dropping the suit. One day it will be necessary for me to become a naturalized American. This is obvious, because I earn my living here, my home is here, and my son is a citizen of this country. If my pending business with Catherine prohibits me from entering my country of origin, that will obviously be very painful for me, but I will reconcile myself to it. I'm asking you not to speak about this to anyone, for if Catherine knows, she would be capable of trying to block the shipment of *Le Chasseur*. Furthermore, I wouldn't want to give Mr Masse the idea that I am losing interest in the lawsuit, which isn't the case.

You have truly cleared up this question about the house servants, and we thank you wholeheartedly. Before you bother yourself anew, we ask you to wait a little longer. Here is what has happened. Dido has an old friend[4] in England who for her whole life took care of the house belonging to her brothers and sisters. Since her last sister just got married, she is alone now and seems to want to come to help Dido. It's a very different solution, and much less brilliant than the house servants, for she will not entirely unburden Dido from all the house work and it will be necessary, without a doubt, to have a housekeeper come in from time to time. But she offers the advantage of security. This friend is an English spinster. Her father worked for Dido's father at the Liverpool Consulate. She is a little like family. With her, if we have to go away, the house and the paintings would be as well guarded as if we were there. She will let us know her intentions about this in a week or two. If she doesn't come, which is very possible, we ask you to start things again on the French couple front.

We've given your regards to the Slades. They send you their best and we send our love.

Jean Renoir

1 This subject was eventually filmed as *The Naked Maja* (Henry Koster, 1959), with Ava Gardner.
2 Mother of Catherine Hessling and grandmother of Alain Renoir.
3 *La Grande Illusion* was re-released in France in 1946, but with two censor cuts.
4 Elizabeth ('Bessie') Smith (1899–1967) became housekeeper for the Renoirs until 1961.

To Louise Chevallier-Munier
Essoyes

1 October 1946
Hollywood

My dear Louise,

[...]

I am no doubt repeating in this letter some of the things I told you in a previous letter, but I don't know if this last one arrived. Allow me then to tell you how much I am touched by this posthumous sign of friendship to my father by the people of Essoyes. This makes the old country even more dear to me. You asked me when I plan on returning there. Frankly, I don't know. I will admit to you that Europe makes me 'fearful' now. I do not mean a physical fear, nor a fear of having nothing to eat, nor of a lack of comfort. No, I am afraid of ideas which swirl at such a speed that I can no longer follow them, and which are absolutely alien to me. During the last five years I've lived in America among people who rather resemble the French before the first war. My preoccupations, like those of my neighbours, were simple. Would we be victorious? Would our sons return from the war without too many injuries? In what sector would they be fighting? Etc. etc. Of course, this love of money, for which you reproach the French, exists here as well. It's a world-wide crisis. The industrialists and the merchants reduce production in order to make prices rise, and the workers strike in order to obtain better wages. The American government, in the middle of this disorder, is showing itself to be as incoherent as our French ministers were in similar circumstances at the time when we were happy. But ultimately, all this is relatively simple compared to the sudden jolts which mark poor Europe's convalescence.

The most serious thing you tell me is that farming is being carried out by German labour, and that you wonder what will happen when the prisoners have been sent back.

Alain has entered the University of Santa Barbara, a little city located along the ocean roughly 160 kilometres from here. He is doing very well. His studies seem to interest him.

Excuse my ramblings. I hope to have the pleasure of reading something from you soon. My wife, who hopes to get to know you, joins me in sending to you and your family our kindest regards. (Don't forget Bielle.)

Jean Renoir

To Randolph Weaver[1]   5 October 1946
New York   Hollywood

My dear Randolph and Dorothy,

It's been ages since we've written to you. You are not the only ones of our friends whom we have abandoned this way. Alain's return, the problems that his presence brought, and above all a film which I haven't yet succeeded in shaking off, are the causes of this. This film, *Woman on the Beach*, began with huge problems. Then the shooting started in an excellent atmosphere. Alas, it was the calm before the storm. The previews were bad. And now, after months spent trying to fix the situation in the editing room, my bosses have asked me to reshoot parts of the film. Therefore, it will be more than a year spent on the same production. This abnormal situation really upset me and gave me a great desire for solitude. But now I'm back on it. Without abandoning this film, which I must complete, I have seriously set myself to writing a book. This independent work brings me great relaxation. And this relaxation gives me the desire to converse with my friends. Hence, my dear Dorothy and Randolph, this short letter.

[. . .].

Dido is still very active and busy. That's to say, we haven't gone out this year. I don't believe we've seen more than two or three films. Also, she has to keep the house in working order. One of her friends from England is coming to help her. This daughter of Albion will be our *housekeeper*.[2] That's to say, if you pass by here, the lunch we offer you will consist of lamb stew and desserts full of ginger.

That's another way in which things seem to be taking a good turn. The only cares which trouble us are those concerning the general situation. Are they going to start another war, once more without any excuse? I'm dying from worry, for if men commit such a folly, it's the end of all that we love in Europe. The harmonious streets of Paris will be transformed into piles of pebbles. Italian palaces reduced to ashes. It's the end of a civilization which, after all, is ours, with people reduced to living in landscapes of *drugstores*[3] and *gasoline stations*.[4] As for myself, I'm getting by because I don't leave my house, where I've hung on the wall some small paintings by my father. If I didn't have this oasis, my life would be unbearable.

I think I've said enough. Excuse my ramblings, and my best wishes to you and Dorothy.

Jean Renoir

PS. When are you going back to Cagnes?

1 Randolph Weaver was an old friend of Jean Renoir. With his wife Dorothy he would later translate *Renoir My Father* (1962).
2 Originally in English.
3 Originally in English.
4 Originally in English.

To Albert André

25 October 1946
Hollywood

Dear Albert André,

Thanks to you, and especially Maleck,[1] we now have an idea about what's going on over there, and it's hardly encouraging. I would have liked to take a trip there, but I am in the middle of legal proceedings with my former wife, and as long as that hasn't been ruled on, I risk going to prison for bigamy if I set foot on French soil. I miss my old friends. One curious thing is that, since I've been in exile, the only language I understand is that of the people of my generation or the previous generation. I've tried to see some French films. Except for one – *La Bataille du Rail*[2] – which I found extraordinary, the others bore me. The films that are being made in Hollywood aren't any better. They are probably even worse, but they are made by fine arse-licking businessmen who just simply and clumsily try to make money. In each new French film, I seem to feel in every frame the ambition to change the world. I've felt the same sensation when reading some new books which fell into my hands. You recall when my father said that he didn't like Victor Hugo[3] because he had undone the simple way the French people spoke? What would he say today, with this false simplicity more pretentious than the romantic overemphasis?

Here in the American West, there is no 'artistic life'. Instead, people form groups for political or religious reasons, or even because they enjoy being together. There is a small, rather amusing group mainly composed of Germans who emigrated a long time ago, such as Feuchtwanger,[4] Thomas Mann,[5] the musician Hanns Eisler,[6] and, around them, people such as the American writer Clifford Odets,[7] the Englishman Aldous Huxley,[8] Charlie Chaplin. Dido and I sometimes mix with them, and so have had the chance to spend several wonderful evenings in their company. The system adopted here for get-togethers is called the 'party'. That means one doesn't sit at table but one serves oneself in the dining room, where the table is transformed into a buffet. At rich people's places, the table collapses under the weight of food, while the poor get by with a lot of coffee and cakes that are a little hard to swallow. The advantage is that in Hollywood, people don't attach any importance to the question of 'economic circumstances'. All they ask of you is not to be boring. An amusing poor person makes the 'parties' more successful than a boring rich person.

I don't like these 'parties' very much, as I prefer the old notion that a good dinner, the behind well wedged in a good chair before a pretty white tablecloth, and with the help who takes away your dishes and fills your glass, is worth more than sitting on a cushion balancing one's plate. We have a good friend, Al Lewin, who is in the same line of work as myself; for the simple reason that he's been doing it in this town, he's been able to amass a rather splendid fortune over some thirty years. He shares my opinion on these 'parties' and puts on absolutely perfect dinners: French champagne, Russian caviar, authentic *foie gras*, not to mention an unbridled love of garlic, which is very agreeable. His dinners remind me a little of the ones Palazzoli used to give. We always find ourselves there with the same friends, who belong to a whole range of professions: a German doctor very knowledgeable in anthropology and his feminist American wife, a musician from the operetta who came to bury himself at Metro-Goldwyn-Mayer and his very funny and passionately anarchist wife, one or two actors, Man Ray,[9] and loads of others not at all illustrious, but good drinkers and good people.

From time to time, we have friends over to our place. Dido cooks and everyone raves about it. Each of these get-togethers is an expedition, because this city is so big; in order to see a neighbour, it's a little like going from Loudon to Avignon.

All this to tell you that the way we live here is a lot like the way we would live if we were to return to a normal France. I hope that this evocation of Hollywood life doesn't bore you too much. Maleck seemed to want to know a little about how things are here. If it amuses you, I can tell you all you want to know. The subject is inexhaustible.

I hope that your domestic problems are resolved. Your painting-wine exchange was very funny. Let us know if the wine was good. Thanks for the little card with my father's roses. Has Maleck received the fountain pen? Do you still need some canvas?

With all our love to you both.

Jean Renoir

1 Maleck André, wife of Albert.
2 *La Bataille du Rail* (René Clément, 1946).
3 Victor Hugo (1802–85), author of *The Hunchback of Notre-Dame* (1831) and *Les Misérables* (1862).
4 Lion Feuchtwanger (1884–1958), novelist and playwright whose works included *Jud Süss* (1925).
5 Thomas Mann (1875–1955), author of *Tonio Kroger* (1903), *Reflections of a Non-Political Man* (1918), and *The Magic Mountain* (1924).
6 Hanns Eisler (1898–1962), composer whose credits include *Le Grand Jeu* (Jacques Feyder, 1934) and *Woman on the Beach*. He was deported in 1947 by the House Un-American Activities Committee and settled in East Germany, whose national anthem he eventually composed.
7 Clifford Odets (1906–63), playwright, director and screenwriter. His most famous plays were *Waiting for Lefty* (1935), *Golden Boy* (1937), and *The Big Knife* (1949). His film credits included *None but the Lonely Heart* (directed by Odets in 1944), *The Country Girl* (based on his play and directed by George Seaton, 1954) and *Sweet Smell of Success* (Alexander Mackendrick, 1957).
8 Aldous Huxley (1894–1963), author of *Crome Yellow* (1924), *Brave New World* (1932), and *Doors of Perception* (1954).
9 Man Ray (1890–1976), painter, photographer and maker of avant-garde films, among them *Le Retour à La Raison* (1923) and *L'Etoile de Mer* (1928).

To Fernand Bercher[1]

9 November 1946
Hollywood

My dear friend,

For some time now, I should say several years, I've been losing my interest in the cinema. I still make films, because it's the only way I know to earn a living. During the making of these films, I do everything possible to supply my employers with a quality product. But I fear that

21 Jean Renoir with his dachshund, Kiki, on the lawn at Martel Avenue

the period when everything to do with the cinema was great fun is now over. What if I told you that the only films I see are those that I must watch for professional reasons and are screened for me at the studio! The idea of sitting down in a real cinema no longer enters my thoughts. For the moment, I am committed to a very long job which I haven't been able to get out of yet. When it is finished, perhaps I will try to write a book. But for me, the prospect of making other films is completely unbearable.

I'm not telling you all this to bother you with my personal problems, but to explain to you why I took so long to answer your letter. Since I can't find the right direction for myself, what would be the worth of the advice that I could give to my friends.

If you were just anybody, I would tell you anything, or rather, don't come to Hollywood because you won't have any luck here – or even come on over, because one can manage to get along fine here.

The truth is that America is still America, that's to say, the land of success stories. Here there is always a public of several million inhabitants ready to be as enthusiastic for the best as for the worst, for the banal as for the special. I assure you that I regret not having immigrated earlier, at a moment in my life when I felt driven by a huge energy and prepared to overcome all obstacles. This said, I believe there is a better chance for a newcomer here in the theatre than in the cinema. Although I live far from New York, echoes arrive constantly from the theatrical activity in the big city, which doesn't exclude new names, actors and writers who one hears about for the first time. Here in Hollywood, it isn't the same. The reason for this stagnation is that the importance of film production hasn't increased, and has even perhaps diminished, since the silent film days. The talkies have been very favourable to national industries. You know what happened in our country. Before 1930, the French didn't, so to speak, exist. The public much preferred American productions. As soon as our national actors began speaking, it was easy for them to supplant their Hollywood colleagues.

Right after this change, American film artisans went back into their shells. One rarely sees newcomers in the Hollywood studios. Breaking in is forbidden both by producers, who prefer to make their product with the help of their usual people, and also by the unions, who try to limit the risks of unemployment for their members. The best way they have found so far is to close the doors to newcomers. It would be easier to reach a compromise with the producers, who are still fairly anxious to use new talent, than with the unions, who show themselves to be inflexible diehards.

[196]

You will remember Lourié, who was my production designer on *Les Bas-Fonds*. He was the last to be accepted by the union for his particular skill, in 1942. Thanks to this lucky break (due to absences in the studios caused by the war) he is getting along brilliantly now, always working, and able to design sets with great artistic freedom. Lourié is a happy example. On the other hand, my son Alain, who was a cameraman before the war, tried to join the union in this capacity after the liberation of the American army, and they told him that he would have to wait several years before there was a place. Please understand that he didn't sign up as a top cameraman but as a second assistant. In general, the French who came here because of the war haven't been very successful. The only job which allows such a person to scrape a living is as a technical adviser on films with a French atmosphere. This craft, which isn't really one, consists of advising the props and costume people to help them commit fewer errors in films which don't take place in America. This craft has no union whatsoever because these technical advisers are, in general, imported for the duration of the film from the country they want to represent on the screen. Only once, since I've been here, was I able to find a job for one of my friends as a technical adviser.

A gentleman I know who is the president and owner of a studio and several film production companies wanted to have his son work as a third assistant director. The director agreed. The other assistants agreed. At the union, they replied that there were more than fifty veterans who were waiting their turn, and that if an assistant director was required, they would have to take the first person on the list.

I'm giving you these examples in order to illustrate my point that your chances of penetrating any branch of American cinema are, at the moment, terribly uncertain. It is possible that this industry will win new markets, construct new movie theatres and new studios, which will change things. But for the moment, there's no chance of that, and my advice to all my friends asking me the question which you asked, is not to attempt this adventure. That's also the advice I gave to my son, who made the decision to go to university and to finish his English studies there.

This is the bad side of the matter. I'm now going to try to show you the good side. In my opinion, this good side only exists for two categories of individuals – writers and actors. Our industry never turns down a writer with ideas for films and never turns down a good actor if, to start with, his claims are modest. Francen[2] is a shining example of this. When he arrived here, he knew he should accept, with good grace and intelligence,

[197]

the fact that although he was a big star on the stage and screen in France, here he was totally unknown. So in the beginning he applied for small roles. At the same time he perfected his English. Quite quickly, directors and producers noticed him. An actor who knows his craft offers one advantage at least: that he is economical, that he costs less time than others. Now Francen earns a small fortune every year, playing roles which appeal to him, in an atmosphere of respect and cameraderie.

I am convinced that any good actor with a little money to support himself, a lot of patience, and no vanity, can sooner or later make himself appreciated in Hollywood. (I suddenly remembered that Mrs Pitoeff,[3] that great actress, couldn't even find a role here as an extra. Without some theatrical performances in Canada, she wouldn't have had enough to buy herself even the small piece of daily bread needed for her survival.)

Now that I've answered, and confusingly, the practical side of your letter, let me tell you how happy I was to have the news from you and Claire Gérard.[4] The compliments you gave me on *The Southerner* touched me all the more as this is the only film I've been able to make up till now that corresponds a little to my ideal. I believe that it's also my only American work deserving of the hour and a half lost in watching it.

I'll pass on your regards to Alain when I see him. He is at the University of Santa Barbara, three hours from here, and we see him once a month.

I thank you for your photographs. I'll take good care of them. If you want me to pass them around to other people, let me know. Please stay in touch. I fear that the only way for you and I to work together again would be for me to return to Europe. But that's another story.

Forgive me for this long ramble. You must blame the happy memories I have of you, and the respect in which I hold your talent.

Best wishes,

Jean Renoir

1 Actor who appeared in *Las Bas-Fonds*.
2 Victor Francen (1888–1977), actor whose credits included *Hold Back the Dawn* (Mitchell Leisen, 1941) and *Mission to Moscow* (Michael Curtiz, 1943).
3 Ludmilla Pitoeff (1896–1951), wife of Georges Pitoeff (1884–1939), who together were the leading classic actors of the French stage, with only very occasional film appearances.
4 Claire Gérard (1893–1971), actress who appeared in Jean Renoir's films *Le Crime de M. Lange*, *La Bête Humaine*, and *La Règle du Jeu*.

To Charles Einfeld [*Original in English*]   *19 November 1946*
Enterprise Productions Inc.   *Hollywood*
Hollywood

Dear Mr Einfeld,

Since I made *The Southerner*, I have been desperately looking for a really good story that I could suggest to David Loew and yourself. I believe I have found it in the recently published book *The River* by Rumer Godden.[1] An excellent review, appearing in the *New Yorker* about three weeks ago, brought it to my attention. I read the book, and became so enthusiastic about it that I asked my agents Phil Berg–Bert Allenberg to buy the rights for me, and am now awaiting an answer from London.

I know that few people are going to realize the wonderful possibilities contained in this story, but I feel that it is exactly the type of novel which would give me the best inspiration for my type of work – almost no action, but fascinating characters; very touching relationships between them; the basis for great acting performances; and an unexpressed, subtle, heart-breaking, innocent love story involving a little girl and a physically broken-down, morally sick, but still hopeful, wounded officer.

I am going to see David tomorrow, and am very sorry that I shall not find you too. It so happens that Monday next I start to reshoot several scenes of my perennial *Woman on the Beach*, and this is going to keep me busy for several weeks. If you could find time to read the book, which I have told Brentano's[2] to send you, or have someone read it for you, I would appreciate it very much, then I could call you from Pathé Studios where I shall be working, and ask you how you feel about it.

I have not mentioned this project to anyone but my wife, David Loew, yourself and my agent.

Sincerely,

Jean Renoir

PS. The action takes place in India, within the limits of a garden. It would not be an easy picture, but at the same time would not involve any insurmountable production problems.

1 Rumer Godden (b.1907), author whose works include *Black Narcissus* (1939), *An Episode of Sparrows* (1955), and *In This House of Brede* (1969).
2 Book store chain.

To David Loew [*Original in English*]　　　　*1 December 1946*
Enterprise Productions Inc.　　　　　　　　　*Hollywood*
Hollywood

Dear Dave,

Thank you for giving me your answer so quickly. As a matter of fact, after we had this meeting at your studio, Dido and I started to think that my *River*, without any star possibility, was probably not at all fitting with your programme at Enterprise.

Our Thanksgiving dinner consisted of steak as we believe that in all probability the pilgrims, beside turkeys, may also have killed a few buffaloes.

I am terribly busy at Pathé but confident my picture is going to be greatly improved. I am very lucky to have Frank Davis with me. Our work together is so easy we are thinking of making a team in the future.

We hope to see you soon, and Meta before she leaves for New York.

Sincerely,

Jean Renoir

To Robert Flaherty [*Original in English*]　　　*21 December 1946*
Black Mountain Farm　　　　　　　　　　　　*Hollywood*
Brattleboro, Vermont

My dear Bob,

I know you are somewhere in Louisiana, but since I don't know the exact spot, I am sending this to your farm address in Vermont. Dido and I also know that your fellow-workers and some of your family are with you, and that you are shooting a picture,[1] more or less as the spirit moves you – which is great news. We miss your pictures terribly. You know, for me they have been milestones in the development of our profession, and they have helped me enormously to find my dead reckoning, and to try to understand where we have arrived. If I ever become the complete man of Hollywood, I shall build a house here; in it there will be a projection room where I can see your various works whenever I feel in the mood for them.

I am just finishing a picture the subject of which is insignificant but which has been the means of my getting to know some worthwhile actors, and a writer whom you know. His name is Frank Davis. He is a friend of Al Lewin. He used to write with his wife, Schlesinger – they were a team. Her death two years ago hit him very hard. His work with me is the first he has done after a long retirement from which he could not make up his mind to emerge. Our getting together is very important for me because I think that in him I have found my ideal collaborator. He, for his part, seems to think that I also am a good fellow-worker. Here in Hollywood it is pretty hard to fight single-handed for the pictures one would like to make. Two minds with same tastes and ideas are better than one when it comes to defending the thing desired.

Dido and I are terribly anxious to see you again, and to exchange ideas with you. We hope to go east when I have finished cutting my picture, and if so, whether you are then in Vermont or Louisiana, we are absolutely determined to make a detour and spend a few moments in your company.

My boy, Alain, is at the University of Santa Barbara. His hair and his political opinions – the one as red as the other – seem to win popularity for him in that ultra-bourgeois crowd. He appears to be enjoying himself. In English he is one of the three best in the whole school. I suspect him of wanting to write stories.

All our best wishes to you, Bob, for a very merry Xmas, and in the New Year good health and happiness to you and all your family. For ourselves we wish that we shall soon see your picture.

Sincerely,
Jean Renoir

1 *Louisiana Story* (1948).

To Richard Griffith[1] [*Original in English*] 23 *December 1946*
The National Board of Review *Hollywood*
New York City

Dear Mr Griffith,

I am terribly happy and proud to have had my picture, *The Diary of a Chambermaid*, mentioned by your organization as being among the ten best of the year.

I am all the happier about it due to the fact that certain Hollywood trade papers gave it as their opinion that this picture was scandalous, and that those who made it should blush for shame at having done so.

In doing me this honour, your members have given me the greatest encouragement. I love my profession, and I should like to be able to practise it with perfect integrity. To this end it is necessary that I stand firm against certain harmful commercial ideas of which you and your organization are well aware, and against which you are fighting the good fight. It isn't always so easy. Thank you for being on my side.

Sincerely yours,

Jean Renoir

1 Richard Griffith (1912–69), executive director of New York's 'National Board of Review' 1946–49, critic and film historian, whose books included *The Movies*, *The World of Robert Flaherty*, and *Anatomy of a Motion Picture*.

To Louis Guillaume
Paris

25 *December 1946*
Victorville

Dear Mr Guillaume,

I received your letter of 18 December informing me that the ruling was not favourable for me. I am impatiently waiting for you to see Mr Masse and for you to write to me about the outcome of your visit so that I know what I must do. If I understand correctly, the tribunal refused to allow my request to transform a separation of fifteen years into a divorce. But I'm eager to know if the same tribunal indicates what I must do in order to be correct according to French law:

Would I be condemned to a fine or some other form of indemnity? Or go to prison? And once this formality was accomplished, would I be allowed to reiterate my request for a divorce? Or must I divorce Dido so that, finding myself again in admissible circumstances by French law, I would be authorized to resubmit said request for a divorce?

The second procedure would be ridiculous and furthermore impractical. According to the law of the state where I live, California, Dido and I have no valid reason authorizing us to file, she against me, or myself against her, a request for divorce.

I therefore hope that the letter informing me of your interview with Mr Masse will give me some indication as to how a French citizen, who finds himself against his will in such an impasse as I do, can hope to get out of it.

[. . .]

Dido and I send you our love and wish you a Happy New Year with few problems of any sort, without lawsuits and without paintings to send off.

Best wishes,

Jean Renoir

PS. We are in Victorville, in the desert, for a few days' vacation. Dido and I are trying to get rid of a lingering cold.

1947

To Pierre Braunberger   *14 January 1947*
Paris   *Hollywood*

My dear Pierre,

Don't be ashamed for not having written to me. I've been no better, and my circumstances were certainly a lot easier than yours. But after the events which overwhelmed our poor world, one feels a little overcome and one doesn't feel the need to communicate the details of one's petty life.

I am very moved by the warm welcome given to *La Partie de Campagne*, and I wish you all the success possible with this old friend. I would, of course, be delighted if the Museum of Modern Art wanted to send a copy of the film.

I don't know when I could think of going to work in France. I've lived these war years with the feeling that I've been waiting for something, and that all I was doing was only provisional. Now that the war has ended, I've got it in my head not to leave Hollywood without having made at least one film that satisfies me entirely. It's a very arduous enterprise. Not because production is more difficult here than elsewhere. On the contrary, I have the feeling that if one knows what one wants, one can try anything in the framework of American cinema. What's stopping me is the difficulty of gathering together my own ideas in a world and a language new to me.

Alain is well. He is at the University of Santa Barbara.

All my best wishes.

Jean Renoir

To Claude Renoir Jr   *4 February 1947*
Paris   *Hollywood*

My old friend Claude,

[. . .]

I have a project this year, but so far, unfortunately, I'm afraid I have it to myself. The studios and independent producers don't at all share my enthusiasm for a book for which I bought the rights and which is called *The River*. It's written by an English lady living in India, Rumer Godden. It's a film I cannot make in France. To tell the truth, the best place to make it would be in India. It's a simple and passionate subject, almost all of it takes place outdoors, and I believe that you would love to be the *cameraman*[1] on it. Unfortunately, I don't even know if I will do it, and if I do, you know the practical barriers which prohibit a technician from one country shooting in another. Here in America, the unions are particularly ferocious. It's one of the reasons which led Alain to study at university rather than try to take up his craft again. It really worked well for him, by the way. I am waiting for him at this very moment. Soon it will be two months since I last saw him. He has just finished his final exams of the semester, but doesn't know the results yet.

Your Franco-Swiss proposition is very nice, but I don't want to leave America right now for many reasons, some personal (you are no doubt familiar with my dispute with Catherine) and others professional (before taking off, it would be good for me to have a real success here).

No doubt you are without Denise, but I send my love to you three nevertheless. Dido and Gabrielle send their best.

Jean Renoir

1 Originally in English.

To Pierre Lestringuez   *6 May 1947*
Paris

My dear Pierre,

[...]

I've just had a letter from Koch in Berlin. I was very pleased.[1] It's frightful, but all that's happened, the massacres and the tortures, haven't succeeded in awakening a nationalistic feeling in me. The destruction of the old parts of Cologne and Monte Cassino continues to upset me. When I try to point out the guilty, my first impulse is to accuse all of humanity and the imbecilic times in which we live. When I express these ideas, I am told that they have photographs of the plans and measurements of Monte Cassino, and that the reconstruction will be better. Can you believe it?

Here there is a cry of indignation against the last Chaplin film.[2] Dido and I adored it. But to the modern man's eyes, it was wrong in being the expression of a personality. And that is one thing which is no longer wanted. Down with the individual, and up with salads made with mayonnaise bought at the grocer and in which it's impossible to recognize the ingredients. On both sides of the barricade which is soon going to separate the Orient from the Occident, the main activity is to make everything 'level'. If one wants to live, one must dance in a circle with others, and join in a kind of collective *boogie-woogie*[3] by putting one's feet in the footprints of the neighbour who came before you.

Send me news about *Cartouche* and *La Fille du Géolier* and about yourself and your family ...

With love,

Jean Renoir

1 Jean Renoir had been told, in a letter from his brother Claude, that Carl Koch had committed suicide in Berlin to escape being taken prisoner by the Gestapo. Koch and his wife, Lotte Reiniger, were actually safe in Berlin and soon moved to London.

2 *Monsieur Verdoux* (Charles Chaplin, 1947).

3 Originally in English.

To Walter Wanger [*Original in English*]   *10 May 1947*
Universal Studio[s]   *Hollywood*
Universal City

Dear Walter,

For some personal reasons which I shall explain some day to you, my friend, I still did not take the decision of becoming an American citizen. And I don't think it is right for me to take part at your reception for Mr Snyder and for the woman I admire the most in this country, Mrs F. D. Roosevelt.[1] As a foreigner I prefer to stay away from any political manifestation. All my best wishes to you.

I hope that some day when you are not too busy with *Joan of Arc*[2] we can get together for lunch. I heard that the *Reporter*[3] and some other trade papers are going to be very severe for *Woman on the Beach* and its director but very kind to the interpreters. That makes me happy for Joan.[4] My consolation in joining the group of those who are so often bitterly attacked will be to find myself in very good company.

Sincerely,

Jean Renoir

1 Eleanor Roosevelt (1884–1962), widow of President Franklin D. Roosevelt and cam-
paigner for human rights.
2 *Joan of Arc* (Victor Fleming, 1948), with Ingrid Bergman in the title role.
3 *The Hollywood Reporter.*
4 Joan Bennett, Wanger's wife.

Woman on the Beach *opens in New York on 8 June with disastrous results. Jean Renoir's contract with R K O is terminated.*

To Edmond Renoir Jr[1]   *20 August 1947*
Viroflay   *Hollywood*

My dear Edmond,

Dido and I are very happy that you were able to use the little things which we sent to you. Let us know what you need and Dido will be pleased to get it for you.

[...]

I am happy that you are so busy. This proves that you are doing well, and it's also probably the best way of being happy.

I'm not thinking about returning to France, at least not for the moment. In Paris I would have a much better situation than here, but I admit that the old world scares me a little. Seven years spent in a country put together by immigrants and where one rubs shoulders with all races, all accents, all religions, has made me quite indifferent towards questions about which I was once passionate. There is one thing about which I'm pretty sure: that 'progress' has been an error, and the more material things we possess, the more our situation on earth becomes complicated. One of my friends wrote a play about Galileo[2] which has been much talked about in this town. My opinion is that the Church was very wrong not to burn this dangerous innovator swiftly, and that things worked much better when the earth was flat.

Don't forget to give Helène[3] and all your family our love.

Fondly yours,

Jean Renoir

1 Edmond Renoir Jr, cousin of Jean Renoir.
2 Presumably Bertolt Brecht (1898–1956), whom Jean Renoir had met in Berlin in September 1933 and was then reunited with in Hollywood in July 1942. Brecht's play *Galileo*,
starring Charles Laughton in the title role, was produced on the Los Angeles stage by
Joseph Losey in 1947.
3 Helène Rivière Renoir, wife of Edmond Renoir and daughter of Georges Rivière.

To Claude Renoir Sr
Paris

My dear Claude,

[...]

Practically speaking, my Hollywood career, as a European director arriving here loaded with the reputation of past films, has not been a success. I haven't given up the battle, and I want to try something else. I might have the chance to produce my own films for a small organization. Here, when one says 'small organization' that signifies a lot. It almost means that one enters a different world from that of the big studios, and a world that is inevitably rarely paid any attention. My various experiences seem to prove that I am incapable of working in the framework of big organizations; I prefer to try to find low-budget films which are my idea, rather than well-financed films based on other people's ideas. If this works out, it is going to take all my time. That is why I definitely want to settle down here.

I am in a period of important decisions. I have even requested my American naturalization papers. Among the reasons which pushed me, and which I have discussed for a long time with Dido, there is one I can tell you in two words: it's Alain. He is doing brilliantly and I am very pleased with him. But I believe that he still needs me. He has become a complete American, in his heart and in his habits.

What I've told you about my projects doesn't mean that it's impossible for me to find work in a big studio. But the subjects which we talked about aren't attractive to me, and I feel a little like Julius Caesar who, when passing by a poor Gaulish village, said to his generals that he would rather be number one in this village than number two in Rome.

[...]

You must see the Cézannes. Tell us about them.

Christmas is coming, Dido and I wish you and your family a happy New Year and send our love.

Jean Renoir

To Pierre Lestringuez
Paris

My dear Pierre,

I wish you the traditional Happy New Year and good health to you and your family. Here we are enjoying a winter with thirty-plus degrees in the shade and glorious sunshine. Alain hasn't come to see me for Christmas. He stayed in Santa Barbara with Lucretius, plus a part-time *job*[1] at a *gasoline station*[2] where he makes a few dollars, which to him seems better than getting them from his old folks. I'm going to see him one of these days, and won't miss the chance to have him fill up my car.

The Hollywood studios are practically closed. They say that it's because of the 75 per cent tax which the English put on American films. The truth is that, because films cost too much, they hope to shoot them at a better price by getting painters and plumbers to bite the bullet and accept lower salaries. Of course, they hold on to the $300,000-a-year stars and $400,000 executives. These pleasantries don't make anyone laugh, in fact there is a sort of wind of panic blowing through the city.

Here we are doing well, and hope the same goes for you.

With love,

Jean Renoir

1 Originally in English.
2 Originally in English.

1948

Jean Renoir, in despair at the machinations of the studio system, attempts to find an independent route to production. In January he forms the Film Group, at first intending to shoot classical and modern plays on a low budget. But his projects fall through when the government stops giving loans to small businesses.

To Georges Simenon[1]   *2 March 1948*
Tucson, Arizona   *Hollywood*

Dear Georges,

I have read *Lettre à Mon Juge*,[2] which gave me a lot of pleasure. I love your murderer, as does my wife. And we were deeply moved by your way of taking us by the hand and leading us down the streets of a little French village.

Charles Boyer has read *Trois Chambres à Manhattan*.[3] He found the book impressive, but he's worried that the Hays Office would ask for too many changes in a film adapted from the story. His reasons are not entirely convincing to me, and I would like to talk it over with a few friends who, I believe, know the rules of American censorship pretty well. Could you tell me if the book has been translated into English, and if so, where I could find a copy?

I can't reply to your letter of the 18th because we don't know yet whether we can get out of Hollywood. I have been very preoccupied with organizing the finance for the first film from my little production unit. I think it's done at last. In a few days I hope to create a company which can sign up with a bank, a studio, a laboratory, etc. If this comes together quickly enough, perhaps Dido and I could come to see you. We really want that to happen. It was a great joy to me when you came back, and I would like to see you more often.

Tell Miss Denise[4] [sic] that we also look forward to getting to know her better.

Fond regards,
[Jean Renoir]

[209]

1 Georges Simenon (1903–89), prolific author celebrated for his thrillers featuring Inspector Maigret. Renoir's *La Nuit du Carrefour* was based on a Simenon novel, with Pierre Renoir as Maigret.
2 First published in 1947. English translation: *Act of Passion*.
3 First published in 1946. English translation: *Three Beds in Manhattan*. For a long time Renoir attempted to set up a film of this book, with the title translated as *Three Rooms in Manhattan*, especially with Leslie Caron – see later letters. It was eventually filmed by Marcel Carné in 1965.
4 Denyse Ouimet, companion to Simenon.

To Robert Flaherty [*Original in English*]

New York City

26 May 1948
Hollywood

Dear Bob,

Dido and I do not expect to go east as soon as we wished. The reason is that I am too busy trying to organize a small independent company. The idea would be to produce my future pictures with a very limited budget, but with more freedom than in a studio. My partners are: a young businessman, a young actor, a young writer, a very old attorney, and my friend Lourié whom you certainly remember. I have an agreement with a studio who shall provide me with the shooting space and the equipment, with a laboratory, with the bank, and more important than the rest, I have a release. The name of this distribution company is Allied Artists. (Do not confuse it with United Artists.) Allied Artists is the branch 'de luxe' of a company which makes only western and gangster pictures, and whose name is 'Monogram'. They are the only ones who seemed to be willing to leave me alone. Furthermore, I will have nothing to do with them, except for the release. I will do the shooting at General Service (which is, as you know, a very good studio), and my films will be presented under our own trade mark, which is 'The Film Group'.

Later, if we are successful, we even intend to have our own salesman travelling in the various states, and establishing connections with the local distributors and important exhibitors. His name is Harry Stern. He has been with United Artists, and has a great deal of experience in selling unusual pictures. As he is now going to New York, I took the liberty to give him your address. I suppose that you are probably beginning to think of the distribution of your film, and he might possibly give you a useful advice.

My dear Bob, we miss you very much. Dido and I think more and more about you as the years go by. And we are dying to see your film.[1] I saw

Benoît-Lévy[2] who is raving about it. Knowing the story, his enthusiasm did not surprise us.

I hope we will see your picture on the coast. Maybe Stern will give us some information about that.

Give our kindest regards to your family. Dido and I send you our love.

Jean Renoir

1 *Louisiana Story* (1948).
2 Jean Benoît-Lévy (1888–1959), producer and director, whose credits included *La Maternelle* (1933) and *Altitude 3000* (1938).

Telegram to Robert Flaherty [*Original in English*]   22 July 1948
Hotel Chelsea
New York City

JUST SAW YOUR MAGNIFICENT FILM.[1] DO THIS AGAIN AND YOU WILL BE IMMORTAL AND EXCOMMUNICATED FROM HOLLYWOOD WHICH IS A GOOD FATE. CONGRATULATIONS.

OONA[2] & CHARLES CHAPLIN — ESTA & DUDLEY NICHOLS — DIDO & JEAN RENOIR

1 *Louisiana Story* (1948).
2 Oona O'Neill, daughter of playwright Eugene O'Neill, who married Chaplin in 1943.

To Robert Flaherty [*Original in English*]   26 July 1948
Hotel Chelsea   *Hollywood*
New York City

Dear Bob,

Already three days have gone by since we saw your picture and every frame is still present in our minds. Dido and I love *Louisiana Story*. To us it is very close to a work of art of old Greece – a perfect expression of pantheism. This wonderful boy is the god of the realistic fairyland you have created with the camera. In this dangerous and poetic world he is surrounded by some other gods of lesser importance but as definite as their ancestors in the Greek religion when a brook, a tree, a swan, a bull, were possibly the possessors of a divine personality. That is the way we felt when we met the little raccoon, the alligator, the workmen, and even the little bird who seems to be drawn by an ancient Japanese painter.

[211]

Thank you for this picture, dear Bob, we hope everybody in the world will be able to see it. I was starting to doubt of the value of our medium and you gave me a good injection of energy and hope.

With our love,
Jean Renoir

To Jean Renoir [*Original in English*]   *1 September 1948*
Hollywood   *Savoy Hotel*
                                                          London

Dear Jean and Dido,

Now and then Ruth[1] writes me that she saw you, and you are well, and I miss you so much. But I never get to writing you, because when I come from work I have all those business letters and social letters, and I never get time for the nice letters of little importance, but still of the utmost importance, to your friends! So far I have not written a word to Signe Hasso[2] or Frank and I am afraid I never will.

How is the new house coming along? So silly of me to be so excited about you moving so close to us, because we probably won't see each other more than we used to.

I hope your film plans are moving too, and you begin to work soon. While in Paris (and I have gone there for many weekends) I heard your name mentioned so many times by various people and I was proud to say: 'He is a very good friend of mine.' (Isn't that right?) How you would have laughed if you could have seen Peter[3] and me, last weekend, on our own in Paris. Two nights in a row we went home at 5 in the morning, Peter clutching the book *What you Want to Say and How to Say it in French*. Now Peter and Pia[4] are in Sweden and I am trying to finish the picture so I can join them, and go back home, and see you.

With love,
Ingrid [Bergman]

1 Ruth Roberts, Ingrid Bergman's dramatic coach.
2 Signe Hasso (b.1915), actress whose credits include *Heaven Can Wait* (Ernst Lubitsch, 1943), *Thieves Holiday* (Douglas Sirk, 1946), and *I Never Promised You a Rose Garden* (Anthony Page, 1977).
3 Peter (or Petter) Lindstrom, Ingrid Bergman's husband.
4 Pia Lindstrom (b.1939), Ingrid Bergman's daughter.

To Clifford Odets [*Original in English*]   *1 October 1948*
New York City   *Hollywood*

AS. (ante-scriptum) If you are working, please ask Bette[1] to read this too long letter.

Dear Clifford,

   I am so happy to know that your play is brutal and strong, scandalous and shocking. The only way in our days to escape from the proper, careful line adopted by modern writers is either to read an old book or to read one of your plays. Our language nowadays is perhaps more free, but about the fear of real passion we are becoming more Victorian than they used to be when the dear old queen was alive. Same thing with acting, and more in the movies than anywhere else. The big preoccupation is to avoid any expression which could suggest that there are maybe some bitter tears or some warm blood outside of the sweet tears and the cold blood accepted in our so-called realistic dramatic art. We can hardly wait to read your new play.

   My independent production[2] is a complete failure. After months (I should say years) of useless talks, after having found the private guarantees asked by the bank, the same bank decided to reject my bid for a loan. No money, no pictures. My partners and I are going to have a meeting very soon to decide whether we dissolve the corporation or not. I am also going to ask Herzbrun to take care of the necessary formalities in order to release *Night Music* from any possible impediments. I don't feel unhappy. The reason given by the bank is that they act according to the new policy recommended to the Federal Reserve by the Congress. But I believe that even without this contrary circumstance there was a worm in the nut, and that I will some day find a better way to put on the screen one of your works.

   Meanwhile I will try to make some money. I have a vague possibility here and a more definite one in Europe. Since my personal picture enterprise is stillborn, I try to work as much as I can on a stage play I mentioned to you. It's a new version of *Amphitryon*.[3] But it is very difficult after twenty-five years of movie making not to be impressed by each phone call which may mean a hope for a new film; and that breaks the fragile walls defending the little world where I am trying to give some appearance of life to my characters. I am afraid the only way to help them to grow would be to abandon Hollywood for a while.

   A good thing about my new possible jobs is that to go to Europe one has to pass through New York. If it happens very soon Dido would have to stay supervising the building of our house. But she would certainly escort me up to New York, we would see you, and that's a very pleasant side of the question. If my trip is for later she would probably come with me all the way through. I am hungry for a long evening with you, around a table, not only for the sake of listening and talking, but also for the sensual luxury of feeling myself close to the people I love; like puppies of the same litter in a nice warm dog-house. Dido feels like me, and what we feel is about both of you.

Dear Cliff, and dear Bette, we sent you *la bise* as we say in the south of France. It is just a quick family kiss on the cheeks.

Jean Renoir

1 Bette Odets, wife of Clifford.
2 'The Film Group'.
3 Jean Renoir had first worked on a contemporary version of the Greek legend in 1939, following the example of Jean Giraudoux in his play *Amphitryon 38*, in which Pierre Renoir had played Jupiter.

To James Mason[1] [*Original in English*]   24 *October 1948*
Beverly Hills   *Hollywood*

Dear James,

Thank you for your nice letter. Even having lost the hope of directing *Trilby*,[2] I have won something infinitely precious: more self-confidence due to the fact that an actor of your class considered I could be of some help to him and to his partners. I know how difficult are things for Mr Lasky.[3] I myself just wasted nearly two years trying to settle an independent enterprise of my own, and I didn't succeed in spite of many concessions.

I am quite sure *Trilby* will be a good picture. Miss Jane Wyman[4] seems a very gifted actress, and the script is good enough to serve well its interpreters. I wish the greatest success to this production.

Dido and myself are very anxious to know how is your wife. We send her our love. Our best to Johnny. We hope to see you all very soon.

Sincerely,

Jean Renoir

PS. Our little dog Kiki died, murdered by a vet, and we are very sad.

1 James Mason (1909–84), actor whose credits included *Odd Man Out* (Carol Reed, 1947), *Desert Fox* (Henry Hathaway, 1951), and *Lolita* (Stanley Kubrick, 1962). He

collaborated with another European director in exile, Max Ophuls, on *Caught* (1949) and *The Reckless Moment* (1949).

2 Unrealized project, apparently based on a story by Charles Nodier, but more likely to be adapted from the novel by George du Maurier.

3 Jesse L. Lasky (1880–1958), film executive and producer. His company, Famous Players-Lasky, eventually became Paramount Pictures.

4 Jane Wyman (b.1914), actress whose credits include *The Lost Weekend* (Billy Wilder, 1945), *Johnny Belinda* (Jean Negulesco, 1948), and *Magnificent Obsession* (Douglas Sirk, 1954).

To Clifford Odets [*Original in English*]   *15 November 1948*
Hollywood

Dear Clifford,

Dido and I love your play[1] and believe it is perhaps your best. This opinion doesn't diminish our admiration for your pre-Hollywood work, but it seems you are talking now from a higher platform. Strangely enough Hollywood, this town you dislike so much, did you a lot of good. I heard several times your admirers affirm that your destiny is to remain inside your own range, meaning New York. And why not. You would be in the fine company of Molière,[2] Courteline, Jules Renard, and so many others, who by plowing stubbornly the little bit of ground on which they were born finally grew a crop generous enough to cover the needs of the whole world. But there are also good artists who reach the universal by the use of a universal language about universal problems. It is a dangerous technique when it fails. The result is as cheap as a Hollywood movie. When it succeeds it is the classical tragedy: Racine,[3] Giraudoux.[4] Some authors like my Father, Shakespeare, belong to both categories. With your new play, showing your ability in using any type of tool, you join them.

Your Hollywood background becomes as rich as the court of Denmark or Venice in the fifteenth century. And your hero is the brother of all those kings, generals, great lovers, who talk in the Latin or Greek verses we had to translate in school.

Thank you for this great contribution to the theatre.

Our love to all of you,

Jean Renoir

1 Presumably *The Big Knife*.

2 Molière (1622–73), French author of such classic plays as *Tartuffe* (1664) and *Le Misanthrope* (1666).

3 Jean Racine (1639–99), the great French tragic dramatist in the neoclassical style, author of plays such as *Phèdre* (1677) and *Bérénice* (1670).

4 Jean Giraudoux (1882–1944), distinguished French dramatist whose plays, most of which were produced on stage by Louis Jouvet, included *Amphitryon 38* (1939), *Ondine* (1939), and *The Madwoman of Chaillot* (1945).

To Bert Allenberg [*Original in English*] 16 November 1948
Beverly Hills *Hollywood*

Dear Bert,

Here are some precisions about my possible deal with Mr McEldowney,[1] Oriental-International Film Inc, Hal Roach Studios, Culver City.

The following propositions were made to Mr Forrest Judd:[2]

Mr McEldowney takes care of the rights, knowing people connected with Mrs Rumer Godden, the author of *The River*. The option I had taken about two years ago would be reimbursed.

The picture would be shot in India with a budget of $500,000– $200,000 in American money, the rest in Indian money. The cost of production in India is supposed to be the third of what it is in Hollywood.

The picture would be in Technicolor.

My salary would be $25,000 cash – $25,000 deferred – and paid after the reimbursement of the American dollars and before the Indian money. I am also entitled to 33 per cent of the profits. The rest of the profits being divided in: 33 per cent for Mr McEldowney, and 33 per cent for the financing.

Out of my share I must give an interest to Forrest Judd who brought me the deal.

The production would be a Jean Renoir picture, presented by Oriental-International. I would be the producer, Mr McEldowney the executive producer, Forrest Judd assistant to myself.

No stars. Release to be found after the shooting.

The River would go into production in winter 1949. Winter is the only good season over there and it is too late this year for me to be ready on time with a very delicate screenplay. But Mr McEldowney insists that I go now, before Christmas, to India for several weeks in order to meet some useful people, collect documentation for the script, and supervise the filming of a certain elephant round-up, an event which happens only every ten years and which would be incorporated in the picture.

Mr McEldowney is going to call again very soon and I shall then ask him to get in touch with you.

Thank you, dear Bert,

Jean Renoir

1 Kenneth McEldowney, a former florist turned producer.
2 Forrest Judd was assistant director on *The River*.

To Louis Guillaume   *3 December 1948*
Paris   *Hollywood*

Dear Mr Guillaume,

You must have received my letter telling you about my possible trip to
Paris. I add to it Dido's suggestion that she herself might avoid going through
France. Journalists have lists of passengers on planes, and she thinks that
finding 'Mr and Mrs Renoir' could excite their dangerous curiosity.

If things work out, we will leave Los Angeles on the 18th of this month.
This will only be a preparatory trip, as the film is to be shot in India in the
fall of 1949. Nothing has been done yet. My agents are busy sorting out the
business side. They are worried that I have taxes to pay both in India and
here, and these could absorb most of my salary. I'm not doing this film for
a studio, but for an individual financed by the Hindus and aided by
Nehru's[1] government, who seem keen to see a film about India which has a
chance of getting a good distribution in the United States. If this happens, it
is equally possible that I will make my stopover in Paris on my return trip,
that's to say on 15 January. But I would like to take advantage of the
opportunity 'on the way' since I am not sure that my return wouldn't be via
the Philippines and Honolulu. It's almost the same distance either way. In
any case, as I am still thinking of going to Italy around February, the details
you will give me will be of help to me now, even if the India business
doesn't come off.

I enclose for you a translation of the reply from my *attorney*[2] to the letter
from Catherine's *attorney*[3], a copy of which you have no doubt received in
one of my earlier letters.

[. . .]

Thank you for the diligence with which you have sorted out the question
of payment for the transportation of the furniture. We have sent a telegram
to you so that you can judge for yourself the speed with which everything
happened. I might add that we were lucky, as the dockers' strike is over
and our furniture can be unloaded at Los Angeles. Dido and I are very
happy that you have freed us from this great worry. All that now remains is
to wish that my divorce follows the same course.

Kind regards,
Jean Renoir

---

1 Jawaharlal Nehru (1889–1964), disciple of Gandhi who became Prime Minister of India
with independence in 1947 and served until months before his death.
2 Originally in English.
3 Originally in English.

To Forrest Judd [*Original in English*]   *31 December 1948*
Metropole Hotel   *Hollywood*
Mysore City, India

My dear Forrest,

Just a few words for you, McEldowney, de Vinna and Hartman to wish you a happy New Year. I hope you are successful with the shooting of the elephant round-up. I am sure it is going to be a very interesting documentary picture.

I didn't send any news before because I had none. Finally I didn't write to Miss Godden. I still feel uncomfortable with her freezing wire, and I am afraid to say something which would harm instead of helping. The best is maybe for McEldowney to explain our problems directly when he sees her in London. During a conversation you can switch, find new ways of approach if you feel no response to your first attempts. But when a letter is written it is for good and you cannot change it.

I saw *Enchantment (Take Three Tenses),*[1] the Goldwyn picture, and it is very bad. The screenplay and the direction are poor and Teresa Wright[2] is not believable in the part of a Rumer Godden character. This mistake shows us how important is the casting of Harriet in *The River*. The success of our picture will depend primarily on the little actress we have to find, and after seeing Teresa Wright's performance I am inclined to believe that such parts are wrong for American actresses and that we should have an English (or Hindu-English) girl. I hope you will come back with some good suggestions and interesting tests.

I am terribly anxious to know about your different researches, enquiries for the locations, etc. The picture can be great if we do it properly, and very much depends on the preparation work you are doing now. Don't forget that having no screenplay, for the moment being the book is your Holy Bible. It is so easy, when confronted by the amazing and beautiful things which surround you during such an exciting trip, to forget the real basis of our future work and to allow your imagination to run wild. Please be careful and hold the book in your hands as a talisman against temptations.

Nothing new about my other projects. Walter Wanger asks me to direct a picture with James Mason. That would be immediate. I still don't know about *Goya*.

We saw Pookie. She sent us your nice Christmas present. Thank you so much.

My best thoughts to all of you.

Sincerely,

Jean Renoir

1 *Enchantment* (Irving Reis, 1948).
2 Teresa Wright (b.1918), actress whose credits include *The Little Foxes* (William Wyler, 1941), *Shadow of a Doubt* Alfred Hitchcock, 1943), and *The Best Years of Our Lives* (William Wyler, 1946).

1949

To Pierre Braunberger   3 *January 1949*
Paris   *Hollywood*

My dear Pierre,

I hope in fact to pass through Paris this year and one of the things which will mean the most to me would be to see you again. I will finally have the chance to see *La Partie de Campagne* and *Paris 1900*.[1] Concerning *La Partie de Campagne*, could you strike me a copy in 16mm, for which I could remburse you through Mr Guillaume in Paris?

Now let's talk about my chances of making a film in France. I have had several propositions but I didn't accept them because before returning I would like my situation with Catherine to be straightened out. It's the only reason which until now has prevented me from making the trip, and which prevents me from renewing my collaboration with the French cinema. No matter how this ridiculous situation turns out, any production will have to wait until I'm free. Actually, I must in principle either shoot a film here for Walter Wanger or a film in Italy for Schulberg,[2] and definitely shoot a film in India next winter (*The River*, a novel by Rumer Godden). Therefore my first post-war film in France won't be for at least a year. I want to write the story and screenplay, and I will do whatever I can to make it something out of the ordinary. I wouldn't want it to cost too much, preferring to shoot only a French version. Nevertheless, I'll try to find a subject and an 'approach', as they say in English, allowing for not-too-limited distribution in the United States. Here the situation is currently as follows. There are truly two publics: on one side a kind of élite, and on the other the masses, consisting principally of kids. If one is looking for wide distribution, it is necessary to accept working for twelve-year-olds. If one looks to the élite, one can make films for them just as well, and even in a foreign language. I have here a certain reputation among this élite. As for the masses, they are only interested in the names of certain actors. I would like to benefit from this situation, and also from the fact that now I know America and Americans well enough to make films for them in French — maybe with a little bit of English, and in any case with very few subtitles — which they would like.

My dear Pierre, these few thoughts aren't even projects yet. Rather, they are a means to regain contact with you by discussing problems which interest us both.

Dido and I wish you a Happy New Year and good heath, as well as to your family and our mutual friends who you may encounter.

Sincerely,

Jean Renoir

1 *Paris 1900* (Nicole Vedrés, 1948), a vivid compilation of actuality and newsreel shot in Paris in the pre-World War One period.
2 B. P. Schulberg (1892–1957), former producer with Paramount Studios from 1925–32, then worked as an independent.

To Louis Guillaume
Paris

22 January 1949
Hollywood

Dear Mr Guillaume,

We leave on 26 January and not having received a letter from you, I ask you to write to me care of Mr Salvo d'Angelo, 'Universalia', via del Traforo 146, Roma, Italia.

I hope to be in Rome between 17 and 21 February. Then Dido and I will go to Paris, so before we leave Rome, we ask you to reserve us a room in a hotel that's comfortable but not too plush. Something like the Terminus-St Lazare or the Lutetia. I would like to avoid the George V and the places the Hollywood people descend upon. We would stay two days, enough time to see you as well as my brothers, the Cézannes, and some friends.

In the course of my trip, I will inform you by telegram about my principal changes so that you can send me a telegram yourself if necessary. From now on, my address will be: Grand Hotel, Calcutta, India, where we're arriving on 1 February.

[. . .]

On the advice of an official at Pan American airlines, we will make sure we meet the costs of our trip by taking with us some hard currency (dollars). If you have some advice to give us on this subject, let me know at one of my vacation addresses. We will probably stay two weeks in India.

At last we have the great pleasure of seeing you soon. Dido and I send our best.

Jean Renoir

In February Jean and Dido Renoir travel to India with Kenneth Mc-Eldowney and Forrest Judd to make production arrangements and to look for locations for The River.

To Clifford Odets [*Original in English*]   *15 February 1949*
New York City   *Great Eastern Hotel*
                                              Calcutta, India

Dear Clifford,

We have been in India two weeks including two days in Pakistan. I won't tell you all about it because we still know nothing. The only thing which is certain is that in our whole life we never were in a country with ways of living so completely different from ours. We feel very much attracted by the Hindus, and the few experiences we had in the preparation of our work are very encouraging. I shot tests with a Hindu cameraman and an India crew. I cut them with an Indian editor. They are all skilful and have for our trade a respect I wish I could find among many white technicians. We met young people, students, and they are fascinating. The strange part of it is that even in so-called scientific fields they don't try to look European. Hollywood people would take an Indian director or a writer for a beggar and would hardly believe that they have any education. On the other hand the Hindu intellectuals are probably more broad-minded and don't consider our clothes too silly.

Calcutta is a good copy of a suburb of London including the fog and the smoke. Huge old-fashioned factories maintain the town in a kind of black cloud. Sometimes a little breeze from the sea chases this screen and you are delighted by the sight of a charming little temple which would be painted by Matisse[1] or an Indian apartment house with fancy shutters by Dufy,[2] or a bit of garden where you wouldn't be surprised to meet Sheherazade[3] resting under a mango tree.

We will tell you all our impressions when we see you in New York. I suppose that now you are very close to the premiere of the play. We are with you with all our hearts in this novel adventure. If such a play is successful I will feel more proud to be a Westerner.

We are in Calcutta for two more weeks. Plenty of work. I believe I found a little girl[4] for my picture. She is an ugly duckling and that's not so bad. I also found an Anglo-Indian girl[5] who is maybe not a good actress, but who is so nice that I would like to bring her to the States as a wife for an unmarried best friend. But my best friends are married with wonderful girls and my project is not very practical.

[222]

Calcutta is a very remote provincial town and I am anxious to be in London and to know about your play. I give you a tentative travel schedule, leaving Calcutta 1 March, then Bombay, Rome and London, 8 March. [. . .] New York about two weeks later.

Dear Clifford, dear Bette, it's too bad we are not having this adventure of meeting the East together. We are anxious to see you.

With all our love,

Jean Renoir

1 Henri Matisse (1869–1954), artist particularly drawn to the East.
2 Raoul Dufy (1887–1953), artist and member of the Fauve group.
3 Sheherazade, one of the wives of Sultan Schahriah, and narrator of tales from the *Arabian Nights*.
4 Patricia Walters, who played Harriet in *The River*.
5 Radha Sri-Ram Burnier, Theosophist and dancer.

On their return to USA, Jean and Dido Renoir move into their newly-built home on 1273 Leona Drive, off Benedict Cañon, Beverly Hills. On a plot chosen by him, Jean had the one-storey house built to his specific instructions, and olive trees planted around it to remind him of Les Collettes.

To Mr Schlamm
[*Original in English*]

14 April 1949
Oriental-International Film Inc.
Culver City, California

Dear Mr Schlamm,

I was very happy the other day to see your interest in our project in India. May I add, which I consider as a very important step in my life. As a matter of fact, this adventure is maybe equally important to our whole profession.

You know very well the evils which are slowly (?) destroying us. The star system, which makes us the prisoners of forms decided by publicity. The credit system, which makes us so afraid of not being 'safe' that we voluntarily accept the tyranny of distributors, exhibitors, intermediaries of all sorts, plus legions of clerks, departments, 'Gallup polls'[1] etc.

The first reason which impelled me to accept McEldowney's proposition to shoot in India was that he was proposing a picture with all the money in the bank, which meant <u>freedom from fear</u>. Also, I didn't realize that I was going to find in India one of the greatest inspirations in my life. Something as important to me as my discovery in France, with the coming of sound. I didn't know how to see until about 1930 when the obligation of writing dialogue brought me down to earth, and established a real contact between the people I had to make talk and myself. In silent pictures, dealing with only outward forms, the imagination can allow you to live in a world that doesn't exist at all.

What I discovered now is the beauty and the quality of the ancient world. I had always imagined that the contemporaries of Ramses II[2] or of Socrates[3] were walking, sitting down, eating, making love with a great nobility of attitudes, but that was only a supposition. In India I saw them, because practically India didn't change in four thousand years, and is still living with an aristocratic style which has about completely disappeared in our mechanized civilization. To be confronted every day with boatmen working their oars in the Ganges River who are directly stepping out of an Egyptian bas-relief, or with a girl dressed in a sari just buying in a market, looking like an animated Tanagra statue, believe me, that's exactly the shock I was needing after eight years in Hollywood.

Practically our projects are: #1, *The River*. That's the novel by Rumer Godden. I owe [it] to the *New Yorker*[4] to have bought an option on it several years ago. By chance I read such an enthusiastic review about this book in this magazine that I decided to read it, and after reading it, to use it as a basis for making a picture. It is a magnificent story about a twelve-year-old girl growing up in a garden on the bank of the Ganges River. No apparent plot, but an intense, may we say, 'inner action'. Exactly the type of picture I couldn't do in Hollywood. As a background we will have the life on this fantastic river, with the ugly factory chimneys reminiscent of Liverpool or Pittsburgh, and the delicate temples that are the perfect evocation of the *Arabian Nights*. They do everything around this river. From immersion at birth, to blessing at marriage, to the holy place where the ashes are scattered at death, with every day worship of their gods, the washing of their laundry, and the rubbing away of dirt from their bodies and their sins from the souls, this holy water is the life.

Rumer Godden, who is a little disappointed with the two pictures *Black Narcissus* and *Enchantment*, has accepted to collaborate with me in writing the script. She will join me in Hollywood very soon.[5] This is the first time she will be in America.

The shooting time being between monsoons, that means from October to April, we will probably shoot another picture the first year and two the second year.

The pictures being in Technicolor, it is the first time anything of this kind will be done in India. We bought the necessary material, or made arrangements in London and in New York, and will be as free technically as we will be financially and artistically.

Kenny McEldowney is the president of our film organization. Its name is Oriental-International Films Inc, and the address is the Hal Roach Studios in Culver City. He will be the producer of the pictures. Forrest Judd is the associate producer. I will have around me some of my old partners like Eugène Lourié, who has designed all my sets since 1935.

Our work will be done in close collaboration with Indian crews. They are remarkable. We will bring here this summer a young Bengali cameraman, Ram Sen Gupta,[6] for training at Technicolor in Hollywood, and possibly a young sound man from Mysore for training with the new Western Electric, including the magnetic.

Knowing the influence, sometimes dangerous, certain distributors have on the shooting of pictures up to now, we didn't make any arrangement for the release, and maybe won't make any until the picture is finished. This leaves us entirely free on casting. We will choose the actors we believe the best ones for the parts without any consideration for their commercial importance. We have already chosen a little girl in Calcutta, Patricia Walters, twelve years old. We found her in school. She will play the lead.

I believe that's all. I certainly will see you again on my way back to India, probably in August, and hope I will have more time to talk about your literary projects which I'm so glad and so proud you have decided to include me in.

Sincerely,

Jean Renoir

1 Polls taken to judge public opinion on current issues.
2 Ramses II, King of Egypt, 19th Dynasty (1304–1237 BC)
3 Socrates, philosopher (469–339 BC)
4 *The New Yorker*, literary magazine.
5 Rumer Godden co-wrote the script for *The River* with Jean Renoir at his Beverly Hills home.
6 Ramananda Sen Gupta worked as assistant cameraman on *The River*.

To Rumer Godden [*Original in English*]   *19 April 1949*
Buckinghamshire   *Beverly Hills*

Dear Rumer,

We found California as pleasant as in our recollections. Only you are missing. We saw McEldowney yesterday. He is waiting for Curtis Brown's[1] letter and hopes that all the questions will be easy to solve. We are so anxious to see you arrive.

After several talks with newspaper people, distributors, etc, we believe that it will be difficult to keep the title *The River*, already used. On the other hand the publicity, bigger than we were expecting, [has] started already around our project. It is no good to leave [sic] it grow around a title we will have to change when we show the picture. This makes it imperative to find a new one right now.

McEldowney suggested an Indian word *Pukka Sahib*, applied to Captain John (ironically by Valerie, seriously by Harriet). To me the general idea is good. I am always attracted by mystery, and the less a title explains the more I like it. About *Pukka Sahib*, I don't know. Maybe it is too 'comedy', but in the range of Indian expressions perhaps something could be found.

Here are some other quick suggestions: *Krishna's Flute*, applied to Harriet's literary gifts. *Diwallis Night* in honour of what could be the first meeting, or the first important scene between Captain John and the girls. *River India* not very elegant, but sounding all right for a movie audience. *The Garden in India*, banal, but the word India is very important in this adventure. I believe more in an Indian title (*Pukka Sahib?*) with a beautiful sound meaning nothing for an American audience but obviously Indian.

Dear Rumer, drop me a note with only one word: the title. Then when you feel like it, write us a few lines bringing us a little more of you. Dido and myself send you our love and to Jane, Paula, and Simon. I go back to the big task of organizing our new house. We found everything in a kind of mess and we want it ready for your arrival.

[Jean Renoir]

1 Literary agent.

To Rumer Godden [*Original in English*]   *29 April 1949*
Aylesbury, Bucks

Dear Rumer,

Ganga Nadee or *Gunga Nahdee* is a beautiful title. I doubt it is possible to find anything more appropriate to a story originally called *The River*. I believe it is even better than *The River*. It does suggest India without being explanatory and it has a lovely mysterious sound.

Dido and myself are very excited at the idea that very soon there will be one more novel by Rumer Godden. We can hardly wait to see it published and to read it.

Our love to the children and to you,
Jean Renoir

To Ram Sen Gupta [*Original in English*]   *7 June 1949*
                                                              Beverly Hills

Dear Ram,

I found your letter the day we got back to Hollywood, and my answer is this late because I wanted to give you some information about your future trip for Technicolor training and also about the results of our work on *The River*.

Unfortunately, things have gone slower than I expected. About your training – we cannot decide anything before having a talk with our future head-cameraman. When I left you, I thought it was going to be Schuftan[1] but during our sojourn in London, Mr McEldowney was convinced that it would be a good thing to have our picture be an English quota one. That would ensure us a wide release in England. This advantage carries with it added assurance of benefit to the backers of our enterprise. To be an English quota picture, we must have on salary seventy-five per cent actors, technicians or other workmen who are citizens of nations belonging to the British Commonwealth, but it is bad for our possible American co-workers. Schuftan is an American citizen and that may prevent us from taking him. In case we have to take an American actor for the role of Captain John, this actor would probably absorb the whole of our twenty-five per cent remaining for salaries of people who are not part of the British Commonwealth. We are now in touch with Boradel, a Canadian (also British Commonwealth). He shot *Elephant Boy*[2] with Robert Flaherty in Mysore, in the old days, and loves India. We hope to have an answer very soon, and should we reach an agreement with him, the first matter we would bring up would be your situation. I have no doubt that with him, everything would work out fine, but I don't like to anticipate before being sure.

About the stuff we shot together, you will hardly believe that I haven't seen it in colour. I've seen it in black and white but would like to have seen it finished in colour, to give you my final impressions. The reason we are still waiting for the final process is that Technicolor doesn't print in colour any film if you cannot give them proof that you have a release and as yet, Mr McEldowney hasn't signed an agreement with any distributor. It is possible that in a few days we will see our stuff, since Mr Mc-Eldowney hopes he will have an agreement for a documentary picture about an elephant kedda he shot, in Mysore, and then our film might be printed in colour together with the kedda film.

Dido and I think and talk about you and Minu[3] everyday. Minu is so beautiful on the pictures you sent us – as beautiful as she is nice and good. We are very happy at the idea that in a few months we are going to see her again, and that maybe before then, you will be with us. Your apartment, the nice painting Minu had done on the floor with rice flour, her touching voice when she sings – all these remain alive in us. As for your very interesting brother and his wise and friendly wife, we are very fond of them and are very anxious to be with all of you again.

The description you gave of the festival at the Tagore University caused us great nostalgia. We hope that some day we will be in Bengal for such an event. In the Kalpana picture, we remember a dance depicting this spring celebration with the throwing of colours. What you say about certain exaggerations in the streets of Calcutta doesn't surprise us. It is the same everywhere. In Italy and in Southern France at about the same time, we have what we call 'carnival'. People in the streets get drunk and throw coloured pieces of paper and even coloured, small balls of plaster. When an old bag of this plaster is thrown from a high window, it can very easily crush some passer-by. You can also imagine the mishaps with women who are thus assaulted right in the middle of the street. The older I grow, the more I've come to believe that just about the same things exist all over the world, with perhaps one difference in favour of India. That is the great 'reluctance of killing' which unfortunately remains unshared by most of the other countries . . . That must be the result of your wonderful religious faith. The few things you told me about that in your letter are perfectly beautiful and I must say the description of your day at the Tagore University is very colourful and gives a clear picture of this festivity. I'm anxious to see it on the screen.

Dear Ram, I will write you again after seeing this film as well as the other things, and as soon as I know more about our deal with Boradel and the different projects concerning yourself.

This letter has no practical purpose and is just by way of a little chat with you and Minu. We send our love to both of you. Please don't forget to tell your brother and sister-in-law that we are thinking of them.

Sincerely yours,

Jean Renoir

1 Eugene Shuftan (originally Eugen Schufttan) (1893–1977), important cinematographer who invented the 'Shuftan Process' for photographing miniatures. His credits included *Quai des Brumes* (Marcel Carné, 1938), *Les Yeux sans Visage* (Georges Franju, 1960), and *The Hustler* (Robert Rossen, 1961).
2 *Elephant Boy* (Robert Flaherty/Zoltan Korda, 1937)
3 Minu Sen Gupta, wife of Ram.

To J. K. McEldowney [*Original in English*]

The Great Eastern Hotel
Calcutta, India

1 July 1949
Beverly Hills

Dear Kenny,

We saw the rushes of Pat[1] again last night, and the Kodachrome ones and the black and white talking tests, and the more we see of her the more we like her. Rumer was anxious to hear her voice, to imagine her speaking some of the lines, and she found it surprisingly good and thinks it has the quality we need. She also thinks Pat has a perpetual interest in that she can vary from looking exceedingly plain and becoming almost beautiful. Few girls, including Margaret O'Brien,[2] can say a line of poetry without being ridiculous, but Pat's saying of the little lines about the crimson rose and plop-apart were so excellent in the test that we feel that with her we can include lines of this sort in the script. The only question is her size. Has she grown a great deal in the heat? On the other hand, Margaret O'Brien is taller and Pat has this long-legged, coltish quality that is very young. We cabled you after seeing the projection because we both felt very strongly that if we can keep her as she is, no one could be better for Harriet. If the production could afford the expense of sending her to the hills, we do feel it would be a very good thing as she needs to keep her colour and be well.

I, Jean, had a letter from my nephew, Claude Renoir. He is interested in making our film, but as he has certain other projects in view, he would like to know as soon as possible if you are definite. If you really intend to pass through Paris and see him, could you wire or write him in advance because, having just finished a picture, he may be with his family in the south of France but would go to Paris to meet you. I gave you his address. I answered his letter, giving him all the possible information about the story, the dates of shooting, etc.

Last night, by chance, I met Kay Harrison[3] at a friend's house. He is very much in favour of Claude and prefers a cameraman of his class used only to black and white, to a secondary cameraman knowing Technicolor. Of course, Claude will have to take a course at Technicolor, London. Maybe Harrison would also advise that we take with us a kind of mere technician who would be able to advise Claude and us on the question of light as well as on the use of the new cameras, etc. I also told Claude about Ram Sen and suggested that he himself and Ram could take their training at Technicolor at the same time so they will get acquainted before the real shooting. If you could see Ram in Calcutta, and tell him about these latest developments, I believe you would make him very happy.

Harrison is still very enthusiastic about our Indian projects.

Concerning our friend, Cleghorn, I am going to write him a letter but I think your explanation would do a lot of good. The facts are that all the purely descriptive scenes we planned before having started our collaboration on the script seem now to be unnecessary. If we need a break with the spring sequences at the end of the picture, we have it and we can always supplement it with some shots taken right here in California. The only thing that remains is that description of the Ganges River from the Himalayan Mountains down to the delta. In any case, it will be shot, and I prefer to take all the necessary shots myself. In such a quick evocation, the angle must be very exact, and I don't believe that a cameraman can do them alone. The only part of this scene which might be difficult is the beginning, concerning the mountains themselves, with glaciers, mountain flowers, mountain lakes, etc. They are probably impossible to approach in winter and even in summer they are very expensive to get to. I see the following solutions – 1) to have Cleghorn shooting them now and if you feel this is the best solution, send me a wire and I will send him a list of shots and a copy of it to you.

There is another solution – 2) Rumer knows that every year there used to be an Indian film unit that went to Kashmir and it is likely they would have these shots in one of their films, or if they go now not to Kashmir but elsewhere in the Himalayas they could add our shots to their shooting schedule. Rumer thinks they were in Bombay.

A third solution, and probably the best one, would be to ask Claude, if he makes the picture, to shoot this stuff in Switzerland or in the French Alps where this type of scenery is about the same and where we would find roads, telefarics,[4] funiculars exist, helping us to approach the peaks. This could be done in a few days needing only a few shots, while the first solution would take weeks or a month.

We saw again the test of Mrs Naidu's sister and heard her speak in the part of Nan, and though we like her, we feel that she may be too regal for the part and would detract from the Mother. In the script we are rather sinking Nan down and bringing the Mother up. Though the latter's part is not a big one, it is important.

We do hope you got off safely. We heard from Forrest that you only just caught the plane.

We believe that you must feel uncomfortably warm. In spite of that, Jean regrets very much not being with you. If by chance you see Prince Fateh Singji,[5] tell him that Dido and Jean think of him very often and send him their best regards. In Calcutta don't forget to tell the same thing to any of our good friends – Cleghorn, Ram Sen, Hari. We are anxious to see them soon.

Good luck on your trip. Come back soon.

Yours,

Jean & Dido Renoir

1 Patricia Walters, who played Harriet in *The River*.
2 Margaret O'Brien (b.1937), actress whose credits include *Jane Eyre* (Robert Stevenson, 1944), *Meet Me in St Louis* (Vincente Minnelli, 1944), and *Little Women* (Mervyn LeRoy, 1949).
3 Kay Harrison, head of Technicolor.
4 Renoir is attempting an English spelling of *télépherique*, meaning cable car.
5 Prince Fateh Singji of Limbdi, Indian financial backer of *The River*.

To Claude Renoir Jr
Paris

2 July 1949
Beverly Hills

My dear Claude,

I have your letter and I am delighted that my project interests you. I will try to tell you in a few words all that I know.

The production company is called Commonwealth. The producer is K.J. McEldowney, c/o Hal Roach Studios, Culver City, California.

This producer found some money in India and very little outside that country. He obtained authorization from the Indian government for several technicians and actors to take their salaries out and convert them to foreign currency.

It's his first film and it's been agreed that he will be responsible for business matters and I will have complete artistic and technical freedom. He's a very pleasant and practical man, and so far, we have worked together in a very agreeable way on all questions relating to the film.

The story I will film is *The River*, a novel by Rumer Godden of which a translation appeared in *La Nef* in July, August, September and October 1947 under the title *La Fleuve*. Rumer Godden is here, and we are working on the screenplay together.

The interiors and exteriors will be filmed in Calcutta.

I hope to be there with Lourié, and if it can be arranged on your side, with you at the beginning of October. We will need a good solid month for preparation. The work threatens to be rather long and I believe that it is wise to count on the shooting not finishing before the middle or the end of February.

I saw Kay Harrison, the head of Technicolor, yesterday. He knows *Monsieur Vincent*[1] and would be very happy for you to shoot our film on the condition that you spend some weeks at Technicolor in London. Perhaps he will also ask us to bring along a technician from their end who would assist you.

We would love it if your second or third assistant were a young Hindu operator in whom we have great confidence, and we could maybe arrange for him also to train in London and, in this way, make contact with you.

The film will be an Indian production, that is to say, it will satisfy the English quota. Concerning your situation with the union, I haven't studied the problem, but I believe that the Guild of Bengal Technicians will gladly accept you taking into account that the shooting of our film in their country presents certain advantages and that the training of one of their men in Technicolor will interest them.

McEldowney is in India at the moment. I am going to write to him after today insisting that he stops over in Paris on his return in three or four weeks and sees you. If it's possible for him to make this hop over to Paris he will be in touch with you by letter.

We will have the new three-strip camera, which will be ready in September and is a lot lighter than the old one. McEldowney bought a generator and some new Mole-Richardson carbon lamps in London. The

Calcutta studios are only equipped for black and white, and only have alternating current. They are rather primitive but sufficient for this film, which includes a lot of exteriors and no large sets.

I am ending this letter quickly so it can be sent as soon as possible.

Much love. The best to Denise and your family.

Jean Renoir

---

1 *Monsieur Vincent* (Maurice Cloche, 1947) was photographed by Claude Renoir Jr.

To J.K. McEldowney [*Original in English*] *11 August 1949*
c/o Christopher Mann *Beverly Hills*
London

Dear Kenny,

[...] James Mason read the script. He is very complimentary, even declaring that it is the best screenplay he has had in his hands since he is in Hollywood. Unfortunately, he is afraid of going to India with his baby daughter and will be busy for perhaps the entire winter with the *Duchess of Langeais*, the Greta Garbo[1]-Walter Wanger picture.[2] As I told you, Bob Ryan[3] loves the script, but there is practically no chance of obtaining him from RKO, his future schedule being very heavy. Mason suggested Lew Ayres.[4] I'm going to see him in *Johnny Belinda* and I already gave a script to his agent, who is also Van Heflin's[5] agent and who fortunately is also in love with the script. This morning I saw different bits of pictures with Lawrence Tierney,[6] a very good actor. I'm afraid he is not the type. I hope to see him in his last picture made in Portugal where according to what Melvina[7] has heard, he is very good and behaved very well. Tomorrow, I'm going to see *The Rope*[8] [sic], because of John Dall[9] in it. Other suggestions – in America: Glenn Ford,[10] Robert Walker,[11] Mel Ferrer.[12] I saw the latter in *Lost Boundaries*[13] and am terribly impressed. I'm going to get in touch with him through Elizabeth Dickinson who is not his agent but who admires him greatly and also admires the script. Unfortunately, he has just signed a director-actor contract at RKO.

Here are some suggestions in England and perhaps you could see about them while you are in London: Michael Redgrave[14] (tied up with the Old Vic) – I believe he would be wonderful, I don't know the others. Sam Wanamaker,[15] American, but just finished *Christ in Concrete* in London, played opposite Ingrid Bergman in Broadway's *Joan of Lorraine*; Roger Livesey[16] (*Colonel Blimp*) – according to some information, too old.

22 Jean Renoir and Rumer Godden working on the script of *The River* at the
newly built house on Leona Drive

[. . .] Dear Kenny, that's about all. I'm sure one of us will find the ideal Captain John.

Dido and I send our love.

Jean Renoir

1 Greta Garbo (1905–90), actress whose credits included *Flesh and the Devil* (Clarence Brown, 1927), and *Queen Christina* (Rouben Mamoulian, 1933).
2 The film was never made. Garbo retired from the screen in 1941.
3 Robert Ryan (1909–73), actor whose credits included *Woman on the Beach, Act of Violence* (Fred Zinnemann, 1949), and *The Wild Bunch* (Sam Peckinpah, 1969).
4 Lew Ayres (b.1908), actor whose credits included *All Quiet on the Western Front* (Lewis Milestone, 1930), *Holiday* (George Cukor, 1938), and *Johnny Belinda* (Jean Negulesco, 1948).
5 Van Heflin (1910–71), actor whose credits included *Santa Fe Trail* (Michael Curtiz, 1940), *Johnny Eager* (Mervyn LeRoy, 1942), *The Strange Love of Martha Ivers* (Lewis Milestone, 1946), and *Shane* (George Stevens, 1953).
6 Lawrence Tierney (b.1919), actor whose credits include *Back To Bataan* (Edward Dmytryk, 1945), *The Greatest Show on Earth* (Cecil B. De Mille, 1952), and *Reservoir Dogs* (Quentin Tarantino, 1992).
7 Melvina McEldowney, wife of Kenneth, and press agent for Esther Williams.
8 *Rope* (Alfred Hitchcock, 1948).
9 John Dall (1918–71), actor whose credits included *Rope* (Alfred Hitchcock, 1948), *Gun Crazy* (Joseph H. Lewis, 1949), and *Spartacus* (Stanley Kubrick, 1960).
10 Glenn Ford (b.1916), actor whose credits include *Gilda* (Charles Vidor, 1946), *The Blackboard Jungle* (Richard Brooks, 1955), and *Superman* (Richard Donner, 1978).
11 Robert Walker (1918–51), actor whose credits included *Since You Went Away* (John Cromwell, 1944), *The Clock* (Vincente Minnelli, 1945), and *Strangers on a Train* (Alfred Hitchcock, 1951).
12 Mel Ferrer (b.1917), actor whose credits include *The Brave Bulls* (Robert Rossen, 1951), *Eléna et Les Hommes*, and *The Longest Day* (Ken Annakin, 1962).
13 *Lost Boundaries* (Alfred L. Werker, 1949).
14 Michael Redgrave (1908–85), stage and film actor whose credits included *The Lady Vanishes* (Alfred Hitchcock, 1938), *The Captive Heart* (Basil Dearden, 1948), and *The Importance of Being Earnest* (Anthony Asquith, 1952).
15 Sam Wanamaker (1919–93), actor whose credits included *Give Us This Day* (Edward Dmytryk, 1949), *Those Magnificent Men in Their Flying Machines* (Ken Annakin, 1965) and *The Spy Who Came in From the Cold* (Martin Ritt, 1965).
16 Roger Livesey (1906–76), actor whose credits included *Rembrandt* (Alexander Korda, 1936), *The Life and Death of Colonel Blimp* (Michael Powell/Emeric Pressburger, 1943), and *I Know Where I'm Going* (Michael Powell/Emeric Pressburger, 1945).

To J.K. McEldowney [*Original in English*]   *13 August 1949*
Great Eastern Hotel   *Beverly Hills*
Calcutta, India

Dear Kenny,

[. . .] Today I'm going to try to write down a kind of ideal schedule which could help all of us to understand our future problems.

[. . .] This ideal schedule is, of course, purely arbitrary, our real shooting date depending on the one big fact of the availability of the right 'Captain John'. I assume that concerning the other roles, we will get the actors to fit our schedule.

[. . .] SUGGESTED SCHEDULE:

25 AUGUST – Lourié and Vreeland join you in Calcutta – Technical preparation based on script and breakdown ensues – They go through each scene and determine precisely where and how to shoot, which material we need, how to have the best possible sound and the best possible lighting, whether a whole set or only a bit of set has to be built, or a real location used, or a combination. In other words, analyse, number by number, all the complex problems of the shooting of this picture and try to find the most adequate answers. All of this was impossible to do before having our actual script and breakdown. I'm very much in favour of this preparation now and not just prior to the shooting of the picture because if Lourié and Vreeland discover that we need some building or some piece of equipment which would take time to have done or delivered, by knowing this too late, we risk being delayed while having an expensive actor, the rest of the cast, and the crew on our payroll as well as the hotel and other overhead expenses going on.

10 SEPTEMBER – If Vreeland has no material to buy in Europe or if Lourié can take care of it himself, Vreeland returns to Hollywood. Lourié accompanies you to Europe. At this point, let me add that the purpose of the whole thing will be defeated unless you stay with them during this entire technical preparation, in order to take the responsible decisions together. In Europe, Lourié should have technical meetings with

a) Technicolor London
b) the cameraman
c) some other key technicians
d) make-up (or no make-up?), costumes, etc.

and occasionally advise you in the buying of some material such as screens, or reflectors, or muslins, rock wool for additional insulation (sound proofing), etc. I hope we find all these things in India. Here again, I believe that you should be with Lourié to take the final decisions.

If, as I wish, this film is a British quota picture, Lourié, knowing so many technicians in Europe, could also help you in completing the non-Indian crew.

Meanwhile, in Hollywood, Melvina, Judd and I will continue exhausting every possibility to find the right 'Captain John'. Its not as easy as it might seem, and it takes an awful lot of time to see films, get in touch with actors, acquire information about their availability, etc.

1 OCTOBER – You and Lourié are back in Hollywood, with the technical questions resolved. If, as I hope, we have a Captain John by then, that would give you the possibility of making a release deal, this distribution problem depending very much upon the importance of the actor who is going to play this part.

Now, let's suppose that here in Hollywood, very soon, we find the right 'Captain John', and asking your advice via cable, we start to open negotiations with some distributor – Let's also suppose that this Captain John is at our disposal when we want him – In this case, the schedule could continue in the following way.

15 OCTOBER – You and I go to London. Forrest Judd and Lourié go to Calcutta. In London, you and I complete the English cast. In Calcutta, Judd gets busy with the general organization, and the Indian cast; Lourié starts building the sets.

1 NOVEMBER – You, Rumer (I hope she will be able to do it), and I arrive in Calcutta. Probably the sets will be half-built and we will have built just enough not to have wasted any time and to add modifications if necessary. During the finishing of the sets and the completion of the organization which we could personally oversee, I, with the help of Rumer, could adjust the script to the personalities of our cast, which would be more clear to us after the first rehearsals. We could then make any alterations in the script suggested by this personal contact with our cast.

15 NOVEMBER – WE SHOOT!!

Our script is a great one and everybody who has read it is crazy about it, but even to this perfect script it is possible that Rumer's first acquaintance with the making of a picture and her reacquaintance with India will give her unexpected inspirations for certain scenes or maybe even for another picture.

15 FEBRUARY – END OF SHOOTING SCHEDULE

I suggest two weeks longer in Calcutta, allowing us to think of another picture and look at possible future locations, maybe also some retakes after seeing our rushes.

1 MARCH – We leave India and go to London for the cutting, which must be done close to Technicolor labs, dubbing, scoring, etc. You go back to Hollywood to get busy with business questions, promotion, publicity, build-up of the picture for release.

1 JUNE – I join you in Hollywood with a print of the picture.

Dear Kenny, I established this prospective schedule with Forrest. Then I asked Lourié, then Dido, then Melvina to check it. I believe, as with any human work, it is subject to improvements, but as it is it can help us.

We are all here in my house and send you our love.

Yours,

Jean Renoir

Telegram to Ingrid Bergman

[*Original in English*]

14 August 1949

Beverly Hills

RKO Radio

Rome

GREETINGS AND REASSURANCES FROM YOUR FRIENDS EVERYONE HERE KNOWS YOUR INTEGRITY ARTISTIC AND PERSONAL AND YOUR POSITION IS SECURE IGNORE NEWSPAPERS.[1]

DUDLEY DIDO JEAN RENOIR.

1 When it was revealed that Ingrid Bergman had begun an affair with Roberto Rossellini during the making of *Stromboli* (1949) and that she was pregnant by him, the ensuing scandal was broadcast world-wide.

To Ingrid Bergman [*Original in English*]

15 August 1949

Beverly Hills

RKO Radio

Rome, Italy

Dear Ingrid,

Dido, Dudley, I and many of your friends cannot help reading the papers. When we see your name in large headlines, we know that the end of any privacy is part of the contract an actor signs with the public when he decides on a profession whose aim is to provoke audience emotion. Even so, it must be quite unpleasant and that's why we decided to send you a wire.

Dido and I are now living close to your house. From our terrace, we can even see your roof through the trees. Peter comes to see us quite often, and we hope we will also see Pia. We like our new home very much. I'm sorry to have to leave it soon to shoot my picture in India. On the other hand, I'm terribly happy to have the opportunity to do a good picture. I finished the script with the collaboration of the author of the book, Miss Rumer Godden. She is a magnificent writer, certainly one of the two or three great ones living in England now. I intend to continue collaborating with her. After the shooting of our picture, we will rewrite together a screenplay I did in French one year ago. If ever you feel the desire to say, in front of a camera, some good lines, sensitively carved in a delicate English, you just make a little sign and you join us.

I hope your picture, which I believe must be about finished now, will be a great success. That would make everybody forget that they maybe talked out of turn.

Dido and I send you our fondest love,
Jean Renoir

To Rumer Godden [*Original in English*]   *22 August 1949*
MacDowell Colony   *Beverly Hills*
Peterborough, New Hampshire

Dear Rumer,

[. . .] Van Heflin has now read the script, likes it, and wants to make the picture. I am afraid his good will is very encouraging but not very practical. I doubt that MGM would give in so easily. Before asking Metro, I want to see, with you, whether we shouldn't first try to find an actor really young. By young, I mean between twenty-four and thirty. The trouble is that some of the characterizations we gave to our Captain John are very rare in young actors. The bitter irony, the sarcasm due to his bad wound which made him mature before his time are, as a rule, non-existent in youth. This mature state of mind might perhaps be generated by this ablation of somebody's leg, but it wouldn't be so easy to find a young man so overly enthusiastic about his art as to make such a sacrifice. I am auditioning a very handsome one, Gar Moore. You may have seen him in *Paisan*.[1] He was the GI in the very sentimental sequence about a Roman girl who becomes a prostitute because of the American victory. I am also going to see some other young actors. Please let me know how you feel about this question so vital to our picture.

[. . .] We miss you terribly. I don't know whether it is because he feels the same, but during the past few weeks, our dog, Tambeau, is becoming very bad with strangers. He beat [sic][2] Lourié's daughter, then Lourié himself, and more recently tried to do the same with Milene, Stravinsky's daughter.

With our best love,
Jean Renoir

1 *Paisan (Paisa)* (Roberto Rossellini, 1946).
2 'bit'.

To Clifford Odets [*Original in English*]   *22 August 1949*
Oliver Cromwell Hotel
New York, New York

Dear Cliff,

We have your book with the nice note you added on the first page. Both the book and the note tell so much about you that for a few minutes after we received them we forgot about the distance and were warmed by the feeling that the front doorbell had rung and that you and Betty were going to step in. You must be with the Chaplins now and the two girls must have wonderful days going around the town together.

Have you finished writing your Philadelphian Jewish play? I am through with the first readable draft of my Indian picture. People seem to like it, which doesn't mean one thing. I had a great time working with Rumer Godden. Probably I will stop in England on my way to India, see her again and rewrite scenes to fit the actors who, except for the young girls, we still don't know. Mel Ferrer and Van Heflin seem anxious to play the part of the man. I am wondering if I shouldn't take a good, unknown young actor. If you know of one ... He has to be very Anglo-Saxon as a contrast to the Indian surroundings, and tall to make the children shorter. I believe if the man looks <u>really</u> young, his problem of how to accept life in a world he despises would be more touching. The difficulty is that he also has to be sarcastic, with a certain bitter sense of humour and that is a quality actors acquire only with years of experience.

In about six weeks, perhaps two months, I shall start my trip, the first stop being New York; that means you, Betty [sic] and the children. I hope Dido will be with me, unless for some practical reasons she decides to join me later.

A big kiss to all of you

Jean Renoir

To Jean Renoir [*Original in English*]   *22 August 1949*
Beverly Hills

Dear Jean and Dido!

How very happy your wire made me! Thank you for the encouraging words. I don't hear much from friends. I don't expect to.

The picture[1] finally finished 2 days ago. It was lucky, because I don't think I could have hold [sic] out much longer. If I had not had all that emotional upset, it would have been a wonderful experience. So much I have seen and learned being with all these primitive people on Stromboli, then later in the women's camp outside Rome. All those lost souls that after 4 years of peace have no place to go and are wanted nowhere. And to work for Rosselini² [sic] is something entirely different. He is a man of extraordinary quality and talent. But it will be my last film for a long, long time. I thank you for wanting to give me some good lines to say. But I prefer to be silent from now on. I have also given my last interview and taken the last stills!! To quit working I decided already when Petter came to Messina. I could then already feel how my strength and nerves were thin bare. For the last years it has been nothing but difficulties. Difficulties to find a good thing to do and when you find it, there are fights with studio, writer, publicity, director, producer. Difficulties all the time. Then the picture is a failure. I don't give up now just because I have had bad publicity for some months. It goes deeper. I need to heal my body and soul and try to find some peace.

I hear your house is wonderful. How sad I cannot see it. It makes me so happy to hear Petter is often with you. Take care of him. Maybe you, Jean, whose life I am sure has been difficult, confusing and maybe tossed like a shipwreck, maybe you can explain to Petter that sometimes people leave and they don't go back.

Give also Dudley my regards and thanks.

I embrace you with all my love,

Ingrid [Bergman]

---

1 *Stromboli* (1949). Ingrid Bergman had written to Rossellini asking to be in one of his films; she found his semi-improvisatory way of working and the supporting cast of non-professionals a severe challenge.
2 Roberto Rossellini (1906–77), Italian director credited with creating 'neo-realism' with his war trilogy *Rome Open City* (1945), *Paisa* (1946), and *Germany Year Zero* (1947). His films with Ingrid Bergman, especially *Voyage in Italy* (1953), were a great influence on the French New Wave. In the 1960s, he turned to making television films on important historical figures.

To Ingrid Bergman [*Original in English*]   29 *August 1949*
RKO Radio   *Beverly Hills*
Rome, Italy

Dear Ingrid,

Dido and I read your letter together and feel very sad, not because you seem decided to abandon your film career, but because of the feeling of exhaustion which is even stronger than your words. We hope it is only temporary and now that your big work is over, you will be able to take some rest. After the over-excitement of a picture certainly very different from anything you have done up to now and which we hope will be very successful, you probably find yourself a little lost, and that is very normal.

About renouncing your film career, before doing it, you must be sure that you are not influenced, subconsciously, by the bad results of *Arch of Triumph*[1] and *Joan of Arc*.[2] The lives of great artists are always made of many errors. Maybe the ordeal of *Joan of Arc* was even sent to you by the Gods. They certainly love you and wanted to teach you that in Art, 'only the form counts'. They know that the cult of great ideas is dangerous and may destroy the real basis for great achievements, that is the daily, humble work within the framework of a profession.

Dear Ingrid, we had many amusing arguments together and I was the first one to defend, stupidly, the importance of 'great subjects'. I wasted a large part of my life by becoming uselessly busy with 'the significance' of my pictures. In Hollywood, we also use the word 'message'. Today, I regret not having busied myself with the endless, ant-like work of small, cheap pictures of a definite style, like 'westerns' or 'murder' stories.

In a structure that is always the same, you are free to improve what alone is worthwhile, the detail in human expression. My son, Alain, has a teacher who told him something that proved a revelation to me – it is that the Classic Greek theatre was very much helped by the fact that the authors were dealing with the same stories, the same characters, and having to tell them to a public who already knew the action from A to Z, and was intimately acquainted with the characters. When the Athenians sat down in the theatre to listen to *Oedipus* and what was going to happen to him, they knew very well beforehand who he was and what would ensue. Hence, Sophocles[3] didn't have to get busy with the useless explanations which are just about the only content of any drama today. He was free to deal with the details of human expression.   Excuse this useless talk, but we miss you and are just trying to make up for the distance.

With all our love,
Jean Renoir

1 *Arch of Triumph* (Lewis Milestone, 1948).
2 *Joan of Arc* (Victor Fleming, 1948).
3 Sophocles (497–406 BC), Greek tragic dramatist.

To Rumer Godden [*Original in English*]   *25 October 1949*
Aylesbury, Bucks   *Beverly Hills*

Dear Rumer,

Well, it's done! We have a Cousin John and a Captain John. As you know, the first is Breen[1] and the second is a very wonderful Irish actor, Arthur Shields.[2] He was at the Abbey Theatre for years. Everybody here admires him but strangely enough this admiration has rarely manifested itself in concrete parts.

I believe that we will decide, together, everything concerning the script and the rest of the cast, when I come to London, which means the first week of November. We leave Monday, but Kenny has to stop for two days in New York, and I would like to see Alain at Harvard.

If I bother you now with my suggestions, it is because I'm anxious to begin the fascinating and indispensable arguments. Out of them, the cygnet will become a swan [. . .] Any trustworthy person who has read the book or the script has understood it as a poem, maybe not directly about Harriet but in any case about the world Harriet is going to digest and transform into written words. In this world seen by Harriet belong human beings, landscapes, animals, trees, among them and probably in order of importance, the river, Captain John, Bogey, Bea, Mother and then the others. This doesn't mean that Bea's problem is not very important. Everything is important in this film and even an Indian gardener passing by must be a star for a few seconds.

[. . .] I had to make the final decisions about Tommy Breen and Arthur Shields, and I decided on the former in spite of my fear of taking any road you may be reluctant to step on. I did it because I still believe that it is possible to keep the barrier between a very young Bea and a Captain John who still has his whole life before him.

Excuse this rambling on and don't take it too seriously. I'm anxious to see your Valerie, which will change the script. We are just at that point when changes can be excellent and add those subtle changes that make a picture really successful. We have digested our first draft now and are free to judge in a minute what is necessary and what is superfluous, what is powerful and what is weak, what is funny and what is dull [. . .].

Dido and I are so sorry to know you were not well. We hope we will find you and Jane and Paula[3] in good shape when we arrive. We are ready for our French conversations with Jane.

All of us send you our love,

Jean Renoir

[243]

1 Thomas Breen, son of censor Joseph Breen, and who, like his character in *The River*, had lost a leg in the war.
2 Arthur Shields (1896–1970), actor whose credits included *She Wore a Yellow Ribbon* (John Ford, 1949), *The River*, and *The Quiet Man* (John Ford, 1952).
3 Rumer Godden's daughters.

At the end of the year, Jean and Dido Renoir travel to London; and then, for a few days, Jean makes his first visit to Paris in November, re-establishing his residence there at 7 avenue Frochot. They then travel on to India, where filming on The River *begins at the end of December.*

23 Jean Renoir with his actresses in *The River*: from left to right, Patricia Walters (Harriet), Adrienne Corri (Valerie), and Radha Sri Ram (Melanie)

1950

Telegram to Jean Renoir [*Original in English*]   *21 January 1950*
Great Eastern Hotel   *London*
Calcutta

RUSHES ALL RIGHT[1] COBRA SCENE CONVINCING BOY ESPECIALLY
EXCELLENT HARRIET MUCH IMPROVING HER LIP MAKEUP IN TESTS
DANGEROUS NOW ALL RIGHT WHY IS SHE SO MUCH FROWNING RAM
AND NAN CONGENIAL RHADA [SIC] IN SPITE OF MARVELLOUS EYES
DISAPPOINTING IN NOSTRILS MOUTH AND CHIN RIVER SHOTS SEN-
SATIONAL CAPTAIN JOHN BETWEEN THE BEAUTIFULLY COLOURED
INDIAN BODIES QUITE JUSTLY LIKE A SPECTRE VEGETATION
COLOURS IN GARDEN SHOTS SOMETIMES DISTRACTING FROM
ACTORS ON THE WHOLE DOCUMENTARY CHARACTER OF SHOOTING
MOST PROMISING REGARDS
   [CARL] KOCH

1 Because Technicolor was new to India, the film stock had to be processed in Britain, and
the rushes viewed by Carl Koch before being shipped over to India.

To Dudley Nichols [*Original in English*]   *24 March 1950*
                                                  Great Eastern Hotel
                                                  Calcutta, India

Dear Dudley,

   When we receive one of your letters we don't open it right away. We
first go to our room, wash our hands, very dirty after a long day on
location, order a cool drink, and then we read it. We don't want the
exterior noises and interruptions to spoil the magic trip you offer us so
generously. Then we talk about you and Esta and our life back home. We
imagine our first reunion, probably with the Slades. Time is passing, and
slowly I am adding one foot after one foot to this film. We are in a period
of optimism partly due to the work of my nephew Claude who is making
a little revolution in the Technicolor world, very much helped by the
encouraging comprehensiveness of the London lab people.

Some time ago I wrote you that I had an idea that could maybe interest you. Perhaps I already told you about it in Hollywood because it is not new in my mind or in itself. But my discovery of 'colour' on the screen convinces me more and more that there is a possibility for a good picture with this idea which consists in redoing what the Middle Age and Renaissance painters, sculptors, illustrators, toy-makers did with the story of Christ; treat it according to the most accepted traditions but with modern clothes. The Medici contemporaries accepted very well to see the Roman centurions dressed as Florentine Knights, Mary Magdalene as a fifteenth-century kept woman. They were keeping a longer dress for Christ himself, anxious to make him eternal even in his clothes. But the apostles were often copied from the real fishermen the painter took as models, and in the religious *mystères* the actors were often just dressed with their Sunday clothes.

We film people shouldn't forget that we are the possible modern illustrators of great stories, and I don't see why we shouldn't do what our ancestors did. My project consists in shooting a Life of Christ in our days in a modern surrounding, with the apostles dressed as modern fishermen and St Joseph dressed as a modern carpenter. The soldiers surrounding Golgotha would be modern policemen.

I see several possibilities for the spot where the action could take place. The more impressing [sic] would be an American industrial town. This solution would make clear to the public the fact that the story is not a fairy tale but a profoundly timely story as good for our present time as for the past or for the future. It would make the most powerful picture ever done.

The opposite solution would be to locate it in a country where people still keep a biblical simplicity – India would be great. We could find here people as noble in their attitudes as the Jewish subjects of Herod. A solution in between would be to go to a colony like Cuba where the Americans would play the part of the Romans. I am sure you would find many other solutions.

It is useless to tell you too much about this project. You can see in one second what it means. Either you will like it or not. I need to know your reaction. And I believe that my interest for this idea is greatly increased because it seems to be a possibility of putting us together again. That would be wonderful.

My love to Esta and you,
Jean Renoir

To Jean Renoir [*Original in English*]　　　　　*11 April 1950*
Great Eastern Hotel　　　　　　　　　　　　*Rome*
Calcutta

My dear friends,

Many thanks for your letter. It was so nice to hear from you. Yes, from all the things that you can read in the newspapers lately this much is true; I have a son. Probably you don't read so much in India and you are lucky. My little son is very strong and fine, and I am very happy about him. I forgive him gladly the terrible 'scandal' he brought with him. It would surely be nice if the American people would not be such hypocrites. It has gone so far that now they talk about me in the American Senate, calling me 'an apostle of degradation' and trying to ban me from the country. Roberto has been called 'Swine' by this Senator[1] and cocaine smuggler, Nazi collaborator and black marketeer. He has been refused a visa, which we have never <u>asked</u> for yet. Strange things happens [sic]. If he had not been in the senate we could have sued him for libel, but now there is nothing to do, but laugh. It is a little hard sometimes to laugh, though.

And you should see the open letters in the press! Everybody has something to say about this extraordinary thing; a baby out of wedlock!! The letters I receive run all kinds of advice from: 'Come back to your husband – Go on the radio and ask the American people for forgiveness – Marry the man you love, forget the world – Don't marry that Italian who doesn't love you – Don't marry, but live together in free love like free people – Write your Swedish king to help you go back to Sweden – Leave both men and become a nun – Take enough sleeping pills to kill yourself.' Most letters are full of Christian religion and forgiveness for my sin. The trouble is that I don't feel so sinful. I am unhappy so it almost breaks my heart for what Pia must go through, and also Petter, though he could have helped and finished this thing. I spoke to Pia yesterday and she sounded very cheerful on the phone. I don't know if she puts it on or not. After all she is [the] daughter of an actress!

How is it going for you? I guess it is not too easy to make a film in India. I hope so much that you are happy. When are you coming this way? I long to see you again. Ruth and I have great hopes to meet soon. When Roberto has finished St Francis[2] in about three weeks we plan to go to Paris and Ruth will probably be there at that time. I just have to have a cup of coffee with her!

Hoping soon to see you and speak FRENCH to you!!
Love,
Ingrid [Bergman]

1 Sen. Edwin Johnson.
2 *Francesco giullare di Dio (Flowers of St Francis)* (1950).

To Prince Fateh Singji of Limbdi   *23 April 1950*
[*Original in English*]   *Calcutta, India*
Bombay, India

Dear Prince Fateh,

Amina, after having been called by Your Highness from Bombay, asked me to write you a letter expressing my feelings about the inner situation of our picture. I couldn't find any time to do it before today. Please excuse the delay.

First I would like to relate the very small incident which, all of a sudden, made me understand (I hope I do understand) so many important things. One day Amina inquired from my wife Dido why she and myself had asked the McEldowneys to obtain from Your Highness a decision against her. The truth is that before going to Bombay Kenny explained to us that his wife had to accompany him to perform the very unpleasant duty of dismissing Amina. Dido and I thought that Mrs McEldowney just wanted to take a trip at the expense of the picture, and I jokingly suggested that if they wished to fire one of our two wardrobe girls for reasons of economy, they should keep Amina who was the prettiest.

But this inquiry from Amina to Dido made clear an incomprehensible state of affairs. Up to now in any country where I directed or produced pictures I got along very well with the actors and the crew, not because of my personal qualities or behaviour, but just because of the fact that I know my job and actors and technicians respect professional people. In this picture, for the first time in my life, I was feeling a strange and vague hostility which bothered me very much and made my work extremely difficult. Amina's revelation gave me the idea to talk openly with some members of the crew. I am quite sure now that Kenny's policy was to gossip with me against the crew then to gossip with the crew against me trying to represent me as the villain and himself as the hero.

How to explain this strange attitude of a producer whose interest is to provoke good spirit and good will in order to obtain good work? Probably vanity. It is also the only explanation I see for a strange publicity which seems mainly aimed at the glorification of his name – for his sojourns in expensive hotels in London while putting me in a hotel in Windsor where the thick fog of winter made transportation to and from London to interview actors exhaustive and expensive using up a great deal of my time better utilized for the preparation of the picture – for his refusal to deal with honourable, well-established people preferring dubious specimens who knew how to flatter him.

Up to now I thought: 'His Highness likes this man and wants to make him a producer. It will cost a great deal of money because Kenny who was in the flower business ignores[1] everything about picture making, but that is His Highness's business.' The end of the shooting approaching, my mind is more free and I realize that it is also my business. I am mostly paid with interests in the benefits of the picture, the largest part of my salary being deferred. I also understand that this deferment of the salaries of some of us constitutes the American capital of the company.

I am not complaining, and even consider that we were very lucky. I mentioned my nephew's name for a cameraman, and by playing with Kenny's vanity made him believe he had discovered Claude whom he ignored[2] before. I also brought Lourié who picked up in London first class technicians, and by disregarding Kenny's decisions practically went on successfully up to now through the production's problems. And all together, actors, crew members and myself, we arrive at the end of the shooting in spite of the amazing ignorance of an amateur producer. This ignorance will cost the picture maybe 30 per cent of the expenses (the 30 per cent is not the result of calculation but only a guess) but I pretend[3] that finally everything is for the best. Kenny bothered me with petty questions of administration and general policy, but he left me entirely alone for the real making of the picture. With a regular, severe, highly-organized producer, you would perhaps have saved 30 per cent, but we would have a great chance of ending with a good, dull, picture which would lose money at the box-office. If our picture is successful and brings us good benefits we will forget Kenny's foolishness and the useless expenses. I am very enthusiastic and hope that we will succeed if the last operations of the picture are properly managed.

May I add that Kenny promoted the whole affair. If I had tried to convince you that a film is an interesting enterprise probably you wouldn't have believed me. I am not a good salesman. As a matter of fact Kenny probably started a new type of business which can be very profitable: the making in India of pictures for the American market.

Perhaps it is better to forget all the errors more or less explainable in a first attempt. I am even convinced that Kenny can help you very much in the future. I don't believe he will ever learn how to produce a film but he is a good promoter and a good public relations man. He has the patience and the right attitude to run along the halls of public buildings, he loves to talk with official people, political men; he knows how to travel and does it himself easily. If you don't use him for the direct making of pictures he can be very useful. Mrs McEldowney is an excellent woman. She has a good education and knows her job. She is probably just blinded by her love for her husband, and that is very natural.

I arrive now at the most important part of this letter. The two last operations are the cutting and the distribution of the picture. A bad cutting can ruin a good film and many bad pictures were rescued by a good cutting. To do a good cutting you need calm. It is a kind of meditation. I am a little afraid of a noisy Kenny bringing amazing visitors to the cutting room, showing projections which should be kept secret up to the moment when you are sure of the tempo of a scene, etc. In other words forcing me, in order to resist his crazy suggestions, into a fighting spirit which is not the right one for this editing period. May I add that I would like to see the money we have to spend during this period applied to the improvement of the picture and not to useless expenses in London hotels and cocktail parties with newspapermen.

The distribution of the picture is even more dangerous. If the best picture remains in a drawer and is not shown to the public it is a meagre consolation to accuse the exhibitors. Those exhibitors have to be convinced to buy a picture by men who belong to certain organizations called the distribution companies. Some of them are good and small and reach many theatres because of the ability of their salesmen. Some other ones are big and good because of the fact that indirectly they own the most important theatres in the world. Some are good for the business in general but bad for the independent producer because they take too much percentage. And some of them are absolutely crooked. I don't know very much about all this but Kenny knows even less than I do. And if we take the wrong decision about distribution it is the end of our hope of seeing one penny of benefit. I believe that Kenny is too impulsive to supervise such an operation. May I add that in spite of being built up by several months of expensive publicity he is still a little man. We would be better represented by somebody who could [be] treat[ed] as an equal with the distribution companies. I have several suggestions, one would be to take a good representative [such] as this Mr George J. Schaefer who wrote me a letter. I know several other good men in the same branch. Another one would be to find an association between your Indian company and a serious American group. I wouldn't advise a regular studio who would absorb you but a banking organization like Peter Rathvon, former president of RKO, or David Loew, the son of Marcus Loew of the Loew Circuit. I am at your disposal to talk about those questions.

Maybe all of this is useless and you have no way of taking the picture out of Kenny's hands during this delicate period. In this case let us pray [to] God.

If Your Highness wants to show this letter to Kenny I don't see any inconvenience to it. He will probably be very much surprised that somebody doubts his universal ability, maybe that could do him a lot of good.

I am very happy to see Your Highness in a few days as Amina told me.

I am sincerely yours,

Jean Renoir

1 Meaning 'is ignorant of'.
2 Meaning 'didn't know about'.
3 Meaning 'believe'.

To Robert Coryell [*Original in English*]
[Berg-Allenberg Agency]

7 May 1950
Great Eastern Hotel
Calcutta, India

Dear Bob,

I never write because I am too busy, but this Sunday I really see the end. The shooting will be finished within the coming week. The recording of sound will keep me busy during the following week, and we intend to leave Calcutta 21 May. We will spend some days in Madras, Bombay, Constantinople, Athens, Paris, and be in London in the beginning of June. If you have anything to tell us please write c/o Christopher Mann.

Since I left France ten years ago I never worked so hard. Fortunately I had Claude, my nephew, who is a magnificent cameraman, and Lourié for the art direction. I also have a very co-operative English sound-man, Charles Knott, who has been with me for one month, and the English crew was fine. The Indians were very good but I had no production organization at all. The ignorance of McEldowney and Judd is unbelievable. If we add that they were deeply despised by the Westerners as well as by the Indians because of their not too scrupulous way of handling money you can imagine in which disorder I had to shoot the picture. I will tell you more when I see you, but it is beyond all imagination.

Well, the most important step is done, now the cutting time will probably see another sort of fight but I am determined to defend a picture which I believe is the first good one I did since I left France.

Remind me to Phil and Bert. I am anxious to see you all again.

With my best regards,

Jean Renoir

Telegram to Carl Koch and   *May 1950*
Rumer Godden [*Original in English*]   *Great Eastern Hotel*
Chalfont St Giles, Bucks   *Calcutta, India*

I WILL NOT RECEIVE LAST RUSHES AND WILL LOSE CAMERA AND CREW MAY FIFTEEN PLEASE ADVISE QUICKLY IF RETAKES NECESSARY YOUR OPINION BEING FROM NOW ON MY ONLY GUIDE

LOVE JEAN

Telegram to Jean Renoir [*Original in English*]   *May 1950*
Calcutta   *Calcutta*

RUSHES ALLRIGHT [SIC] HEAR [SIC] DONT GO BACK WHAT ABOUT BENGALI STORY CAN YOU DO IT WITHOUT SEEING RUSHES REGARDS

KOCH

Telegram to Carl Koch [*Original in English*]   *May 1950*
London   *Calcutta*

GREAT HANDICAP FOR ME NOT TO SEE RUSHES BUT IMPOSSIBLE DO OTHERWISE PLEASE ADVISE IF ANYTHING WRONG URGENTLY I LOSE CAMERA AND CREW MAY SEVENTEEN

RENOIR

24 Jean Renoir filming *The River* with his nephew, Claude Renoir Jr

Telegram to Carl Koch [*Original in English*]   *19 May 1950*
Chalfont St Giles   *Great Eastern Hotel*
Bucks, England   *Calcutta, India*

KRISHNA MAKEUP SO DIFFICULT NECESSITY SAVING TIME COM-
PELLED ME HAVE DIFFERENT ACTOR[1] HOPE IT WONT HARM PICTURE
LOVE YOU AND RUMER
    RENOIR

1 Koch had queried if a different actor had been used in the dance sequence during the
transformation from man to God.

To Claude Renoir Jr   *17 June 1950*
Paris   *Beverly Hills*

Dear Claude,

I couldn't wait for you, being eager to catch up with the film in
Hollywood. It seems also that Kenny has become wiser. The sound was
delivered to Western Electric right away. Now we are in the process of
developing and printing the film. I will have the positives Monday and
will begin editing. In London, Bill anticipated this operation would take
five months, here it seems I can do it in two. Kenny hasn't yet decided
where we will do the music, but he still swears to me that the titles and
possible additional shots will be done in London and, if you are free,
under your supervision. I imagine that this could be at the beginning of
September.

    [. . .]

All that you told me about Kenny is fine. It can only help to keep on the
right track. Prince Fateh would like us, and I believe he's right, not to
make any waves before the film is in the hands of a distributor. From my
side, when I see the depression into which Hollywood has plunged, I feel
very indulgent towards Kenny, who unconsciously allowed us to make a
film that we couldn't have done in the confines of a regular production.

It's television which is killing the cinema here, and what is strange is
that the murderer isn't rich enough to buy himself well-made films. All
the studios are full of producers who in two days make lamentable films
intended for this new master. The public loves television, which allows
them to stay at home in their bath robe, have some drinks, and not to
watch when something bores them; which keeps the kids occupied and
makes you popular with your neighbours; and which finally ends up

costing much less than going to the cinema with the whole family. [...]

I agree with you about *La Peste*.[1] It's because of that I'm taking on *L'Etranger*.

I'm passing on your best wishes to the Slades.

Dido and I send our love,

Jean Renoir

1 *The Plague* (1947), novel by Albert Camus (1913–60), author of *L'Etranger (The Outsider/The Stranger)* (1942).

To Jean Dewalde
Paris

2 July 1950
Beverly Hills

Dear Jean,

My letter about the possibility of filming *L'Etranger* in the fall must have expressed my thoughts badly. I would simply like to say that to my mind this project wasn't limited to the spring. Since Gérard Philippe[1] [sic] has worked it out so he would be free in the spring, tell him that it's agreed and that until further notice I will keep this period free for *L'Etranger*. This project is closer to my heart than anything else. I believe I can make a film with Gérard Philippe which will satisfy all of us.

Claude is right. I too would like to stay in my house and try to work there as a writer, but I am first of all a film-maker and what interests me most at the moment is to make *L'Etranger* with Gérard Phillipe. There, my dear Jean, you have what I really feel. Therefore, reassure our friend and tell him that since our discussion at the Hotel Lutetia, I haven't changed my mind.

As far as Claude is concerned, I am delighted about this collaboration and it would be wonderful if we could have him for *L'Etranger*.

[...]

On the question of salaries: I believe that it is better to film *L'Etranger* in one version only. An English version would not be better distributed in America than a French version. In both cases, exhibition would most likely be limited to the 'art houses'. This kind of exhibition can also yield a lot. I also think that Gerard Philippe 'would lose' something in a language new to him.

You must then handle my affairs as for an exclusively French film, with the slight difference that, as I am in a position to be useful to

American exhibition, perhaps the producers will understand that it is normal for me to be involved in said exhibition either with a percentage on the American returns, or a small sum in dollars, or a combination of the two. It would also be necessary to consider my travel and other expenses, as well as those of Dido who helps me a lot with the preparation of my films. Besides, these sorts of costs can be settled in France and in francs. I will write more to you one of these days. The American exhibition question is very delicate. Today I mainly wanted to tell you swiftly to reassure Gérard Philippe to whom I also writing today.

Our best to you and Mrs Devalde [sic].

Jean Renoir

1 Gérard Philipe (1922–59), actor whose credits included *Le Diable au Corps* (Claude Autant-Lara, 1947), *Une Si Jolie Petite Plage* (Yves Allegret, 1949), and *La Ronde* (Max Ophuls, 1950).

To Clifford Odets [*Original in English*]   *30 July 1950*
                                                                                Beverly Hills

Dear Cliff,

We will miss a little your lost in the sky apartment when we go to New York. But what is an apartment, what is a view – nothing. The important items are the people connected with the apartment and the view. What we want is to see you, and around you to see Bette and the children. It can be on a cloud or in a basement; circumstances are just secondary.

You will start your rehearsal very soon, that is great news. Your natural living quarters are on a stage or on a screen. I am dying to see the result of your work.

Complete silence from France about Camus' *L'Etranger*, but I have no time to worry about that being more busy with the cutting of *The River* than I ever was with any picture.

Please tell Bette all our love and take for yourself a big part of it.

Sincerely,

Jean Renoir

To Gérard Philipe

Dear Gérard Philippe [sic],

I am delighted about your good news. I received your letter today and I'm answering you quickly so that you can relay to Mr Gordine some of my thoughts on *L'Etranger*.

L'Etranger will never be a comedy and it is obvious that only the death of the hero of this adventure can give us an ending conforming to the spirit of the book. Furthermore, as in the book, the film (if we succeed at it) will be full of a sort of bitter irony. Absurdly comic details abound in Camus, and we must build them up in the film. Perhaps we have the opportunity in this project of creating a drama with a style and dialogue that sometimes borders on the burlesque. For me, that, when it is successful, is the ultimate in cinema as in theatre.

After our hero meets the priest, it will be necessary to try to find something that at present I can glimpse only vaguely; a kind of cinematic and poetic translation of his new and unexpected contact with the exterior world. This should be the outcome of the film, its reason for existing. Of course, the intoxication of this strange encounter with a world where our hero, up to that point, feels a stranger, would lift up the spirits of the audience. This would be a sort of 'happy ending'. Even so, it is still necessary to accept the idea that this happy ending is only provisional, and that no one can ignore the fact that our man will die after this great joy. As in the book, it isn't necessary to show the execution, but it is too inevitable for people not to know how things stand.

There you have, my dear friend, some random thoughts which came to mind while reading your letter and which I share with you before taking the time to sort them out. If by a 'dark film' Mr Gordine means one of those stories which are too slow, where the heroes speak with a feeble voice and where the dialogue never raises a smile, let him be reassured. I dream of making *L'Etranger* in completely the opposite way. On the other hand, there is a note of poignant despair in the book which we can't ignore, and if we didn't find it in the film as well, we would very much risk deceiving the audience.

Hope to hear from you soon, dear Gérard Philippe.

Kindest regards,

Jean Renoir

To Pierre Braunberger
Paris

21 October 1950
Beverly Hills

My dear Pierre,

I received word from Dewalde, who let me know that *L'Etranger*[1] will not be made because of the cost of the rights. He asked me to find another subject for Gérard Philippe [sic] and I'm going to work on it. During my time in Paris, I saw Philippe and we agreed on doing something together. You seem reticent about him; that's because you've seen too many of his films, some of which, such as *L'Idiot*,[2] were rather badly done. I'm attracted by the Philippe of *Le Diable au Corps*[3] and I believe that if I find the right subject, I can make a beautiful film with him. My best to Desfontaines. I am pretty near the end of editing *The River*.

Very truly yours,
Jean Renoir

1 *L'Etranger* was eventually filmed by Luchino Visconti in 1967, with Marcello Mastroianni.
2 *L'Idiot* (Georges Kampin, 1946), based on the Dostoevsky novel *The Idiot*.
3 *Le Diable au Corps* (*The Devil in the Flesh*) (Claude Autant-Lara, 1947), based on the novel by Raymond Radiguet.

To Clifford Odets [*Original in English*]

9 December 1950
Beverly Hills

Dear Clifford,

Our phone number is Crestview 13897 and we wish to hear and see you very soon. We are anxious to read the script (in the spirit of Verdi),[1] we have a great weakness for Verdi.

Of course I would love to direct *Clash by Night*.[2] It could be a wonderful movie and I am terribly attracted by your woman in it.

We enjoyed the good news of your show for many reasons, a very important one being that it gives us definite chances to see it one day.

I am through with the cutting of my picture but for minor details concerning the sound. We may send the cutting print to Technicolor London around the end of this month and receive the first colour print beginning of February.

We saw Chaplin last night, brilliant. We heard a little bit of the music for his film[3] recorded on tape and he sang, but not enough for our taste. I believe his picture will be good and also successful.

We will give your telephone number to our little Indian friend Radha

Sri Ram. We love her, and if you meet her you will do the same. She will arrive in New York beginning of January but I don't know whether she will stay one or two days or come directly to California. This is her first trip out of India.

I am suddenly wondering if you know about Slade's[4] death. It happened last September and was a great shock for Gabrielle and Jeannot. Now they recovered and life goes on.

We miss Bette very much. Her picture by Man Ray is on our wall but that is only a substitute.

We love you both.

Jean Renoir

PS. I have ideas for movies, just too many, I must first put some order in them before writing you about it. It would be magnificent if we could make a film together.

1 Guiseppe Verdi (1813–1901), Italian opera composer.
2 *Clash by Night* was eventually directed by Fritz Lang in 1952.
3 Presumably *Limelight* (1952).
4 Conrad Slade.

To Georges Simenon   *16 December 1950*

Dear Georges,

You are certainly blessed by the Gods. Not only do you have an adorable wife, exceptional children, but even more, Jupiter has given you the energy to fight for the success to match the gifts he has given you. You were born to write and you write. If the distribution of functions could always be as successful as it's been for you; if each person on the Earth could know what is his true place, occupy it and maintain it, all problems would be solved; there would no longer be war in Korea, no more Russian menace, no more revolutions and maybe even – and this would be the most beautiful thing – each person finding themselves satisfied, there would perhaps be no more progress. I'm eager to read the four novels so elegantly created and to see what the old New England windmill brings your way.

We would like to see your abode, Denise,[1] the elder boy, the little one, and you. Perhaps certain business problems with my Indian film will bring me nearer to you. That's my wish. I have only just finished editing. This operation has taken a ridiculously long time. My excuse is that, being unable to correct my faults with the usual *retakes*,[2] I had to make do with the tricks of editing. Another reason for this long delay is that, instead of entrusting the film music to a skilful Hollywood manufacturer, I used classical Indian music and also Mozart, Schubert, Schumann, Weber. And the marriage between these masters' works and my scenes and characters was not achieved without long and meticulous preparations. Now I am going to proceed with the final sound mix, and at the beginning of January, I hope to send my work to London so Technicolor can cut the negative and proceed to make a colour print.

I am rather happy with my film. What is too bad is that dealings with India can't be treated in a playful tone. Either you reject the Orient because it irritates you, or you accept it with open arms. Then that becomes such a huge matter that, if one has other preoccupations, it's better not to start with it.

Dido and I are happy to know that you have recovered from the flu. We wish you good health and much happiness, and we all send our love to you.

Jean Renoir

1 Denyse Ouimet married Simenon on 22 June 1950 in Reno, Nevada, one day after his divorce. He then changed her name to Denise. Their son Johnny was Jean Renoir's godson.
2 Originally in English.

1951

To Clifford Odets [*Original in English*]   *21 January 1951*
                                             Beverly Hills

Dear Cliff,

Dido and I read *The Country Girl*.[1] I don't understand the little doubt expressed in the note you sent with the play. To me it is an extraordinary play and Dido shares my opinion. I know several works treating the subject of the artist and more precisely of the actor. I don't remember any giving me such a wide description. You succeeded with a mean[2] common to all great artists: the study of very precise local conditions. By digging a narrow delimited hole you go very deep, and as always when the hole-digger is a great artist you finally join the universe. People whose work is only based on general ideas often remain superficial. It is a strange contradiction that only creators who cultivate a very little bit of ground finally plow the entire world. Your actor and his wife are typically New York stage and still I knew them in Paris, in Berlin and in Rome. Their reactions are common to every married couple not only of actors but of artists in general in any occidental country.

One night has gone since I read *The Country Girl*. This morning she is haunting me and will do so for a long time. Men are fascinated by truth as snakes by the sound of a flute. Thank you, dear Cliff, for having given us one more masterpiece.

I must add another unimportant thought: in our days good Anglo-Saxon authors try to break with the nineteenth century melodramatic tradition by a come-back to the Shakespearean tradition. With your play you didn't attempt any revival of an old style. But if I had to find a comparison for some lecture I would probably chose Molière. His characters: Tartuffe, the Would-Be Gentleman, the Cheated Husband, were as Parisian as your actor and his wife are New Yorkers, and they were also universal. Bette must be very happy. We think of her very much. As a matter of fact, in our imagination New York is now entirely identified with Bette, the children, and you.

We asked our little Indian friend Radha Sri Ram to pay you a visit. This idea is merely based on the belief that people you like are the best messengers between people who love each other. She will be in New

York the first of February for a few days and will live with her father with Theosophists somewhere around town.

With love,

Jean

1 *The Country Girl* was written for the stage in 1950. It was filmed in 1954 by George Seaton.

2 Meaning 'method'.

To Rumer Godden [*Original in English*]

29 January 1951
Beverly Hills

Dear Rumer,

[...] The work print of *The River* is gone to London. I hope to convince Kenny that he should send the editor George Gale to watch the cutting of the negative. Of course, as soon as he arrives, George will get in touch with you and, when you have time, make you acquainted again with our picture. A little later, probably in three or four weeks, Claude will also go to London to supervise the colour.

I don't know what I will do now. The movie business is not an easy one for an independent. I abandoned *Amphitryon*. The horrors of the war in Korea don't help me to find jokes based on the great conflict between West and East.

When you are settled and feel like sending us news you will make us happy. We are expecting Radha very soon and are delighted to see her.

Many things [sic] to James,[1] Jane and Paula. Our love to you and your whole family.

Jean Renoir

1 James Haynes-Dixon, husband of Rumer Godden.

Telegram to Jean Renoir

28 March 1951
Paris

Beverly Hills

WOULD YOU BE INTERESTED DIRECTING CARROSSE SAINT SACRE-MENT[1] IN ITALY SEPTEMBER GREETINGS
DORFMANN[2]

1 *Le Carrosse du Saint-Sacrement*, play by Prosper Mérimée, author of *Carmen*. In the adaptation, the title was changed to *Le Carrosse d'Or* (*The Golden Coach*).

2 Robert Dorfmann (b.1912), producer whose credits include *Mayerling* (Anatole Litvak, 1968), *L'Armée des Ombres* (Jean-Pierre Melville, 1969), *Trafic* (Jacques Tati, 1971), and *Papillon* (Franklin J. Schaffner, 1973).

Telegram to R. Dorfmann

Paris

30 March 1951
Beverly Hills

IN WHICH LANGUAGE DO YOU PROPOSE MAKING CARROSSE STOP
HAVE YOU AN ACTRESS IN MIND STOP GOING TO REREAD BOOK
BEFORE MAKING DECISION GREETINGS
  RENOIR

Telegram to Jean Renoir

Beverly Hills

2 April 1951
Paris

FRENCH AND ENGLISH ANNA MAGNANI[1] ENGAGED GREETINGS
  DORFMANN

1 Anna Magnani (1908–73), actress whose credits included: *Rome Open City* (Roberto Rossellini, 1945), *L'Amore* (Roberto Rossellini, 1948), and *Mamma Roma* (Pier Paolo Pasolini, 1962).

Telegram to Dorfmann

Paris

3 April 1951

AM VERY INTERESTED BY MAGNANI AND CARROSSE SEE JEAN DEW-
ALDE MY AGENT LETTER FOLLOWS GREETINGS
  JEAN RENOIR

To Jean Dewalde

Paris

3 April 1951
Beverly Hills

Dear Jean,
    As you know, my most recent proposal to raise the possibility of collaborating with Gérard Philippe [sic] and Braunberger was Zola's *La Faute De L'Abbé Mouret*.[1] I had a reply from Braunberger, who seemed to love the subject and asked Desfontaines to reread the novel. That was some time ago, and since then there has been complete silence. If Dorfmann's proposal seems serious to you, perhaps Braunberger, Desfontaines

and Gérard Philippe ought to be asked to make a decision – unless we decide on Dorfmann straight away. In any case, I believe it would be good for you to make contact with the latter and let me know his reaction to some of the ideas expressed in this letter and in a letter that I'm sending him at the same time.

Dorfmann's proposal interests me for several reasons: I would love to make a film with Magnani, who I admire very much; I believe I can make a good film with Le Carrosse, for reasons which I'll explain to you later; the film being in two versions, English and French, it is possible that you could secure the profits for me in dollars, and this last consideration is no small matter.

There are two conditions under which I could make Carrosse a good film: first, I must have considerable freedom in adapting a fascinating but difficult subject. Please explain to Mr Dorfmann that I always write my screenplays, sometimes in collaboration with an author of my choice, but this operation, as much as the shooting and editing, has always been my responsibility. In order to make a good film, I must be the author of it.

The second condition is a certain luxury in production. If we want to make Carrosse a studio version of a sweet play that at an hour and a half is a little thin, we must play up the problems of occupation in a country of American Indians. This means showing the roads, the churches, the bull-fights, and military parades. I'm even convinced that the only Way [sic] to bring together such an enterprise would be to film some establishing shots in a Latin American country.

Finally, I think that colour would give enormous value to the film. Claude Jr probably spoke to you about the Technicolor system, which really makes the shooting easy. There is obviously the question of making an agreement with Technicolor, who don't like giving their process to non-English or non-American productions. But I think that I can help Dorfmann in this matter.

Now let's talk about the financial conditions. For the French version, you know better than I. You expressed your feelings on this matter when we discussed making L'Etranger. For the English version we will need to reach a compromise. Perhaps a certain number of Dollars in cash, to be decided between you and the producer, and a percentage of the distribution in English-speaking countries.

The date proposed by Dorfmann is fine for me. It will give me time to help in the negotiations for the distribution of The River. I am full of hope about it. The publicity was excellent and people are looking forward to the film. But, as you know, I have a huge percentage of the profits, and I like to keep an eye on these matters.

If negotiations start, please don't forget the travel arrangements and expenses for Dido and myself, the question of taxes, etc.

I hope that you and Mrs Dewalde are doing well. Dido and I send you our best.

Jean Renoir

PS. Of course, if things work out with Dorfmann, I would like to have Claude for the photography and Lourié for the sets.

PPS. I would like to know if Dorfmann already has a deal with an American studio for the distribution of *Carrosse* here.

1 *La Faute de L'Abbé Mouret* (*The Sin of Father Mouret*) was eventually filmed by Georges Franju in 1970.

To Robert Dorfmann
Paris

3 April 1951
Beverly Hills

Dear Mr Dorfmann,

I am writing by the same post to my agent Jean Dewalde. I am already having talks with other people about a film to be shot in France. It's possible that these talks are too advanced for me to accept your proposal. Jean Dewalde knows the situation better than me.

Moreover, I have also started talks for a film here and I need a few days to clear up the situation.

As I told you in my telegram. I would be delighted to make a film with Magnani, and *Le Carrosse du Saint Sacrement* is a subject that thoroughly appeals to me. I had already thought about doing it a few years ago with Paulette Goddard.

If I could, I would go to Paris to discuss with you the way in which we could treat this story. Unable to do so, I will here try to convey my reaction in a few words:

Le Carrosse could be an extraordinary film, a little in the vein of *La Kermesse Héroique*,[1] and could have the same international success as Feyder's film.

But it's a short story, and any normal-length film based on a short story risks appearing a little shallow.

I have several ideas myself that will not 'water it down', which would be bad, but will add substance to the story.

My ideas are obviously based on the description of the Pericole lovers, but also, above all, on the general situation. This general situation is the Spanish occupation of an Indian country. From this situation are born habits, obligations, duties, hypocrisies, goodness and cruelty; all that's necessary to make a good film.

It's a shame you won't be shooting this film in a Latin American country. Streets full of real Indians would give enormous value to the production. There is also the style of the churches, the bull-fights, etc. Perhaps you could envisage the possibility of filming establishing shots in Mexico, for example.

I also believe that colour would add a lot to this film. You know that Technicolor now has a process which doesn't require special equipment. My nephew Claude Renoir, who shot *The River* with me in India, could give you information on the subject.

Dear Mr Dorfmann, I hope that the omens are favourable to me, and that I will soon find myself busy preparing this film with you.

My very best wishes.

Jean Renoir

1 *La Kermesse Héroique* (*Carnival in Flanders*, 1935) was Jacques Feyder's greatest international success.

To Jean Dewalde
Paris

10 April 1951
Beverly Hills

Dear Jean,

I have just received your telegram and I'm delighted that the negotiations with Dorfmann went so well. You must have already received my response by telegram. I am adding to it some details that I ask you to pass on to Dorfmann:

1) I believe I have a good idea which will make *Carrosse* a richer and longer story.
2) I'm waiting for the first copy of *The River* any minute now, and I will have to be in New York for the first negotiations with American distributors. I think that I will be free to link up with Dorfmann in Paris at the beginning of May to work on the adaptation.
3) I suggest in my telegram a research trip to Mexico before my

departure for Paris, because Mexico is very near here and this wouldn't mean a huge expense for Dorfmann. Obviously there are certain differences between Peru and Mexico, but there are also many points in common between the two Spanish colonies. I've never visited Latin America and I believe that a short stay in a town where Spanish and Indian civilizations are superimposed would be an excellent preparation for the adaptation of *Carrosse du Saint Sacrement*.

I hope to have a letter soon from you with details of the financial conditions. The question of dollars worries me a little.

Don't forget to explain to Dorfmann how much collaborating with Claude and Lourié could help me. Moreover, he knows Lourié, as he worked on his film with Errol Flynn.[1]

Without any commitment on his part, perhaps Dorfmann could even pay for a trip to Mexico for Lourié as well, who would return with information useful for set construction; unless Dido, who has the advantage of speaking Spanish, could come with me.

There is also the question of travel arrangements, the trip and the stay of Dido's. I don't doubt that you've settled all these matters for the best.

I am very happy that you've conducted these negotiations so promptly, and I thank you for it.

Best wishes,
Jean Renoir

PS. If Magnani is in Paris, please would you tell her my great pleasure at the idea of working with her.

1 *The Adventures of Captain Fabian* (William Marshall, 1951).

To Robert Dorfmann
Paris

13 April 1951
Beverly Hills

Dear Mr Dorfmann,

I have just received your letter of 9 April.

I will be in New York, along with the producer of the film, at the beginning of next week to work on the distribution of *The River*, which I shot in India and the first colour copy of which I should receive any day now. I hope that my presence in New York won't be required for too long and that I can join you in Paris at the beginning of May or later.

I don't know the conditions of film-making in Italy nor the difficulties of preparation in France, but it seems to me that it won't be too difficult to be ready to start with Anna Magnani on 15 September.

Concerning the choice of actors and technicians, it seems to me that apart from the collaborators who are definitely necessary, we should wait for the first draft of the screenplay. We could agree right away upon my nephew Claude as cinematographer. His work on *The River* is considered by those who have seen the film to be the best Technicolor to date. Lourié, whom you know, has worked with me since 1935. He is used to organizing everything on my films to do with the sets, the exteriors, and the costumes. Apart from his considerable talent, he would win us time in the pre-production and the shoot. I don't have any preference concerning the line producer and the assistant, and I am sure that you have very good people with you.

Concerning the writer, I suggest that you put off this decision. Once in Paris, you could furnish me with an office and a good secretary, and in two weeks I would give you a first draft, very rough but sufficient to allow us to choose the appropriate actors and writer. Perhaps this writer could be English or American since we are making a version in English. I'll be in charge of the French version. An intelligent assistant, literary-minded with a good education, would be sufficient for me to 'kick the ball about' with, and would be my partner in the exchange of ideas so needed in this line of work.

Concerning the question of American actors, I propose the following method: after the first draft, and while the line producer and, I hope, Lourié would be busy setting up the production, I could return to America to work on certain actors I know and, as I've already suggested to you, make a quick research trip to Mexico. That could happen in June. Then I would come back and rejoin you and, with the collaboration of an English-language writer, fine-tune the screenplay. If you decide that the inclusion of a French dialogue writer could add something, there will always be time for that. The last stage of screenplay writing, and the preparation, can take place wherever you want, either in Paris or Rome.

At the time of my arrival in Paris, I could also give you up-to-the-minute information on the current conditions of film distribution in America. It seems that it's not too difficult a problem. Nearly everyone is interested in my film *The River*. That must be because the few distributors who handle independent productions are lacking in films. In any case, the situation of *The River* and the future situation of *Le*

Carrosse are very similar, and perhaps the experience I and my producer are currently acquiring may be of help to you.

Concerning Technicolor, it is obvious that colour would add enormously to the commercial value of such a subject.

Dear Mr Dorfmann, all these ideas perhaps seem a little confusing to you. This disorder comes from my eagerness to respond to you. These are nothing but suggestions, and I believe that the real decisions can only be made when our collaboration has effectively begun. That's why I think that my trip to Mexico can be postponed until later. What matters now is to hasten our meeting and I will do my best in that regard. As soon as I know it, I will give you my address in New York, where I am to arrive on Tuesday night.

Yours sincerely,
Jean Renoir

To Dido Renoir   *9 May 1951*
Beverly Hills   *Paris*

Dear Dido,

I have not yet received your telegram. While waiting, I am writing you this little note to tell you that I love you, that I miss you terribly, that I had a good trip, and that my brief meeting with Dorfmann and Alliata[1] (I think that's his name) has left me with a good impression.

I'd hardly arrived when I had a telephone call from Pagnol,[2] who I saw – very considerate and sweet.

Dined with Pierre, Claude and Paulette – very nice.

At the airport – Jean Dewalde, Claude, the producers, journalists – I don't know why. One big hilarious party.

The officials had held everything up by laughing at my American passport – 'an American with a Parisian accent' – the customs officers didn't want to open my suitcases, but asked me for autographs.

At avenue Frochot some anonymous youngsters had covered the sidewalks and walls with chalked inscriptions: 'Vive Jean Renoir' – 'From *La Petite Marchande d'Allumettes* to *The River*, thank you', etc. It seems they have not forgotten me in Paris.

Mr Guillaume, more charming than ever, is well and is anxious to send me quickly to Italy.

Regards to Bessie.[3]

All my love,
Jean

PS. I got your telegram just this instant and am very happy.

1 Prince Francesco Alliata, production manager for *Le Carrosse d'Or*.
2 Marcel Pagnol (1895–1974), playwright and film-maker famous for his 'Marseilles Trilogy' *Marius*, *Fanny*, and *Cesar*.
3 Elizabeth Smith, the Renoirs' housekeeper in Beverly Hills.

To Dido Renoir   *10 May 1951*
Beverly Hills   *Paris*

Dear Dido,

Nothing definite concerning my work, except that I am about to go to Italy – at the beginning of next week – to the great relief of Monsieur Guillaume, who is afraid that Catherine[1] will only cause me problems in Paris.

In Rome, the producers have stacks of paper, screenplays already written by at least a dozen different writers. They aren't asking me to use them, but think that if I glance over them, it might help me in the elaboration of my own screenplay.

My impressions are very good – Dorfmann and Alliatta[sic] seem like producers who want to follow my ideas – anxious to know them, if necessary to discuss them, and to help me. I hope that this will continue. For the moment, I am very pleased.

The two questions pending are Lourié and the American version. As for the latter, what is preventing us are questions of budget and of course, legality. The film is subject to certain Franco-Italian trade-union and governmental agreements, and these agreements are embellished with masses of decrees, laws, obligations – it's insane. I myself might be passed off as a French director. It is more difficult not to categorize Lourié as 'American'.

But be sure to tell him that Dorfmann has good intentions on his behalf, and that I think that, once in Italy, I will be able to convince the producers to take him on. This is obviously just a wish, but I hope it will happen.

As for the American version, I am almost sure it will be made. But we mustn't mention it, or the advantages of the Franco-Italian agreements will no longer be conceded.

Before starting to work in Italy, the real reason for my trip here is to have some French films screened that I should see. I think it is important for me to be up to date.

Last night I dined with Pagnol, and at the last moment I brought Ingrid (who had telephoned) and, of course, Rossellini. Tonight, I'm dining with my brothers. I will tell you about that in more detail later, and of Ingrid in another letter.

All my love,
Jean

1 Catherine Hessling, Jean Renoir's ex-wife.

To Dido Renoir

Beverly Hills

Dear Dido,

Everything seems to be going well. I am more busy receiving journalists and friends than dealing with *Carrosse* problems. I think that it was necessary. Otherwise the Parisians could have shown their disappointment. So I have received each journalist and I have given him long explanations. I will not leave until Thursday for Italy. I am only stopping in Milan for one day, for a press conference with Italian journalists, and will leave during the night for Rome, where I will be on Saturday morning. It amuses me to think that I am going to spend two nights on the train after all that time flying around on planes. The journalists, radio people, and friends of various political persuasions are extremely kind. But I still feel a great reticence vis à vis America, and to avoid stirring up sensitivities in a superficial way, I have to be careful of what I say.

Braunberger and Desfontaines have offered to make a film with me after *Le Carrosse*, on no matter what subject. I think everyone is glad to see me again. Everything would be better if you were with me. I am very lonely without you and I miss you enormously.

With all my love,
Jean R.

To Dido Renoir

Beverly Hills

Dear Dido,

The hustle and bustle is still going on, old friends or new ones from morning to night. This week in Paris, I hope to get the joy of seeing them again out of my system. Tomorrow I leave for Rome. Down there I hope that I will be able to work, and that on my return to Paris in five or six weeks, I will cease to be a curiosity, that the loving kindness of my friends will have abated and I will be left alone to get some work done.

But this disruption was necessary, and I must say it has given me immense pleasure, spoiled only by the fact that you are not with me. In future, we shall have to arrange things to avoid these terrible separations. [...]

All my love,
Jean

PS. I am stopping in Milan and will only be in Rome on Saturday or Sunday – Alliata is already there. I'm leaving on the train with Dorfmann.

To Dido Renoir
Beverly Hills

20 May 1951
Hotel Hassler
Rome

Dear Dido,

This is the hotel Michel Simon[1] stayed at,[2] but it's been completely refurbished in a very luxurious style. I have an apartment with an astounding view. It is so beautiful that I don't know how to describe it. If only you were here. In Milan I showed *La Petite Marchande d'Allumettes* and extracts from *La Grande Illusion* to some journalists under the auspices of the 'Cineteca'. I also dined with some film backers who are very emancipated young girls – daughters of rich industrialists. An associate of Alliatta [sic] is Renzo Avanzo, brother-in-law of Visconti.[3] I just had lunch in Rome with another group including Alliatta's[sic] wife. She resembles Dulce, your sister. Dorfmann came with me from Paris. Everyone is amusing, affectionate, well-bred; what a change from Kenny. Tonight I am showing some of my films at the home of some particularly rich people who have a screening room. The French Ambassador is coming. If only you were there. You would have fun, and my happiness would be complete. Love to Bessie and Ga and Jeannot.

With all my love,
Jean

1 Michel Simon (1895–1975), actor whose credits included *La Chienne, Boudu Sauvé des Eaux, Panique* (Julien Duvivier, 1947), and *Blanche* (Walerian Borowczyk, 1971).
2 Presumably during the shooting of *La Tosca*.
3 Luchino Visconti (1906–76), director whose credits included *La Terra Trema* (1948), *Senso* (1954), *The Leopard* (1963), and *Death in Venice* (1971). He is credited as an assistant on *Une Partie de Campagne*.

To Dido Renoir
Beverly Hills

(Write to me at Panaria – I might be changing hotels)

Dear Dido,

Rome is even more like Rome than when we were here together. The night that I presented *La Grande Illusion* – at the home of some people whose name I have forgotten [. . .] was incredible. The French Ambassador, a Borghese princess, La Magnani, charming and tired (I think that I will work well with her) and Visconti's little sister, now Baroness Avenzo, and her crazy husband – she is delicious, lives with fourteen dogs, six cats, some rabbits, and a parrot. Surely you remember her. The father, Duke Visconti, is dead. I have not yet had the time to see Luchino. He is constantly sending me messages, but I barely have time to relax. And when I do relax, it's to think of you. Despite all the excitement of seeing again this city that we love, I do not take to the idea of seeing it without you. And I get lonely when I stop to think.

I had your letter today, and one from Koch. I think that, as for this passport question, the best thing to do would be to pay a friendly visit to the French Consulate in Los Angeles. Tell him that I don't know anything about this law which deprives me of my French nationality because I am more than fifty years old, that I did not anticipate this shock, and ask him what must be done to get this resolved. Perhaps he might return the passport, and maybe the young New York employee had not reckoned on certain exceptions – the best thing would be to leave it up to the new Los Angeles Consul who, from what we know of him, is a very honest man.

The bad news about Kenny's[1] $3,000 stuns me. How are we going to live? Maybe you could exchange francs for dollars with the Slades. I have made an arrangement here so that you can receive some dollars in Beverly Hills from *Le Carrosse*. But not right away. My contract is not even signed yet. I wonder if Coryell is right. How does he know that we won't get this money from India? In any case, I think that before attacking Kenny we must wait for the contract for *The River* with United Artists to be signed. And we can find that out from David Loew or from Coryell.

I don't know what else to tell you except that I love you. Love to Bessie and Ga and Janot [sic] and everyone.

I love you,

Jean

[274]

1 Kenneth McEldowney. Jean Renoir made *The River* on a deferred salary basis. It took him several years to see any money from this film.

To Dido Renoir
Beverly Hills

28 May 1951
Rome

Dear Dido,

A quick note before starting work. Yesterday was like a sentimental American film. First a newsreel with Magnani and a *public welcome*[1] – for the screen – to the great artist who has come to honour Italy . . . etc. Although they clearly exaggerated their sentiments a little before the camera, it pleased me all the same.

Then Ingrid, the kid (Robertino)[2] and . . . (wait for it) Ruth, on vacation here and returning to Hollywood where she will see you. She seems worn out but delighted with her work with the Quakers. Tears of joy, emotion, bottles of champagne. Then Rossellini arrived. I am his brother . . . no less. Moreover, very kind.

Then Magnani and Radha.[3] [. . .]

Today I am going to speak to the 'Centro Sperimentale'.[4] I will tell you how it went. And I send you all my love. Regards to Bessie, the Slades and to the dogs.

Jean

1 Originally in English.
2 Robertino Rossellini.
3 Radha Sri Ram, actress in *The River*.
4 'Centro Sperimentale di Cinematografia' (CSC) is the oldest film school in Western Europe, having been founded by Benito Mussolini in 1935.

To Dido Renoir
Beverly Hills

7 June 1951

Dear Dido,

Yesterday, I finished dictating the first draft of my treatment. I told my secretary to type it at home. I am going to have a meeting today with Alliatta [sic] and Avanzo. All the Alliattas [sic] have gone to vote in Sicily and have to return tomorrow night.

I am happy enough with my work. The film will have a lot of action and some real conversations of the *Règle du Jeu* type. What bad luck not to have Lourié with me. Before writing to him I want to see Alliatta [sic] again to be quite sure that nothing can be done. I am afraid the producers were impressed by the work already done by the Italian designer (Chiari,[1] who had worked on sets with Visconti and against whom – alas – I have nothing to say). Well, this enormous amount of work, costumes, watercolours, photos, and set designs, will not help me at all. It relates to screenplays which I have read but not used.

[. . .]

I will leave for Sicily at the end of the week, and will probably have little opportunity to write. I imagine that I will be carted around from place to place. During the evenings, instead of having a little time with you, I will discuss affairs with the producers. I will also go to see a little Calabrian town built by the Spanish.

I saw, with Dudley amd Esta, a private screening of *Miracle in Milan* by de Sica.[2] It is one of the most beautiful films I have ever seen in my life. Dudley wept. The Italians hated it. Alliatta had organized the screening and invited Dudley and Esta to dinner. Dudley had wanted to see de Sica the next day, but preferred to flee to Florence, for Esta, he told me, is becoming more and more impossible. His trip had been terrible. And he is constantly afraid of a scene. However, during the Alliata dinner, she had been perfect and had impressed everyone with her wit and good humour. She even adored little Princess Alliata – the one who looks like Dulce. In sum, for Dudley it was one of the rare good evenings of his trip. Alliatta had even found him some *lire* at a good price.

I also saw Radha again, and Raymond[3] and Alain[4] but briefly. Alain continues to drive around in a Peugeot which he bought – despite his disgust with our era and Western civilization. Radha and her husband have left for Cannes [. . .]

As for Ingrid – you'll see Ruth who will tell you that Ingrid is perfectly happy – I don't think so. Rossellini – who is charming – is not a 'spouse'. Everyone here knows that things cannot last with his attitude – he had arrived after lunch under the pretext of business, not hungry because he had already eaten a sandwich. I even ask myself if he doesn't already have his eye on someone else.

Tonight I am dining with his aunt – my old pal the Baroness Avanzo – she will tell me all the gossip.

[. . .] I'll leave you now, for I could chat with you for hours. Tomorrow or the day after I will reply to you about the passport and I will

[276]

concentrate on practical matters. Thanks for all you've done. You must be exhausted. Hello to Bessie.

With all my love,
Jean

1 Mario Chiari (1909–?) art director, whose credits included *Miracle in Milan* (Vittorio de Sica, 1951), *War and Peace* (King Vidor, 1956), and *King Kong* (John Guillermin, 1976).
2 *Miracle in Milan* (Vittorio de Sica, 1951).
3 Raymond Burnier, Swiss husband of Radha Sri Ram, a photographer.
4 Alain Daniélou (1907–94), friend of Raymond and Radha Burnier, a specialist in Indian music and literature.

To Dido Renoir
Beverly Hills

12 June 1951
Rome

Dido darling,

Yesterday the kind Mrs Alliatta [sic] telephoned me through her husband to say that she had decided to take me to see the Pope.[1] At noon we were received, she, her husband, and I. A private audience is an enormous honour. You must tell Bessie this. I was very affected and did not know how to respond to the questions of the Holy Father. He gave me a small medallion that I will give to you. The Pope seems to me in good health – very lively and looking younger than in his photographs.

I am leaving right away for Sicily, so I will not be writing to you for a few days.

With all my love,
Jean R.

1 Pope Pius XII (1876–1958), reigned from 1939–1958.

To Jean Renoir

23 June 1951
Beverly Hills

Dear Jean,

The screening[1] last night was a complete success, you would have been happy to have been there. It was the first time that I had seen your film without you, but you seemed to be there all the same, right next to me. It all looked so beautiful that the second copy didn't seem to me to be really superior to the first, and there are even some things which pleased me

[277]

more in the first, but as I have not seen the first copy since New York perhaps my judgement is poor. The shots in which Pat and Nan's faces had been very red, for example when they watch Capt John and Valerie on the veranda, were much improved. Anyway, you will see for yourself. I'll tell you about my evening. The Lewins picked me up at the house and all three of us dined at Catherine's with Johnny Walsh, then Al took all five of us to the screening at the Goldwyn studios. There were hordes of people I didn't know invited by Kenny, who also made a stupid little speech. Al was furious. For my part, I had invited Ruth Roberts, her son Jim and his wife, Peter[2] came with Pia and three of her little friends, the Marions, the Stravinskys[3] and the Huxleys.[4] All of them were genuinely enthusiastic. After the screening Ruth, Peter, and the Lewins came over to have a drink at the house and stayed until one in the morning. Al said that *The River* will have the same career as *La Grande Illusion* and that it is a film which will go down in the annals of film history. What really amazed me was Peter's love of the film. He was astounded. As you can imagine, I was happy and so wanted to have you there with me.

But now, alas, I don't have any good news to give you. I saw the Consul. New York had sent him back your passport and he thought he had the situation well in hand, but this vice-consul in New York is a bastard, and suspecting what Mr Bertrand wanted to do, he tied his hands by warning the Minister of Foreign Affairs in Paris about your American naturalization before getting hold of your passport. Mr Bertrand seemed truly sorry not to be able to help. He regretted your actions in New York. If you had gone to him, he would have given you the passport without any difficulty. He told me that the only thing you can do is make a request for reinstatement of your French nationality, which can be done at the préfecture de la Seine after residing in France for three months, or by presenting a receipt for rent, made out in your own name. After that, they will give you a French passport, but he thinks that if you take this action, you will lose your American nationality. I am sorry all this has turned out so badly, especially since Mr Bertrand had given me so much hope. This has really upset me. Thankfully I got your very sweet letter from Sicily. I needed that. It must be a paradise, maybe one day we will go there together.

Dido

1 Screening of *The River*.
2 Peter Lindstrom.

3 Igor Stravinsky (1882–1971), Russian-born composer of such important works as *The Firebird* (1909), *Petrushka* (1911), and *The Rite of Spring* (1913).
4 Aldous Huxley and his wife.

To Dido Renoir
Beverly Hills

29 June 1951
Paris

Dear Dido,

I think that I will soon have found my actors for *Le Carrosse*. I have made the Viceroy a younger man, and Jouvet[1] or Pierre[2] would definitely not be able to play him. I think I have found a rare bird: a Mediterranean singer, a magnificent fool when he read the lines that I had provisionally written for some tests I am going to make on Tuesday and Wednesday. Maybe we have a young Raimu[3] before us.

I don't understand anything about the cut (or change) in *The River* that Lourié spoke about. I saw Arthur Krim here and he assured me that United Artists had not asked for any changes. They like the film as it is.

I am very happy that our friends like *The River* so much. I have received a telegram from Peter, Pia and Ruth.

Radha and Raymond are here once more. She has asked me to help her with her dance recital, which I am going to do. I will introduce her. It will be the debut of a beautiful tuxedo that Princess Alliatta [sic] has had made for me – 'What a love!' as you say. But I prefer that to people not being able to show their feelings for us. I am constantly being stopped in the street by former technicians or workers who used to know me. We often end up in tears. It's wonderful and horrible.

I add that there is extreme misery here. However, the general impression of Paris is much better than the last time. Mr Guillaume is coming to take me to be finger-printed. At Silverfilm they think that I will get a new passport.

Don't work too hard. Come to me well-fed and very pretty. I don't have time to see Renée.[4]

With all my love,

Jean

1 Louis Jouvet.
2 Pierre Renoir.
3 Raimu (Jules Muraire) (1883–1946), actor best known for his work in Marcel Pagnol's films *Marius* (1931), *Fanny* (1932), *César* (1936), and *La Femme du Boulanger* (1938).
4 Renée Rivière Cézanne, wife of Paul Cézanne Jr.

To Dido Renoir
Beverly Hills

Dear Dido,

Last night I went to Tabarin with Claude Sr, Braunberger, his wife and his wife's daughter, a very sweet, very lively girl of seventeen. The girl had never seen a show like it, and was astonished. So was I – I even danced – the tango? – with Mrs Braunberger. A month ago, when I was passing through Paris, a journalist saw me in a restaurant (La Grille, where I used to go in the old days with André Gide[1]) with all the Braunbergers, but had only remembered the girl. And a little piece of gossip resulted, that I had returned to Paris to resume my Don Juanesque activities with a very young girl – and they published her name (which I don't even know myself). Of course everyone had a good laugh. This (rather flattering) little jab at me was the only sour note since my return. I cannot account for it, but it's unique, as the people here like me very much: I go to a theatre to see some actors, and on the stage the people were speechless and sputtered with emotion to see me there. And not only old friends but young people whom I had never seen before. It's even dangerous, for such emotional outbursts often bring about reactions, and I ask myself what these reaction will be [. . .]

I have taken on the role of confidant, or I should say Father Confessor, especially with women. It must be my age which bestows this position on me. They know, or sense that I'm not a candidate for their favours – they also know that I love you – and, perhaps, with age, I have acquired the gift of listening.

All this doesn't get in the way of preparations for the film. On Tuesday and Wednesday I am going to make some tests. If they are conclusive, I will return to Italy and polish up my scenario. I'm going to see Cortegianni[2] today. His *confidences* will be about fire-arms – for him, to change from muzzle-loading to breech-loading is more important than a love affair. He's been waiting to talk to me about it for ten years.

With all my love,

Jean

---

1 André Gide (1869–1951), major French literary figure of the twentieth century, whose works included *Fruits of the Earth* (1897), *The Immoralist* (1902), and *Strait is the Gate* (1909).
2 Antoine (Tony) Cortegianni, firearms expert who worked on *La Marseillaise* and who appeared in *La Règle du Jeu*.

To Dido Renoir
Beverly Hills

Dear Dido,

I am very annoyed because my tests have not revealed any actor capable of bringing some grandeur to the role of the Viceroy. I have a big reputation here, and it's dangerous, for people think I can make a good actor out of anyone. You can try that out in a 'realist' film, or get by by relying on the natural qualities of a gifted individual. That's what I did with Flamant in *La Chienne*. But in *Le Carrosse* I must have real actors, capable of gracefully speaking a text I must try to write as a pastiche of the classics – a text which is a little like that of *La Règle du Jeu*. You remember how Nora Gregor's[1] blunders nearly killed that film.

We've begun, naturally, to envisage Pierre Brasseur[2] in the role, for he is the only French actor who isn't too old, is capable of playing with words, ideas and who can wear a costume with truculence. I saw him in a play by Sartre.[3] He parodied Jules Berry,[4] but it was probably a natural parody due to the fact that his professional development had brought him to the same point that Jules Berry had reached.

Have I told you this play by Sartre – *Le Diable et le bon Dieu* – was the biggest bore I've had to put up with, except for Wagner's *The Flying Dutchman*, which I saw with Koch in Berlin in 1933. But Sartre's dialogue is right, and resembles a little what I would like to do for *Le Carrosse*. It's just that he [Sartre] repeats himself, and is too long – he never forgets that he is in charge. I'll try to avoid these pitfalls.

I'm waiting for Claude Junior to talk to him about the film.

With all my love,

Jean

---

1 Nora Gregor (1890–1949), actress who starred in *La Règle du Jeu*.
2 Pierre Brasseur (1903–72), actor whose credits included *Quai des Brumes* (Marcel Carné, 1938), *Les Enfants du Paradis* (Marcel Carné, 1945), and *King of Hearts* (Philippe de Broca, 1966).
3 Jean-Paul Sartre (1905–80), philosopher, literary critic and playwright, whose works included *Huis Clos* (1944), *Les Chemins de la Liberté* (1949), and *Les Main Sales* (1948).
4 Jules Berry (1883–1951), actor whose credits included *Le Crime de Monsieur Lange*, and *Le Jour se Lève* (Marcel Carné, 1939).

To Dido Renoir
Beverly Hills

Dido Darling,

Yesterday I put Bessie's card in the post. I hope you received it. I continue to swim in the midst of Viceroys, some more unbelievable than others. I hang about, I get irritated, and when I think I have it in my grasp, it becomes like sand which slips through my fingers. I am going right away to see Pierre Brasseur at his home. A pointless quest, as all the good actors are busy indefinitely. Last night I dined with Sam Levin.[1] Tonight I see Braunberger. Tomorrow I make new tests. Apart from my worry over trying to find this actor, I am having a good time in Paris. Friends are more than kind. I only miss you at these little get-togethers.

With all my love,

Jean

[1] Sam Levin, photographer who worked on the set of *La Grande Illusion, La Bête Humaine* and *La Règle du Jeu.*

To Dido Renoir
Beverly Hills

Dear Dido,

I have a Viceroy – he's a singer at the Lapin Agile. His name is Caussimon[1] – he did a stunning test for me. He's a man of around thirty-five, maybe younger, but very distinguished – tall, thin, bald – very dashing in a Louis XV costume. He has certain intonations which he can get rid of, for he is as sly as a fox, and a certain tendency to do too much, but he's the first one that I've encountered who tried to portray a character and not play himself.

I am going to leave Paris next Tuesday.

Last night, or rather tonight, I staggered around until three in the morning. I was allowed to crash the Technicians Ball, outside in the Place Vendôme. There I met loads of people. A good time was had by all, but there too I missed you.

With all my love,

Jean

[1] Jean-Roger Caussimon did not eventually play the Viceroy – the role went to Duncan Lamont – but Renoir cast him in *French Cancan.*

To Dido Renoir

Beverly Hills

17 July 1951

Paris

Dear Dido,

Three letters from you arrived together – as a result of the 14 July holiday. Tomorrow morning I leave for Rome – 10 o'clock in the morning – Air France – Orly. The Tambeau-Niki drama really upset me – especially your own injuries.[1] Poor Dido, I can see you with your bleeding hands, still continuing to do everything around the house. I am anxious to see you get here and for you to relax in Rome in our little apartment, rue Jacopo Peri – too warm, I'm afraid.

[. . .] My work is really difficult. I think I'll be able to bring with me a marvellous 'script girl, secretary', Mrs Doynel[2] – and Maurette[3] as assistant. Maybe de Bretagne[4] for the sound [. . .] How I would like to see Lourié working. [. . .]

With all my love,

Jean

---

1 Apparently the two dogs fought and Niki, Tambeau's puppy, was killed. Dido seems to have been injured while trying to separate them.
2 Ginette Doynel, who had worked as scriptgirl on several films, and would later become secretary and general manager of La Compagnie Jean Renoir, J.R.'s company in France.
3 Marc Maurette, assistant on *La Vie est à Nous* and *La Marseillaise*. He later became an assistant director for Orson Welles, Vincente Minelli and Stanley Donen, among others.
4 Jo de Bretagne, who worked as soundman on several of Jean Renoir's films: *La Chienne, La Nuit du Carrefour, La Marseillaise, La Grande Illusion*, and *La Règle du Jeu* among others.

To Dido Renoir

Beverly Hills

20 July 1951

Rome

Dear Dido,

I have just posted the papers for Tannenbaum as well as a quick letter to you. Since my return the day before yesterday I have not had the time to write you. Francesco Alliata wanted to know what I had done in Paris and why I had been so long. Today he is leaving for Palermo, but yesterday and the day before we had a meeting and established a much-needed work plan. Unfortunately, the customs rules don't allow me to show my tests with Caussimon here and I had to explain everything verbally in place of screening them. Before leaving Paris, I wasted my last three days persuading Madame Dorfmann that Caussimon was very good. She will play the role of the Marquise Altamirano. As you know, I had made the cast younger, but her imagination was racing ahead of mine and she envisioned a Viceroy like an Adonis. She made me waste three days in Paris and I only left after I'd seen the Caussimon contract drafted and ready to be signed.

[...]

I found several letters from you. They have allowed me to follow the saga of Tambeau, the unnatural father. I hope that your hands have healed up well and that the scars have disappeared. Your letter of 16 June also informed me of Bessie's return, which will allow me to expect you around the beginning of September. It's not too soon! [...]

I had a less agreeable trip to Paris than the first. The test and the problems on *Le Carrosse* took up all my time. Despite that, I had a very good time on 14 July. I went into the street and I met up with lots of comrades, technicians, electricians and others. There were all terrified to see me drink Coca-Cola. They are convinced that a few drops of the stuff could provoke an immediate heart-attack.

I've seen Radha several times, mostly at events for the television, radio, etc. I rediscovered my former pleasure in her company. I have also had the pleasure of the company of a young Persian woman, a total cinephile. Accompanied by her young male friend, she hardly ever leaves my side, making telephone calls for me and ordering taxis. Finally, as still happens in the Orient, I have virtually adopted her. Her name is Parvine and the name of her young friend is Jean Claude See. As you see, it is not as easy to detach oneself from the Orient as one believed. Besides, I have put her on to Radha and the two, I think, have become close allies.

[...]

I have not seen a copy of *The River* in colour. That idiot Kenny didn't know how to benefit from my trip to Paris, nor Claude's free time, for one of us to have a last look at the film before the 250 copies that United Artists have requested are made. Strangely enough, despite what he said in his letters, he has not taken the necessary steps for the Venice Film Festival. In the end, it is United Artists who will take care of it. Their Italian director is in touch with me here. As the quota of authorized English or American films has already been filled the film will be presented as an Indian film.

Some news in passing: Sartre, through the intermediary of Pierre Brasseur (who is currently the most successful of French actors), has sent to me a script conceived for Brasseur, Marlene Dietrich and China, but which would also suit Brasseur himself, and perhaps Radha and India. Sartre wanted to have lunch with me last Sunday. He couldn't make it because at 11 o'clock he decided to leave for Greenland. He telephoned Brasseur from Oslo, asking him to ask me if I would have dinner with him on 12 September at 8 o'clock in Rome. As you no doubt already know, he is a very precise man.

Dorfmann's office is still busy sorting out my passport. [. . .]

Here are the latest developments on *Le Carrosse*. As for Technicolor, I have a telegram from Kay Harrison who hopes to succeed in getting a guarantee for the laboratory costs from New York financiers. But, up to now, plenty of hopes but no definite response.

[. . .]

I really want to chat with you and I could go on to write volumes. I'll leave you now, but not before sending you all my love,

Jean

PS. Don't forget to give my love to friends who I really want to see again, Bob and Jessica [Ryan], the Pecks,[1] Al and Millie [Lewin], Dave and Meta [Loew]. Of course, lots of love to Ga and Jeannot [Slade]. Have the Nichols' returned? [. . .]

---

1 Sedley and Flo Peck, who owned the Peck Mine in Azusa, California.

To Dido Renoir
Beverly Hills

21 August 1951
Rome

Dear Dido,

I have your letter of 14 August – seven days to get here – and also that of the 16th. I can see you – fighting single-handed – against that luxuriant grapevine – David and Goliath. What size will it be in January? The film's editing will definitely be done here. As for the Buick, since it is like new, we should keep it like an old friend.

I have started the English screenplay with a nice guy who does dubbing here – (Kressel[1]) [sic] – he is studious and lacks a sense of humour. Luckily my American Viceroy, Tor (Michael) has enough to spare. I see la Magnani sometimes – everyone is scared stiff of her. Up to now our relationship has been cordial.

[. . .] Mrs Doynel has helped me to save *La Grande Illusion* from Rollmer's bankruptcy. I will update you on this when you get here. To write about it would take volumes [. . .]

My leg is better. I am walking with a stick. But the pain has

[285]

disappeared. The young girls have also disappeared. They come and they go. Only the Persian girl from Paris stays faithful and writes me long letters. I respond from time to time – she is very sweet but has a little difficulty understanding that the harem has yet to become part of our culture. She has a boyfriend who also writes to me. I get loads of letters from young people. If I were more cunning, I could start a cult and become the Annie Besant[2] of the cinema.

I have written to Alain to ask him what day the baby is due. As he cannot have time to write, tell me yourself.

Now I know that you are coming – at last – soon after you reply to this letter. My dates have not changed. I will return to Rome on 5 September (even before). If you arrive on the 6th, you can be sure to find me at the airport in our new *mille quatro cento Fiat*.[3] I will be in the midst of making tests with actors – black and white – with Claude.

One of the reasons that I so much want to have you here is that I am eating too much. I am lonely without you and – as you know very well – when I am lonely I eat and I drink. It's one of the reasons I am anxious to see you – there are several others – to sum it all up in a word – I desperately need you here.

Each time that you tell me about the Loews, I am more touched. Let's hope that Coryell can stop Kenny's expenses. He is living like a prince in Venice. On the other hand, maybe he's right. The festival is important and an element of intrigue plays a big part in winning the prize.

See you soon, dear Dido – on the 6 September. If my Venice programme changes I will send you a telegram – I have sent one to Stravinsky saying that we are not going to see his opera[4] – (11 September – the very day I have a chance to make a test with Magnani).

With all my love,

Jean

1 Lee Kresel, director of US versions of Italian films in the 50s and 60s.
2 Annie Besant (1847–1933), social reformer and Theosophist, President of the Theosophical society 1907–33.
3 Originally in Italian.
4 Stravinsky's opera *The Rake's Progress* was given its première in Venice on 11 September 1951.

Jean Renoir attends the Venice Biennale for the world première of The River. *It shares the International Critics prize with Bresson's* Le Journal d'un Curé de Campagne *and Wilder's* Ace in the Hole.

To Dido Renoir
Beverly Hills

22 August 1951
Venice

Dear Dido,

Could you slip in your suitcase one of the boxes of fifty Gillette razor blades that have accumulated in my bathroom cabinet?

The Venice [Biennale] approaches. It's an enormous event here – and in all of Europe. I am rather curious to see this carnival.

I'm happy to think that this letter is one of the last I will send you.

[...]

I am in the middle of correcting my screenplay before sending it to be duplicated. The first results of the English translation are excellent.

Can you believe that the only way to heat the bath water in our apartment is on a wood stove? Just like Les Collettes. It's so inconvenient that I wash in cold water. I will wait to decide with you how we are going to deal with this situation. I'm terribly afraid that you will not approve of my choice of apartments and will find it a little rustic.

Give my regards to Maurice[1] and maybe to Bessie, whose return must be approaching.

With all my love,

Jean

---

1 Maurice Renoir, son of Jean's cousin Edmond, became a paediatrician in Northern California.

To Dido Renoir
Beverly Hills

27 August 1951
Venice

Dear Dido,

Venice bores me. I'd like to talk to you about it but I don't know what to say. Thankfully, I have Macchi[1] with me – my dear Macchi. I hope you will like these Milanese, who are in love with the South. His wife has a house in Venice and they are going to show me the non-tourist parts of the city.

This note, if it reaches you, will no doubt be the last, judging by the time it takes for letters to travel the distance between Rome and Los Angeles. Give my love to Bessie and tell our friends who come to say good-bye that I think of them and thank them for the attention that they have paid you. No doubt you will see the Louriés, the Als [Lewin] and the Davids [Loew] and dear Bob Ryan and his family – and the Dudleys

[Nichols] – maybe the Hartwells and the Pecks. The cousins I doubt. Give my love to those you do see. If you have the time, call Chaplin and Una [sic] and say hello for me.

Another seven days and you will be here. Hope the weather will be beautiful and you will have a good trip.

With all my love,
Jean

Love to the doggies.

1 Giulio Macchi, assistant director on *Le Carrosse d'Or*. Later worked in Italian television.

To Lester Cowan [*Original in English*]   *20 September 1951*
Cinema Productions Inc.   *Rome, Italy*
New York City, New York

Dear Lester,

Thank you very much for your interest in *The River*. It encourages me immensely. As you guess the picture wasn't easy to make and I knew it before starting, but I needed a complete change in my style and hoped that this unusual story could bring me a good springboard for this change.

I would love to work with you but my Hollywood experiences taught me several things, among them that I cannot make a good picture if I am not the author of the script, if possible of the story, and if I'm not also the editor of the picture. The part of my job concerning the direction is not as important for the success of my enterprises as the building up of the drama, and I'm entirely lost when I have to base my shooting on situations and lines not invented by myself. I want and love collaborators, but I frankly recognize that they must follow my line. In *The River*, I was entirely at ease because Rumer Godden accepted to reinvent another story together with me. We were both faithful to the spirit of her novel, but she left me free to imagine the situations, the dramatic progression, the contrasts, and even to add new characters. She helped me immensely in this creation and brought me her beautiful English language.

Every picture I didn't make with such a liberty was a failure. It is why I am not a good Hollywood employee.

I am explaining myself very frankly because I remember our meetings in Hollywood and would like very much to do something in the frame of your organization. It could not be too immediate, I am tied for a while with my present projects, but that is not important; what is important is to have a complete understanding before dreaming of a possible collaboration.

I hope you will come to Europe and that I will see you in Rome.

My best wishes to your productions.

Sincerely yours,

Jean Renoir

To Clifford Odets [*Original in English*]   *1 October 1951*
Rome, Italy

Dear dear Clifford,

I would like so much to be near you and of course I am unhappy, and more for Bette who is the real loser.[1] What a foolish little girl, but she suffers perhaps from a sickness of our time: 'dissatisfaction'. Often only late in life one realizes that real happiness lies in forgetting oneself and living for the man one loves, a little bit as his shadow. How lucky when this man is someone like you. I often told Bette that after living beside you, and I know how difficult you must be at times, she will never be happy or satisfied with anyone else. But Clifford, if you cannot function it is better to make a clean break, nevertheless it is a very sad thought.

Jean is adding a few lines. For a week now he is bedridden and in great pain, his old war wound bothering him again, neuritis, etc. etc. It is a bad time for this to happen during the preparation of the film, and somehow sickness away from home and in discomfort becomes even more unbearable.

I hope you have cast *The Country Girl* and that you are deep in work. Chaplin also seems to doubt Lena Horne's[2] ability to act. I don't know. Perhaps you will manage to come to Rome, that would be wonderful! When Jean is better we shall see Ingrid and ask her if she wants to act in a play in the US. We had dinner with her some time ago and Jean mentioned *The Country Girl* and what a good part it was for her. With her usual 'flair' she dislikes the play. Poor girl, she is rather pitiful.

Dear Clifford, we think of you all the time and we love you *molto molto*.[3]

Dido

Dear Cliff,

I don't know what to say, the separation between you and Bette is like a natural catastrophe. Two days ago we were terrified by one of those

[289]

Roman storms with clouds and lightning like in a Michael Angelo[4] dramatic composition. There is nothing to say, just to wait and afterwards to count how many houses were destroyed. The only thing I can do is to wish that with your present ordeal no houses will be destroyed.

I hope to convince my brother Pierre who was the temporary boss of Louis Jouvet's theatre to put on *The Country Girl* on the Athénée stage. He would like to talk about it later. Now he is very depressed by the death of his old friend and seems unable to plan anything. Of course he was terribly interested by the idea of showing your play in Paris but too tired to start the necessary work.

Dear Cliff, I wish we find each other very soon around a nice job. Maybe *Camille* will be this job, if it's not *Camille* we must find something else.

Good luck dear Cliff and my best wishes to you, the kids, and Bette.

Jean

1 The Odets had temporarily separated.
2 Lena Horne (b.1917), singer and actress, whose films include *Stormy Weather* (Andrew L. Stone, 1943), *Till the Clouds Roll By* (Richard Whorf, 1946), and *The Wiz* (Sidney Lumet, 1978).
3 Originally in Italian.
4 Michelangelo.

To Clifford Odets [*Original in English*]   29 October 1951
Rome, Italy

Dear Cliff,

I am still in a bed in a clinic on my way to recovery. Since a surgeon opened my leg and cleaned the infection I feel a little better every day. But it is terribly slow. The wound is a very big one and when I look at it the day it will be completely healed seems to be very far away. I don't know whether I will be able to make my Italian picture. My only hope is that the obtention [sic] of importation licences for cameras, equipment, and Technicolor film from London will require more than a month of red tape, formalities, etc.

I am very fortunate to have Dido with me. She spends about all her time at the clinic which is a very uncomfortable, freezing place. Italians have a strange gift for discomfort. They don't know what is a decently heated place or an electric light allowing you to read in bed. But that's nothing. I am primely [sic] deeply bored of suffering and lying down for six weeks now. I don't suffer any more but during the daily dressing which is a very unpleasant ceremonial. If the comfort of the place is not what it should be I believe that the surgeon is good and the nurses and servants, all females, are amusing and friendly.

I hope the casting of *Country Girl*'s road show is now completed and that your mind is free to think of a new play. I am anxious to see you and hear what you have in mind. And more and more I would like so much to do something with you.

Dear Cliff, this is not a letter but just a small part of one of the many conversations I have with you in imagination. I am very weak and spend a part of my days and nights in a strange state between waking and sleeping; and in a kind of half dream I have sometimes the feeling that some of my friends are close to me and that you and I listen to records or look at paintings. Since I was very much impressed by the new turn in your life most of those meetings are with you.

Well, I don't feel like telling you too precise things. I just want to enjoy the warm feeling of our friendship.

So long, dear Cliff, I would like to know that you are rested and happy. If there is a God I ask him to bless you,

Jean

I just add my love. As always,
Dido

To Clifford Odets [*Original in English*]   *17 November 1951*
                                                     Rome

Dear Cliff,

Dido and I am going to Paris to consult a surgeon who will tell me whether I can work or not.

So often we thought of having a good time together in Paris. Well, we still have to wait a little.

In ten days or two weeks we shall be back here.

Dido and I send you our love.

Jean

Excuse the writing. I am still lying down.

1952

To Jean Renoir [*Original in English*]   *2 January 1952*
Rome   *Los Angeles*

Dear Dido, dear Jean,

There, that is the first time I have written 1952! What better way to begin this year than to sail a note in your direction? We have staggered through the holidays and get back to normal with a sense of relief – though God knows there was no wild social life.

I enclose a cutting from the Hollywood paper. You will have had the news. You can see how close you came to winning the N[ew] Y[ork] award, which means more than the Hollywood awards because it is disinterested – no studio pressures. You were squeezed out by only one vote, and I know what idiot lost you that vote – Bosley Crowther,[1] who is blind, deaf, impervious to poetry, and cannot even write grammatical English! He was 'agin' *The River* and gloated over his obtuseness – the silly ass! Which, of course, only proves again the greatness of your film, because any work of art judges the judge even more than the judge judges it. There is so little film criticism of any account in America, alas!

There were psychological advantages for *Streetcar [Named Desire]*[2] too, bear that in mind: it was released later than *The River* (weak memories among weak critics!) and contained those quantities of violence, rape and viciousness which the barbarous adore in 'movies'.

We wonder how you both are. I am sure Rome is cold, but brrrr! so is Los Angeles this morning. Rosie[3] had to break ice in the bird's bath out in the garden, and our more tender vines and shrubs have been frost-bitten. We had heavy rains, more than three inches in the one three-day storm which flooded areas to the south and west as usual. Then the cold moved in. But the sun sparkles and the world looks grand. A beautiful New Year's day yesterday too. We had seen the old year out with much champagne and a few people and my head ballooned when I rose, so we hung around here listlessly till three in the afternoon when we decided to start the new year right by touring the universe: we drove up to the Griffith Park observatory and spent an hour in the planetarium, where we entered a spaceship and travelled much faster than light to

Andromeda Nebula, 700,000 light years distant. What is faster than light? Thought, of course. It was a grand journey but we felt dreadfully small gnats among clouds of stars in infinite space, and I realized I know <u>absolutely nothing</u> and I felt very meek confronting this mask of God, and was glad to think myself back hastily from the terrible journey and get out of the domed darkness and walk out on the terrace and look down on the comforting small world of Hollywood and Los Angeles and the sea shining like a gold band along the coast to the west. But it was a good way to begin the year, don't you think?

We embrace you,

Dudley (+ Esta) [Nichols]

PS A card from Jane[4] this morning tells us there is a young <u>John</u> Renoir in the world, very healthy and strong, starting at 7½ pounds and determined to add weight and grow into the wonderful but fearsome adventure of becoming a Man! Alain 'bones up' for his exams! He knows what the adventure is, huh? To have a son and a son's son – I envy you!

1 Bosley Crowther was an important film critic at the time.
2 *A Streetcar Named Desire* (Elia Kazan, 1951).
3 The Nichols' maid.
4 Wife of Alain Renoir.

To Prince Francesco Alliata

28 January 1952
Rome

Dear Francesco,

On the eve of starting *Le Carrosse* I think it is appropriate I should describe the exact frame of mind in which I am beginning this work.

I have great hopes and many doubts at the same time. I will go into my doubts first: the English dialogue needs polishing. It has been written, but it is not as 'amusing' as it should be. You know that I don't think I am good enough to write dialogue in English, which is why I had requested a collaborator. Upon the recommendation of trusted friends (Pierre Fresnay)[1] I had suggested Jack Kirkland, whom you hired. However, instead of polishing the dialogue, Jack wrote an entirely new screenplay. His work has not been useless, since it has allowed me to tighten and polish my own script, but it has not helped as far as the dialogue is concerned.

To remedy this situation, I suggest Lee Kresel be allowed to work exclusively with me and that he only deals with the dialogue. Since

Pamela Matthews will be occupied entirely with her work with Magnani, I am asking you to hire a third dialogue coach to work with the other actors.

Since the English dialogue will be fine-tuned as we shoot, the fewer actors we have who find difficulty remembering lines in English, the better it will be. While I agree completely on having an Italian actor play the procurer, who doesn't have much to say, I do not feel the same about the toreador. I could manage with Rioli, of course, but I fear this may be time-consuming and be detrimental to the overall quality of the film. It occurred to me, why not ask Alexander Knox[2] to play that part? He is a character actor; he can be very funny when the occasion demands, and he might bring to the film a comical note which might be helpful for its success.

I don't think it is necessary to underline the fact that the less dubbing we have in the film, the more chances we have of pleasing American audiences.

I have told you what I thought of Magnani. I agreed to come on this project partly because of her. Since then I have discovered that her successes are based on last-minute inspiration instead of preparation. This works wonderfully in her native language. In a foreign tongue, I am not sure it can work. During my conversations with her, I felt that Anna did not really understand the screenplay. Furthermore, she has been so busy lately that she has had no time to work on her English. It is such a handicap that I feel quite discouraged before we start.

In spite of Mario Chiari's and Maria de Mattei's talent, the sets and costumes only remotely match the aesthetic concepts I have tried to maintain in all my films. I do not pretend that all my ideas are superior to those of others, but the few people who take an interest in my films, the critics and cinephiles, expect even the sets and costumes to be consistent with what I have shown them until now. I am not saying they will be disappointed with this one, but they might be puzzled by it.

Dear Francesco, I merely want to point out the obstacles standing between us and a successful film. They are so great that I often regret the doctors have found me fit enough to stay on this project. I overlook some minor drawbacks like Michael Tor, who only thinks of his good looks, or shooting a tropical story in Arctic cold. Those are part of film-making.

However, we have a few trumps in hand: your extraordinary patience and energy, without which the film would not be made, and without which I would have given up long ago. We also have the music from the eighteenth century, which will be a discovery in foreign countries.

Finally, even if the English dialogue is not perfect, the screenplay itself is now in fine shape.

And then there is also divine providence, which always counts, even in film-making.

Jean Renoir

1 Pierre Fresnay (1897–1975), actor whose credits included *Marius* (Alexander Korda, 1931), *La Grande Illusion*, and *Monsieur Vincent* (Maurice Cloche, 1947).
2 Alexander Knox (b.1907) actor best known for his portrayal of Woodrow Wilson in *Wilson* (Henry King, 1944).

To Mr Brosio
Panaria Films
Rome

30 January 1952
Rome

Dear Mr Brosio,

Following our conversation yesterday about the shooting schedule, I realize you are not as aware of my feelings about dubbing as Prince Alliata.

I may be wrong, but I have always refused to make dubbed films and I won't give in.

Therefore, I find it necessary to reiterate what I told you yesterday. Should I be confronted with the impossibility of recording the lead character live, I will be compelled to withdraw and will ask you to find another director for the film.

Sincerely yours,
Jean Renoir

To Prince Francesco Alliata
Panaria Films
Rome

3 February 1952
Rome

Dear Francesco,

Thank you for your letter. It really put my mind at ease to learn that all concerned are now willing to present *Le Carrosse d'Or* using the lead actor's direct sound recording.

Be assured that I fully appreciate your sacrifices to save our film. Furthermore, I am also very grateful for your agreeing to keep the French crew on the film. Were it not for my respect for you I would not have stayed on the project after my surgery. I am still in pain and I would have liked to have gone home to convalesce. Besides, I still have some important concerns in America, and my prolonged absence will end up being quite costly if they remain neglected for long. I am merely mentioning this to impress upon you the depth of my commitment to the picture and our relationship. As for my inflexibility with regard to the sound, it merely reflects my conviction that I do not believe I could make a good film otherwise. Many directors can handle dubbing. Even Duvivier is working with it now. (However, since I have not seen any of his latest films, I can't really say whether they are as good as *Carnet de Bal*[1] or *La Bandera*.)[2] Some directors are indeed able to excel with dubbing. But so far, each time my films are dubbed they become ridiculous. Few men can succeed in everything.

I would also like to say that I am available to discuss my contract whenever you find it convenient. I'd rather take care of this myself than go through Dewalde, who is not really closely in touch with me, and therefore not fully aware of my concerns.

While I am praying for our success with *Le Carrosse*, I also want to express how happy I am that circumstances have brought you, Teresa and me together. I only hope with all my heart that our collaborations will be long and friendly.

Jean Renoir

1 *Carnet du Bal* (1937).
2 *La Bandera (Escape from Yesterday)* (1935).

To Prince Francesco Alliata
Panaria Films
Rome

23 April 1952
Rome

My dear Francesco,

Your three letters reached me and between shooting scenes I will reply succinctly, hoping my comments will give you some ideas.

1) With regard to Kay Harrison's letter rehashing the notorious problem of Anna's cleavage,[1] I think he is right that it would be unwise not to reshoot some of the scenes again, as it would cost less now than later. We could do them when production is over, in a corner of the stage, at lesser cost, and I hope in one day.

2) Thank you for your suggestions about what I am supposed to tell the press.

25 Jean Renoir and Anna Magnani (Camilla) during the filming of *The Golden Coach*

3) I don't see how we could finish shooting before 15 May, which is the date on the schedule I had Maurette give to Brosio. As for trying to save on production costs, I am at your disposal to meet with you and go over what can be done. Unfortunately, we have scheduled the scenes that present the most technical difficulties for the end. Yesterday I barely managed to shoot three scenes and I don't think I could have done more.

I think we need to meet under quiet conditions as soon as possible. You know I am determined to do my best to help you deal with the situation.

Warm regards,
Jean Renoir

1 The American censor objected to the amount of cleavage that Magnani's costume exposed.

To Clifford Odets [*Original in English*]

4 May 1952
Panaria Films
Rome, Italy

Dear Cliff,

Did you start the new play which was germinating a month ago when you wrote us one of your notes we love dearly because they are like a bit of conversation with you? We are approaching the end of our shooting. It was a big job and we still have ten difficult days to go. To make a picture here is fascinating but slow. I enjoyed all the advantages of no production at all. I am sure that the producers never read my script. They ignore entirely[1] what I am doing and that is great. On the other hand it makes the organization of a period picture with costumes, wigs, crowds, and technical precision, a very daring enterprise. I was saved by the extreme good will of the crew, the cast, and in a strange way of the production. I am terribly anxious to show you my work. Alas, it won't be before several months.

Rome is beautiful as ever. Dido and I are spending our first peaceful Sunday since ages curing a cold. In three weeks we hope to take a short trip to France, see again the house of my father near Nice and pay a little visit to our Burgundy village[2] and its tiny cemetery where my father and my mother and my brother Pierre[3] are resting. We will drink there a little village wine and go back to the Roman cutting room. That is the type of trip we would like to do with you.

[298]

A big kiss to the children. Our congratulations to Bette for her part in *Golden Boy* (I always found it a classic).

To you our love,
Jean & Dido

PS. Alain will become a teacher of English at the University of Athens, Ohio.

1 Meaning 'are entirely ignorant of'.
2 Essoyes.
3 Pierre Renoir died on 11 March 1952.

To Robert Coryell [*Original in English*] 30 July 1952
Beverly Hills *Rome, Italy*

Dear Bob,

Thank you for your letter of 25 July. You know better than I do what is the best way for us to get a few pennies out of *The River*, so I rely entirely on you. I hope that Krim and the United Artists people will understand our position. Here enclosed the signed authorization for Lefkowitz and Berke.

I completed the cutting of *The Golden Coach* and am recording the music. It is a big job. As a matter of fact everything here is a big job. The producer is involved only with financial problems; all the production problems are for me. It's hard work but I like it because there is not even the idea of an interference. I believe I will have a two-track print of the film with a rough mixing in about two weeks; enough for a few previews. If those previews are satisfactory we will ask Technicolor to cut the negative. Meanwhile I would polish the sound. Technicolor being very busy they may only deliver the first standard colour print in November. I think we will go back home before that. They can send me the print for checking.

After reading your gloomy description of the state of affairs in Hollywood I decided to make a picture in France next spring. My agent in Paris is setting up a deal with a very safe producer.

Dido and I send our best to Bert, to you and to everybody around you.

Sincerely,
Jean Renoir

To Clifford Odets [*Original in English*]

2 *June 1952*
Rome, Italy

Dear Cliff,

We cannot stop thinking of poor Julie Garfield.[1] We loved him for this almost blind Americanism you mention, this real national quality which shows at its best in your plays and comes out from the pavements of New York; this quality at its best becomes universal, at its narrowest remains local but is always the necessary condition for great art. It is the same thing in Paris, or in Calcutta, or anywhere. Strangely enough, in any country, people who pretend to wave the flag of nationalism are unable to locate it. The same type of rootless academic paintings are praised by the same type of reactionaries as well in Russia as in the US.

We think of poor Julie as we would think of a beautiful tree broken down by one of the devastating hurricanes rather common in the new world. Fortunately those calamities of nature don't last, and after the tempest we look with more love at the familiar trees which managed to remain alive.

Dido is very well. We hope to leave for Paris around the 15th and be back in Rome at the end of the month. We wait anxiously for a short note telling us that you are in the middle of a writing spell and ready to give birth to a new play.

With all our love,
Jean and Dido

---

1 John Garfield (Julius Garfinkle) (1913–52), actor whose credits included *The Postman Always Rings Twice* (Tay Garnett, 1946), *Body and Soul* (Robert Rossen, 1947), and *Force of Evil* (Abraham Polonsky, 1948). He had recently died of a heart attack, which was said to have been brought on by his being blacklisted after refusing to denounce friends as Communists to the House Un-American Activities Committee.

To David Loew [*Original in English*]

1 *October 1952*
Panaria Films
Rome, Italy

Dear Dave,

[...] I am proceeding with the final mixing of my picture. The only good mixing place in Rome is Metro but it is free only at night. We go to bed around five o'clock every morning and Dido refuses flatly to go home without me. But the noisy Italian life starts at eight. We feel like a young couple burning the candle at both ends. The truth is we prefer a mixing room to a night club. Every reel done is one more step toward

[300]

home, and now we can think of the day when we are going to see you again.
Our love to Meta and you,
Jean Renoir

To Clifford Odets [*Original in English*]

5 *October* 1952
Panaria Films
Rome, Italy

Dear Cliff,

In spite of the difficult times you look wonderful on your picture. It gives us the certitude that you are going to create once more in your life something unexpected and delightful. Too bad you cannot base it on Chaplin. You know him better than he does. But I don't believe that after thirty-five years of film-making he can renounce the advantages of constructing his own comfortable screen situations. I am starting to be a little bit like that myself. It can be compared with the case of an old bachelor unable to sleep in a bed not made up by himself. I am afraid your only way is to find a young man and to invent your own 'Chaplin'. You discovered already so many actors. You are used to this kind of exercise.

I am still busy with the editing of my picture. My error was not to insist for hiring a good American cutter. My Italian producers were terrified of the expense and finally we took a young Englishman who had the advantage to live in Rome and to ask a salary only slightly above the Italian standards. But he has no experience, and practically I had to do everything myself with the help of my French assistant who fortunately talks English, and of an Italian girl cutter who doesn't. What I missed in *The Golden Coach* is an important American partner – writer or producer – somebody closely connected with the American public. A young actor, Lee Kresel, who is living in Rome helped me a great deal. As a matter of fact he was the only good English talking help I found. But it is his first work of the kind. Jack Kirkland was with me a couple of weeks in the beginning and disappeared like a meteor. You cannot do a film alone and I did this one in complete solitude. It's why I am afraid *The Golden Coach* won't be exactly an Anglo-American picture but the translation of a French picture in the Italian style.

The worst part of it is that during this cutting I had very little time to dedicate to the real problems of editing. Italians ignore[1] about entirely what is quality in sound. Fortunately during the picture I had my old French soundman who did a wonderful job on magnetic. But the transmission of this magnetic into photographic or into another magnetic track, which is no problem in America, here represents days of quarrels, fights, menaces, under the astonished eyes of the producers who cannot hear the difference between a good and a bad sound. For instance the electric current never being the same the recording machines never turn at the same speed and I had to re-record several pieces by Vivaldi which were passing through different pitches in a few seconds. Some Italian pictures are great because of the individuals. Rosselini [sic] or de Sica² do everything alone, and they gave up long ago about the technical quality of their products. Of course if I had to choose between Rome and Hollywood I would choose Rome. The highest standard in technique without liberty of creation means nothing.

We wish Bette will be happy with her psychiatrist but are quite sure that she will be very quickly bored to death. We hope to see you beginning of November.

With all our love,

Jean

1 Meaning 'knowing nothing'.
2 Vittorio de Sica (1902–74), important Italian director whose films included *Shoeshine* (1946), *Bicycle Thieves* (1948), and *Miracle in Milan* (1950).

1953

To Clifford Odets [*Original in English*]   *17 February 1953*
                                              Beverly Hills

Dear Clifford,

   Time is passing and very soon we will have the great joy of seeing you. We are enjoying our sojourn in California very much. The weather is gorgeous; our house very pleasant. Jeannot Slade is having a vacation and brings Gabrielle over very often, which is for us a wonderful thing.

   If we stop to examine the details of our lives, the situation is under control. But we feel in the air that something is wrong. Maybe it has to do with the appearance of this new madness of the moment, the third dimension. The few short contacts I've had with film people here, have terrified me. They are convinced that with a technical trick they are going to solve the problem. And of course this is a magnificent occasion to return to the same old stories and to reject anything different. I didn't try and I don't want to try. My feeling is that it is becoming more impossible than ever to make a good film in Hollywood.

   I saw one. I don't know whether you saw it. It is *High Noon.*[1] Columbia and UA had a big fight <u>not</u> to have this picture which today is a big money maker.

   We read in the papers that Chaplin wants to sell his house.[2] To me it is like a symbol. I cannot forget a certain date of the winter of 1915. I was then in a very exclusive French air squadron. One of our buddies was the son of the famous Professor Richet. He was just back from a furlough and his father had taken him to see a short film with Chaplin in it. Professor Richet had declared that it was great art. A few months later the whole of France thought the same way, and also the rest of the world. People like Elie Faure started to write about Charlie in books which included studies of Cézanne or Debussy. Partly because of this, the movies business graduated from the nickelodeon theatres to palaces and the public accepted to pay one dollar for a seat instead of a nickel. And yet today not one of the big bosses of the movie industry has the idea to cable him and to beg him to return to our town.

   Dido and I are very anxious to see you. That will be in about five or six weeks. We wish to find you in good shape and bursting with inspiration.

[303]

The art of films looks like it is disappearing so that more than ever we need good theatre.

With our love.

Sincerely,

Jean Renoir

1 *High Noon* (Fred Zinnemann, 1952).

2 Chaplin had been hounded by the House Un-American Activities Committee, slandered in the papers as being a Communist, and denounced for never having requested American citizenship. When he left the country for a vacation with his family, he was informed by American officials that he would not be let back into the United States. Chaplin settled with his family in Vevey, Switzerland, which would be his permanent residence until his death in 1977.

The Golden Coach *opens in the French version,* Le Carrosse d'Or, *in Paris on 27 February.*

To Amos Vogel[1] [*Original in English*]   *30 March 1953*
Cinema-16 Inc.   *Beverly Hills*
New York

Dear Amos,

I don't even know where Chaplin is living now. Last time I saw him in London he was determined to come back to the States. But recently I met a real estate girl who is in charge of selling his house.

I wouldn't dare to ask him anything which might result in any sort of publicity in the United States. It may be his policy to remain in the background for the time being. I am convinced that he could go through any investigation and that he would get his re-entry permit easily. He is certainly the victim of an unconsidered campaign and one day the American people will discover that there may be smoke without fire. But the issue is very delicate and I don't believe I have the right to attempt to influence him one way or the other.

Excuse me, dear Amos, for not being able to help you in these circumstances. I hope I will be luckier next time.

With my best wishes.

Sincerely,

Jean Renoir

1 Amos Vogel was the founder-director of *Cinema-16*, the most prestigious film society in the US.

To Ram Sen Gupta [*Original in English*]   *31 March 1953*
Calcutta   *Beverly Hills*

Dear Ram,

I'm terrified by the speed of the passing time. In your last letter you mentioned your niece Ratna and when I think of her I still imagine the little girl who danced so nicely the day Minu had decorated the floor of your house with rice flour to welcome us. Probably now Ratna is a big girl and the next time I go to India there is a possibility I might find her already married. She must be very happy not to be a child any more. When you are very young you believe that any added year is an advantage. I've arrived at the time when the days are too short. There are so many things I would like to do. I make so many unworkable plans and the time goes and goes, giving me the feeling of water you try to hold in your hand and it dribbles through your fingers. One of the things I want to do before it is too late is go back to India, and mostly to Calcutta. But how and when? I miss the feeling of your warm friendship.

[...] I am a little bit in the dark concerning my French picture. I must see the producer tomorrow. He came from Paris. The American film industry is very much disturbed by the unbelievable success of television and also by the arrival of several three dimensional systems.[1] I must say that television is very interesting. You can see many things – news, sports, listen to lectures and even attend films without leaving your house, and we cannot blame the public for deserting the movie theatres. The three-dimensional systems are of two sorts. One with coloured glasses which give you a perfect impression of depth. But the exhibitors think that the distribution of glasses to the audiences won't be easy and also that many people won't like to watch a film through glasses.

The other systems are more panoramic than three-dimensional. One – the Cinerama[2] – is a three camera system with three screens, giving the impression that you are in the middle of the projected landscapes. I don't believe this system will succeed because it's too expensive. Another system has just been adopted by the 20th Century-Fox and Metro. The film is shot with only one camera with a special lens added. The proportions of the screen are about three times the width of the present screen and one time the height. It is curved. The name is CinemaScope.[3] It was brought here by a French engineer named Chrétien.[4] It is not as impressive as Cinerama but it is more practical. Maybe it is the CinemaScope which will be finally adopted by everybody. The only thing I know is that these different changes are very bad for our profession. Studios are

[305]

almost idle. Myself I don't know what will happen to my French picture. The producers hesitate to start anything of importance before knowing which system is going to be the winner. I think the big studios can afford such experiments and as you know, I'm not working with the big studios. It is why I consider very seriously to switch to the writing of books or of stage plays.

You know how anxious I am to make another picture in India. But I don't want to do something which wouldn't bring a benefit. That's why before thinking of shooting in India I must know more about the future of the movie business and also about my own future.

[...] I don't give you any news about *The River*. We had the best possible reviews. Many people wrote and talked about this film and if we could live on glory that would be perfect. Not only the critics but the public loved the picture and the Indians who financed it should have obtained a handsome benefit by now. Unfortunately, our producers left something to be desired and I'm afraid Prince Limbdi and his friends and myself will never see one penny. This business is a very strange one and if I ever do a picture again in India I want to be sure to be represented in America by the proper people.

All our best thanks to your brother and to Tom and Ratna. Our love to Minu and you.

Sincerely,
Jean Renoir

1 The first studio-produced 3-D feature film released was *Bwana Devil* (Arch Oboler, 1952).
2 The first feature film released in Cinerama was *How The West Was Won* (several directors, 1962).
3 The first film released in CinemaScope in the U.S. was *The Robe* (Henry Koster, 1953).
4 Henri Chrétien (1879–1956), inventor of the anamorphic lens which was first displayed in 1927.

To Eliot Gibbons[1] [*Original in English*]   *1 April 1953*
                                                          Beverly Hills

Dear Eliot,

Dido and I had dinner with Irene last night. We met at the Sameks and went all together to have dinner at your Club. Of course we talked a great deal about you. With Dido I had hoped very much to see you in Rome. The time when the days will be more than twenty hours long is probably approaching for you. Alaska must be a strange place.

Hollywood is also a strange place. It seems that I came back just to witness the last gasps of a dying medium. You loved this medium as I did and its death must make you as sad as I am. Now we will have to tell stories through television, which is not so bad but completely different, or through some three-dimensional system which is even more different. Some producers believe in the old system with glasses. You certainly saw it – at least with stills. I even saw it myself with real people on the stage of the Olympia in Paris in 1913. There were two sources of light of different colours and the spectators wore glasses with a different colour in each lens. One of the numbers was a drunken man throwing a bottle in the direction of the audience. The bottle fell close to the footlights but all the women screamed believing that they had gotten the bottle right on their skulls. Many other numbers followed, all based on the throwing of objects or brandishing of weapons toward the terrified audience. The grand finale was a girl on a swing, with a very short skirt and the legs slightly open. When she swung over the footlights you can imagine the effect on the men.

Apparently we won't go back to those innocent entertainments, the exhibitors believing that their patrons will not accept the idea of glasses. And our new master will be the Cinerama or the CinemaScope, which is just a panoramic system, the first with three cameras, the second with one camera and a different lens. The screen, instead of being almost square, becomes very low, very wide and curved. It is the end of the close shot, the width of the new screen making it very difficult to avoid the other fellow. I saw a comedy scene[2] with Miss Monroe,[3] Miss Bacall[4] and Miss Grable[5] trying hopelessly to fill the width of the screen, walking uselessly, lying down on a chaise longue – very ill at ease. A documentary shot of the harbour of New York, with the skyline in the background, was very beautiful.

Bob Ryan, who is shooting a picture of this sort, tells me that the technicians have taken the situation entirely over. The Director is no longer allowed to say one word, the writer has to shut up, and the actors are considered as useless strangers. They all keep silent, watching the technicians fiddling with the lenses and sometimes looking at them impatiently as Einstein might if he had to lecture before an audience of Zeigfield [sic] Follies[6] girls.

I am supposed to go back to Paris within a few weeks and shoot a picture over there but with all these new developments I don't know what will happen. Dido and I thought of you each time we took an airplane and believe me that was very often. We would like very much to see you. Let's hope it will be very soon.

With our love,
Jean Renoir

1 Eliot Gibbons, screenwriter and husband of Irene Gibbons, known as 'Irene' (1902–62), Hollywood costume designer.

2 *How to Marry a Millionaire* (Jean Negulesco, 1953).

3 Marilyn Monroe (1926–62), actress whose credits included *All About Eve* (Joseph L. Mankiewicz, 1950), *Bus Stop* (Joshua Logan, 1956), and *The Misfits* (John Huston, 1961).

4 Lauren Bacall (b.1924), actress whose credits include *To Have and Have Not* (Howard Hawks, 1944), *Key Largo* (John Huston, 1948), and *Murder On the Orient Express* (Sydney Lumet, 1974).

5 Betty Grable (1916–73), actress whose credits included *Tin Pan Alley* (Walter Lang, 1940), *I Wake Up Screaming* (Bruce Humberstone, 1941), and *When My Baby Smiles At Me* (Walter Lang, 1948)

6 *The Ziegfeld Follies* was a famous New York revue which featured scantily-clad showgirls.

To Clifford Odets [*Original in English*]   *19 May 1953*
Beverly Hills

Dear Clifford,

We just returned from our mailbox which is down on Benedict Canyon. There we found an envelope with red ink. It was a great excitement for Dido and I. We rushed to the living room, sat down comfortably, and Dido read it aloud.

It's good to know that you are well, that you are writing a play about Noah,[1] and that the kids are in good shape. As for the girl friend that's something too easy to fix.

We should have seen you a month ago and be preparing a picture in Paris. Unfortunately the French producer wanted absolutely a deal with an American distributor. He didn't find it; and gave up.

I almost forgot my Magnani picture. The Italian producer, I believe, had arguments with the Italian distributors in USA; Burstyn who wanted the picture is apparently in trouble. The result is that the print of my film is hidden in a drawer somewhere in New York. Probably it will never be shown in America. I insisted several times to have this film shown to you not to impress you with a work which is probably merely an attempt to [do] something but because you are my friend and you have the patience to consider my products with kind eyes.

This commercial nonsense added to the fear of my new producer of three dimensions, wide screens, etc. seems to put me out of film business for this year; maybe for always. I feel such a stranger to the Hollywood industry that I don't see why they shouldn't feel strangers to me.

I started a few weeks ago what I should have started long ago. I gather notes for a book about my father. I do it now with Gabrielle. At the end of summer I'll go to France and pay a visit to the several spots where I used to live with my father.

I am also writing a stage-play and have an idea for another one.

I stay in touch with people who could vaguely bring me the possibility of shooting a film but wishing that they won't succeed and that I won't have to interrupt my new type of work.

Dido is very well. She works very hard in the garden and gets extraordinary results. The roses are gorgeous. We are surrounded by geraniums and all sort of plants. It makes me think of Zola's *La Faute de l'Abbé Mouret*. We don't see anybody. You are in New York, Dudley is out of town and Chaplin, as you know, is far away. Alain, his wife and our grandson are happy and busy in Athens, Ohio. Next year Alain will teach at Williams College.

Tell us where you will be in summer. We are terribly anxious to see you and to know more about Noah.

With all our love.

Sincerely,

Jean Renoir

1 *The Flowering Peach*.

To Bennett Cerf[1] [*Original in English*] 30 May 1953
Random House Inc. *Beverly Hills*
New York

Dear Mr Cerf,

I will be delighted to meet you in New York and tell you about my project of writing a book on my father. I may go East in the beginning of August or in October depending on a film assignment. For the time being I am merely gathering information from Gabrielle who is also living in Hollywood. I don't intend to present a new 'life' of Renoir. That was already done excellently by several good authors; nor a technical or 'artistic' explanation of the painter's work. In this last field nobody can beat Barnes.[2]

I would like to attempt to give form to my own recollections of the conversations I had with my father mostly at the end of his life. I won't quote the exact dialogue which I don't remember, but try to give an idea of my past impressions of such meetings and of the way they influence me today.

Those conversations were about anything: his past experiences, his childhood, our family, his friends, his admirations, and also very much about his suspicions regarding the fast changes of our modern world.

I intend to visit again the different spots in France where I went with my father when I was young. Maybe I will take some photographs of different houses where we used to live and of landscapes which inspired him.

I am looking forward to the pleasure of meeting you.

Sincerely,

Jean Renoir

1 Bennett Cerf (1898–1971), publisher, founder of *The Modern Library* series and a television personality on the popular panel show *What's My Line?* from 1952 to 1966.
2 Albert Barnes, founder of the Barnes Foundation in Philadelphia, which houses a large collection of Impressionist work.

To Clifford Odets [*Original in English*]   *9 August 1953*
New York   *Beverly Hills*

Dear Clifford,

How is Noah? Dido and I should be acquainted with your interpretations of this biblical drunkard since ages. The spring disappeared and summer nearly reaches its end. Our trip to Europe with a stop in New York was always for next week. Then the hope of shooting a film in France vanished. I wrote a kind of experimental stage play, *Calla Lilies*. I did it to acquire a very necessary stage discipline: one set, five characters. I missed the twenty-four hours.

Your Noah, lucky offspring of your enthusiasm, must be grown up by now. We have a good chance to hear you talk of him before the New York papers start to rave about 'fall's golden leaves in New England'. The practical reason for our trip this time will be Ibsen's *Lady from the Sea*¹ to be filmed in Norway: midnight sun, whale fishing, reindeer roundups, aurora borealis; and the exciting perspective of a few hours with you in New York. Your 'spring' letter makes us expect many developments in your life. We are anxious to know about them and wish you as much happiness as nature allows to a sensitive creator.

With all our love,

Jean Renoir

1 Unrealized project.

To Jean Dewalde   *21 September 1953*

Dear Jean,

I merely want to add a few words to my last letter and inform you of a project which has taken shape these last few days. It has occurred to me that I would like to do a biography of Van Gogh.[1] I would like to shoot the film in France on locations where Van Gogh lived and painted. I already have an agreement with the actor Van Heflin who looks a lot like Van Gogh. I would like the film to be done on a small budget but without so-called commercial compromises.

Van Heflin's salary would be deferred. He and I could make our profit from the English version. He could also do the French version in spite of the fact that he doesn't speak French, because there won't be much dialogue in the film.

This project is triggering quite a bit of excitement around here. Metro had already thought about it, but had given up. In order to work without interference I am set on doing this without an American studio. I am sure a French producer could be interested in this. I am asking you to think about it, and send me your thoughts as soon as possible. Unless there are some problems that escape me, you might inform the press. It would give us some kind of priority on a subject matter I am probably not the only one to think about.

Looking forward to seeing you again soon.

Warmest regards,

Jean Renoir

PS. Maybe you will notice the contradictions between my previous letter and this one with regard to 'English versions'. I am very much in favour of an English version of *Van Gogh*, because it is a film with a special character and a strong enough subject matter to allow me to make no concessions to a distributor.

---

1 Vincent Van Gogh (1853–90). The first major biopic was *Lust for Life* (Vincente Minnelli, 1956), starring Kirk Douglas as Van Gogh.

To Van Heflin [*Original in English*]   30 *November 1953*
Los Angeles   *Paris*

Dear Van,

I received your nice letter and I am happy to answer with some good news. As you know I had been impressed by the fact that several other companies wanted to do *Van Gogh* and argued about a certain moral right for having started the preparation before me. After consulting experts in such matters, among them a very well-known lawyer named Rappoport, I am entirely convinced that we must just go ahead without hesitation. I am going to put some order in my notes concerning the treatment and ask a specialist to establish an estimate based on this treatment. I hope to be able to send this work to Willis[1] in a very near future. Of course as soon as I have the treatment I'll send it to you. I found wonderful material here, much better than *Lust for Life*.

The ideal combination is to shoot it with Radford and a French producer. If Radford can bring a big participation the French producer would be of no importance but very necessary for our relations with the French Government including financial help. We should nevertheless stick to the United Artists release.

Van, it is wonderful to have a friend like you and I am so happy to think that we are going to attempt something really great together. A big kiss to the girls and the wife. Dido sends her best wishes to the whole family.

Sincerely,
Jean Renoir

1 Willis Goldbeck (1900–69), screenwriter, *Freaks* (Tod Browning, 1932), *The Man Who Shot Liberty Valance* (John Ford, 1962); and director of many of the *Dr Kildare* series of 'B' pictures in the 1940s.

To Albert Lewin [*Original in English*]   9 *December 1953*
                                                        Paris

Dear Al,

I received the book *Un Roi Tout Nu*[1] but I didn't do very much about it for two reasons, first I am involved with such a complicated situation concerning *Van Gogh* that I found very little time for anything else; also the different producers I met here didn't seem to be interested in my French-American project.

[312]

As I told you I had a meeting with the boss of the Centre Cinématogra-phique (he is the new one). He confirmed my impression that the French producers are, for the time being, interested only in the European market. It is easy to settle a French-Italian or French-Spanish or French-German combination. It seems almost impossible to get anybody interested in the English version of a French film unless the cost of this English version is paid by an English or an American group.

All of a sudden, a few days ago, while I was discussing *Van Gogh* with a very smart agent named André Bernheim I learned something new and very important had happened. Bernheim and Feldman signed an agree-ment for their agent business and they intend to promote French-American films. The French producer who will finance and release the films in Europe is Loureau. He is the most important one here, recently he was very successful with Clouzot's *Le Salaire de la Peur*,[2] Duvivier's *Don Camillo*[3] and some of the best late French films. He is also the best distributor in France and in several other European countries. I am wondering whether the Lourau-Feldman group is not what you need for your *Un Roi Tout Nu*.

Of course that would mean going through Feldman or Bernheim. If you are not against it I could tell them about your project. Please drop me a note quickly. Feldman will be in Paris for one or two more weeks. If I miss him, and if you are interested, you could see him in the States.

That is the only sound issue I have to suggest. Forgive me if it took so much time to come. I must confess that during this first month here I was very much bewildered by a very confused situation.

Give us more news about *Saadia*,[4] the previews, and your hopes. Dido and I love your picture and are convinced that it is strong enough, even with stupid cuts, to have great success.

Millie is probably delighted to be in New York, both of you must at last enjoy quietly your beautiful apartment. We wish you will give birth to *Un Roi Tout Nu* here in Paris, that would be a wonderful occasion to be together again.

Tonight we have dinner with Man Ray.

With our love.

Sincerely,

Jean Renoir

1 *Un Roi Tout Nu* – novel by Albert Ades.
2 *Le Salaire de la Peur (The Wages of Fear)* (Henri-Georges Clouzot, 1952).
3 *Le Petit Monde de Don Camillo (The Little World of Don Camillo)* (Julien Duvivier, 1951).
4 *Saadia* (Albert Lewin, 1953).

1954

To Dudley Nichols [*Original in English*]   *12 January 1954*
Los Angeles   *Paris*

Dear Dudley,

Just a few words to ask you (once more) to help me. Bessie sent me a circular of the SWG,[1] dated January 4, concerning the future publication by Calstate of a list of persons named within the reports of the California Legislative Committee of Un-American Activities.[2]

Apparently I was named, and probably my 'activity' is the article I wrote about Chaplin's *Monsieur Verdoux* in *The Screen Writers Magazine* in 1947. This 'publicity' cannot harm me practically. I am not seeking a job in Hollywood. But I dislike to be mixed up with a bunch of American Communists which I always tried to avoid, and who profess philosophical ideas exactly opposite to mine.

What do you advise me to do? Should I write to Senator Hugh M. Burns as suggested or should I drop the whole thing?

Thank you in advance. Dido and I send you and Esta our love.

Jean Renoir

1 Screen Writers Guild.
2 A state-run version of the House Un-American Activities Committee. It is curious that Jean Renoir thought his only suspicious 'activity' was this article written about Chaplin. It is even more surprising that, with the FBI's meticulous scrutiny into the backgrounds of those in the entertainment business, Renoir's left-wing activities in the 1930s were never discovered, an 'offence' which could easily have led to his deportation or being blacklisted.

The Golden Coach, in the English version favoured by Jean Renoir, opens in New York on 21 January.

To Albert Lewin [*Original in English*]

Dear Al,

It was really nice of you to have seen *The Golden Coach* and then to have sent us the cable, the letter, and the reviews. This act of friendship made us extremely happy not only because it gave us precious informations, but also because it brought us closer to you. Thank you for being such friends.

I am still working on my play. It is more difficult than I expected. I rewrote it twice entirely. Before the end of the week I hope to have it in sufficient shape and I will attempt a reading to a group of three or four friends.

Very often we go to the little restaurant rue Condorcet across Metro and we see a big poster of *Saadia*. It means it will be shown very soon dubbed in French. We are anxious to see the result of this naturalization. We are terribly upset about the suppression of the essential sequence of the beginning. Could you tell us how were the reactions during the presentation tour?

Film people are all the same. In *The Golden Coach* I worked very hard to give it a rhythm and to introduce not only Magnani's character but Magnani's accent to an English talking audience. With some very bad cuts, which I only learned about now, they jeopardized this attempt. Strangely enough they didn't cut those shots in Italy nor in France where Anna has not to be introduced. The distributors and producers refuse to recognize the notion of authorship in film-making and that is our trouble.

We are happy to know that your new screenplay is progressing to your satisfaction. Concerning the production of *A Naked King*[1] in France by the group Loureau-Feldman-Bernheim, I am its worst defender because the same group is also interested in the production of a *Van Gogh* and are obviously avoiding me. Did you see Feldman in America?

I asked a certain Mr Gergély, a sort of agent, to talk to a friend of his, a French producer named Barr, who could be interested by the production of an English talking picture in France.

I also had a meeting with Mr Flaud, the head of the official film centre. He says the general trend in France is now toward French-Italian, French-Spanish, or French-German combinations. They exaggerate here the difficulties of the film business in the US and believe more in European markets. I must see him again for some other questions and will ask him whether, besides Barr, he could suggest the name of a producer.

Paris is freezing but extremely gay. Dido is typing this letter and for a while we imagine to be together with you. Let us hope very soon it will be reality and not imagination.

    With all our love to Millie and you,

    Jean Renoir

1 *Un Roi Tout Nu.*

To Van Heflin [*Original in English*]   *12 February 1954*
Los Angeles   *Paris*

Dear Van,

    The last time I saw Dowling in New York in October we talked a great deal about our *Van Gogh* project. He didn't say that he was interested. A month before, in Hollywood, I had seen him with Fefe Ferry and asked him whether he could help us in the producing of the picture. He was very vague and I understood, maybe wrongly, that he could have considered the production of this film only if the budget had been kept very low. After some other attempts with different producers, and after receiving the last letter from Willis I am now convinced that we must give up, at least for this year, our project of a film about Van Gogh. Time is passing, spring will arrive in a few weeks, and nothing is settled. I postponed the writing of such a pessimistic statement to you because this project was so dear to my heart. But I have no right to ask you to keep your time free for nothing, and what I have in front of me now is exactly nothing.

    You know the reasons of this failure. Willis Goldbeck who is the most courageous partner and who tried every American possibility can explain them to you better than I can. Obviously it is dangerous to go ahead without the Metro Goldwyn situation being cleared. That would mean a big amount of money added to the budget. This extra expense may be understandable in a high budget picture where $150,000 of difference doesn't mean very much. A high-budget picture is now as expensive in France as it is in America. Apparently American finance people are not ready to take such a risk. On the other hand French or European finance people are not interested in the present American market. Several of them asked me to shoot *Van Gogh* in French with a French producer, a French star and dubbed German and Italian versions.

    I started the *Van Gogh* adventure with you, Fefe Ferry, Lagache, Willis Goldbeck. A French film would mean for me to have to reconstruct the whole thing with different partners. I cannot do it. I got used to a Vincent looking, walking, acting, like Van Heflin. I cannot conceive another Van Gogh and I prefer to give up.

I will send a copy of this letter to Willis. I wish you and I will find a way to go back to our original idea which was: the hell with the studios, the distributors, etc. Let's make pictures with a little bit of film, a few technicians and electricians and our talent, as we would write a book. I don't know when that will be possible but let's try to make it possible. What I know is that it cannot be done with over $100,000 already spent foolishly by a major company on screenplays and projects.

Dido and I miss you and Frances[1] very much. We hope the nice offsprings [sic] are in good shape. I am just finishing a stage-play in French. I don't know whether I should make a French picture. I would like very much to start to take notes for the book about my father. We are still living in my old apartment in Montmartre, crumbling, dilapidated, rather charming. Give me some news of your health, hopes, activities.

With our best wishes.

Sincerely,

Jean Renoir

1 Frances Heflin, wife of Van.

From Dudley Nichols [*Original in English*]   *14 February 1954*
Paris   *Los Angeles*

Dear Jean and Dido,

You have been in my thoughts and my conscience has been shrieking at me, but it was no use, I just couldn't write a line, I don't think I have written so much as a note since Xmas, I have simply been sweating over a script at MGM and getting nowhere, and I'd get home at the end of the day, have a drink, flop into a chair, eat and go to bed, hoping for a better tomorrow which hasn't come. I really think I can no longer write for the studios and I must get back to my own work and sink or swim with it. And the misery of trying to do the sort of thing they want isn't worth the reward. I have just grown out of it, I guess. I cannot work on things that go nowhere and have no meaning to the inner me. Forgive my starting this note with a lament. Your letter asking about the fascist insanity should have been replied to at once. I hope you did not write a damn word to that committee. I received the same sort of letter, I daresay every member of the SWG did, and I got so mad I wrote the SWG they ought to be ashamed of themselves, suggesting people crawl before these committees, that I had nothing I was ashamed of or regretted, and that their business was to have some backbone and find out what legal redress the SWG would have if those bastards published for profit what was privileged material under congressional imprint. The man who headed that California committee at the time was an ex-radical named Tenney, a fascist bastard if there ever was one, an anti-Semite, friend of Gerald Smith etc., I believe he even included the SWG on his 'subversive list'. We are in strange times over here, Jean. The irony is that the true liberal here has become the conservative, almost the reactionary in the American sense, for he wants to conserve what Washington, Jefferson and Lincoln, along with the other American forefathers, struggled for if you will; and a new breed of 'Americans', who are anti-American and subversive, are calling themselves the true Americans and everyone else 'anti-American' and 'subversive'. I don't like the way things are going. Was there ever a 'safer, sounder' man than Gov Warren,[1] and now some of our Senators are demanding an FBI[2] report on him and refusing to approve his nomination as chief justice of the Supreme Court. It is hard to believe such a time would come. No one is immune to attack. And these smug, foolish little heads of film companies sit around and play along with the fascists who are out to eliminate every free, liberal, independent-minded man in the film world. Can no one remember what happened in Germany? Our President is a respected man, but so was President von Hindenburg[3] – who went along with Hitler. I remember something from Santayana:[4] 'those who cannot remember the tragedies of the past are doomed to repeat them' . . . Studio life is very sad. Men fearful to open their mouths. Conversation is all trivia. I believe Nero was a film writer and that he *did* fiddle while Rome burned, but he fiddled very badly. I am a little ill with it all. No doubt because I love my country and its great liberal tradition so deeply . . . Well, I shall not concur with the men who are out to wreck it, never! Of course I keep believing we are not hearing from the best people and that the good American core cannot be destroyed. We may see a swing when things get worse and the real voice of America, growing a little wrathful, is heard.

Stevenson[5] is a man of great sense and character, and I believe is a conservative in the American sense I speak of. Civilization, I suppose, is the gradual process of the highest individual conscience working on the mass of men and getting them to strive to express the good within them

[318]

and reject and overcome the evil. But the evil is always there in the collective unconscious, in the individual's collective unconscious as in the mass unconscious, and there are certain voices that can woo it all out again and give it power over the good that is always struggling to be born and show itself. The Hitlers are the brilliant brute voices conjuring forth all this hate, fear and savagery which civilized men have striven to put down in the dungeon. The powerful 'haves' who fear the collectively powerful 'have nots' are always ready to use these conjuring voices of the devil, and they always think they can remain the master, though of course they cannot. They don't know what immense savage forces they play with, the forces of nihilism and destruction.

But I must not depress you just because I am depressed. A sort of paralysis lies on my spirit lately. I think I can only free myself by getting back to work on my own and writing about it.

[...] I wish we were with you in Paris. I could perhaps for a while forget the things that make life painful. I am going to work another week on this damn script, and if nothing comes of it I am going to throw it over – *sans* pay – it doesn't matter. I think the era of film-making is over in Hollywood. Now it is a sort of circus business. Who can make a bigger noise or swing on a higher trapeze.

You had wonderful reviews of *The Golden Coach* and I meant to send them to you, but I was just too paralysed to manage it or even cut them out. Forgive me. I tried – useless. But it gave me joy to see how you are praised and respected as an artist in this perverse film world. You will have had some of the reviews I know, especially *Time* magazine. They carry your film at the top of their preferred list now. Even *The New Yorker* grudgingly unbent – and you know their business is to hate all films. Well, you cannot make a bad film! No matter what happens or what obstacles you meet, it is always your own film, individual, or your own blood and spirit and absolute honesty. That is a great thing in this day, Jean – it is something almost nineteenth-century, more rightly of the Renaissance. You, Chaplin and maybe a couple of others will be the 'last of the great film-makers'. Lord bless Chaplin. Now he is gone, you can see more vividly how his presence stimulated Hollywood in the art of film-making. Everyone unconsciously wore a bit of his artistic glory, and now they look rather foolishly naked. Not that they know it yet. Charlie had neither political interest nor political activity, he was too much of an artist for that. His concern was with artistic truth, and what he was hated for (by fools) was that he remained a free, creative, independent-minded *individual* – and they did not. Ah, well – why talk about it. There is something mortuary about the great studios here now, there is no laughter and people speak softly and a little fearfully, as in a house of the dead ... Yet death cannot conquer life for ever – life will always break out in another place. Yet one's life is so fleeting, one cannot live in eternity with the comfort of the vast historical view. Perhaps scholars can, artists cannot: they live in time and only try to meet the obligations of eternity.

I must cut off this elegy. I am going for a walk with Esta and we shall feel better – or I'll have a drink – it's Sunday and the rain seems to be over and the sun glitters suddenly and the wind blows and everything outside my window is gold and green. I should take heart from Rosie's little canary. One died, but the blind one remains. He lives in absolute darkness but has learned to peck his seeds from the cage floor, to measure his confines, leap to a perch, find his water, be quick and alive and interested; and in broad daylight he will suddenly tuck his head under his wing and sleep, for it's always night in that cage. A brave little fluff of feathers, and Rosie (and all of us) love him for the will to live, without moping.

Forgive my silence, we embrace you both.

[Dudley Nichols]

1 Earl Warren (1896–1974), former Governor of California who served as a Supreme Court Justice. He is best known for heading the 'Warren Commission', which investigated the assassination of President John F. Kennedy.
2 Federal Bureau of Investigations, headed by the notorious J. Edgar Hoover.
3 Paul Von Hindenburg (1847–1934), former President of Germany who relinquished his powers to Adolf Hitler.
4 George Santayana (1863–1952), writer and critic.
5 Adlai Stevenson (1900–1965), former Governor of Illinois and UN Ambassador under the Kennedy administration.

To David Loew [*Original in English*]   24 *February* 1954
Paris

Dear Dave,

If you and Meta decide on a trip to Europe you will certainly find us here.

I abandoned my *Van Gogh* project because of the Metro situation (as you know they own *Lust for Life*).[1] I am still rewriting my French stage-play and I am thinking of an original story to replace *Van Gogh* and to be shot here in summer. And I don't want to go back to the States without having gathered the notes, information, recollections, which could help me with the book about my father.

The other day Dido and I took a little walk around the Sacré Coeur.

From the street downhill, this monument, which in itself has not architectural value, was extremely charming. In front of it there is a green slope with many little paths where children of the district like to play. Against this green background, which with the perspective looked almost vertical, crowds were walking in lines. Every little figure was very precise. Some red balloons were added just for contrast. With Dido we couldn't help thinking of you. When you come we would like to take you there a Sunday afternoon. Perhaps it will be an inspiration for you.

We are still involved with McEldowney's 'fantasies'. Now he wants to make me responsible for the high cost of *The River*. Ackerman, at Morris-Allenberg Agency, is looking after my interests. I took the liberty to tell him that if he needs an advice before starting legal action he may phone you. Thank you in advance.

We are also expecting a grandchild in May. Isn't it an amusing coincidence?

All our best wishes to the whole family without forgetting the newly-weds.

With our love.

Sincerely,

Jean

1 *Lust for Life*, Irving Stone's 1934 biography of Van Gogh.

To Jean Renoir [*Original in English*]　　　　　*9 March 1954*

Dear Ones,

I was lonely enough not knowing your address in Europe, but when [on] 22 February (have you had this news?) Bette died in the hospital of severe pneumonia, I was very lonely indeed not to be able to write to you both. I sent the Chaplins (have you seen them yet?) a cable immediately, but you two I did not know where to find and it was part of the deep hurt and shock and daze of that week.

The worse thing was to have to tell Nora and Walt[1] – I thought I would faint and my body and arms felt to be made of soft dough with iron nails in them. But the children took it very well and just now seem (<u>seem</u>, I say) just as before. A big help is myself, of course, for I moved right into the old apartment and stayed with them so constantly that actually I must have become a nuisance to them. Also we have Helen, the old nurse back: they love her.

26 Jean Renoir walking in the avenue Frochot, the private road in Montmartre
where his Paris apartment was located

If there is more news it will be sent to you when I've heard from you that both of you are well and happily and fulsomely at work. (Finally I got this address of yours by writing to your Miss Smith in California. Once before, after Xmas, I addressed you to Paris 'c/o Claude Renoir' but that letter returned).

This week I return to work and hope to have two plays on Broadway next season, *The Flowering Peach* and *The Seasons*.

What else shall I write? I feel purged, empty. Poor Bette was about to make a very good marriage in the week of her death. As it always is, I can't believe the poor dear tender girl is gone. But, of course, gone she is. She was thirty-three and on the threshold of life. Too much death have I seen this past year. It blurs my eyes and is not something I take easily. But who does?

And so here, on a bright March morning I sit, listening (very much alive) to Bellini's *I Puritani*, so naive and melodic and lovely.

I love you both dearly and want to have a few words from you soon.

Many kisses

Clifford

1 Nora and Walter Odets, children of Clifford and Bette.

To Clifford Odets [*Original in English*]   *13 March 1954*

Dear Cliff,

We cannot imagine that we won't see any more this sweet girl – unfitted for modern life. Almost an anachronism in a big town, making elevators, streetcars, neon lights look indecent – born to be Nausicaa and chatter with the King's servants around the well, with Mount Olympus in the background. The last time we saw her was in a taxicab. In my memories this banal background – cheap set-up – disappears replaced by an olive tree and the broken column of an ancient temple.

With our love,

Jean & Dido

To Van Heflin [*Original in English*]   *29 March 1954*
Los Angeles   *Paris*

Dear Van,

Back from Switzerland I find your letter. It is wonderful to think that all the difficulties haven't diminished your enthusiasm. I also am still dreaming of this Van Gogh picture and cannot see it without you. What you say about Stone is very encouraging. An understanding with him would be for us a magnificent opportunity. Besides, after working on the subject, I realize his book is a good bridge between the art of Van Gogh and the public. A collaboration with him would solve many of our problems.

I finished the writing of my French play *Orvet*.[1] I am not absolutely satisfied, probably I was too much preoccupied by Van Gogh while writing it.

Now I am going to try to do a picture here. I don't know which one, I have several ideas. That will bring my return to the States close to the date when Irving Stone will be free with his Van Gogh and will have to take decisions.

Shane[2] was shown everywhere in Paris and the French public is very impressed by your performance.

In Switzerland we saw Chaplin who is working hard and hopes to do a picture in England. His children talk French with a Swiss accent.

Dido and I hope that Frances and the children are well and that you are happy with your work. We miss you and we also miss California but I think I needed this contact with the Old World in order to refresh my imagination.

Our love to all of you,
Jean Renoir

1 *Orvet* was originally a character in a screenplay written by Jean Renoir with Dudley Nichols called *Les Braconniers* (*The Poachers*). The character Orvet is a young girl who lives among the people of the Burgundy forest.
2 *Shane* (George Stevens, 1953).

To Van Heflin [*Original in English*]   *3 May 1954*
Los Angeles   *Paris*

Dear Van,

I just received your letter and answer it immediately to advise you not to miss *Van Gogh* with Clement.[1] He is a wonderful director, the best in

France among the younger generation; and I must insist on the fact that I don't see any consistent hope for myself to do *Van Gogh*, in English.[2]

That is the main thing I wanted to tell you.

As for the rest, I am very happy with Dido in Paris. Our sojourn in this old district gave me a bit of inspiration for a story, and I am probably going to make a film with it. I am also going to direct a stage show of Shakespeare's *Julius Caeser* [sic] in the Roman arenas of Arles. The 10 July is supposed to be the two thousandth anniversary of the foundation of the city by Caeser [sic].

Maybe *Van Gogh* will bring you to this part of the world and we will see you, and Frances, and the kids. That would be great.

Our best wishes to all of you.

Sincerely,

Jean Renoir

1 René Clement (b.1913), director whose credits include *La Bataille du Rail* (1946), *Jeux Interdit* (1952), and *Is Paris Burning?* (1966).
2 Van Heflin never made *Van Gogh*.

To David Loew [*Original in English*] 13 *June 1954* *Paris*

Dear Dave,

Dido and I had been very much impressed by a wire of Bob Coryell explaining that he had reached a kind of understanding with McEldowney who will give his OK to the payment of my deferred salary by United Artists if I reimburse him the cost of Radha's trip. I agreed knowing that it is just a way to put a couple of thousand dollars in his pocket, and I sent a cable of congratulations to Bob. After reading your wonderful letter, which we just received, I realize that I owe these congratulations to you. I don't know how to thank you. What a letter! You managed to be perfectly insulting, to let the man know how much you despise him; without being ever vulgar and without putting yourself in a wrong position. Mr Foster Dulles[1] should take some lessons of diplomacy with you.

I am living with Julius Caeser [sic]. He is not a bad companion and teaches me many good tricks which will help in the stage-plays I dream to write. What terrifies me is that my players still don't know one word of the dialogue. In a film, when they stumble over a difficult word, you just say 'cut' and you start the scene again. In the arenas of Arles, in front of

20,000 people, I would be probably unwelcome to apply this method.

I finished a treatment for the first film I am going to shoot here. It may be amusing.

I am no more with William Morris. I signed for three years with the agents who brought me two pictures here. That puts me, in the States, with their American associates, MCA.

Did you find new material for your paintings? If not are you going to come here and gather some new impressions?

How are Meta and Virginia and the other kids and grandkids? We miss you.

Our love to you all,

Jean Renoir

1 Foster Dulles was Secretary of State under the Eisenhower administration.

On 10 July, to mark the 2,000th anniversary of the city of Arles, Jean Renoir directs Shakespeare's Julius Caesar. *The play is performed for one night only in the Roman arena to an audience of 8,000 people. The cast includes Paul Meurisse and Jean-Pierre Aumont.*

To Leslie Caron[1]
Los Angeles

19 July 1954
Paris

Dear Leslie,

My producer, Mr Deutchmeister[sic],[2] cannot wait [any longer] for you to start *French Cancan*. He has offered to make another film with you later. I will try to come up with a story befitting the talent of our dear little Leslie. Françoise Arnoul[3] will play the part I had written entirely for you. I am lucky. She is not Leslie Caron, but she is a very skilful actress. It saddens me that I won't be working with you, but this little mishap will prompt me to find a story even more beautiful and noble, on which I hope we work together soon.

I have no clues as to the mysterious disappearance of the two manuscripts of *Orvet*. Perhaps they never arrived or perhaps, since they were sent registered, the mailman did not find you at the hotel and they are sitting in some nearby post office. Fate has been against us here as well. Since we had not heard from you, Blanche Montel my agent (and yours, indirectly) has begun investigating the possibilities of getting the play performed on stage in Paris, and I don't know what will happen. If you find these manuscripts, only read the one numbered seven. The other one is almost certainly full of gross mistakes that would embarrass me if you read it. Afterwards, would you be kind enough to have them delivered to my home address: 1273 Leona Drive, Beverly Hills? If you call your agents, who are now also mine, they will send a messenger. Very few people have read *Orvet*, maybe four or five. Reactions have been quite positive. Blanche Montel is very hopeful and advises me not to give it to anybody else to read.

I am very happy to hear that you are starting *Daddy Long Legs*.[4] I remember the film with Mary Pickford.[5] It is a good part for you, a good story. Afterwards you'll be right where you deserve to be. You'll be a big star.

Dido, who is writing this letter with me, has just come out of the hospital where she underwent surgery to the abdomen. It all went as well as can be expected. She is obviously tired but well enough to start pottering around the apartment.

We think about you a lot, and are happy to see you are so busy. Maybe this will help you forget your personal difficulties in some ways.

Dido and I send our fond love.

Jean Renoir

1 Leslie Caron (b.1931), dancer and actress whose credits include *An American in Paris* (Vincente Minnelli, 1951), *Gigi* (Vincente Minnelli, 1958), and *Damage* (Louis Malle, 1992).
2 Henri Deutschmeister, French producer responsible for such 'quality' films in the post-war period as *Madame de . . .* (Max Ophuls, 1953), *French Cancan, Eléna et les Hommes*, and *La Traversée de Paris* (Claude Autant-Lara, 1956).
3 Françoise Arnoul (b.1931), actress whose credits include *French Cancan, Napoleon* (Sacha Guitry, 1955), and *Le Petit Théâtre de Jean Renoir* (1969).
4 *Daddy Long Legs* (Jean Negulesco, 1955).
5 Mary Pickford (1892–1979), silent film actress, whose credits included *Little Annie Rooney* (William Beaudine, 1925) and *Taming of the Shrew* (Sam Taylor, 1929).

From 4 October to 20 December, Jean Renoir films French Cancan *in Paris. He also works on revisions of his play* Orvet.

To Jean Renoir

Dear Sir,

I am so happy the opportunity has arisen for me to work with you. I find the play fascinating, the characters appealing – it radiates warmth, simplicity and charm, and I'm sure that *Orvet* will have a great artistic impact.

Orvet herself is a very sweet character – I really like her from the start – she is wild, honest and direct with a lot of heart – I like the slang she's given to speak, it's very poetic.

Robert told me that you will make some changes for me, and so here's what I have in mind – see if it suits you. In the second act I would like to take an active part in the departure scene – I feel Orvet is a bit lost among all these characters from her childhood – perhaps by announcing to her father she's said goodbye to her friends and by making the scene principally between Orvet (as much as Olivier) and Georges; a scene in which she hesitates, in which she declares her heartbreak over the idea of leaving the forest, her friends, and then finally chooses to follow Olivier.

Also at the end of the third act I feel Orvet's dilemma is swamped by the other characters and their own dilemmas. Orvet and Olivier could find themselves again by overcoming the obstacles Georges imposes on them. To tell the truth, I find myself a little neglected at the end, and I wonder if it wouldn't be possible for me to play a more active part at the close of the play.

See if it's possible for you to make these changes without losing the dramatic line that you've created for yourself.

I believe I can confirm that I'll be free after 20 January. I know that doesn't give much time for rehearsal, but my film will hold me up till then.

I anxiously await your reply. I want you to know I'm bubbling over with excitement to go on stage – I'm beginning work [on the play] between scenes on the set.[1]

Love to you and Dido,

Leslie Caron

1 The set of *Daddy Long Legs*.

To Leslie Caron   *12 December 1954*
Los Angeles   *Paris*

Dear Leslie,

I have finished shooting the *real* scenes of my picture. I only have three days on location left, with many extras and some close-ups of important but episodic characters. The difficulties are behind me now and I am going to be able to dedicate my time almost entirely to *Orvet*. Starting the middle of next week, I'll only spend mornings working on *French Can-can*, in the editing room. By then you will have arrived and we shall have the small dinner you had promised Dido and me.

I fully agree with you that Orvet should play a more active part in the outcome of the play. I am not quite sure yet, but I think the changes I will make in Georges' part will provide some additional vitamins to our young heroine. Here are the changes:

The drama of Orvet is the same as Pygmalion, complicated by the fact that Galatea-Orvet also exists in real life. Instead of loving a statue Pygmalion-Georges is in love with an idea, a character obviously inspired by a real live girl, who nevertheless is his own creation. I need an obstacle between Georges and Orvet; otherwise there won't be any story, Orvet and Georges would love each other and all would be said. The obstacle I had imagined in the version you read was the age difference. Several decades stood between the old Georges and the young Orvet. The obstacle I am considering now is Puritanism. Georges is not older any more, and his relationship with Orvet is humanly acceptable. However, he is a puritan, and he is afraid of what would be said about him if it was known he is involved with a young beggar, despised by all, daughter of an ignoble father, and whose sisters shame the town. That is why he is so nice to Orvet when he meets her in the woods, but prefers not to see her enter his house.

Writing this play is a form of release for him. He hopes that by creating Orvet as a stage character, he will purge his love for her. Unfortunately, this love will turn into a burning passion, and when he realizes that the character he has created and loves so much prefers Olivier (whom he has also created), he will decide to erase their existence by tearing up his play. Fortunately, the real Orvet, the one from the woods, is real and the short final scene will make us understand that Georges' love will win over his prejudices.

In Georges' case we are dealing a little with a Dr Jekyll and Mr Hide [sic]. Instead of doing what he doesn't dare to do under Mr Hide's (sic]

[329]

different appearance, Georges surrenders to his passion in the imagination. It is his craft as a writer which is his Mr Hide [sic].

This explanation must seem quite stern for a story which is supposed
to be funny and poetic. It's because I still have one foot in my film and
need to refamiliarize myself with our play. Don't be afraid, it will
happen. I wrote *Orvet* thinking of you. Thinking of you and your
presence will be the magic wand that will make my ideas blossom.

Dido and send all our love,
Jean Renoir

1955

Orvet opens on 12 March at the Théâtre de la Renaissance in Paris, with Leslie Caron and Paul Meurisse in the lead roles. Despite mixed reviews, the play runs for 400 performances.

To Clifford Odets [*Original in English*]   *21 April 1955*
New York   *Paris*

Dear Clifford,

It seems years since we have heard from you. We miss your letters. How are you and the kids? It is wonderful all we read about *Country Girl*. It will open in Paris soon. We are leaving for Brittany tomorrow and will only see it upon our return at the end of the month. We have a hectic last day in Paris so I will write and give you all the news later. This little note in haste [is] to ask you whether you would be interested in an attempt to produce *The Big Knife* in Paris. Jean feels it might go over well here. If you have no commitments could you send us the play; we could have it roughly translated; and if a theatre gets interested Jean would adapt it when we return to California. It is a project for in two years time, maybe too long for you to wait.

We miss you dear Clifford. All our love as always,

Dido and Jean

French Cancan, rejected for competition in the Cannes Film Festival, opens in Paris on 27 April.

To Jean Renoir [*Original in English*]   *18 May 1955*
Paris   *Hollywood*

Dear Jean,

I will write briefly now and at greater length when next I hear from you. This is the story. I have been in Hollywood for three months. The children were here with me for most of the time and only this Saturday

[331]

past have flown back to NY. I am rather heavily involved in the writing of *Joseph & His Brethren*[1] for Columbia, the amusing and laboured history of which you will hear (have to wait until we are together again). I will be here for another month and then go east, but will return in the early fall to write a movie from original materials, directing it, too.

The Flowering Peach,[2] the Noah play, opened and closed after about sixteen weeks. It was received very warmly by half of the press and coldly by the others. I was, as usual, disgusted and immediately took this Hollywood job when it was offered, knowing I should need money again, and how right I was!!! It may give you some pleasure to know that I won't need money again because now I'll just sit down and earn it (for at least another year) and keep it! I can't be nagged by it any more !!!!!!!!

Did you see *Country Girl* in Paris? I hear it's a big hit there. Now, about *The Big Knife*, do whatever you want in the way of producing it as a play there. But you must let me know so that I can inform my agent. I trust your judgment in everything. Just take what you want, only it is the agent we must tell to keep the accounts straight – I don't mean money but rather who is doing what.

But I must tell you that a motion picture (independent, to be released thru United Artists) was just finished of *Big Knife*. This may make you feel differently about a stage show of the same, but do as you want.

Let me [be] brief and not too sentimental: Hollywood has been empty without you! When are you returning? I long to embrace you both and eat dinner and talk with you. It is very dead here. This is my address:

Chateau Marmont,

8221 Sunset Blvd, LA, 46

Why don't the three of us just get married? Then we can be together all the time. If not for the children, I would be living in Europe, anyway. They, I must say, are flourishing and growing very well.

Please write to me here in Hollywood and,

With dearest love,

Clifford [Odets]

I'll send a copy of *The Big Knife* in a day or two.

1 *Joseph and His Brethren* was eventually directed by Irving Rapper in 1962.
2 In 1970 this became a successful Broadway musical, *Two by Two*, starring Danny Kaye.

In the autumn, Jean Renoir and Jean Serge work on the screenplay of Eléna et les Hommes, *which will star Ingrid Bergman. Filming begins on 1 December.*

1956

On 17 March, shooting is completed on Eléna et les Hommes.

To Clifford Odets [*Original in English*]   *19 March 1956*
                                                        Paris

Dear Clifford,

The shooting of our picture is supposed to be finished. Actually it isn't. I still have a few days of locations without actors including letting loose an old-fashioned balloon. We are happy to be nearly through with this job. We didn't imagine that the shooting of a picture in winter in Paris could be so uncomfortable. When the weather is nice the lack of organization is rather funny. It costs only time and a little extra money to the producer. But when you have to wait hours on an unheated stage you find it less amusing.

I don't know what I have as a picture. I started the editing, and during the next few days will get better acquainted with it. The only thing I am sure of is the tremendous strength and beauty of Ingrid. I must say the actors around her are first class. In Paris well heated studios and good organization are unknown but talent is plentiful.

Dido and I envy your parents to be with their grandchildren. It is exactly the dream of our life to live closer to Alain's sons.

We have no suggestions for a wife. We feel no one is good enough for you, at least no one around us at present. Girlfriends, here in Paris, I could take care of, but they are just as easy to find in Hollywood.

Thank you for *The Big Knife*. I am anxious to see your play well staged in Paris. I thought of several candidates for the part of Castle. All were good; now I have a great actor: Daniel Gélin.[1] You probably know him. As a matter of fact he is a sort of French John Garfield. During several years he was the top star in the French movie business. No producer imagined a picture without him. In six months he lost everything. His wild life was supposed to be a little too wild and movie people had decided that he wasn't reliable. Now Paris is discovering that he never ceased to have talent they love him again. I am sure with him your play could be a hit.

I hesitated very much before making up my mind on the style of the translation. My first idea was to have your characters talk the slang of French movie people. I was afraid of Hollywood exotism [sic]. After two years in Paris I discovered that this exotism still attracts the French people.

We had here a very successful adaptation of Bernard Shaw's *Pygmalion*. The play ran for one year and a half and is still running. The dialogue is not French slang nor a translation of English slang or Oxfordian language. It is the conception of an intelligent Frenchman concerning English slang or Oxfordian language. I believe this success is a good indication for the adaptation of *The Big Knife*.

Practically the play could be staged at the Théâtre des Mathurins in September. Unfortunately I will be back in the States and won't direct it. I could start a preparation right now with the help of Jean Serge[2] who was my assistant in *Julius Caesar* and helped me to write my last screenplay. Now, with the work left to be done on my picture we would be ready too late in the season.

If you could ask your agent to give me an option up to the end of the year that would help me to deal with the theatre, Gélin, and some others. La Société des Auteurs here is a very safe organization, they will protect your interests. I must show them some proof of our understanding. A letter written by you or your agent is sufficient.

Dear Clifford, I have to stop in New York for the editing of the English version of my picture. That means three or four months before seeing you. It's unbearably long.

With all our love,
Jean & Dido

1 Daniel Gélin (b.1921), actor whose films include *La Ronde* (Max Ophuls, 1950), *Le Testament d'Orphée* (Jean Cocteau, 1960), and *Le Souffle au Coeur* (Louis Malle, 1971).
2 Jean Serge was Jean Renoir's assistant on several ventures: the plays *Julius Caesar* and *The Big Knife*; and the films *Eléna et les Hommes* and *Le Testament du Docteur Cordelier*.

To Charles Spaak[1]

9 September 1956
The Royalton Hotel
New York

Dear Charles,

My work on *Eléna*[2] which was supposed to keep me in New York for three weeks has kept me longer, as I expected. Dido and I have not seen our second grandson yet, and cannot hope to leave for California before 29 September. We have taken advantage of our stay here to see several plays. Broadway remains active during the summer and we have been to several excellent performances. Tonight, we are going to see a revival of Brecht's *The Threepenny Opera*. It is showing off Broadway, in an old part of town. It has been playing there for over a year and is very successful.

I received a letter from Renée Lichtig[3] informing me that the negative of *La Grande Illusion* has been restored, and that the sound is weak in parts. I'll screen the print they have at the Museum of Modern Art on Tuesday. They have agreed to let me transfer some of the sound on tape so that I can send it to Paris to replace the defective parts in our soundtrack. I will write to Renée to ask her to let me know exactly which scenes are defective.

With regard to a theatrical release in America, we must wait. The art theatres have all the new European films they want. However, if I am to believe the specialists, if we pick the right time, *La Grande Illusion* could still attract audiences in art theatres in New York. As for the rest of the country, I will ask for advice from the exhibitor in Berkeley when I get back to California. He is the one who gave me some information about the prints being circulated. As for television, it is better to wait until a re-release or a publicity event has stirred some renewed interest in the film. If the re-release in Paris is successful, it could be of tremendous help here.

It seems that MGM would be interested in the re-release of the film in France and maybe the rest of the world, except the US. At least, this is what transpired during an informal conversation over lunch with some of the top studio executives. Loureau would probably do a better job with the film, but we should still consider their offer. According to Deutschmeister, the best distributor in France would be Morgenstern.

It occurred to me that if I were asked to do a film here, I should suggest *Les Bas-Fonds*, which I could adapt and shoot in a rundown part of Los Angeles. This might be a chance to use parts of our old screenplay and get some money for it. In order for me to bring this up I have to make sure it would not create any problems with the producers of the film and the writer who did the original adaptation. Would you make some kind of discreet investigation? This may be a viable idea, and I would not want it to be spread around. I doubt good old Kamenka[4] would create any difficulty, and we might be able to obtain some kind of compensation for him. As for the other one, whose name I have forgotten, he can get nothing more out of *Les Bas-Fonds*. What I would like to get is some kind of an option for two years, so that I can explore all possibilities.

At the same time would you mind asking Kamenka whether he might let me have a 16mm print of *Les Bas-Fonds* for my personal film library?

You must have returned to Paris. How is your wife? I hope that warmer climates have been beneficial to you both. Dido and I send you both our fondest regards.

Jean Renoir

PS. Once I am back in Los Angeles, I'll ask my lawyer about the best way to stop screenings of *La Grande Illusion* and get the prints back.

J.R.

1 Screenwriter who worked with Renoir on *La Grande Illusion*.
2 *Eléna et les Hommes*.
3 Renée Lichtig would become Jean Renoir's film editor on *Le Déjeuner sur l'Herbe, Le Testament du Docteur Cordelier*, and *Le Caporal Epinglé*.
4 Alexandre Kamenka (1888–1969), producer whose company Albatross was famous for films made by White Russians in Paris, including *Le Brasier Ardent*. He also produced *An Italian Straw Hat* (René Clair, 1927), and *Les Bas-Fonds*.

To Charles Blavette[1]
Manosque, France

11 September 1956
The Royalton Hotel
New York

My dear old Blavette,

I am still in New York working on the English version of my last film. It was over a year ago now that I started writing *Eléna*. It is most discouraging. You'll recall that we shot *Toni* in two months, and that the editing only took a month and a half. In fact, I think I am working faster than I used to, but it's all the technical aspects that have become cumbersome.

I hope to leave New York to go to California by the beginning of October. I must meet my grandson, who was born while I was in Paris. I must also get back to the house and see the dogs, and undergo some minor surgery. Finally, I can't postpone the book I want to write about my father any longer. It is becoming imperative because time goes by, people forget and false information on Renoir is accumulating. All this will delay my return to France and any film project I may have. Therefore, before even talking about making another Giono,[2] I must be sure I won't be pressed for time and that I can make something worthwhile.

Did you contact the people I had suggested in Paris? Deutschmeister, Loureau, Desfontaines? You must really start working with serious people and find another director besides me, one who will be available within a reasonable amount of time to dedicate himself to adapting a Giono piece. Nowadays, great films are based on great stories, and Giono has many great stories to offer for films. I have always dreamed of collaborating with him and three years ago, upon my return in France, I tried to do *Le Chant du Monde*, but it didn't work out. I am so tied up now that you must consider somebody else. We'll meet again, I'm sure. When I come back to France, God knows when, I'll call on Giono, who was kind enough to invite me when I called him.

I guess I am pouring out my immediate thoughts without thinking much about what I'm saying, because of my admiration for Giono and our old friendship. I also have two plays in mind. I find myself quite attracted and yet bothered by the theatre.

Thank you for your letter. Beginning October write to my California address: 1273 Leona Drive, Beverly Hills.

Please give my best wishes to Jean Giono.

Fond regards,

Jean Renoir

---

1 Charles Blavette (1902–67), actor whose credits included several Renoir films: *Toni, La Marseillaise* and *Le Déjeuner sur l'Herbe*.
2 Jean Giono, writer, whose stories share the same locale – Le Midi in France – as those of Pagnol, who adapted some of them for the screen, such as *Angèle* (1934).

On 12 September, Eléna et les Hommes *opens in Paris. In the same programme appears a short film,* L'Album de Famille, *in which Jean Renoir talks about his childhood and introduces the themes of* Eléna.

To Blanche Montel and Lucienne Watier[1]   *24 September 1956*
Ci-Mu-Ra   *The Royalton Hotel*
Paris   *New York*

Dear Blanche,

First of all, thank you for your news about *Eléna*, which rather surprised me. It was such a difficult film to shoot. I had to give up so many 'necessary precautions', so many close-ups that would have accentuated the actor's performance. I had to improvise so much to simplify the

English dialogue for the French actors and Ingrid's French dialogue that it is impossible for me to think of this production as anything but an ordeal. To this day, Deutschmeister's choice of the New York dubbing company, a small place with well-meaning people not used to projects of this size, has kept me here against my interests. My son had pneumonia in California and I could not go to see him. Our old dog[2] has just died without us seeing him again.

I am convinced that Deutsch[3] is acting in good faith when he says that, besides all my efforts to finish *Eléna*, I still owe him the film of the first part.[4] I am sending him a note to tell him I disagree. It is true that I mentioned it. He had asked me for some advice regarding the film of the first part. Right now, I am talking to a publisher about my book on my father. Does that mean I have to give this publisher my book for nothing?

I of course shot that television film[5] before the editing of *Eléna* was finished. But I was not paid by the week. I was paid for *Eléna* and *Eléna* only.

There is nothing you can do before you familiarize yourself with the terms of my contract with the television production company, which I have forgotten. Ginette Doynel will show it to you and will explain what happened when she returns from Germany at the end of the month. In the meantime I ask you to <u>stall</u> Franco-London and Paris Television. I am not concerned about the monetary aspects, and if there is any money to be paid to me, I ask you to give it to a charity.

The problem lies in the fact that I improvised a text after discussion with the producer from the television company, and that I assumed this text would only be used for television. This text is being used otherwise, and I intend to keep my copyright and to be paid according to French custom. The same thing applies to the soundtrack album. If I did not act on this, I would be betraying the cause of other authors who are my colleagues. The position taken by the other side, claiming that I surrendered <u>all rights for all media</u> on my text, which was memories of my father and of myself, seems to me to be untenable. I don't blame Deutsch, who has enough problems to solve, and who has difficulty in understanding an author's point of view. In other words, I find impossible to accept such treatment from a moral standpoint.

My first thought is to consult Kohlheim of the Société des Auteurs. But you and Ginette may come up with a better idea.

Would you be kind enough to fill in the copyright forms with Ginette? She has a power of attorney allowing her to sign for me.

I hope everything is going well for you in Paris. Here the upcoming theatrical season is bound to be fascinating. We bumped into Claude Dauphin,⁶ who has a very pretty wife.

Dido and I send our most affectionate thoughts to all three of you.

Jean Renoir

PS. Your secretary wrote down our address wrongly.

Dear Lulu,⁷

Thank you for your letter. My experience with *Eléna* has led me to think that in order for me to work in France, I will have to produce my own films. Deutschmeister is probably the best producer in France and my feelings for him are one of friendship. However, I am emerging from *Eléna* as if I had just been through the retreat from Russia. I can't imagine how this would have been with somebody less intelligent and whom I did not like as much. What I'll need you to find for me when I come back is a partner. I would add that through my contracts in New York, I feel confident I will get support from a major American company.

Dear Lulu, I hope I can give you more details in a few months. We are leaving for California on 13 October.

Fond regards,

J.R.

1 Agents.
2 Tambeau.
3 Henri Deutschmeister.
4 Evidently a contractual agreement for two films.
5 *L'Album de Famille de Jean Renoir*.
6 Claude Dauphin (1903–78), actor whose credits included *Salute to France, Casque d'Or* (Jacques Becker, 1956), and *The Tenant* (Roman Polanski, 1976).
7 Lucienne Watier.

To Borys Lewin¹

9 October 1956
The Royalton Hotel
New York

Dear Borys,

Your letters gave me a lot of pleasure. The last days of work have made me regret even more that Borys and his men could not handle *Eléna*'s American naturalization. The men from Titra were very devoted. In the end, and despite certain problems with the production company I will choose to ignore, they gave their heart and soul to *Eléna*'s cause. Unfortunately, it is not an easy one and it needed your talent to ensure her safe introduction into the world. I am afraid the last two reels are far from being perfect. But I also know that we can't do any better in New York.

In order for me to check the final work, Titra has made a 16mm copy of the master. With this I'll be able to see and listen to the film, reel by reel, this afternoon. However, this won't allow me to check the optical soundtrack.

I feel I am just coming out of a nightmare. I had some good moments on *Eléna*: working with Ingrid, Jean Marais,[2] Jouanneau,[3] and most of the actors, my collaboration with your crew, and the preparation with Jean Serge. Yet in contrast to these bright memories, so many shadows, so much trouble.

We are leaving for California on Saturday. I'll see my children and only one of my dogs (the other one did not wait for us and has just died); I have to undergo surgery, write my book, and think about a picture which I'll talk to you about as early as possible. In other words, life is sweet.

Dido and I send our best regards to Rally and Cocotte. Remember us to Mrs Lewin and her children.

Fond regards,

Jean Renoir

1 Borys Lewin, editor on *French Cancan* and *Eléna et les Hommes*.
2 Jean Marais (b.1913), actor whose credits include *La Belle et la Bête* (Jean Cocteau, 1946), *Orphée* (Jean Cocteau, 1950), and *Eléna et les Hommes*.
3 Jacques Jouanneau, who also acted in *Le Caporal Epinglé*.

To Henri Deutschmeister   *10 October 1956*
Franco London Film   *New York*
Paris

My dear Deutsch,

I have checked the sound on *Eléna*, or rather I have tried to check it. After the screening, Shapiro called to tell me he would send you a wire. Nevertheless, I think it would be useful to let you know what I think in a letter.

Overall, my feelings are rather negative but probably wrong, since I only had a 16mm print, with a magnetic soundtrack transferred from the final mixing track. In other words the sound quality was uneven. It was too weak in parts, and too strong in others. I will pass over some errors of details I agreed to overlook because you felt the work was going too slowly. But now I consider it was too rushed and botched up. I also recognized some weakness in the performances due to my absences from the set to meet journalists. Maybe all this will pass inspection if the general effect is outstanding and if the sound is powerful enough to lift the whole sequence. During the screening nothing was in synch, which really bothered me.

I am really annoyed by the fact that you don't have a black-and-white print of the film in Paris, because you could assess it after just one screening, synchronized with the sound. You will have to wait until the colour answer print arrives in Paris. On the other hand, in case you were thinking of redoing some scenes, we need the black-and-white print in New York, as the actors are here. I had a long talk with Lee Kresel about the elements I feel are the weakest. He knows the film thoroughly and could be put in charge of any changes you might feel are necessary.

All I wish is that you get a better impression of the film than I have. So much is at stake on this picture: a lot of money, the reputation of several people, and in some ways the reputation of French cinema, for which it is so hard to find distributors in America. Shapiro thinks my pessimism is due to my state of fatigue resulting from all the strenuous work I have done. I hope he is right. However, as I feel obliged to tell you the truth, I must say that *Eléna* as I saw it yesterday bothered me a lot.

I would appreciate your writing to me in California and letting me know your reaction to the screening. Maybe you could also show the film to a couple of American friends.

My best wishes are with you. I am not questioning the wisdom or necessity of your decisions and send you my warmest regards.

Jean Renoir

PS. Walter has just called me and I want to tell you what he said: attempting to make a dubbed film sound like a film with direct sound is an enormous undertaking, quite different from conventional dubbing, and would require a lot of time and money if we want to do it right.

J.R.

PPS. Second phone call to Walter: I discussed something Lee had reminded me about. In the tenth reel, when Ingrid walks away from the window, her line 'Let's have an intermission' is totally lost. Walter and I think the tenth reel should be re-mixed because of this line. However, he would rather wait for your comment in case you notice other problems in reel 10. I would not be surprised if the sound of the crowd has to be redone as well.

In order to assess the sound, why don't you strike a black-and-white print? You already have reels 1,6, and 10.

J.R.

To André Bazin[1]
Nogent-sur-Marne, France

My dear Bazin,

We enjoyed your letter very much. It gave us the impression that despite your bothersome health problems, your work is going full steam ahead. Maybe it will be a blessing. I am flattered that you are once more considering doing this book about my work. You may use my interviews, after getting agreements from the various publishers and interviewers. I will ask you also to let Ginette Doynel know what you will be using. I will inform her of your project. The only published conversations that interest me right now are those concerning my father, about whom I am currently writing a book. Besides, they have no bearing on your project.

Unfortunately, I am sure I won't have the time to write the article our friends from *Cahiers* were requesting. Give them my apologies. The unrewarding and badly-organized work I did on the English version of *Eléna* kept me in New York until the end of October. I have not been able to go and see my children in San Francisco yet. I must also go and stretch out on an operating table. Nothing major, but between all this and the fact that I cannot think of anything else but the book about Renoir, I could not possibly fulfil any commitment I would make.

Would you believe we are having a heat wave? Dido is spending the time running around the garden with a hose in her hand.

We hope your winter won't be too harsh. We think a lot about you both and send you our warmest regards.

Jean Renoir

1 André Bazin (1918–58), leading French film critic, co-founder of the journal *Cahiers du Cinéma*, and father-figure of the New Wave.

To Lucienne Watier
Ci-Mu-Ra, Paris

30 November 1956
Beverly Hills

Dear Lulu,

I apologize for replying so late to your letter of 19 November, but we have been terribly busy. We also had the pleasure of having our son, daughter-in-law and grandchildren visit us for several days.

I thank you for your news about *La Grand Illusion* following the screening. Dido and I are most heartened by your positive comment. Ginette has informed us that Loureau is still interested and that we should have some kind of decision very soon.

Thank you for asking Fresnay to volunteer his help for the scene to be redone. For my part, I'll write to Stroheim. I can't wait to see *La Grande Illusion* in the hands of a professional distributor.[1] Before going into any recording expenses, perhaps we should check with this potential distributor and see if we're all in agreement. I must confess that I am beginning to feel the pinch as far as my accounts in France are concerned. I understand Charles Spaak has to meet huge personal expenses, but I was counting on his participation and on income from *French Cancan*. As you know, I should receive a percentage on the profits of this picture, which has done well. This might be the right time to ask Deutsch for some explanation of this. You reported that he becomes agitated whenever you mention my modest requests relating to *L'Album de Famille*. I hope this odd nervous state won't let him forget he owes me some money, in particular the last payments on *Eléna*.

Thank you so much for all your trouble. The suggestion of seeing René Clair is excellent. Dido and I send you our fond love.

Jean Renoir

1 The rights on *La Grande Illusion* had lapsed and Renoir had just reacquired them.

To Erich Von Stroheim [*Original in English*]   *30 November 1956*

Dear Eric [sic],

I was told you were unwell.[1] I hope it is not serious and that we will find you in great shape when we return to France. During my last sojourn I was foolishly involved in so many different tasks that I had to give up the pleasure of seeing my friends. I was also submitted to little health inconveniences which kept me home when I wasn't at the studio.

You may know that Charles Spaak and myself bought the commercial

[343]

rights of *La Grande Illusion* with the intention of showing it in the original version. De Bretagne, who kindly checked the sound of the new print, wishes to rerecord a few lines of the scene of Boieldieu's death. I am far away and I didn't see the print myself, but you know how reliable is Jo. May I ask you, if he does the re-recording of this scene, to help our picture by saying again the few lines.

Dido and I send you our warmest wishes.

Sincerely,

Jean Renoir

1 Erich Von Stroheim was dying of spinal cancer and could not leave his bed. He bravely offered to re-record the dialogue if a soundman could be brought to him. He died on 12 May 1957.

1957

To Jean Renoir

12 January 1957

Dear, dear Jean,

You have no idea what a profound mark you have left here by going to India.[1] Everything which lives in the Indian cinema comes directly or indirectly from you – so I feel your close presence. Here, things are going well for me. I have been travelling through India for three days with Nehru. He is an extraordinary man.

Eléna is having a very, very big success in Italy at the moment.

I hope to see you again soon – How long will you stay in the USA?

With all my heart I send you my love, my dear Jean – and to Dido, too.

Roberto [Rossellini]

1 Rossellini was preparing to film *India '58*.

To Pierre Gaut[1]

14 January 1957
Beverly Hills

Dear Pierre,

It seems you had a lot of trouble and a lot of pleasure at the same time in helping your children buy their sumptuous property. I was not aware that residences on such a scale could still be found just outside Paris. It will be heaven for the children.

We were very distraught also to hear about Braque's[2] bad health. We hope he and Marcelle are getting better.

I haven't yet resumed my usual activities. We visited the kids in San Francisco, and I have started to write again. But we have not been in touch with the industry people as of yet. Besides my feeling rather tired, we have been worried about the health of our old friend Gabrielle. She can't really leave her house, and Dido and I call on her whenever we can. In other words, we are living on our hill in Beverly Hills, as isolated as monks in a monastery. But it's a very pleasant monastery. Dido has resumed working in the garden. On rare occasions, I give her a hand by pruning the olive trees which are gorgeous but tend to grow too high.

Tomorrow, I'll try to prune the grapevine. We only have four plants and the grapes are eaten by the *mockingbirds*[3] and squirrels before they have a chance to ripen. After a long dry spell and intense heat, the gardens were delighted to get some rain.

My isolation has kept my mind off *Toni*. I realize that the film doesn't stand a chance in cinemas. However, there may still be two ways to get some money out of it: by selling the story (it would be most helpful if you had a synopsis I could translate into English); or television. However, we may have a problem there, because the major studios are all selling their pictures dating a few years back to television.

It would be helpful if I could have a print of the film. By the way, I could not see Brandon in New York. He was ill. Anyway, since my lawyer in New York is currently in touch with him about *La Grande Illusion*, I will ask him to tell Brandon to send me his print. You can't imagine the kind of tricks these salesman pull on us. Here in Los Angeles there is a guy who did manage, God knows how, to get a 16mm print of *La Grande Illusion*. He had promised me in writing to give it back to me, but when the time came, he merely told me he had lost it. I am sure he is renting it out to clubs and schools on the sly, and pockets the money.

We went to see my film.[4] Berkeley is on the other side of San Francisco Bay. It is rather humid there. The university is very pleasant, surrounded by beautiful gardens. I don't think Alain intends to stay there very long. He has his own ideas on how to teach medieval literature and dreams of a place where his methods would be welcome. Everything looks fine to laymen like Dido and myself. The level of his students is certainly high enough, and they apparently follow his teaching most enthusiastically. I guess each profession has its own mystery.

The grandchildren are gorgeous, spoiled – but not excessively – and very sweet. They seem to be catching colds all the time and, according to Alain and Jane, it is because of the climate in Berkeley. Their paediatrician is Dr Maurice Renoir, grandson of one of my father's brothers. He settled here six years ago and now has a very successful practice in a Kaiser hospital.

Thanks to Gabrielle I am gathering a lot of information for the book on my father. I have already written the rough draft of several chapters. They will have to be rewritten, of course, but at least they got me started. I have written a few scenes for a play as well. I wish I could wake up full of stamina one morning, and be able to complete these two undertakings without too much procrastination.

When you see the Braques, tell them we think about them a lot. The apples are in a very simple frame, hanging between a sculpture in high relief and some of Renoir's anemones. They look very good there. The room is very bright and their golden tones are well enhanced. Dido and I are thrilled by them.

Love to Maud and you,
Jean Renoir

1 Producer of *Toni*.
2 Georges Braque, artist.
3 Originally in English.
4 Presumably *Eléna et les Hommes*.

To Erich Von Stroheim [*Original in English*]   15 January 1957
Maurepas, S. et O.
France

Dear Erich,

Dido and I are terribly sorry to know that you are not well. We wish that your spine can be cured by one of those amazing discoveries which are almost common in modern medicine. We would like to be in Paris and pay you a visit. Alas, Hollywood is very far away. We hope you or Denise[1] will soon give us better news.

As for the recording of *La Grande Illusion*, there is no hurry. The only person who knows about this question is Ginette Doynel, my secretary. I will ask her to get in touch with you, and with Jo de Bretagne, as soon as she returns from a vacation in La Martinique.

I don't know how to thank you for your kindness. I would hate to bother you. It is possible that the lab will improve sufficiently the quality of those few lines. Ginette Doynel will enquire about that.

I don't doubt we will meet again one of these days, in Maurepas or at my place, 7 avenue Frochot. You will have forgotten your ordeal and it will be a wonderful reunion.

Our warmest wishes to Denise and you,
Jean Renoir

1 Denise Vernac, actress and companion to Erich Von Stroheim.

To Jean Serge

Dear Serge,

Ivan must be a big boy now. I hope Morane has fully recovered from the exhaustion of bringing him into the world, and that you have a lot of fun with this new character. As for us, we paid a visit to our children in Berkeley, and I must confess it perked me up. Alain's house is small and rather modest, but it is constantly buzzing like a beehive: friends and colleagues from the university drop in at all times, stay for dinner, spend the night. There was Alain's wife's brother, a sailor whose ship is anchored in the San Francisco Bay; our cousin, Maurice Renoir, a doctor who practises in one of the local Kaiser Hospitals, is often there as well. All these people from various walks of life meet there and get along brilliantly, generating so much electricity that it made me completely forget 'Moby Dick' and his letters. He certainly succeeded in murdering the American *Eléna*. But let's wait and see. Sometimes, last minute reprieves do happen.

Ingrid triumphed in New York, and Hollywood is once more at her feet. If she wanted, she could really give all the Marilyn Monroes a run for their money. I am sure of this, one can feel these things. I must add, I am particularly thrilled that her really big success is happening on a Parisian stage. I hope to write a play that she will like enough to agree to come on board with me for the adventure. I am working on an idea I think is good. In any case, the worst is over, and Dido and I are very happy to see her coming out of the bad patch she had been in.

Please try, as soon as possible, to send me as much detailed information as you possibly can on *The Big Knife*. I really don't know what to tell Clifford Odets. Tell me what you think of the Gallimard edition as well. Clifford Odets has not heard a thing.

I have just finished the first chapter of my book on my father. It took me some time to find the 'tone', but now I think I've got it.

Kiss Morane and Ivan for us. Tell us about their projects, mostly Morane's. Our best to the eldest two.

Kind wishes,

Jean Renoir

We think about your family in Sceaux.

To Jean Renoir [*Original in English*]   *25 January 1957*
Beverly Hills   *Paris*

Dear friends,

Wasn't it wonderful with New York and my trip!![1] I was so calm, that is what amazes me, with all that press and TV and that is why, thank God, I came through it. If one only can take a deep breath when the curtain goes up, everything will run smoothly, said Mercure before *Tea*'s[2] curtain went up. I did the same before the NY curtain went up. The only cloud was that Roberto was violently against my going. He sent letter after letter and telegrams and even phoned! He wired Skorous,[3] I would not come, the same day I wired I <u>would</u> come. I think he was completely wrong and for the second time went against his wishes. The first one with *Tea*! Now he is very unhappy. I hope you don't mind I sent your sweet letter, that arrived today to him. He loves you, and if you say it was good I came back, and that I behaved with dignity, maybe that will help him. Everybody tried to wire and write him that it was good for me to go, but they were all *cretini* he said. Marcella[4] and his brother[5] were on his side and telephoned and wrote from Italy. Now I am afraid I have cut off my ties with them. I have not heard from anyone since I came back. It is funny how they always stick together. Even the second generation, I mean even Fiorella, who has always been on my side in earlier situations of disagreement between Italy and Sweden, took their side this time. I think this was THE BIG STEP and if I took it meant I was – finally – independent! Well, that is how we stand today. I am happy about my trip and as I said to Renzo when he thought of persuading me that it was bad for Pia that I went. I feel she was happy I came, and that now the wind has turned. She was so sweet over the phone. She understood, what the family here didn't. They said I could not go to USA for the first time and not see her. I felt it had nothing to do with a publicity stunt, and I would not have wanted to see her under such circumstances. She understood and she said: 'Don't worry, I don't mind being an actress' daughter. I am used to the press now! I will see you this summer.' Don't tell anyone, because Peter might then stop her from coming. But if I gave her the money, she said, she would come. I have given her the money!!!

Eléna is a tremendous success in Rome. Much bigger than here. 'No one prophet in' and so on. I am enclosing some clippings. I hope you can read them. I am sorry I didn't with the French ones, but I was sure you had them.

Even Deutsch was happy I went to NY but that of course is understood as it also gives his picture publicity! I have not seen him at all. I can't get over the way he told you the picture went bad here and sent you only bad clippings. I have one more pic to do. Roberto wants me to do *Adorable Julia* for him. What do you think? I think I am too young to play an actress of forty!! I am so happy for what you wrote about America. Roberto's last letter was full of how he hates America and Americans. I can't understand it, it is like saying 'I hate Jews'. And even if Spellman, Sen. Johnson and many of the press were mean, so many, many were good to us. But he remembers, it seems, today only the bad.

Ingrid [Bergman]

1 Ingrid Bergman had returned to the United States for the first time since the Rossellini scandal to accept the New York Film Critics Award for *Anastasia*. She later won the Academy Award for this performance.
2 Ingrid Bergman was appearing on the Paris stage in *Tea and Sympathy*.
3 Spiros P. Skorous (1893–1971), (President of 20th Century-Fox from 1942 to 1962).
4 Roberto Rossellini's sister.
5 Renzo Rossellini, composer.

To Lucienne Watier   28 *January 1957*
Ci-Mu-Ra, Paris

Dear Lulu,

Thank you for your letter of 10 January. Let's hope your good wishes will bring us lots of work we can do together.

I can't wait to see *La Grande Illusion* in the hands of Loureau or a distributor. Here, despite the assistance of Mr Lewy, attorney for the French Film Office, I have not been able to get back the prints that have been circulating. The film is still being shown in film clubs, schools, and so on. This is all second-rate stuff, paying maybe $25 to $50. But I suspect the showings are frequent enough to make illegal owners of these prints unwilling to surrender them. My last experience was quite typical: one of these bogus distributors had sworn in writing to give me the print back. I was weak enough to let him use it one last time for a showing he had already advertised in his cinema. Now, he claims he gave it back to me, and I don't know what to do.

Deutschmeister is made from the same mould. I received a strange letter from him, in which he accuses me of having refused to show *Eléna* to Mr Warner. I'm quoting from his letter: '. . . In America, the film was shown to WARNER Bros by our co-producer, Mr BERCHOLZ. We deeply deplore your refusal to show the film yourself to Mr Warner in Holly-wood. It would have been better because now, after screening the film

27 Jean Renoir relaxing with Ingrid Bergman and Roberto Rossellini

film with his top executives, Jack Warner requests that the film be cut, and that we change the title as well. They are also asking for the right to show the film in ART THEATRES, because they don't feel confident enough to release it on the normal circuits.'

I am afraid Deutschmeister is only looking for excuses not to pay me the $10,000 he still owes me. Since my contract to direct the picture was signed with his American partner Mr Shapiro, I have asked MCA, and particularly Kay Brown in New York, to take care of this.

I would rather not reply to Deutschmeister. If you have no objection, I suggest you write to him and explain that your client, Jean Renoir, is puzzled by the terms of his letter of 4 January 1957, claiming that your client refused to show the film to Mr Warner. Deutschmeister must have misunderstood parts of my letter of 6 October 1956, dealing with this matter.

'. . . I'll arrive in California on the 16th. You asked me to show the film to Mr Jack Warner. I'd be glad to do it. However, I'd like to point out that it will be impossible for me to pretend that Jean Marais speaks with a New England accent, and that Morel and his buddies speak with a Brooklyn accent. I would have to be a really clumsy technician to spend nearly three months in New York merely to resolve some minor technical problems. The time spent on the dubbing makes the explanations you asked me to give unbelievable. If you are so adamant about presenting *"the film as done in direct sound instead of dubbed"*, it might be better to choose a more anonymous emissary; one who is not too familiar with all the work that was done, and most of all, one who is more diplomatic than I am.'

Would you tell him that I see no problem in having the picture open in art theatres? This is what MGM did with *Lust for Life* (Van Gogh), and the film is doing extremely well. With regard to the cuts requested by Mr Warner, please tell him that I'll be his disposal for any assistance, as always. All the more so since it has always been understood that I will have to agree to any cuts being made.

Deutschmeister's attitude with regard to *Album de Famille* is quite suspect as well. Like he did with *Eléna*, he is distorting the truth when he claims that I asked him to take it. I did suggest it to him, merely because he was complaining about the difficulties of finding an introduction to *Eléna* done by me. But terms were never discussed, and I was waiting for him to bring it up after he saw the material in Paris. Let's suppose that, upon hearing I was looking for a house in the country, Mr Deutschmeister came to me and told me: I have one which I am trying to get rid of, maybe you should consider it. That would not mean he intends to give it to me as a gift.

I am sorry to hear that Ingrid still has one film to do for him. It's a real shame. His conduct and his lies really got to me. The work I had to do in New York under impossible conditions and in tropical heat had drained me already. But his behaviour finished me. I am barely beginning to get back to work now, and think about the future. Ginette will keep you informed of some of my projects as they go forward.

Thank Paulette for us for her lovely letter. And express my gratitude to Blanche for her assistance. Don't forget to give our best to David as well. We often think about your friendly team on the avenue Hoche.

Fond wishes to the three of you,

Jean Renoir

To Ingrid Bergman
Paris

8 February 1957
Beverly Hills

Dear Ingrid,

Dido and I have read your letter several times with the same pleasure as if we were chatting with a dear friend.

I think the reluctance Roberto and your family have expressed about your trip to New York stems mostly from their desire to protect you from the temptation to return to the canary cage. I know that if you have left it, it is not to go back to it. But nothing should keep you from coming back once in a while. Just make sure the door is still open, so that you can fly away wherever you want after having eaten some of the good seeds Hollywood feeds to its canaries. Ingrid, you are very strong because you are very honest. I am convinced that now you'll be able to preserve your independence.

We were deeply touched by the orderly way in which you disposed of the Italian bad press in your letter. It is indeed a great proof of friendship to take care over information you send to friends. We are still shaken by the wave of support you received during your stay here. People worship you and some of this worship is rubbing off on us.

I have just learned that Warner, in agreement with Deutschmeister, has re-edited *Eléna*, and that a print of this new English version is being struck at Technicolor. This strikes me as a very dishonest way to proceed toward myself and you as well. It was in my contract that I would have to approve all editing.

[353]

Claude reports from Bombay that Roberto loves India. I bet he'll bring us back a masterpiece.

I may have an idea for a project for you. It is an old book (1920) that may be a bit dated. Yet it suddenly occurred to me that with a few changes it could become a great vehicle for you. It is rather downbeat. It takes place in London. I have asked Kay Brown to find a copy of the book and send it to you.

I'm ploughing along with my play. I'll give it to you to read before I give it to anybody else. It would be a blessing if you liked it and agreed to do it. One set – four to five characters – in French – on the sad side.

The way you handled Pia was excellent. You are under a lucky star, and at this time everything you do is well done.

It's a shame you have one film left for Deutsch. You should try to get out of this commitment, and we could make a film together for an American company.

Some friends are ringing at the door. Regretfully I end this letter. Dido is shouting from the kitchen. She sends her love. Me too.

Jean Renoir

To Ingrid Bergman   *25 February 1957*
                                                      Beverly Hills

Dear Ingrid,

Eléna has been released in Buffalo with a new title that I find obscene: *Paris Does Strange Things*. The editing is quite different. I also hear that Warner Bros have added a voice-over narration by Mel Ferrer. The sad truth is that you and I are being held responsible by the audience for a product we had no control over whatsoever. We owe it all to Deutsch-meister, whose attitude toward me has been inexcusable since we finished the dubbing at Titra. On the other hand, a telephone call from one of Mr Jack Warner's assistants convinced me they were quite willing to work with me. When I return to France, I'll ask my colleagues at the Société des Auteurs to give me a hearing and I'll expose Deutschmeister's behaviour toward me. If it can be of any use, I'll explain my case in the Screen Directors Guild newsletter as well.

I don't know if all the reviews are bad, but the only one I have read, in the *Hollywood Variety* [sic], is a complete hatchet job. Fortunately you are not the victim. I am. I think your reputation will remain unblemished.

This picture was the trickiest to edit of all my pictures. By depriving me of any control over this re-editing, and not even informing me that such an editing was in progress, Mr Deutschmeister has damaged my interests and could have easily damaged yours as well.

I have just received a phone call from Mr and Mrs Edwards, who are Deutschmeister's legal representatives in New York. They are delightful elderly people, very devoted to their boss. They are genuinely honest, but they tend to get too enthusiastic too easily. They told me the picture was well received in Buffalo. They said the theatre was packed, and that the audience laughed and applauded on several occasions during the film, and even more at the end.

Let's forget *Eléna*. Dido and I congratulate you on your nomination for the Academy Awards. It's really great. You will surely get the Oscar; and even if you don't get it, you'll have been so close to it that it will be the same thing. Don't feel you have to reply to this letter. It is only an excuse to chat with you, the friend we both like so much.

Fond wishes,
Jean Renoir

To Jean Renoir [*Original in English*]   *26 February 1957*
Beverly Hills   *Paris*

Dear Jean,

Your letter was so wonderful and so understanding, and I thank you for being my friend.

You are so right about my wanting to go in and out of *la cage* and I feel honestly I can pick from inside and outside, at least for a couple of years, while it is good eating on both sides.

Here all is well; the theatre always packed and I will continue the play probably until 14 July. I hope that Pia will come to Europe in July and I will wait for her here.

They want me to pick up the play in September again, but I think by then I rather do the Deutchmeister [sic] picture. They are thinking of *Adorable Julia*, the play that ran here in Paris with Madeleine Robinson. I am not too keen on the idea, but nothing better has come up. It will probably be shot in Cinecittà.

I have had my difficulties with Deutchmeister again. My lawyer from Rome was here and they had a big fight. Peggy is always crying, as she likes me and she wants me to like her husband. I try, but it is not always easy. It might happen and that is what my lawyer wants: that the picture will be done without Deutchmeister. Deutch has understood this and is

[355]

now on no speaking terms with me. He who lives will see!

A little man without teeth came to my dressing room saying he was a friend of yours and he worked with you in *Madame Bovary*. Maybe in those days he had teeth and you will never know whom I am speaking of. I could not catch his name, he insisted that you had gone to India. I kept saying you were in Hollywood. Now I understand why he thought Renoir was in India, it is Claude!

Roberto has just started his picture, will travel all over India and will not be back until 1 July. Robertino[1] has been operated for appendix and Isabella[2] has the mumps. Otherwise everything is fine.

I am delighted about the play and the picture that you write for me. Send them on when they are ready. I enclose two clippings, news about your actors and much love,

from your actress,

lovingly,

Ingrid

1 Son of Rossellini and Bergman.
2 Isabella Rossellini (b.1952), one of twin daughters, now an actress whose credits include *Il Prato* (Tavianis, 1978), *White Nights* (Taylor Hackford, 1985), and *Blue Velvet* (David Lynch, 1986).

To Lee Kresel [*Original in English*]   4 *April 1957*
                                                        Beverly Hills

Dear Lee,

Dido and I received your letter and feel very sorry for this idle period you are going through. Thank you for the news of *Eléna*. Don't send us the reviews. I am not sure that the critics would have liked it as it was. But Warner's big mistake is their stubborn decision to present the picture as a sentimental drama. The film was shown in Los Angeles but I didn't want to see it. Some friends of mine told me about the cuts, the new beginning, and the new ending. I also know that the Warner people never liked the picture, being convinced that the American public was expecting only a sad, sentimental Ingrid. The best thing I have to do is to forget about the whole thing. It's not easy. Strangely enough my agent here doesn't seem to be impressed by this bad reception. I am still hoping they will find the possibility for me for a production with Leslie Caron. I am not too sure they will succeed. Maybe several statements in the papers about *Eléna* being dubbed will help me. A foreign film remains for

Hollywood something which doesn't count very much.

I certainly owe you some money for your work on *Orvet* and *La Grande Illusion*. Please let me know how much.

I am working on my book and on a stage play. The book progresses very slowly. I am still with Renoir as a child. I am correcting the fifty first [sic] pages, and, in a few days, will read them to Dido. I am anxious to have her impression.

I think my play is good. I may be wrong but I am so confident in it that my disappointment concerning *Eléna* is almost forgotten. I was so impressed by Deutschmeister's mistakes when I arrived here that it took me three months to find the strength to start to work again.

[...] We love *The Thirteen Clocks*.[1] I don't believe that Hollywood people would like it for a film. As for myself, I think after *Eléna* I must shoot a drama. This story could make an extraordinary musical. We don't know *The Voice at the Back Door*. We will buy it.

Deutschmeister still owes me money.

We don't know very much about the work situation in this town. I think the only opportunities are with television. The film industry is shrinking. The only opportunity I know for you is to join me in my next production. But there are still many 'ifs' and a big 'when'. Myself, I would like to finish at least the first draft of my book and a, if not final, more polished version of my play.

Our best regards to your brother, his wife, and children; to your father and your mother.

With our fondest wishes and our love,

Jean Renoir

PS. Ingrid sent me several Italian reviews of *Eléna*. They rave about it. Jean Serge sent me Spanish and Belgian reviews, also excellent.

1 Play by American humorist James Thurber.

To Dido Renoir
Beverly Hills

11 September 1957
Paris

Dear Dido,

On my arrival I went to the theatre.[1] That night we rehearsed. In bed at two in the morning to be ready to discuss sets, costumes.

Gélin remarkable. Cast good. I think that we will have a very beautiful show. Group of actors, directors and others very enthusiastic.

Everyone asks me anxiously if Clifford will come. Telephone him and inform him of my good impressions.

The play, in French, is incredibly *violent*. I am surely going to p... people off. All the better. It's better than indifference.

This morning, woke up at nine o'clock. Truffault² [sic] was on the telephone.

The plane was two hours early. No one was there. I had expected Ginette and Jean Serge at the airport. She had called Pierre Gaut, who came to avenue Frochot. The avenue is very pretty, not ruined at all; there's a pretty path covered with reddish sand.

I am going to have lunch with Paul Meurisse³ and Micheline.⁴ He really wanted to give me his Jaguar to use during my stay. I'm not very tired.

Ginette saw some 'practical-documentary' errors in *Judith*.⁵ I'm going to correct them. I am going to give the manuscript to Paul to read. Ginette had typed seven copies of everything.

Much love to you. Give my love to Ga and Jeanot [sic].

Jean

1 Théâtre des Bouffes-Parisiens, Paris, where Renoir was directing *The Big Knife*, translated into French as *Le Grand Couteau*.
2 François Truffaut (1932–84), director whose films include *Les 400 Coups* (1959), *Baisers Volés* (1968), *La Nuit Américaine* (*Day for Night*, 1973), and *Le Dernier Métro* (1980). While a critic writing mainly for *Cahiers du Cinéma*, he had strongly supported Renoir and worked as an assistant on *French Cancan*.
3 Paul Meurisse (1912–79), stage and film actor. His film credits included *Les Diaboliques* (Henri-Georges Clouzot, 1954), *Le Déjeuner sur l'Herbe, Le Deuxième Souffle* (Jean-Pierre Melville, 1966), and *L'Armée des Ombres* (Jean-Pierre Melville, 1969).
4 Micheline Gary, actress and wife of Paul Meurisse, who was also in *Le Déjeuner sur l'Herbe*.
5 *Judith* was the working title for Renoir's play *Carola*.

To Dido Renoir   [?] September 1957
Beverly Hills   *Paris*

Dear Dido,

As I write, Bessie must be arriving. Give her all my wishes for a good homecoming at Leona Drive and tell her of my pleasure in knowing she is with you.

I am leading a very interesting life because work is going well, but also a mind-destroying one because I am not sleeping enough. Rehearsals finish at around one in the morning, and hearing Claude get ready to leave at 9 am gets me out of bed. With the time it takes to get home and clean up a little at night, I get about six hours sleep. This fatigue also makes me eat, which is bad for 'my figure'.

I miss you enormously. I really want to see you here, more than rejoining you at Leona, for the simple reason that here, I am able to find work. They are making films, despite the lamentations of producers. The one that Claude is shooting, directed by young Astruc,[1] nephew of your dress-designer, has a dream budget. But (this is the most attractive thing) one can also shoot simple subjects, without stars – like Bresson's latest film[2] – and yet they benefit from good distribution.

I'm anxious for rehearsals to finish to correct *Judith*, to present it (to the French, Paul Meurisse told me) – to write quickly a film project with Ginette, and return to have a chat with you and prepare for the future – (But of course, also and especially to be with you and see Alain and his family again!)

I saw *Pauvre Bitos* by Anouilh[3] at the Comédie des Champs Elysées. It's a violent and petty indictment of the French in general – but a great play which proves that the Parisians are ready to swallow <u>anything</u>.

I think of Ga and Jeannot a lot. All my love.

Jean

1 Alexandre Astruc (b.1923) was filming *Une Vie*.
2 Robert Bresson (b.1907) had just made *Un Condamné à Mort s'est Echappé* (*A Man Escaped*, 1956).
3 Jean Anouilh, playwright.

To Dido Renoir[1]   *17 September 1957*
Beverly Hills   *Paris*

Dear Dido,

Saw Ingrid. I was embarrassed. Claude had told me that <u>everything the papers say</u>[2] is true. And Ingrid told me about all the money that these films in India had cost <u>them</u>. She must do films in London to pay the expenses.

The rehearsals continue to go well. With all my love,

Jean

1 Handwritten footnote to a formal letter from Ginette Doynel.
2 Scandal had broken out over Rossellini's relationship with Sonali Das Gupta, the wife of producer Hari Das Gupta, who had been the Indian assistant director on *The River*.

To Dido Renoir
Beverly Hills

Dear Dido,

Last night we had the first nearly complete rehearsal. The sets are not finished, we don't have costumes, and the actors still forget parts of the text. Apart from that, my impressions are good ... I had to modify the ending but there's no point in telling Clifford, as these modifications consist of a few cuts which will help Claude Genia[1] (Marion) and which allow for a more dramatic use of the spiral staircase. Christine[2] came to have dinner with me. By chance she stayed during the rehearsal. She is practically the only outsider who has seen the play until now. She seemed very impressed. This chance presence has given me confidence.

[...]

Ginette and I are very affected by the absolute despair of Sylvie Gélin.[3] We had her working on costumes but now that work is nearly completed, once more she has time to think of the death of her child. Last night at a restaurant (Brasserie des Bouffes Parisiens) she literally collapsed and went to hide. Apart from that, she is very decent and doesn't exhibit her sorrow.

When you get the chance, ask Clifford Odets to send me a copy of a resumé of his life and his artistic activities, which his agents ought to have made. I will often be asked to speak about him, in interviews. I would prefer not to make mistakes on dates and not to omit important facts. At the same time, you might speak to him about the question of French language television and radio rights. Until now we have only done recordings for publicity but something more serious might present itself and it would be good to know whether he has already signed an agreement about this type of broadcast including the entire world.

The rehearsals are prolonged right through the night and my Beverly Hills habits drag me out of bed rather early. Thus, I have very short nights, but despite that I am holding up well. It's because my work is very active. However, I am not completely satisfied because you are not here. I am very unreasonable, and want to have professional activities and your presence at the same time.

[...]

Depending upon Ginette's projects, financial resources and activities, we will see if I can keep her with me for my return. But let's talk about the future before knowing the reaction to *The Big Knife*.

All my love to Gabrielle and Jeannot.

My tender love to you.
Jean

1 Claude Genia, actress.
2 Christine Burnier, sister of Raymond Burnier.
3 Wife of Daniel Gélin. Their young son had died after swallowing pills he had found in his mother's purse.

To Dido Renoir   *9 October 1957*
Beverly Hills   *Paris*

Dear Dido,

Thank you for your telephone call this evening. Hearing your voice has given me the irresistible desire to see you again soon.

I have established a 'programme' with Ginette and tomorrow or the day after I hope to see my problems clearly. I already know that the reviews will be mixed. Some are embarrassed by what they consider to be an unreal situation: 'a producer prepared to commit murder!' There will also be the crudity of my language.

It doesn't matter! Or rather, it will not have the importance it might have had if the 'opening night crowd' had been cold – as with *Orvet*. Thus it was a triumph. Maybe more of a success for the actors than the play! But who can tell? The essential fact is that the audience were on their feet and cheering.

Whatever the reviews are like, this production has put me back in the 'news'. And, barring a complete demolition job, I can probably profit from this to put the case for *Judith*, after shedding the improbabilities caused by my ignorance of the wartime situation. Not bad at all.

With all my love,
Jean

To Clifford Odets [*Original in English*]   *10 October 1957*
                                         Paris

Dear Cliff,

We are running since 5 October and every night the play is more successful. Yesterday we had the terrifying *générale*, the equivalence of the press-show in New York. The public was a mixture of actors, authors, producers and of course newspaper people. They applauded vigorously many times during the show and ten good minutes after the end of the play. That doesn't mean that the reviews will be good. I am even convinced that the theatre critics will be rather reluctant. It is the fashion now in Paris to be nasty and to try to present every event with a kind of acid, destructive sense of humour and this Jean Renoir just arriving from California to open a successful show in the most Parisian of all the theatres is a good target. But even if some reviews are deceiving I won't be depressed because I know that we won the game with the public.

I am anxious to see you and to talk with you about the wonderful and exhausting week I spent now in Paris. The feeling that every word, every gesture of the actors is followed with passion by the audience is simply enchanting. *The Big Knife* is perhaps the happiest experience I had up till now, including my own films.

To go back to the critics, *Bitos*, the last play by Anouilh, received the worst reviews of the year. After ten months it is still running and the theatre is packed.

I wish you [could] find the time to help Leslie Caron and myself with the *Three Rooms in Manhattan*. We need your collaboration very badly. The story is weak but could be the basis for an unusual film and I am convinced that this part was created for Leslie. She would be out of the world in it.

My love to the kids.

When I have the reviews I will send them to Dido.

With all my love,

Jean Renoir

To Dido Renoir
Beverly Hills

10 October 1957
Paris

Dear Dido,

I have just finished reading the reviews of *The Big Knife*. As I had expected, they are not all good. Jean Serge and Jean Mortier, who read the reviews of almost every play, think that, given the habitual ferocity of our judges, the situation is in our favour. We are obviously a long way from the critical drubbing we got for *Orvet*. I should add that the veterans of Parisian first nights perhaps sensed that Daniel Gélin was a bit shaky because of his unfamilarity with the stage. This shakiness will disappear and the public will not see it. On Tuesday night they gave him an ovation. Yesterday he was very upset by Favalelli's review and had a memory lapse. He started again and the audience really applauded him at the end.

I too ought to be angry, because this same Favalelli says that I don't have the lyricism of Bob Aldrich.[1] I really couldn't care less, as by all reports I think the situation is favourable to me and I am benefiting from it. The fuss made about *The Big Knife* firmly classifies me as a theatre director and prepares the way for *Judith*. I am in our living room in the midst of dictating this letter to Ginette. From time to time we stop ourselves to 'get our bearings'. Our gut reaction is that the author Jean Renoir has improved his standing. I don't feel nervous at all. I am very calm and very optimistic. Simply a little tired.

I am now going to try to establish a work plan with Ginette. At the end of this week and the beginning of next, I will see journalists. I will lunch with Ingrid on Saturday. Sunday I will go to Brussels. Probably I will not find the time to work on *Judith*. Next week we must choose a day to close the door and turn off the phone and play 'absent from Paris'. If I can concentrate, I might be able to make the corrections to *Judith* in a week. Then I will read it to useful people.

[. . .]

I will try to read the play to Ingrid, but I think more and more that it would be better if Carola[2] didn't have an accent. What's more, Ingrid has signed for several films in London and will not be free for at least two years.

With *Judith* rewritten and 'read' to interested parties, I would like to do these things again before returning:

– go to Essoyes.

– go down to the Midi, with a stop at Arles for my Van Gogh story, which is ripening in my mind, stop at Manosque to say hello to Jean Giono, two days at Cagnes to see Les Collettes again and to get myself back in the atmosphere of the book. One day at Menton and at Nice to see Claude and the Fighieras.

I might go on the train as far as Avignon and rent a Dauphine there.

Back to Paris and, after *Judith*, I would like to help Ginette definitely settle the questions of distribution for *La Grande Illusion*; get back the rights to *Boudu*, and see Jonas.

[. . .]

To return to the reviews of *The Big Knife*, I'd like you to decide if the bad ones ought to be shown to Clifford Odets. I wrote warning him that the Parisian critics would carp at us. Despite this warning, maybe it would be better for him to avoid reading the bits which are too malicious.

I am expecting young Truffault [sic], always so faithful. I never cease to think of you and I send you all my love

Jean

1 Robert Aldrich (1918–83) directed the film version of *The Big Knife* in 1955, with Rod Steiger and Jack Palance. His other films included *Vera Cruz* (1954) and *The Dirty Dozen* (1967). He was assistant director to Renoir on *The Southerner*.
2 Carola is the lead character in the play *Judith*, later titled *Carola*.

To Dido Renoir
Beverly Hills

12 October 1957
Paris

Dear Dido,

A little note to say hello. I adored your letter by return of post from Berkeley. Did you know that John and Peter[1] have sent me two autographs?

Paul Bernard[2] is ill and will be replaced tonight by a nice kid who barely knows his lines. It's a catastrophe, since attendance was going up after the première. Paul will not be able to return before Wednesday. Gélin brings in more business than he does, but I ask myself if it isn't Paul who has 'made' the play. He's a magnificent actor.

Lunched with Ingrid and Paul Meurisse. I think that she 'knows' and has no more illusions about Rossellini's activities in India. Above all, not a word! I am pursued by American journalists (mostly of Russian origin) who are convinced that Claude and I are hiding Sonali in a closet at avenue Frochot. (The French are going crazy over the story!)

According to Truffault [sic], the word on Roberto's work in India is excellent – I find all this terribly sad for Ingrid, and I don't know what to do to make her happy. I play the 'I don't know anything and everything's fine' game with her. I would like to see her more often, but there just isn't time. How I'd like the opportunity to see you!

Ginette, happily, is coming with me tomorrow to Brussels. I send you all my love. *Love*[3] to Bessie. Love to Ga and Jeannot.

Jean

1 Sons of Alain Renoir.
2 Paul Bernard, stage and film actor. His film credits include *Les Dames du Bois de Boulogne* (Robert Bresson, 1946).
3 Originally in English.

Dear Dido,

I have just received your letter of 14 October. Rather, I received it yesterday, but I was immersed in *Judith* and I had to put off until the peace of the next morning the pleasure of conversing with you.

Obviously, the critics are not singing our praises. But they have done enough to create a favourable climate in Paris.

Apart from Marcel Achard's *Patate*, which has a full house every night at the Saint Georges, *The Big Knife* is probably the most successful show in Paris. I should say in that type of theatre, for obviously, the Folies Bergères or the *Strip-Teases*[1] are jammed.

We've made almost 400,000 every night and approach 600,000 on Saturdays. Looking back to my memories of *Orvet*, I feel a very distinct improvement in my rapport with the public and also in my commercial success. One black mark – I invited to the first night Miss Schneider and Darthea and also an attaché. No reply. Maybe they had been shocked by the violence of the hero's anti-American imprecations. If that's the case, then they are wrong. Clifford Odets' free use of language is, on the contrary, taken by a lot of people whom I have spoken to as the proof of liberty of speech – and thought – in the United States. And some of them are stunned and disturbed.

[. . .]

Ginette is going to announce my (faked) departure for the Midi in four days. In reality, I will stay at home and work on *Judith*. Because of the fake voyage, I have refused invitations from Loureau and from Paul Louis Weiller for me to join the Chaplins for the première of his film and to have supper afterwards. Too bad – *Judith* comes first.

I could make sure of some films for myself here in the future. For example, my Arles story. But I am putting all that back for another trip so I don't hold up my return and don't compromise a film with that dear little Leslie, whose sincere friendship touches me profoundly. Yet something tells me that no American producer will take on *Three Rooms in Manhattan*.

[. . .]

Dear Dido, give my love to Ga and Jeannot and also our friend Bessie. I often think of Jeannot and Ga and I imagine you all here, especially you, in the kitchen at avenue Frochot. That doesn't stop me from dreaming of Leona Drive – even more beautiful seen from Paris.

All my love.

Jean

1 Originally in English.

To Dido Renoir
Beverly Hills

Dear Dido,

It's late. Ginette has gone home. The nephew is in the country. Eva[1] has not yet arrived from Rome. I am alone in the apartment and I must admit that it rather pleases me. All the better to think of you. Tomorrow, Ginette and I will take advantage of the Sunday to make progress with *Judith*. Maybe we will get to the end of the first act. The changes seem fine to me. They correspond to those I made to *La Grande Illusion*, once the screenplay was established, by collating it with the results of my conversations with prisoners of war.

You are right. I must beware of the [Comédie) Française.[2] If I could guarantee a good role for Paul Meurisse in a film (but I haven't one in mind) and *Judith* – Jean Serge claims he would leave the [Comédie] Française. But I am afraid of that responsibility.

Phone call from Edith Piaf.[3] She wants me to shoot *Irma La Douce*[4] with her, when I want, with the budget I want. I think that I should stay faithful to my programme, but am touched by this confidence.

[. . .]

Wednesday, fake departure for the Midi – clever me! Tuesday night dinner at the Rouarts. Sunday night fake return from the Midi with, I hope, the second act – at least – of *Judith*. Tell Ga and Jeannot that I really miss them. Affectionate regards to Bessie.

I love you very, very much,

Jean.

1 Evangèle, second wife of Claude Renoir Jr.
2 Long-standing theatrical institution priding itself on pure traditions and with a tenacious attitude towards its members.
3 Famous French singer who made a cameo appearance in *French Cancan*.
4 *Irma La Douce*, Broadway musical eventually filmed by Billy Wilder in 1963 with Shirley Maclaine.

To Dido Renoir
Beverly Hills

23 October 1957
Paris

Dear Dido,

I received your letter of the 17th and I'll reply to it when I am a little more calm. For the moment, I am troubled by the return of Rossellini. Ingrid telephoned me and said that Roberto really wanted to see me. She left me alone with him and he told me the whole story. This man is in the ridiculous and lamentable state that romantics call *la passion*. For the authors of *fabliaux*[1] in the Middle Ages, it was the subject of jokes. Let's simply look at the facts: he is very unhappy. Sonali is hiding in Paris and he doesn't dare see her. He has explained the situation frankly to Ingrid. He is looking for a retreat for Sonali and is thinking of Haut de Cagnes.[2] Ingrid pretended to take this all <u>lightly</u>, but when Roberto left to wash his hands, she had a brief collapse in my arms which distressed me. Both of them have asked me to keep completely silent about all this, but they know that I can't keep anything from you and I have taken Ginette into my confidence (she is typing this letter), for I need the support of friends to see things clearly. Rossellini is going to return to finish his film in India. Then, when the fuss has calmed down, he and Ingrid will arrange their separation. Probably Santa Marinella will remain as a sort of common ground with the children. Roberto dreams of not making any more films but writing and living in a shack in the South of France with Sonali. We are swimming in s... but they are both very unhappy and deserve our genuine sympathy. Under the bonds of secrecy, you might tell all this to Gabrielle.

With all my love,
Jean Renoir, happy not to be Roberto Rossellini and to have Dido.

1 Secular, often bawdy tales popular in medieval France.
2 Town next to Cagnes-sur-Mer, clearly visible from Les Collettes.

To Dido Renoir
Beverly Hills

26 October 1957
Paris

Dear Dido,

I have had such a sweet letter from Leslie.[1] But tonight I am too tired to send her a reply. Despite that, I feel myself full of the desire to work with her, and to let her know how much I was touched by her kind – wonderful – affection.

[367]

To be frank, being away from home makes me selective. And there isn't a big place in my heart for non-familial affections. My thoughts are too occupied by you and Alain, the kids and Jane. I also miss Ga and Jeannot.

I finished, a few minutes ago, the corrections to *Judith*. I think that there is still a little work to do on this play. But it is now sufficiently precise from the 'Occupation' point of view for me to read it to people.

Tomorrow, Sunday, nothing can be done. I see Ingrid in the afternoon – the theatre in the round (in bad shape) tonight.

Monday – lunch with Bazin in the suburbs, regarding his book on me – he is introducing me to a new collaborator – I blush at the importance given to my lucubrations in suburbia. Afternoon, conversations on this book, the evening, seeing several films at the Cinémathèque – for my TV appearance *Joie de vivre*[2] and to get back some 16mm copies.

Tuesday – rendezvous which I couldn't get out of with the heiress to the Countess of Ségur – then more screenings – then *Irma La Douce* (Piaf project).

Wednesday morning – radio – afternoon reading *Judith* to Herbert. Time is passing, Dido, and each obligation puts back my return. But once I have a solution for *Judith*, I will cancel all my engagements and I will come home.

Lunch with Peck, Floflo, Pierre Gaut, Maud – Tuesday. We shall eat 'Jewish'. I read *The Waltz of the Toreadors*[3] – it's amazing – exactly the story of Esta and Dudley. A thousand *loves*[4] to Bessie – my very affectionate thought to Ga and Jeannot. All my love to you.

Jean

If I don't restrain myself, I'll be writing you a ten-page letter.

1 Leslie Caron.
2 Broadcast on 12 November, a television show made at the Théâtre de l'Alhambra, in which Renoir recreated famous scenes from his films with the original actors.
3 Play by Jean Anouilh, filmed by John Guillermin in 1962.
4 Originally in English.

To Dido Renoir
Beverly Hills

30 October 1957
Paris

Dear Dido,

At last! I haven't written to you in three days. I've been missing it. Tonight I am alone at the house and I've settled down in the kitchen with you and that's my greatest pleasure!

If I'm not careful, I will allow myself to be caught up in 'obligations' again. That is to say, swallowed up from nine in the morning until one the next morning by radio interviews, lunch with friends, elegant dinners (Paul Louis Weiller tomorrow night), group screenings. This life has its compensations. The first is the pleasure of knowing that people in Paris willingly accept me. The second is . . . (wait for it) . . . but I must tell the story from the beginning: Screening of an old print of *La Grande Illusion*, in a theatre which the Cinémathèque is allowed to use at the Musée Pédagogique, rue d'Ulm at the Panthéon. The old print was in excellent condition – perfect 'sound' – after examining it, I concluded that it's the print that had disappeared 'in Germany'. After the screening, I took it off with Ginette in the *macchina* to the main gate at LTC (laboratory) Saint Cloud and left it in the hands of Faidherbe. The slackness at the Cinémathèque had made us lose our property. But because of its chaos, we got it back. Not bad!

[. . .]

I said *au revoir* to Ingrid today. She is going to be in London for eighteen months. Did I tell you that I saw *Tea and Sympathy*, and that she is magnificent?

[. . .]

Today I read *Judith* to some 'non-professionals'. Very good reaction – I can see some corrections. Bika[1] was clearly moved.

Titra have offered to let me make a film on 'whatever subject I wish, provided it includes some great crowd scenes'. Bika isn't happy about it.

I will stop the news, because it is less important than my love for you. I want to have at least these last three lines to say how much I love you.

Jean

1 Bika Reed, former assistant to Vittorio de Sica, who worked as Renoir's assistant on *Orvet* and the films *French Cancan* and *Eléna et les Hommes*.

To Dido Renoir
Beverly Hills

Dear Dido,

I am waiting until tomorrow to wire Mr Smith at Berkeley University. Maybe the night will bring some inspiration. However, I have made a decision. Ginette suggested I put everything on paper, with the pros on one side and the cons on another. The pros are the children, fame, the English version of *Judith*, money. The cons are Gabrielle, my need to be with you in our house for a few months, Nenette, preparing the next film. This last reason is not the major one, but it is important nevertheless. I am getting old. In a few years I'll still be able to give lectures to students; and the older I get, the more impressed they'll be by the moronic statements I'll utter. But while I'm still standing, I'd like to make a few more films and plays.

I'll try finding an Englishman or American to help me write a nice letter to Mr Smith. I am very touched and honoured by his offer, and I am genuinely sorry I have to pass it up this time. It would have been fun for you and I to be on campus, and we could have seen the children every day. Besides, there was the certainty of getting $7,500, which is not the case with my film project.

If *Three Rooms in Manhattan* does happen, and if we shoot at the beginning of the summer, as Leslie suggested, I will have to make several trips to New York. Between pre-production there and pre-production in a studio, probably in Hollywood, I could not possibly find the time to be in Berkeley. If the project doesn't happen, I won't leave Paris until I have made an agreement with a producer for another picture with Leslie Caron. I've just got some new ideas which could make a far more interesting picture than *Three Rooms in Manhattan*.

I'll try to get these ideas down on paper and send you a synopsis in a few days. I have just given Ginette a rough account of the various themes of the story. Without having looked for it I found one which is the opposite of Chaplin's *The Kid*. A very young girl and a very old and senile grandfather who are starving. The real theme of the film would be hunger. My enthusiasm may fade, but once more I hope I am seeing the positive results of some sort of unconscious gestation, whereby ideas I had been playing around with for Leslie are brought out under different forms. Another advantage would be that the film could be almost entirely narrated in voice-over, which would facilitate the making of an English version. What worries me the most is the question of my passport. I'll try to get an American distributor interested, and ask them to get me hired by their parent company in New York.

This is how I see my time schedule:

– Complete *Judith*;

– Read it to Herbert (this has not been done yet) and Meyer of the Comédie Française;

– Help Ginette to settle *La Grande Illusion*, Jonas, Daber, Rudier, Lejeune; problems relating to prints of old films; and if possible, get the rights of *Boudu* for 'Les Films RS'.

– Make a trip to Essoyes and Cagnes.

The last part of these plans would probably coincide with Leslie's return from New York. I'll stop by in London on my way back to see her.

Concurrently with my filmic preoccupations, life goes on. I received a call from Inspector Isnard from National Security. His men have just recovered a bunch of forged Renoirs and he needs my help to have them legally locked up. First I'll look at them, to make sure they are all forgeries, which is the consensus from the experts at the Louvre. I was careless enough to use this phone call as an excuse for being late in the presence of a journalist. He wasted no time in reporting it, and the news appeared in *France-Soir*.

I was also careless enough to mention Kurt Jurgens'[1] visit to Hollywood to the press, and now all the papers are claiming I am remaking *La Grande Illusion*, which did not help in our relations with Cinédis. They even printed a photograph of Kurt wearing Stroheim's uniform! . . .

I keep being hounded by American journalists, who are convinced I'm hiding Sonali Dasgupta [sic] in the apartment. Their curiosity has sharpened since I showed up for dinner at Paul-Louis Weiller's with a ravishing eighteen-year-old girl from India. She was actually dumped on me by Ingrid when she left for London, and she is the wife of the owner of about twenty hotels in India, including the Grand Hotel in Calcutta. Her company gave me the aura of a sly devil at Weiller's, where I met a bunch of delightful people: a certain Prince Massimo and his wife Dawn Adams[2] [sic], who co-starred with Chaplin in his latest film. Massimo is one of the funniest Italians I have ever met. The lesson to be drawn from the events of this past week: never talk in front of a journalist. (In this last sentence you'll recognize Ginette's style.) Mary Meerson is still calling me 'the bard of Modern Times'. I have here a note from Ginette, so it's her rather than me who is quoting Mary Meerson's claim that I was 'the dynamite which exploded the theatre of the Institut Pédagogique at a screening of *Diary of a Chambermaid*.'

Dearest Dido, I'll leave you now to open the door to Paul Meurisse, who has been suggesting I read *Judith* to Danielle Darrieux.[3] Ginette thinks it's an excellent idea.

The only thing left to do is to send you my love.

Jean

1 Kurt Jurgens (1912–82), German actor whose films included *The Devil's General* (Helmut Kautner, 1955), *Et Dieu Créa la Femme* (Roger Vadim, 1955), and *The Inn of the Sixth Happiness* (Mark Robson, 1958).
2 Dawn Addams (1930–85), actress whose credits included *The Moon Is Blue* (Otto Preminger, 1954), *A King in New York* (Charles Chaplin, 1957), and *The Thousand Eyes of Dr Mabuse* (Fritz Lang, 1960).
3 Danielle Darrieux (b.1917), French actress whose credits include *La Ronde* (Max Ophuls, 1950), *Madame de ...* (Max Ophuls, 1953), and *Les Démoiselles de Rochefort* (Jacques Demoy, 1967).

1958

To Leslie Caron

Dear Leslie,

Dido and I saw *Gigi*[1] the night before last. I had an important meeting with Arthur Freed yesterday. But let's talk about *Gigi* first. The picture is excellent and should be most beneficial for you. I can't think of any film better than this one in the 'musical comedy' genre. It was made by people of taste, and it is never boring. The two hours the screening lasted went by like a half-hour for Dido and I. What delights us most is that, even though your part is not more important than Jourdan's and Chevalier's, you really emerge as the lead of the story. In spite of the beautiful score, the beautiful sets, the beautiful costumes, and some very successfully executed special effects, like the various arrivals at Maxim's, this pleasant spectacle might have been too lightweight were it not for you. It is Leslie, the little mosquito, who gives some depth to the whole show.

In our wire we used 'extraordinary', which means unlike anybody else. Your performance in *Gigi* convinces me further that you bring to the screen a quality that has not been seen before. You showed glimpses of it on stage, at certain moments of *Orvet*. You showed it two or three times in *Gigi* also; when you forget your surroundings, your technique, any intended grace or clumsiness in your moves, and surrender yourself to genuine emotion. Forgive me for this old cliché: it's when you see red! When you are no longer yourself, or maybe even better than your ordinary self, when your gestures have lost all self-consciousness and are dictated by a demon within yourself, which is probably only your own *alter ego*.

We were very entertained by your gags and the faces you made, and by the ways you played with your hat. But these are not enough for me any more, because I know you can reach deeper into my heart as a spectator.

The outcome of my meeting with Freed[2] is the following: he now seems willing to do *Three Rooms*, but still thinks that a good writer should be put on the project to fatten up the story.

In *Gigi*, your scene in front of the mirror more than ever makes me want to do an introspective film with you. This could be accomplished if

[373]

Three Rooms in Manhattan was done from the woman's point of view instead of the man's. After all, this is how Chaplin's films succeed: by identifying with the audience. We could do the same thing with you.

Arthur went to New York. He'll be back on 2 April, and he hopes he'll be able to give me a definitive answer before my departure to New York on the morning of the 6th. I have an appointment with Mr McKenna, head of the Story Department, on Monday. I met him with Arthur Freed and I must give him the synopsis of *Three Rooms*.

In other words, for the first time since we dreamed of doing this picture together, there is a glimpse of hope, and this is thanks to your courage and your insight. I feel most enthusiastic, and hope that with your collaboration I'll make a picture that will be a step ahead of my other films. I wish we were already shooting the sequences in front of your mirror when you take a merciless look at yourself.

Dido and I send our warmest thoughts to Peter[3] and Christopher.

Fond wishes,

Jean Renoir

1 *Gigi* (Vincente Minnelli, 1958), which starred Leslie Caron, Louis Jourdan and Maurice Chevalier.
2 Arthur Freed (1894–1973), producer most famous for MGM's quality musicals.
3 Peter Hall (b.1930), noted stage director, knighted in 1977, who was married to Leslie Caron from 1956 to 1966. They had a son, Christopher, and a daughter, Jenny.

To Clifford Odets [*Original in English*]   24 April 1958
Paris

Dear Cliff,

We spent our first week in Paris shooting a new trailer for the reissue of *La Grande Illusion*.

I met several people involved with *The Big Knife*. We had to stop in spite of a very big success. Every night the theatre was packed. But the new owner (a lady) had already postponed her own show about two months. Finally we had to make room for her. The play she presented to the Parisians lasted two weeks. A second one was also a flop. The backers of *The Big Knife* tried to rent another theatre. Unfortunately meanwhile Gélin had accepted a deal for a picture. *The Big Knife* would start again if they can find a male star, preferably a film star. It is difficult. Actors don't like to follow something already started by another one.

As for the money, the Société des Auteurs did not hear from Rotschild [sic] who still holds your money. Even if he had sent it back (the money of *The Big Knife*) to the Société des Auteurs, the rule of this Association is that they cannot accept two 'powers of attorney'. If you decide to give your power of attorney to Ginette Courtois-Doynel (my representative in Paris), you should cancel the authorization you gave to Mr Rotschild. It is probably better to keep Rotschild as your representative, since the power of attorney you have to give only to one person is for not only *The Big Knife* but all your works represented in France. Rotschild is an established agent with a permanent office in Paris. Mrs Courtois-Doynel may have some work outside of France. I may take her to help me in some picture in Italy or anywhere else. Of course if you prefer to have her represent you instead of Rotschild, she would do it gladly. As for myself I don't think it would be wise to choose me as your representative since I am too often in America. Another difficulty is my American citizenship.

Dido and I think of you often. We found Paris beautiful: exactly as you would like it.

We hope you and the children are well and that we will see you very soon.

With all our love,
Jean Renoir

To Clifford Odets [*Original in English*]

17 May 1958
Paris

Dear Clifford,

We are so happy with your letter received this morning, Jean even more than I because you liked his piece in *Art News*. As for the book it is difficult to work on it here, too many distractions, projects, friends, trips, newspaper people, radio, tv, etc. And in California no French secretary! Still it will work out somehow.

Jean is going to make a film over here, also an original story, that is if the dates work out without hindrance to his film with Leslie Caron.

The distributors of *La Grande Illusion* (Cinédis-Lourau) are so confident with the results of a referendum all over Europe that they have decided to show the picture at the Brussels Fair and also to postpone the reissue to September–October which is a better season than now.

Concerning the royalties of *The Big Knife* everything is in order. Mr Rotschild [sic] talked to Jean over the telephone and has the money at his disposal. At the first opportunity Jean will go to collect it and then buy the musical supplies and instruments you want. Also the stamps. But I have been told one is not allowed to send them by mail and we will be staying in Europe for some time. Should this be so, do you wish me to buy them nevertheless, keep them for you, and bring them back when we return?

Your last envelope shows you are now at 20th [Century-Fox], that is good and we hope you are happy and working hard at your movie, written and directed by you it is bound to be exciting. How are the kids? We miss you all and mostly you.

All our love,
Dido

PS. According to the newspapers we are supposed to live in the midst of a political turmoil. But the Parisians are used to revolutions and outside of the streets surrounding official buildings or symbolic landmarks like the Arch of Triumph life goes on as usual. Dido just discovered a new kind of goat cheese which is a dream. Those are the important news.

Love,
Jean

To Jean Renoir [*Original in English*]   *27 June 1958*
Paris   *Los Angeles*

Dear Jean and Dido,

[...] I'm clearing out of the studio today, Friday. I'll go home, do neglected chores, and Esta and I will see about getting reservations for London. She won't fly, so it may be a while before we can get away. She's not too well and I'm secretly worried about her. Physically she's all right, psychically no. Doesn't sleep, very nervous – all that. I'm afraid my being away from her every day for so long hasn't been good for her. Anyway, that's over.

I haven't been able to do a thing about rendering your play for America. You'll understand why. And Esta didn't want to go ahead, she wanted to wait until I could work along with her. So I told her we'd be getting a rough literal version from your man in New York, but so far nothing has arrived. Do you know if he's done it?

I'll get to the version as soon as I can now, but I'd like to wait till we have the literal translation, as something to work from. As I cannot really translate myself, what I can give to it is an American style to match your French and personal expressiveness. I know your style, even in English, is sharp, exact, pithy and paradoxical. When thought is paradoxical, and

the temperament behind it too, the verbal style must match it and catch it
... We shall see. More about this later.

I know you are all very busy. Anyone around Jean is busy, for he is like
the great whale, always swimming through new seas and throwing up
great spouts – sounding and surfacing. It is hard to keep up. Dido and
Ginette, my sympathies! Also I know it's grand too, no matter how hard
you work; for there's never a dull moment around Jean.

The news we get of Paris and France is never too clear. De Gaulle seems
to have support and is doing a good job. But can he handle everyone by
mere prestige and soft speaking? I think he'll have to put his foot down, as
we say, in time. The news of the world is confused everywhere. Fireworks
everywhere. 'Double, Double, Toil and Trouble' – as Macbeth's witches
chant. I find I know nothing about the world. I only know it is in chaos and
is changing. I wish I could believe it changes for the better. But no one
knows the future. Hollywood is whistling in the dark. They started drilling
for oil here at Paramount [Studios] yesterday! Now you see oil drillers –
but no actors. Nothing shooting. Twenty big stages idle. The gate looks
like Forest Lawn.[1] No, not quite, for they're doing business at Forest Lawn
– people are dying to go there (they say). The film industry is waiting for
'Pay-TV'. What a delusion. MGM loses a couple of million a month. They
don't know where they're going, nobody. Me, I sit off and smile. So what?
I'll write you a better letter as soon as I get squared away at home.
Meantime love to you all from both of us.

Dudley [Nichols]

PS. I hope the political air won't hold up for *Carola*. I'm sure it will be a hit
... A here-and-now filmed Day-in-the-Country sounds fascinating!

1 Cemetery chain.

To Dudley Nichols [*Original in English*]   8 *July 1958*
Los Angeles   *Paris*

Dear Dudley,

It's good to know that you are happy with your screenplay. We admire
your surgical courage to have cut more than one third of your original
work. We wish the producer and director won't disappoint you. The way
you talk about this script makes us feel that it must be good and we are
anxious to see it on the screen as you conceived it.

We are stuck in Paris by my different projects. Now I foresee the possibility of a film in early spring and of the showing of *Carola*[1] in the middle of winter. That gives us a chance of seeing you when you come to Europe. If you decide to stay in England we may find a couple of days to fly to London. We miss you and Esta and a few hours with both of you would do us a lot of good.

There is one thing which is dearer to my heart than any other project and that is to have *Carola* adapted in English by you. The trouble is Lee Kresel hasn't finished yet the rough translation I asked him and which he was supposed to deliver beginning of May. I will ask Alain to have it done by somebody in Berkeley. It is too bad to think that we are delayed by the lack of this mechanical work. On the other hand the play was also delayed in Paris not only by the political events but also the fact that Paul Meurisse has been appointed partner in the 'Comédie Francaise' and cannot act in any other theatre. I think I found another actor to replace him but he will be busy with a film at the end of the year and I will have to start the production later than I expected. I also decided to reverse my policy concerning the type of theatre. Instead of a huge showplace I aim now at a small elegant one very near your Grand Hotel.

In any case I am dreaming of the day when we will be together, trembling of fear, behind the wings of a New York theatre.

Here everybody seems to agree with de Gaulle's decisions, probably deep in their hearts the politicians do not, but the public is so enthusiastic about the General that they don't dare to open their mouths. I must say those twelve solitary years in a little village on the border of Champagne and Lorraine seems to have been beneficial. Even physically he improved. His voice is better and his speeches perfectly sensible.

We didn't see Mr Marty Melcher[2] and wish he will appear. I would be delighted to shoot *Noblesse Oblige*.[3] We should change not only the name of Orvet but also the title [as it is] used in several countries for the Alec Guinness picture *Kind Hearts and Coronets*.[4]

Ginette is beside us and joins us in sending love to Esta and you.

Jean Renoir

1 *Carola* was never to receive a professional theatrical production. An English adaptation by James Bridges was produced by Norman Lloyd on US television and broadcast on 3 February 1973. Leslie Caron played the lead role opposite Mel Ferrer.
2 Martin Melcher (1915–68), producer and husband of Doris Day, with whom he made such films as *Calamity Jane* (David Butler, 1953), *Pillow Talk* (Michael Gordon, 1959), and *Move Over Darling* (Michael Gordon, 1963).
3 *Noblesse Oblige* was another title for *Les Braconniers*.
4 *Kind Hearts and Coronets* (Robert Hamer, 1949). In France it was called *Noblesse Oblige*.

To Jean Renoir [*Original in English*] 20 *July 1958*
Paris *Los Angeles*

Dear Jean and Dido,

I am trying like mad to get off a dozen scribbles that are owed but I keep getting interrupted every five minutes by Esta who is also trying like mad to get her luggage ready and do all the things which must be done before we can leave. We take the train out Thursday next and I have a full schedule of things to be done every day until then.[. . .] I am sorry *Carola* has been delayed but it will work out better for my chore, which I can't start now until we return in late September. I cannot work while travelling and wonder if anybody ever has, really. I managed it only once in my life, when I did *The Informer* script on Ford's[1] yacht, during a slow cruise to Mexico and back; but I remember I had to lock myself in a stateroom for eighteen hours a day, for there were other gay carefree passengers on board! And I wasn't on the Pacific at all, at least I don't remember it – I was in Dublin! ... You are very busy I know. I am sorry you will not have Paul Meurisse, though glad he has the prestige of the new appointment – he's such a fine artist. I am sure you will find a good substitute; you have the flair; after all, you found Meurisse. I rather like your shift of theatre, to a small elegant one. I loathe big theatres for a good play. Most of our N[ew]Y[ork] theatres are too large, the London theatres are so much better. A big theatre is a place for spectacle, for music, not for thought and passion and the communication of individual personality and character and feeling. As you know better than I. Perhaps the major difference between stage and film is that film is for large theatres while stage plays should be presented in small intimate theatres. At least it is one difference. Film is stentorian, no? (Of course film can be anything.)

Yes, it was a nuisance that Kresel did not make a rough translation as promised. I hope Alain can get it done. [. . .]

Our love to you all and to Ginette. I don't know if we'll be able to cross to Paris or not. We shall be at I think the Green Park Hotel in Half Moon Street. We shall have to take Esta's sister to the seaside for a couple of weeks. I am also hiring a car for a two weeks' drive in rural England which I've always wanted to ramble through. In any case I shall write you as soon as we are settled in London and tell you my plans and whether we can cross the Channel. [. . .]

We embrace you!

Our love to you all,

Dudley (& Esta) [Nichols]

[379]

1 John Ford (1895–1973), director famous chiefly for his classic Westerns. Nichols wrote the scripts of some of his finest films, including *Judge Priest* (1934), *The Informer* (1935), and *Stagecoach* (1939).

To Dudley Nichols [*Original in English*]

7 *August 1958*
Paris

Dear Dudley,

You must have arrived in England by now. It is exciting and frustrating to know that Esta and you are so close. Dido, Ginette and I hope you had a pleasant trip.

I have interesting news for *Carola*. Kurt Jurgens, who is very much in demand in America, was asked to appear on Broadway. He has the possibility of choosing the play and believes that the best thing for him would be *Carola*. I also believe that no actor could be better than Jurgens in the part of 'the General'. This opportunity changes all my plans since Jurgens does not want to open on Broadway if the play has been shown in Paris first.

It is too bad Lee Kresel did not keep his promise to send you the rough translation in May. You would probably have found the time to polish it and we could have grabbed this unexpected chance.

In order to save a little time, I asked my son Alain to have the rough translation done in Berkeley. This work is already started.

Your letter suggests that your schedule in England will be pretty busy. I am not sure to have the time to go to England before 18 September. Probably we'll have to go to Venice to present *La Grande Illusion*. But our plans are extremely vague and all our moves are completely unpredictable. Perhaps we will find the possibility to cross the Channel. Please let us know where you are.

Dido, Ginette and I send our love to Esta and you.

Jean Renoir

To Charles Spaak

Roquebrune-Cap Martin

22 *August 1958*
Paris

Dear Charles,

Just a brief note to wish you, Claudie and the girls an enjoyable time, and to give you some news.

– Ledoux[1] must have written to break the news to you about the great event: *La Grande Illusion* is among the twelve selected films. This information is still confidential. Not a word to the press.

Moreover, in the future Bosc asks us to refer to Mr de la Mazelière, at the publicity department of Cinédis.

Due to some indiscretion I have learned that our film is the only French film of the twelve.

– I saw the new credits sequence. It is gorgeous, and gives the impression that the print of *La Grande Illusion* is new.

– I'll go to Brussels for the screening of the picture at the Exhibition and for its première in a cinema whose name I don't know on 17 October.

– Chabert is completely enthusiastic and co-operative. He is still pushing Broadway for Paris.

– Dido and I will go to Venice on 30 August. We'll stop over in Lausanne to try putting a stop to the clandestine showings reported by the buyer.

– In Venice, a tribute to Stroheim. Screening of two reels and speech by yours truly.

– We hope we'll be able to pass by Menton to see you all, around 7 September.

– Besides the problem of illegal showings in Switzerland, we still have the problems of other film clubs. Ginette will send you copies of letters she has been writing to all concerned. Dido and I will go to the Centre as well. Bosc will try to have Loureau intercede with Flaud, whom I'll see in Venice.

– The Cinémathèque is lending us a precious hand in our fight against illegal showings.

– Bosc requested we cut the number of photographs I used in the trailer. His reasons make sense: he is afraid it will make people in the audience feel they have already seen the film and decide not to see it again. On the contrary, by not showing too much, we might lead them to think they may have seen the picture but don't remember it too well, and decide to see it again.

The problem is that these small changes will cost a little more money. The final decision will be taken at the beginning of next week. At the same time Mr Bert will give us an estimate. Ginette is planning to ask Cinédis for an advance to pay the expenses.

That is all for now.

My fondest regards to you all,

Jean Renoir

1 Jacques Ledoux, curator of the Cinémathèque Royal de Belgique for forty years until his death in 1988.

To Dudley Nichols [*Original in English*]   *September 1958*
Los Angeles   *Paris*

Dear Dudley,

Dido and I are anxious to have some news.

You must be back home and enjoying the Californian heat wave. Esta is certainly happy to work again in her nice study with the sight of the growing [h]edge which hides so conveniently your neighbours' activities.

Alain told me that the rough translation of *Carola* is about finished. He will send it to you in a very near future.

Here the weather continues to be unfriendly.

I work like a beaver on a TV film.

Tomorrow we'll go to Normandy to see Georges Braque. On our way back I'll deliver a lecture for the Red Cross in Rouen.

La Grande Illusion will be released in less than a month. Luckily this film is amongst the twelve best pictures of all times at the Brussels fair[1] and perhaps that will help our business. Unfortunately the French distributors and exhibitors are only interested in 'naughty stories'. There is practically one star left in the sky of the French movie industry and that is Brigitte Bardot.[2] I confess she is fascinating. Maybe the public likes her as a reaction against over-acting players. After Kirk Douglas pulling faces in *Van Gogh* [sic][3] it is a rest to watch an actress who does not act at all. Unfortunately some good directors have decided to make her 'an actress'. I am afraid she will succeed and she will join the crowd of the forgotten stars.

A little note would make us happy.

We miss Esta and you very much and hope that we will be together in a not too distant future.

With all our love,
Jean Renoir

1 *La Grande Illusion* was voted one of the twelve greatest films of all time at the Brussels World Fair by an international conference of 117 critics.
2 Brigitte Bardot (b.1934), actress and one-time sex symbol, whose films include *Et Dieu Créa la Femme* (Roger Vadim, 1955), *La Vérité* (Henri-Georges Clouzot, 1960), and *Le Mépris* (Jean-Luc Godard, 1963).
3 Kirk Douglas starred as Vincent Van Gogh in *Lust for Life*.

To Dudley Nichols [*Original in English*]   *7 October 1958*
Los Angeles   *Paris*

Dear Dudley,

We received your letter and it was for all of us, including Ginette, a great relief since we were longing for some news. We are happy to know that you feel well now and wish you a pleasant rest in your beautiful house.

You probably received the rough translation of *Carola* made in Berkeley. I had not time to read and correct it. Since it was done in a hurry there must be many mistakes. I noticed on page 8, act I, second line from the top, which should be read the following way:

'Carola
... end of the coal
                    Campan (proudly)
end of the coal ... It would be too stupid if your impudence were to compromise everything.
                    Mireille (practical)
Rather than ... '

There must be many others.

May I add that nothing is more deceiving than a rough translation. But Esta will give you the real spirit of the play and this work will be only a practical help for you: a kind of dictionary.

La Grande Illusion starts again on the Champs-Elysées. Exactly as twenty-two years ago, the distributor, the last minute, lost confidence in this picture. The first time they said the picture was too new, now they considered the picture as too old. Result: the biggest queue on the Champs-Elysées and the audience likes the film more than any other one shown presently. It is a kind of revolution around the offices of the noble avenue. The distributor is now very confident ... (I always said it ...).

Dido, Ginette and I are delighted with this adventure but we have to check carefully the distribution business in provincial towns.

A beautiful sunshine warms our apartment and also our house, bringing us closer to you and Esta and sunny California. We would like to see you. Something is missing in our lives when we remain too long far away from you.

The three of us send our love to Esta and you.

Sincerely,

Jean Renoir

To Clifford Odets [*Original in English*]   *10 November 1958*
Paris

Dear Cliff,

Back from Nice and on our way to Lille we stopped two days in Paris. On the wall of the living room in our old apartment we found the tree with the tempting golden fruit. We don't need it to think of you but it made us long for a little chat. It is why Dido and I send you this note. Too bad it is a one way conversation. We miss your voice and your eyes which become entirely round with the eyebrows very high when you want to affirm something evident; evident for you or for us but not always for the other ones.

We hope you will change your decision and make your fingers dirty again painting. The little tree is too nice. It is the expression of a part of yourself. Your plays being the expression of another part of yourself.

I would love to make a film with Noah, but when! I got involved with too many things. A TV show which I have to write and direct, a ballet for a charming girl named Ludmilla Tcherina,[1] and a film in spring. I believe I found a good story, a kind of serious comedy which should be acted by dignified actors not too conscious of the silliness of the situation. I am also happy with the title: *Le Déjeuner sur l'Herbe.*

We are anxious to know more about your script for 20th Century-Fox. You seem pleased with it so it must be good. And we have a feeling that you may work very freely with Jerry Wald[2] who likes you.

Tell the kids that we are happy they are well. We don't wish you to find the time for a vacation knowing too well that you will never take it. Mozart is your real vacation, and after all he is as good as the Grand Canyon or the pinewoods of Oregon.

My old picture *La Grande Ilusion* is very successful. We have the most impressive queue on the Champs-Elysées and we do better than any picture in provincial cities. But it isn't easy to be a businessman. This new task added to the other ones will keep us here until next fall. That means many many months before being with you unless you come to see us. It would be wonderful!

With all our love,
Jean & Dido

PS. Mme Doynel is delighted with the stamps and thanks you.

---

1 Renoir wrote the argument for the short ballet *Le Feu des Poudres*, performed by Raymond Rouleau, as part of Ludmilla Tcherina's ballet, *Les Amants de Teruel.*

2 Jerry Wald (1911–62), producer whose credits included *They Drive by Night* (Raoul Walsh, 1940), *Key Largo* (John Huston, 1948), and *An Affair to Remember* (Leo McCarey, 1957).

To Pablo Picasso[1]   *28 November 1958*
Cannes   *Paris*

Dear Mr Picasso,

I have written a ballet for Ludmilla Tcherina. Enclosed with this letter is a synopsis of the project in question. As you will see, it is an allegory. However, as you might find the synopsis rather long to read through, here is a brief summary of it:

A country of military dictatorship and scientific progress decides to conquer a country where life's charms are the only law. On the one side industrial organization, arid mountains stuffed with uranium, derricks, factories, a divinity which is none other than the atom, and a high priestess who transmits to the faithful the orders of the Divinity. On the other side, an earthly paradise, or maybe a golden age. In the shade of palm trees or rose bushes couples make love, sleep or do nothing at all.

The first country attacks the second with the aim of saving it from turpitude. The inhabitants of the second country respond to this attack with smiles and flowers. Single combat betwen the high priestess of the first country and the chief of the second country will conclude the argument in the time-honoured manner: the male conquering the female with his sexual brutality. The soldiers of the two camps follow their leaders' example.

Although I know that you have several projects in hand and that you will probably not have time to devote to my ballet, I nevertheless want to ask if you might agree to design the set. My nephew,[2] who you know well, thinks that your daughter might be able to follow through and supervise the making of the set and the costumes.

I hope that you are in good health and I send you my sincerest wishes and compliments.

Jean Renoir

1 Pablo Picasso (1881–1973), Spanish-born artist of huge influence in twentieth-century art, especially in his Cubist period. He did not work on the ballet as proposed by Renoir.
2 Claude Renoir Jr photographed Picasso at work in H.-G. Clouzot's *Le Mystère Picasso* in 1955.

In November, Jean Renoir forms the Compagnie Jean Renoir, to be run in equal partnership by him and Ginette Courtois-Doynel, his representative in Paris.

1959

To Leslie Caron   *10 January 1959*
Los Angeles   *Paris*

Dear Leslie,

We received a letter from Bessie telling us about the fire in Benedict Cañon and about how much your presence had comforted her when on two occasions you were in our house while it was under threat.

Dido and I are moved to tears at this new proof of friendship which you have shown us. Your dear little face which we love so much is, if possible, even more close to us, more engrained in our thoughts. It's very nice to allow oneself to be overcome by this wave of warm affection.

With our very dear love,
Jean & Dido

In January, Jean Renoir shoots Le Testament du Docteur Cordelier.

To Alain Renoir   *16 March 1959*
                                                   Paris

Dear Alain,

After thinking it over, I can tell you that I will be very happy to spend the semester from February to May or June 1960 in Berkeley.

Could you tell me if I should write to Mr Henry Smith, and what kind of letter should I write?

My decision is largely motivated by the experiment I have just completed in agreement with French Television. This experiment consisted of applying the same methods as live television, with a few exceptions, to a movie made for television. It meant the screenplay had to be written differently, and the rehearsals had to be as thorough and precise as if we were working on a play (we even rehearsed outside in freezing weather). We had to use several cameras simultaneously (from three to eight, depending on the scene), with sets built on three sides like stage sets. Even outside, I had placed the cameras ahead of time to record the actors walking by. Regardless of which scene we were doing, the master shot, middle shots and close-ups were recorded at the same time. I could never have done this with a movie crew. Television crews are used to live shows during which the audience don't sit around and wait, as we know.

I chose to adapt *Dr Jekyll and Mr Hyde* by Stevenson. I tried to follow the original story as closely as possible; which means I did not add a female character, as in the several versions done by Hollywood. However, I set the story in Paris, in the present. I changed the title to *Le Testament du Docteur Cordelier*.

Rehearsals excluded, I shot the whole film, which is of normal length, in eleven days. If we don't take into account the salaries paid to several actors, Jean-Louis Barrault,[1] Vitold,[2] to some of the technicians, and myself, who will get a percentage on the income from the theatrical release (I am co-owner of the film with French Television), the film cost 31 million francs. If we had shot it in Paris as a regular feature, the budget would have been about 125 million.

I am waiting for a rough cut to assess whether the picture is as interesting to watch as it was to rehearse and shoot. Meanwhile, my experiment did stir up a lot of controversy. Many people in the film industry rose up against me, calling me a traitor. Some even started a campaign demanding that the government ban the showing of the film. However, in the past week the mood has changed, and it appears that many producers, technicians, or salesmen, are reconsidering their position.

What interested me in this enterprise, and I was able to verify it when I screened the dailies (I watched them in sequence order, and it took two entire days), is that this method allows the actors to perform in a progressive manner, and rely on their own inspiration. The equilibrium of each scene rests more on direct interaction between the actors, and less on the director's planning, thereby allowing moments of genuine intensity. Of course his 'natural' progression only exists within each scene, and they last from three to six minutes. It would be interesting to plan shows such as this so that they are shot in order of sequences, within the time-frame of a live performance. But already this rigorous application of a scene-by-scene method appears to lend a new style to the picture on screen. I must also add that this method gives the advantage of allowing the crew a more active participation in the process. The many cameramen who follow a scene with their cameras are constantly required to make on-the-spot visual choices, instead of merely following the preconceived and often wavering instructions given by the director of photography, or the director. This is the reason why I decided to work with several newsreel cameramen. They know when they shoot a horse race, for instance, that they can't ask the winning horse to run the race again because they missed their shot.

I am trying to apply part of this method to the film I'll shoot this summer.[3] It will be a colour film in which the photography will have tremendous importance.

These experiments might be of interest to the students when I get to Berkeley. In any case, because they are so fresh in my memory, I'll be able to approach the subject matter of my 'lectures' in a less theoretical manner. I might even attempt to recreate such an experiment at Berkeley.

Dido and I cannot stop thinking about Gabrielle.[4] In a way, we are relieved that we were not there. Thus her death remains unreal. Somehow, I am convinced she'll never leave and that she'll stay with us until it is our turn to go.

Bessie tells me that you have a cold. I hope it's over now.

We are very proud of John's[5] grades in school.

In this Parisian climate, Dido thinks about Jane[6] with gratitude every day, when she puts on her nightgown.

I came out of the clinic, minus a hernia, last Thursday. I need to rest for two weeks. Everything went fine.

We have heard from Dumas, but not from Travis Bogard.[7]

Dido is fine. She has found a charwoman who is a 'cleanliness maniac'. But she still has to handle the rest of the household chores, beginning with feeding your dear father who lives like a prince.

Dido and I send our love to Peter,[8] John, Jane and you.

Jean

1 Jean-Louis Barrault (1910–94), distinguished stage and film actor whose credits included *Les Enfants du Paradis* (Marcel Carné, 1945) and *La Ronde* (Max Ophuls, 1950).
2 Michel Vitold (b.1915), Russian-born actor whose credits include *L'Entrée des Artistes* (Mark Allegret, 1938), *Judex* (Georges Franju, 1964), and *L'Aveu* (Costa-Gavras, 1970).
3 *Le Déjeuner sur l'Herbe.*
4 Gabrielle Renard Slade died in Beverly Hills on 26 February 1959.
5 John Renoir, Alain's elder son.
6 Alain Renoir's wife.
7 Travis Bogard, professor in the Theatre Department at UC Berkeley.
8 Alain Renoir's younger son.

To Jean Guilhem   *21 April 1959*
Administrateur du Festival de   *Paris*
Théâtre Amateur, Cahors

Dear Mr Guilhem,

I doubt whether the pre-production work I have to do for a film I am starting in June will leave me any spare time in May. Therefore, do not count on me. Nevertheless, should some unfortunate event defer my project, I would be available and would certainly come to see you. I hope you won't mind if I wish this won't happen, in spite of my desire to attend your performance of *Orvet* in Cahors.

I am very happy and flattered that you chose this play. Amongst all my wild imaginings, this is the one which remains the closest to my unrealized dreams. This is how it came to be:

After my father's death, I went to live in a house on the fringes of the Fontainebleau forest. It was because of the stories he had told me that I decided to go there. When he was young, before the war in 1870, he stayed in Marlotte and painted with Bazille, Sisley and Claude Monet. He had told me so many times about the tall beech trees that looked like 'ship masts', and the bluish light under the canopy of trees. And what I found there was as beautiful as his memories had described. I only gave up my daily walks along its mysterious paths because my career pulled me towards different horizons.

One brisk winter morning, I was travelling at a good speed in a car driven by my best friend.[1] He lost control and we ended up in a ditch. He was killed instantly. I fainted.

I came to under strange circumstances: I found myself in some sort of small square box which jerked around constantly and inexplicably. Weird shapes were stacked up around me. As I regained more consciousness, I realized these were the bodies of animals. Feeling around with my hands I could touch their fur. I was in a small van going rather fast, and I was lying in the middle of dead game. A rather large stag lay next to me. A deer stared at me with dead eyes.

The van stopped. Upon seeing I was awake, the driver told me what had happened. He had found me unconscious and had brought me to the hospital at Fontainebleau. He asked me not to mention the game that was in his car.

In fact, he dropped me in front of the entrance of a clinic, sounded his horn and sped off before they opened up.

Some weeks later, during a walk in the woods, I came face to face with this obliging poacher. This encounter was followed by many others. He became known to me, or rather he allowed me to know a little about this strange population of sylvan tramps who haunt the forests that surround the capital. The company of these last 'unassimilated people' struck my imagination. Twenty-five years later, this memory materialized in the shape of the play which you have chosen to perform.

I realized full well the problems that you are encountering in the direction of the play, having had to resolve them myself when I was rehearsing the actors on the stage of the Renaissance. In my opinion, the principal difficulty comes from the fact that many actors believe they have to speak a text regarded as 'poetic' in a tone that is supposed to be 'poetic' in itself. Well, I am almost certain that the characters in *Orvet* express themselves better if they avoid this tone and revert to its opposite, the style of everyday speeches. The language of Orvet is the most typical, and I even had to ask Leslie Caron to avoid inflections and to try out a way of speech that is almost on one note, without going so far as to affect the monotone particularly noticeable in certain interpretations of Maeterlynck [sic].[2] *Orvet* is the opposite of this style. The characters must remain perfectly natural in their language and their gestures. To help Leslie Caron, I found a little trick in the accent which, in her case, achieved good results. It was to adopt the opposite of a 'precious' way of pronouncing words. Take for example the word *bois*. An affected person would pronounce it in a rather dry manner with a shrill voice. Leslie Caron adopted a large, deep voice and added a strong circumflex accent. *Les bois* didn't completely become *boas*, but almost. In her mouth, the deep resonance of this word made one think of the echo in a valley.

My collaborator Madame Doynel is busy trying to find one or two photographs to send you. She will also be in touch with Kosma[3] about the music.

If this letter can play the part of the text you asked me for, that would suit me.

I take this opportunity to thank Cahors for having given me the pleasure of receiving a letter from Marcel Aymé,[4] who I greatly admire.

My best wishes to you, to your actors, to all those who are participating in this work and also to the public at the Cahors Festival.

Jean Renoir

1 Pierre Champagne. For full description, see *My Life and My Films*.
2 Maurice Maeterlinck (1896–1949), French playwright famous for his symbolist dramas.
3 Joseph Kosma (1905–69), composer who scored many of Renoir's films: *Le Crime de M.*

Lange, Une Partie de Campagne, La Grande Illusion, La Règle du Jeu, Eléna et les Hommes,
Le Déjeuner sur l'Herbe and *Le Caporal Epinglé.*
4 Marcel Aymé (1902–67), novelist and essayist.

To Alain Renoir

Dear Alain,

I have received your letter of 21 May, announcing my nomination to the position of Regents' Professor of English and Dramatic Arts. Would you tell Mr Henry Smith I am very grateful to him for having made this nomination possible? I'll write to him today, and to Mr Clark Kerr, whose letter I have just received. Dido and I are thrilled by the idea of spending a few months near the children, Jane and you.

We'll arrive in February. I will ask you or Jane to find us a place to live. A small apartment with two bedrooms and a living-room would be ideal. One bedroom with two beds may be enough, but we need a living-room to entertain guests. Dido would like to find a place in a hotel, or motel, or any other kind of apartment building where services are available.

Jeannot[1] is staying with us at the moment. Tomorrow, I will show him my film *Le Testament du Docteur Cordelier.* The day after tomorrow he'll visit his cousins in Troyes. If I can find the money for my next film, I will shoot it mostly at Les Collettes. If nothing else, this will give us a chance to get some photographs of the place before it changes too much. Right now, after years of neglect, it looks more beautiful than ever.

Our fondest love to all of you.

Jean Renoir

1 Jean Slade.

In July, Jean Renoir shoots Le Déjeuner sur l'Herbe *in twenty-four days, with exteriors filmed at Les Collettes and around Cagnes-sur-Mer.*

To Alain Renoir

My dear Alain,

I have received a lovely letter from Mr Henry Smith. It was passed around all over the set of *Le Déjeuner sur l'Herbe* before catching up with me. I am deeply touched and honoured by the trust your organization puts in me. I'll reply to Mr Smith in a few days, as soon as I begin to see my way through the problems of post-production. In the meantime, would you mind acting as my go-between and convey my reaction to his interesting suggestions? Bessie has found a literal translation of *Orvet*. I could stage this play and polish its dialogue with the help of one or several students during rehearsals.

Since this would be a time-consuming undertaking, I doubt I'd be able to schedule seminars on a regular basis. However, during my spare time I would make myself available to students who might seek information.

On the other hand, since they don't require lengthy preparation, I will be able to give the lectures that are requested.

I'll agree of course to any kind of curriculum, and I'll welcome any suggestion. However, I must confess that I'd be thrilled to be able to direct *Orvet* at the university.

I'll ask Bessie to send you the only existing copy of the literal translation of *Orvet*. Could you look it over? Unless it presents too much difficulty, could you also get enough copies typed, so that I can start working on it as soon as I get there?

We are going to make bronze copies of your grandfather's statues: *La Vénus* and *La Laveuse*. To avoid paying prohibitive customs duties and transportation costs, we will loan these pieces for a period of five years to museums. They won't have to pay any duties, but they must take care of transportation expenses. We are counting on the Los Angeles museum[1] for *La Laveuse*. They already have a *Vénus*. Do you think Berkeley University [sic] might be interested in the latter?

Dido and I hope Jane and the children are well, that the heat is bearable, and that you are in good shape.

Our love to all of you.

Jean

1 Los Angeles County Museum of Art.

To Alain Renoir

9 September 1959
Paris

Dear Alain,

I have had a very interesting letter from Travis Bogard and before replying to him I would like your advice. Let him know that my reply will be delayed a little.

I understand all the difficulties surrounding *Orvet*. However, I haven't the heart to repeat *Julius Caesar*, which was a stroke of improvisation. I relied on the help of the inhabitants, who provided a Roman crowd with Meridional accents, on the Camargue herdsmen, who were delighted to dress up as Roman horsemen, and also on a location in a two-thousand-year-old arena.

Moreover, my theatrical experience is limited, whereas my cinematographic experience will soon cover forty years. Perhaps by using my knowledge of the cinema, I might try being useful to the students of the Dramatic Arts Department.

Travis Bogard seems to be suggesting that I could make a film. If this is possible, I would like to look at doing a series of interviews with students. The overall picture would give an idea of some of the problems of today. The students we interview could work on a given topic and when they are ready, the recording could be done without insisting on a compulsory text and using a lot of improvisation. This could be done on 16 mm.

I'm throwing this idea out at random so that you can tell me whether Mr Smith and his colleagues would like to see me working in this way. This would in no way rule out the 'readings', meetings, discussion groups and all forms of exchanges of ideas with the students.

We have just come back from Venice. *Le Testament du Dr Cordelier* was given an 'information' screening in a little theatre and was a big hit. This didn't prevent the French Cinema Union from vetoing the film's release. We also showed the complete, reconstructed version of *La Règle du Jeu*.[1] It was quite a triumph.

The children, Jane and you are always in our thoughts and we're delighted at the prospect that we will soon all be together. With all our love.

Jean Renoir

1 *La Règle du Jeu* was restored in 1958 to 112 minutes, almost its original length, by Jean Gaborit and Jacques Durand.

Le Déjeuner sur l'Herbe *opens in Paris on 11 November.*

1960

To Leslie Caron   *17 January 1960*

Dear Leslie,

Do you remember you once showed a particular interest in the role of *Irma La Douce*? A New York distributor (Continental-Reade) is offering me a deal which would allow me to shoot the film in Paris, perhaps in the autumn. On the other hand, I have an understanding with Pathé and I've written to them about this subject. Alas, all this is very vague, as are all my projects involving you. Where are the *Three Bedrooms in Manhattan*? Let me know if *Irma La Douce* interests you in any way.

Dido and I had to rush home to Beverly Hills without passing through London. This deprived us of spending a few amiable hours with you. Perhaps you will make a film in Hollywood? Let's hope that this won't coincide with a trip I must make to Berkeley, where I've been invited to The University of California in the capacity of Regents' Professor.

Give my best to Peter.[1] With all my love to your mother and the kids.

Jean Renoir

1 Peter Hall.

To Ginette Doynel   *22 January 1960*
Paris   *Beverly Hills*

Dear Ginette,

Dido and I are most worried thinking of the cold you and our dear Antoinette are enduring, as you described in your letter. If it turns out that you cannot heat the apartment, you should perhaps think about moving your offices elsewhere and just call in to collect the mail. Your own apartment is perhaps less glacial. If you think that business will stand an interruption, it would perhaps be best to declare it time for a holiday. But we hope that the temperature has risen a little and that by dint of gas, electricity and Mirus, you will escape freezing.

Here the weather is rather fine. At the moment the sun is hiding behind fog which is perhaps the famous *smog*.[1] Dido is very busy and despite a terrible cold, which is almost over, she's getting reacquainted with our American problems.

As for me, I'm completely exhausted. The flu is in part to blame, but now I'm no longer in the middle of the storm, I'm realizing the extent of my commercial failure with *Cordelier* and *Le Déjeuner*. This is giving me the courage to take up my work at Berkeley; working on my various plays; and on the book. But it also gives me an unhealthy distaste for anything to do with films or television. I have the impression that this field is not only foreign to me but hostile, and that I'll receive yet more blows to the head if I try to enter it again. Your news from Belgium about *Le Déjeuner* only serves to confirm my scepticism.

Nevertheless, I enclose with this letter a copy of a letter to Mr Bézard. I should already have met with Yves Montand and written to Leslie, but up until now I've put these things off. In any case, the idea of *Irma la Douce* may not interest Bézard at all.

I have done nothing at all about the *Fantôme de l'Opéra*, even though it would make a very amusing film. I have obviously not received confirmation of participation in a film that Mr Michel must have asked Mr Bézard to send me. [. . .]

Dido is going to try and collect all the information which would enable me to get a Motion Picture Industry Pension Plan. The information you have gathered for the Capric will be indispensable to her. Please send this to her as soon as possible. [. . .]

Clifford Odets is very ill, but his eyes lit up when we gave him the stamps. On Monday we shall go and see the Pecks and your name will be repeated often by the echo of the San Gabriel Canyon. Bessie is wonderful as ever. Nenette has a cold.

All our love to Nicole, to the children and to Madou. Tell Mr Michel that we are always thinking of him and that his protective presence near you gives us a feeling of security. Tell Serge that we haven't forgotten him, but that we're too worn out to write. Greetings to Antoinette.

Warmest love,
Jean Renoir

1 Originally in English.

In February, Jean Renoir is appointed Regents' Professor of English and Dramatic Art at the University of California at Berkeley, for the Spring semester. This enables him to mount a student production of Carola.

To Yves Montand[1]　　　　　　　　　　　8 February 1960
Beverly Hills Hotel

Dear Yves,

A chance conversation in New York with Mr Walter Reade, an importer of French films, gave me the idea of adapting *Irma La Douce* to the screen. To tell you the truth, I've been thinking of the idea for a long time. Just in case, I submitted the project to René Bézard at Pathé, who discussed it with his colleague Mr Cabaud and told me that it interested them. Would you like to make a film of *Irma La Douce* with me? I suppose you are committed to many projects for several years, but I want to try to work with you at least once.

As for practical matters, Mr Reade is trying very hard to obtain the film rights from the theatrical producers who are staging the play on Broadway. We should probably produce the film ourselves, financed by Pathé on one side, and an American group led by Mr Reade on the other.

Dido and I hope that Marilyn Monroe's health problems are over.[2] We still have very pleasant memories of the short time Simone[3] spent at our place.

Best wishes to you both,

Jean Renoir

1 Yves Montand (1921–91), French singer and actor whose credits included *Le Salaire de la Peur* (*Wages of Fear*) (Henri-Georges Clouzot, 1953), *La Guerre est Finie* (Alain Resnais, 1966), and *Z* (Costa-Gavras, 1969).
2 Yves Montand was filming *Let's Make Love* (George Cukor, 1960) at Fox with Marilyn Monroe, with whom he was having an affair. She suffered various mental and physical illnesses during production.
3 Simone Signoret (1921–85), actress and wife of Yves Montand. Her credits included *Casque d'Or* (Jacques Becker, 1952), *Les Diaboliques* (Henri-Georges Clouzot, 1955), and *Room at the Top* (Jack Clayton, 1958).

To Yves Montand　　　　　　　　　　　19 February 1960
　　　　　　　　　　　　　　　　　　　　　　　　[Berkeley]

Dear Yves,

I would very much like to go to Beverly Hills and give myself the great luxury of a nice long chat with Simone and yourself. But the Dramatic Arts department at Berkeley has overwhelmed me. Even more, I am translating a play into English which I wrote in French and I barely see the possibility of a free moment coming soon.

As for *Irma La Douce*, you are probably right and the lead male role is perhaps not the one which I vaguely remembered and had seemed to me very amusing. I am trying to obtain either the play, or a very complete summary of it. I will read it and send it to you.

What you said about the possibility of working with me touched me profoundly. It would have to be something which would bring the three of us together with the hope of each having something to say. There is a story which has been following me around for a long time, and I would be curious to know what you think of it. It is *Chair et Cuir* by Félicien Marceau, which he adapted for the stage under the name *L'Oeuf*. But *Chair et Cuir* is much better than *L'Oeuf* because of its perceptiveness, which could make it a phenomenal film. I am obviously thinking of it as a French film, but the idea of it as an American film is not out of the question. It would be necessary to find a great writer such as your friend Miller[2] to write it in English. I believe that I could properly bring this subject to the screen. But it is possible that the character doesn't correspond to the film industry's expectations of you. On the other hand, don't you already play all characters from the theatre of life in your concert tours?

Dido and I send you and Simone our love.

Jean Renoir

1 Arthur Miller (b.1915), eminent American playwright whose works include *Death of a Salesman* (1949) and *The Crucible* (1953). Married to Marilyn Monroe from 1956 to 1961.

While Jean Renoir is at Berkeley, he hears of the death of Dudley Nichols. Esta Nichols dies in 1968.

To Jean Renoir
Beverly Hills

31 October 1960
Paris

Dear Sir,

I learnt of the recent birth of your granddaughter[1] and I wanted to send you my congratulations. I also wanted to ask your forgiveness for never having thanked you for the piece you sent to *Cahiers*[2] following the death of Jacques Becker. The staff of *Cahiers* is so disorganized that it's possible you never even received the issue in which your text appeared!

Today is All Saints' Day and I'm stuck at home for a few days because I had to have some nasal surgery (a deviated septum which had caused me to breathe through my mouth for the past twenty-eight years). Anyway, I'm not supposed to poke my nose outside the door for another four days. But this allows me the leisure to begin a letter which I know will be a bit long,

28 François Truffaut with Jean Renoir during the filming of
Le Déjeuner sur l'Herbe

because my eagerness to chat with you (a one-way traffic, perhaps) is very great.

As you know from what you read in the newspapers, the current political situation in France is appalling – everyone would like to be another year older so they could see the Algerian conflict resolved, without being subjected to the diplomatic circumlocutions that are as tiresome as the final plot revelations in a bad detective film.

Early this year, I went to America for the first time – I was invited by the American distributor of *Les 400 Coups* and by the New York critics. But as I hadn't finished my second film (*Tirez sur le Pianiste*[3]), I could only stay for ten days, in New York and Chicago. I hope to return soon, finally to get a look at Hollywood – even if it's on strike.

Jeanne Moreau[4] asked me to direct a film version of *Madame Bovary*, which she intends to produce and star in, but I turned down her offer (just as I turned down *Le Journal d'une Femme de Chambre*[5] for the Hakim brothers last year) because, knowing your films almost by heart, I would not be able to stop myself from copying entire scenes, even unconsciously. I do have another project with Jeanne, though – it's called *Jules et Jim*.[6] It takes place between 1900 and 1930, and is about the friendship between two men and the love they both have for the same woman; each of them in turn marries her and has children with her. It's about their life together in different places. The story is taken from a little-known novel published eight years ago by a writer named Henri-Pierre Roche, who died two years ago. He was seventy-six years old when he wrote the book, which explains his extraordinary perspective: the female protagonist was inspired by Marie Laurencin. All his life, Roche was a lover of painting and of women, a dilettante. From the standpoint of chronology – of dates, physical ageing, the separation of war – the film will be very fluid, very vague, but the feeling of years passing will be expressed through the ongoing presence, in each setting, of reproductions of works of Picasso. As the film progresses, the paintings will become more and more abstract; we will quickly recognize various movements in art as the images go by. This film will be horribly difficult to make, because any self-indulgence must be avoided as far as the eroticism goes, any mawkishness as far as the comedy goes, as well as any literary references or clichés that have to do with 'Bohemian Artist Trios'. In short, it will be through the process of successive elimination that the film's form and structure will emerge.

The film I have just finished, *Tirez sur le Pianiste*, did not go down at all well with exhibitors. It's based on an American crime novel by a writer whose work I enjoy enormously (David Goodis[7]). I was able to transpose the story to France and still keep it relatively intact. It's a portrait of a timid Armenian (Charles Aznavour[8]) whose brothers are gangsters, and, while not putting Goodis in quite the same league with Simenon, or Truffaut with Renoir, my friends think *Tirez sur le Pianiste* has a certain connection with *La Nuit du Carrefour*. Braunberger produced the film, which was finished some months ago but still hasn't been released. I must give Braunberger credit for loyalty – he holds up his end very well, seems very pleased with the film, and, in spite of everything, has confidence in it.

Blavette, whom I admire a great deal (I met him during the shooting of *Le Déjeuner sur l'Herbe*), has given me a script he wrote. According to him, it's the 'ultimate gangster film', the definitive work of the genre. It's called *Le Caïd sera Tondu!*[9] It's awfully bloody – maybe a bit too bloody. I'm going to try to steer it towards a couple of producers . . .

We're all busy making films right now, so *Cahiers* is having its ups and downs. I didn't hear the radio broadcast you did about your *Voyages*,[10] but I did get in touch with Madame Tournaire to have her send me either the text or a tape of the show; I then would have asked you for your permission to reproduce certain passages in *Cahiers*. But the tape got lost at the radio station, which was especially distressing for Madame Tournaire, because apparently this particular interview was supposed to be the subject of a book. I told your secretary Ginette Doinel [sic][11] about all this, and they will let us know when the tape has been found and the text transcribed ...

I heard that you finished your book about Auguste Renoir, and I am very eager to read it. For the launch of your book, if you want to have any excerpts reprinted in either specialized art publications or the mainstream press, it will be easy to do. (*L'Express*, for example, has twelve times the circulation of *Arts*.)

I haven't really kept up-to-date on what you're doing these days (teaching cinema courses?), but if any of your current activities might result in your writing something which you would entrust to *Cahiers*, I can assure you that we would be extremely grateful for it. All of us at *Cahiers* have had to resort to 'begging for alms', as it were – you see, we (Godard,[12] Rivette,[13] Doniol[14] and myself) are so shocked by the gap between our ideas as cinephiles and our discoveries as film-makers that we don't dare write anything any more. Nevertheless, so much journalistic attention has been paid to the 'New Wave' that the magazine is selling better than ever.

The situation with French cinema is very strange at the moment – the number of films produced has doubled within a year, and in last year's euphoria, many young film-makers jumped in feet first and made films without producers. And what's more, some young producers have also thrown themselves into the water the same way, by producing films without having distribution for them. What this means is that right now, distributors (and especially exhibitors) are in a very advantageous position: they can just sit back and let the films pile up – and collectively depreciate. Then they can pick and choose the ones they want, only taking what they think is sure to do well at the box office. And so, for most films, the market is totally closed off – the only films which get released are by major directors, with big budgets and stars. Perhaps the revolution in film production happened too quickly, too roughly, or perhaps what's to blame is that no restructuring took place at the level of distribution and exhibition. In any case, the 'New Wave' is currently coming under such attack – from all sides – that in order to survive, it needs to come up with a big hit every three months. The most recent one, last February, was Jean-Luc Godard's *A Bout de Souffle*. Ever since then, we've been massacred: Godard's second film, *Le Petit Soldat* (about torture), was completely banned by the censors, and everything else has either flopped or was never released in the first place – even some really lovely films, like Eric Rohmer's[15] *Le Signe du Lion*.

I don't know if you find these bits of news and gossip amusing or not; maybe you're quite relieved to be away from the confusion and turmoil of the Parisian film scene. In Switzerland, Godard saw *Le Testament du Docteur Cordelier*, which he considers one of your most beautiful films, and, apparently, quite extraordinary in its violence. Everyone here is asking about your future plans: have you considered starting up again on *Trois Chambres à Mannathan* [sic]? It seems like a very worthwhile project to me, although I wonder if Marguerite Duras,[16] in writing *Hiroshima*, didn't borrow here and there from that very same book: the foreign city, jealousy of the past, etc. Of all the anti-intellectual popular novelists, no one is more plagiarized by the most exclusively highbrow (and most ambitious) essayist than Simenon – I know of other cases that are just as unsettling as *Hiroshima/Mannathan* . . .

Sunday, 20 November

I let this letter go unfinished for a couple of weeks, feeling doubtful that the one-way chatter I'm imposing on you is even worth sending. But, as I'm leaving Paris the day after tomorrow and will be gone for a number of days, I decided that I might as well send it after all. My film, *Tirez sur le Pianiste*, is opening here in Paris next Friday[17] – that's why

I'm escaping to where it's warm and sunny, because I predict the worst. It's a small, tight-lipped film without laughs and at times sad, and is in no way suitable for a big first-run house on the Champs-Elysées; in a cinema like that it's bound to be buried. Besides, it's so depressing having to deal with all the various publicists about everything. In the South, I'll have a chance to work on *Jules et Jim*.

I am well aware how precious Ginette Doinel is to you; nevertheless, if there is anything at all that I can do for you in Paris, please don't hesitate to ask. And of course, a word or two from you, at your leisure, would please me greatly.

My best wishes to Madame Renoir. To you, as always, sincere regards from your admirer,

François Truffaut

1 Anne Renoir, born 12 September 1960.
2 *Cahiers du Cinema*, founded by Andre Bazin in 1951, is the influential cinema magazine for which the New Wave directors (Truffaut, Godard, Chabrol, Rohmer, and Rivette) wrote.
3 *Tirez sur le Pianiste* (*Shoot the Piano Player*, 1960).
4 Jeanne Moreau (b.1928), actress whose credits include *Les Amants* (Louis Malle, 1958), *La Notte* (Michelangelo Antonioni, 1961), and *Chimes at Midnight* (Orson Welles, 1966). She has also directed films: *Lumière* (1976) and *L'Adolescente* (1979).
5 The film was directed by Luis Buñuel in 1964.
6 *Jules et Jim* (*Jules and Jim*, 1961).
7 David Goodis, American thriller writer.
8 Charles Aznavour (b.1924), singer and actor whose credits include *Le Testament d'Orphée* (*The Testament of Orpheus*) (Jean Cocteau, 1960) and *The Tin Drum* (Volker Schlöndorff, 1979).
9 Possible translation *The Big Boy Will Be Fleeced!*
10 *Voyages et Rencontres*, broadcast in October 1959, a series of interviews with Renoir about his Hollywood years.
11 Ginette Doynel. Throughout the 1960s, Truffaut continued to misspell 'Doynel' as 'Doinel', coincidentally the surname of his *alter ego* Antoine Doinel in *Les 400 Coups* and the films that followed.
12 Jean-Luc Godard (b.1930), director whose films include *A Bout de Souffle* (*Breathless*, 1960), *Alphaville* (1965), and *Pierrot le Fou* (1965).
13 Jacques Rivette (b.1928), director whose films include *Paris Nous Appartient* (1960), *Céline et Julie Vont en Bateau* (*Céline and Julie Go Boating*, 1974), and *La Belle Noiseuse* (1992).
14 Jacques Doniol-Valcroze (1920–89), co-founder of *Cahiers du Cinema* and director whose films included *L'Eau à la Bouche* (*A Game for Six Lovers*, 1960) and *Le Viol* (*The Rape*, 1967).
15 Eric Rohmer (b.1920), director whose films include *Ma Nuit Chez Maud* (*My Night at Maud's*, 1969), *Le Genou de Claire* (*Claire's Knee*, 1970), and the cycle 'Comédies et Proverbes'.
16 Marguerite Duras (b.1914), writer whose works include *Hiroshima, Mon Amour* (Alain Resnais, 1959). As a director, she has made several films, including *India Song* (1975). Her novel *L'Amant* (*The Lover*) was filmed by Jean-Jacques Annaud in 1992.
17 *Tirez sur le Pianiste* opened in Paris on 25 November.

1961

To Rumer Godden [*Original in English*]   *7 February 1961*
                                              Beverly Hills

Dear Rumer,

The big wordy Viking book will be welcome on Leona Drive. To read your lines is for us the nearest thing to being with you.

I had a very exciting phone call from David Selznick. He thought that I had an option on *Kingfishers Catch Fire*. I didn't tell him the real reason why I have no option which is that I am not in position to produce a film. But I told him the rest of the truth which is that I expressed several times my love for this novel and my confidence in it as a vehicle for the screen. That is why he thought I had an option. David Selznick has Jennifer Jones[1] in mind for the part of Sophie and myself for the direction. Both left for Mexico and I am supposed to meet them when they return in about a week. I am so used to live with dreams which all of a sudden crumble that I am trying to protect myself against a disappointment by repeating constantly: it won't happen, it won't happen. But perhaps it will. How wonderful it would be to collaborate with you again.

Radha and Raymond wrote us about their divorce. We are sorry for them.

We found in the bushes near the vegetable garden a small black kitten which now looks like a miniature panther. Her name is Minou. Nennette adores her.

We are anxious to see James in his happy new life. The good part of improving a house is that it never ends. It is why we like Leona Drive.

Dido and I have a premonition that we will see you before the end of the summer.

Our love to both of you, to the daughters and to the grandchild.

Jean Renoir

PS. We saw Lee Siegel[2] who asked many questions about you and wants to be remembered.

1 Jennifer Jones (b.1919), actress whose credits include *The Song of Bernadette* (Henry King, 1943), *Duel in the Sun* (King Vidor, 1946), and *The Man in the Gray Flannel Suit* (Nunnally Johnson, 1956). She was married to David Selznick from 1949 until his death in 1965.
2 Lee Siegel, Jean Renoir's doctor and friend.

To Carlos Serrano
Film Studio, Madrid

23 February 1961
Beverly Hills

Dear Mr Serrano,

Forgive me for responding so late to your letter, which had gone astray between Paris, the University of California at Berkeley and finally my residence in Beverly Hills. I am very flattered that you are interested in my work. It is difficult for me to answer your question about whether my style is realism, naturalism, or lyrical since I've never deliberately adopted one style or another. It would be very pretentious of me if I believed myself capable of determining in advance a film's tone. What happens each time is that the film imposes its tone on me. For each individual who tries to express himself through the medium of art or literature, there exists a constant struggle between the need for self-expression and the desire for self-effacement before the wonders of the world in which we live. The struggle also exists between the tendency toward exterior realism and that toward interior realism, whose most pure expression was perhaps in the *commedia dell'arte*.

I believe that my attempt to give an explanation may answer all of your questions except the one concerning the New Wave which I consider to be the continuation of the same search for reality which had inspired the great classic authors whether they be Cervantes,[1] Shakespeare or Molière. Each period has had its own new wave which tried to dissipate the fog that surrounds us.

Kind regards,
Jean Renoir

1 Miguel de Cervantes (1547–1616), author of *Don Quixote*.

To R. Bézard   *27 February 1961*
Consortium Pathé   *Beverly Hills*
Paris

Dear Mr Bézard,

I received your letter dated 17 February as well as the treatment by Charles Spaak, which I read, and the book by Jacques Perret[1] which I haven't finished reading yet. I haven't received a response from my letter to Mrs de Carbuccia.[2]

I believe I know enough about it now to give you my impression of *Caporal Epinglé*. The subject thrills me to bits and Spaak's treatment seems to me to be an excellent starting point. What I'd like to do is to give each of the elements more resonance, and try to go further than mere anecdotes and bring out the essence of a situation the importance of which in world history is beyond doubt. Spaak could help me with this. It's what we did with *La Grande Illusion*.

Thank you for the good news about *Testament du Docteur Cordelier* and I hope that we won't run into any new obstacles.

My wife and I send you and Madame Bézard our best.

Jean Renoir

1 Jacques Perret, author of *Le Caporal Epinglé*.
2 Adry de Carbuccia, producer at Films du Cyclope.

To Charles Spaak   *3 March 1961*

Dear Charles,

Our letters in fact crossed. What I tried to say in mine is more or less what you expressed very clearly in yours.[1] If we succeed in depicting that certain 'I-don't-give-a-damn' attitude, we will have made something that no one else has yet made. It's indicated in the works of the New Wave, but with a slight anarchistic bent which is short of the truth. This tranquil and ironic way of destroying the gods which for many are still the gods of this century, goes beyond anarchy. This is the wave that is going to change the world. Even here in America, one smells the salty air which precedes it.

I am thrilled at the thought that together we are going to try to clarify a tremendous upheaval which is all the more difficult to express because its nature is, at the same time, individual and universal.

    With love,
    Jean Renoir

1 Renoir wanted Spaak to collaborate with him on the script of *Le Caporal Epinglé*. They eventually abandoned their first draft.

To Ginette Doynel
Paris

7 March 1961
Beverly Hills

Dear Ginette,
    [...]
    CAPORAL EPINGLE: It's a great subject. The book might serve as the basis for a unique screenplay. If I am left alone I might be able to give *La Grande Illusion* a successor it won't be ashamed of. It's precisely because I believe in *Caporal Epinglé* that I ask you to be uncompromising in your negotiations. If these fine people don't understand what I can do with this book, especially with Spaak's help, then they can go fly a kite.

    Thus I think that we can't ask for less than the following: 25 million old francs plus some interest or another, as I believe in the film. Regarding the shooting schedule, I agree with Spaak. He wants as much time to refine the editing of the Michel Simon film as to refine the *Caporal* screenplay.

    Concerning the eight or nine weeks of shooting, I am convinced that if we shoot in France it will take me less time. But I don't want to take another engagement where the producers are responsible for organizing, like Deutschmeister was for *Eléna*.

    Changes during the shooting. It's thanks to these changes that *La Grande Illusion* became a world-famous film. To calm the apprehensions of the producers, I propose: to rehearse before shooting and to make the principal changes, if possible all the changes, during the rehearsals. If after this preparation, some changes during shooting seem to me necessary to improve the film, I will promise to adopt them only in agreement with Spaak and with the production.

    YUGOSLAVIA: I can shoot where they want, on condition that the countryside can pass for German countryside and that I have a prison camp with prisoners who are really French and guards who are really German.

    GUY LEFRANC:[1] The Guy Lefranc situation will probably make all the negotiations futile, for I refuse to take the place of a young colleague. Only if the producers have absolutely decided not to make the film with Guy Lefranc, that's to say if I find myself not replacing a colleague but filling a hole, will I consider being the director, and again I must be very sure that there is no double-crossing. The idea of being a supervisor seems to me highly impractical. But if, one way or another, we can encourage them to bring Guy Lefranc back into the film, I beg you to proceed with it or to tell me what I can do.

[...]

DEJEUNER SUR L'HERBE: I'm glad finally to have some good news about this film. I did not expect this reaction from the Germans. Here it's complete silence. Obviously Pathé have failed me.

A. R. [AUGUSTE RENOIR] BOOK:[2] I will check your corrections later. When the pages have been numbered, it seems that we will have finished. It's marvellous news. You know the importance of being able to discuss the book with Helen Strauss[3] during my stop in New York.

All this gives us the hope of seeing you soon. We will go to Berkeley at the end of next week and will stay there for two or three days. Thanks again for the way in which you have handled things. Our best wishes to Antoinette.

We send you all our love,

Jean and Dido

1 Guy Lefranc became assistant director and co-writer of *Le Caporal Epinglé*.
2 *Renoir* was published by Hachette in 1962. The English translation by Randolph and Dorothy Weaver, *Renoir, My Father*, was published by Collins in the same year.
3 Jean Renoir's agent at William Morris.

To Jean Renoir [*Original in English*]   *26 July 1961*

Dear Jean and Dido,

Four times I started to write to you, but writing in any shape seems to revolt me. On my uneventful birthday, the 18th, I actually started a letter to you and finished several passages – it was a sort of birthday present to myself to write to you – but it wasn't continued. So here I am, still without news, nothing new, not working but anyway reading voraciously in the best and the cheapest thriller books I can lay my hands on. Now it is between day and evening cool and I have something in the oven for the kids' supper – I can write in the breakfast room and smell if something is burning in the kitchen.

There is no news – it is a dead summer of a dead year for me. When I want a movie writing job with an unholy itch I can't get one and my plans for writing a play by the fall seem badly bent. I feel like a Céline[1] character, to give you some idea – hateful, resenting and burning – but none of this shall interfere with my play plans – the plays will get written in spite of my temporizing and caution and incompetence – some way, somehow, nevertheless, in spite of all! Just imagine this fisherman's luck – to want for once to joyfully write a movie for what is at stake and lo! Oh! So! No movie is offered me! A man's skin is only so elastic, his heart only so expandable: I am ready to jump out of this skin or am already skinless, I can't say which. Anyway, as I say, the first play, and after it some others, will get written.

The children are in good and happy shape, I believe. Growing, of course; swimming, schooling, dentisting, inventing, dreaming – they are doing well. Next week I send them to camp for a month and the mutual absence will be good for all of us. I will be alone in the silent house, drink the grand and girlish and delicate Beaujolais of '59 alone and watch its ruby glowing darker and darker in the cool dusk of the living room, alone, pondering, thinking, with my own dreams and hopes: a terminal point is being reached in my life, I think, I am sure. Full tide is here and I must not delay with the oar-locks or the boat. I am not happy – I am not happy, but I am clear, if not refreshed.

Last night the President[2] made a speech here on TV. It was a very serious talk and made a deep impress, I learn by phone, on all sorts of people. Probably you read about it; he virtually told the American world and its allies that they must tighten their belts and prepare for war, altho [sic] on any level he is willing to negotiate. It was a mature, sober statement from the Young Man, very carefully considered; he took the bit in his mouth EXACTLY, if you know what I mean. Everything was calculated to the inch and comma. Myself, I believe we are far away from anything as serious as a showdown, for it seems to me that K[hrushchev] will wait and let the prerogative and 'absolute' of history assert themselves without cost of a war. Max Lerner was here with me, from N[ew] Y[ork], and we listened to the speech together. He wrote and telegraphed off his column to *The Post* while I prepared our dinner; he would not let me read what he had written, the nerve of him! One thing is sure: the name of a new war would be Nameless, as the ancient Hebrew did not mention His Name; Jaweh or Ellim were not spoken, as you know.

As for you, you are in France, working and happy, I am sure. Wherever you go my love goes with you. I miss you both very much. Not only you but your very atmosphere I miss. You are to me friends in the classic sense of that word. Does the work go well? Did you settle for Steegmuller to translate the precious book? He seems best to me, with real feel for the subject itself; it will be something dear to him, if I know the man.

Think of me when you lift next a glass of good wine.

Clifford O[dets].

PS. Things are not as bad as they sound. These complaints, this cry, these depressions and oppressions, this pain, all are a way of getting in touch with myself (it is the curse of the poet!)

Love again,

C.

PPS. I will tell you the names of the next plays, altho [sic] I don't know the order in which they will come out.

An Old Fashioned Man
I Heard the Music Start!
Poor John or Beau John
Private Treaty
Valse Triste (Probably)

Next stop, Nobel Prize Station!

C.

1 Louis Ferdinand Céline (1894–1961), author of such novels as *Journey to the End of the Night* (1932) and *Death on the Instalment Plan* (1936). His characters are noted for their misanthropy and sense of nihilism.
2 John F. Kennedy.

To Clifford Odets [*Original in English*]   *1 August 1961*
                                                               Paris

Dear Cliff,
An old fashioned man named Jean Renoir
tired of his own war
will be the first fan of *Beau John*
who to be *Poor* never can
being the son
of Clifford the rich.
And I am ready to sign a *Private Treaty*
with the Cabbala against the guarantee

[409]

of a comfortable audition of your *Valse triste*.
As for the Nobel Prize station
your train will stop along its platform
a certain sunny day of Autumn
just when you will forget
that a thing like the Nobel Prize does exist.
At the end of this good day
we will open together a bottle of Bouzy,
light blond of the hills of Champagne,
witty and meaningful product of a difficult soil,
firestones and lime just like one of your plays.
This celebration will be a short interlude in your worrying life,
since you were born with the divine gift
of suffering and rejoicing more than the others
and this for the delecation of the others.
    We love you,
    Jean & Dido

To Dido Renoir
Beverly Hills

23 October 1961
Parkhotel Schönbrunn
Vienna, Austria

Sunday – eve of shooting

Dear Dido,

Everything seems to be getting itself back to normal. Georges Leclerc[1] (in between two attempts to obtain a vehicle to transport his equipment) sends you his regards. Gigi[2] is coming and little Jean[3] and many others.[. . .]

You must be without Bessie now. I know what peace this departure gives you, but knowing you are alone in the house revives my regret not to be with you. You did the right thing to spoil Bessie and to help her leave contented.[4]

The Carbuccias' son seems very interesting. He might be an untapped resource.

My personal adventures included getting stuck in the elevator between floors (the hotel is being extensively renovated) and two changes of room. At first I was lodged on the third floor in a smaller and more pleasant room. In sitting on the lavatory I broke a water-pipe and started a flood. They explained to me that all the new installations were like that:

'*progress ... schrecklich!*' ... and brought me back down to the first floor in an enormous room, noisier than ours but with heated bathrooms. I am writing to you in the décor of a notary's drawing room at the time of François-Joseph [sic]. Give Jeannot my love. All my love to you.

Jean (room 62)

PS. Don't be surprised if from tomorrow, I don't write very often. We are leaving at seven in the morning and after work we will be screening the dailies.

1 Georges Leclerc, cinematographer on *Le Testament du Docteur Cordelier*, *Le Déjeuner sur l'Herbe*, *Le Caporal Epinglé*, and *Le Petit Théâtre de Jean Renoir*.
2 Nickname for Gilbert Chain, camera operator.
3 Jean-Louis Picavet, also camera operator.
4 Bessie Smith had recently returned to England.

To Dido Renoir
Beverly Hills

24 October 1961
Parkhotel Schönbrunn
Vienna

Dear Dido,

I've returned from my first day's shooting. How we floundered about! The crew is not yet working as a team. But at the end of the day I perceived favourable signs. I think everything will go well. Jean-Pierre Cassel[1] and Claude Brasseur[2] are excellent and delightful in their work. Mrs de C[3] is very co-operative, thanks, I believe, to her son.

Leclerc sends his best. The crew speaks of you a lot.

Renée Lichtig arrived today.

I send you all my love.

Jean

1 Jean-Pierre Cassel (b.1932), stage and film actor whose credits include *Those Magnificent Men in Their Flying Machines* (Ken Annakin, 1965), and *Le Charme Discret de la Bourgeoisie* (*The Discreet Charm of the Bourgeoisie*) (Luis Buñuel, 1972).
2 Claude Brasseur (b.1936), son of Pierre Brasseur and Odette Joyeux, actor whose credits include *Les Yeux Sans Visage* (*Eyes Without a Face*) (Georges Franju, 1960) and *Une Belle Fille Comme Moi* (*Such a Gorgeous Kid Like Me*) (Francois Truffaut, 1973).
3 Adry de Carbuccia.

To Dido Renoir
Beverly Hills

25 October 1961
Parkhotel Schönbrunn
Vienna

Friday – I received your letter of 21 October. I received all the first ones in a packet about seven days after your arrival in LA. They are my best company – I should say my only reason for real joy for, except for rare moments during work, I am a little bored. I'm now in room 62 – with a big bed on which the chambermaids piously fold the minuscule covers and sheets for pygmies. I try and sleep despite the noise. I had to choose between the *tramways*[1] and a bad bed. I took the *tramways*. I am wondering about the change that Bessie's departure will bring to our lives. But it's of little importance. We will stay together at *maion*,[2] limiting if necessary our way of life and trying to take things logically, 'untangling' ourselves from what's unimportant. Alain earns a living. That's a great comfort to us. We owe him a lot.

[. . .]

Mrs de C is superficial (all the ferocious faults of a socialite), but more bearable than many others. One can work with her. What irritates me the most is the slowness of Guy Lefranc and Gigi, which unfortunately counterbalances the rapidity of Leclerc and Picavet.

If you write to Bessie, give her my love and thank her for the rose bushes.

All my love,
Jean

1 Originally in English.
2 An imitation of a child's way of saying *maison* (home).

To Dido Renoir
Beverly Hills

27 October 1961
Parkhotel Schönbrunn
Vienna

Dear Dido,

Good day's work – I reshot what I had done yesterday but much better. We were shooting the end of the film. The French peasant is not peasant enough. He's a 'theatre' actor – I should say 'bad theatre'. By contrast, the female peasant, a Viennese, is superb and I am enchanted with Cassel, Brasseur, and Carmet[1] (Pater, the other peasant and the greedy prisoner).

Your letters delight me but don't feel obliged to write. I myself often go without writing to you when the rhythm of shooting becomes more demanding. I was very interested in the photo of tanks from the 32nd division.² My greetings to Nenette and Minou who have begun once again to collaborate with you on the typewriter. My best to Jeannot. I send you all my love.

Much love to all the *smala*³ from Berkeley when you telephone them.

Jean

---

1 Jean Carmet (1921–94), stage and film actor whose credits included *La Rupture* (Claude Chabrol, 1970), *Violette Nozière* (Claude Chabrol, 1977), and *Buffet Froid* (Bertrand Blier, 1979).
2 Dido Renoir had sent Jean a photograph of tanks from the *Los Angeles Times*.
3 Arabic word describing an extended family – in this case Alain, his wife and children.

To Dido Renoir   *29 October 1961*
Beverly Hills   *Parkhotel Schönbrunn*
                                              Vienna

Dear Dido,

Last night, [I] shot the French camp behind the church that we had visited on our arrival. First contact with Ballochet – Claude Rich.¹ I was impressed with him. I think the film will be very well acted. And, after all, the little inconveniences which you know about, differences of conception, obstinacy, etc., are really nothing compared to the tyrannical rigidity of a film in a Big American Studio.

I'm getting over a cold, almost completely. I'm responding by telephone to the swarm of young girls (alerted by an idiotic interview with Glass) who wanted to play the little dentist. All shapes and sizes of baby-dolls patterned after the same model! Brigitte Bardot has also taken over Vienna! I'll probably end up taking little Kiefer who easily learnt the French text.²

Mrs Guy LeFranc will arrive today. I'm having lunch with Leclerc. He's a first-class cameraman and a very interesting man – an island in the middle of an ocean of banality. On the set, he lights a shot in five minutes. Then I have to wait a half hour for Gigi.[...]

All my love.

Love also to our dear Jeannot.

Jean

1 Claude Rich (b.1929), stage and film actor whose credits include *La Mariée était en Noir* (*The Bride Wore Black*) (François Truffaut, 1967) and *Je t'aime, je t'aime* (Alain Resnais, 1968).
2 The part was eventually played by Cornelia Froboess.

To Dido Renoir
Beverly Hills

10 November 1961
Parkhotel Schönbrunn
Vienna

Dear Dido,

Yesterday I received your letter announcing Minou's[1] disappearance. It makes me very sad. That little animal brought us a lot of happiness – I don't know how we are going to replace that bizarre and affectionate presence. It's like a relative going. I continue to hope that Minou, with her sense of the dramatic, will return when you stop waiting for her. The news of the fire given by the European papers is horrifying.[2]

I'm anxious to receive details and learn how you've borne this trial. We mustn't ever be separated again.

Perhaps you could send me the *Los Angeles Times* to give me the details?

With all my love,
Jean

1 Minou was the Renoirs' black cat.
2 Wide-scale brush fires in Los Angeles burned thousands of acres and hundreds of homes very close to the Renoirs' in Beverly Hills. Minou had disappeared in the confusion, and was believed to have been either burned or eaten by one of the coyotes which populated the Benedict Canyon area of Beverly Hills.

To Jean Renoir
Vienna

10 November 1961
Beverly Hills

Dear Jean,

I have just received the letter you wrote on Sunday. The mail is taking a long time between Vienna and Los Angeles. The week at the brickyard is nearly over. I hope you will be pleased with the work you have accomplished there, and that it did not tire you too much. I wish so much that I could be with you!

I had sworn that I would not mention Minou any more, but only a week ago she was still here. While I was writing to you, I watched her happy and proud, playing with a rat she had caught, and which I buried

29 Jean Renoir surrounded by his young cast in *Le Caporal Epinglé*: clockwise
from top left, Gérard Darrieu (Medee), Mario David (Caruso), Jacques
Jouanneau (Penche-à Gauche), Jean Carmet (Guillaume), Claude Rich
(Ballochet), Jean-Pierre Cassel (The Corporal) and Claude Brasseur (Pater)

later. I can still see the little hole where she did her business. The house is sad without our little Minou. I have lost all hope and cancelled the advertisement in *The Los Angeles Times*. I got a call about a black cat that had been found on Edinburgh and Santa Monica, two blocks west of Fairfax. I went with Nenette.[1] I was sure it couldn't be Minou, but the people had told me they had found it hanging on their screen door, like Minou used to do. I nearly adopted the little cat I saw there to save it from the pound.

I guess I misunderstood your wire, which must have been about Minou and not about the fire. But since I was getting calls about the fire from all over (Pierre Olaf,[2] Helen Strauss, etc., etc.), I *jumped to conclusions*.[3] The fire has been under control since yesterday, but the total losses are awful: 456 houses were destroyed, including 447 in Bel Air and Brentwood;[4] and more than fifty were seriously damaged.

With all my love.

Dido

Love from Nenette.

I have just received a note from Renée Lichtig. Will you thank her for me?

1 The Renoirs' dog.
2 Pierre Olaf (b.1928), stage and film actor whose credits include *Le Diable au Corps* (Claude Autant-Lara, 1947), *French Cancan*, and *Camelot* (Joshua Logan, 1967).
3 Originally in English.
4 Areas in West Los Angeles next to Beverly Hills.

Le Testament du Docteur Cordelier opens in Paris on 16 November. It was shown in only one cinema.

To Dido Renoir
Beverly Hills

17 November 1961
Parkhotel Schönbrunn
Vienna

Dear Dido,

I have returned from work a little tired. I'm going to dine in my room and go to sleep.

I received your letter of 12 November recounting Minou's return. What a happy event. I'm more relaxed knowing that noble Egyptian has returned home.

[416]

Your party at the Loews' pleases me. I'm sure they love us very much and for my part, I feel such affection for them.

[. . .]

I told Ginette to come and look for me. I got her telegram about the premiere of *Cordelier*:[1] 'Film well received'. If the film was a success, 'La Gourde's'[2] tone would have been dithyrambic. But I don't care. I'll try to make a beautiful *Caporal* and afterwards I'll write. Even if it yields little, it will permit us to stay together. You were right not to rent the house, even to sweet Annie Farge. It is 'our *maion*'.

Mrs de C continues to be full of touching attention. Her son is very interesting. My two great pals are Leclerc and Marc Maurette. The actors are excellent and delightful companions – they make me forget the cold and the woollen underwear that makes my legs itch.

All my love.

Jean

1 *Le Testament du Docteur Cordelier*.
2 Nickname for Ginette Doynel.

To Dido Renoir
Beverly Hills

22 November 1961
Parkhotel Schönbrunn
Vienna

Dear Dido,

Would you believe Gigi has become very co-operative? And when he is in that state of mind he is of course the most precise framer in the world. Mrs Chain wrote me a charming letter deploring your absence in my work.

The results on the screen seem to me good. I still have some serious problems. Marc Maurette, Leclerc, etc . . . Mrs de C . . . do their best to help me resolve them.

I won't talk about *Cordelier*, for its failure leaves me cold and seems to me natural. One doesn't cling for two years to a film made in a brief moment's enthusiasm.

I'm leaving in a few minutes and send you all my love.

Jean

To Dido Renoir
Beverly Hills

28 November 1961
Parkhotel Schönbrunn
Vienna

Dear Dido,

Hard day's work – I believe I have shot everything 'exterior' concerning stations and trains. Mrs de C is a genial *slave driver*[1] with her innocent air and absurdly stupid ideas. She ends up making her minions sweat better than a Deutschmeister. That said, she is very nice and I think maybe perhaps sensitive to the grandeur of cinema.

I have your letter from Wednesday, preceding the arrival of the children. I feel near you, ready to receive them – the irony of distance, since when you receive this letter, they will have left. I hope to be in Paris at the end of next week.

I am surprised and pained by the news concerning the little Bergman[2] – I had the impression that the couple might 'function'. And Francen's daughter![3] And Hugh's daughter. The Indians (from India) are right (I should say the old ones, the orthodox people) who marry off their children without asking their opinion. Great waves of emotion often turn out to be short-lived. What luck we have with Alain and Jane – what luck, of course, we have with ourselves!

How can one accept the intimacy of conjugal life if it isn't for life? I, myself, made attempts before having the good luck of meeting you. But I have only realized spiritual intimacy with you. The Indians, I insist, are right – if it's just a physical affair, why not go to a professional prostitute – more skilled and often very beautiful. We are lucky. Pardon! I am lucky! I know it and really want to take advantage of it with you.

All my love,
Jean.

1 Originally in English.
2 Pia Lindstrom, Ingrid Bergman's daughter, who had separated from her husband after a year of marriage.
3 Leno Francen, daughter of actor Victor Francen.

[418]

To Dido Renoir
Beverly Hills

29 November 1961
Parkhotel Schönbrunn
Vienna

Dear Dido,

I have the Thanksgiving card signed by Alain, Jane, John, Florence,[1] her kids, Peter, and you. I couldn't read Alain's kind thoughts. The card gave me real pleasure.

The technicians are in the middle of having a 'meeting'. No doubt they are going to ask Mrs de C to pay their expenses in advance, fearing she might rip them off. She is insensitive, and her sharp opinions don't make things easier.

That said, dear Dido, remember that I don't need to do any more production work. Good old Vouattoux [sic][2] doesn't know which way to look. Everyone's making demands – the question of food plays a large part. Luckily I am beyond all that. However, the cinema is a crazy profession, because a film brings together too many egos. Vanities clash, they collide. It's like the intrigue at the Chinese court. I really want to start my next book with you!

I dined alone in my room and treated myself to an enormous bottle of Hungarian wine – present from Mrs Brody – it's already three weeks since I saw her. She must be in Paris with Mary Meerson.[3]

Dear Dido, my love, everything will work itself out. One more week of shooting and that's it. I really am anxious to finish, so I must fight not to 'hack' it. I am encouraged not to let go by the touching confidence that the actors (also the technicians, and even Mrs de C) have in me. I can't allow myself to let them down.

I think of Ga. I had an actor that she would have loved (Jean Carmet); he plays the sly and greedy peasant.

I'm going to sleep, cheered up by this little chat with you.

All my love,

Jean.

1 Florence Homolka, photographer.
2 René G. Vuattoux, production manager on *Le Caporal Epinglé*.
3 Mary Meerson (1900–93), co-founder of the Cinémathèque Française with Henri Langlois.

To Dido Renoir
Beverly Hills

5 December 1961
Parkhotel Schönbrunn
Vienna

Dear Dido,

Except for an epilogue which I will add to the film – I believe it's necessary – and except for certain retakes, the *Caporal Epinglé* is in the can – in thirty-six days. I am very happy. Once more, I don't know whether I have added a commercial success to my numerous failures. But I believe I have turned out a film of good quality, if sufficiently unusual not to ruin the good opinion some friends have of me.

I am enthusiastic about Leclerc's work – so crazy and daring! In brief, I am happy and I believe you will be too and will love *Le Caporal*. I still have quite a few dailies to see. In the meantime, I am going to see the Breughels at the museum.[1] Mrs de Carbuccia, amicable and kind as ever, is going to leave today by plane – Voittoux [sic], his wife, Marc,[2] and I will be the last fighters at the abandoned fortress.

I am happy with what you've told me about the kids and their kindness with the neighbours.

I have received the William Morris contract – they want me to sign it, and they hope that the film in England will be made. I'm going to sign. Because of Helen Strauss, it would be better to be with William Morris than anyone else.

All my love,
Jean.

1 Kunsthistorisches Museum, Vienna.
2 Marc Maurette.

To Dido Renoir
Beverly Hills

8 December 1961
Parkhotel Schönbrunn
Vienna

Dear Dido,

Last day in Vienna. I've seen everything we've shot here except for an unimportant bit which I shot twice anyway. I'm leaving with a general idea of the film and the hope of writing an epilogue on the train. I went to see the Velásquez paintings: they are Renoirs *avant la lettre*,[1] that's to say that they stop where the young Renoir begins. It is unsettling to sense a real continuity [between them] and to have to state that Renoir went much further. But if I had to designate a spiritual father for my father, I would not hesitate in proposing Velásquez.

The lab in Vienna has caused us a lot of problems – scratches, dirt, bad prints. But all this is reparable.

My next letter, without a doubt, will be from avenue Frochot.

All my love,

Jean

PS. *Le Caporal* is not 'sewn up' yet. But I have the weapons with which to defend this film – above all the excellent acting, which is completely accessible to people – just as Barrault in *Cordelier* is too ethereal for our clod-hopping audience.

1 Meaning 'before the term was invented'.

To Dido Renoir   *13 December 1961*
Beverly Hills   *Paris*

My dear Dido,

Would you please ask Clifford Odets for his help in finding the correct translation of the following excerpt from my book (page 249 in the most recent version, and page 213 in the previous).

'A la fin de sa vie je l'ai entendu faire la réponse suivante a un journaliste qui s'étonnait de la déformation de ses mains. 'Avec de pareilles mains, comment faites-vous pour peindre? – Avec ma q ...' répondit Renoir pour une fois grossier. Ça se passait dans la salle à manger des Collettes. Une demi-douzaine de visiteurs l'entouraient. Personne ne rit de la boutade. Car cette réponse était la saisissante expression de la vérité, un des rares témoignages, si rarement formulés dans l'histoire du monde, du miracle de la transformation de la matière en esprit.'[1]

Here is what Randolph wrote to me on this matter:

'I wonder whether Renoir's reply to the journalist implied any reference to the phallus worship of antiquity, as a symbol of creation? If so, it might be more appropriate to translate this for Anglo-Saxon readers as: "the work of any true artist is created out of his whole being", or something of that order.'

In his postscript to the letter, Randolph adds: 'Here is what Dorothy suggests in regards to the text on page 249 (page 213 on the previous drafts):

'Have we interpreted the text correctly? We feel that it would give the English and American reader a better idea of what Renoir was really referring to. As we all know, "penis" (*queue*) is the phallus, or "phallic symbol", if you like, which of course stands for creation (in both senses of the word stand!), in this case *creation of art*. But if you would prefer, we shall stick to your original phrasing. Just let me know which would suit you best. Randolph.'[2]

I find these comments from Randolph rather alarming, because they show he doesn't quite grasp the meaning of some of Renoir's dialogue. The weight of Renoir's jest comes from the fact that it sounds like a crude joke but has a deep, hidden meaning. Maybe at the time, he was not even aware of this hidden meaning. I think it would be best to keep the jest in English as it is in French, and translate the word *queue*, referring to the male sexual organ, by a slightly slang, or childish, American expression. The main thing is that this expression be understandable by the majority of readers.

While Ginette was taking this letter in dictation, she noticed a repetition in the same sentence on page 149: '... un des *rares* témoignages si *rarement* formulés ...'

I suggest the following change: 'car cette réponse était la saisissante expression de la vérité, un des rares témoignages dans l'histoire du monde du miracle de la transformation de la matière en esprit.'[3]

I have not started editing yet. Renée's[4] room at Billancourt will not be ready for two to three days. But since I am a bit tired, I enjoy the chance of a rest.

I have heard about Marie Lestringuez's death. What can I say? This event is prompting me to take a nostalgic walk into the past.

I think I have already mentioned my fur cap, or rather yours – since I am convinced it will fit you very well. Thanks to it, I have been able to shoot outside without a catching a cold. Since I did not have time to buy canned *grape fruit*[5] [sic], I got into the habit of taking Vitamin C. These vitamins are easy to swallow now, and they work marvellously well.

I apologize for repeating a question that I have already asked in one of my recent letters. Must I send you the children's clothes, your cape and the fur cap? With the mail getting really busy, they may not reach you in time for Christmas.

Love from Ginette and I.

Jean

PS: I fell in Vienna. I slipped on the clayey ground at the studio, and my leg is covered in the most harmonious shades of blue. I saw Jamoil and also another gentleman who took X-rays of my leg. Nothing is broken. I must only refrain from doing any *striptease*[6] until my leg is back to its normal colour.

Much love,
Jean

1 Translation by Randolph and Dorothy Weaver, published by Collins, reads:
'Once, towards the end of his life, I heard him make the following rejoinder to a journalist who seemed to be astonished by his crippled hands:
"With such hands how do you paint?" the man asked, crudely.
"With my prick," replied Renoir, really vulgar for once.
It took place in the dining room at Les Collettes. There were a half dozen or so visitors present. No one laughed at the quip. For what he said was a striking expression of the truth; one of those rare testimonies, so seldom expressed in the history of the world, to the miracle of the transformation of matter into spirit.'
2 Originally in English.
3 Evidently the use of 'so seldom expressed' in the English translation avoided the proximity of 'rare' and rarement (rarely) in the original French that Renoir was worried about.
4 Renée Lichtig.
5 Originally in English.
6 Originally in English.

To Jean Renoir

Vienna

21 December 1961

Beverly Hills

Dear Jean,

I spent a nice evening at Clifford's yesterday. He made some 'coudrou' in his *pressure cooker*.[1] We also had good cheese, and drank an excellent bottle of Bordeaux. He sent me home with the usual calendar and a handful of small cigars. One never leaves Clifford's house empty-handed.

This is what he suggests for the translation of 'Avec ma q ...' If we wish to remain proper, we could say: 'WITH MY ORGAN'[2] otherwise we could say: 'WITH MY COCK.'[3] He and I prefer the second version, which is closer to the French text. Clifford has offered to read Randolph's translation, if you have an extra copy, and to make suggestions. It is most kind of him, and I wonder if we should agree. He was most insistent, and said: 'That will give me the chance to brag about being the first to have read Jean's book.' Your Christmas card made him very happy. He asked me to send you this small fox's head because of its great beauty. Yesterday, it was very hot during the day. But the evening brought a thick fog and the temperature dropped tremendously. I was not prepared and consequently this morning I woke up with a very bad cold. I have been taking Bromo-Quinine to get rid of it. The fog is still with us this morning, so I don't think I'll see Irene and her *yammi*[4] today.

To get back to Clifford. He still has no work and things are getting pretty bad. [. . .] I was very thrilled to receive your picture with Jouanneau and my fur cap. It looks gorgeous. Clifford said it makes you look like a *Russian Commissar*[5] and he'd love to get one, too.

JAGUAR: I'll order it after the holidays. You told me you expected to be back by the end of March. Do you agree if I plan on getting it by then? You have plenty of time to let me know. It would be better if it was not delivered before your return. I would not use it, and we could save on the insurance, which has gone up a lot.

At the same time, please confirm that light grey for the body and natural leather for the seats is your final choice.

I'll try to get it without the small chrome jaguar. Since wire wheels are much nicer, I'll order them if you agree.

I still have some important things to tell you, but I think it is enough for today. Jeannot and I had a lot of fun with your verses about the demise of the little wine from Apremont. They are really quite hilarious. Nenette and Minou send love to their pappy, and so do I.

Dido

1 Originally in English.
2 Originally in English.
3 Originally in English.
4 'Yummies'. Irene cooked as well as cleaned for the Renoirs.
5 Originally in English.

To Dido Renoir   26 December 1961
Beverly Hills   *Paris*

Dear Dido,

I received your letter of the 20th where you told me about your night out at the Sicard's. I am anxious to know the contents of the package from little Francen.[1] This morning I went to the dubbing of some rainy scenes in the film. The skill of these young actors – J.P. Cassel, Claude Brasseur, Costelli[2] – is extraordinary. Obviously it's just something they pick up, but the fact they pick it up well is a sign of natural adaptation to this means of expression called cinema. Renée Lichtig has given me a beautiful tie – exactly the kind of accessory I never wear – perfect for Roland Girard or Mr Blum. Tonight, I'm dining at the Louis XIV with

Cassel and the young Brasseur. Mrs de C telephoned me from Sainte Maxine to give me an idea – a childish one – for the next film. She knows that I don't want to make another film – I haven't hidden from her my desire to write – and my resistance annoyed her. When she wants something, she wants it badly.

But I am really determined not to be diverted away from Leona Drive, and to write a book with you. The problem is that the intensity of making films – even the editing – isn't conducive to the deep thinking required before writing a book. But a few weeks at '*maion*' will put my imagination back to work – or rather my ability to order my thoughts and clear my memory, which falters when I have too much on my mind.

With all my love,

Jean

1 Leno Francen.
2 Philippe Costelli.

1962

To Dido Renoir
Beverly Hills

2 February 1962
Paris

Dear Dido,

Before going to sleep, I just want to say a brief goodnight. I had lunch with Bézard, and Girard and Mrs de C joined us at the café. They pestered me to make another film. I told them that I was returning to Beverly Hills as soon as I could, that I would write a project and that we will see when we have resolved our house problems. The fact is, I am glad that this gave me my excuse. I don't want to be separated from you any more, and the weeks that remain seem to me to be taking a long time. I reread one of your old letters, from 17 January, and I feel guilty that I can't respond to you on the subject of the purchase of *tax free municipal bonds*.[1] It's just that I don't have a brain for all that. In principle, it seems very good to me. I fear inflation, but securities are so high that these bonds are maybe the wisest thing. I'll skip to your letter of 25 January, where you tell me about the insurance taken by the museum for the works of art that we have loaned. The bronzes don't run a great risk. What seems inadequate to me is the insurance on the paintings. On the other hand, there is the tax risk. The taxman might rely on the insurance to make an estimate for this famous tax on personal objects.

I have your letter of 28 January – I have not yet studied Vincent Cronin's report on Randolph's translation. I will do it Sunday. Tomorrow, Saturday, I will correct all that I can of the book in French, with Ginette, then I will go busy myself with the film's music with the Kosmas. In the evening, dinner at the Carbuccias – with neither Girard nor Bézard.

I hope that Irene will start work again soon – here I am starting to despair of finding a solution to the '*maion*' problem. For better or for worse! That way we will stay at home!

But if I am once again obliged by the money question to make another film in France, I would regard this obligation as a catastrophe. I ask myself if it would be better to sell Le Chasseur since we aren't able to enjoy it at home. All this is really annoying. Life in two different countries is too complicated for a man of my age. Not that I feel old! But I have arrived at a point where I know the value of a peaceful life. This intense activity prevents me from gathering together ideas which might be good for a book. And what's more, I'm lonely without you!

With all my love,

Jean

1 Originally in English.

To Dido Renoir

Beverly Hills

24 January 1962

Paris

Yesterday I did not write to you, and I had something very important to tell you. But I had to run from Génévilliers to Billancourt – still looking for my newsreels – and I arrived just in time to dine with Braunberger who had taken me to see *Jules et Jim*, the film by Truffaut – very beautiful, but with the same impression of boredom as a lot of the new products of French cinema. We are in the midst of late nineteenth-century bourgeois literature with its grace, its fragility and its emptiness – the 'modern style' genre, like the entrances to the Metro stations.[1]

What I really wanted to tell you is that it's not going to work with Lowery, who has had his doctorate project accepted by the Sorbonne and must write his thesis. I think that he has found me a very good young English writer to replace him, whom I will meet the day after tomorrow. I see things now as they really are. Weaver is a very good base. I must work on it. And, as I don't speak English sufficiently well, I need a 'language assistant'. If I had finished the film, I would have gone to do this correction at '*maion*' with Florence. The film will keep me in Paris, so I must do it with someone else.

Another chapter: For the '*maion*' I saw a woman friend of Jacqueline André's.[2] It won't work. She's an intellectual! I am going to see another candidate early this afternoon. At least, I hope so. (A small advertisement appeared in *Le Figaro*). Ginette was suitably impressed with her voice.[3] I will keep you posted, and I send you all my love.

Jean

1 A reference to the art nouveau entrances to Paris Métro stations, designed by Hector Guimard.

2 Jacqueline André, daughter of Albert and Maleck André.
3 The Renoirs were trying to find a permanent housekeeper.

To François Truffaut

8 February 1962
Beverly Hills

Dear François Truffaut,

I want to take this opportunity to let you know that I consider *Jules et Jim* the most accurate portrayal of modern French society I have yet seen on the screen.

Since modern ideas and behaviour are contemporaries of automobiles adorned with shiny brass, by setting your film in 1914 you have really enhanced the exactness of your description. That some of our colleagues would hint at some kind of immorality on your part is baffling. Stating an outcome cannot be immoral. Rain is wet; fire is hot. The resulting humidity and heat have nothing to do with ethics. In just a few years we have jumped from one civilization to another. This jump is more impressive than our fathers' between the Middle Ages and the Renaissance. On each side of the gap, people relate to one another in different ways. The stone-cutter who built Tournus did not think of love in the same way as the man who put up the cornices at Versailles. For the Knights of the Round Table, sentimental escapades were a laughing matter. For the Romantics they were an excuse for excessive outpouring of tears. For the characters in *Jules et Jim* they mean something else again, and your film contributes to our better understanding of what this 'something else' might be. It is very important for us, for men to know where we stand with women, and equally important for women to know where they stand with men.

You help to dissipate the fog surrounding the core of this question. For this and for many other reasons, I hope your film will be widely shown.

I hope to see your sequel to *Les Quatre Cents Coups* soon. Please give my best regards to your charming wife.

Most sincerely,

Jean Renoir

To Dido Renoir
Beverly Hills

15 February 1962
Paris

Dear Dido,

I received your letters of 10 and 11 February and would really like to know that the 'monsoon' rains have stopped soaking California. I know that the slopes are solid, but still I find this persistent deluge disturbing. I understand Nenette and Minou's disgust.

Don't do anything about the film on the Protestant revolt under Louis XIV – I have glanced through a work on this matter. It was a succession of horrors and violence on both sides, and I refuse to show such real provocations to murder on a screen. I lunched with Pierre Gaut. Maud is not well. Great weakness and persistent fever. It's really annoying that 'old Irene' (as Ga used to call her) let you down. Make sure Minou cannot climb up as high as the finches. Ginette, sad that you have got rid of your trousers, wanted to send you a 'zipper'. I am going to try to dissuade her. Your good relations with the neighbours really please me. Don't be worried by the news from France. People are really too well off to attempt to overthrow things here. It's the repercussions of the Algerian situation, which the French in France care less about. I have tried to use my time wisely for the rest of my trip to Paris. The film will, in principle, open in Paris on 11 April. I don't think I'll be able to leave before then. I had intended to, but it's now more the book which will keep me here. I don't want to leave Europe without seeing the final translation by Cronin. I am going to turn down the Swiss lectures, but I would still like to take a trip to Les Collettes. Maybe I will take notes for a project. I would like to write another book at '*maion*'. It's my most ardent wish. Nevertheless, I don't dare reject film projects which come up without being sure of my situation, because this might be my last chance. I feel old and maybe sooner than I think I will have to stop running around cameras.

With all my love,

Jean

PS. Besides, these future film projects depend on our personal affairs and the discovery of another Bessie.

To Dido Renoir
Beverly Hills

17 *March 1962*
Paris

Dear Dido,

Last night, a screening of copy B at Billancourt for about fifty invited guests. I don't know how it will do in front of a real audience, but before this small group it went very well. I think that the majority of people were genuinely moved.

Pierre Gaut, his granddaughter and Maud were very impressed. Braunberger and Truffaut liked the film a lot. People were no longer disappearing [afterwards] and I sensed — Ginette too — this undefinable impression of a complete accord between the screen and the audience.

Only discordant notes: a nephew of Mrs de C, named Chiappe, who having pretensions of technical knowledge, suggested a cut. 'What are you interfering for?' Ginette barked at him. And, the day before yesterday, Maurette and his wife hadn't liked Claude Rich.

I spent today carrying out little technical improvements, and especially cutting out some subtitles. I had invited Renée, her assistant and Ginette at the end of the film to lunch in the bistro which faces the church at Auteuil.

Michael Arnold, who I will see at the screening of *Le Caporal* at Le Mans (it's 80 km from Angers) told me that Pathé had already praised *Le Caporal* as much as *Ben Hur*. And they had allowed *Le Déjeuner Sur l'Herbe*, which they despised, to fail! Ginette won't bother [with them].

I hope to see Raymond tomorrow. I will talk to him about Uncle Zizi. I am anxious to learn whether you are burning up the road in the Jag[uar].

With all my love,

Jean

Le Caporal Epinglé *opens in Paris on 23 May.*

To Duncan McGregor
Pathé Cinema Corporation, New York

9 July 1962
Beverly Hills

Dear Duncan,

Thank you for your letter. Regarding which version of *Le Caporal Epinglé* I wish to be shown in America, there is only one version as far as I am concerned: the version I edited myself, before it was cut after my departure from France. The unfathomable stupidity of these cuts turned this farce which needs to be serious to work into mere buffoonery. Some shots of planes preceding the final scene were even cut. Consequently, the melancholic mood they helped convey in that scene has been obliterated, and with it, any hope that the audience might take home a more lasting impression.

With regards to the English title, I think that just *Le Caporal* might be fine. I find this title even better than *Le Caporal Epinglé*. I am very happy that you are releasing the picture. In Paris, these cuts deprived me of the kind of success one can only have on rare occasions in a whole lifetime. They were probably prompted by fear of certain reactions in the audience resulting from Jacques Perret's performance. They tried to lessen the impact of the film. In New York, where the critics are even hungrier for powerful films, these cuts would be even more detrimental than in Paris.

Dido and I hope you are in good health, that the New York summer heat doesn't make you perspire too much, and Denise will come back soon to help you withstand its rigour.

With our warmest regards,
Jean Renoir

PS. Have you heard anything about *Cordelier* on television?

To Adry de Carbuccia
Paris

14 July 1962
Beverly Hills

Dear Adry,

I hope your trip to Berlin[1] with Jean-Luc[2] was pleasant in spite of the jury's verdict, which was not what we had hoped for. I am sorry I was not determined enough to oppose any cuts when Gérard approached me. I could not guess the cuts they were planning would be so clumsy. Because of the humorous content of certain scenes, I was already expecting some criticism and being accused of 'selling out', or 'self-indulgence'. Consequently, I had carefully balanced the picture in the editing to reduce the possibility of such criticism. One of the new cuts which strikes me as particularly awkward is the one removing a few seconds of aeroplanes at the end. This wartime imagery, supported by the soundtrack blending into the sound of a barge under the Tolbiac bridge, lent to the final scene a meaning which can only exist if related to its framework. These planes provided an aura of heroism to the two characters, and their goodbyes became more touching. Whoever recommended this cut

[431]

must be unable to feel. And without the ability to feel, we can't possibly touch the hearts of audiences. These cuts denied us an opportunity which seldom arises in the lifetime of a producer or a director. Neither you nor I will stumble upon it again, for it will be impossible to regroup elements that had as much potential as those of *Caporal Epinglé*. Since I am a strong believer in divine equity, I am holding no grudge against Films de Cyclope. If success eluded me with *Le Caporal*, it is probably because I'm enjoying too many privileges in other domains. One can't have everything. It may also be a sign that I should write what I have in mind. I just started working on a book and I feel lucky I've found a story I'm dying to tell.

The editing of your Roman picture must be completed by now. I'd love to hear that you are happy with it. And I'd also love to hear about where you are with your novel. Unfortunately, Beverly Hills is rather far from the avenue du Bois and I could not possibly invite you for dinner and a pleasant chat afterwards. Would you tell Mr de Carbuccia and Jean-Luc that I often think about them? My wife and I won't miss the opportunity to knock on your door as soon as we return to Paris. The question is, when? We are immersed in the daily problems that are part of being a 'resident' anywhere. If things keep up as they are, the only way out of these administrative aggravations will be to live in a hotel, and reduce the extent of our possessions to a few clean shirts in one suitcase.

Dido sends her best.

Fondly,

Jean Renoir

1 The Berlin Film Festival.
2 Jean-Luc de Carbuccia, Adry's son.

To Adry de Carbuccia
Sainte-Maxime, France

22 August 1962
Beverly Hills

Dear Adry,

I have finally been able to show *Le Caporal* to Dido and to my son. They liked it a lot. The few Americans I had invited were enthusiastic as well. And I take this opportunity to let you know how happy I am to have made this film I am very proud of with you.

I am enclosing a copy of my letter to McGregor. I hope that the problem of translating the narration into various languages has been under consideration.

Fond wishes,
Jean Renoir

To Jean Renoir   *23 October 1962*
Beverly Hills   *Paris*

Dear Mr Renoir,

The manager of EUROPE No 1 (Lucien Morisse) has asked me to direct the radio broadcast of a play – if possible, one which has not been staged before. The actress we have in mind to play the lead role in this production (unless we choose a play whose heroine would require different casting) is Marie Dubois, whose performance you liked, I believe, in my film *Tirez sur le Pianiste*.

Although I am only familiar with excerpts of your *Carola*, it is my feeling that the characters and dramatic tone of this work would correspond quite well to what I am looking for. I would be very proud to make my début on radio with a production of *Carola*, and would make every effort to serve your text well.

The management of EUROPE No 1 has assured me that this broadcast of an unproduced play would in no way endanger any future staging of that play in a French theatre, but this too is something you really have to judge for yourself.

Of course, I would be very pleased if you agree to this request; if you feel, however, that you must refuse, I certainly understand your reasons for doing so. After all, as Octave says in *La Règle du Jeu*: 'The terrible thing about this world is that everybody has their reasons.'

I am not going to ask you for news of yourself because, before writing to you, I spoke on the 'phone with Ginette Doinel [sic]. She is convinced that you are hard at work on a new screenplay.

I've heard reports that your book on Auguste Renoir will be published some time between now and the end of the year. Is this true? Do you think it might be possible that *Cahiers du Cinema* could reprint a chapter from the book, or part of one?

I eagerly await your response regarding *Carola*. Until then, Madeleine[1] joins me in sending you and Mrs Renoir our best wishes.

Yours faithfully,
François Truffaut

1 Madeleine Morgenstern, Truffaut's wife.

To François Truffaut
Paris

26 October 1962
Beverly Hills

My dear Truffaut,

I would be very happy in the knowledge that you are directing my play *Carola* for EUROPE No.1. But before you begin the project, I would like you to read the version of *Carola* closest to my English adaptation of it. Mrs Doynel might have a copy of it. I'll write to her about this. You might also get in touch with her from your end.

Don't hesitate to give me your true reaction when you've read this play. I've fiddled about quite a lot with it and it's far from the spirit of the extracts of the original version that I'd given to *Cahiers*.

Concerning publication in *Cahiers* of extracts from my book about Renoir, this depends on Hachette. On this, too, please put the question to Mrs Doynel, who represents me with publishers.

I hope that you and your wife are well. Give her Dido's and my best regards. Let me take this opportunity to tell you again how much I liked *Jules et Jim*, which I saw again here.

Yours sincerely,
Jean Renoir

To Ginette Doynel
Paris

28 October 1962
Beverly Hills

My dear Ginette,

Our reaction, confronted with the menace of war which hangs over us,[1] is that Dido and I regret not being with our children and you at the same time. Catastrophes seem easier to bear when you have your family around you. That said, I think it is all a diplomatic game, dangerous but not inevitably fatal, and that the Russians have placed their missiles in Cuba in highly visible areas so that their discussions will draw the world's attention to the question of American missiles in Turkey. Maybe the Russian missiles in Cuba are fakes. Remember Potemkin and Catherine [the Great].

ACCOUNTS: Thanks.

FILMS DU CYCLOPE: You ought to have received my handwritten letter acknowledging receipt of the $5,000.

As for the cuts [to *Le Caporal Epinglé*], I think that we must avoid working with Cyclope in the future. These cuts have seriously hurt, perhaps not the film's <u>business</u>, but my position regarding the prime

[434]

problem: my only hope of success is in a certain alliance on certain issues with a certain public, especially the young. If I lose that, I will have no purpose. The next time (with another producer) we must think about putting a clause in the contract regarding the editing.

[. . .]

TRUFFAUT: Enclosed is a copy of my response. As I no longer have any hope of producing *Carola* in a theatre, it's possible that this radio production will inject new life into that poor forgotten [play], in which, I swear to you, I have completely lost interest.

[. . .]

Dido and I send you our dearest love.

Jean Renoir

1 Between October and November 1962, the United States and the USSR were on the brink of nuclear war over Soviet missiles in Cuba that were pointed at the US. Moscow finally backed down and removed the missiles when President Kennedy pledged not to invade Cuba again.

To Jean Renoir
Beverly Hills

27 *December 1962*
Paris

Dear Mr Renoir,

Thank you so much for your quick and kind reply regarding *Carola*.

It's a truly beautiful play, and in a completely different genre than that of *Orvet*, which is just as powerful a work and often very moving.

I am very glad I had the chance to read *Carola*, even though it will not be possible for me to use it for the broadcast that was proposed to me by EUROPE No 1.

What happened is that the people undertaking this enterprise let me know recently that the programme will feature hour-long 'dramatic pieces', which of course changes my approach completely. These people couldn't care less about such matters, however – they see nothing wrong with cutting a half-hour of text from a good play that's ninety minutes long!

I still don't know whether I'm going to give up this project altogether, or if I'll do it anyway, finding a play in some lesser genre – a crime drama, for example – which could be condensed without too much fuss.

If you don't have any plans for mounting a stage production of *Carola* in the near future, I think it would be a good idea to give it to

Gallimard, for their collection *Le Manteau d'Arlequin*, in which *Orvet* was also published.

I started reading your book *Renoir*, and it really is extraordinary.

The other night, a dozen or so of us were spending Christmas Eve at Jeanne Moreau's. We all exchanged gifts, and four or five different people gave each other your book.

Of course, all the cinephiles think you ought to write the same sort of memoir about the making of your films, and I share their opinion.

Don't go to the trouble of writing back to me if you are too busy, because every so often I telephone Ginette Doinel [sic] and she gives me news of you.

My wife and I wish both of you a Happy New Year.

F[rançois] Truffaut

1963

To Ginette Doynel   *25 January 1963*
Paris   *Beverly Hills*

Dear Ginette,

According to our paper this morning, the cold weather is still persisting in Paris. Will you come and see us?

I'm enclosing a few lines about Braunberger. I wrote them for a small brochure the Cinémathèque is publishing for a screening honouring him. I was happy to write these lines, but in view of the bad blood between us and the Cinémathèque, I'll leave it up to you to forward them to the interested party, or throw them in the waste-basket. I guess I should clarify that it was Braunberger who requested these lines, and not the Cinémathèque.

[...] We were considering going to New York to appear on TV to promote the book. At the same time, we would have attended the première of *Le Caporal*, which has been retitled *Liberty* by the American distributors. I find this title completely idiotic, but McGregor gave me a call to convince me it is good. I am not convinced.[1] I am not convinced either that my chatting on television will help the book. Therefore, I am not going to New York. A decision that will benefit my next book. Could you contact McGregor in Paris? You'll find him at Pathé. Could you please warn him that I won't have the time to write the 1,200-word article he had asked me to do! I'd love to do this for him because I like both him and Denise very much, but this interruption would be quite detrimental to my book. I think it will be good, but I'm having a hard time with it.[2]

We have received a postcard from Belle Ile en Mer, which reminded us for a brief moment of the time when Maud, Pierre and you had gone to Brittany in freezing weather. Fortunately there had been that great lunch at Le Play. All this makes us long to see you again.

Still no trace of the money from Fayard.

The drought persists.

Dido and I send you our love.

Jean Renoir

1 Ultimately, the film's title in the US was *The Elusive Corporal*. In Britain, the title was *The Vanishing Corporal*.

2 Renoir was writing *Les Cahiers du Capitaine Georges* (*The Notebooks of Captain Georges*, 1966).

To Adry de Carbuccia

Paris

13 April 1963
Beverly Hills

Dear Adry,

Dido, Ginette and I have come back from San Francisco where we saw the première of *Le Caporal* and we can't wait to share with you our disappointment, in the hope that you might ensure that the film is better championed in other parts of the world. I do not know who is responsible for the distribution in the United States, but this person was wrong to give the film to a local cinema that the owners will surely decide to modernize, but which at present is in a pretty sorry state. I'm quite well known in the Bay Area, that is San Francisco and the neighbouring towns. With my presence, a smart salesman could have found a brighter movie theatre. The reviews that came out on the morning of the Première were excellent. Enclosed is one of them, from Knickerbocker, San Francisco's Jean-Jacques Gauthier. Despite these favourable conditions, the cinema was not absolutely full. Many people think twice about going to this out-of-town theatre which has no parking lot and where you have to go miles to park your car. This last circumstance is crippling in California, where the success of any business, restaurant, novelty store or theatre, depends in part on parking facilities. I even felt a little ashamed to appear in person in these circumstances. Happily, this whiff of vanity quickly subsided as the audience proved receptive.

I'm afraid that the bad launch of the film in California might close off to us the good theatres in the other cities in the West.

My dear Adry, I have been thinking of you all the time. You made a big effort for this film, you participated in its development and shooting, you had the intelligence to insist on a young cast that everyone finds remarkable. From my side, I feel that I worked well. We don't deserve to be so badly supported. It seems to me that our product is worthy of presentation not in a village grocers, but in luxury boutiques. I even think that it is strong enough to take on the customers of a department store.

We used this trip to show Ginette something of California. We saw the thousand-year-old sequoias and the umbrella pines at Monterey, visited some missions[1] and climbed to the top of a San Francisco skyscraper.

These successes didn't diminish our regrets about the bad launch of *Le Caporal* in the west, but did help us to bear it.

All our kind regards to Mr de Carbuccia and to Jean-Luc.

Best wishes,

Jean Renoir

1 Churches built by Spanish missionaries.

To Otto Halpern [*Original in English*]

Pacific Palisades, California

20 April 1963
Beverly Hills

Dear Mr Halpern,

I read with the greatest interest your work *On a Nuclear Test Ban*. As a matter of fact I read it several times and after each reading I had the intention to take the telephone and to tell you how impressed I was. I did not do it because such matter demands reflection.

Your argument is so brilliantly logical that it does not leave room to [sic] any contradiction. Still I am not absolutely convinced. To be more precise I should say that sometimes I am convinced and sometimes I am not.

Your belief in the necessity of going on with atomic tests is based on your belief in the inevitability of a war between our world and the communist world. Of course the only solution to the obvious apparent quarrel of our days seems to be a war. But often I wonder if this quarrel is the only one. Our capitalistic world has nothing in common with the capitalistic world of our fathers and Lenin would probably be very much surprised if he could visit Moscow today. I believe very much in history and history teaches me that the most successful human enterprises do not last for ever. The most stable Roman governments: Septime Sevère, Marc Aurèle or even Constantin[1] lasted a few decades. Our democracy is now loaded with socialistic regulations. I assume that one of the traditional basis of our Western society was the family. Our ways of living are destroying this institution as surely as do the communist ways of living in Russia. Since in many cases the wife has to work outside the house, the children grow in kindergartens. The influence of the school in many cases becomes more powerful on the shaping of our future citizens than the one of the father and mother. May I add that the taxes are destroying the idea of succession. Only a very rich man today can afford to keep the house of his parents. Very soon we will all be living in furnished apartments.

The fact that very complex and sometimes dangerous technical devices

[439]

are now a part of our life forces the State to interfere with our ways of living. There are regulations for the use of automobiles, airplanes, guns, chemicals. We must stop in front of a red light and in certain parts of the world the pedestrians have to walk on the right side of the street. I wonder why the Russians should fight for the cause of the omnipotence of the State since we seem ourselves ready to accept this omnipotence. Such are some of my arguments in favour of the test ban. I have many other ones.

Against them I have only one thought. It is that the most horrible wars started for foolish reasons. A war with Russia or perhaps with any other nation, or perhaps a civil war and why not a global civil war could start for no reason at all. In this case I see two alternatives: either we use our atomic weapons and the world will experiment[2] a new version of the Flood, instead of being wet it would be hot. Noah's ark would be an underground shelter, or at the last minute men will be terrified by such a perspective and will go on with centuries of clumsy compromises. This last solution is probably a better hope and requires that the most reasonable one be also the strongest. Everybody believing in such a possibility must agree entirely with the content of your report.

With my sincerest compliments,
Jean Renoir

1 Septimus Severus, Marcus Aurelius, Constantine.
2 Meaning 'experience'.

To Georges Simenon

17 June 1963
Beverly Hills

Dear Georges,

I have just finished Les Anneaux de Bicêtre,[1] and it is with my head filled with this novel that I am writing to you. Of all your books, this may be the one that has impressed me the most. God knows I loved Pedigree[2] with its wealth, its vitality, its style: it was a 'chronicle of an era'. It is the bare simplicity of Les Anneaux de Bicêtre that I find so compelling. It is as much of a confession as Pedigree was, but focusing on emotions and feelings of a different order. In it I can detect the statement of an author who is able to limit himself to the essential. Moreover, it is impossible to single out one of your books from the others, because your work represents a whole, like Balzac's.

Dido and I were thrilled by the news about the house you're building above Lausanne. Since you and Denise have experienced all types of construction from Arizona to Lake Geneva, you must know what a house should be, and yours will certainly match your aesthetic and practical needs.

From time to time Dido and I wonder if we should not move to Switzerland. Dido is very unhappy in cold weather, but we could consider the Italian part of Switzerland which is more temperate. We looked on the map and saw there are only 250 kms between Locarno and your place. These considerations have become more pressing recently, since the County of Los Angeles has decided to introduce taxes on paintings and pieces of art. What this means for us is that we will have to get rid of ours. In any case, the income tax situation makes life very difficult in America. At least for someone who has an irregular income as I do.

Dido and I still can't believe Marie-Jo[3] is going to boarding school. She must be lovely. We are pleased to hear that Johnny is leaning toward classical studies. It's a lucky break for him and for you. I could not see Marc the last time I was in Paris. We hope to catch up with him the next time we are there, and get acquainted with his son. We will pay you a visit also, most probably; and play with merry and peaceful Pierre. We are planning this for the end of the coming winter.

We have a pretty good idea of what Denise must be going through with the construction of the house, and how tired she must be. Some rest in the mountains will do her good. We have just returned from Berkeley where we spent a few days with the children. They are all well. John is eleven, Peter is nine, and Anne is two.

Our fondest regards to the family. Our love to you, dear Denise, and to you, dear Georges.

Jean Renoir

1 In English, *The Patient (1963)*.
2 *Pedigree* (1948).
3 Marie-Jo Simenon (1953–78), daughter of Georges Simenon.

To Ginette Doynel
Paris

17 *June 1963*
Beverly Hills

Dear Ginette,

We have received both your letter of 13 June and your telegram of the 15th. I immediately rushed to Larousse to fish out some information on the Charles Blanc Prize. I learned that Charles Blanc (brother of Louis

Blanc) was an engraver and art critic who died in 1882; he was the author of a grammar of art and design, a highly appreciated work, and was in charge of editing the great *Histoire des Peintres*. So, I suppose that this prize by the Académie Française is thus named because it is intended for a work on painting. I am very proud and very happy. This distinction will help gain some respect for my work.

[. . .]

NUIT CARREFOUR [sic]:[1] Impossible for me to remember a single name. Those who had participated in this film are, alas, no longer here. My brother Pierre, Becker,[2] Gehret.[3] Simenon, the author of the book, might remember.

[. . .]

PROBLEMS: We are very worried by a measure which has been taken by the *County Assessor*[4] of taxes for Los Angeles. He has just disinterred an old law which would impose on art-collectors a tax on said art. In addition to the paperwork, which asks us for an evaluation of our paintings, sculptures, furniture, miscellaneous objects, this tax would be beyond our means, which as you know are not large. It is possible that this measure will be applied with discretion, and that we will not suffer too much. It is also possible that it will hit us hard and force us to make a serious decision. This decision would be to flee Los Angeles County and put our little collection in a country where they take into account the non-commercial nature of our collection. We are prepared to go so far as considering leaving America. With *jets*[5] it would be easy to go to see Alain and his family where he is teaching. We wouldn't like to go to a country with a cold climate, which Dido can't stand. I remember her freezing in Paris. An idea, which might be a little crazy, would be for us to move to the Italian part of Switzerland by one of the lakes. We were impressed by Paulette Goddard's stories about her residence by Locarno. George Simenon and Denise would give us all the details [. . .]

With all our love,
Jean and Dido

1 *La Nuit du Carrefour*.
2 Jacques Becker.
3 Jean Gehret, actor.
4 Originally in English.
5 Originally in English.

To Raymond Burnier

1 July 1963
Beverly Hills

Dear Raymond,

Dido and I hope that you have left the care of doctors and that the memory of your little cardiac inconvenience has now faded. We also hope that you have finished with the painful formalities of your divorce. We write to you in Italy on the off-chance. The newspapers inform us that it's hot in Rome. The temperature must be most agreeable on your hill. Life carries on here. We went to see my son Alain and his family in Berkeley, and they came to see us here. We adore our grandchildren but are obliged to admit that we are a little old to bear bravely living with these forces of nature. The boys, John, eleven, and Peter, nine years old, have become well-behaved, but two-year-old little Anne does not let herself be left out. She is in love with me, which proves that she has good taste. She follows me about, murmuring with a voice trembling with passion, 'Papa Jean'. Dido and I are quite upset at the idea that we shall be some time without seeing them. Alain is going to take on an important post at Berkeley, but only in a year's time. Meanwhile, he's teaching at Seattle, then he'll go to Madison, Wisconsin and will even give a lecture at Fribourg in Switzerland. On the subject of Switzerland and the question of American taxes (there is talk here of taxing paintings and works of art), we are vaguely thinking of retiring to your country where we could probably live off our little income. Dido's and my aversion to the cold would point us to the Italian part of Switzerland. But it's really only a very vague idea.

We hope to go to Paris in March or April. Ginette is rushing about to organize a couple of films for me. This time round we really don't want to put off our visit to your beautiful house. Christine gave us an enthusiastic account, which I am sure is realistic. We hope to find you in fine form. As for ourselves, we're well. I had some gall-stones, but they're being sorted out with a diet.

Fondly yours,
Jean Renoir

[443]

To Ginette Doynel
Paris

Dear Ginette,

[. . .] We go every day to see Clifford Odets and each time we return more upset by our visit. They are in the midst of prolonging the life of Lourié's mother by tube-feeding and artificial respiration. Poor Lourié asks why, but the doctors are all-powerful. The Carthaginians sacrificed human beings to their gods. We do the same in the name of the new religion: science.

We hope that you will take a vacation, that you will have beautiful weather, and that you will send us good news of a well-earned rest.

We are also very anxious to see you. While waiting, we send you all our love,

Jean and Dido

[. . .]

PPS. We have received your letter of 9 August. We'll respond to it later. We agree on the salary increase. Clifford Odets is dying.

To Pierre Olaf
Paris

20 *August 1963*
Beverly Hills

Dear Pierre,

We have been most upset by the death of Clifford Odets. His disappearance leaves a great emptiness, at least for us. It also leaves problems: two children at an awkward age. To take some comfort, we reread your letter telling us that all is well with you and that your mother has recovered her strength. We saw the Curtises[1] and talked about you a lot. They were supposed to come for dinner, but we put them off because of Clifford's death. All that day we stayed with him. He was unconscious. We left him quite late in the evening. He died an hour later. Happily for his children he has some very good friends, notably Lee[2] and Paula Strasberg[3] who you must know and who are admirable.

The heat here is bearable, but Dido was worried that its fierceness might be a bit much for the chervil. Your seeds await a more favourable moment. We're going to Aspen from 31 August to 5 September. Our children are on their way to Madison, Wisconsin. I still have gall-stones and use this excuse not to do anything. I'm being asked to do a television programme in which I would only have to present short stories grafted on to classical or other paintings. I said yes, but with the firm determination to have my projects for Parisian films take precedence.

Dido is a bit tired by events, by the garden, the heat and Nenette, who with age refuses to go outside to do her business.

The film you're shooting in 104 Fahrenheit must be finished now. We hope that you are happy with it and that your purple complexion matches the set.

Fondly yours,
Jean & Dido

1 Tony Curtis and his wife.
2 Lee Strasberg (1901–82), artistic director of the Actors Studio which produced a generation of 'Method' actors.
3 Paula Strasberg, wife of Lee, also a director of the Actors Studio.

To Ginette Doynel   *23 August 1963*
Paris   *Beverly Hills*

Dear Ginette,

As you know, Clifford Odets is dead. He was buried at Forest Lawn, or rather his ashes were placed in a small niche. Paula Strasberg has taken Nora[1] to New York. The house is still rented for a month, Walt will live there under the care of Kim Stanley's husband, who is here to direct a television show. You can understand the great void left by Clifford's departure.

[...]

We miss you terribly.
We send you all our love,
Jean and Dido.

1 Nora Odets, daughter of Clifford Odets.

To Bosley Crowther [*Original in English*]   *7 November 1963*
The New York Times   *Beverly Hills*
Times Square
New York

Dear Mr Crowther,

I certainly feel honoured to have my film *La Grande Illusion* mentioned in your book. I will do my best to give you the information you request.

The idea of *La Grande Illusion* came to me in 1933 while I was shooting a picture named *Toni* in the south of France. Close to my location was a military airfield and the pilots, attracted by our reflectors, were constantly flying in circles above us making the work of our soundman impossible. I decided to pay a visit to their commander and found myself in front of an old friend, General Pinsard. During the war he had been a magnificent fighter pilot. He had saved my life while I was myself, humble reconnaissance pilot, under the attacks of German fighters. Pinsard had been shot down and made a prisoner seven times and escaped seven times. I asked him to tell me more about his adventures thinking that they could provide a springboard for an interesting motion picture. Since several years I had been looking for a convenient frame which would help me to tell my belief in the vanity of war. I was also irritated by the successful cliché representing the soldiers of the First World War as stock characters. The *poilu* with his crude language, his easy common sense, was a product of the imagination of writers specializing in heroism. My friends in the trenches and later on in the air force were normal human beings, ready to do their duty but hating war and impatient to resume civilian life with their wives and children. Such are, I think, the main ideas which impelled me to realize a project which in those days wasn't yet named *La Grande Illusion*. I wrote a first treatment, then I got involved with other pictures up to the fall of 1935 when, during the preparation of *Les Bas-Fonds*, I met Charles Spaak. He became excited by my story and we decided to write the screenplay together. Jean Gabin who was playing the main part in *Les Bas-Fonds* shared our confidence. After *Les Bas-Fonds* was finished we started to peddle unsuccessfully *La Grande Illusion* to all possible producers of any possible nation. We met Albert Pinkewitch, an assistant producer, who was trying to convince a stock-market man who had been extremely lucky to invest some of his benefits in a motion picture. Fortunately this gentleman wasn't a professional producer. He ignored the fashions of the

[446]

film world at the moment and liked our story. He was also impressed by the success of *Les Bas-Fonds* and decided to finance the picture. I don't remember the budget of *La Grande Illusion*. I believe that it was a normal budget rather on the economical side.

My first idea was to ask Louis Jouvet who had been excellent in *Les Bas-Fonds* to play the part of *le capitaine de Böildieu*. Unfortunately he was too busy with Giraudoux in his own theatre. I quickly changed the part and asked Pierre Fresnay to play it. Encouraged by his acceptance and knowing that Eric [sic] von Stroheim was in Paris I convinced the producer (Mr Rollmer) to have him play the part of Herr Hauptman von Raufenstein. At the moment it was a very small part but I knew that with a man like Stroheim I would find ways to make it important. This addition forced me to bring considerable changes to the screenplay during the shooting. Charles Spaak being involved in another picture with Duvivier I asked my assistant Carl Koch who had been in the German army during the war to help me. Albert Pinkewitch, the assistant producer, brought me many Jewish expressions for the part of Rosenthal acted by Marcel Dalio.[1] When the picture was completed what we had on the screen was very far away from the screenplay which had convinced the producer. Several times, upset by my improvisations, he menaced to stop the production. We owe to the eloquence of Albert Pinkewitch to have finished *La Grande Illusion*.

At no moment had I thought of *Les Croix de Feu*, my description of army people being more ambitious and I hope more timeless.

Eric von Stroheim contributed to the creation of the character he played but mostly about his presentation, for instance the uniforms. (By the way, the uniform Jean Gabin is wearing was my own. We were exactly the same size.) Concerning the German spirit and its influence on the behaviour of the Germans I owe about everything to my collaborator Carl Koch.

La Grande Illusion was presented to the public in May 1937 with great success. I must say that when Charles Spaak and myself decided to release the picture again three year ago it was equally successful.

I am at your disposal for any further informations you might wish.

Sincerely,

Jean Renoir

1 Marcel Dalio (1899–1983), actor whose credits included *La Grande Illusion*, *La Règle du Jeu*, *Casablanca* (Michael Curtiz, 1943), and *Gentlemen Prefer Blondes* (Howard Hawks, 1953).

To Ginette Doynel
Paris

1 December 1963
Beverly Hills

My Dear Ginette,

[...] Dido wants to remind you that Christmas is approaching, and that we remember you'll soon be one year older. We would like you to choose a beautiful gift for yourself. You are so young in spirit and body, you could easily forget time is going by. We really want you to pick something that you like a lot. At the same time, and without waiting for the last-minute rush of Christmas shopping, could you take care of the gifts situation by getting something for our lovely god-daughter? Dido asks you to keep the receipt of your own gift (and any others that are justifiable) and enclose them with the papers to be sent to Blum for our income-tax return. We know for sure that the American Internal Revenue Services will accept the deduction for gifts to a *business manager*.[1]

Here, people have not recovered from Kennedy's death.[2] Not only in his own country, but all over the world, people have responded with great dignity to the death of this young prince. I found the reactions of heads of state and people in the streets remarkable. We were very touched by the several letters we have received from France, including yours.

Good news: Alain is arriving Saturday at about 7 pm. He'll spend the night with us and will leave in the morning. We are trying to find some *boudin* and we'll get some champagne.

With love from both of us,

Jean Renoir

1 Originally in English.
2 President John F. Kennedy was assassinated in Dallas, Texas, on 22 November 1963.

To Radha Sri Ram Burnier
[*Original in English*]

2 December 1963

Dear Radha,

Dido and I are at the same time happy and sad to read your letter, happy because we love to be with you and your letters always bring us very much of yourself, sad because we know too well how much not only India but the whole world is deteriorating. Progress is a terrible thing and the advantages of streetcars, aeroplanes, iceboxes, anaesthesia and conservation of food are dearly paid by the disappearance of wonderful habits and traditions. We cannot have everything, the possibility to reach London in a few hours and also the art of the potter who used to make masterpieces just for the purpose of helping people to drink a mouthful of tea. India will be one of the rare countries where the unconscious genius of craftsmen still allows human beings to enjoy the immense benefit of being surrounded by handmade objects. In spite of their hi-fi talking machines modern men are not gay because machine-made objects generate a great sadness. But we won't change this state of affairs. Perhaps the destruction of our barbarian world is the only solution. Dido and I don't wish it. We would like to see again some of our good friends before it is too late. Often we think of you and have to admit that we miss you.

Christmas is approaching. Since it is the custom of our age we wish you a joyful holiday. We also wish you and your dear parents a happy New Year with good health and good achievements.

With our affection,

Jean Renoir

To Christine Burnier

2 December 1963
Beverly Hills

Dear Christine,

Dido and I are writing to you at the same time. She is at the typewriter, and we are both thinking about what we want to tell you. First of all, we are flabbergasted by the work you're accomplishing. India, Africa, and to top it all the delightful translations of Tagore's[1] writings. We have seen the two films that S[atyajit] Ray[2] made from the works of this author. The longest one is based on a story you included in your book: the one about the wild girl. It is always dangerous to adapt masterpieces. Ray is a great director, but despite his talent, I was not able to find on the screen the breadth of Tagore's tale. Dido has not had the time to read it yet. She has been helping me by going through the mass of projects submitted to me, none presenting any interest whatsoever.

We'll be happy to see you again and listen to your African stories. From the various, and rather superficial, conversations I've had with Africans, I fear that they are rushing after progress instead of preserving the few traditions that have not been destroyed by the white man. It is even possible that the new governments will be even more destructive of the past than the French bureaucrats. Dido and I thank the current administration for its wisdom in choosing you. From your letter we deduce that you won't get away without a little trip to Africa. That's all for the best for the Africans.

We are very pleased at the good news about Raymond and Alain. What they are doing in Berlin must be fascinating.

My classes at the University are not entirely satisfying.[3] I wonder if film-directing can be taught, and if it would not be better for all aspiring directors to acquire a solid general culture instead. Knowing a couple of good books, a few good paintings and a few pieces of music, understanding them, absorbing them and digesting them may be the best preparation to becoming a film-maker.

Your reference to Kennedy's death has touched us deeply. Maybe his death won't be in vain. Worthy causes need martyrs, and peace is a worthy cause.

We are expecting my son Alain at the end of the week. He and his family are in Madison, Wisconsin until the end of next summer. He has arranged to make a slight detour to see us for a few hours.

Christmas decorations are already up in the streets of Los Angeles, including this horrible white-bearded man who looks like a drunk. I can't find any connection between this satyr and the child Jesus. I close my eyes and remember the manger scenes of my childhood. Dido and I wish you a Merry Christmas. Even if the symbolism of Christmas has been vulgarized, what it attempts to evoke still remains the most important event in the history of the world. We wish you a Happy New Year, with lots of success in your work and good health,

Jean Renoir

1 Rabindranath Tagore (1861–1941), Bengali writer who won the Nobel Prize for literature in 1913. Several of his stories were filmed by Satyajit Ray.
2 Satyajit Ray (1921–92), Bengali director whose films included *Pather Panchali* (1955) and *Charulata* (1964). He helped find locations for *The River* and observed the filming.
3 Jean Renoir taught a directing class at UCLA in the autumn of 1963.

To Pierre Gaut

11 December 1963
Beverly Hills

Dear Pierre,

Knowing that we shall not see Braque[1] again when we visit Paris is very painful for both of us. Dido and I have some reservations about the appropriateness of all the public demonstrations, speeches and military parades that have surrounded his funeral. These are fine for men like

Kennedy, who was a public figure, or Louis XIV, but for Molière or Chardin, whose influence was more limited, we feel this is inappropriate. What do you think? What does Maud think? What does Marcelle Braque think?

The Kennedy assassination has shocked us deeply. We had a 'prince' for president, with all the grace and elegance of a prince. Johnson will probably do a good job, but with him, we are stepping back to a more humdrum routine.

We imagine you are still very involved in managing your business and that it must be very exciting.

I thank you for your concern about my gall stones. I never received the medication Maud sent to me. In any case, my doctor has given me some enzymes which compensate for the reduced action of the bile and help digest whatever has become hard to digest. They seem to be quite effective.

Alain has just spent a day with us. He and his family had just been in a car accident, in which they suffered only minor contusions, thanks to the effectiveness of safety belts and the sturdiness of their Volkswagen. Dido is fine. The garden is overpowering her. Everything is growing so fast that the whole house is surrounded by a jungle. It is quite nice, actually. We hope that the beneficial results of the sea-baths of last summer will persist and Maud will completely recover from shingles. We think about her a lot and we also think of you, and we hope to see you both again next Spring. But first we must celebrate Christmas and the New Year, which always brings us closer in thought to those we love. Dido and I wish you a Merry Christmas, a Happy New Year, and good health.

With much love,
Jean Renoir

1 Georges Braque had died on 31 August 1963.

1964

To Ginette Doynel   *3 February 1964*
Paris   *Beverly Hills*

Dear Ginette,

[...]

LEVER DU RIDEAU:[1] I cannot prevent Pozner [sic] from selling his story to Delannoy,[2] since I haven't been able to stir up any enthusiasm for this subject when I've spoken to cinema people about it. Only Leslie has understood the value of this story, and I sincerely regret having to abandon the hope of shooting this film with her. But I can't bleed myself dry again by purchasing rights. We took risks with *Hunger*[3] which amounted to nothing.

[...]

My prospects for future films, as you can see, seem compromised. Perhaps it is Providence which makes me stop and pushes me to write books rather than plunge myself into the complications of the film business. We must thank you for all the help that you have given us and we send you all our love,

Jean and Dido

1 *The Curtain Rises*, novel by Vladmir Poznar.
2 Jean Delannoy (b.1908), director whose films included *L'Eternel Retour* (1943) and *La Symphonie Pastorale* (1946).
3 *Hunger*, novel by Knut Hamsun which Renoir wanted to film with Oskar Werner. It was eventually filmed by Henning Carlsen in 1966.

To Ginette Doynel   *22 February 1964*
Paris

Dear Ginette,

[...]

LEVER DU RIDEAU: Despite the subject's quality, I continue to think it best not to get involved in anything and to avoid any risks. Leslie[1] has left for London. We didn't see her.

I learned yesterday that Jeanne MOREAU is going to shoot *Le Journal d'une Femme de Chambre*, directed by BUÑUEL.

Dido and I have attended the *Charter Day*[2] ceremony marked by the meeting of the Presidents of the United States and Mexico, who had received a *Doctor's Degree*[3] as Eisenhower and I did last year. We then went to a reception consisting of introductions and hand-shaking. Mrs Lyndon Johnson[4] has read my book on Renoir.

[. . .]

I have not taken up my book again – too many excursions – too many honours – and above all too many film projects. It is only when I have completely renounced making films that I will be able to write seriously. What absorbs me the most is not really the making of the film itself but the preparation, the meetings and the disappointments.

[. . .]

We send you all our love,
Jean and Dido

1 Leslie Caron.
2 Originally in English.
3 Originally in English.
4 First Lady of the US.

To Ginette Doynel   *27 April 1964*
Paris   *Beverly Hills*

Dear Ginette,

We have received your letter of 18 April. I have not responded sooner because my health is giving me problems. I am doing a little better and this (relative) recovery allows me to stand the operation. I am going on Thursday to Cedars of Lebanon[1] and Friday morning they will take out my gall-bladder. The surgeon doesn't guarantee that this operation will cure all my ills. No doubt it will cure some, and anyway there is the risk this infected gall-bladder could become dangerous.[. . .]

LA CANNE: I think you were the one who sent me a book entitled *La Canne* by Vahé Katcha (published by Julliard). I read it. It might make a good film, but this really doesn't interest me. It might make a good subject for a beginner like Becker's son.[2]

This operation is obviously going to change all my plans. It is wise to renounce *Aspects of Love*[3] this year. As for *La Célestine*, it's a big piece that we shouldn't think about doing before spring '65. *Le Lever du Rideau* could be shot in the winter.

[453]

Dido and I hope that all your *smala* are well. Give them our regards [...]. We think of you all the time and hope that this operation will not slow down our reunion.

We send you all our love,

Jean Renoir

1 Hospital.
2 Jean Becker (b.1933), son of Jacques Becker, director whose films include *Un Nommé la Rocca* (1961), *Tendre Voyou* (1962), and *L'Eté Meurtier* (1985).
3 A novel by David Garnett, subsequently turned into a musical by Andrew Lloyd Webber.

To Klaus Piper
Munich

22 *September 1964*
Beverly Hills

Dear Mr Piper,

My wife and I were delighted by your flowers. Besides being gorgeous, the chrysanthemum also has the advantage of being a plant which we'll put in our garden after we've enjoyed it inside our house.

I have been considering writing my autobiography for a long time. But each time I started working on it, I was stopped by the fear of hurting people who are still alive, or their relatives. On the other hand, if I limit myself to the mere telling of trivial stories, and do not use my memories to put certain human frailties in perspective, this autobiography might end up being dull.

This constant rehashing of my memories has allowed me to extract a few characters and, by changing their identity, I intend to use their adventures in a novel. I'm just starting to work on this now.

I wish you a good trip to Sicily. It is a fascinating land.

My wife and I thank you for your invitation, which we hope to be able to accept in the future, and send you our best wishes.

Jean Renoir

To Helen Strauss [*Original in English*]
William Morris Agency Inc.
New York

31 *October 1964*
Beverly Hills

Dear Helen,

I am answering your letter of October 20, 21 and 27. Thank you for the copy of the royalty report of the Danish edition of *Renoir My Father*.

We received to date only two copies of the Swedish edition of the book.

The completion of the first draft of my novel[1] will perhaps take a little more time than I expected. I may need three more weeks.

Thank you for your enquiry regarding the photocopy of this first draft. We will send it to you, as you suggest, ahead of our trip and would go to New York after Elinor [sic] Wolquitt gives you an idea of the content. Could you ask your secretary to take care of this Xerox business and to bill us. Since I will make corrections and additions with Mrs Doynel in Paris, I think two copies are sufficient at this time.

Basically this book is about a great love between a young rich bourgeois and an extremely young prostitute he finds in a brothel. Outside of a kind of introduction in England the action takes place in France before, during and after the First World War. It ends during the Second World War. The most important backgrounds are the Paris of highly successful kept women and the French cavalry. It is a touching and sad story which I am trying to tell lightly and to stuff with as many funny anecdotes as I can remember.

I am going to answer Bob Knittel's[2] nice letter. We plan to go to Europe and I could see him in London. The introduction and the end of the story being told by an English gentleman, we will need an English collaboration for their translation. The story itself is told by the hero of the adventure, Captain Georges, who is French. A good American translation would be adequate.

The book is a short book, probably around 250 pages.

If you see Elinor [sic] tell her our best. Dido and I send you our affection.

Sincerely,

Jean Renoir

1 *Les Cahiers du Capitaine Georges.*
2 Robert Knittel, publisher and husband of actress Luise Rainer.

1965

To Judd Boynton

7 February 1965
Beverly Hills

Dear Judd,

Thank you for your concern about my health. It was just a short alert. Now I am almost back to normal.

I am not surprised by your confused impression of Paris. It is a difficult city, more difficult than when young Raymond Duncan arrived there. The artistic or intellectual groups, may I say the casts, were in those days more obvious. After a few experiences it wasn't too difficult to find a centre of attraction among the many existing centres. Today everything is mixed up, the daughters of bankers are actresses. To think or to be an artist is no more the privilege of people dedicated exclusively to a vocation. But perhaps there is still something to be gained from the contact with the people of Paris. Some Frenchmen still have a direct and realistic approach to the problems of life and one may discover that to be surrounded by such clear minded people may have helped a Modigliani or a Picasso born in other countries. Of course, as you say, the indispensable bridge is the language but I don't doubt that you will master it very soon. It is not so much a question of talking, it is a question of understanding which is more difficult. In any language, beyond the meaning of each word there are other meanings which express a personality more than the academic translation.

Dido and I hope to go to Paris in spring and perhaps you will be there and we will see you. It will probably be a short sojourn but we will manage to spend a few moments with you. We are anxious to know how you progress in this adventure within the mysterious world of the old city.

Our best wishes.

As ever,

Jean Renoir

To Pierre Olaf
Paris

5 May 1965
Beverly Hills

Dear Pierre,

I waited for a few days before replying to you about *The 13 Clocks.*[1] I needed to think. I understand your enthusiasm for the project. Fairy tales are your territory. Dido and I pass our time regretting that film-makers and theatre producers have not been struck by the blinding truth, which is that you were made to give reality to dreams as much as to communicate a dream atmosphere to reality. As far as I am concerned, I cannot help you with *The 13 Clocks*, as I am working on a theme also based on fantasy characters. Ginette (Durandal)[2] is trying to work out an agreement to make this film with the accomplice of my first efforts, who goes by the name of Pierre Braunberger.

As for work, all I've produced so far is a fifty-page treatment, but this sketch makes me hope that I can show on screen some situations that are still fresh. There will be a series of short stories linked by a central situation, a little bit like a revue. There will probably be many characters. My dearest wish is that one of them will please you, and that you will be free at an appropriate moment so that we might have the opportunity of working together. But all this is still nothing more than a wish. Apparently the cinema is unwell in France, and appeals for money fall on deaf ears. Despite these difficulties, I don't want to give up this project which I care about, before proving that it really is in the realm of the impossible.

Dido and I desperately want to see you. We know that this will happen one way or another, in the meanwhile we send our love,

Jean Renoir

1 Originally in English. A play by James Thurber, famous American humourist.
2 Pierre Olaf's nickname for Ginette Doynel.

To Audrey Wood [*Original in English*]
AFA
New York

5 May 1965
Beverly Hills

Dear Miss Wood,

I won't leave California in the immediate future. I plan the shooting of a film in Paris but I don't believe that I would have to go there before June.

I was thrilled when, in London, Rumer Godden told me that she had written a musical comedy. The result of her association with Hans Christian Andersen will certainly be a masterpiece. It would be for me a rare pleasure to read the text of *The Feather Duster* and also to hear the score. Strangely enough I am myself working on an old film project comprising several short episodes, one of them inspired by an Andersen fairy tale.[1]

With my best regards.
Sincerely,
Jean Renoir

1 This would evolve into *Le Dernier Réveillon*, the first episode of *Le Petit Théâtre de Jean Renoir*. It harks back to *La Petite Marchande d'Allumettes*, which was based on Andersen's *The Little Match Girl*.

To Randolph Weaver

24 May 1965
Beverly Hills

Dear Randolph,

Our trip to France went fine. We were lucky enough to have good weather. We only spent a few days in Paris, where we saw some old friends again including Renée Cezanne with her children, a few grand-children and even a few great-grandchildren. We stopped by Essoyes where, as you know, my father, mother and brother are buried. We went to Les Collettes. Since there are no paintings exhibited there, the museum is rather meaningless. Nevertheless, we did at least manage to save the olive trees by converting this private property into a public property. Once again, they look like they used to when my parents were alive. And this alone has made the creation of this museum worthwhile.

You are asking me to describe the state of mind of the French people. Dido and I have found that they appear to have overcome the anxiety left over from the Occupation. We have met a lot of helpful and kind people, in particular a mechanic who fixed our windshield wipers for practically nothing. The cost of living is very high in Paris, and not that much lower in the country. I hope this state of things will keep the tourists away. Their money is welcome, but I don't think their presence does any good in lifting the spirit of a nation.

Dido and I often think about the too-brief moments spent with you in New York. Your welcome was so kind. We are sorry we didn't have time to take a meal with you, and I deeply regret having had to pass on the good liqueur Dorothy had given me.

Thank you for the article from the *New Statesman*. My fate is rather odd, I'll have to wait another thirty years before my work is really appreciated.

Many thanks to Dorothy for her very beautiful postcard, and especially for what she wrote on the back.

My book about my father has been published in German, Italian, Danish, Japanese, Swedish, Finnish, Polish, Spanish, Dutch, and is about to come out in Czech and Russian.

Alain is too busy teaching to have taken part in the events at Berkeley. I think his position is the following: he approves of the students' motivations, but not their methods.

We hope to have another chance to stop in New York, and spend more time with you then. In the meantime, we send our fondest regards to both of you.

Jean Renoir

PS. I shot *Madame Bovary* in 1933 or '34; *Toni* at about the same time. *La Charette Fantôme* was made by Stiller,[1] a wonderful Swedish director who died after a disappointing sojourn in Hollywood. It was he who brought Greta Garbo to America.

1 Maurice Stiller (1883–1928), Swedish director whose major films included *Erotikon* (1920) and *The Gosta Berling Saga* (1924). *La Charette Fantôme (The Phantom Carriage)* was actually directed by Victor Sjostrom in 1921.

To Albert Lewin [*Original in English*]   26 May 1965
                                                         Beverly Hills

Dear Al,

Dido and I enjoyed our little telephone talk last Sunday. We are deeply moved at your idea to give us a practical souvenir of Millie.[1] We don't need it to have her in our thoughts, but beside our spiritual evocation, it is good to feel something you can touch and see.

We are anxious to spend again a few days with you and to talk freely about the past.

Dido and I started the week looking at paintings: an exhibition of etchings at the Lytton Centre with a few good things – an exhibition for an auction at the Acosta Gallery with a beautiful small bouquet by my father, about 12″×10″, but the price is as big as the size is small, $45,000 – then the Museum. There, the two big statues by my father, the Venus and the Washerwoman, are beautifully presented outside on a terrace. That is the right place for bronzes. My portrait as a huntsman, a bouquet of roses and a landscape are also exhibited. The lighting from the ceiling is perhaps a little cold, but I don't see any other alternative. Dido and I were terrified at the sight of the crowd invading this museum. Children and teenagers could very easily scratch a painting just for fun. And no wardens! We met the daughter-in-law of Stendhal very busy explaining the works of art to a flock of visitors gathering around her like chickens around the mother hen. She told us that she is in charge of guided tours.

This museum is certainly a great achievement, still if I was a painter I would prefer to have my audience limited to Duke Alexander de Médicis, King Francis the first, and Pope Julius the second.

We saw David about a week ago. We have the feeling that he is recovering nicely.

With our love,
Jean Renoir

1 Millie Lewin had recently died.

To Ingrid Bergman

5 July 1965
Beverly Hills

Dear Ingrid,

It was really kind of you to send me the *New York Herald Tribune* article on *La Règle du Jeu*. We knew nothing about it, and Dido and I were delighted.

You must know, of course, that poor Selznick is dead. I miss him. He really was somebody, and his absence will be felt in the film industry.

Your film[1] is presently showing in Los Angeles. According to the comments we've heard from friends, it is very successful and you are excellent. We'll go and see it as soon as we have a chance.

We received a phone call from Ruth when she came through town. Swedish women strike me as being travellers. Ruth never ceases to surprise us. And you, you keep turning improbabilities into probabilities. We would not be surprised to hear one day that you have become queen of a cannibal tribe in Congo; or that you have decided to settle in Nepal.

We hope the Tourguenev [sic] play you are doing with Redgrave[2] is going well.

It is nice to hear that your children are doing fine. Ours, too. They don't travel as much as yours, though. Alain is quite happy teaching this summer in Boulder, Colorado.

Finally, I think I'll see you in Choisel. I hope to have a chance to go to Europe by the end of the summer or in the Fall. Unfortunately, I don't think Dido can come with me. In fact, we both dislike travelling, except for the fact that it is an excuse to see old friends again. We are becoming Los Angeles suburbanites, and we are more concerned by the health of one of our olive trees whose leaves are turning yellow than by the political situation in the world. However, this doesn't prevent us from having have a raging desire to see you again. In the meantime, we send you our love. Don't forget to give our warmest regards to Lars.[3]

Jean Renoir

1 Presumably *The Yellow Rolls Royce* (Anthony Asquith, 1965).
2 Ingrid Bergman starred in Ivan Turgenev's *A Month in the Country* with Michael Redgrave on the London stage.
3 Lars Schmidt, Swedish theatre impresario, who had married Bergman in 1958.

To Ginette Doynel
Paris

20 *August 1965*
Beverly Hills

Dear Ginette,

Dido and I are deeply touched by your concern for us. The revolt of the blacks seems to have ended, at least for the moment.[1] Will it start again one day or another, here or elsewhere? Many people fear it will. This type of trouble, if one believes history, happens in regular cycles. We hope that the epidemic will be stopped.

HUNGER: Dido and I dined last night with Oskar Werner[2] and Stanley Kramer,[3] the producer-director of big, successful films. The latter offered to present the project to one of the major distribution companies, probably Columbia. He didn't hide from us the fact that film industry executives wouldn't understand a thing about the subject. Our best hope would be to shoot the film in Europe with frozen money. I suggested Ireland. Nevertheless, things still seem too vague to me for us to shell out any money for a new option.

[...]

We send you all our love,

Jean Renoir

1 Renoir is referring to the Watts riots of August 1965.
2 Oskar Werner (1922–84), actor whose credits included *Lola Montes* (Max Ophuls,

1955), *Jules et Jim* (François Truffaut, 1961), and *Fahrenheit 451* (François Truffaut, 1966).

3 Stanley Kramer (b.1913), producer, director, whose films include *On the Beach* (1959), *Judgement at Nuremberg* (1961) and *Guess Who's Coming to Dinner?* (1967).

To Ginette Doynel
Paris

27 August 1965
Beverly Hills

Dear Ginette,

[...] You will probably get a phone call from Warren Beatty[1] and Leslie Caron. Warren is very eager to make a film with me, and once more I'm thinking of *Les Bas-Fonds* (the Gabin part). Would you arrange a screening for them? You might also explain to them that it is a very old film, which I am not considering remaking faithfully, but rather using as a source of inspiration. You might point out to Warren as well that this part had a decisive impact on Gabin's career.

Hunger with Oskar Werner looks like it may go ahead. I'll set the story in Dublin.

I'll end this letter now, so that it won't miss the post.

Dido and I vacillate between deploring the fact that your vacations are over, and hoping to see you again soon.

Love,

Jean Renoir

PS: The idea about *Les Bas-Fonds* came to me after Warren's phone call informing me of his departure. I'll try to reach him, but most probably I won't succeed. Consequently, when you talk to him about it, it'll all be news to him.

1 Warren Beatty (b.1937), actor, director whose films include *Splendour in the Grass* (Elia Kazan, 1961), *Bonnie and Clyde* (Arthur Penn, 1967), and *Reds* (1981).

To Albert Lewin [*Original in English*]

14 September 1965
Beverly Hills

Dear Al,

Dido and I are really delighted to know that *The Unaltered Cat*[1] will be printed. Personally it makes me particularly happy to think that we are starting a new career almost together.

I know Bob Knittel very well. As a matter of fact we talked a great deal about you with Luise[2] and himself during my last sojourn in London. I had told them that you had written a novel about a cat and they appeared to be interested by this turn in your artistic life. They have a beautiful daughter who is working at Sothebys. Bob published my two books in England.

Thank you for Maillol. It reminds me of the man. He loved my father and my father loved him. He came to our home in Essoyes to work on a bust of Renoir. He didn't bring his wife because the lock of his door was broken and he had found it less expensive to leave Clotilde watching the house than to buy a new lock. The book is beautiful. Dido and I love it.

There are good chances that we will see you and Angna[3] in the middle of next month. Little, Brown asked me to go east at the time of the publication of my novel. That would be wonderful. We would land at the old Westbury and spend many hours with you. There are still good things in life.

We will phone to you on the day of your anniversary.[4] We want to hear your voice and drink to your good health. We won't send you any gift. You are surrounded by so many beautiful things in your house that it is about impossible to find anything to match.

With our love,
Jean Renoir.

1 *The Unaltered Cat*, novel by Lewin, published in 1966.
2 Luise Rainer (b.1910), stage and film actress whose credits include *The Great Ziegfeld* (Robert Z. Leonard) and *The Good Earth* (Sidney Franklin, 1937).
3 Angna Enters, artist, became Lewin's companion after the death of his wife Millie.
4 Meaning 'birthday'.

To Robert Knittel [*Original in English*]   *21 September 1965*
Collins Publications   *Beverly Hills*
London

Dear Bob,

The best title for my book[1] would be *L'Education Sentimentale*. Unfortunately a certain Flaubert used it already. I thought of several other titles but I don't like them:

Death of a Horse, makes me think of a depressing stage play.
La Douceur de Vivre, but I don't believe it is good in English.(x)
The Constant Prostitute, too much like Sartre.
The Embarkation for Cythera, too much XVIIIth Century.
I would prefer something simple like *Les Amours du Capitaine*

Georges or the old title *The Notebooks of Captain Georges*.
    Our affection to Luise and you,
    Jean Renoir

(x) *La Douceur de Vivre* is an expression used by Talleyrand, who pretended[2] that those who had not lived in France before the Revolution ignored[3] what is *la douceur de vivre*. We could apply the same thought to the pre-1914 period.

1 *Les Cahiers du Capitaine Georges* was published by Gallimard in 1966. The English translation, *The Notebooks of Captain Georges*, was published by Collins in the same year.
2 Meaning 'claimed'.
3 Meaning 'did not know'.

To Ingrid Bergman

30 September 1965
Beverly Hills

Dear Ingrid,
    Dido and I share your happiness. The English critics are good people. With a part like this, you could not be anything but dazzling, and it is apparently obvious to everyone. We are terribly happy to know you, first of all because we love you. We would love you just the same if you were not as successful, but it is comforting to see that people understand you so well. We also appreciate the fact that you are a complete actress. And it is always comforting to watch someone like you fulfilling her destiny completely. A beautiful cherry tree will produce cherries; a good wheat-field will produce good bread. You, you produce good theatre. Thank you.
    You are so kind to send us the little clipping on *Boudu*. In return, we are sending you one about yourself.
    We would love to see Pia acting on stage. It is lucky that she is so passionate about the theatre. If you write to her, send her our love. What is also fortunate is that your personal life and the lives of those closest to you are under a peaceful sign.
    Our best to Lars.
    Lots of love,
    Jean Renoir

To Oskar and Annie Werner

Dear Oskar, dear Annie,

They say that cities are inhabited by human beings. What a mistake! Cities are inhabited by feelings, talent, spirit. Since you and Annie have moved on to new horizons, the Los Angeles sky covers only emptiness. It is like the lid of a pan in which the cook has forgotten to put the food he was going to prepare. Fortunately, Ditty will be back soon. She will dispense to Dido and I the warmth emanating from a group of which we are so happy to be a part.

It looks like we won't make this film now. I have not heard from Schaeffer. Even so, this project was a success since it brought us closer. We should not let distance separate us for too long. If I come to Europe, I'll manage to see you both, wherever you are.

I hope you have seen our dear Ginette Doynel, and that you got along with her. I am going to ask her to come here to help me put down on paper the screenplay of my French film. As far as our health is concerned, we are fine, and we hope it is the same for you. Let's hope these travels and long hours spent on aeroplanes have not been too taxing for you. My leg is not bothering me too much. No surgery, no more penicillin! I'm dreaming about the film (whatever it may be) that will bring us together again.

Dido and I send you both our love,

Jean Renoir

To Leslie Caron

Dear Leslie,

Thank you for the review of *Boudu*. Most of all, thank you for your wonderful friendship. I'm happy you had a chance to see *Les Bas-Fonds*. I'd love to make it as an American film. I would set it in a *slum*[1] in Los Angeles. Warren[2] would discreetly burgle houses in Bel Air. It would be a completely free adaptation, and nobody would recognize *Les Bas-Fonds*. But Gorky's work would still provide the backbone to the whole. It is always better to lean on a masterpiece, even if one strays away from it.

Love from Dido and I,

Jean Renoir

1 Originally in English.
2 Warren Beatty.

To Tony Curtis[1] [*Original in English*]

26 October 1965
Beverly Hills

Dear Tony,

Your letters are like a bit of yourself. As always with good things, they make us wish to have more. To tell you the truth we would like to have all of Tony, all of Christine,[2] and all of Alexandra.[3] We were terrified with your story of chickenpox and hope it is entirely over now. We are moved by the way you reacted in front of the landscapes and buildings of the south of France. In spite of the efforts of modern architects who go on trying to destroy this delightful country, and in spite of the tourists, motel keepers, asphalt layers, sign painters, etc, La Provence is still there. What makes us particularly happy is your reaction about the garden of my father. You are right. As [with] everything connected with Renoir, the impression one can gather from such a visit is one of peace. Soon we will talk about it – in French.

Dido and I are very pleased to know that your work is going on successfully. We think constantly of the three of you.

Jean Renoir

1 Tony Curtis (b.1925), actor whose credits include *Houdini* (George Marshall, 1953), *The Defiant Ones* (Stanley Kramer, 1958), and *Some Like It Hot* (Billy Wilder, 1959).
2 Christine Kaufman (b.1945), actress who was married to Tony Curtis from 1963–7. Her credits include *Taras Bulba* (J. Lee Thompson, 1962), *Lili Marleen* (Rainer Werner Fassbinder, 1980), and *Bagdad Café* (Percy Adlon, 1987).
3 Alexandra, the Curtises' daughter.

To Pierre Braunberger

Paris

29 November 1965
Beverly Hills

Dear Pierre,

Ginette has just finished typing the first draft of *C'est la Révolution.*[1] We are sending it to you as it is, in order to save time. I am going to spend three days with Alain in Berkeley, and my absence would delay any polishing of it till the end of the week or the beginning of next week.

Like all my screenplays, this one will undergo many changes after we have had a chance to talk about it, and after I have got to know the cast. It would be good if you could get a few more copies typed in Paris. Here it is impossible.

But read it first. I can't wait to hear your reaction.

I thought of an opening in the form of a song which we would use again, maybe three times during the picture, and which would reinforce its cohesiveness. This song would say that on earth there are big people and small people, and that sometimes small people get angry.

Below are a few suggestions for the cast. They are quite vague, and only meant to give you an idea of my conception of the characters. As you know, all this is flexible.

LA DUCHESSE: Magnani, Popesco.[2]

CREME DE BEAUTE:[3] Geneviève Page,[4] Piccoli,[5] and for the part of Mathilde, the best in the film, I suggest Gisèle.[6]

LA GRANDE CUISINE: Parédès,[7] Jouanneau.

LE ROI D'YVETOT: Michel Simon, Claude Rich.

LA CIREUSE ELECTRIQUE: Pierre Olaf, Marguerite Cassan, Albert Rémy.[8]

LA GUERRE: Oskar Werner, Jean Carmet.

How is Gisèle's pregnancy? I hope she doesn't suffer too much from morning sickness.

We give her our love, and you too.

Jean Renoir

1 *C'est la Révolution*, a project by Renoir which, in its condensed form, became *Le Petit Théâtre de Jean Renoir*.
2 Elvira Popesco, Romanian-born theatre actress whose film credits included *Ils Etaient Neuf Célibataires* (Sacha Guitry, 1939), and *Plein Soleil* (René Clement, 1960).
3 Possible translations: *The Duchess, Beauty Cream, Grand Cuisine, The King of Yvetot, The Electric Wax-Polisher*, and *War*.
4 Geneviève Page (b.1927), actress whose credits include *Fanfan la Tulipe* (Christian-Jaque, 1952), *El Cid* (Anthony Mann, 1961) and *Belle du Jour* (Luis Buñuel, 1967).
5 Michel Piccoli (b.1925), actor whose credits include *French Cancan* (1955), *Belle du Jour* (Luis Buñuel, 1967) and *Le Mépris* (Jean-Luc Godard, 1963).
6 Gisèle Braunberger, wife of Pierre.
7 Parédès, comic actor whose credits include *Fanfan la Tulipe* (Christian-Jaque, 1952), *French Cancan* (1955) and *What's New Pussycat?* (1965).
8 Albert Rémy, actor whose credits included *French Cancan* (1955) and *Eléna et les Hommes* (1956).

To Ingrid Bergman
Choisel

16 December 1965
Beverly Hills

Dear Ingrid,

Dido and I are thrilled to hear about your tremendous triumph. The interest the Royal Family is taking in your performance only proves they have good taste. Long live the Queen, and her husband![1] What can we say about the vacations you have arranged for the people who are working in your show and for yourself? That's what glory is all about; real glory. And we are happy that you have had this happy break. You deserved it.

I hope this letter will reach you in time to convey our best wishes for your reunion with the kids and Lars in Choisel. Kiss them for us and give them our best wishes. We are sorry we can't be in Paris to pay you a visit and attend these merry festivities. May the coming year be as auspicious.

We hope Pia will find an interesting part. I would really like to see her either on stage or on the big screen.

Lars must be very happy with the Montparnasse Theatre. It is a wonderful place, loaded with illustrious memories. *La Dame de Chez Maxim* is an excellent play, and considering the current rage for the 1900s it seems quite timely as well.

I sent a wire to Charles Boyer when his son died,[2] but I did not dare to visit him in person. Should anything like this happen to me, I know I'd rather be left alone, and this is why I did not show myself. This doesn't prevent me from sharing his grief sincerely. He is a very good man whom I love dearly, and it hurts me to know he's in pain.

Much love from Dido and I. Ginette Doynel who is staying with us sends her best wishes.

Jean Renoir

1 The Queen of England turned up unannounced at a performance of *A Month in the Country*. It was her 'night off'.
2 Michael Boyer, son of Charles Boyer, committed suicide in 1965.

To Oskar Werner [*Original in English*]   *19 December 1965*
Triesen   *Beverly Hills*
Liechtenstein

Dear Oskar,

I asked Braunberger to send you a copy of *La Guerre*, thinking that it would save time.

As soon as I had finished to write the script, my first idea was to mail it to you, but I had only two copies. I need one for corrections, the present form being only a first draft.

I decided to send the second one to Braunberger who enjoys the advantage of having an office with secretaries and for whom the question of typing is a mere detail. For me it is always a problem. I don't type myself, Dido is very busy and my assistant Ginette Doynel, after helping me with this first draft, must go back to Paris.

My English is too poor to attempt myself a translation of the story, but I thought that Annie could give you an idea of *La Guerre*, her French and her English being both so perfect.

Anyhow the details of the story have to be worked out and I hope I could do it with you.

The script is now divided into five stories (in the beginning of my work I had ten). *La Guerre* is the last one and, I hope, expresses clearly the significance of the film. According to Braunberger I can shoot this episode any time of the year which could be convenient to you. The general title of the film would be *C'est la Révolution*.

Dido and I think of you constantly. We hope your work will bring both of you in California very soon. We did not see Ditty yet: health troubles in her house, bad colds in ours, but we intend to get in touch with her after the holidays. We are very much attracted by this lovable woman.

I am expecting the galleys of my next book in January. After correcting them I will probably go to Paris to prepare *C'est la Révolution*.

Again we wish you and Annie a good, healthy, prosperous and creative New Year.

With our affection,
Jean Renoir

To Daniel Losset   20 December 1965
Paris   Beverly Hills

Dear Mr Losset,

I received your letter of 9 December, which was forwarded to me. I read it with great pleasure. Your confidence in me is most touching. I would like to reply by giving some advice which might be helpful to you in your pursuit of the career in the film industry which attracts you so much. I get the feeling that you are sincere, and that it is not the dazzling side of the industry that is attracting you. Unfortunately, this side is more often than not a mirage, and I know an incredibly large proportion of people working in the cinema who are terribly unhappy. Success is rare and, strangely enough, even among those who have succeeded, I often detect an undeniable bitterness. I have to say that this bitterness is more frequent among actors, and especially actresses. These comments are purely theoretical on my part. I am not too familiar with the current state of the industry. I will probably make more films, but I live outside the film world, and I am totally ignorant of what is going on. It is impossible for me to give you the key that will open the door to the profession of your dreams.

In answer to your question: Vaugirard or IDHEC?[1] My feeling is that IDHEC probably offers a wider range of studies. It may not be a 'hands-on' school, but it is probably the best of its kind in France. And it compares advantageously to some I know in foreign countries. As you know, quite a few of the good French directors now working have come out of IDHEC.

What more can I say? Maybe you should mingle with people in the industry. Human activity takes place in a kind of current, and in order to be part of it, one must find a way to dive in and be carried along. It doesn't mean that all the swimmers in these private waters will succeed, but at least they will learn the language of their profession.

But I'm chatting away, and not saying anything useful about a craft in which practical and technical knowledge play an important part. I apologize for having nothing better to tell you.

Yours sincerely,

Jean Renoir

1 Institut des Hautes Etudes Cinématographiques, the leading French film school, was founded in 1943. It is now called FEMIS.

1966

To Oskar Werner [*Original in English*] 7 *January 1966*
Beverly Hills

Dear Oskar,

Dido and I are jubilant at the news of the Film Critics Award given to you. It is certainly the most important award in our profession. We also think that the critics were right to honour Julie Christie. She was perfect in *Darling*.[1]

Concerning the possible dates for the shooting of *La Guerre*, the only thing I know is that Braunberger agrees with me about shooting it when convenient to you. Your idea to do it after *Andersonville* is probably the right one. I will write to Braunberger asking him to plan it that way.

I also still believe in *The Master Forger*.[2]

According to your address, Annie and you are in the country. We hope your work gives you a little time to enjoy it and that Annie takes advantage of the beautiful English countryside and doesn't regret too much her California.

What Dido and I regret is you and her, our conversations, our projects, an atmosphere of quality you don't often find in life.

With our love,
Jean Renoir

1 *Darling* (John Schlesinger, 1965).
2 One of the several projects that Werner and Renoir tried to realize.

To Oskar Werner [*Original in English*] 12 *February 1966*
Beverly Hills

Dear Oskar,

I will write to Braunberger telling him that September, October, would suit you for the shooting of my sketch *La Guerre*. According to what he told me, the fact that my picture will be divided into several bits helps him to be quite free with the schedule. I intend to go to Europe in early spring and to give to the project the last push that will make it a reality.

We didn't see Stanley Kramer. We didn't even see our dear Ditty. I was too ill to have any pleasure in meeting friends. Now I am much better and in a few weeks I will be as well as many months ago before my troubles started.

My old project *Aspects of Love* seems to wake up. I wish *The Master Forger* could give us as much hope. I dream to do something with you, not only because I am convinced that together we could do a good job, but for the mere pleasure of our collaboration. I miss your presence and the presence of Annie. Dido feels the same.

With our love to both of you,

Jean Renoir

To Ginette Doynel   *3 March 1966*
Paris   *Beverly Hills*

Dear Ginette,

We received your letter of 26 February. The strike must have slowed it down a little. We are sorry to know that you have hurt your left arm. May the beautiful season be beneficial to you and chase away this arthritis.

THE SOUTHERNER: I received a very affectionate letter from Pagnol, in which he states that my films and his are practically the only ones which have held up over the years. Perhaps Pagnol's distribution company could see a way to release *The Southerner* and re-release *La Marseillaise*. I throw out this idea, just in case. What do you think?

ASPECTS OF LOVE: Strictly between us, Columbia, after much hesitation, has decided not to make the film. United Artists are delaying their response. I expect a refusal from them. Chuck Sachs has had very advanced discussions with Hellman (*Le Caporal Epinglé*) in Munich. If he decides to back out of Europe, why not [use] Braunberger and his English contacts? But would the latter be able to handle both *C'est la Révolution* and *Aspects of Love*? As you know, I set more store by the first than the second.

TRIP: Dido and I think that it is time to set a date for our trip. The proofs of the American edition of *Les Cahiers du Capitaine Georges* will be ready at the end of April. I could stop off in Boston for the corrections, but I am afraid that if I arrive too late in Paris it will compromise the start of *C'est la Révolution*. Don't you think that the beginning of April would be a marvellous date for this trip? If you think that we could leave later without it being inconvenient, I will stop in Boston for the corrections; if

[472]

not, I will ask Little, Brown to send me the proofs in Paris.

C'EST LA RÉVOLUTION: I have received a letter from Braunberger enclosing a note from Aznavour, who declares that there is only one good role in *La Guerre*, the enemy corporal. He's right. Ideally, I would consider Aznavour for the lead role if Werner isn't able to play it.

This letter has been a pleasure for us to write because it makes us think of our reunion.

We send you all our love,
Jean and Dido

To Ingrid Bergman   *25 August 1966*
                                                     Beverly Hills

Dear Ingrid,

I am back with Dido and we want to tell you how often we think about you, and about our gatherings of long ago in your old house, the roof of which we can vaguely see through the trees. On the occasion of your birthday all our wishes go to Isabella.[1] We know you'll be happy if her health improves. I took your letter with me to show it to Dido upon my return to California. She was nearly in tears at the thought of what you must be going through and your anxiety while waiting for the second term of six months, at the end of which Isabella will be totally upright and able to live like a normal young lady. It was fortunate that Roberto was with you when you fainted. I tried to get in touch with him at the Hotel Raphael before I left Paris. I also tried to find out where he was through friends of mine in television. I wanted to tell him how much I sympathize with Isabella's trouble. But he was probably shooting outside Paris. I was told that his work for French television has been difficult, and that he could not get what he wanted. It is fortunate that Isabella's tragedy will end well. Speaking of drama, I am terribly happy to hear that you like my book.

Since my film projects are more than doubtful, I have started to write a new novel, which I find enthralling. I think I was destined to be a writer. I just discovered it a bit late.

Dido is fine. We miss you a lot. However, we still hope we'll make it to Europe and see you with Isabella, who will be running about on your lawn by then. Give our best to Lars, Pia, and the children. If you see him, our regards to Roberto. Our warmest wishes to Isabella.

Much love,
Jean Renoir

[473]

1 Isabella Rossellini had contracted scoliosis, which resulted in her spending eighteen months in a cast to correct her spine.

To Maurice-Jacques Keller
L'Ecran Lorrain
Nancy

6 September 1966
Beverly Hills

Dear Mr Keller,

It is only now that I am replying to your letter which I found waiting for me in Beverly Hills. I am deeply touched by your friendly expression of sympathy following my failure to get my French project going. The Centre's refusal to help me make the film I was planning doesn't surprise me.[1] It has been the same pattern for most of my films. I am not very skilful when it comes to submitting a project, and most of the time the initial reaction I get to these submissions is a denial. I don't see why the members of the Commission de l'Aide au Cinéma should react differently from the producers in all the various countries in which I submitted *La Grande Illusion* for nearly three years; that was despite Jean Gabin and Charles Spaak's support, which should have helped to convince them. The only help I can get is from people who trust me and who know that my screenplays, although precisely written, are merely a springboard, a point of departure. It is from the excitement generated by my work with the actors and technicians that I finally come to grips with the real direction my theme should take. I can't give any kind of shape to my pictures until I have explored the quality of the material with which I'm working. But I can't possibly hold it against people if they prefer dealing with directors who are less inclined to delayed discoveries than I am.

So I am staying here with my wife at my home in Beverly Hills, where I am starting work on a new book. Consequently, it won't be possible for me to join you and introduce a couple of my films to the members of the Lorraine Film Association.

You ask me what I think of the current situation of the French film industry. I have no definite thoughts on the subject. I can only vaguely guess what direction motion pictures are taking in general. I think that, in order to compete with television, films will have to be more and more lavish. In America, the films that are successful have cost millions of dollars. Consequently, caution prevails in their production, and they rely on precisely-written screenplays, something which I am unable to accomplish. Probably there will be a kind of 'alternative', non-professional film-making, which will maintain the sense of exploration and experiment without which cinema could not exist.

I am still saddened by Carette's passing.[2] Not only because I loved the man, but also because, as an actor, he had come to symbolize a certain aspect of the French spirit which is vanishing. I think that the actors who played the magnificent character of Pierrot in the eighteenth and nineteenth centuries were Carette's ancestors.

My wife and I are sorry to hear your health is bothering you. Please accept our wishes for your improvement, and give our respects to your family.

Kind regards,

Jean Renoir

---

1 *C'est la Révolution* was refused a subsidy – the *avance sur recettes* (advance on receipts) – by the Centre Nationale du Cinéma on the grounds of 'obscenity'. This provoked an outcry in the press, but to no avail.

2 Julien Carette (1897–1966), actor who appeared in several of Jean Renoir's films: *La Marseillaise, La Grande Illusion, La Bête Humaine*, and *La Règle du Jeu*. Carette died of severe burns in July 1966 after falling asleep while smoking.

To Claude Beylie[1]

22 *September 1966*
Beverly Hills

Dear Claude Beylie,

Your article has reached me in Beverly Hills and reading it gave me great pleasure. Even if I am switching from camera to pen, I still remain a man of the cinema. I was moulded by cinema, and I realize that if I had not been a film-maker, my novel would probably be very different. Consequently, the opinion of someone who is totally immersed in film knowledge is important to me. After all, it is quite possible that films may be not only a way to record images and sound, but also a state of mind. I think the new generations are largely shaped by the cinema, while those who preceded them were shaped by literature and theatre.

I hope to have the pleasure of meeting you next time I come to France. My respects to your wife.

Kind regards,

Jean Renoir

---

1 Claude Beylie, film critic and historian.

To Pierre Braunberger   *26 September 1966*
Les Films de la Pléiade, Paris   *Beverly Hills*

Dear Pierre,

I am delighted by your response to my novel. To tell you the truth, I have received quite a few favourable comments, and I was particularly moved by the letters I received from Truffaut, René Clair and Duvivier. I am presently getting ready to confront the New York press. Ten days of interviews with journalists, as well as radio and television. It will be exhausting, but probably very helpful. My publisher, Little, Brown from Boston, is planning to launch the book on a large scale. It will be out on 19 October.

I am not planning to make any films at the moment. My dealings over *C'est la Révolution* were too disappointing, and I have no intention of getting my fingers burnt again by the formidable machine which dominates our profession.

I hope we shall have the opportunity to see each other again soon. Dido and I send our love to Gisèle and the children.

Much love,
Jean Renoir

1967

To Raymond Burnier   *20 May 1967*
                                                Beverly Hills

Dear Raymond,

[. . .] We were planning to go to Europe at the beginning of the summer. The truth is, I have been suffering from some kind of chronic tiredness; making the smallest move becomes an ordeal, and the tiniest molehill turns into a mountain. I have nevertheless decided to write a small film project, which our dear Ginette will attempt to set up in Paris. If she succeeds I'll go to Europe. Dido will come with me. At least, she's hoping to, even if she has to leave me in Ginette's hands later on.

What you told us about Chaplin's film[1] is quite interesting and not surprising. An artist of his stature is impervious to decadence. He might make a few mistakes from a commercial standpoint, but the quality of his work can only improve as his knowledge of life expands. In Chaplin's case, his mistake was probably in not acting the part himself. We wanted to see the film, but could not find the time. We'll catch up with it soon, I hope.

We are living here in the midst of great turmoil. Even toned down, the news of all these demonstrations is forcing us to take an interest in what is going on in the world. Personally, I find these young men and their long hair rather compelling, and I can sympathize with the disgust the younger generation feel about the hypocrisy of those who preceded them. My son Alain, who lives in Berkeley, is right in the middle of this agitation. But since his preoccupations seldom go beyond the scope of medieval literature, he remains unperturbed by the tempest.

We will make sure we see you if we come to Europe. In the meantime, we send you our love. Our best regards to Alain.[2] He must have brought back some interesting stories from Moscow. His brother just gave a lecture here.

Jean Renoir

1 *A Countess from Hong Kong* (1967).
2 Alain Daniélou, friend of Burnier.

To Arthur Knight [*Original in English*] 27 May 1967
Los Angeles

Dear Arthur,

I will try to answer the questions Hollis Alpert and yourself decided to ask to several readers of your so interesting *History of Sex in Cinema*.

1 I don't believe that a production code can do anything for controlling the morals of our movies. As a matter of fact I don't see why 'sex' should be controlled. The only thing which should be forbidden on the screen is violence. I am not bothered by the sight of people loving each other on the screen or anywhere else. I am bothered by the sight of people killing each other.

2 I am against any classification. A good picture is good for new-born children as well as for crumbling old people.

3 I feel that the screen should be entirely free. The reason for my opinion is that I am concerned with morality. Let's take, for instance, the question of nudity. When the public will be used to the sight of nude bodies they will consider them as something absolutely normal and the general attitude will be very close to perfect chastity. Immorality during the precedent centuries was greatly helped by the mania of hiding the human body. I am convinced that this concealment of our persons was the invention of sex maniacs.

4 The area which is still closed to the film-maker is 'quality'. Of course there are good films but such exceptions are the result of some miracle. The truth is that the organization of the film business makes imperative the necessity to recuperate the invested capital as quickly as possible. The author of a film in order to comply with this 'must' is tempted to bow to the taste of the public. He has to follow the crowd instead of preceding it. In the field of the other arts, the [in]novator can afford the luxury to be unsuccessful in the immediate future and to have his revenge only after years of patience. The real artist is often ahead of his time.

5 I don't see great differences concerning this question of treating ideas and situations between the countries I know and the US.

Sincerely yours,
Jean Renoir

To Marshall Lewis [*Original in English*]   *15 August 1967*
Montreal International Film Festival
Montreal

Dear Marshall Lewis,

Several years ago I used to carry with me a little elephant – Ganesh – given to me by an Indian friend when I was shooting *The River*. Later on I gave it to a friend who had to undergo a dangerous operation. The place was vacant. Octave[1] will fill it. He will also remind me that I have a friend somewhere in the world and that I must meet him again.

Such exchanges give a certain value to life. Thank you for having initiated this one.

Mon souvenir ému à Bruno,
Jean Renoir

---

1 Renoir was given a stuffed bear called Octave, named after the character he plays in *La Règle du Jeu*, who during the party scene wears a bear costume.

To Ginette Doynel   *31 August 1967*
Paris   *Beverly Hills*

Dear Ginette,

[...]

JULIENNE ET SON AMOUR. I've thought hard about this matter, and I wonder if we were not wrong to reject the idea that Braunberger present the project to the people he alludes to in his letter, without however giving us their names. [...] It's undeniable that *Julienne* was the springboard for *Capitaine Georges*. But closely analysing the question, I come to the conclusion that *Capt G.* is a good novel (between us I can even confess that I'm very proud of it) but almost impossible to adapt as a film. I'm thinking about the age of the protagonists: Georges is twenty, Agnes eighteen. We could probably find good actors young enough for these roles. But these debutants would not give us any chance to finance what could be a very expensive film. Captain Georges would have to be treated in the same way as *Dr Zhivago*.[1] I maintain that the film should be made in French, and the French market is too small to command a comparable budget.

The second reason which would make it difficult to adapt *Capitaine Georges* for the screen is that it's a purely 'interior' story. It's the sincere confession of a man who discovers the world, women, the war, love, and

[479]

life in general. *Julienne* is a much more exterior story, and consequently easier [to film].

I must add that the final screenplay would certainly involve situations and expressions of feeling that are very different from those in *Capitaine Georges*.

I believe, as long as you don't have any fundamental objection, we ought to agree that the people Braunberger talks about should read my treatment. But I insist on one point, that this project doesn't damage the Jeanne Moreau project. I consider her as my associate in this venture, and as such, this has priority over all my other projects.

PROJECTS IN GENERAL: I have to tell you that since my return from Europe (July 1966) I have started many projects but hadn't had the courage to give a definitive shape to any of them. I blame my health for this. I am pretty much in the same state I was in when I left you. My head is better, my ideas are very clear, but the aches and the weakness in my legs make my movements difficult. It is possible that the stairs at avenue Frochot are the stumbling-block, and I confess that the idea of living alone doesn't appeal to me. Despite these difficulties, I have decided to ask you to work with me and help me formulate the ideas which have haunted me for several years. I would like to make a film (at least one more) before it is too late. I would also like to revise a pile of projects which you know about and which I can look at now with a keener eye. I think that I can do something really good with my Jeanne Moreau project.[2] I think I could also be successful with *Julienne et son Amour*. The problem will be to organize my material life. From a spiritual point of view, and with your help, I think I can take it on. It's in this state of mind that I am going to rejoin you in Paris. Dido might come with me. In any case, if my trip is prolonged, she will come to see me from time to time, and if necessary I will go to see her. She knows that I can work well with you, and because of this, accepts the idea of a momentary separation.

My intention would be to join you after the children's visit, that's to say the beginning of October. Tell me if this date suits you. Given that my projects have piled up over a long period, we won't be ready for a week or two.

Dido and I ask you to give our love to the children. At the same time, we send our love to you.

Jean Renoir

1 *Doctor Zhivago* (David Lean, 1965).
2 In addition to *Julienne et son Amour*, Renoir had written *En Avant, Rosalie!* for Jeanne Moreau.

1968

In January, Jean Renoir takes part in a 22-minute film called La Direction d'Acteur par Jean Renoir, *in which he directs Gisèle Braunberger
(wife of his producer friend Pierre) in a scene adapted from a Rumer
Godden story,* Breakfast with the Nikolaides.

*On 9 February, André Malraux, then Minister of Culture, fires Henri
Langlois from his position as artistic director of the Cinémathèque
Française. This provokes a scandal, and many French film directors join
forces to boycott the new administration. Jean Renoir is appointed
Honorary President of the Committee for the Defence of the Cinémathèque Française. On 16 February, he takes part in a press conference at
which he pleads for the reinstatement of Langlois. The government does
allow Langlois to return to his office in April, but withdraws his subsidy.*

With the outbreak of the évenements de mai, *the Cinémathèque is
closed down, as is the film industry, while students riot in the streets. Jean
Renoir's immediate hopes of setting up a film with Jeanne Moreau are
postponed once again.*

To Ginette Doynel   *9 May 1968*
Paris   *Beverly Hills*

Dear Ginette,
   Your letters of 6 and 7 May have taken two days to reach us. Before
responding I have to tell you some sad news; Albert Lewin died this
morning in hospital. Angna had called us. She is distraught. We believe
that Al succumbed to pneumonia.
   [...]
   VENICE BIENNALE: I am very flattered by Prof Chiarini's offer, but I
wonder if a trip to Venice at the time of the Festival doesn't risk
compromising our film projects. Give me your feelings on this matter.
   [...]
   CINÉMATHÈQUE: What you have told me about the Cinémathèque is
hardly encouraging. On the other hand, I don't want to disappoint those
friends who have always been true to me. I would like to know what

Truffaut thinks about this matter. The article in *L'Aurore* is worrying. In any case, I will wait until you have taken a closer look at the matter before making a decision.

[...]

JULIENNE: Tony Curtis is in the Bahamas. I let him know through his secretary that he shouldn't have misplaced the English screenplay of *Julienne* and that he should get it back to me in a week.

Omar Shariff's [sic] lack of interest in the role of Henri and Mastroianni's silence are disturbing.

[...] I am beginning to fear that *Julienne* will be impossible to set up. To return to the question of actors, several people here have suggested Louis Jourdan for Henri.

[...]

We'll close by hoping you will avoid the tumult that surely won't spare avenue Kléber. All the same, the Majestic is further away than the Palais Rose. Dido joins me in sending you all our love,

Jean

To Ginette Doynel   *15 May 1968*
Paris

Dear Ginette,

We received you letter of 9 May. The news you give us is relegated to the second row. We are worried above all about how you got through the events of the past few days. We are somewhat reassured by the fact that you're not too near the thick of the fighting. According to the newspapers here, the encounters between the students and the police take place mostly on the Left Bank. Our greatest regret is not to be with you and not to hear what you have to say.

[...]

CINÉMATHÈQUE. I'm a bit embarrassed about not having replied to Langlois'[1] letter. It gives the impression that I'm in hiding. Could you not give him to understand that I'm waiting until I've talked to him in person before taking the decision, and that I shall be back in Paris soon? This will allow me to look at the question with you from every angle. Alain still has a mind to get Langlois invited to Berkeley. Perhaps you might be able to discuss this with him. Alain has two questions about him: how old is he, and does he speak English?

We end this letter with all our affection, hoping that you've come through these troubled days without too much inconvenience for you and yours.

Best regards to Nicole, Madou, Marie Louise and Ghislaine.

Jean Renoir

1 Henri Langlois (1914–77), co-founder of the Cinémathèque Française, was responsible for nurturing the New Wave and had supported Renoir through repeated screening of his films. Following his dismissal and reinstatement at the beginning of 1968, Langlois had written to Renoir asking him to be Honorary President of the Cinémathèque.

To Ginette Doynel
Paris

16 May 1968
Beverly Hills

Dear Ginette,

Dido and I spoke to Mike Zimring[1] who's back from New York. He's agreed completely to abandon the representation of *Aspects of Love* and to leave it to Lebovici[2] as far as I'm concerned. It's up to you to judge whether this development will help things along. Nonetheless, I would remind you that it's *Julienne* with Jeanne Moreau which interests me above all else, and that *Aspects* should in no respect harm *Julienne*. All the more so as I'm not sure whether I'll be up to it physically for two films. If you think this is right, I'll leave it up to you to inform those concerned of this decision. I'm letting neither Chuck nor Lebovici know.

These considerations about a film which is still very vague are of little consequence compared to our worries about you. Dido has just opened the papers and tells me that the students have taken the Odéon. If this carries on, you'll have to come and take refuge in California.

Most affectionately,

Jean Renoir

1 Mike Zimring, agent at William Morris.
2 Gérard Lebovici, French agent, producer and publisher.

To Ginette Doynel
Paris

18 May 1968
Beverly Hills

Dear Ginette,

Dido and I are very worried about you. The American papers speak of numerous strikes and the complete shutdown of some services, including Orly airport. We know that newspapers tend to exaggerate and that seen from afar, the situation sometimes seems more unbearable than it is. Despite this, we would like to know that you're out of these troubles. All our wishes to you and your relations. Let the revolution pass you by without touching you.

We received your letter of 14 May. In principle, I'll follow your advice and will leave on 6 June or thereabouts, unless the situation is so troubled in Paris that my presence will only add to your worries and the disruption of business makes our activities too difficult. [. . .]

We send our love, all the more so as we think of your difficulties and worries, but in haste so that we can post this letter.

Jean Renoir

To Ginette Doynel
Paris

20 May 1968
Beverly Hills

Dear Ginette,

The newspapers reassure us somewhat as to your fate. There is no doubt a great upheaval in France, and perhaps elsewhere, but it seems that as far as Paris is concerned the period of violence must give way to a period of strikes, stoppages of services and difficulties in getting supplies; in other words, a lot of unbearable inconvenience but less dramatic than fighting in the streets.

It is more than probable that the Centre's decisions and perhaps even Guino's court-case[1] will be postponed, so I'll wait to hear from you before deciding the date of my departure. André Marion has booked me flights just in case, on Air France on 5 June and on Pan American on 6 June (this latter stops over at London). What makes me hesitate in coming to join you is that I find walking difficult. Travelling itself is not a big problem, as I only have to take a few steps from my seat to the toilet. But it's the lack of transport facilities in Paris that worries me. All the more so as I'll be asked to participate in meetings, rallies and other activities which involve walking or standing for long periods.

On this subject, I don't think I can decently postpone any longer accepting Langlois' offer to appoint me Honorary President of the Cinémathèque. I intend to take your advice and to talk directly to my friends in Paris after my arrival. But my arrival will probably be put back, and it doesn't seem to me very natural to delay my reply any longer. Would you therefore try and contact Langlois and tell him that I agree and that I'm honoured by this distinction?

So I shall wait to hear from you before moving and confirming the date of my departure to Marion. I don't know whether this letter will get to you. We're sending a copy to avenue Frochot.

Dear Ginette, we never stop thinking of you, and we ask you, if business stagnates, to think about turning our plans around and coming to see us here. It would perhaps be best after my visit to France.

All our love,

Jean Renoir

---

1 Richard Guino was a sculptor who collaborated with Pierre-Auguste Renoir in his last years, leading to a protracted legal dispute over who was responsible for 'their' work.

To Ginette Doynel
Paris

14 June 1968
Beverly Hills

Dear Ginette,

What a joy! We have just received a pretty religious image from our god-daughter Anne and your telegram about the Guino court case. These two messages prove that you are well, that you are busy and that nothing unfortunate has happened to your family or to our mutual friends. Please thank Anne for her message, which is all the more precious as it breaks a long silence. It also makes us hope that this involuntary silence is nearly over and that the French post is working again. We are delighted with the good news in the despatch and are crossing our fingers so that the second session might confirm your hopes.

I feel that my presence in Paris could only be useful when life has nearly got back to normal. I share your fear of me being obliged to take part in demonstrations and to sign petitions on issues about which I know little. The only clear position that I believe I should take is accepting the Honorary Presidency of the Cinémathèque, and this precisely because they've got problems. I shall write a note to Langlois.

I will not mention business affairs, as I shall only be able to get an idea when I receive your first letter, which I hope will be soon. We had a letter from the American colonel and the day before yesterday had the letter of 17 May. The first gives us an idea of the state of Paris at the moment, but leaves us a bit in the dark as to how you are personally. Thank you for the cutting from *Le Figaro*, 20 May 1968. We enclose with this letter a cutting from the *Los Angeles Times*, a conservative paper, which gives a different point of view which might be of interest to you.

Today's paper informs us that the French government has adopted a measure permitting the expulsion from France of foreigners involved in subversive movements.

[. . .]

I shall send Alain the information about LANGLOIS and if you have the time, perhaps you could speak to the British Film Institute about the 16 mm copy of *Le Carrosse d'Or*.

What bothers me most when thinking about my different projects is that I cannot walk better now than when I left you. Walking is an ordeal and the slightest physical effort gives me insurmountable fatigue. I wonder whether I am physically capable of shooting a film.

Dido and I now watch out for the postman, our hearts beating. Your first letter can't be delayed much longer. Anne's little image only took three days. Dido and I often think that if the Compagnie J.R. and your family gave you enough of a break, you might perhaps come here and take some California sun.

With all our affection.

Jean Renoir

PS. The card-holder put aside by my old Alpine Chasseur friend arrived safely.

To Henri Langlois
Cinémathèque Française, Paris

15 June 1968
Beverly Hills

Dear Henri Langlois,

I had hoped to reply in person to your letter of 27 April. The breakdown of communications prevented me from doing so. The aircraft are now flying again, but I'm waiting for news from Ginette and about my projects before abandoning a book I'm trying to write here. I am very honoured to have been chosen as Honorary President of the Cinémathèque. I hope that we will soon be able to celebrate this inauguration together with a good lunch in Paris with our dear Mary,[1] to whom I send all my kindest wishes for every success and to you also.

Jean Renoir

1 Mary Meerson.

To Ginette Doynel   *16 June 1968*
Paris   *Beverly Hills*

Dear Ginette,

JULIENNE: We received your telegram yesterday announcing that the Centre is giving us an advance of 500,000 francs for *Julienne*. Thank you for having telegraphed this good news straight away.

We are looking forward to your comments on this agreeable result. You have already told us that this advance will greatly help Lebovici to find a producer or an organization which could put up the amount outstanding for this production.

Obviously, there are also other interests. Could you in your next letter give us your feeling about the possibilities of producing *Julienne*? One piece of information I would like to have is the amount of the estimate as you reckon it now.

This aid will probably make my presence in Paris more urgent, though I'm putting off my return as long as I can because of the political situation. If I'm in Paris it will be impossible for me to shy away from demonstrations for the new cinema. All the more so because when I see the names of the producers who represent 'the Establishment', I find those who made my career so difficult. I have not been helped by 'the Industry', whereas I have always received great moral support from the younger generation. Now, from what I read in the papers, the country will increasingly be cut in two. On one side the reactionaries, on the other the revolutionaries. And in a public profession such as the cinema, one has to take sides. It makes me wonder whether I should set about making *Julienne*.

Given that I have all the necessary means to make this film, could you try and tell me when you'll see me? The Air France flights are still a bit irregular, and there is a better chance of sticking to schedules on Pan American, via London.

VENICE: As you will see from reading the copies of the letters enclosed, I have agreed in principle to go to Venice. Mr Chiarini gives the date of 7 September for the Prize-giving. Even given that everything goes well for *Julienne*, I doubt that we will have started shooting by that date. Could you therefore envisage the possibility of making this trip, you and I, and let me know whether this suits you and fits in with your other commitments?

LETTERS: We only received ONE letter from you (posted by an American officer) during the period when the post was interrupted.

[487]

Dido and I have a thousand things to say to you. There are heaps of questions pending, like Agel, about which decisions will have to be made, but I cannot overburden you with these preoccupations. You have enough problems with *Julienne* and Venice as it is. Perhaps we will have news from you tomorrow.

All our love,
Jean Renoir

To Henri Langlois
Paris

29 June 1968
Beverly Hills

Dear Henri,

Thank you for your letter of 21 June. I contacted Fritz Lang, who had also had a communication from you. When I went to see him I took with me Philip Chamberlin[1] of the Los Angeles County Museum, who reckons he can organize performances which will be useful for the Cinémathèque. We are waiting for Truffaut in order to sort out the different aspects of this proposal. In the meanwhile, don't be surprised if you receive a communication from Philip Chamberlin directly.

Don't forget to remember me to Mary.

Kind regards,
Jean Renoir

1 Philip Chamberlin was the film curator at the Los Angeles County Museum of Art.

To Robert R. Gitt[1] [*Original in English*]
Dartmouth College
Hanover, New Hampshire

18 July 1968

Dear Mr Gitt,

I am sorry not to be able to join you for the presentation of a series of my films at Dartmouth this summer. Temporarily, I hope, my health is not too good and I would like to keep my strength for a trip to Europe which may be unavoidable.

I am extremely flattered to have so many of my films shown at your festival.

I remind you the name and address of my business manager in Paris who may help you: Mme G. Doynel, 7 avenue Frochot, Paris 9.

As for *La Chienne*, I am afraid the difficulty comes from the family of the late author of the novel. They don't agree with my interpretation of this work.

I didn't direct *La Tosca*. I just wrote the script and directed one or two scenes. The job was done by my old partner Carl Koch.

I can only wish you all possible luck in your enterprise.

Sincerely yours,

Jean Renoir

PS. This postscriptum, if it doesn't arrive too late, could perhaps serve as the short introduction you requested:

I would like to attract the attention of the students on the vanity of planning. When we study the history of science we are impressed by the fact that the great discoveries were made by chance, Newton and the apple are a good example. In art it is the same thing. The artist as well as the scientist carries all the elements of his invention inside himself without knowing it. When I produced *La Grande Illusion* my purpose was just to make a successful escape picture. It is only while I was shooting that I discovered the real meaning of my subject: a confrontation among men of different casts. As a matter of fact I am wondering whether during my long career it is not the same story I constantly told. This story may be presented with different people and different backgrounds but it always expresses my constant preoccupation which is *how can men meet each other*. I don't believe that I am able to give the recipe to erase the differences among human beings but at least I tried to show how superficial and dangerous they are.

1 Robert Gitt, subsequently renowned for his work in film preservation at the UCLA Film and Television Archive.

To Ginette Doynel   *19 August 1968*
Paris   *Beverly Hills*

Dear Ginette,

Here is the copy of a snippet from this morning's *Los Angeles Times*:

A SMALL BOMB EXPLODED IN ONE OF THE GATES OF THE CINEMA PALACE WHERE THE VENICE FILM FESTIVAL IS SCHEDULED TO OPEN SATURDAY. THE BOMB APPEARED TO BE THE FIRST MANIFESTATION OF THE ANGER DIRECTED TOWARD THE FESTIVAL BY THE COMMUNISTS AND OTHER LEFTIST GROUPS WHO CONSIDER IT

This news makes me look at our trip to Venice in a different light. My name is associated with left-wing movements. If my presence at the festival can be interpreted as approval for right-wing movements, I'm in danger of appearing as a renegade. I expected 'round table' discussions with representatives of revolutionary movements and I accept this, but on no account do I want to enter into a phalanx of defenders of commercial cinema.

The situation seems incomprehensible to me. On the one side the producers and distributors are withdrawing their films because the Festival is too left-wing, on the other the Socialists and the Communists accuse said Festival of being capitalist.

An ideal came to Dido and me: whether rightly or wrongly, I accepted the Honorary Presidency of the Cinémathèque. Under pain of being taken for a weathervane, I believe the best decision for me is to follow the Cinémathèque's policy at least in so far as it concerns the question of my presence in Venice. If later the Honorary Presidency of the Cinémathèque seems likely to draw me towards a position that I don't approve of, there will be time enough for us to go our separate ways.

According to Fritz Lang, Lotte Eisner[2] will be in Venice where she'll be taking my films. You would do me a great service by asking Langlois' advice on this question and by cabling me as soon as you can. It's in Langlois' interest to keep the Honorary President of his association above the mêlée. Furthermore, he copes better in this kind of situation than you and I, and he has information that we don't. Don't worry about writing an over-long telegram, as I'd like your advice on this. Your telegram should get here in time for me to get in touch with Alitalia if need be. I will write by letter the content of this message, as the question is difficult to express in a telegraphic style.

Dido and I send our fondest greetings.

Jean Renoir

PS. Could you let me know whether the Hitchcock retrospective is still on the programme and whether he's going to Venice?

PPS. The advantage in consulting Langlois is that the decision will be the Cinémathèque's and not mine.

1 Originally in English.
2 Lotte Eisner (1896–1983), distinguished film historian who wrote *The Haunted Screen*, and books on Fritz Lang and F. W. Murnau. She was head archivist at the Cinémathèque Française from 1945–75.

To Dido Renoir   *5 October 1968*
Beverly Hills   *Paris*

Dear Dido,

I am going to make the corrections to the Macchi project[1] myself, so I have written the first draft. The visit to the house used in *La Partie de Campagne* was very sad. House falling down, nettles invading the orchard, a lamentable state of affairs! It was so beautiful in Marie Verrier's[2] time.

With all my love,

Jean

1 Giulio Macchi, former assistant, who was then working in Italian television.
2 Anne-Marie Verrier, friend of Jean Renoir, whose husband was a forest ranger. Their house was situated by the bridge at Sorques on the River Loing. It is still standing.

To Dido Renoir   *22 December 1968*
Beverly Hills   *Paris*

Dear Dido,

How sad to start next year far away from you. In three days it's Christmas and we won't be together. I ask myself if it is too high a price to pay for the chance to make one or two films.

How fortunate that nothing may stop the march of time and that one of these days, here or in the next world, perhaps we will be reunited. 'Perhaps' seems false to me – I should say 'certainly'.

Merry Christmas to everyone at home, not forgetting Minou.

With all my love,

Jean

1969

To Georges Simenon   *12 May 1969*
Epalinges, Switzerland   *Paris*

Dear Georges,

Il y a encore des Noisetiers[1] had not yet arrived in Los Angeles when I left
town, so as soon as I arrived in Paris I bought myself a copy and have just
finished reading it. I was overwhelmed by it. I'm exactly the same age as
your hero and I find in your book the expression of many of the doubts
that crowd in on me. What is amazing is the precision with which you
have built a character much older than you are.

Your book will remain with me for a long while. It's stamped on my
mind. I would like to make it into a film in which I would play myself. It
seems to me that I would only have to appear, get up, sit down, look out
of the window and drink my glass of port to play your banker just as you
conceived him.

Dido accompanied me to Paris. She will be returning to Los Angeles in
a few days to deal with the practical problems that are submerging us and
which I shrug off. She sends her love.

Ginette Doynel was very touched by your greetings and sends you hers.

I hope that your little health problems are not persistent and that they
already belong to the past.

With all my affection,

As ever,

Jean Renoir

1 Simenon novel published in 1969, as yet not translated in English.

From June to September, Jean Renoir shoots Le Petit Théâtre de Jean
Renoir, *with production financing from Italian (RAI) and French
(ORTF) television.*

30 Jean Renoir films the 'Christmas' episode – *Le Dernier Réveillon* – of *Le Petit Théâtre de Jean Renoir*

To Alexander Sesonske[1] [*Original in English*]   *2 August 1969*
Department of Philosophy   *Paris*
University of California
Santa Barbara, California

Dear Alex,

Dido wrote to me about the projection of your film. She certainly enjoyed it very much.

About my plans concerning *Julienne et son Amour* I have nothing definite. I don't know if Dido told you that I have some troubles with an old war-would. It makes me walk with more difficulty than ever and it may be unwise to take the responsibility of a full length film. I advise you not to count too much on my realization of *Julienne*.

I have asked the producers of my present film *Le Petit Théâtre de Jean Renoir* if they could allow you and your partner to film me while I will be shooting the third episode of this production: *Le Dernier Réveillon*.[2] This shooting will start on the first of September and should last a little more than one week. It seems that they already have in mind a similar work by a crew belonging to the French TV. That would kill any other possibility. If not there may be a possibility for you to follow this shooting. I will let you know. Please tell me if you are interested or not.

I have no objection to have your film shown at the New York Film Festival.

Concerning the printing of the text of this interview, could you be so kind as to give a ring to Mike Zimring at William Morris in Beverly Hills.

The first sketch of my TV film is almost edited. I believe it is OK.

Please convey my kindest regards to your wife.

Sincerely yours,

Jean Renoir

---

1 Alexander Sesonske, professor of Film Studies and Philosophy, and author of *Jean Renoir, The French Films 1924–1939* (1980) and editor of *Lettres d'Amérique* (1984). He shot footage for a documentary on Renoir, to include scenes of the making of *Le Petit Théâtre*, but it was never finished.
2 This became the first episode in the finished film.

To Ginette Doynel
Paris

Dear Ginette,

I have started to take care of my health. Lee Siegel suggested I have a complete check-up at the Sansun clinic in Santa Barbara. He himself has diagnosed severe anaemia.

The time draws near when I will receive the 16mm copy in colour of *Le Petit Théâtre*. It would perhaps be a good idea for you to ensure that this copy is not a low-quality dupe print but is taken from a reduced negative. I'll try to project provisional English subtitles, using a small machine that exists to do this job. The copy must be good, as my screenings can affect the reputation of the film in the United States. There should be a list of the dialogues in the film (or a screenplay modified after shooting). Send them to me so that I can work on the subtitles before the film arrives.

[. . .]

Have you had any feedback after the screening of the film?

Love from Dido and me.

[Jean Renoir]

To Jean Renoir
Beverly Hills

13 November 1969
Toledo, Spain

Dear Sir,

I received news of you through Jeanne, and Ginette Doinel [sic] gave me your address. I'm sorry I didn't get a chance to say goodbye to you before you left, but I was caught between my weekly visits to Spain and the preparation (which proved more demanding than I thought it would be) for the television broadcast *L'Invité du Dimanche*.[1]

I would like to thank you for having participated in it, and with so much patience and goodwill. All in all, the show went pretty well: Jeanne performed a song by Charles Trenet, Rossellini appeared 'live' to talk about didactic cinema[2] and his film on Socrates; we also had Henri Langlois and Jacques Robert (both of whom you know well), a selection of film clips, and to end the programme, a montage of photographs, which I narrated, evoking memories of three people whom you knew and loved a great deal: André Bazin, Jacques Becker and Françoise Dorléac.[3]

Cahiers du Cinema is having a difficult time at the moment, the result of a conflict that is almost entirely 'ideological' and which pitted the management against the editorial staff. They may be able to work things out by means of a separation (the way the problems at the Cinémathèque were dealt with) if they can get several publishers (Le Seuil in France, Grove Press in New York) and certain wealthy individuals, such as Jean Riboud etc, to buy 'shares' in Editions de l'Etoile and so forth . . .

Rivette is running around night and day trying to find a solution to these problems, and so is Jacques Doniol – he is even going to New York. You'll be able to read about the outcome of all this in *Cahiers* – that is, if future issues even get published.

Here in Toledo, I have found the peace and quiet I need in order to write the sequel[4] to *Baisers Volés*, which will portray Antoine Doinel as a young husband and father. The title they plan to use for the American version is *Bed and Board* – of course, I have no idea whether that's any good or not . . . I absolutely must start shooting this film by the beginning of the year; then I really need to put the brakes on for a while, so I can take a rest, and try once again to learn English.

[. . .]

I tried to write a song for Jeanne but it wasn't very successful; it's about a couple who call each other *vous*, then *tu*, and then go back to *vous* again, in order to preserve an element of gentility in their relations. I think my nature is too prosaic to allow me to write poetry . . . I'm going to keep working on the thing, even through I'm afraid the word 'work' doesn't really have much to do with the word 'song'.

I have never been able – or have never known how – to tell you how much *La Règle du Jeu* (which I saw over and over again between the ages of thirteen and fourteen, when everything in my life was going so badly) helped me to keep going, to understand the motives of the people around me, and to get through those awful years of my adolescence, up until the precise moment when I met Bazin and he saved me for good . . . I will always feel that <u>my life is connected to the film you made</u>. All this is rather awkwardly explained in this letter, but it would be even more awkward to try to express it verbally. Anyway, the main thing I'm trying to confide to you is to what extent it became necessary for me to feel that I was a part of your family, in the truest sense of that word. I have a feeling that I have said either too much or too little here, but I know you understand everything.

I hope you have a pleasant winter, there in the land of 'Champale', which is apparently what they call Californian champagne (fortunately, this is also the country that gave us D. W. Griffith).[5] I'll be back in Paris around 20 November, and I'll call Ginette Doinel to ask her to let me know when the next screenings of *Le Petit Théâtre* are.

My best wishes to Madame Renoir, who might well have me confused with Jacques Rivette, because when *French Cancan* and *Eléna* came out, everyone called us the 'inseparable Truffette and Rivaut' . . . For both of you, warm and sincere regards from

François Truffaut

1 *Sunday Guest*, a regular Sunday-afternoon television show in which a celebrity would be fêted with visits by friends in the studio as well as special performances.
2 Rossellini had turned away from the cinema in the 1960s to make television films about important historical figures.
3 Françoise Dorléac, who starred in Truffaut's *La Peau Douce* (1964), was the sister of Catherine Deneuve. She was killed in an automobile accident in 1967 at the age of twenty-five.
4 *Domicile Conjugal* (1970).
5 D. W. Griffith (1875–1948), the most influential of film directors whose *Birth of a Nation* (1915) was the first important feature-length film. His other films included *Intolerance* (1916) and *Way Down East* (1920)

To François Truffaut

Paris

22 November 1969

Beverly Hills

Dear François Truffaut,

Thank you for your good letter. Like Janus it has two faces. One side expresses the sweetness of friendly relations, the other the hideousness of destruction. Because the *Cahiers* matter is a real demolition job. If from time to time there is a film that means something, we owe this to a great extent to *Cahiers*. It seems to me that *Cahiers* should come through this ordeal in one piece. It couldn't be otherwise. We need them: they're the cinema's conscience.

I hope you'll find in Toledo the calm you need to produce your screenplay. I don't know if *Bed and Board* is a good title. I don't speak English well enough to judge. I like it, and if I saw it posted up outside a cinema I'd go in without hesitation.

I'm thinking of the two songs Jeanne asked me for. Up until now my mind's been occupied by my check-up. It was done at the Scripps Clinic at La Jolla about 200 kilometres from here. They examined me all over and declared that I needed rest. I'm going to rest in the hope that I'll be able to walk normally again.

I do not agree with you about your talents as a song-writer. Perhaps it's the rhymes that bother you. If that's the case, why don't you write in prose?

Please send Dido's and my best regards to Jeanne Moreau. She's won over my whole household. When you see Rivette, tell him that I haven't forgotten his film.

With my affectionate wishes,
Jean Renoir

To Giulio Macchi

Dear Giulio,

I hope that you've got through the difficulties that must have followed your mother's death. It's the fate we have to accept with the flight of time. I'm surrounded by corpses, and when you get to my age it'll be your turn. We imagine that the world in which we live is unchanging. The truth is that with each second we're another second older. I wonder whether Adam and Eve once used to be eternal. If that were the case, the Eternal opened a door for them into a passionate world by subjecting them to the law of time.

I spent a few days in hospital for a check-up. It would appear that I'm in good health, just a little tired.

Dido and I send Adèle[1] our love and to you, too,
Jean Renoir

---

1 Adèle, wife of Giulio Macchi.

To Robert Knittel
Collins Publishers, London

11 December 1969
Beverly Hills

Dear Bob,

I've been in California for a bit over a month. After finishing my film *Le Petit Théâtre de Jean Renoir*, I felt very tired. Dido took me for a check-up at the Scripps Clinic in La Jolla. It seems that I'm in perfect condition. That makes me want to work, and I'm gently beginning to collect my memories together. I don't use the word *memoirs*, because it seems to me to suggest a complete list of events that I've lived through and which I witnessed. There are some I don't want to mention. It seems to me that the title *Souvenirs d'un Faiseur de Films* (Recollections of a Film Maker[1]) would suit these reminiscences. In other words, I would make a choice and would not proceed chronologically.

Dido and I take the opportunity of this letter to send to Luise and to you our wishes for a Merry Christmas. We have not forgotten Francesca. We hope that the coming year will mark the end of Luise's physical problems.

With our love to you all,
Jean Renoir

1 Renoir's own English translation.

To Ginette Doynel
Paris

17 December 1969
Beverly Hills

Dear Ginette,

First of all, Dido and I wish you a pleasant Christmas and a Happy New Year. [. . .]

We read in the paper that it's cold in Paris. We hope that the cold won't spoil your celebration of the holiday with your family.

JULIENNE. I received both screenplays, one in English, the other in French. Helen Strauss is making a few Xerox copies of the English version.

LE PETIT THEATRE. Do you think it would be possible to reassemble the editing trims for Sesonske to use to illustrate the book he has written about me? I am afraid it will be complicated, unless the trims were provisionally stored after the negative was cut. He is coming to see me today and we will work on the temporary sub-titles.

I note Pierre Long's[1] agreement to show the film to journalists and distributors. It would be best to keep in contact with the latter group until Pierre Long judges that the time has come to talk '*business*'.[2] What I'm counting on here are one or two screenings for people who are interested in my work, and this in the hope of provoking a receptive climate for the film. When Pierre Long goes into action, the screenings must be organized by professionals. It would be best if there already was a sort of understanding before the screenings begin for the toughest customers. Besides, the kind of subtitles which I am currently making require special screening facilities. The only ones I know of are at the Museum. Pierre Long certainly knows that the sale of a film in the United States is no small task. Personally, I am completely incapable of taking charge of it. Forgive me for repeating it, but the only thing I can do is to stir up favourable word of mouth in the little world of Hollywood. It is even possible that the distribution of *Le Petit Théatre* will be decided in New York. But that's no reason not to profit from my presence here to encourage this word of mouth.

[. . .]

JEANNE MOREAU. I'm working on another version of *La Clocharde*.³

[. . .]

I hope that Ghislaine and you are not freezing too much in the avenue Frochot apartment. Have you lit the oil stove? Is the gas heater working? Here the cold (relative) has just arrived.

Dido and I send you our love,

Jean Renoir

1 Producer of *Le Petit Théâtre de Jean Renoir*.
2 Originally in English.
3 *La Clocharde* was a project in which Jeanne Moreau was to play a female 'Boudu'.

1970

To Ginette Doynel   *9 March 1970*
Paris   *Beverly Hills*

Dear Ginette,
   [. . .]
   HEALTH: I am perhaps doing better, but am far from regaining my
agility. Dr Wolf, as well as the other doctors I have consulted, didn't see
that it is a mild case of Parkinson's Disease. Finally it was Lee Siegel who
noticed that my legs were shaking. More than likely my case, if not
curable, can at least be stabilized. At the moment I am very satisfied with
the results, but I must not expect a spectacular recovery. All that I ask is
to be less sleepy and to walk better. That will come. You know what it's
like; you have pretty much recovered from a similar illness by courag-
eously dealing with it.[1] Anyway, I don't want to throw myself in the
direction of a film if I'm not feeling better. I refused a film for TV based
on my book about my father, as well as a film for the big screen based on
a good story about a truck driver which Mike Zimring brought to me.
What bothers me the most is the thought that this state of things is
disastrous for the film with Jeanne Moreau.
   [. . .]
   Dido and I send you all our love,
   Jean Renoir

1 Ginette Doynel had overcome polio through her self-determination.

To Guy Cavagnac[1]   *20 April 1970*
Paris   *Beverly Hills*

Dear Cavagnac,
   Your letter has assumed an important place in my life and in my wife's,
too. We have re-read it several times, and without asking ourselves
whether your praises were justified or not. I don't think that many
film-makers (or picture-makers or novel-makers) have enjoyed such a
reward for their efforts. I recently explained to some young, aspiring

[501]

American film-makers that you can't make a film without encouraging yourself with the thought that you're reaching out to the public. But you also have to impregnate yourself with the idea that this public might be made up of millions of viewers or of just one viewer. What's important is to speak to someone who's listening.

I don't know if my *Petit Théâtre* will be successful. Perhaps it will be badly received by the critics and certain audiences. This no longer has any importance for me. Your letter gives me the certainty that there is a bridge between you and me and that by shooting *Le Petit Théâtre* I didn't waste my time, because my language touched you. Your letter is all the more important for me as it reminds me of a thought dear to my father. It was that a painter doesn't work for the crowd, but for other painters. If the crowd follows, so much the better. If it sulks, too bad. Thank you for saying to me what you said.

My wife and I sincerely hope you have overcome the difficulties you mention in your letter. We hope that the work you talk of will bring you great satisfaction. Let's hope that little Céline will stop causing problems.

We send you and your wife our sincerest wishes.

Jean Renoir

1 Former assistant to Jean Renoir on various unrealized projects.

To Ginette Doynel
Paris

22 April 1970
Beverly Hills

Dear Ginette,

HEALTH: Lee Siegel has succeeded in having me treated by another doctor (Randall Parker) who can get for me the drug which Dr Wolf spoke about (Dopamine, here El Dopa [sic][1]). Unfortunately, I must remain at the disposal of this specialist for observation and daily tests, and all this for a minimum of four months. The administration of this drug needs painstaking care as it has not yet been accepted for public sale. Besides, the price is astronomical. It's a big decision to make but I am ready to try anything to regain the use of my old body, which apart from this nasty blow has held up well.

[...]

Dido and I send you our love,

Jean Renoir

1 L-dopa is a drug used in the treatment of Parkinson's disease.

To Ginette Doynel
Paris

27 April 1970
Beverly Hills

Dear Ginette,
I am replying to your two letters, of 20 and 23 April, which we have just received.

LE PETIT THEATRE: I have received a very kind letter from Mrs Fée Vaillant (Festival of Bad Ems). I ask you to make sure that the copy sent to this festival is complete. I place great importance on showing complete versions of my films at festivals.

I am thinking about the screening which Langlois is organizing in New York in July. You must insist that the film be shown on this occasion not only in a good 35mm copy but also with normal subtitles. By 'normal' I mean subtitles printed at the bottom of the screen. I'll remind you that the subtitles Phil Chamberlin is going to use on 15 May are simply projected above the screen on a little screen. It's better than nothing, and I am grateful to Chamberlin, but the method is terribly amateurish. If the principle of these normal subtitles were adopted, as I hope, we shouldn't forget that Sesonske's subtitles might be used, which would save time and money.

What luck that my film should be so well supported. I am delighted that you rejected the date of 2 May and the first channel. The film ought to be screened in colour. In this you will have an ally in Langlois. I am anxious to know what he has told you regarding the screening in New York.

You might also suggest to Jaigu and those with whom the fate of the film rests that cinephiles would not let pass without protest the news that the TV people didn't feel it necessary to present my film correctly. After the first refusal from 'l'Aide au Cinéma' this new attack on my work will not go unnoticed. I am curious to know what people like Truffault [sic] and Beylie think.

[...]
Dido and I send you our love,
Jean Renoir

To Pierre Long
Son et Lumière, Paris

19 May 1970
Beverly Hills

Dear Pierre Long,

I hope that this little note will find you nimble and that your pains are no more than a memory.

Le Petit Théâtre was shown at the Los Angeles Museum on 15 May. The film theatre is very beautiful. Dido and I are still full of emotion when we think about the unique reception my film had, and this despite the handicap of provisional sub-titles which Mrs Doynel must have mentioned to you. The audience started reacting favourably right from the beginning of the screening. At the end they gave me a standing ovation which lasted several minutes. People were jostling each other to come and tell me how much pleasure the film gave them. I can't resist telling you about this success. I only regret that the film does not yet have an American distributor who could have profited from this favourable wind.

I explained to Mrs Doynel the question of the sub-titles. The only remedy is to wait until circumstances allow the expense of proper sub-titling.

The texts of the provisional sub-titles were produced by Sesonke, the Santa Barbara professor who came to see my work on set. They could be improved, but give a solid basis for the final draft.

Apart from that, this screening gives us hope that *Le Petit Théâtre* can have a good career in America. I do not believe that we'll break down the barrier of the big companies, but the independent art cinemas are now sufficiently numerous in the United States to ensure us honourable takings.

Dido and I send best regards to Mrs Long and to you our wishes for good health,

Jean Renoir

To Jeanne Moreau

8 June 1970
Beverly Hills

Dear Jeanne,

We received your letter of 4 June and have read and reread it. It has transported us to the sweet fragrances of Provence. It's very pleasant to roll around in the rosemary and thyme, especially when in your company.

Dido and I are always talking about you. You give us the comfort and certainty of being friends with a real human being. Men and women, children and old people are so numerous on this Earth, but they are difficult to make out. They wear a mask. They aren't really responsible for this. It might come from their parents, the way they were brought up, from their class, or from their wealth. Forgive my desire to evoke your presence, but it's not difficult in your case, because you don't wear a mask. Your true identity is not hidden. For many, a mask is necessary because what it hides isn't always pleasant. Furthermore, let's be honest, the world is composed of little groups, human families that have created themselves regardless of our wishes or laws. But they exist, nevertheless. Dido and I have the feeling that behind your borders, there perhaps exists a place for us.

I have gone back to work. Our tramp[1] seems to me to be taking shape. At the moment, the ground that she gazes out on is a desert, the wind that she breathes comes from the Sierra Nevada, the sky which looks down on her is unsparing in the most extraordinary displays of colour.

Once the character is familiar to me, I will write and give you the news about her and will present her to John Calley.

Dido and I ask to be fondly remembered to Anna and Quick by you.

With all our love,

[Jean]

1 The heroine of Renoir's project, *La Clocharde*.

To Jean Renoir   *22 July 1970*
Beverly Hills   *Paris*

Dear Sir,

I have asked Janine Bazin to lend me the manuscripts that André wrote which were to have comprised his book about you. My secretaries – who are also your secretaries, since they are working for Les Films du Carrosse[1] – have started to type up this material: Bazin's early articles, his unpublished texts, his notes, etc ... I myself would like to organize and index all these texts and to put them in chronological order (the chronological order <u>of your films</u>, not the order in which the articles were written).

There will no doubt be gaps in what he wrote about you, which I propose to fill in myself – working with Rivette – and putting our own texts in italics, for example, to distinguish them from Bazin's. Does this idea meet with your approval, or would you suggest another solution? I would like to send you the completed manuscript, possibly in September, so you can look it over before the publisher does. Perhaps when you go over the material, it will inspire you to write a few lines which could serve as a foreword to the book, about your relationship with Bazin or about his way of seeing your films?

Jeanne gave me some news about you – she told me about your lovely evening together in Los Angeles. Right now she's staying at her house in the south, watching the fires that are devastating the region. She's been writing some wonderful songs, too – I hope she sent you the record she made.

And so, dear Mr Renoir, that is everything I wanted to tell you. It would be very helpful if you could take a moment to write to me with your thoughts and ideas regarding the Bazin book. If, however, you are hard at work on your own projects and simply do not have the time, I certainly understand. In that event, I will consult Ginette Doinel [sic], who I am sure stays in touch with you.

Kindly extend my best wishes to Madame Renoir, and accept my warmest regards,

François Truffaut

1 Truffaut's production company, so named in homage to Renoir's *Le Carrosse d'Or*.

To François Truffaut
Paris

27 *July 1970*
Beverly Hills

Dear friend,

I am enchanted by your decision to complete and publish André Bazin's texts. After the death of this creator of contemporary cinema, I turn to you and Rivette when I hesitate in my opinions. I am very flattered that you've asked me for a preface. I'm working on it.

Your idea to present in italics the texts that you and Rivette are going to write seems to me a good way to preserve the book's clarity.

Dido and I immediately thought of Jeanne when the papers announced the forest fires in her region.

I haven't progressed with the preparation of the film that I'd like to do with her. It's perhaps because, now I can have all the material facilities to do it, the spiritual facilities, alas, are lacking. I feel tremendous admiration for her and I'd like to give her a story worthy of her. I have to admit that up to now it's not been forthcoming.

I'm following a rigorous treatment in the hope of ridding myself of unbearable fatigue. The results are not brilliant.

Your letter pleased me greatly and Dido, too . Give our best regards to Rivette. I still think about his film and am sorry that Dido didn't see it. She joins me in sending you all our affection.

Jean Renoir

To Jean Renoir   22 December 1970
Beverly Hills   *Paris*

Dear Sir,

The other night I finally saw *Le Petit Théâtre* – on a colour television set and under good conditions – and it was a truly lovely evening. I very much enjoyed the Christmas episode, and the fact that it was dubbed didn't bother me at all – in fact, it underscored the 'fairytale' aspect of the piece. Between the hunger, the snow, and the spectre of death, the story was far from lighthearted, but it was told with such familiarity and simplicity that it was absolutely delightful nonetheless. *La Cireuse Electrique* is a dazzling piece of film-making – a bit off-the-wall, superbly executed, and acted to perfection by Marguerite Cassan, Olaf and Dynam. *Le Roil d'Yvetot* is to *Toni* what the Christmas episode is to *La Petite Marchande d'Allumettes* – a philosophical variation on the same theme: that cruelty has nothing to do with our perceptions and everything to do with our actions. The song *Lorsque tout est fini*, sung by Jeanne,[1] was an equally successful blend of fragility and emotion, and I must also mention the brilliant use of the little steel ball that turns into a *boule de petanque*[2] as it passes from the stage to the screen. The whole show was terrific, and the next day, it's all anyone could talk about. In my opinion, *Le Petit Théâtre* should be released in cinemas, where it would have a good chance of success.

Soon I hope to be able to send you a typed copy of *Jean Renoir par André Bazin*.[3]

This letter will probably reach you some time between Christmas and New Year's Day – with the hope that your Christmas Eve was festive, and in time to wish both of you a happy New Year.

Warm and affectionate regards,
François [Truffaut]

1 Jeanne Moreau.
2 The large metal ball used in the French game of bowls.
3 Published by Champ Libre, Paris, in 1971.

To François Truffaut
Paris

Dear François Truffaut,

Your letter is like the morning dew that dispels nightmares. I won't go so far as to say that it restores my health, but it helps me out of a depression caused by my inability to overcome unpleasant dizzy turns. I do however think that I'm coming to the end of my troubles, and that I will be able to look at life and join in with it, instead of contenting myself with being an onlooker, which is a depressing position. Can you imagine, I have not yet started reading *The Adventures of Antoine Doinel.*[1] I'm going to start today to absorb your book not like a passive actor, but like a companion in adventure. I haven't seen your last film either. All my close friends whose opinions I trust dream about this film and consider it a masterpiece. I shall rush to see it at the next opportunity.

So you see that your letter was opportune. I don't thank you for it; it's part of a state of things which unites you and me on the essential points.

When you see Jeanne Moreau, tell her how much my wife and I delight in knowing her. She brings an air of authenticity which is rare in the history of human relations. Nearly all human beings wear a mask. Not her. We hope to see her and to see you this summer. These meetings justify making the trip.

With all my friendship,
Jean Renoir

1 Published in 1970.

1971

To Jean Renoir   *5 March 1971*
Beverly Hills   *Paris*

Dear Mr Renoir,

Today I am mailing you a typed manuscript of *Jean Renoir par André Bazin*. I wrote an introduction to it, which explains how the book was done, what has gone into it, etc. ... It's still missing the filmography (Claude Beylie is still working on it – and anyway, that's not something I want to bother you with) and the 'additional texts' (which we will include only if you have no objections).

In any case, I am going to show another copy of the manuscript to Ginette Doynel as soon as she returns from her trip, so that she can check the whole project. What we would like from you, of course, is a text about Bazin himself and about this book. To facilitate things, I am sending you a copy of an article you wrote when Bazin died, as well as the short introduction you wrote, in English, for the collection of Bazin's writings that were translated in California. These may be helpful to you.

As soon as we receive your text, the entire book will be sent to the printer, because we would like it to be ready by May – to coincide with the Cannes Film Festival and, according to what Jeanne tells me, your next visit to France.

I hope the book will please you, even in this incomplete state. But as it is, I think it's better than most of the various books that have been written about you in France over the years.

I would appreciate it if you could let me know, as soon as possible, when you plan to send me your preface. Until then, I remain faithfully and very affectionately yours,

François Truffaut

To François Truffaut

Paris   *Beverly Hills*

Dear François Truffaut,

I have just – once again – had to have a stay in hospital. It was quite an unpleasant ordeal, although without risk of preventing me from working on the preface for the Bazin book. Now I'm better and am starting to think again about things other than my physical problems. So I tried to settle down to the preface. All that came out of my hospitalized mind are the two pages I enclose with this letter. I think the result is rather meagre. If you think that it's not what's needed, throw it out.

All my apologies for this involuntary delay over something about which I care deeply. Having said this, as soon as I got home I started reading the book and devoured it as if it was about somebody else. It's a great success.

With all my friendship,

Jean Renoir

To Jean Renoir

23 March 1971

Beverly Hills   *Paris*

My dear friend,

I was very pleased to get some encouraging news about your health from Ginette Doynel. The text you wrote about Bazin was wonderful, and your description matched him perfectly. I had forgotten his beret, the way he dressed – it's certainly true that Bazin was completely unaffected in his demeanour.

I think the filmography is pretty good – thanks to Claude Beylie – and the notes on the films (those for the more recent films were compiled by Jean Douchet and Michael Delahaye) are also well done.

If I might be permitted to bother you with a detail, it is this: a young lady who appeared in *Le Petit Chaperon Rouge*,[1] and also in the film *La Petite Marchande* [*d'Allumettes*], is variously credited as AMY WELLS and ANNY XELLS. Which name is correct? Don't worry if you can't find it – it's not that important. A similar question arose with Catherine Hessling's character in *La Fille de L'Eau* – was her name <u>Virginia</u> or <u>Gudule</u> (or both)?[2]

Apart from that, everything is falling into place – Janine Bazin seems happy, as does Gérard Lebovici, who is publishing the book. I hope to see you soon, whether in Paris or in the South. You probably already know that Jeanne will be coming to Hollywood to be a presenter at the Oscars, and she is delighted to have such a pleasant pretext to see you. She is in especially good spirits these days (she is shooting a film, *L'Humeur Vagabonde*) and is also full of energy.

Thanks again for your text. I will send you the galleys of the other sections of the book as soon as they come back from the printer. You needn't worry, though – I won't ask you to perform any tedious proof-reading tasks.

My best wishes to Madame Renoir, whom I have not seen for quite some time, and my sincere affection.

François Truffaut

1 *Le Petit Chaperon Rouge* (1929) was a short film by Alberto Cavalcanti which featured Jean Renoir and Catherine Hessling in its cast.
2 For Renoir's reply to these questions, see his letter of 13 February 1973.

To Orson Welles [*Original in English*]

8 *May 1971*
Beverly Hills

Dear Orson,

I am ill and unable to appear in your show.[1] I am deeply sad and disappointed to miss this opportunity to work under your direction.

With my affection,

Jean Renoir

1 Orson Welles had written to Renoir asking him to play himself in his (then) self-financed film *The Other Side of the Wind*. Though the editing of the film was practically completed, at the time of writing it still has not been released for legal reasons.

To Giulio and Adèle Macchi

3 *November 1971*
Beverly Hills

Dear Adèle and Giulio,

Long live Tiepolo![1] Venice cannot die. A miracle will come from San Marco, Tiepolo and Vivaldi.[2] But it's comforting to think that the powerful people of our era seem set on adding their material aid to the spiritual forces of the past.

Your building projects seem fascinating to us. Your activity is in happy contrast to the boring life I make my family lead because of my fall. I didn't break anything, but the shock was great. My house has been transformed into a hospital. Luckily I have Dido; without her I wouldn't pull through, but it means that she has more work and unending problems. We hope that one day holidays with the Macchi will make us forget all this. Your kindness will never be forgotten. Thank you for the reviews of the *Le Petit Théâtre* and above all thank you for the good opinion you have of it. These reviews really made us happy.

Kindest regards,
Jean Renoir

1 Giovanni Battista Tiepolo (1696–1770), Venetian artist famous for lavish frescoes.
2 Antonio Vivaldi (1678–1741), Italian composer celebrated for his many concertos. Vivaldi's music was an inspiration to Renoir on *The Golden Coach*.

To Ginette Doynel
Paris

8 December 1971
Beverly Hills

Dear Ginette,

I am responding to your letter of 1 December.

OFFICE: What a pity your apartment is not bigger and that it is not possible for you to dedicate a corner to the Compagnie J. R. My health problems mark the occasion of the end of my film career. Of course I am beginning to walk again, but it's the walk of an invalid and my excursions are limited to going around the patio. The most serious thing is that my dizziness has returned and that my ability to work is extremely limited. I would consider myself lucky if I can turn out several literary works. I brought the curtain down on the cinema with *Le Petit Théâtre*. I owe this last joy to you. In organizing the shooting of this film you have helped me to say a decent goodbye to my profession.

Thus we must now renounce all film projects. But you must continue to represent me. I don't know how we are going to make this work if Dido and I don't have you acting on our behalf in Paris.

Until now, I have only shared this state of things with Dido. I didn't want to worry you. But we must see things as they really are, and for me the cinema is over.

Of course we should discuss these things with you. If I find myself incapable of making the trip, I will ask you to come and stay here for a while. Even if it is useless from a business point of view, it would give you a vacation in a climate which, despite everything, remains very pleasant.

Regarding the practical aspects of moving out [of avenue Frochot] I have not changed my mind. I'll think about the details when you have given me your reaction to this letter.

[512]

I'll make an exception and tell you a small detail: the combination to my safety deposit box is 127. I used it because it reminded me of the number of my house on Leona Drive.

[. . .]

As in previous years, we ask you to take care of birthday and Christmas presents. It's really your fault if we ask you to keep representing us. We are so used to you.

We read in the papers that it is cold in Paris. Clearly you must come for a little trip to California.

We send you all our love,

Jean Renoir

To Jean Renoir [*Original in English*]   *26 May 1972*
Beverly Hills   *Pacific Palisades*

Dear Jean Renoir,

I had a letter from Bernardine Fritz the other day telling me you are ailing and perhaps feeling a bit lonesome too. Her letter came a few days after I had finished re-reading your wonderful book – *Les Cahiers du Capitaine Georges*. I think I told you once before that I wish I had been able to write such a book myself. And I mean it most sincerely. Which leads me to ask if you have written any others besides this and the one on your father. I would love to read them, if there are any others.

I don't drive but I could get some [one] to drive me to your place one day if it would be any consolation for you. I almost never visit anyone except women, of course. I seldom feel lonely, but when I do it's frightful. Then I feel I am totally alone in the whole wide world. (And, of course, that's what we really are, when we admit it to ourselves – *alone*.) The thing is to be able to be <u>alone</u> but not lonely, what!

Well, I am expressing myself poorly. All I want to tell you is that you are really in my thoughts very often, and if there is anything I can do to make things easier for you, please let me know.

Meanwhile all good wishes – and to Madame Renoir also.

Give me something – <u>titles</u> – to look up and read, if you can. You should have been a writer, as well as all the other things you are.

Henry Miller[1]

1 Henry Miller (1891–1980), author of *Tropic of Cancer* (1934), *Tropic of Capricorn* (1939), and many other novels.

To Henry Miller [*Original in English*]   *30 May 1972*
       Beverly Hills

Dear Henry Miller,

One of my dearest occupations is to be with you and since I am too ill to visit with my friends, my communications with you consist mainly in reading a chapter of one of your books.

Your writing is for me very close to your real presence. Enjoying the company of a perfect 'honest man' is rare in our days. By 'honest man', I mean '*l'honnête homme du dix-huitième siècle*',[1] I mean Diderot. I don't know how the readers of his time considered him. Probably this philosopher was misunderstood as you are.

The question is, of course: why is Henry Miller interested in sex? The question is stupid. In our century of *petit bourgeois*, sex is perhaps the only thing people cannot cheat with.

Please forgive my futile statement. I am so happy with your letter that I had to write you anything.

For the time being, I am still in bad health and I prefer postponing our next conversation until I feel in a condition to appreciate it. Although I know a young woman who would be delighted to fetch you or to take me to your place.

I wrote several screen and stage plays, also articles, but my two only books are the one on my father and *The Notebooks of Captain Georges*. For the time being, I am working on a book of recollections.

By the way, when I feel depressed, I think of your comments on these books and immediately, life becomes wonderful.

Sincerely yours,

Jean Renoir

---

1 'An honest man of the eighteenth century'.

1973

To Georges Simenon

8 February 1973
Beverly Hills

Dear Georges,

I have just read in the Los Angeles paper that you have decided to stop writing. I can't believe it's true, unless it is only a temporary halt. God created you to be a writer, just as he created my father to be a painter. This is why both of you have done what you did so well. For you, writing is not a mere sentimental account of your state of mind – it is a duty. I will add that the companionship you provided through your books will be missed by lots of people, and that you must think about them. Maybe your thoughts will no longer reach us by means of novels. Maybe your books will become purely philosophical. But regardless of which form you use, and for the sake of your readers, you must let us know you're here.

Dido and I send our love from the depths of our hearts.

Jean Renoir

To François Truffaut

13 February 1973
Beverly Hills

Dear François Truffaut,

After two years of negligence, I realize that I did not reply to some of your questions regarding an actress who appeared in *Le Petit Chaperon Rouge* and *La Petite Marchande d'Allumettes*. I think, but I am not completely sure, that she was Aimée Tédesco, Jean Tédesco's[1] wife. Amy Wells was only a stage name. If it is not too late, Ginette Doynel can give you Aimée Tédesco's address. As for the name of the character played by Catherine Hessling, I remember neither Virginia, nor Gudule. However, Gudule might be right.

I can't tell you how happy I am to have played a small part in your book on Bazin, and to have contributed, even if it was only on a small scale, to the work accomplished by you, Claude Beylie, Jean Douchet, Michel Delahaye and the other cinephile friends I love.

I still have not received your *Bazin* in English. Perhaps it's not out yet. I would know it if it was.

Dido and I can't wait to see *La Nuit Américaine*.[2] I hope my legs will be gracious enough to carry me to the screening.

If I may take the liberty of giving you a piece of advice, I think you are quite right to learn English. The times when I claimed my faith in folklore are gone. My statements published in *Le Point* reflect what I believed, and still believe, to be of vital necessity for artistic creativity. Nowadays, one can fly from Paris to Los Angeles in about ten hours. Our audience is international and we are working for the audience. Just like the nineteenth-century writers who left their native towns to become Parisians, today one must become a citizen of the world. If one has any talent, what one brings from one's native land will be felt. But the audiences will be from all parts of the world. Today, an artist is not bound by yesterday's boundaries. To avoid remaining insular, he must touch the whole world. It can only be helpful to an artist of your stature to know the language which is the most used worldwide.

Would you tell Jeanne Moreau that Dido and I think of her very fondly? Dido was quite amused by the idea that she could scare you.

Love and best wishes for the success of your new film.

Jean Renoir

1 Jean Tédesco (1895–1958) began an avant-garde cinema in the former Vieux-Colombier theatre in 1924, where he screened the dream sequence from *La Fille de l'Eau* in one of his shows. The attic of the theatre was transformed into a studio for filming *La Petite Marchande d'Allumettes* in 1927. Tédesco made several shorts and one feature, *Mort ou Vif* (1947).
2 Titled *Day for Night* in English, being the same term for the method of shooting night scenes by day with a filter.

To Alexis Minotis[1]
Athens, Greece

1 March 1973
Beverly Hills

Dear Alexis,

Dido and I are sharing your grief. What a loss! Katina Paxinou carried so much weight in the scale of our affections that her disappearance will affect the equilibrium of our world. We know this is not much comfort to you – regardless of how many times you hear it – but the whole artistic community is mourning Katina.

On the day she died, Dido and I had noticed that the camellia she had given us carried more bloom than usual. Its flowers were exceptionally bright and of an extraordinary size. The following day, we saw in the papers that Katrina was dead ... She had sent us this message through this flower she loved so much.

Dido and I send you our love,

Jean Renoir

1 Husband of Greek actress Katina Paxinou (1900–1973), who won an Academy Award in 1943 for her role in *For Whom the Bell Tolls*. She had just died of cancer.

To Ginette Doynel
Paris

8 June 1973
Beverly Hills

Dear Ginette,

We have received your three letters, of 28 May, 2 June and 5 June.

[...]

SOUVENIRS INCOMPLETS:[1] we had a visit from Simon Michael Bessie from Atheneum Publications. I read to him my corrected version. He is enthusiastic but he insists on my adding my remembrances of the American period. I am going to take my courage in both hands and put them in. This addition will make my book a huge work. Bessie is partial to illustrating it with photographs. I have already written asking you to be in touch with *L'Avant-Scène*[2] with regard to photographs. As for the title, he thinks it's good in French but not so good in English.

Of course I will keep Bob Knittel abreast of this visit, and also Norman Denny, who I would really like to have as translator.

Could you get me some information for the book: who are the children that Marcel Pagnol had with the English dancer and what was the colour of the hair of the eldest?

[...]

We send you all our love,

Jean Renoir

1 Provisional title for *Ma Vie et Mes Films* (*My Life and My Films*).
2 *L'Avant-Scène du Cinéma* is an ongoing series of published screenplays in France.

To Ginette Doynel
Paris

22 June 1973
Beverly Hills

Dear Ginette,

[. . .]

SOUVENIRS INCOMPLETS: This title is only provisional. Maybe it will be kept, but nothing is decided. The adjective 'incomplete' applies not to the period (the book is not chronological), but to the fact that the remembrances seem to be taken at random from my past. I won't talk about the question you raised but will explain how upset I was by the failure of *La Règle du Jeu*. There were lots of reasons which led me to become an expatriate, but this one also counts.

[. . .]

We'll close by saying we miss you. We are very anxious to see you and we send you all our love.

Jean Renoir

To Simon Michael Bessie
Atheneum
New York

3 September 1973
Beverly Hills

Dear Mike,

I have just finished the first draft of *Souvenirs Incomplets*, and I am starting the first revisions. As far as I can say, the final version should be ready by the end of September. Could you come here to read it before we send it in for typing? The book is now about 380 pages long. I hope this increase in size will be matched by an increase in quality. [. . .]

I apologize for taking so long in finishing this book, but adding a second half gave it a relevance I did not expect. As for the title, we can talk about it when you come. I like *Flash Back*, but I like *My Life in Film* even better.

Give our regards to Mrs Bessie.

Warmest regards.

Jean Renoir

To François Truffaut
Paris

9 December 1973
Beverly Hills

Dear François,

Many thanks for Jean-Claude Maillet's interview with Claude Renoir. Thank you also for the paperback of *The River*. How do you manage to keep so well-informed with all the work you're doing? Even the Spanish translation of *Bazin* found its way here thanks to you.

I am most grateful to you for helping Ginette Doynel resolve the problems she's having with publishing my book. She had forwarded your objections relating to *Boudu*, and I think I have done what is necessary; also with regard to *Le Déjeuner Sur l'Herbe*. Chasing after photographs might be more difficult for her. Without disturbing you too much, she might be able to find a good portion of what I am asking her to get at Durand-Ruel.[1]

I am revising the segments dealing with Chaplin and Burgess Meredith.

Jacqueline[2] has not only brought us some news about you but also herself, in person. Dido and I are very touched by her kindness, which we feel is genuine. We hope to see her often in the future. In the meantime we are happy about her big success.

We are really sorry to hear the bad news about Jeanne Moreau's father and son. We really like Jeanne, and her troubles touch us very deeply. It is fortunate that she is working, because it is the best remedy.

You may be missing Leona Drive, but Leona Drive misses you as much. We are impatiently awaiting your next visit, and we are dying to meet your daughters. Give them our best.

Love from both of us,

Jean Renoir

---

1 Art dealers. The founder, Paul Durand-Ruel, championed the Impressionists. His son Georges was Jean Renoir's godfather.
2 Jacqueline Bisset (b.1944), actress who had recently starred in Truffaut's *Day for Night* (1973).

1974

Ma Vie et Mes Films is published by Flammarion. An autobiography loosely constructed around reminiscences of friends and anecdotes, it is dedicated to the New Wave. The English translation, My Life and My Films, *is published by Atheneum in the United States and by Collins in Britain.*

To François Truffaut   *27 February 1974*
Paris   *Beverly Hills*

Dear François,

Ginette's recorded message on the answering machine gives a rather grand impression of the Compagnie Jean Renoir. Dido and I could not stop laughing. Ginette has informed us, by means of a letter and not by means of an automatic recording, that you have agreed to read the final proofs of *Ecrits 1926–1970*.[1] I am delighted and very grateful to you, because I could not possibly find the time to correct the galleys before 14 March.

We are still under the spell of *La Nuit Américaine*, at the same time moved and entertained by your painting of so many familiar situations. Such a beautiful film! Thank you for the screenplay.

We have not yet seen Jacqueline.

Thank you for the clipping on Durand-Ruel. I did not have it.

Ginette tells us that you'll be coming here in March. We are thrilled.

Love from both of us,

Jean Renoir

1 A collection of Renoir's writings, edited by Claude Gauteur and published (in French only) by Pierre Belfond in 1974.

To François Truffaut
Paris

Dear François,

My hand trembles but I feel the need to communicate with you without the intermediary of a typewriter, that cold mechanical object without a soul, letters hard as steel, or more like chrome.

May this little note bring you the handwritten expression of my friendship.

– Long live the senses.
– Down with the intellect.
Dido joins me in sending our love.
Vivent les mistons.[1]
Jean Renoir

[PS.] Thanks for your assistance and work on *La Grande Illusion* and for the books. Faithful messengers of your thoughts.

PPS. Your description of the elections is hilarious.

1 *Les Mistons* was the title of Truffaut's first important short film, made in 1957. It was translated in English as *The Mischief Makers*.

To Janine Bazin

Dear Janine,

Thank you for thinking of me when in the settings of Essoyes and the Moulin Rouge. These monuments, spanning various styles from the rustic to the night-club, are the background for a film very familiar to me: the film of my life. Despite the good news about your recovery, I found your letter sad, or rather melancholic. It is due to the passing of time. I am beginning to feel it too. One must not dwell on the past. One must keep living in new settings. The pleasant thing is to grow old at the same time as the people one likes. Our little clan is Bazin. It is on the verge of becoming Truffaut. I reproach myself for not having taken more advantage of friendships such as these.

I am delighted to hear that a cinema is now wearing the name of our irreplaceable friend. I hope I'll be able to see Paris again (there's a song about that) and consequently, you. Don't think that this is a letter. It is

31 Jean Renoir and François Truffaut in the mid-1970s: 'There is something magical about our relationship'

only a small eruption of a disease called friendship.
   Fond regards,
   Jean Renoir

To François Truffaut
Paris

7 July 1974
Beverly Hills

Dear François,

   I have received your letters of 6 and 28 June. They give us the wonderful feeling that we are with you and Ginette, and this without bothering to make plane reservations; and with the possibility of going back many times to the parts we find most interesting. Actually, we are interested by the whole content of your letters. We have read them several times, and following them has carried us from the Mediterranean to the Irish Sea, with a short stop at the Folies Bergères. Between you and I, I don't see why a cardinal should not have the right to call on a little lady of easy virtue in the Bergère district.[1] We'll see each other soon, and then we'll try to figure out together what kind of consequences such a tragic joke may have.
   Our best regards to your family.
   Dido and I send you our love,
   Jean Renoir

PS: Thank you for the article. Thank you for the information. Thank you for your devotion (one might think we are in India). Thank you for everything.

PPS: I haven't received the illustrated book of *La Grande Illusion*, nor *Ma Vie et Mes Films*.

---

1 A reference to a recent scandal in which a leading cardinal expired in the room of a Parisian stripper.

To François Truffaut
Paris

19 November 1974
Beverly Hills

Dear François,

   I am still deluding myself about my illness. I have found out that illness is a well-defined kingdom with its boundaries, its customs, and even its own language. When one is ill, it is a little like becoming a child again. One gets used to being attended to by one's entourage; the more so in my situation where using one leg is strictly forbidden. I find this state of dependence rather hard to get used to.

To top it all, I am a real coward: I cannot stand pain, and when it gets too much, I'd like to be able to scream. Unfortunately, it seems our civilization doesn't approve of screams. It approves of noise, mainly of the mechanical kind. But with the microphone which makes it possible for a singer to whisper, we are forgetting the beauty of the vocal efforts of opera singers, especially the women. Whenever I feel depressed on a rainy day, I think about Florence Mills, a black singer who was with the group 'Blackbirds' [sic] around 1920. She had a very high-pitched, almost shrill voice. A nightingale in the woods. She died of tuberculosis.

I was also madly in love with Carola Neher who sang Brecht and Kurt Weill. She also died of tuberculosis.

Forgive me for these erratic recollections, but as we say in English, *I miss you.*[1]

I hope that Jeanne Moreau's leg is not hurting any more. Fortunately, she is a strong lady. Give her our love. We are haunted by the desire to see her and talk to her.

Love from Dido and I.

Jean Renoir

PS: Thank you for the book on Impressionism. It is very handsome. We have received your letter of 11 November, and we are delighted by the prospect of hearing you tell us all about Adèle Hugo's touching life.[2]

There is a chance this letter will reach you. A friend of my new secretary Anne (it would appear we are surrounded by Annes) is flying back to Paris and has kindly offered to take it.

1 Originally in French: *vous me manquez.*
2 Truffaut was about to film *L'Histoire d'Adèle H.* (*The Story of Adèle H.*).

1975

To François Truffaut   *6 February 1975*
Paris   *Beverly Hills*

Dear François,
   I have just heard that the Motion Picture Academy is giving me an
honorary Oscar.
   You may know about it already, but I wanted you to be the first to
whom I expressed my happiness and pride.
   Jean Renoir

To Jean Renoir   *1/3 March 1975*
Beverly Hills   *Guernsey*

My dear friends,
   Thank you for your telegram regarding the nominations for Uncle
Oscar. I really hope that Valentina Cortese[1] wins one, but in my case, the
best part about the whole thing is that it gives us a chance to find our way
back to Leona Drive.
   We're getting close to finishing the shooting at this location; we'll be
leaving Guernsey next Saturday, 8 March. Then we'll be in Paris for four
days, from the 8th to the 12th, and from there, on to Dakar and L'Ile de
Goré for the last eight pages of the script (the island of Barbados). After
21 March, I'll be able to rest easy, when I can be certain I have all the
elements of the film ready to put together.
   This production has been by far the most difficult, the most nerve-
wracking I've ever done, because of the emotional climate created by our
young actress.[2] I think she is truly brilliant, but she does not know, does
not tolerate, any intermediate state between the mystical exultation she
finds in performing and the absolute anguish of putting herself into a
role. I wish I could describe her to you but in fact it's quite difficult – one
would have to imagine a cocktail of Charles Laughton, Jeanne Moreau,
Oscar [sic] Werner, Jean-Pierre Léaud,[3] Emil Jannings[4] and James Dean[5]
. . . and to that I must add that working with her presents the same
obstacles as does working with children, animals and helicopters! To set

against all these difficulties, though, are results which amaze me almost constantly. To help her performance, she has invented a sort of hostility towards her leading man, towards the crew, and towards me – which leads to many 'final' confrontations, followed by reconciliations that are no less 'final'. Even though she's not yet twenty years old, I decided to treat her like an adult, because I know she suffered a great deal from being treated condescendingly at the Comédie Française (which she left so she could do this film).

If she does indeed cause me to lose my critical bearings, the resulting film will be absolutely hideous – an exhibitionistic tear-jerker that could quite possibly be laughable. Of course I hope this will not be the case; but in any event, if it is, I must blame myself, because she is very eager to take direction, and she seems to trust me, despite her deadly stares. She can't stand watching anyone eating, laughing, whistling, smoking or anyone watching her, or turning away from her, or moving at all. She agonizes over her work and makes us agonize along with her. I am sharing with you some of my impressions of the shoot so far, knowing full well that these feelings will eventually fade away, to the point of making us all absolutely nostalgic for this period, as if the whole thing had taken place in an idyllic atmosphere.

Recently Leslie[6] wrote me a brief note, and in it she said that things are well with you. I think that your Oscar was worth all the Dopa or Eldopa (or Aldopa) [sic] in the world, and that what you need to do right now is simply learn to keep the door to your house open or closed to visitors, depending on how you feel ... On that subject, I am sending you a photocopy of an article that appeared in *France-Soir* last week. Of course, your Oscar will be very helpful for the sales of your book. I hope the new book is progressing well; I am very impatient to read it, and to experience the same emotions I did those nights when I read the manuscript of *Ma Vie et Mes Films* in my room at the Beverly Hills Hotel.

Giscard[7] wants to have the backing of people in the arts. After watching *Le Jour Se Lève* on television, he invited Marcel Carné to have lunch with him at the Elysée Palace, in the company of Paul Meurisse, François Périer,[8] Jean-Louis Barrault, and also Michel Simon who, when questioned by journalists as he was leaving the Palace, told them: 'This establishment is very convenient – it's well-situated, right in the centre of town.' As for Giscard, he counted *La Grande Illusion* among his six or eight favourite films.

There you have it, the only news I've received from Paris, since we are cut off from everything here. Today I was able to find some time to write to you, because we've been shooting for five nights in a row, so we're taking a rest. And I'm expecting a visit from Gérard Lebovici, whom you know.

MONDAY

I had to interrupt the writing of this letter. Last night I spoke to Rivette on the 'phone, and he told me how delighted he was with his lightning visit to LA, about his reunion with you, and the warm reception he got from Leslie. Upon returning to Paris, he learned that the Centre du Cinéma had given him a subsidy of 200 million francs for a six hour-long film he's planning to make; things have certainly changed in the film industry since *La Règle du Jeu!*

I have to leave you now and go to work . . . From my window I can see the sea, the boats, and the little islands that Victor Hugo looked at for seventeen years!

I send my love to both of you – I hope to speak to you by 'phone very soon, and most of all, I look forward to seeing you a month from now.

Yours,

François [Truffaut]

1 Valentina Cortese (b.1924) won the New York Film Critics Award for Best Supporting Actress in *Day for Night*.
2 Isabelle Adjani (b.1955), actress who was the sensation of the Comédie Française in the early 1970s, and whose film credits include *La Gifle* (1974), *The Tenant* (1976), *The Driver* (1978), *Possession* (1980), *L'Eté Meurtrier* (1985), *Subway* (1985), and *Camille Claudel* (1988).
3 Jean-Pierre Léaud (b.1944), favourite actor of Godard and Truffaut, for whom he incarnated Antoine Doinel in four feature films, beginning with *Les 400 Coups*.
4 Emil Jannings (1884–1950), German actor most famous for *The Last Laugh* (1924) and *The Blue Angel* (1930).
5 James Dean (1931–55), cult actor who died after completing only three films in a lead role – *East of Eden* (1955), *Rebel Without a Cause* (1955), and *Giant* (1956).
6 Leslie Caron.
7 Valéry Giscard d'Estaing, President of France 1974–81. In cinema, his main achievement was the relaxation of censorship.
8 François Périer (b.1919), actor on stage and in such films as *Orphée* (1950), *Le Samourai* (1967), and *Z* (1969).

To François Truffaut
Paris

30 April 1975
Beverly Hills

Dear François,

Your book[1] is as essential to any self-respecting home as the history of literature. It also benefits from something unheard-of in literary textbooks; it was written with love. In any case, it places the cinema where it should be, in first position. It makes us realize that our profession is the only one which is not anachronistic. I don't mean to say that the other art-forms are obsolete, but that their success is due to individuals. It has been said hundreds of times that cinema is like the universe. I indulge myself in toying with this idea while thinking about you.

Love from Dido and I,
Jean

1 Truffaut's book, *Les Films de Ma Vie*, a collection of his criticism and writings, was published in 1975. The English translation is *The Films in My Life*.

To Claude Beylie
Paris

30 June 1975
Beverly Hills

Dear Claude Beylie,

In reply to your letter of 24 June, the execution scene[1] was never shot. In this version, which I believe to be the final one, the film ends when Dédé is taken out of his cell and led to the guillotine. My reply to your question relating to the possibility of cuts in the film is that I have no idea. I think some cuts may have been made, short ones in other scenes of the film. Conceding that there was no way he could turn this drama into a comedy, the producer soon gave up on changing my editing. The only scene where I can see some important changes is Lulu's death scene, in which the new editing uses the sound recorded at the studio for the song, instead of the sound recorded in the street. But my memory might be failing me here as well, and it is quite possible that in this scene of Lulu's death, the sound recorded directly was drowned by the street noises.

The final cut must have borrowed a few feet of Denise Batcheff's[2] work, but I can't remember exactly where this happened. I must add that Denise Batcheff did a lot to prevent this manipulation of the sound, and had put my own cut back together before returning it to me.

I don't remember using Viviane Romance[3] in that scene.

The part of the lady working for the gallery owner was played by a Polish actress who was also working in the production, but I have forgotten in what capacity.

The shooting of *La Chienne* was disrupted by Janie Marèze's[4] death. On the one hand, I was grateful to the heavenly powers for allowing this unfortunate accident to occur only after I had completed my work with

[529]

her, and on the other hand, I was terribly distressed, as was Michel Simon, by the news of her death. And now it is Michel's turn. It is so sad! It seems to me that the sun has turned darker. For me, his disappearance has a sombre meaning: the triumph of stupidity over intelligence.

I like your prologue a lot. It is so laudatory that I felt myself blush as I was reading it.

I am happy for the success of your book,[5] and congratulate you on your relentless work.

I'm anxious to know how the exhibition is going.

Pay my respects to your wife.

Fond regards,

Jean Renoir

1 In *La Chienne*.
2 Later Denise Tual. As film editor, she was hired by the film's co-producer Roger Richebé to 'improve' Renoir's cut.
3 Actress who came to prominence in *La Belle Equipe* (1936).
4 Janie Marèze (1908–31), the new 'star' of *La Chienne*, began an affair with fellow actor Georges Flamant during the shooting of the film. He was driving her in his new Cadillac in the South of France when the car crashed, killing her instantly. At the funeral Michel Simon, who also had grown amorous of Janie Marèze, was overcome by emotion and created a scene, subsequently threatening the lives of both Flamant and Renoir.
5 *Jean Renoir, le Spectacle, la Vie*, by Claude Beylie, published by Cinema d'Aujourd'Hui in 1975.

To Janine Bazin

Nogent sur Marne, France

1 July 1975
Beverly Hills

Dear Janine,

These past months, I have been living in a state of expectancy. I wish time would contract and leave me in a better physical shape. I have struck one mark against my illness: I know what it is. One of my thigh bones, which was hit by a German bullet in 1917,[1] has been quietly festering all these years. I have been feeling better for the past few days, and I want to thank you for keeping me apprised of Parisian events that concern you and I. I am delighted to hear that Florent[2] has found his vocation. I am also delighted about your activities in Orléans. On the other hand, I'm rather saddened by your news about the state of French television.

I am going through a phase in my life where familiar as well as unknown friends are manifesting their concern. I am deeply moved by the warmth of their feeling, and more than a little embarrassed. I don't think I deserve such attentions. This is what I would have liked to express in my book. I shall say it another time.

Among the good things that I feel blessed with, there is my friendship with Truffaut. His presence brightened my life while he was in Los Angeles.

Dido is asking me to thank you for your letter, which was so informative, and we both send our love. Say hello to Florent.

Jean Renoir

1 Actually 1915 – see letters from that year.
2 Florent Bazin, son of André and Janine, who became a cameraman.

To Henri Cartier-Bresson[1]
Paris

1 July 1975
Beverly Hills

Dear Henri,

Your photo of Martine and Mélanie[2] makes me want to see them in the flesh. I know that the images you sent me represent the last stage before physical actuality; you even succeed in giving an idea of the sound of voices, but I don't regret that you've given up photography. You made optical methods say all they had to say. You reminded us what is essential in the human being. But at your age you can start studying a new mode of conversation. All my best wishes accompany you in this bold experiment. I'm sure that you'll do great things, as you would with no matter what medium of expression.

All my love to you and Martine and Mélanie.

Jean

1 Henri Cartier-Bresson (b.1908), celebrated photographer who officially 'retired' from the camera in the 1970s. He worked as an assistant to Renoir on *La Vie est à Nous, Une Partie de Campagne*, and *La Règle du Jeu*. See his 'Memoir' below.
2 Wife and daughter of Henri-Cartier Bresson.

To François Truffaut
Paris

1 July 1975
Beverly Hills

Dear François,

What is happening to Adèle?[1] Has this compelling heroine of unrelenting love found some lovers less fickle than her handsome lieutenant among the audience? As far as I am concerned, I am more than ready to bestow on her the passion she deserves. I assume she's been launched into life by now, and I can't wait to hear how life is treating her. I'd love to hear about the children in your other film as well.

I am enclosing an article I wrote on Chaplin in 1947.[2] This little piece was sent to me by a professor, editor of a university journal. He asked me for authorization to publish this article in his journal, and I granted it wholeheartedly. I had completely forgotten about this article, and this professor must be the only person in the world who has found out about it. I thought this little story might entertain you.

Jean Renoir

1 The heroine of Truffaut's *L'Histoire d'Adèle H.*
2 An article on *Monsieur Verdoux* for the *Screen Writers Magazine*. See letter dated 12 January 1954.

To François Truffaut
Les Films du Carrosse, Paris

28 July 1975
Beverly Hills

Dear François,

Dido and I are so sorry we cannot be in Paris to witness Adèle's first steps into the world. I would have liked so much to give my hand to this wanderer. You say some find her sad. It is so fortunate your film can be labelled. Audiences love simple labels. We'll be wanting to hear from you, but we are already certain your news will be good.

I think you are in the midst of shooting your picture in Thiers. I remember this small town very well. From the moment I entered its outskirts. I was impressed by the predominance of the colour black. The houses were black, and at the time of my journey through this town, the inhabitants seemed to favour dark clothes.

I'll finish this in a hurry. Dido and I only wanted to express our deep affection.

Jean Renoir

To Ingrid Bergman [*Original in English*]
Choisel, France

28 July 1975
Beverly Hills

Dear Ingrid,

To open a letter from you is like opening the door to wonderful recollections. You are the type of human being who doesn't need a rich surrounding to be loved by the public and even more by your friends. In the movies they don't trust the power of the actor. For a love scene, they surround the players with a lighting which means love; the background will suggest love. Of course there is also the dialogue which should be sufficient but the motto for the film industry is: 'Let's be safe, don't take risks, don't try anything which wasn't done twenty times before.' In life as well as on the stage you don't need a special background, a special music, special props; you are yourself and could act with the same success dressed by Macy's[1] and in front of a black curtain.

Dido and I thank the Gods who put us together on this planet.

With our love,

Jean

1 High-class department store chain in the USA.

To Henry Miller   *29 July 1975*
Pacific Palisades   *Beverly Hills*

Dear Henry Miller,

This little note is to let you know that Dido and I think about you, and wish you a prompt recovery.

I'm still incapacitated, and if you have had no news from us, it is because we were hoping to bring it to you in person. Until now, this hope has been in vain.

With our fond regards,

Jean Renoir

To Ingrid Bergman   *27 August 1975*
Choisel, France   *Beverly Hills*

Dear Ingrid,

Dido and I are delighted with your letter. It expresses good health and peace of mind. Unfortunately, the miracle that could have brought us back together on a set is not likely to happen. I guess miracles have limited powers. I am envious of Minnelli,[1] but it is a waste of time. I had better concentrate on endeavours I can still manage.

I am still unable to walk and must rely on my entourage. Fortunately for me, this entourage is armed with patient tenderness. So I try to write books. It is fascinating, and I am lucky to have found a way to remain active. I am still ambitious enough to think that people may be interested in my stories. For the moment, I am focusing on introspection. It is a pretentious word, but I can't think of any other; 'confession' would be too portentous.

How I wish I could hold your sixty years in my arms, with Dido participating in the embrace! The affection we feel for you goes way beyond any friendly alliance. Yet we should preserve in it some kind of material element. I feel the need to check the shape of your nose, the sound of your voice, your assertive gait.

We won't ask you to give our best regards to your family, they are too many. But when you see your children, remind them that we are not strangers. Our best to Lars.

With all our love,
Jean Renoir

1 Vincente Minnelli (1913–86), who was directing Bergman in his last film, *A Matter of Time* (1976).

To Henri Langlois
Cinémathèque Française
Paris

26 September 1975
Beverly Hills

Dear Henri Langlois,

Dido and I did not know you had been so ill. We are very sorry, and at the same time we are happy to hear that your problems are now things of the past. But I must caution you: 'Be careful with your legs.'

Dido is as happy as I am by the honours bestowed on me. You have been the driving force behind this gesture in my favour, and we are very grateful. Even though, as my father said, 'it's only when one has no more teeth that one can afford the best steak.' I would have liked to be there in person to savour this steak. Unfortunately, I am still incapacitated and must renounce pleasures of this sort. Therefore, it is only in writing that I thank you for letting me take part in the Cinémathèque's triumphal march.

Some friends who were passing by told me that Mary's eyesight was giving her more and more problems. We can only sympathize and let her know that we think of her as warmly as ever.

Fondly,
Jean Renoir

To François Truffaut
Paris

Dear François,

Since you left, life has gone on here, dull and without any surprises. The news you gave us regarding *Adèle*, *La Chienne* and *Le Petit Théâtre* gave us a boost. Dido is more active than I am. She has to deal with the household problems. As for myself, I keep falling asleep, but your message will wake me up.

I have started going out again. We went to see Woody Allen's *Love and Death*.[1] Our choice was motivated, I'm ashamed to say, by a reason which has nothing to do with motion pictures. The cinema in which the film is showing has no steps, and Greg[2] was able to push my wheelchair there without any difficulty. From now on, this particular feature is going to play a major part in our choices of entertainment. Dido and I enjoyed Woody Allen very much. His work is truly cinematic. We recognized in it something of a kindred spirit to the American primitives. I nearly forgot to mention another outing, this time in a screening room in a studio – *Cabaret*.[3] I am really the wrong person to comment on this film, as I knew Berlin at this period.

They are going to stretch me several times a day, by means of a machine inside which patients are placed like big hot dogs. I hope this ritual will bring closer the day when I am able to walk without a wheelchair.

Dido and I am glad to hear that Anne is happy with her husband. If you see her, tell her we are expecting her.

Through people returning from trips we have had sad news from France. It is mostly the high cost of living which frightens people. They are forgetting inflation. In general, this state of things is good for show business. Let's hope this will help *Adèle*. I have no doubts about the bright future of this film. The reviews I have read indicate an amazement which I think is more valuable than praise. Since you're getting praise as well, the future should be yours. Then there is your actress, who is intriguing and beautiful at the same time. It's a rare combination. Most often, beauty is a smoke-screen for vacancy – *oia kefale*. With these good words, I'll leave you. All our mutual friends in Hollywood join us in sending their fondest regards,

Jean Renoir

1 *Love and Death* (Woody Allen, 1975).
2 Greg Giacomo, a film student at UCLA who acted as nurse to Renoir through the 1970s.
3 *Cabaret* (Bob Fosse, 1972).

To Anne de Saint-Phalle [Ginette Doynel]¹ *3 December 1975*
Paris   *Beverly Hills*

Dear Anne,

You blame yourself for rarely writing to us. What should *I* say! I can only blame my health. I am in an unreal situation. All the medical examinations possible have been tried on me and nothing found. I have the liver of a baby, the spleen of an adolescent, the pancreas of a juvenile, the blood-pressure of a new-born and not a drop of cholesterol, and despite this I continue to be unable to walk and to be subject to dizzy spells which remove the power in my arms and legs as well as my desire to work. I think of you going through experiences similar to mine with a smile. The secret is that God has blessed you with astonishing energy. Me, he has forgotten.

[...]

Dido and I are delighted to read what's in your letters. They bring us a little of the atmosphere of Paris. Our regards to your family.

We send you all our love,

Jean Renoir

1 Ginette Doynel married Claude de Saint-Phalle in 1975.

To Ingrid Bergman   *29 December 1975*
Beverly Hills

Dear Ingrid,

Your Christmas wishes made Dido and I very happy. We thought a lot about you on that day, or rather that night, since Baby Jesus was born at midnight. Truffaut was here with us and we talked a lot about you. If it is true that thoughts do fly, then you must have bumped into us very often, because I know you think about us just as we think about you. Happy New Year and good health to you, Ruth, and your family.

Much love,

Jean Renoir

1976

To François Truffaut

19 February 1976
Beverly Hills

Dear François,

This dinner must have been excellent. Nothing is more exquisite than sharing a great meal. By themselves the dinner guests can transform an indifferent meal into a feast for the senses. As in the case of any work of art, this gathering of palates must have only achieved its full importance when you were polishing it off.

These few lines are only meant to reiterate our fond feelings for you.

Dido and I are impatiently waiting for the screening of *L'Argent de Poche*.[1]

Let me tell you once more how much we loved *Adèle*. It is a picture to which the audience must surrender.

Love from both of us,

Jean Renoir

1 *L'Argent de Poche (Small Change,* 1976).

To François Truffaut
Paris

22 March 1976
Beverly Hills

About the Grand Prix du Cinéma Français awarded to Francis Truffaut on 17 March 1976.

Dear François,

Once more you have done honour to the French Cinema. I regret deeply that I was not by your side to participate in the actual unfolding of this tribute. Either far or near, all those who contribute to the glory of our profession are with you. As well as all those devoted to you – they grow in numbers each day.

[Jean]

To Simone Signoret

Dear Simone,

Dido and I have just seen *L'Armée des Ombres*.[1] We were able to borrow a 16mm copy and screened it at our Beverly Hills home[2] quite alone except for two very close friends who had already seen the film. We were enraptured. I can't speak for our friends. We were struck by the impression it made on us. What a masterpiece! Not to mention how well the actors performed. One had the impression of penetrating into part of their true nature. As for you, you are extraordinary. At the end of the screening Dido was streaming with tears. As for me, I am trying to order my thoughts. I knew that you were a great performer, or rather a great actress. But at that moment, you bowled me over.

All our love,

[Jean]

1 *L'Armée des Ombres* (*The Army of the Shadows*) was Jean-Pierre Melville's 1969 adaptation of Joseph Kessel's book about the French Resistance. Renoir had been approached to make a film version immediately after the Liberation of France, but had to decline the offer.
2 A 16mm projector was installed at Leona Drive, and Renoir would regularly watch his own films and those of others brought to him.

To François Truffaut

Paris

Dear François,

L'Argent de Poche has crashed through the barrier. It is a triumph for the French cinema. With *L'Argent de Poche*, you are opening the door for French producers, who I hope will know how to take advantage of your success. All the Americans I have talked to are unanimous: they love your film.

Here, we think a lot about you and count the days that bring us closer. Leona Drive has not changed. I keep on moving around on wheels. It's not so bad any more. We can't wait to see your next film, I was going to say: your next child.

Love from Dido and I,

Jean

To Charles Chaplin [*Original in English*]   *24 December 1976*
Beverly Hills

Dear Charlie,

Every Christmas time Dido and I as a gift to ourselves, plan a visit to the Chaplins. And each year something happens which jeopardizes our project. We console ourselves with the showing of one of your pictures.

This year it is going to be just the same. My old war-wound decided to interfere and to forbid me to trespass the limits established by my wheelchair.

This little note does not mean very much. We love you and Oona and we feel close to you in spite of the distance.

With our best wishes,
Jean Renoir

To Rumer Godden [*Original in English*]   *30 December 1976*
Beverly Hills

Dear Rumer,

Perhaps it is the influence of Christmas which urges us to get in touch with you. We realize how much you weigh in our life. Fortunately, I own a 16mm print of *The River*. We projected it and the show enchanted us. After the word 'the end' appeared on the screen we remained silent for a long time. Through the images we had been close to you. The distance had disappeared. We did not want to break the magic spell. Somebody suddenly opened the door and turned on a light. And we went back to our present life.

Dear Rumer, Dido and I have no need of a film projection to be with you. We love you and that makes the bridge between LA and London.

With our sincere wishes. Happy New Year.
Jean Renoir

1977

To François Truffaut   *24 January 1977*
Paris   *Beverly Hills*

Dear François,
   We read in the papers that your birthday is 6 February. May this date, as well as all other dates in the calendar, be beneficial to you.
   6 February is also our wedding anniversary.
   With all our love,
   Jean Renoir

Dear François, We have just found your '*Small Change*'[1] on the table in our living-room. What a lovely surprise. Thank you. Dido.

1 English title of Truffaut's *L'Argent de Poche*. Could this possibly be a reference to some 'small change' that Truffaut left behind?

To Herman G. Weinberg[1]   *5 February 1977*
                                              Beverly Hills

Dear Herman,
   I have received your magnificent book on Eric [sic] Von Stroheim.[2] Dido and I have not finished reading it yet, but we are delighted. You know how much I worship this exceptional film-maker. He was the high priest of a cult largely unknown to the public, and kept alive only by a few disciples. You have now become the leader of this cult.
   Stroheim's prominence doesn't lie only in the power of his images, nor does it come from the merciless rhythm propelling the story and the anguish it stirs in us. It stems from a passion for the grandiose; a grandiose beyond bad taste. It is a climate that might seem harsh at first, but once one gets used to it, it becomes the Garden of Eden.
   Dear Herman, your book will help us penetrate this paradise. Congratulations. Our kind regards to Gretchen.[3]
   Jean Renoir

1 Herman G. Weinberg (d.1983), distinguished film historian, whose collected writings were published in *Saint Cinema: Writings 1929–1970.*
2 Weinberg had published at least three major works on Von Stroheim: *The Complete Greed* (1972), *The Complete Wedding March* (1975), and *Stroheim: A Pictorial Record of His Nine Films* (1975).
3 Weinberg's daughter.

To François Truffaut
Paris

29 April 1977
Beverly Hills

Dear François,

Dido and I deeply regret we were not able to attend the opening of your picture. Our thoughts are with you, and we wish a long and brilliant career to this *Man Who Loved Women.*[1]

With our love,
[Jean Renoir]

1 *L'Homme qui Aimait les Femmes* (*The Man Who Loved Women*) (François Truffaut, 1977).

To Ingrid Bergman

3 June 1977
Beverly Hills

Dear Ingrid,

Dido and I share your pain at Roberto's death.[1] We are convinced that your union was, and still is, productive. Two mountain-tops cannot be brought together without causing some damage. It's like attempting to kill a fire with gasoline. For you, the experience resulted in magnificent successes, which enriched the arts of theatre and cinema. It allowed you to reveal the most secret recesses of your soul. Thank you, dear Ingrid, for being so generous to your audience. We bid an emotional farewell to the man who stood faithfully by your side during many trying years. Convey our deepest sympathy to your children.

Love from both of us,
Jean Renoir

1 Roberto Rossellini died on 3 June 1977.

To Anne de Saint-Phalle
Paris

17 June 1977
Beverly Hills

Dear Anne,

It took all your benevolent devotion to hold on and manage the Compagnie Jean Renoir, as well as my personal concerns. It could not last forever. I feel fortunate enough that you will keep me under your protective wings until 31 December of this year. What are you planning to do to secure new leadership for our business? How can we ever replace the tender care you bestowed on our lives?

Dido and I are overcome by sadness at losing such a vital tie with the past.

We won't have many occasions to kiss you any more. And with this brief letter we want to express our deep sense of loss.

Convey our best regards to Claude de Saint-Phalle.

Our love to both of you,

Jean Renoir

To François Truffaut
Paris

12 September 1977
Beverly Hills

Dear François,

Time is passing, and the hope of making a trip to Paris is waning slowly in my mind. So I pray to Saint Jean, my patron saint, to bring you here. Like Americans say: *I miss you.*[1]

The French who visit us here are complaining about the changes Paris is undergoing. Maybe they are forgetting that our native city has lived through worse times. This is difficult to digest.

Dido is dying to see you as well as the girls. We have just seen ours, Anne,[2] who turned seventeen yesterday.

Love from both of us.

Jean Renoir

1 Originally in French: *vous me manquez.*
2 The Renoirs' grand-daughter.

To Georges Simenon

Dear Georges,

I beat you by several years in having my prostate removed. Nothing to boast about really. From the way the doctors were talking about this operation, I was expecting to regain a second youth. Nothing of the sort. With or without prostate, I'm still an old invalid. I don't go out any more, and as a result, Dido is turning into a homebody. Fortunately we still have friends to brighten our retirement. On frequent occasions these friends bring me 16mm copies of their films and I watch them at home.

I have also discovered an idol whose cult is even more demanding than literature or cinema: story-telling. I have produced two books during these past years. I hesitated a lot before launching into this new form of activity, mostly because of you. When I look at the collection of your books you had sent me, I feel inadequate. They fill a whole shelf in my library, and each one is a masterpiece. But after thinking about it, I decided that masterpieces are expressly created to inspire other writers.

As a result of reading your letters, we would really like to meet Teresa.[1] You are fortunate. Working in collaboration with someone you love is a piece of paradise on earth.

May you have a Merry Christmas with Teresa. I know mine will be, thanks to Dido. Happy New Year.

Love from both of us.

Jean Renoir

1 Teresa Sburelin, formerly maid to Georges Simenon, who became his last partner.

To Charles Chaplin [*Original in English*]

Dear Oona, dear Charlie,

Fortunately you made films and every frame of your films brings us a thousand messages of affection. We are happy to play our part in this symphony of love.

Merry Christmas,

Happy New Year,

Jean & Dido

To Oona Chaplin [*Original in English*]   *28 December 1977*
                                                  Beverly Hills

Dear Oona,

Dido and I forget that Charlie was the genius of the century.[1] We think only of the deep sorrow which is ours. For you the trial must be unbearable. Please, dear Oona, accept our sincerest condolences.

Jean Renoir

1 Charles Chaplin died on 25 December 1977.

1978

To Rumer Godden

Dear Rumer,

We have not written very often to give you any news, and we won't pretend we are filling the gap with this short note, which is merely intended to convey our admiration for the work you are doing.

In a few words: Dido and I are still living in Beverly Hills, in the house you know. The furniture is the same. The pets and help have changed. The pets have died. Dogs demand too much attention, even work. As for Minou, the cat, she just disappeared one night and never came back. Dido was really upset by this incident, but it would be difficult for her to replace Minou. The household now includes Greg, a fine boy who is at the same time nurse and general help, and Zeneida,[1] an outstanding caretaker. We also have new friends. They are few in number, but of such quality. I'll conclude this list by telling you that we love you from the bottom of our hearts.

Much love,

Jean Renoir

---

1 Zeneida, domestic help to the Renoirs in the 1970s.

To François Truffaut

Dear François

This morning the symbolic rites took place of putting the last draft of *L'Assassinat*[1] in the post. If you are interested, you could ask Anne de Saint-Phalle to give you a copy. I would not want you to spend too much time taking pleasure in making a friend happy.

It took me a long time to finish this work. It's still my bloody health. It must be pretty bad if it keeps me from letting you hear from me for so long. It is not that what I have to say is of great interest, but it is always a mistake to stay out of touch for too long with friends, spouses, or associates. With you it doesn't matter as much. You sow heroes and heroines in your path, and they spring up on the screens they conquer.

Speaking of conquest, we congratulate Laura on her recovery. As for Eva,[2] she doesn't need encouragement. I can still imagine her running like a rabbit, or rather like a doe. We send them our love and tenderness, and to you too.

Jean Renoir

1 Original title for *Le Crime de l'Anglais*, published by Flammarion in 1979.
2 Truffaut's daughters.

To Anne de Sainte-Phalle   *25 February 1978*
Paris   *Beverly Hills*

Dear Anne,

We will reply to your letter number 85. We have not received numbers 83 and 84. What is most surprising, we have not received my book. I am beginning to think that *Le Coeur à l'Aise*[1] will never reach me. We have had very favourable reactions up to now, among them an admirable letter from Georges Simenon. Dido and I had tears in our eyes. He loves the book and my work. Of course, part of it is due to his great friendship, but even taking that into account the letter is a rare eulogy.

[...]

I take back my praise of Flammarion. What you tell me about the bad publicity at the launch makes me sad, for a book badly launched has little hope of pulling through.

We are happy that *L'Assassinat* pleased you. I would like a more complete account from you. As for the question of length, I could, by adding one or two new bits, bring it up to the content of a normal-sized book, but all that would take time.

TRANSLATION: I would like you to give me some suggestions about the translation. Maybe Flammarion has an agent in America who looks after this matter. I would very much like to go back to Norman Denny.[2]

[...]

We are coming out of a rainy spell. You would think we were in the tropics. The roads were blocked by landslides. There was snow, and there were even deaths. Things seem to have returned to normal. You have the elections, we have the rain. Unfortunately, the elections are just as harmful as the floods. How wonderful it will be to talk about all this with Claude and you! During your trip I will close up shop and give Paulo[3] a vacation.

    We send you all our love,
    Jean Renoir

1 *Le Coeur à l'Aise*, the first of a trio of short novels written by Renoir (through dictation) in his last years. It was published by Flammarion in 1978. Possible translation: *The Heart at Ease*.

2 Translator of *The Notebooks of Captain Georges* and *My Life and My Films*.

3 Paulo Barzman, son of blacklisted screenwriter Ben Barzman, was secretary to Renoir in the late 1970s.

To Jean Renoir
Beverly Hills

3 *March 1978*
[*Paris*]

My dear friends,

    You are with me constantly these days; I am reading *Le Coeur à L'Aise* for the third time, rereading *L'Assassinat*, and discussing both with Anne de Saint-Phalle, Thérèse, Claude Beylie, etc.

    Everyone who has read *Le Coeur à l'Aise* finds it enchanting, and moving — several good articles about it have already appeared here and there. Thérèse will send you things as they come out.

    With regard to *L'Assassinat*, I think it's terrific — the last changes you made were excellent. I had some fun counting up the number of words in it; there are 25,000. That is to say, it is absolutely suitable for publication as is — all the more so, in fact, because Flammarion puts out certain books in a format a little smaller than the one used for *Le Coeur à l'Aise*. I do think, though, that it's a good idea for Anne de Saint-Phalle to wait a bit before submitting it to their editors.

    What I would very much like to know now is this: What are you concentrating on at present? What new project do you have in progress?

    As for me, I'm finishing *La Chambre Verte*[1] — it's going to open at the Biarritz Cinema on 5 April. I'm also preparing a new 'Antoine Doinel' film with Jean-Pierre Léaud, which will start shooting in June. it's called *L'Amour en Fuite*.[2] I am looking forward to visiting you, as always, the day after we crank up the camera for our last shot — which is to say, just in time for Bastille Day!

    Jeanne Moreau is back in Paris, preparing various film projects, especially the one she's planning about her adolescence. She hasn't split up with Friedkin,[3] but I get the feeling she's putting a little distance between them . . . She goes to visit the Countess[4] from time to time.

Nothing new in France . . . just politics – too much politics – and of course, the crisis in cinema that's been going on since . . . 1895!

Thanks to Ginette Auribeau and Patrice Délafaux, a very real bridge is being built between Los Angeles and Paris – a means of communication that's more valuable than Concorde.

I hope both of you are enjoying good health, and are comfortable with the comings and goings of your ever-changing entourage.

I send you a kiss with all my affection,

Yours,

François [Truffaut]

PS. My daughters are fine, they are in Italy with their *boys friends* [sic].

1 *La Chambre Verte* (*The Green Room*, 1978).
2 *L'Amour en Fuite* (*Love on the Run* 1978), the final chapter in the Antoine Doinel cycle.
3 William Friedkin (b.1939), director, to whom Jeanne Moreau was married in the mid-1970s.
4 Anne de Saint-Phalle.

To François Truffaut

Paris

7 March 1978

Beverly Hills

Dear François,

We have finally seen *Close Encounters*.[1] It is a very good film, and I regret it was not made in France. This type of popular science would be most appropriate for the compatriots of Jules Verne and Méliès.[2] Both men were Montgolfier's[3] rightful heirs. You are excellent in it, because you're not quite real. There is more than a grain of eccentricity in this adventure. The author is a poet. In the South of France one would say he is a bit *fada*. He brings to mind the exact meaning of this word in Provence: the village *fada* is the one possessed by the fairies.

These fairies who reside with you have agreed to let themselves be briefly borrowed by the author of the film in question.

Love from Dido and I.

Jean Renoir

1 *Close Encounters of the Third Kind* (Steven Spielberg, 1977), in which Truffaut played the part of a French UFO expert.
2 Georges Méliès (1861–1938), magician turned pioneer film-maker who exploited the tricks of cinema to the full. His classic fantasy films include *Le Voyage Dans la Lune* (1902).
3 The Montgolfier brothers were pioneers in ballooning.

To Jean Renoir   *7 March 1978*
Beverly Hills   *Paris*

My dear friends,

On television last night, several writers were talking about their books, and one young man had high praise for *Le Coeur à L'Aise*. Also there among the guests was a ninety-year-old writer, Marcel Jouhandeau. He asked the show's moderator: 'How old is Jean Renoir?' The host answered: 'He's eighty-three.' To which Jouhandeau replied: 'Only eighty-three? He's just a kid!'

Today I'm sending you the article I did for *Le Nouvel Observateur*. I hope you won't be too shocked when you see that, to describe your present life on Leona Drive, I have employed certain expressions that I had already used for the little booklet in Lyon.[1] It proved difficult, you see, to write about the same thing without using the same words. I very much enjoyed choosing the quotations from *Le Coeur à l'Aise* for this article – I just wish I could have quoted the entire book!

I appeared on a television show about *Close Encounters of the Third Kind*, and the last thing I spoke about was *Le Coeur à l'Aise*, showing the book itself on camera. In my enthusiasm, however, I didn't notice that I was holding the book upside down, so millions of viewers had to bend over and look at the TV screen upside-down to be able to read the title. I don't have to tell you that my daughters were on the floor laughing about this.

Other than that, not much to report. Press screenings for *La Chambre Verte* start next week, which is making me ill, because I've taken the greatest possible care with this film and now it's out of my hands. I'm just waiting for it to open to the public, which is scheduled for 5 April. I think you would agree with me that, in choosing this profession, one must accept the fact that one will be judged by others – but those who sit in judgement should at least buy a ticket!

I hope Todd McCarthy[2] is still coming to visit you, in addition to your other old friends, and that you are having some pleasant screenings at home. Did you replace Minou? I know I will find out the answers to all my questions in July, but if you were to drop me a note from time to time to let me know how you are, it would make me extremely happy.

I think of you constantly and send you all my love and affection.

François [Truffaut]

---

1 Probably a reference to *Premier Plan*, a series of books on cinema published in Lyon.
2 Chief film critic on *Variety*, who at this time took 16mm prints up to the Renoir house for their screenings.

To François Truffaut
Paris

16 *March 1978*
Beverly Hills

Dear François,

I was so entertained by your letter that I laughed aloud while reading it again. Thank you.

I feel very privileged indeed. My parents were very good people and nature blessed me with a robust constitution. And now, as I near the end of the journey, here you are.

There is something magical about our relationship.

Dido and I send our love to you and to the girls, at the same time.

Jean Renoir

To Georges Simenon

17 *March 1978*
Beverly Hills

Dear Georges,

I find it hard to express the deep emotion your letter has stirred in me. It only confirms a fact we both know well: our friendship, which is stronger than the distances between continents, tender like the memory of a love-affair. I love you, Georges, and you love me.

I have been asking a lot from God, but it has not been possible for me to maintain equality between all my prayers. When I think of our destiny as human beings, there is always one item that keeps bouncing to the top. It's our friendship for each other.

Dido and I send all our deepest love.

Jean Renoir

To François Truffaut   29 *March 1978*
Paris   *Beverly Hills*

Dear François,
   I have just read the interview Danièle Heymann and Catherine Laporte
did with you. You come off so well that I could not resist the pleasure of
telling you directly. These two young women have been able to give an
impression of the overall optimism that emanates from your films without affecting what is essential: allowing the readers to know you better.
They know how to step back, and do not forget you are the 'client'.
   I also cherish this interview for other reasons: it showed me that the
French cinema was not killed by machine-guns. It will not only satisfy the
curiosity of aficionados, but it might inspire French film-makers to cultivate a quality essential for the profession: courage. You describe things
and refer to facts as they are. It's most enjoyable.
   Dido and I are dying to see *La Chambre Verte*. Until then, we send you
our love.
   Jean Renoir

To François Truffaut   6 *April 1978*
Paris   *Beverly Hills*

Dear François,
   Dido and I thought about you lovingly when *La Chambre Verte* was
released. Our wishes won't change the destiny of your picture, which we
hope will be brilliant. They are just a way to express our friendship.
   Much love,
   Jean Renoir

To François Truffaut   26 *May 1978*
Paris   *Beverly Hills*

Dear François,
   Such a great letter! As your letters always are. It seems you always have
something to say.
   I am deeply moved by your taking the time to sort out the articles on
Le Coeur à l'Aise. However, what strikes me once more is the power of
your creativity. Dido and I are happy that it is devoted to exciting
subjects. For a long time I believed that subjects did not matter. Well, I

was wrong. The best-told tales may run into difficulties if they are not supported by a larger theme. I am delighted by everything I hear about *La Chambre Verte* . . . This is certainly a great theme.

The truth is that something is happening in the heads of audiences. First of all, they are not the same people, they have matured and grown older. The whole world follows the path of evolution, including the world of man.

We have received *Tant que Je Suis Vivant* and *Un Oiseau Pour le Chat*.

I really like your title *L'Amour en Fuite*. It has an eighteenth-century flavour which touches me particularly.

How are the girls? Remind them of us.

We are eagerly waiting for 14 July. Our gathering is worthy of Bastille Day. You must have enjoyed the Colombe d'Or. Are the owners of that place still alive?

Warmest regards from Dido and I,

Jean Renoir

To Anne de Saint-Phalle
Paris

7 June 1978
Beverly Hills

Dear Anne,

I am replying to your letter No 98 of 25 May. The news that you are postponing your trip to Beverly Hills is sad. But the reason is compelling enough, and we congratulate Anne Jouve[1] on her wedding. We would have enjoyed attending the ceremony and the festivities following it. Unfortunately, it appears the problems I have with my leg will last for ever. This limb has become an appendage which keeps me nailed to the ground. The first victim of this state of affairs is *Geneviève*.[2] I hope that the end of next week will see the completion of the first draft. My leg is not the only worry: my energy level is rather low. Once I get going, work is easy enough. It's getting started which I find difficult. To compensate for these troubles, I hope my novel has more substance than what I have done until now, and that I am getting closer to the writing style of my pictures.

A happier note is brightening this weekend: Paulo is back on form, and he can resume his work with me.

LE COEUR A L'AISE: Thank you for the review. We have received several others. All very good. It doesn't mean the audience will follow the critics' opinions.

The failure of your negotiations with the English-language publishers does not surprise me, even though the English have always been favourable towards me. If the sale of *Le Coeur à l'Aise* proves to be difficult, I won't lose hope. I am used to delayed successes.

L'ASSASSINAT: *Geneviève* has postponed my work on *L'Assassinat*. I found some short stories that could be included. I'd rather have *L'Assassinat* published in the format you know, and that Flammarion be satisfied with it as it is. Later, we could submit *Geneviève* to them.

Thank you for forwarding me the messages from Charles Durand-Ruel. The absurdity of this mix-up is obvious.

I'll end this letter in the hope of seeing you in the not-too-distant future. Give our regrets to Claude.

Much love,
Jean Renoir

PS: Distances make it difficult for us to choose a wedding present for Anne. Once more we ask you to take care of it. We count on your own good judgement.

1 Grand-daughter of Anne de Saint-Phalle, and god-daughter of the Renoirs.
2 *Geneviève* was the last of Renoir's novels, published by Flammarion in 1979.

To François Truffaut
Paris

11 August 1978
Beverly Hills

Dear François,

I am sending you this note for no practical purpose. You know how fond I am of you, and I know how fond you are of me. I am repeating it aloud because I enjoy it. It is like a brief farewell on a station platform. All that is missing is the smell of soot from Victoria Station.

You don't need anybody to help you transport your friends into a world whose citizens are all genuine knights. The New Wave gathers together its barons at a round table.

Dido and I send our love.
Jean Renoir

1979

Jean Renoir dies at his home in Beverly Hills on 12 February. Four days later a funeral mass is held at the Church of the Good Shepherd on Santa Monica Boulevard. Early in March, his body is taken to France, and he is buried in the same grave in Essoyes as his father and brother Pierre.

Dido Renoir continues to live at Leona Drive until her death on 7 May 1990. She is cremated and her ashes placed in Jean's grave.

32 Henri Cartier-Bresson (second from right) as a seminarist in *Une Partie de Campagne* (1936). Behind him on the left is Pierre Lestringuez.

A Memoir by Henri Cartier-Bresson

After leaving Mexico in 1934, I thought I would never take photographs again – I wanted to make movies. I asked both Pabst and Luis Buñuel, but neither needed anybody to work with them. Then I met Jean Renoir, and he agreed to take me as a second assistant on his next film, which was *La Vie est à Nous*. This loose film of sketches was made for the Communist Party, and it has to be seen in the political perspective of its time. Life had changed dramatically after World War One, and the shadow of Fascism – Hitler, Mussolini and Franco – was very close. During the making of this film I met Jacques Becker, and we worked together on Jean's next film, *Une Partie de Campagne*, he as first assistant, me as second. The producer was Pierre Braunberger, who at the end of the film gave us each a wallet as a present. We said, 'Thanks', but next time please put a little something in it! There was no money, but we enjoyed working together so much it didn't matter. It was important for Jean to have a whole network of friends, so that film-making became the pleasure of being part of a community with the same aspirations.

On this film, Jean had immense problems with bad weather. While we were shooting on the banks of the river, two kids were playing around us, who were two grandsons: Alain Renoir and Jean-Pierre Cézanne. I remember Visconti came and watched the shooting, but he remained very silent and didn't really participate. Jean always wanted his assistants to feel what it was like on the other side of the camera, and I was given the role of a seminarist under the guidance of a priest, played by Pierre Lestringuez. I walked along with Georges Bataille, the husband of Sylvie Bataille, who was the heroine of the film, and as she was on the swing I had to look across with amazement at her petticoats!

The third film I worked on with Jean was *La Règle du Jeu*, which for me is one of the summits of his art and a premonition of everything that was to happen in the world. Again I played a tiny role for a second, when I was supposed to be an English butler. As I had made a living in Africa after my military service by shooting game, Jean put me in charge of the hunt scene, along with Corteggiani, who was a specialist in firearms. It was not very easy, because Dalio and the other actors had no idea how to hold a gun, and I had to shoot the rabbits while they were pretending!

None of us who worked with Jean had any special training. It was more like in the Renaissance, a kind of initiation to become a film director. I knew very soon, as did Jean, that I would never be a movie director, and I went on to do documentary films, which for me was closer to *reportage*. As an assistant to Jean, you did a bit of everything. First you would work on the screenplay, and writing the dialogue was a bit like a jam-session, everybody throwing in their words. Jean was only happy with the dialogue if he knew which actor was playing the role. Sometimes he even changed some words in the morning before shooting, which was at times a problem. And if he didn't like an actor, it could be very difficult. On *La Règle du Jeu*, André Zwoboda was first assistant and I was second. It was a great responsibility, as Jean was one of the main actors in the film, and moreover various upheavals were taking place in his private life.

To be Jean's assistant was also psychological work, because he could get very discouraged during the preparations of a film. We would say, 'Why don't we call Pierre Lestringuez to come over and have a drink of Beaujolais,' or, 'Let's play "Ring"', throwing a rubber ring to each other. We had to judge when it was the right time, either some Beaujolais or not too much Beaujolais! Like many a genius, he had his weaknesses, and we suffered along with him when things went badly. He needed all sorts of refreshment, but it was mainly being among friends. Gaston Modot used to sing beautiful songs, sentimental songs of the street, and Jean loved to listen to them. Of course this way of preparing a film is very unusual, but it helped keep the wealth of Jean's inspiration.

In those days, the cameraman on a film was really the top job, but with Jean, though he respected the work of everybody, the aim was not beautiful lighting but simplicity. Jean showed the utmost politeness towards the actors. There was a rule that the assistant was never to tell the actor what scene would be filmed next. They always had to think that their big moment was coming up! On the set, Jean would say to the actor, 'Oh! wonderful, wonderful, wonderful!' But that might even have meant it was lousy. Then he would say, 'Why don't you try something like this?' Jean loathed actors who came from schools. He told me the best actors were those who came from the music hall, because straightaway they had to seize the audience's attention. That's why he adored people like Carette, Jane Marken, Brunius, Gaston Modot and so on.

Carette was a wonderful man, whose wife did not approve of him drinking. I remember during *La Règle du Jeu*, the owner of the hotel where we staying in Sologne was Madame Rat, who was used to dealing with very respectable hunting gentlemen. She went up to Jean in a huff and said. 'Well, I've never been asked such a thing before!' Jean wanted to know what was the matter, and she replied, 'Monsieur Carette has asked me to put two Perniflards in the loo, so his wife won't see them!' (Perniflard was the slang name for a Pastis aperitif.) She was very shocked, but Jean just burst out laughing.

I think *La Règle du Jeu* was badly received because the upper class felt attacked, and people could not decide whether the film was a comedy or a tragedy. Jean was so upset that he went to Italy, and both Becker and I told him this was not the proper thing to do. We said to him, go to America and do a film, but come back, you must keep your roots. A Beaujolais is essential for you! But if the financial disaster of the film affected Jean so much, I think its influence on the new generation, Truffaut and all the others who adored it, in a way paid him back.

In the early days I would visit him at Marlotte, where I mainly remember seeing frames without his father's paintings, because he had sold so many of them to make *Nana*. Then he had a number of apartments in Paris, when he was living with Marguerite, his editor. At one time he stayed on rue de Rome, with the railway lines of the Gare St Lazare just across the street. Compared to places like that, avenue Frochot was very secluded, but he never lived in luxury. In the next apartment lived his brother Pierre, and they were very close, though totally different. He had nothing of Jean's explosive quality. Coco, his younger brother, was very sweet, but less flamboyant than his brothers, who had something majestic about them.

When I saw Jean after the war in Hollywood, I remember most the portrait of him as a hunter painted by his father hanging on the wall. He seemed to me like an exile, and though he was very comfortable, his health was often bad. But Dido took extremely good care of him, and I met there Gabrielle, who had been his father's model, who cooked some very good meals. He spoke a lot about Essoyes, where he had grown up, and which he still felt was his own place.

He was a very warm man, very cultured, but he loathed pretentious intellectuals. You simply had to be cultured to work with him, by which I mean a fundamental culture, like his father, of whom he spoke a lot. Jean had an intelligence about everything, in the way that an animal is intelligent, and not cerebral. He was not a specialist of anything except generosity, and life for him always came first. I owe him a great deal.

Henri Cartier-Bresson
June 1993

Filmography

All films directed by Jean Renoir unless otherwise stated

1924
Catherine (Une Vie sans Joie)
Production Company: Films Jean Renoir
Distribution: Pierre Braunberger
Director: Albert Dieudonné
Screenplay: Jean Renoir
Photography: Jean Bachelet, Alphonse Gibory
Cast: Catherine Hessling (*Catherine Ferrand*), Albert Dieudonné (*M. Mallet*), Eugénie Naud (*Madame Laisné*), Louis Gauthier (*Georges Mallet*), Maud Richard (*Madame Mallet*), Pierre Philippe (*Adolphe*), Pierre Champagne (*the Mallets' son*)
France; 1800 metres; 80 mins(?)[1]

La Fille de l'Eau (Whirlpool of Fate)
Production Company: Films Jean Renoir/Maurice Touzé/Studio Films
Distribution: Maurice Rouhier, (later) Pierre Braunberger
Screenplay: Pierre Lestringuez
Photography: Jean Bachelet, Alphonse Gibory
Production Design: Jean Renoir
Cast: Catherine Hessling (*Virginia*), Pierre Philippe (*Uncle Jeff*), Pierre Champagne (*Justin Crépoix*), Harold Lewingston (*Georges Raynal*), Maurice Touzé (*Ferret*)
France; 1700 metres; 75 mins(?)

1926
Nana
Production Company: Films Jean Renoir
Distribution: Aubert-Pierre Braunberger
Screenplay: Pierre Lestringuez. From the novel by Emile Zola.
Photography: Edmund Corwin, Jean Bachelet

---

[1] Since the projection speeds of silent films vary according to year and country, these durations are necessarily very approximate.

Production Design: Claude Autant-Lara
Cast: Catherine Hessling (*Nana*), Werner Krauss (*Count Muffat*), Jean Angelo (*Count de Vandeuvres*), Valeska Gert (*Zoé*), Pierre Philippe (*Bordenave*), Pierre Champagne (*La Faloise*), Raymond Guérin-Catelain (*Georges Hugon*), Claude Moore/Claude Autant-Lara (*Fauchery*), Andre Cerf ('*Le Tigre*')
France; 2700 metres; 120 mins(?)

1927
Charleston (*Sur un Air de Charleston*)
Production Company/Distribution: Néo-Film (Pierre Braunberger)
Screenplay: Pierre Lestringuez, from an idea by André Cerf
Photography: Jean Bachelet
Cast: Catherine Hessling (*The Dancer*), Johnny Huggins (*The Explorer*), André Cerf (*The Monkey*), Pierre Braunberger, Jean Renoir, Pierre Lestringuez, André Cerf (*Four Angels*)
France; 600 metres; 20 mins(?)

Marquitta
Production Company: Artistes Réunis (Films Jean Renoir)
Distribution: Jean de Merly
Screenplay: Pierre Lestringuez, Jean Renoir
Photography: Jean Bachelet, Raymond Agnel
Production Design: Robert-Jules Garnier
Cast: Marie-Louise Iribe (*Marquitta*), Jean Angelo (*Prince Vlasco*), Henri Debain (*The Chamberlain, Count Dimitrieff*), Lucien Mancini (*The Step-Father*), Pierre Philippe (*Casino Owner*), Pierre Champagne (*Taxi Driver*)
France; 2400 metres; 100 mins(?)

La P'tite Lili
Production Company/Distribution: Néo-Film (Pierre Braunberger)
Director/Screenplay: Alberto Cavalcanti. From a song by Louis Benech
Photography: Jimmy Rogers
Production Design: Erik Aaes
Music: Darius Milhaud (1930 version)
Editor: Marguerite (Renoir)
Cast: Catherine Hessling (*La P'Tite Lili*), Jean Renoir (*The Pimp*), Guy Ferrand (*The Singer*), Roland Caillaux (*The Concierge*), Jean Storm (*The Minister*), Dido Freire (*The Little Cousin*)
France; 15 mins

1928
La Petite Marchande d'Allumettes (*The Little Match Girl*)
Distribution: SOFAR

Producers: Jean Renoir, Jean Tédesco
Screenplay: Jean Renoir. From stories by Hans Christian Andersen
Photography: Jean Bachelet
Production Design: Erik Aaes
Cast: Catherine Hessling (*Karen*), Jean Storm (*Young Man/Wooden Soldier*),
Manuel Raaby (*Policeman/Death*), Amy Wells/Aimée Tédesco (*Mechanical Doll*)
France; 29 mins (with synchronized music arranged by Manuel Rosenthal)

Tire au Flanc
Production Company: Néo-Film (Pierre Braunberger)
Distribution: Armor-Film
Screenplay: Jean Renoir, André Cerf, Claude Heymann. From the play by André
Mouézy-Eon, A Sylvane
Photography: Jean Bachelet
Production Design: Erik Aaes
Cast: Georges Pomiès (*Jean Dubois d'Ombelles*), Michel Simon (*Joseph*), Fridette
Faton (*Georgette*), Félix Oudart (*Colonel Brochard*), Jean Storm (*Lieutenant
Daumel*), Kinny Dorlay (*Lily*), Maryanne (*Madame Blandin*), Zellas (*Muflot*),
Jeanne Helbling (*Solange*), Catherine Hessling (*Teacher*)
France; 2200 metres; 95 mins(?)

Le Tournoi (*Le Tournoi dans la Cité*)
Production Company: Société des Films Historiques
Distribution: Jean de Merly, Fernand Weil
Screenplay: Henry Dupuy-Mazuel, André Jaeger-Schmidt
Photography: Marcel Lucien, Maurice Desfassiaux
Production Design: Robert Mallet-Stevens
Editor: André Cerf
Cast: Also Nadi (*François de Baynes*), Jackie Monnier (*Isabelle Ginori*), Enrique
Rivero (*Henri de Rogier*), Blanche Bernis (*Catherine de Médici*), Suzanne Desprès
(*Countess de Baynes*), Manuel Raaby (*Count Ginori*)
France; 2635 metres; 120 mins(?)

1929
Le Bled
Production Company: Société des Films Historiques
Distribution: Mappemonde Films
Screenplay: Henry Dupuy-Mazuel, André Jaeger-Schmidt
Photography: Marcel Lucien, Léon Morizet
Production Design: William Aguet
Editor: Marguerite (Renoir)
Cast: Jackie Monnier (*Claude Duvernet*), Enrique Rivero (*Pierre Hoffer*), Diana
Hart (*Diane Duvernet*), Manuel Raaby (*Manuel Duvernet*), Alexandre

Arquillière (*Christian Hoffer*)
France; 2400 metres; 100 mins(?)

Le Petit Chaperon Rouge (*Little Red Riding Hood*)
Producer: Jean Renoir
Director: Alberto Cavalcanti
Screenplay: Jean Renoir, Albert Cavalcanti. From the story by Charles Perrault
Photography: Marcel Lucien, René Ribault
Music: Maurice Jaubert
Editor: Marguerite (Renoir)
Cast: Catherine Hessling (*Little Red Riding Hood*), Jean Renoir (*The Wolf*),
André Cerf (*The Notary*), Pierre Prévert (*A Little Girl*), Pablo Quevado (*The
Young Man*), Marcel La Montagne (*A Farmer*), Odette Talazac (*The Farmer's
Wife*), William Aguet (*An Old Englishwoman*), Amy Wells (*The Newspaper
Seller*)
France; 60 mins

1930
Die Jagd Nach dem Gluck (*La Chasse au Bonheur*)
Production: Comenius Film GmbH
Distribution: Deutscher Werkfilm GmbH
Directors: Rochus Gliese, Carl Koch
Screenplay: Lotte Reiniger, Carl Koch. From an idea by Alex Trasser
Photography: Fritz Arno Wagner
Shadow Theatre Effects: Lotte Reiniger
Music: Théo Mackeben
Cast: Catherine Hessling (*Aimée*), Jean Renoir (*Robert, a Businessman*),
Alexander Murski (*Marquand, a Pedlar*), Berthold Bartosch (*Mario*), Amy Wells
(*Jeanne*)
Germany; duration unknown[1]

1931
On Purge Bébé
Production Company/Distribution: Braunberger-Richebé
Production Manager: Charles David
Screenplay: Jean Renoir. From the play by Georges Feydeau
Photography: Théodore Sparkuhl, Roger Hubert
Production Design: Gabriel Scognamillo
Music: Paul Misraki
Sound: D. F. Scanlon

[1] Apparently only the Shadow Theatre sequences of this film survive, preserved in the
Cinémathèque Royale de Belgique.

Editor: Jean Mamy
Cast: Jacques Louvigny (*Bastien Follavoine*), Marguerite Pierry (*Julie Follavoine*), Sacha Tarride (*Toto*), Michel Simon (*Chouilloux*), Olga Valéry (*Madame Chouilloux*), Fernandel (*Horace Truchet*)
France; 60 mins

La Chienne

Production Company/Distribution: Films Jean Renoir, Braunberger-Richebé
Production Manager: Charles David
Screenplay: Jean Renoir, André Girard. From a novel by George de la Fouchardière, and the play adapted from it by André Mouézy-Eon
Photography: Théodore Sparkuhl
Production Design: Gabriel Scognamillo
Sound: Joseph de Bretagne, Marcel Courme
Music: Eugénie Buffet, Toselli
Editors: Denise Batcheff, Paul Fejos; then Marguerite Renoir, Jean Renoir
Cast: Michel Simon (*Maurice Legrand*), Janie Marèze (*Lulu*), Georges Flammant (*Dédé*), Magdeleine Berubet (*Adèle Legrand*), Pierre Gaillard (*Alexis Godart*), Jean Gehret (*M. Dagodet*), Alexandre Rignault (*Langelard, the Art Critic*), Lucien Mancini (*Walstein, the Art Dealer*)
France; 100 mins

1932
La Nuit du Carrefour (Night at the Crossroads)

Production Company: Europa Films
Distribution: CFC
Production Manager: Jacques Becker
Screenplay: Jean Renoir and Georges Simenon. From the novel by Georges Simenon
Photography: Marcel Lucien, Georges Asselin
Production Design: William Aguet
Sound: Joseph de Bretagne, Bugnon
Editor: Marguerite Renoir
Cast: Pierre Renoir (*Inspector Maigret*), Georges Térof (*Lucas*), Winna Winfried (*Else Andersen*), Georges Koudria (*Carl Andersen*), Jean Gehret (*Emile Michonnet*), Jane Pierson (*Madame Michonnet*), Michel Duran (*Jojo*)
France; 80 mins

Boudu Sauvé des Eaux (Boudu Saved from Drowning)

Production Company: Société Sirius (Films Michel Simon)
Distribution: Jacques Haik
Production Managers: Jean Gehret, Marc le Pelletier
Screenplay: Jean Renoir. From the play by René Fauchois

Photography: Marcel Lucien
Production Design: Jean Castanier, Hugues Laurent
Sound: Igor B. Kalinowski
Music: Raphael, Johann Strauss
Editors: Marguerite Renoir, Suzanne de Troyes
Cast: Michel Simon (*Boudu*), Charles Granval (*Edouard Lestingois*), Marcelle Hainia (*Madame Lestingois*), Séverine Lerczinska (*Anne-Marie*), Max Dalbin (*Godin*), Jean Gehret (*Vigour*), Jean Dasté (*Student*)
France; 83 mins

1933
Chotard et Cie (Chotard and Co.)
Production Company: Films Roger Ferdinand
Distribution: Universal
Screenplay: Jean Renoir, from the play by Roger Ferdinand
Photography: Joseph-Louis Mundwiller
Production Design: Jean Castanier
Sound: Igor B. Kalinowski
Editors: Marguerite Renoir, Suzanne de Troyes
Cast: Fernand Charpin (*François Chotard*), Jeanne Lory (*Madame Chotard*), Georges Pomiès (*Julien Collinet*), Jeanne Boitel (*Reine Chotard*), Max Dalban (*Emile*)
France; 83 mins

Madame Bovary
Production Company: Nouville Société de Film (Gaston Gallimard, Robert Aron)
Distribution: CID
Production Manager: René Jaspard
Screenplay: Jean Renoir. From the novel by Gustave Flaubert
Photography: Jean Bachelet
Production Design: Robert Gys, Eugène Lourié, Georges Wakhevitch
Sound: Marcel Courme, Joseph de Bretagne
Music: Darius Milhaud
Editor: Marguerite Renoir
Cast: Valentine Tessier (*Emma Bovary*), Pierre Renoir (*Charles Bovary*), Alice Tissot (*Old Madame Bovary*), Max Dearly (*M. Homais*), Daniel Lecourtois (*Léon Dupuis*), Fernand Fabre (*Rudolphe Boulanger*), Pierre Laquey (*Hippolyte Tautin*), Robert Le Vigan (*Lheureux*), Romain Bouquet (*M. Guillaumin*), André Fouche (*Justin*)
France; 120 mins

1934
Toni
Production Company: Films d'Aujourd'hui
Distribution: Films Marcel Pagnol
Production Manager: Pierre Gaut
Screenplay: Jean Renoir, Carl Einstein. From a true story found by
Jacques Mortier
Photography: Claude Renoir
Production Design: Léon Bourrely
Sound: Bardisbanian
Music: Paul Bozzi, Joseph Kosma
Editors: Marguerite Renoir, Suzanne de Troyes
Cast: Charles Blavette (*Toni*), Jenny Hélia (*Marie*), Celia Montalvan (*Josefa*),
Max Dalban (*Albert*), Edouard Delmont (*Fernand*), Andrex (*Gabi*), André
Kovachevitch (*Sebastien*)
France; 85 mins

1935
Le Crime de Monsieur Lange (*The Crime of Mr Lange*)
Production Company: Obéron
Distribution: Minerva
Producer: André Halley des Fontaines
Production Manager: Geneviève Blondeau
Screenplay: Jacques Prévert, Jean Renoir. From a story by Jean Castanier
Photography: Jean Bachelet
Production Design: Jean Castanier, Robert Gys
Sound: Guy Moreau, Louis Bogé, Roger Loisel, Robert Teisseire
Music: Jean Wiener, Joseph Kosma
Editor: Marguerite Renoir
Cast: Jules Berry (*Batala*), René Lefèvre (*Amédée Lange*), Florelle (*Valentine*),
Nadia Sirbirskaia (*Estelle*), Sylvie Bataille (*Edith*), Marcel Levesque (*The
Concierge*), Maurice Baquet (*Charles*), Jacques Brunius (*M. Baigneur*), Henri
Guisol (*Meunier fils*), Marcel Duhamel (*Louis*), Paul Grimault (*a Typesetter*)
France; 85 mins

1936
La Vie est à Nous (*Life Belongs to Us*)
Production Company: Parti Communiste Français
Distribution: L'Avant-Scène Cinéma (from 1969)
Directors: Jean Renoir, Jacques Becker, André Zwoboda, Jean-Paul Dreyfus/
Jean-Paul Le Chanois
Screenplay: Jean Renoir, Paul Vaillant-Couturier, Jean-Paul Dreyfus, André
Zwoboda

[567]

Photography: Louis Page, Jean-Serge Bourgoin, Jean Isnard, Alain Douarinou, Claude Renoir, Nicholas Hayer
Music: The 'Internationale', Shostakovich
Editor: Marguerite Renoir
Cast: Jean Dasté (*teacher*), Jacques Brunius (*President of the Administrative Council*), Pierre Unik (*Marcel Cachin's Secretary*), Julien Bertheau (*René*), Nadia Sirbirskaia (*Ninette*), Emile Drain (*Gustave*), Gaston Modot (*Philippe*), Charles Blavette (*Tonin*), Marcel Cachim, André Marty, Maurice Thorez, Jacques Duclos (*themselves*)
France; 66 mins

Une Partie de Campagne (*A Day in the Country*)
Production Company: Films du Panthéon, Films de la Pléiade
Distribution: Films du Panthéon (from 1946)
Producer: Pierre Braunberger
Production Manager: Roger Woog
Screenplay: Jean Renoir. From the story by Guy de Maupassant
Photography: Claude Renoir
Production Design: Robert Gys
Sound: Marcel Courme, Jopseph de Bretagne
Music: Joseph Kosma
Editor: Marguerite Renoir
Cast: Sylvie Bataille (*Henriette Dufour*), Jane Marken (*Madame Dufour*), Gabriello (*Cyprien Dufour*), Georges Darnoux (*Henri*), Jacques Brunius (*Rodolphe*), Paul Temps (*Anatole*), Gabrielle Fontan (*The Grandmother*), Jean Renoir (*Papa Pulain*), Marguerite Renoir (*Servant*)
France; 40 mins

Les Bas-Fonds (*The Lower Depths*)
Production Company: Albatross (Alexandre Kamenka)
Distribution: Les Distributeurs Français, S.A.
Production Manager: Vladimir Zederbaum
Screenplay: Eugene Zamiatine, Jacques Companéez. From the play by Maxim Gorky
Photography: Fedote Bourgassof, Jean Bachelet
Production Design: Eugène Lourié, Hugues Laurent
Sound: Robert Ivonnet
Music: Jean Wiener
Editor: Marguerite Renoir
Cast: Louis Jouvet (*The Baron*), Jean Gabin (*Pepel*), Suzy Prim (*Vassilissa*), Vladimir Sokoloff (*Kostileff*), Junie Astor (*Natasha*), Robert Le Vigan (*The Actor*), Gabriello (*The Inspector*), René Genin (*Luka*), Jany Holt (*Nastya*), Maurice Baquet (*Aliocha*)
France; 90 mins

1937
La Grande Illusion (Grand Illusion)
Production Company: RAC (Frank Rollmer, Alexandre and Albert Pinkowitch)
Distribution: RIC
Production Manager: Raymond Blondy
Screenplay: Jean Renoir, Charles Spaak
Photography: Christian Matras
Production Design: Eugène Lourié
Sound: Joseph de Bretagne
Music: Joseph Kosma
Editor: Marguerite Renoir
Cast: Jean Gabin (*Lieutenant Maréchal*), Pierre Fresnay (*Captain de Boeldieu*), Erich von Stroheim (*Captain von Ruffenstein*), Marcel Dalio (*Rosenthal*), Julien Carette (*Traquet*), Dita Parlo (*Elsa*), Jean Dasté (*Teacher*), Gaston Modot (*Engineer*)
France; 113 mins

1938
La Marseillaise
Production Company: CGT
Distribution: RAC
Production Managers: André Zwoboda, A. Seigneur
Screenplay: Jean Renoir, Carl Koch, N. Martel Dreyfus, Mme Jean-Paul Dreyfus
Photography: Jean-Serge Bourgoin, Alain Douarinou, Jean-Marie Maillols, Jean-Paul Alphen, Jean Louis
Production Design: Léon Barsacq, Georges Wakhevitch, Jean Périer
Sound: Joseph de Bretagne, Jean-Roger Bertrand, J. Demede
Music: Lalande, Grétry, Mozart, J. S. Bach, Joseph Kosma, Roget de L'Isle, Sauveplane
Editor: Margeurite Renoir
Cast: Pierre Renoir (*Louis XVI*), Lise Delamare (*Marie-Antoinette*), Louis Jouvet (*Roederer*), Andrex (*Honoré Arnaud*), Ardisson (*Fernand Flament*), Nadia Sirbirskaia (*Louison*), Jenny Hélia (*The Interrogator*), Léon Larive (*Picard*), Gaston Modot and Julien Carette (*Volunteers*)
France; 135 mins

La Bête Humaine (The Human Beast)
Production Company/Distribution: Paris Film Production (Robert Hakim)
Production Manager: Roland Tual
Screenplay: Jean Renoir. From the novel by Emile Zola
Photography: Curt Courant
Production Design: Eugène Lourié
Sound: Robert Teisseire

Music: Joseph Kosma
Editors: Marguerite Renoir, Suzanne de Troyes
Cast: Jean Gabin (*Jacques Lantier*), Simone Simon (*Séverine*), Fernand Ledoux (*Roubard*), Julien Carette (*Pecqueux*), Colette Régis (*Victoire*), Jacques Berlioz (*Grandmorin*), Jean Renoir (*Cabuche*)
France; 105 mins

1939
La Règle du Jeu (The Rules of the Game)
Production Company/Distribution: Nouvelles Editions Françaises (Camille François)
Production Manager: Claude Renoir Sr
Screenplay: Jean Renoir, Carl Koch
Photography: Jean Bachelet
Production Design: Eugène Lourié, Max Douy
Sound: Joseph de Bretagne
Music: Joseph Kosma, Mozart, Monsigny, Saint-Saëns, Johann Strauss
Editor: Marguerite Renoir
Cast: Marcel Dalio (*Robert de la Chesnaye*), Nora Gregor (*Christine*), Roland Toutain (*André Jurieux*), Jean Renoir (*Octave*), Mila Parély (*Geneviève*), Gaston Modot (*Edouard Schumacher*), Julien Carette (*Marceau*), Paulette Dubost (*Lisette*), Odette Talazac (*Charlotte de la Plante*), Pierre Magnier (*The General*), Pierre Nay (*M. de Saint-Aubin*), Richard Francoeur (*M. La Bruyère*), Claire Gérard (*Mme La Bruyère*)
France; 112 mins

1940
La Tosca
Production Company/Distribution: Era-Scalera Films
Production Manager: Arturo Ambrosio
Director: Carl Koch
Screenplay: Jean Renoir, Carl Koch. From the play by Victorien Sardou
Photography: Ubaldo Arata
Production Design: Gustavo Abel, Amleto Bonetti
Sound: Piero Cavazzuti
Music: Puccini
Editor: Cino Betrone
Cast: Imperio Argentina (*Tosca*), Michel Simon (*Scarpia*), Rossano Brazzi (*Mario Cavaradossi*)
Italy; 90 mins

1941
Swamp Water
Production Company/Production Manager: Twentieth Century-Fox
Producer: Irving Pichel
Screenplay: Dudley Nichols. From the story by Vereen Bell
Photography: Peverell Marley, Lucien Ballard
Production Design: Thomas Little, Richard Day
Music: David Rudolph
Editor: Walter Thompson
Cast: Dana Andrews (*Ben Ragan*), Walter Huston (*Thursday Ragan*), Walter
Brennan (*Tom Keefer*), Anne Baxter (*Julie*), John Carradine (*Jesse Wick*), Mary
Howard (*Hannah*), Ward Bond (*Jim Dorson*), Guinn Williams (*Bud Dorson*),
Virginia Gilmore (*Mabel*)
USA; 86 mins

1942
The Amazing Mrs Holliday (*Forever Yours*)
Production Company/Distribution: Universal
Producer/Director: Bruce Manning
Screenplay: Frank Ryan, John Jacoby, Boris Ingster, Leo Townsend. From a story
by Sonya Levien
Photography: Woody Bredell
Production Design: Jack Otterson, Martin Obzina
Music: Charles Previn, Puccini
Cast: Deanna Durbin (*Ruth*), Edmond O'Brien (*Tom*), Barry Fitzgerald
(*Timothy*), Arthur Treacher (*Henderson*), Harry Davenport (*The Commodore*),
Grant Mitchell (*Edgar*)
USA; 96 mins

1943
This Land is Mine
Production Company/Distribution: RKO
Producers/Screenplay: Jean Renoir, Dudley Nichols
Photography: Frank Redman
Production Design: Eugène Lourié, Albert d'Agostino, Walter F. Keeler
Sound: Terry Kellum, James Stewart
Music: Lothar Perl
Cast: Charles Laughton (*Albert Lory*), Maureen O'Hara (*Louise Martin*), Kent
Smith (*Paul Martin*), George Sanders (*George Lambert*), Walter Slezak (*Major
von Keller*), Una O'Connor (*Mrs Lory*), Philip Merivale (*Professor Sorell*), Nancy
Gates (*Julie Grant*)
USA; 103 mins

1944
Salute to France
Production Company: Office of War Information
Distribution: United Artists
Screenplay: Philip Dunne, Jean Renoir, Burgess Meredith
Photography: George Webber
Music: Kurt Weill
Editor: Helen Van Dongen
Cast: Burgess Meredith (*Tommy*), Garson Kanin (*Joe and Commentary Voice*), Claude Dauphin (*The Narrator and various Frenchmen*)
USA; 20 mins

1945
The Southerner
Distribution: United Artists
Producers: Robert Hakim, David L. Loew
Screenplay: Jean Renoir, Hugo Butler. From the novel *Hold Autumn In Your Hand* by George Sessions Perry
Photography: Lucien Andriot
Production Design: Eugène Lourié
Sound: Frank Webster
Music: Werner Janssen
Editor: Gregg Tallas
Cast: Zachary Scott (*Sam Tucker*), Betty Field (*Nora Tucker*), Beulah Bondi (*Grandma*), J. Carrol Naish (*Devers*), Percy Kilbride (*Harmie Jenkins*), Norman Lloyd (*Finlay*), Charles Kemper (*Tim*)
USA; 92 mins

1946
The Diary of a Chambermaid
Distribution: United Artists
Screenplay: Jean Renoir, Burgess Meredith. From the play by André Heuze, André de Lorde, Thielly Norès, adapted from the novel by Octave Mirbeau
Producers: Benedict Bogeaus, Burgess Meredith
Photography: Lucien Andriot
Production Design: Eugène Lourié
Sound: William Lynch
Music: Michel Michelet
Editor: James Smith
Cast: Paulette Goddard (*Célestine*), Burgess Meredith (*Captain Mauger*), Hurd Hatfield (*Georges Lanlaire*), Reginald Owen (*M. Lanlaire*), Judith Anderson (*Madame Lanlaire*), Francis Lederer (*Joseph*), Florence Bates (*Rose*)
USA; 91 mins

1947
The Woman on the Beach
Production Company/Distribution: RKO
Producer: Jack J. Gross
Screenplay: Jean Renoir, Frank Davis, J. R. Michael Hogan. From the novel
None So Blind by Mitchell Wilson
Photography: Harry Wild, Leo Tover
Production Design: Albert d'Agostino, Walter E. Keller
Sound: Jean L. Speak, Clem Portman
Music: Hanns Eisler
Editors: Roland Gross, Lyle Boyer
Cast: Joan Bennett (*Peggy Butler*), Robert Ryan (*Scott Burnett*), Charles Bickford
(*Tod Butler*), Nan Leslie (*Eve*), Walter Sande (*Vernecke*)
USA; 71 mins

1951
The River
Production Company: Oriental International Film Inc., Theatre Guild
Distribution: United Artists
Producers: Kenneth McEldowney, Kalyan Gupta, Jean Renoir
Screenplay: Jean Renoir, Rumer Godden. From the novel by Rumer Godden
Photography (*Technicolor*): Claude Renoir
Production Design: Eugène Lourié
Sound: Charles Paulton, Charles Knott
Music: Traditional Indian, Weber
Editor: George Gale
Cast: Nora Swinburne (*The Mother*), Esmond Knight (*The Father*), Arthur
Shields (*Mr John*), Thomas E. Breen (*Captain John*), Radha Sri Ram (*Melanie*),
Adrienne Corri (*Valerie*), Patricia Walters (*Harriet*), Suprova Mukerjee (*Nan*),
Richard Foster (*Bogey*)
USA; 99 mins

1953
The Golden Coach (*Le Carrosse d'Or*)
Production Company: Panaria Films, Hoche Productions
Distribution: Corona
Producer: Francesco Alliata
Screenplay: Jean Renoir, Renzo Avenzo, Giulio Macchi, Jack Kirkland, Ginette
Doynel. From the play *Le Carrosse du Saint-Sacrement* by Prosper Mérimée
Photography (*Technicolor*): Claude Renoir, Ronald Hill
Production Design: Mario Chiari
Sound: Joseph de Bretagne, Ovidio del Grande
Music: Vivaldi, Corelli, Olivier Mettra

Editors: Mario Seranderi, David Hawkins
Cast: Anna Magnani (*Camilla*), Duncan Lamont (*The Viceroy*), Odouardo
Spadaro (*Don Antonio*), Riccardo Rioli (*Ramon*), Paul Campbell (*Felipe*), Nadia
Fiorelli (*Isabelle*), Dante (*Harlequin*)
France/Italy; 100 mins

1955
French Cancan
Production Company: Franco London Films, Jolly Films
Distribution: Gaumont
Production Manager: Louis Wipf
Screenplay: Jean Renoir. From an idea by André-Paul Antoine
Photography (Technicolor): Michel Kelber
Production Design: Max Douy
Sound: Antoine Petitjean
Music: Georges Van Parys
Choreography: Georges Grandjean
Editor: Borys Lewin
Cast: Jean Gabin (*Danglard*), Maria Félix (*Lola di Castro*), Françoise Arnoul
(*Nini*), Jean-Roger Caussimon (*Baron Walter*), Gianni Esposito (*Prince
Alexandre*), Philippe Clay (*Casimir*), Michel Piccoli (*Valorgueil*), Jean Parédès
(*Coudrier*), Lydia Johnson (*Guibole*), Max Dalban (*manager of La Reine
Blanche*), Jacques Jouanneau (*Bidon*), Valentine Tessier (*Mme Olympe*), Franco
Pastorino (*Paulo*), Pierre Olaf (*Pierrot*), Patachou (*Yvette Guilbert*), Edith Piaf
(*Eugénie Buffet*)
France; 97 mins

1956
Eléna et les Hommes (*Paris Does Strange Things*)
Production Companies: Franco London Films, Les Filmes Gibé, Electra
Compagnia Cinematografica
Distribution: Cinédis
Screenplay: Jean Renoir, Jean Serge
Photography (Eastmancolor): Claude Renoir
Production Design: Jean André
Sound: William Sivel
Music: Joseph Kosma, Georges Van Parys
Editor: Borys Lewin
English Version: Kay Howard
Cast: Ingrid Bergman (*Princess Eléna Sorokovska*), Jean Marais (*General
François Rollan*), Mel Ferrer (*Henri de Chevincourt*), Pierre Bertin (*Martin-
Michaud*), Jean Richard (*Hector*), Magali Noel (*Lolotte*), Elina Labourdette

(*Paulette Escoffier*), Juliette Greco (*Gypsy*)
France; 95 mins (US version, 98 mins)

1959
Le Testament du Docteur Cordelier (*The Testament of Dr Cordelier*)
Production Company: RTF, Sofirad, Compagnie Jean Renoir
Distribution: Consortium Pathé (1961)
Production Manager: Albert Hollebecke
Screenplay: Jean Renoir. From the novel *The Strange Case of Dr Jekyll and Mr Hyde* by Robert Louis Stevenson
Photography: Georges Leclerc
Production Design: Marcel-Louis Dieulot
Sound: Joseph Richard
Music: Joseph Kosma
Editor: Renée Lichtig
Cast: Jean-Louis Barrault (*Dr Cordelier/Opale*), Teddy Billis (*Maître Joly*), Michel Vitold (*Dr Lucien Séverin*), Jean Topart (*Désiré*), Micheline Gary (*Marguerite*), André Ceres (*Inspector Salbris*)
France; 100 mins

Le Déjeuner sur l'Herbe (*Picnic on the Grass*)
Production Company: Compagnie Jean Renoir
Distribution: Consortium Pathé
Production Manager: Ginette Doynel
Screenplay: Jean Renoir
Photography (*Eastmancolor*): Georges Leclerc
Production Design: Marcel-Louis Dieulot
Sound: Joseph de Bretagne
Music: Joseph Kosma
Editor: Renée Lichtig
Cast: Paul Meurisse (*Professor Etienne Alexis*), Catherine Rouvel (*Nénette*), Fernand Sardou (*Nino*), Ingrid Nordine (*Marie-Charlotte*), Charles Blavette (*Gaspard*), Jean Claudio (*Rosseau*)
France; 92 mins

1962
Le Caporal Épingle (*The Vanishing Corporal/The Elusive Corporal*)
Production Company: Films du Cyclope (Adry de Carbuccia, Roland Girard)
Distribution: Pathé
Production Manager: René G. Vuattoux
Screenplay: Jean Renoir, Guy Lefranc. From the novel by Jacques Perret
Photography: Georges Leclerc
Production Design: Eugene Herrly

[575]

Sound: Antoine Petitjean
Music: Joseph Kosma
Editor: Renée Lichtig
Cast: Jean-Pierre Cassel (*The Corporal*), Claude Brasseur (*Pater*), Claude Rich (*Ballochet*), Jean Carmet (*Guillaume*), Jacques Jouanneau (*Penche-à-gauche*), Cornelia Froeboess (*Erika*), Mario David (*Caruso*), O. E. Hasse (*Drunken Passenger*), Guy Bedos (*The Stutterer*)
France; 105 mins

1969
Le Petit Théâtre de Jean Renoir (*The Little Theatre of Jean Renoir*)
Production Company: Son et Lumière, RAI, Bavaria, ORTF
Producer: Pierre Long
Production Manager: Robert Paillardon
Screenplay: Jean Renoir
Photography (*colour*): Georges Leclerc, Antoine Georgiakis, Georges Liron
Production Design: Gilbert Margerie
Sound: Guy Rolphe
Music: Jean Wiener, Joseph Kosma, Octave Crémieux
Editor: Geneviève Winding
Cast: 1) *Le Dernier Réveillon* – Nino Formicola and Milly-Monti (*Tramps*), Roland Bertin (*Gontran*), Robert Lombard (*Maitre D'*)
2) *La Cireuse Electrique* – Marguerite Cassan (*Emilie*), Pierre Olaf (*Gustave*), Jacques Dynam (*Jules*), Jean-Louis Tristan (*Salesman*)
3) *Quand l'Amour Meurt* – Jeanne Moreau (*The Singer*)
4) *Le Roi d'Yvetot* – Fernand Sardou (*Duvallier*), Françoise Arnoul (*Isabelle*), Jean Carmet (*Feraud*), Dominique Labourier (*Paulette*)
France; 100 mins

Theatre Productions

1954
Jules César (Julius Caesar)
Playwright: William Shakespeare, translated by Grisha and Mitsou Dabat
Stage Manager: Jean Serge
Cast: Jean-Pierre Aumont (*Marc Antony*), Loleh Bellon (*Portia*), Yves Robert
(*Cassius*), Françoise Christophe (*Calpurnia*), Paul Meurisse (*Brutus*), Henri Vidal
(*Julius Caesar*), Jean Parédès (*Casca*), Jean Topart (*Octavius Caesar*), François
Vibert (*The Soothsayer*), Gaston Modot (*Ligarius*), Henri-Jacques Huet
(*Flavius*), Jacques Catelain (*Decius*)
Venue: The Arena at Arles
Performance: 10 July only

1955
Orvet
Playwright: Jean Renoir
Stage Manager: Maurice Fraigneau
Production Design: Georges Wakhevitch
Music: Joseph Kosma
Cast: Leslie Caron (*Orvet*), Paul Meurisse (*Georges*), Michel Herbault (*Olivier*),
Catherine Le Couey (*Mme Camus*), Raymond Bussières (*Coutant*), Jacques
Jouanneau (*William*), Marguerite Cassan (*Clotilde*), Yorick Royan (*Berthe*),
Suzanne Courtal (*Mother Viper*), Pierre Olaf (*Philippe, the Clubfoot*), Georges
Saillard (*The Doctor*), Georges Hubert (*The First Huntsman*), Henry Charrett
(*The Second Huntsman*)
Venue: Théâtre de la Renaissance, Paris
Performances: from 12 March

1957
Le Grand Couteau (The Big Knife)
Playwright: Clifford Odets, translated by Jean Renoir
Stage Manager: Jean Serge
Production Design: Fred Givone
Cast: Daniel Gélin (*Charles Castle*), Claude Génia (*Marion, his Wife*), Paul
Bernard (*Marcus Hoff*), Paul Cambo (*Smiley Coy*), France Delahalle (*Patty
Benedict*), Vera Norman (*Dixie Evans*), Teddy Billis (*Nat*), Andrea Parisy
(*Connie Bliss*), Robert Moncade (*Hank Teagle*), Jacques Dannoville (*The

Gardener), François Marie (*Buddy Bliss*), Andrès Wheatley (*Russell*)
Venue: Théâtre des Bouffes-Parisiens, Paris
Performances: from 30 October

Books

1955: *Orvet* (Play in Three Acts)
Publisher: Gallimard

1962: *Renoir* (Biography of Pierre-Auguste Renoir)
Publisher: Hachette
Renoir, My Father
English Translation: Randolph and Dorothy Weaver
Publisher: Collins

1966: *Les Cahiers Du Capitaine Georges* (Novel)
Publisher: Gallimard
The Notebooks of Captain Georges
English Translation: Norman Denny
Publisher: Collins

1974: *Ma Vie et Mes Films* (Autobiography)
Publisher: Flammarion
My Life and My Films
English Translation: Norman Denny
Publisher: Atheneum (USA), Collins (London)

1974: *Ecrits 1926–1971* (Articles, Speeches, Tributes)
Editor: Claude Gauteur
Publisher: Pierre Belfond

1976: *Carola* (Play in Three Acts)
Publisher: L'Avant-Scène Théâtre

1978: *Le Coeur à l'Aise* (Novel)
Publisher: Flammarion

1979: *Le Crime de l'Anglais* (Novel)
Publisher: Flammarion

1979: *Geneviève* (Novel)
Publisher: Flammarion

Note on Editors

David Thompson worked in film distribution and exhibition before becoming a freelance journalist and joining the BBC in 1983. There he has programmed film seasons and produced the series 'The Film Club'. Since 1990 he has directed documentaries on Roberto Rossellini, Peter Greenaway, Michael Powell and Jean Renoir, as well as contributing reports to the series 'Moving Pictures'. He was co-editor of *Scorsese on Scorsese* and editor of *Levinson on Levinson*.

Lorraine LoBianco received her MA in Critical Studies from the UCLA School of Film and Television in 1992, and has taught an extension class in film at Chapman University. This is her first book.

Index

Figures in italics refer to illustrations.

[582]

Faye, Alice, 99, 100n
FBI, 314n, 318
Feather Duster, The, 458
Federal Reserve, 213
Feld, Robert, JR letter to, 145–6
Feldman, Charles K., 89, 90, 92, 96, 313, 315; JR letters to, 94–5, 98–100
Feldman Blum Agency, 80, 82, 117, 148; JR telegram to, 83
FEMIS, 470n
Femme Nue de Goya, La, 188
Ferrer, Mel, 233, 235n, 240, 354, 378n
Ferry, Fefe, 316
Festival of Bad Ems, 503
Feu des Poudres, Le (ballet), 384n
Feuchtwanger, Lion, 193, 194n
Feydeau, Georges, 21
Feyder, Jacques, 37n, 149n, 266, 267n
Field, Betty, JR letter to, 170–71
Fighiera, Alice, 104, 106n, 363
Fighiera, Pierre, 84, 363; JR letters to, 104–6
Fille de l'Eau, La, 16, 17, 18, 176n
Fille du Geolier, La, 205
Film Group, 209, 210, 213, 214n
Films de Cyclope, 432, 434
Films de Ma Vie, Les (*The Films in My Life*), 528–9
Films du Carrosse, Les, 505, 506n
Films RS, Les, 371
First Regiment of Dragoons, 4
Flaherty, Barbara, 62
Flaherty, David, 85, 87, 91, 135, 145
Flaherty, Frances, 90
Flaherty, Monica, 64, 82
Flaherty, Robert, 54, 56n, 75, 81, 227, 229n; Dido's letters to, 55–6, 64, 67, 69, 70, 72–3, 73–4, 78–80, 82, 89–90; letters to Dido, 57, 62, 87; JR letters to, 70, 71–2, 77–8, 89, 135, 143–4, 200–201, 210–11; telegrams to JR, 71, 73, 80, 86; JR telegrams to, 71, 73, 80, 211; Dido telegrams to, 83; letter to JR, 144–5
Flamant, Georges, 125n, 530n

Flammarion, 521, 546, 547, 553n
Flaubert, Gustave, 179, 180, 181n, 463
Flaud, Mr (of official film centre), 315, 381
Flechteim, Captain Alfred, 35
Fleming, Victor, 117n, 206n, 242n
Flowering Peach, The, 309n, 323, 332
Flynn, Errol, 268
Fonda, Henry, 99, 100n
Fontainebleau, 389
Foolish Wives, 16, 37n
Ford, Glenn, 233, 235n
Ford, John, 95n, 100n, 101, 115n, 118n, 138n, 244n, 312n, 379, 380n
Forever Yours (started by JR, finished by Manning as *The Amazing Mrs Halliday*), 129n
Fosse, Bob, 535n
Foster, Henry, 140n
Francen, Leno, 418n, 424
Francen, Victor, 197–8, 418n
Francesco giullare di Dio (*Flowers of St Francis*), 248, 249n
Francis of Assisi, St, 154
Franco, Francisco, 557
François, Camille, 52, 55; JR letter to, 57, 59–60
Franju, Georges, 229n, 266n, 388n, 411n
Frankenheimer, John, 177n
Franklin, Sidney, 463n
Freed, Arthur, 373, 374
Freire, Dido, *see* Renoir, Dido Danin-Freire
Freire, Dirce, 73n
French Cancan (JR), xix, 43n, 282n, 326, 327, 329, 331, 340n, 343, 358n, 416n, 467n, 497
French Cinema Union, 393
French Communist Party, xix
French Flying Corps, 14, 15
French Research Foundation, 115n
French Television, 386–7
Fresnay, Pierre, 30, 293, 295n
Friedkin, William, 548
Fritz, Bernardine, 514

Froboess, Cornelia, 414n
Front Populaire, 29
Fuller, Sam, 95n

Gabin, Jean, 29, 42, 43n, 76, 77, 112,
  143, 152, 160, 446, 447, 462
Gaborit, Jean, 393n
Gale, George, 263
Galileo, 206n
Galileo Galilei, 206
Gallimard, 436, 464n
Gallimard, Gaston, 23, 24n, 27
Gandhi, Mahatma M.K., 217n
Gang, Martin, 184, 189
Garbo, Greta, 233, 235n
Gardner, Ava, 190n
Gare St Lazare, Paris, 48
Garfield, John, 300, 333
Garnett, David, 454n
Garnett, Tay, 300n
Gary, Micheline, 358n
Gaulle, Charles de, 128, 178, 377, 378
Gaullists, xix, 128
Gaumont Company, 55
Gaunt, Maud, 368, 429, 430, 437, 451
Gaut, Pierre, 41, 358, 368, 429, 430,
  437; JR letters to, 345–7, 450–51
Gauteur, Claude, 521n
Gauthier, Jean-Jacques, 438
Gehret, Jean, 442
Gélin, Daniel, 333, 334, 357, 361n,
  362–3, 364
Gélin, Sylvie, 360, 361n
General Service, 210
Geneviève (JR), 552, 553
Genia, Claudia, 360, 361n
Gérard, Claire, 198
Gérardmer, 9, 10
Gergély (agent), 315
Giacomo, Greg, 535
Gibbons, Eliot, 308n; JR letter to,
  306–7
Gibbons, Irene, 306, 308n
Gide, André, 280
Gigi, 373, 374n
Gilbert, Louis, 177n
Gilmore, Virginia, 117, 118n

Giono, Jean, 336, 337, 363
Girard, Roland, 424, 426
Giraudoux, Jean, 148, 214n, 215, 447
Giscard d'Estaing, Valéry, 527, 528n
Gish, Lillian, 106, 107n
Gitt, Robert R., JR letter to, 488–9
Giverny, 157
Godard, Jean-Luc, xiii, 24n, 400, 401,
  402n, 467n, 528n
Goddard, Paulette, 160, 163, 166,
  182, 188, 266, 442; JR letters to,
  165, 167, 168–9
Godden, Jane, 243
Godden, Paula, 243
Godden, Rumer, 118n, 199, 204, 216,
  218, 220, 224, 225n, 229–32, 234,
  237, 238–9, 240, 288, 457–8, 481;
  JR letters to, 226–7, 239, 243, 263,
  403–4, 539, 545; JR telegram to,
  253
Goering, Hermann, 176n
Goetz, William, 116, 117n
Goldbeck, Willis, 312, 316, 317
Golden Boy, 299
Golden Coach, The see *Carrosse
  d'Or, Le*
Goldwyn, Samuel, 111, 218; JR letter
  to, 48
Goodis, David, 399, 400, 402n
Gordon, Michael, 378n
Gorky, Maxim, 465
Goulding, Edmund, 104n
Goya, 218
Grable, Betty, 307, 308n
Grace (housekeeper), 92
Grand Couteau, Le, see *Big Knife, The*
'Grand' Louise (Renoir family cook),
  12
Grand Magasin Dufayel, 3
Grande Illusion, La (JR), xx, 28n, 30,
  45n, 46, 47, 50, 51n, 77n, 94, 98n,
  100, 112, 137, 177n, 273, 274, 278,
  282, 283n, 285, 295n, 336, 343,
  344, 346, 350, 357, 363, 366, 371,
  391n, 405, 474, 475n, 489, 522;
  and Major Pinsard, 15; and
  accusation of plagiarism, 31–43; JR

holds screening in Lisbon, 85; revival of, 189, 190n; restoration of negative, 335; screening of an old print (1957), 369; trailer for reissue, 374; and Brussels fair, 380–81; release of (1958), 382–4; and changes during shooting, 406; and Bosley Crowther, 446–7; illustrated book, 524; and Giscard d'Estaing, 527

Grant, Cary, 122, 125n

Gregor, Nora, 281

Griffith, D.W., 107n, 496, 497n

Griffith, Richard, JR letter, 22, 201–2

Gringoire, 39

Grove Press, 496

Guerre, La, 468–9, 471, 473

Guignol puppet theatre, Tuileries gardens, 3

Guild of Bengal Technicians, 232

Guilhem, Jean, JR letter to, 389–90

Guillaume, Louis, 176n, 220, 270, 271, 279; JR letters to, 174–5, 183–5, 188–90, 202, 217, 221

Guillermin, John, 277n, 368n

Guimard, Hector, 427n

Guinness, Sir Alec, 378

Guino, Richard, 484, 485n

Guitry, Sacha, 327n, 467n

Hachette, 407n, 434

Hackford, Taylor, 356n

Hakim, Robert, 48, 149, 152, 153, 159, 182; JR letter to, 179–81

Hakim brothers, 399

Hal Roach Studios, 215, 225, 231

Hall, Christopher, 374

Hall, Jenny, 374n

Hall, Sir Peter, 374

Halpern, Otto, JR letter to, 439–40

Hamer, Roger, 378n

Hamsun, Knut, 452n

Harrison, Kay, 230, 231n, 232, 285, 296

Harry (housekeeper), 92

Hartwell family, 288

Hasso, Signe, 212

Hatfield, Hurd, 169

Hathaway, Henry, 214n

Haussman Films, 50, 51

Haut de Cagnes, 367

Hawks, Howard, 101n, 118n, 125n, 308n, 447n

Haynes-Dixon, James, 263

Hays, Will H., 144n

Hays Office, 144, 209

Hefling, Frances, 317

Heflin, Van, 233, 235n, 239, 240, 311; JR letters to, 312, 316–17, 324–5

Helen (Odets' nurse), 321

Hemingway, Ernest, 93n

Hess, Rudolf, 108

Hessling, Catherine (JR's first wife; *see also* Renoir, Andrée), 20, 171, 190n, 204, 220, 271, 272n; character, xix; in JR films, 15–16, 18, 21; acts in Cavalcanti film, 21, 511n, 516; JR separates from, 21, 28n; divorce, 171, 174–5, 185, 187, 217; and *Le Chasseur*, 189

Heuschling, Mamée (mother of Catherine Hessling), 188

Heymann, Daniele, 551

High Noon, 303, 304n

Hindenburg, Paul Von, 318, 320n

Hiroshima, Mon Amour, 401, 402n

Hirschmann, André, JR letters to, 40–41, 44–5

Histoire d'Adèle H., *L'*, 531–2, 535, 537

History of Sex in Cinema (Knight and Alpert), 478

Hitchcock, Alfred, 116, 117n, 119, 138n, 140n, 147n, 151n, 219n, 235n, 490

Hitchcock (publisher), 142

Hitler, Adolf, 62, 69, 318, 320n, 557

Hold Autumn in Your Hand, 151n, 153, 157; see also *Southerner, The*

Homme à abattre, L' (*The Marked Man*), 40, 41n

Homme qui Aimait les Femmes, L', 541n

Homolka, Florence, 419

Macchi, Giulio, 287, 288n, 491; JR
    letters to, 498, 511–12
McCrea, Joel, 149, 151
McEldowney, J. Kenneth, 216, 218,
    222, 223, 225, 226, 227, 228,
    231–2, 249–53, 255, 263, 273, 274,
    275n, 278, 284, 286, 321, 325; JR
    letters to, 229–31, 233–8
McEldowney, Melvina, 233, 235n,
    236, 237, 249, 251
McGregor, Duncan, 437; JR letters to,
    430–31, 432
Mackendrick, Alexander, 194n
McKenna, Mr (head of Story
    Department), 374
Maclaine, Shirley, 366n
McLeod, Norman Z., 125n
Madame Bovary (JR), 22, 23, 24n, 26,
    27, 28n, 98n, 179–80, 182, 356,
    398, 459
Maeterlinck, Maurice, 390
Magnani, Anna, 264, 265, 266, 268,
    269, 274, 275, 285, 286, 294, 296,
    297, 308, 315, 467
Magnificat, Le (JR), 77
Maillet, Jean-Claude, 520
Malle, Louis, 327n, 334n, 402n
Malraux, André, 481
Mamoulian, Rouben, 56n, 104n,
    115n, 235n
Man Who Loved Women, The, 541
Mankiewicz, Joseph L., 104n, 138n,
    308n
Mann, Anthony, 467n
Mann, Christopher, 252
Mann, Thomas, 193, 194n
Manning, Bruce, 129, 131, 133, 134
Manson, Frances, 80
Marais, Jean, 340, 352
Marc Aurèle (Marcus Aurelius), 439
Marceau, Félicien, 397
Marécage, see Swamp Water
Marèze, Janie, 529–30
Margoton La Gardeuse de Poules
    (Poultry Meg's Family), 122
Marin, Ned, 94
Marion, André, 484, 485

Marken, Jane, 558
Marlotte, 15, 16, 29, 55, 70, 189, 389,
    559
Marquitta (JR), 21
Marseillaise, La (JR), 28n, 43, 44–7,
    50, 66n, 149n, 280n, 283n, 337n,
    472, 475n
Marseilles, 73, 83, 84
Marshall, George, 152n, 466n
Marshall, William, 268n
Martha Richard au Service de La
    France, 40, 41n
Martigues, Les, 27, 28
Mason, James, 218, 233; JR letter to,
    214
Masse (JR's French lawyer), 184–5,
    189, 202
Massimo, Prince, 371
Master Forger, The (project), 471, 472
Mastroianni, Marcello, 259n, 482
Mathot, Léon, 41n
Matisse, Henri, 222, 223n
Matras, Mr (cameraman), 37
Mattei, Maria de, 294
Matthews, Pamela, 294n
Maurette, Marc, 283, 298, 417, 420
Mazelière, Mr de la (of Cinedis), 381
MCA, 326, 352
Meerson, Mary, 371, 419, 486
Melcher, Marty, 378
Méliès, Georges, 548
Melville, Jean-Pierre, 264n, 358n,
    538n
Memo from Darryl F. Zanuck
    (Behlmer), 125
Meredith, Burgess, 149, 150, 153n,
    160n, 182, 520; JR letters to, 165,
    167–9
Mérimée, Prosper, 263n
Metro-Goldwyn-Mayer (MGM), 83,
    85, 193, 239, 278, 305, 311, 316,
    317, 320, 335, 352, 374n, 377
Meudon, 24
Meurisse, Paul, 326, 331, 358, 359,
    364, 366, 372, 378, 379, 527
Meyer (of Comédie Française), 371
MGM, see Metro-Goldwyn-Mayer

Water, 101; and Esta Nichols, 106;
enjoys staying in the house, 139;
marries JR, 148, 150n; and *Diary of
a Chambermaid*, 172; and JR's
divorce from Catherine, 185, 202; in
India, 222; move to Beverly Hills,
223; and *The River*, 277–8; and
JR's naturalization, 278; letter to
Odets, 289; and JR's hospitalization
in Rome, 290; as a gardener, 309,
445, 451; and pension for JR, 395;
and Los Angeles brush fires, 414,
416; and Switzerland, 441; JR
letters to, 69–70, 83–5, 270–77,
357–72, 410–14, 416–27, 429–30,
491; letters to JR, 277–8, 414, 416,
423–4
Renoir, Edmond (JR's cousin), 36,
206, 287n
Renoir, Evangèle, 366
Renoir, Helène Rivière, 206
Renoir, Jacques, 177n
Renoir, Jane (Alain's wife), 293, 388,
418, 419
Renoir, Jean: letters of, xvii–xx;
importance to him of marriage to
Dido, xviii–xix; political standing,
xix; birth, 3; first experience of the
cinema, 3; and Guignol puppet
theatre, 3; attends Ecole Masséna,
Nice, 3; in First Regiment of
Dragoons, 4–7, 8; transfers to
Chasseurs Alpins, 9; leg wound,
9–12, 15, 49–50, 79, 92, 96, 113,
131, 134, 285–6, 290–91, 465, 530,
539, 552; transfers to the French
Flying Corps, 14, 15; crashes his
plane, 15; returns to live at Les
Collettes as the war ends, 15; works
as a potter and ceramist, 15; marries
Andrée Heuschling, 15; buys Villa
St El, 15; son Alain born, 15; prefers
American to French cinema, 15;
shoots first film, 15–16; opens shop
to sell his pottery, 18; forced to sell
several of father's painting, 21, 559;
acts in Cavalcanti film, 21, 511n;

directs last silent film, 21; separates
from Catherine, 21; first sound
production, 21; first major film, 21;
lives with Marguerite Houllé, 28;
contributes articles to *Ciné-Liberté*,
29, 66n; wins Prix Louis-Delluc
with *Les Bas-Fonds*, 29; Goldwyn
offer, 48; applies for admission to
the army film corps, 49–50; and
panchromatic film, 50; sets up La
NEF, 52; and Technicolor, 56; takes
up residence at 7 avenue Frochot,
61; enters Service Cinématographique de Armée (1939), 62, 63;
in Italy (1940), 67, 69–70; and
Nazis, 71; plans to go to America,
67, 69, 71–83; goes to US via
Lisbon, 83–7, 88; moves into house
in Hollywood, 90, 91–2; signs
contract with Fox, 90; tries to
arrange contract for Alain, 90–91,
93, 97; terminates contract with
Fox, 125; signs with Universal, 127;
appendicitis, 138–9, 140; marries
Dido, 148, 150n; changes agent,
148; on dubbing of French films,
160–62; divorce, 174–5, 185, 187,
202, 217; and *Le Chasseur*, 175,
185, 188, 189, 426; forms the Film
Group, 209; in India, 222–3, 244;
move to Beverly Hills, 223, 238; re-
establishes residence in Paris (1949),
244; attends Venice Biennale, 286,
287; on sound recording, 301–2,
340–41; and three-dimensional and
panoramic systems, 305, 307; and
forged Renoirs, 371; as Regents'
Professor of English and Dramatic
Arts, 391–6; makes bronze copies of
father's statues, 392; fall in Vienna,
422–3; and Cuban crisis, 434;
Charles Blanc Prize, 441–2; gall-
stones, 443, 444, 451, 453; and
Kennedy's death, 448, 450, 451;
directs class at UCLA, 450;
doctorate, 453, Charter Day
ceremony, 453; and Langlois

reinstatement, 481; and student riots, 482–4; asked to be Honorary President of Cinémathèque, 483n, 484, 485, 486, 490; Parkinson's disease, 501, 502; honorary Oscar, 526, 527; prostate removed, 543; death and funeral, 555

Renoir, John (Alain's son), 293, 364, 388, 419, 441, 443

Renoir, Dr Maurice, 287, 346, 348

Renoir, My Father (translation of *Renoir*) (JR), 7n, 192n, 308, 309–10, 342, 407, 421–3, 426, 433, 434, 436, 453, 455, 459

Renoir, Paulette (wife of Claude, Sr), 18, 270

Renoir, Peter (Alain's son), 364, 388, 441, 443

Renoir, Pierre (JR's brother), 3, 164, 176, 177n, 270, 279, 290, 298, 555, 559; in *La Nuit du Carrefour*, 21, 442; in *Madame Bovary*, 22; and Aron, 23; in *Amphitryon 38*, 214n; dies, 299n

Renoir, Pierre-Auguste (JR's father), *xxvi*, 3, 5, 347; affinity to his father's art in JR's films, xiii; buys house in Essoyes, 3; purchases Les Collettes, 3; crippled with arthritis, 3, 6, 7; finds new model, Andrée Heuschling, 15; dies, 15; JR forced to sell paintings, 21, 559; and *Le Chasseur*, 175, 176n, 185, 188, 426; forged paintings, 371; bronze copies of statues, 392; and Velásquez, 420–21; phallus jest, 421–2, 423n; work exhibited, 459–60; bust of, 463; garden of, 466; and Guino, 485n; JR letter to, 12

Report from the Aleutians, 165

Resnais, Alain, 396n, 414n

Reverdy, Mr, JR letter to, 49

Riboud, Jean, 496

Rich, Claude, 413, 414n, 415, 430, 467

Richard, Mr (president of League of Wartime Escapees), 32, 38

Richebé, Roger, 530n

Richet, Professor, 303

Richthofen, Manfred, Baron von, 33, 35

Ringel, Mr, JR letter to, 65

Ritt, Martin, 235n

River, The (JR), 98n, 181n, 199, 200, 203–4, 216, 218, 220, 222–44, 245, 246, 249–53, 254, 259, 260–61, 263, 265–70, 274, 275n, 278n, 279, 284, 286n, 288, 292, 299, 306, 321, 359n, 479, 539

Rivette, Jacques, 400, 402n, 497, 498, 506, 528

Rivière, Georges, 14, 206n; Aline Renoir letter to, 9–10

Rivière, Renée, 9n

RKO, *see* Radio-Keith-Orpheum (RKO) Studios

Robert, Jacques, 495

Roberts, Jim, 278

Roberts, Ruth, 147, 212, 248, 275, 276, 278, 279, 460

Robinson, Edward G., 125n

Robinson, Madeleine, 355

Robson, Mark, 372n

Roche, Henri-Pierre, 398

Rochemont, Richard de, 67, 69n, 75, 79, 80, 82, 85; JR letter to, 81

Rohmer, Eric, 401

Roi Tout Nu, Un (*A Naked King*), 312, 313, 315

Rollmer, Frank, 42, 43n, 44n, 285, 447; JR letters to, 44, 48

Romains, Jules, 148

Romance, Viviane, 529, 530n

Roosevelt, Eleanor, 205, 206n

Roosevelt, Franklin D., 128, 206n

Rope, 233, 235n

Rosie (Nichols' maid), 293

Rossellini, Isabella, 356, 473, 474n

Rossellini, Marcella, 349, 350n

Rossellini, Renzo, 349, 350n

Rossellini, Robertino, 356

Rossellini, Roberto, 238n, 239n, 241, 248, 264n, 272, 275, 276, 302, 349, 350, 351, 353, 354, 356, 364, 473,